Korean War Comic Books

Korean War Comic Books

LEONARD RIFAS

McFarland & Company, Inc., Publishers

Jefferson, North Carolina

LIBRARY OF CONGRESS CATALOGUING-IN-PUBLICATION DATA

Names: Rifas, Leonard, author.
Title: Korean War comic books / Leonard Rifas.
Description: Jefferson, North Carolina : McFarland & Company, Inc.,
Publishers, 2021. | Includes bibliographical references and index.
Identifiers: LCCN 2020050986 | ISBN 9780786443963
(paperback : acid free paper) ∞
ISBN 9781476640488 (ebook)
Subjects: LCSH: Comic books, strips, etc.—United States—History—
20th century. | Korean War, 1950–1953—Literature and the war. |
Censorship—United States—History—20th century. | War in literature.
Classification: LCC PN6725 .R55 2021 | DDC 741.5/973—dc23
LC record available at https://lccn.loc.gov/2020050986

BRITISH LIBRARY CATALOGUING DATA ARE AVAILABLE

ISBN (print) 978-0-7864-4396-3
ISBN (ebook) 978-1-4766-4048-8

Front cover design by the author

Printed in the United States of America

*McFarland & Company, Inc., Publishers
Box 611, Jefferson, North Carolina 28640
www.mcfarlandpub.com*

Table of Contents

Table of Contents

Preface

Pulled in by my longstanding love for comic books and by atomic-age feelings against war, I have become fascinated by a widely misunderstood chapter of comic book history and its part in the larger stories of American popular culture and American militarism. This book looks at how comic books represented the Korean War, as a way to understand both American comic books and the Korean War more deeply. It compares some of the stories that comic books made up about that war with stories that journalists reported at the time and with stories that historians have written about it. Beyond merely describing some differences between stories made to inform and stories made to entertain, this book examines various forces that shaped the material that appeared in American comic books in the early 1950s. Those shaping forces included both general alarms over the threats of nuclear war and totalitarianism and, more directly, an alarm over violent comic book content. I am especially interested in how those who fought against that period's "crime comic books" thought about Korean War comic books. This includes Dr. Fredric Wertham, who, more than anyone else, agitated against comic books' alleged brutalization of the imagination.

In the United States, the Korean War has long been called "the forgotten war"—and yet, measured by the number of Americans who died or were wounded, it was a larger war than the Revolutionary War, the War of 1812, the Mexican War, the Spanish-American War, the Gulf War, the Iraq War and the war in Afghanistan added together.[1] Like the Vietnam War, the Korean War killed tens of thousands of American soldiers, hundreds of thousands of Asian soldiers, and possibly millions of Asian civilians.[2]

The short, dramatic, visual stories in old war comics help to illuminate a crucial transformation that happened in American culture in the early 1950s. At that time, the United States rapidly built a huge military establishment on the recently laid foundations of our still-existing war economy.[3]

The war in Korea, which made this fast military buildup possible, was strongly supported by the core members of the American "Establishment" (that small group of men who decided America's Cold War policies), but it became highly unpopular.[4] How did comic books, perhaps the *least* elite, *least* censored and *most* controversial of the mass media, handle these changes and tensions? How did people use this then-popular medium to promote their favored ideas? How did they keep material that they disagreed with from being published in comic books?

Those who led the attack on comic books in the late 1940s and early 1950s regarded the stakes of their campaigns as immensely consequential. Although misremembered as people who were simply panicking over juvenile delinquency, their published criticisms of comic books returned again and again to a deeper question. These critics asked how the United States could prevent socially irresponsible, profit-driven publishers from inadvertently encouraging the nation's slide into a barbaric future of dictatorship and endless war. To put this more positively, we might ask how could the United States build a popular culture appropriate to a peaceful and democratic society?

In this book, I have focused primarily on those stories that I could match to nonfiction accounts. These include stories about the origins of the Korean War, germ warfare charges, brainwashing, POW riots, atrocities, and comics with nuclear warfare themes. Focusing on these stories often turned out in practice to mean concentrating on comic book fictions that defended America's self-image as a moral nation from enemy propaganda charges.

To understand the pressures that put limits on the comic book versions of the Korean War, I have closely studied the record left by those who took an active interest in what messages the comics were teaching. These included critics, journalists, researchers, citizen activists, government investigators, and comic book industry cartoonists, editors and publishers.

Most comic book representations of the Korean War appeared in ordinary newsstand entertainment comics of the "war comics" genre.[5] The words "war" and "comics" make an abrasive combination. As Geoffrey Wagner noted in 1954, "you are apt to be rather surprised [...] when you see a soldier plunging his bayonet hilt-deep into the squashy chest of another under the word 'comic,'" and to be struck by a similar incongruity when *Famous Funnies* shows on its cover "reds being burnt alive by napalm bombs."[6] These jarring juxtapositions resulted from an accident of the English language, which calls works in this medium "comics" whether they are intended primarily for humor or for something else. Call the medium by another name (for example, comics creator Will Eisner proposed calling such works "Sequential Art") and that problem disappears.[7]

Most of my examples come from American war comics of the early 1950s, but at the time of the Korean War, comic books were recognized as a mass medium with many uses. I have also included examples of Cold War content from government-sponsored propaganda comics, political campaign comics, superhero comics, and educational comics. In addition, I have traced Korean War themes as they have appeared since the armistice was signed in 1953, including in underground comix, history comics, graphic novels and webcomics. I use just a few examples from comics published outside the United States.

The first comic book to respond to North Korea's June 25, 1950, invasion of South Korea carried a cover date of December 1950 (*War Comics #1*). Most of the major events of the war had happened in those six months between June and December. In the first days of the invasion, the United Nations passed a series of resolutions to support South Korea. By August 1950, the North Koreans had swept through 90 percent of South Korea.[8] In September, General MacArthur landed UN troops at Inchon, behind enemy lines, reversing the tide of the war.[9] UN soldiers then swept north through almost all of North Korea, reaching the Yalu River border with China. On Thanksgiving, the Americans still dreamed that they would be home for Christmas, and that they would leave behind a united Republic of Korea. Then the Chinese entered the war, and with the North Koreans, pushed the UN forces out of North Korea. By the dates printed on the first Korean War comics, the battle line lay close to the original line separating North and South Korea, at which point the war became stalemated for over two years of deadly fighting.

The 1953 armistice included plans for a peace conference, but when that conference was held in 1954, the diplomats failed to agree on a peace treaty. For years, the United States has resisted signing a Peace Treaty to end the war, and Koreans in the North and South have persisted in their dreams of ending the division of the Korean Peninsula.[10]

According to Fredric Wertham (whose words seem particularly relevant to the case of Korea's unfinished "forgotten war"), "Wherever violence is disregarded and forgotten, it perpetuates itself. Wherever it remains unresolved, it persists as a focus of infection." Wertham compared a "war without a proper peace" to "a murder which remains undetected, unpunished, and ununderstood." He warned that when past violence is not recorded, lamented, condemned and elucidated, "the seeds of future violence are sown."[11]

Although I have had a long time to think about Korean War comic books, this subject has many more aspects than I have had time to investigate. I say little in this book about how the fictions in Korean War comics compared to the inconceivable hells (and occasional joys) experienced by the soldiers who fought on its battlefields.[12] Most comic book stories about the war were combat stories, and they were appreciated by readers who could tell when an artist was accurately portraying the uniforms and weapons in the battles he drew. I did not develop the expertise to understand these comics on that level.

Also, I do not deal at length with the formal features of the comic book medium. Except in the captions to this book's illustrations, I have barely discussed the visual art of cartooning and the vital ways that graphic choices having to do with layout, composition, perspective, character design, body language, facial expressions, costuming, staging, panel transitions, backgrounds, lettering, inking, coloring, and so forth communicate the meanings of these stories. As a cartoonist and a cartooning instructor, I could have said more about these aspects of the work, much of which would have been complimentary to the skilled artists who drew many of these pages. Close descriptions of this type, though, would require another book as long as this one.[13]

I have mostly omitted discussion of other visual and entertainment media. I do discuss a few of the newspaper comic strips and cartoons that were especially influential on the look of war comic books. Comic strips reached a much larger readership than comic books, and several military adventure strips were popular during the Korean War. I look only briefly at short stories and novels, and mostly ignore television programs and movies.[14]

The images in Korean War comics differed greatly from those in films and photographs. For example, as far as I know, no photographer captured a shot during the Korean War of an American engaged in hand-to-hand combat with the enemy. In comic books, these scenes appeared often.[15] On the other hand, comic books very rarely showed cannons being fired, a predictable bit of excitement that appeared regularly in Korean War newsreels.

Of all the comic book genres, war comics most closely followed current events. This topical content makes them of particular interest as historical evidence, and yet more often than not, when comics historians have listed the comic book genres of this period, they have not mentioned war comics. The most controversial comics of that time were crime comics, superhero comics, romance comics and horror comics.[16]

In the years I worked on this manuscript, much of that generation of cartoonists and critics who lived through and participated in this history has died. Regrettably, I did not conduct more than a few interviews when I still had the chance. Through long experience as a comic book fan, I did have opportunities to sit down with or correspond with about a half dozen of the people who played an important part in this story, and I describe some of those brief encounters, sometimes in my notes.

I began my research in the 1980s in what seems like a different world. I traveled to great libraries when I could, including the New York Public Library, the Library of Congress, and

Michigan State University's Comic Art Collection, and eventually I practically moved into the University of Washington's libraries in Seattle. I found only small scraps of information that explicitly referred to Korean War comic books. Writing about this subject felt, at times, as though I were building a house out of twigs.[17]

I returned to this project after the Internet and World Wide Web had arrived. "Key-word searching" turned out to be perfectly suited to my method of picking up small bits of information from here and there. Through such searches, I uncovered a lot of material that has not previously been cited in histories of American comic books. The Web has also brought together an international community of comics scholars, which has helped me greatly.

The early generation of comics scholars had little alternative to assembling personal research collections. Fortunately, many of these comic books have now entered the public domain and are freely shared on the Web through The Digital Comic Museum and through Comic Book +.[18] The most serious omissions from these Web-posted collections are the comics published by the company now known as Marvel (which published the most war comics titles), the comics published by the company now known as DC (which published the most popular war comics), and the comics published by EC (which published the most critically acclaimed war comics).

This book differs from both histories of comics and histories of the Korean War. General histories of comic books have given very little space to war comics or ignored them completely. Also, many histories of comic books have taken a defensive approach (as can be determined most quickly by noticing how they describe the anti-comic book activism of Dr. Fredric Wertham). Focusing on war comics puts a different light on this pivotal period in the history of American comic books. In recent years, scholarly books on the subjects of propaganda and ideology in comic books have become plentiful. Even when these books focus on Cold War comics, though, they usually say little about the Korean War.[19] The few books specifically about war comics have also given little or no space to the Korean War.[20]

Just as the Korean War has been largely absent from histories of comic books, the many comic books about that war have been almost entirely missing from Korean War history books. Historian Paul M. Edwards, for example, has surveyed the representations of the Korean War in the press, radio, magazines, television, film, novels, poetry, essays, popular music, paintings, memorials and monuments, without ever mentioning comic books.[21] As far as I know, Jon Halliday and Bruce Cumings are the only authors of books about the Korean War who have mentioned these war comic books even in passing.[22] Adding the evidence from comic books into a history of the war can help bring to life how ordinary Americans tried to make sense of this conflict while it was being fought.

In my master's thesis (the first version of this book), I thanked my parents, Bert and Bernice Rifas and Mizue Fujinuma, each of whose love and support made this possible; my committee chair, Roger Simpson; my committee members; and Pat Dinning. I thank them again. I thank Denis Kitchen for instigating this project. Rather than simply listing those to whom I am gratefully indebted for their help in writing this book, I have scattered most of their names through the notes. Assembling them here would have shown that the community of researchers that I identify with most strongly has been comics scholars. In particular, I thank the participants in the Comics Scholars listserv for our many stimulating discussions.[23]

I thank Christine Hong for helpful comments on the entire manuscript, after I had completed my thesis but still many drafts ago. I enjoyed two years of stimulating e-mail correspondence with comics-scholarship gadfly Michael Feldman. I am glad to thank my old "Project Gen" friends, independent-scholar Fred Schodt for his comments on my draft, and arts-journalist Alan Gleason for editing help. I also feel honored to have received advice from John Lent, pioneering comics scholar and founding publisher of the International Journal of Comic Art (even if I did not act on most of his suggestions).

I thank some of my students at Seattle Central College and at the University of Washington in Bothell who have improved this book by advising me on the clarity of one or more of its chapters: Karen Taylor, Nicholas Rice, Huy Pham, Kitty Slocum and Dalia Swellum.

I have relied most heavily and gratefully on the libraries and librarians of the University of Washington, Seattle Central College, and the Seattle Public Library. I also thank the archivists and librarians in distant places who answered my e-mailed requests for information.[24]

Above all, I thank my wife and best friend, Mizue Fujinuma. She enriches my life beyond words. Thank you, Mbon.

I have never served in the military, never worked for a New York comic book publisher, am too young to remember the Korean War, speak only English, and took my first very short trip to Korea after I had already completed almost all of my research. My book ranges over a wide territory, much of which has been new to me, so if I have accidentally made some claim that will turn out to be scandalously ignorant, I emphasize that I accept full responsibility for the remaining errors, wherever they may be. Please send me a note if you find some.[25]

I have changed my interpretations of some of these comics and events enough times already that I expect I will be reinterpreting them again. I have provided many detailed footnotes to help the interested reader determine how much trust to put in the various parts of this account, and especially to help those who share my interest in continuing to look more deeply at how the comic books of the early 1950s might shed light on issues of our own times.

PART ONE

COMIC BOOKS
AND THE KOREAN WAR

1
◇◇◇◇◇◇◇◇◇

Introduction

American comic books reached the height of their popularity in the early 1950s. At that time, in the brief interval between the temporary collapse of Hollywood's movie industry and the full arrival of television, comic books were a true "mass medium" and were read regularly by most boys and girls and by many adults, both men and women. With stories of romance, talking animals, crime, fantasy, westerns, horror, adventure, and well-groomed teenagers, comic books had something for everyone. When the Korean War broke out in 1950, the comic book industry responded with a flood of war comics The Korean War supplied the subject matter for over a hundred (mostly short-lived) war comics titles, and the setting for probably several thousand comic book stories.[1] Korean War comics provide a rich body of work for studying how details of an ongoing event changed as they were translated into popular fiction and into nonfiction comics.

In recent years, North Korea's growing nuclear and missile capabilities have reminded the world that the conflict in Korea remains unresolved. North Korea, the most militarized nation on earth, never accepted the permanence of the 1953 Armistice Agreement that had established the revised borderline between North and South Korea.[2] South Korea, also refusing to accept the permanent division of Korea, never signed that agreement.[3] The United States still has several tens of thousands of military personnel stationed in South Korea.

People understand a "comic book version" of past events to mean one that includes invention, exaggeration and distortion, but especially oversimplification. By recovering some of the lost puzzle pieces that cartoonists did not know about or did not use when they fictionalized this conflict, we can create a more complete and very different picture of the Korean War. We can also see that even in comic books, American Cold War culture had some complexities of its own.

This project does not describe the Korean War merely as background information for understanding war comics, and does not use war comics merely as a way to introduce readers to a history of the Korean War. It focuses on *both* comic books *and* the Korean War (and, in doing so, it reinterprets the anti-comic book movement). My research project looks at war comic books as a missing piece for making sense of the most dramatic period in the history of American comic books; it sees the Korean War as a national tragedy for Korea and as a turning point in world history.[4]

With "wandering back and forth" between comic books and histories as one's research method, the paths that a study follows will be greatly influenced by the researcher's class background, personal history, tastes and goals.[5] This becomes increasingly true as the focus widens from describing the Korean War comic books themselves to setting them in contexts and interpreting their meaning. I hope that further introducing myself here might help readers understand some of the perspectives with which I began this work. The following self-description emphasizes the roles of war and comic books in my life.

A Long Story of How I Came to Write This Book

I describe myself as a third generation American, born in 1951, and raised in a Northern California suburb in a mainstream-liberal, reform-Jewish, professional-class household. I did not read war comics or play with war toys when I was young. Instead I read Donald Duck comics and played with chemistry sets.

I do not remember how, as a child, I came to think of the whole idea of war as something profoundly horrible. The only military-related object I can remember as being on display in my house when I was growing up was a framed photograph that sat alone for decades on top of my father's dresser. It showed his older brother Leonard, smiling in his U.S. Army Air Corps uniform.[6] My uncle Leonard went missing in action during World War II over the English Channel, and two of my cousins and I were named after him.

In 1968, when I was in high school, I became an envelope-licking volunteer for our local "Peace Center," a small anti-war group which I had discovered by visiting their booth at the County Fair. When I turned 18, I applied to my draft board for Conscientious Objector status. I remember thinking as I wrote the required essay to ask their permission to be excused from military service that the problem of finding a balance between the duties of a citizen and the requirements of conscience had no easy answers.

My anti-war feelings had been strongly reinforced by my fear of the draft, and the first author I encountered who made a principled argument against conscription was the essayist Ayn Rand.[7] (She also wrote novels, but I found those unreadable.)

Ayn Rand's work started me thinking about philosophy, but I lost interest in her writings around the time that I became a Philosophy major at the University of California, Berkeley.[8] I earned my B.A. degree in 1973. The circle of my closest friends in those days was built around our shared love of playing music and drawing amateur comics.

I entered comics publishing through the underground comix movement of the late 1960s, a movement which reinvented comic books as a medium of uncensored personal expression.[9] Beginning in the 1970s, I developed a specialty in creating comics that supported an alternative vision of the future based on a decentralized economy that valued local self-reliance.[10]

When I lived in San Francisco's Mission District, one or more of my educational comic book titles were sold in almost every bookstore in my neighborhood.[11] My comic book about nuclear power could be sold across the political spectrum (from communist to libertarian) because it described a situation in which pursuit of profits, in a market heavily distorted by government subsidies, appeared to be causing serious threats to public health and safety.

Starting in 1978, I spent a year in Princeton, Wisconsin, working for Denis Kitchen's comic book publishing company (Kitchen Sink) as an associate editor while continuing my own publishing company (EduComics) on the side.[12] I've forgotten the details, but that year I read something that described my company as a publisher of "political" comic books. Although this had been accurate, I thought it unfair for the reviewer to stigmatize my comics supporting anti-nuclear protest as "political" while seeming to accept the New York comic books that pictured protesters as dupes or fools simply as "entertainment."[13] The negative image of activists that I saw in mainstream comics felt wrong and definitely "political." This led me to think about healthy and unhealthy ways that "entertainment" acts as a political force.[14]

I soon concluded that the kinds of changes I hoped to see would require not only the small-scale circulation of alternative ideas but a direct challenge to mainstream entertainment, highlighting and criticizing some aspects of the culture that binds us together. I had the idea of writing a history of how entertainment comics have dramatized the Cold War, as a relatively simple way to prove to comic book readers that entertainment comic books *also* had "political" content. As it turned out, though, I did not get to that writing project right away.

About ten years later, Denis Kitchen reminded me of my old plan to write *Cold War Comics*, and invited me to sit down and do it. By then, I was no longer publishing comic books, but I remained very interested in how media shape our lives. I decided to write a history of Cold War comic books under academic supervision as my master's thesis.

My thesis advisor told me that he did not know about comic books, but he did know about master's theses, and that the topic of comic book representations of the whole Cold War had to be cut down to something more manageable. In this way, I came to focus on how American comic books represented the Korean War.

I finished my M.A. thesis in 1991.[15] Denis Kitchen had offered to publish it, but the manuscript spent years in his editor's filing cabinet while I went on to other things.

In 2008, I accepted an invitation to update and revise my thesis for publication as this book. Much had changed since 1991. Most importantly, the USSR dissolved in 1991, and it looked as though the Cold War had finally ended.[16] Comic book scholarship had seemed unusual in 1991, but since then an international network of scholars specializing in the study of comics has sprung into existence with regular conferences, journals, and college and university courses.[17] Thanks especially to square-bound "graphic novels," comics have won recognition as a fully legitimate medium of art and literature. Media studies and cultural studies, including cultural studies of the Cold War, also blossomed, and have illustrated in many ways how popular entertainment expresses political perspectives.[18] The idea that entertainment comic books express political views has become widely understood and relatively uncontroversial.[19] (As I found out, the idea that entertainment comic strips and comic books function as powerful channels of political propaganda had been repeatedly noticed in the 1940s and 1950s.) Still, the sharp contrasts between what historians have learned about the Korean War and what the comic books of that time had said about it can make that point especially clear.

An Organized Collection of Scraps and Asides

Much of what has been written about Korean War comic books has come as small scraps of information. Since the references to my own work, in studies of comic books and elsewhere, have also usually consisted of small scraps, I understand how misleading such tangential remarks can be. A personal example here will illustrate how this method of collecting little bits of information can help us gain insight if we consider each bit critically and do not exaggerate its importance. This example will also show how a history based on a documentary record can come out very differently from history as remembered by those who participated in it.

My own one-man comic book company, EduComics, has appeared only once in the Congressional Record. At a Congressional Hearing on Children's Fears of Nuclear War in 1983, Congressman Thomas Bliley of Virginia challenged those who claimed that America's reliance on nuclear weapons frightens children, asking them to show some concern about "nuclear war curricula" which frighten schoolchildren and immerse them in "fear, guilt and despair." His ultimate "example of just how far this business of scaring children has gone" was a comic book that I had published which was originally written and drawn in Japan by a survivor of the atomic bombing of Hiroshima. Bliley arranged for its six goriest comic book pages to be included as part of the published record of those hearings. He concluded his opening statement by saying that "Anyone concerned with the fears of children, ought likewise to be concerned with such teaching tools as this little book."[20] One might guess that having one of my company's comic books singled out for criticism in this very public way formed a memorable part of my history as a publisher, and it did … twenty-three years later when, to my complete astonishment, I discovered his testimony for the first time while "ego-surfing" in a library database. No one had told me about it before that (and no one has mentioned it to me since then).[21]

Bliley's statement misleadingly suggests that I republished that comic book for American *children*.[22] Although it had no apparent consequences, Bliley's testimony does suggest that if I had attempted to expand my circulation through public schools, I would have encountered resistance—based on the fact that the comics I republished showed nuclear war as *scary*.[23] In a later chapter, I describe a clearer example of resistance to an anti-militarist comic book being made available in schools, the case of *Real War Stories*.

In this book, I collect many small examples of such incidents that show how various kinds of "political" content in American comic books have been supported or resisted, sometimes weakly, sometimes powerfully, by people inside and outside of the comic book industry. Sometimes people have succeeded in keeping material that they don't like from reaching the newsstands. Sometimes controversial comics have found ways to reach appreciative readers.

Sampling Korean War Comic Books

I assembled most of my research collection of hundreds of war comics from beat-up copies that I saw for sale in comic book shops or at comic book conventions, found interesting and could afford to buy. Later I picked up a few more over the Web, including a few from long-time comics retailer Bob Beerbohm.[24] I also looked at a few old war comic books held by libraries, and bought the reprinted boxed sets of Harvey Kurtzman's celebrated series *Two-Fisted Tales* and *Frontline Combat*. Some stories I found posted on the web, and scans or photos of some of the stories that I discuss were shared with me by other comics scholars.

Even in the small literature about Korean War comics, a disagreement has appeared that raises the problem of how to sample this material. William W. Savage, Jr., concluded from his study of Cold War comic books that in Korean War comics American soldiers "dropped like flies." Geoffrey Wagner, as will be described below, complained in 1954 that in American comic books about the Korean War "no one, except the enemy, gets hurt." Their disagreement comes down to whether we should regard these comic books in general as something akin to "the only substantial body of public antiwar literature in the early 1950s" (Savage) or as a literature that could have been "sponsored by draft boards" (Wagner).[25]

Most war comics make their explicit statements about the origins, histories and meanings of the wars they depict only in scattered captions and a few bits of dialogue. When pulled together, the intermittent hints in their words and pictures add up to views of the world. Partly because the stories provide arenas in which different points of view compete rather than fully worked-out and consistent "ideological positions," readers can come away with different ideas of what lessons the comics taught, depending on which examples they read and how they interpreted them.

For any generalization that a critic or scholar might reach about Korean War comic books, exceptions might remain to be discovered. One of the delights in collecting comic books consists precisely in the way that surprising old oddities continue to turn up, even after years of looking. Within their limits, war comics communicated a variety of perspectives.

The Korean War in Other Combatants' Comics

During the Korean War, almost all of the regularly appearing comic book series about that conflict were originally published in the United States. (Some American war comics were republished in Australia, Canada and the United Kingdom.) Other nations participating in that war also produced comic books, and some of them produced comic books about the Korean War.

Korea

The Korean comic book industry barely existed in 1950, but Korean cartoonists did create a few irregularly published, locally popular comic books. These included some that supported the South Korean war effort, for example Kim Jung-rae's *Bool Geun Tang* (*Red Land*), and Kim Yong-hwan's *Tot'ori Yongsa* (*Brave Soldier Tot'ori*), which started in 1952 and lasted for four issues.[26] In 1952, an American photographed a boy in South Korea as he examined a display of Korean comic books that were being sold on the street. The forty or more comic books were hung from their spines on five cords that were strung across a wooden plank fence.[27]

In 1951, one of the founders of the field of Communications Research, Wilbur Schramm, co-authored an article that summarized the comics situation in North Korea this way:

> Comics in sovietized Korea were no more for entertainment than were the other media. [...] Unlike American comics, however, they tended to be single-frame cartoons rather than continued serials. Some of the cartoons were signed by Russian artists; others not signed were in the familiar biting style of *Pravda*. It is reasonable to suppose that in the production of this material considerable help came from the center of the Communist world.[28]

The Korean War eventually became a major theme of North Korean comics, beginning decades later.[29]

In American war comic books, the Americans did almost all of the fighting to defend the recently formed Republic of Korea. Although the South Korean army had more men under the United Nations command than any other nation and suffered far higher casualties than the American military, in American war comics these South Korean soldiers made only infrequent appearances.[30]

China

In the recently established People's Republic of China, another participant in the Korean War, "comic book" sales grew quickly during that conflict. (These were *lianhuanhua*, small, illustrated story books, with one captioned picture on each page.) At first, most of the Chinese publishing industry was still in private hands, and from the revolutionaries' point of view, most of their comics were "feudalistic" and "reactionary."[31] In summer, 1952, the communists confiscated almost 20,000 comics in the capital city of Beijing.[32] By 1953, the Communist Party had gained control of all publishing in China, and their rules required that all politically incorrect comics were to be sent to the Public Security Bureau for burning.[33] In practice, though, their censorship of "reactionary," "absurd," and "obscene" novels and comics remained far from complete.[34] A later chapter describes a Chinese comic book about the Korean War.

United Kingdom

Worldwide, British war comics (focused primarily on World Wars I and II) appear to have been more popular and influential than American war comics.[35] British war comics have not been republished in the United States, or distributed in the U.S. on a large scale.

Britain's *Eagle* helped to inaugurate the "Golden Age" of British comics when it appeared in April 1950. As Adam Riches tells the story, that series began as a project to use this medium "to convey to the child the right kind of standards, values and attitudes, combined with the necessary amount of excitement and adventure," in contrast to American comic books, which were seen as "deplorable, nastily over-violent and obscene." In its early years, the title focused on adventure and fantasy, rather than war fiction.[36]

Of the sixteen members of the United Nations whose military personnel joined with the South Koreans in fighting the Korean War, the United States sent 88 percent and Britain was in second place with 4 percent of the total. (Canada and Turkey sent almost 2 percent each and Australia almost 1 percent.)

Canada

The Golden Age of Canadian comic books ended before the Korean War began. It lasted from 1941 to 1946, thanks to the Canadian government responding to a trade imbalance with the United States by banning the importation of American fictional magazines, including comic books.[37] During World War II, Canadian publishers and cartoonists rushed to meet Canadian children's demand for comics with original material by Canadian cartoonists.

After World War II, the rules changed to allow Canadian publishers to republish American comics, and the publishers found this much cheaper than commissioning new work. By 1948, all Canadian comic books were reprints of U.S. comic books (except for some with original art that Superior Comics commissioned from a studio in New York).[38] That year, a mass movement against "crime comic books" swept Canada. When Canada passed a law against crime comics in 1949, as John Bell comments in his history of Canadian comic books, "everyone from the PTA to the Communist Party of Canada breathed a collective sigh of relief" that action had been taken against "foreign cultural trash."[39]

During the Korean War, some of the republished American comics would include

Two-Fisted Tales, Frontline Combat, U.S. Paratroops, U.S. Fighting Air Force, and *U.S. Tank Commandoes.*[40]

By 1951, the Korean War had stimulated the Canadian economy to the point where the restrictions on the imports of American comic books were removed. U.S. comic books flooded in, which quickly drove the Canadian comic book publishers out of business.[41]

Turkey

American adventure comic strips with speech balloons and continuing stories arrived in Turkey in the 1930s, appearing in children's magazines and newspapers.[42] During World War II, it became harder for Turkish publishers to import American comics, and this allowed some Italian comics of the Western genre to become popular and some local, Turkish cartoonists to succeed. Turkish comic books began in 1951 with one of these Italian Western characters, *Pecos Bill.* The Turkish genre of "heroic" comics provided escapist stories set in the days of Genghis Khan or even earlier, in the time of the Hun Empire, rather than dramatizing contemporary wars.[43]

Turks appeared in several Korean War comic books published in the United States. The story "Flaming Coffin" in *G-I in Battle #8* (1953) emphasizes that it is depicting the Turkish allies in Korea, referring to "Turks" or "Turkey" in six panels of an eight-page story. All we learn about these Turks is that they are apparently devout Muslims, calling on "Allah" in nine panels and the Prophet in an additional two. The star and crescent appear on their helmets and tank.

During the Korean War, members of the Turkish Brigade reintroduced Islam to Korea, and after the war founded the Korea Muslim Society and built the first mosque in South Korea in 1955.[44]

Australia

Very few pages of war comics were published in Australia during World War II, but during the Korean War, Australian comic books were filled with anti-communist war stories.[45] Most of these were reprints of U.S. comic books, but others were made by Australians.

Australian-drawn Korean War comics were created by John Dixon in his popular series *Tim Valour* (circa 1948–1957) and *The Crimson Comet* (circa 1949–1957).[46] Others included Norman Clifford's *Sky Demons* and *Billy Battle* and Terry Murphy's *Sky Hawk.*[47]

As in Canada, World War II restrictions on importation of American comic books to protect currency reserves made possible the rise of a local comic book industry, and as in Canada, the eventual lifting of these restrictions hurt local publishers. As in Canada, anti-comic book campaigns led to censorship of comic books.[48]

In 1953 and 1954, Australian Communist Party members campaigned against American war comics as part of a larger protest against mass media messages that were conditioning children for a future of war, violence and hatred. Comic books such as *War Heroes, Atomic Attack, The United States Marines* and *Soldier* were forced from Australian newsstands.[49]

Formula Fiction

To convert current events into reader-pleasing comic book stories, the vast majority of Korean War comic book stories simply followed the recipe that John Cawelti has identified as the essence of "formula fiction": they packaged together suspense and excitement with reassurance and reaffirmation.[50] War becomes a setting for safely exploring extremes of anger, pain, fear, hate, guilt, competition, sacrifice and duty (and the positive themes of service, self-mastery, fraternity, ecstasy, redemption and victory).

Creators of popular culture have used war as a natural subject for melodramas, told in ways that express people's hopes and fears. We may suppose that the success of a war effort partly depends on how well the nation's popular culture can mythologize that struggle.[51]

Americans had difficulty making the Korean War conform to the requirements of formula fiction. For example, the reluctance to continue pushing for a total victory after being driven out of North Korea made a poor fit with formulaic expectation that in the end, good action heroes will predictably triumph over evil bad guys.[52] Still, the popular fiction formulas had a powerful effect in shaping how the events of the Korean War were transformed into comic book entertainment.

Based on the stories they created, the cartoonists, while giving their readers much to think about, usually intended primarily to stimulate our feelings. To experience their work as "entertainment" means to read the comics on an emotional level.[53] Still, reading old war comics against the grain as commentaries on contemporary events brings them to life in a different way.

2

xxxxxxxxxx

Realism, Harm
and Responsibility

The project of comparing facts with cartoonists' fictions has been open to several long-standing criticisms. In 1965, George J. Lockwood dismissed Daniel J. Leab's examination of the Cold War content of newspaper comic strips with these words:

> Steve Canyon a misrepresentation of actuality? Happy Easter do harm? Dean Wilderness a question of journalistic responsibility? Oh come now, Mr. Leab. Who says that the comics are meant to be factual?[1]

These questions concisely express three challenges to investigations of comics' historical content: first, that we should not expect fiction to accurately represent reality; second, that we have no reason to fear that these stories will have any harmful influence; and third, that fiction authors should not be bound by the same standards as journalists. Since history and fiction pursue different ends by different means, they must be judged by different standards. At the outset, then, some relationships between histories and stories, between fact and fiction, need to be sorted out.[2]

Fact and Fiction

The first of Lockwood's three questions suggested that works of fiction should not be measured by their conformity to the facts. Actually, comic books never had a chance to realistically convey the experiences of those who fought in Korea. For one thing, several memoirs of those who went to Korea to fight emphasize that they were greeted on their arrival by the revolting, inescapable smell of human shit being used to fertilize the fields.[3] By contrast, many older comic fans remember with great pleasure the smell of the colored inks on cheap paper with which these war stories originally were printed, and have an equal fondness for the moldy odor of old comic books.

Fantasy and Reality: "The Adventure of the Flying Discs"

War comics seemed "realistic" mostly by contrast to other comics that seemed "fantastic." Unlike World War II's superhero adventures, Korean War comic books usually tried to keep the two categories of fantasy-based comics and reality-based comics separate. One of the first comic book stories to respond to the Korean War, however, was an imaginative, 12-page Buck Rogers piece, "The Adventure of the Flying Discs." This was published in the first issue of a series of Buck Rogers comic books with a cover date of January 1951.[4] Looking at it closely shows how even some very fictional stories took inspiration from and made comments on the news of the day.

It seems appropriate that the science fiction comic strip character Buck Rogers would take an interest in the Korean War. That character's long history with Asian villains began in his first comic strip adventure in 1929. In that origin story, he awakes 500 years in the future to find that Mongols from the Gobi Desert have conquered America, forcing the Americans to flee into the woods where they are hunted for sport by the Oriental invaders.[5] When Buck Rogers, a World War I veteran, revives in 2429, he quickly joins the war against the "Mongol Reds," whose "Chink Emperor," immodestly self-described as "Buddha's gift to women," has directed his lascivious attention to Buck's friend Wilma.[6]

In the 1951 comic book story "The Adventure of the Flying Discs," Buck Rogers joins a scientist in an experiment to "fly faster than time dimension speed." When "coming in over Korosa," to their surprise, they are greeted with enemy fire from "some strange, primitive people ... using weapons that went out of date 500 years ago." Buck Rogers realizes that they must have arrived in 1950, when, in "the last war ever fought in Korosa," history records that "the United Nations were fighting the Communist invaders!" (The uncredited writer apparently thought that the Korean War would end before 1951.) Buck Rogers sets his ray gun on atomic blast and blows a hole in the fence of a prisoner of war camp. He is surprised when the American soldier he has rescued turns out, under her helmet, to be a sexy girl reporter.[7] In 1950, Buck Rogers finds other flying saucers which had traveled back in time and, without a scientist to help them, had been unable to make their way back to the 25th century. Since they have found themselves back in 1950, Buck Rogers decides they can end the Korosan war by using 25th century technology. The captions explain that:

> That night ... the strangest battle in the history of the world took place ... a battle in which not one person was killed or injured! Flying saucers came down out of the sky.... Communist artillery shells exploded harmlessly on them.... Then the "Bombs of Peace" fell ... exploding high in the air! A strange sweet-smelling gas floated toward Earth, and men fell asleep at their guns!

Buck Rogers then contacts General Douglas MacArthur at United Nations Supreme Command in Japan, to ask the initially incredulous general to:

> Order your armies to advance ... but do not fire! All the Communists are asleep ... and will remain asleep for one week! Destroy their arms and peace will rule on Earth! All nations will live in peace now ... because if anyone else tries aggression, I will return and make short work of them!

Although a science-fiction fantasy, this use of gas was possibly inspired by recent news stories. In April 1950, General Anthony C. McAuliffe's revelation that the United States was working on a new generation of chemical weapons that attacked the nervous system had set off a wave of speculation, which included the widespread misconception that these new weapons caused temporary incapacitation rather than death.[8]

In May 1950, *Time* magazine imagined that these weapons:

> ...would be sprayed over enemy cities by planes in the same way that whole areas are sprayed with mosquito-killing DDT, paralyzing the whole population. Then the attacking army, equipped with protective masks, would march in and take over.[9]

Juxtaposing a news item and comic book fiction in this way does not prove any direct influence. Paralyzing gasses had already made an appearance in Buck Rogers' very first comic strip appearance on January 7, 1929. There Buck explained that he had been preserved in a state of suspended animation for 500 years by a "peculiar gas which had defied chemical analysis."[10]

When the Korean War began, the United States, over the objections of its Army and Air Force, reaffirmed its "use in retaliation only" policy for chemical weapons.[11] At the same time, the United States rapidly expanded its chemical weapons program to be prepared to retaliate against Soviet first use if necessary.[12]

The recent arrival of the atomic bomb in 1945 and the beginning of a wave of "flying saucer" sightings in 1947 had made the lines between science and science fiction more uncertain.[13] Sightings of flying saucers in Korea by American pilots were reported as news in 1951 and 1952.[14] The flying saucers that appeared in several stories drawn in the "realistic" genre of war comics were American or Russian experimental weapons, and not arrivals from distant planets or the far future.[15] The most entertaining comic books about flying saucers in Korea, though, were those few that strayed further into worlds of the imagination, such as Buck Rogers' "Adventure of the Flying Discs" or, especially, "Captain Marvel and the Riddle of the Space Reds."[16] That Captain Marvel story begins with flying saucers shooting American soldiers in Korea and goes on to show that these saucers are from the Planet Pluto, whose inhabitants have formally allied themselves with the communists in Korea because they "despise freedom and democracy such as your America has."[17]

Fiction and Propaganda: "Panmunjom Treachery"

War and espionage comics, especially during the early 1950s, frequently situated themselves at the crossroads between fact ("a true war story") and fiction ("any resemblance to persons living or dead is coincidental"). With the benefit of hindsight, we can often sort out these two strands better than the comics' original readers could. A few comics stories set out to reveal as accurately as they could what had happened in a particular incident. Other stories took news reports only as starting points for works of the imagination. Only a few cartoonists felt a need to create a truthful picture of the war. Even those who did have a passion for accuracy continued to see themselves primarily as entertainers and not as documentarians.

Because American soldiers have not fought on American soil in living memory, people in the U.S. depend to an unusually large degree on media images to understand the realities of war. If the extent to which these images falsify, prettify, idealize, oversimplify, and distort war remains unclear, this confusion can encourage unending catastrophes.[18]

Comic book fictions can be criticized for getting their factual elements wrong without arguing that they should have been more "realistic." If anything, the ideas, metaphors, and images of Korean War comics resembled those presented as factual by journalists, historians, and politicians of that time *too closely*. A body of stories becomes "excessively realistic" when it fails to explore alternative perspectives, to challenge prevailing ideas, to provide a refuge for escape or to light a path to liberation.

Surprisingly often, cartoonists invented stories that turned current examples of anti–American propaganda into anti-communist propaganda presented as entertainment. For example, the plot of "Panmunjom Treachery" in *U.S. Fighting Air Force #3*, January 1953, goes like this:

> A jet with American markings strafes the tents at Panmunjom, Korea, where the Chinese, North Kore-
> ans, and Americans are negotiating to end the war. This threatens to cause a breakdown of the peace

talks, but it turns out to have been "MIGs bearing American markings! Looks like another stinking Gook trick to prolong the talks." The Americans disguise their own jets as MIGs, and shoot the enemy planes down when they return to repeat the deception.[19]

In fact, American planes strafed the truce talk sites in Korea on several occasions. The first time, the Americans denied responsibility and claimed that the communists had fabricated the evidence.[20] On subsequent occasions the United States apologized for strafing the negotiation site, and called it an accident.[21] When deciding whether to understand a series of strafing attacks as a deliberate American attempt to sabotage the peace talks or a hoax staged for communist propaganda purposes, a cartoonist will tend to accept the views of his or her own side.[22]

People commonly argue that fiction cannot harm readers because the readers can recognize the difference between real facts and make believe. This example and many like it, however, suggest that a reader might either underestimate or overestimate a story's factual content and also that news stories can appear to confirm fictional information.

During the Korean War, American readers frequently accused the newspapers of not printing the truth about what was happening in Korea.[23] In 1952, Korean War reporter Robert C. Miller told the Nevada Editors Conference that these dissatisfied readers were correct. Miller informed them that military censors (who took over in Korea after a half year of "voluntary censorship" had failed to adequately protect military security) were inappropriately suppressing stories that the public had a right to know; that most Korean war news originated from the military's self-serving public relations offices; that reporters, swayed by "excellent food, good companionship and good liquor freely poured" by military publicity agents, held back from writing stories that would endanger their continued access to these privileges; and even that some of the articles that they submitted for publication were simply fiction:

> There are certain facts and stories from Korea that editors and publishers have printed which were pure fabrication.
> You didn't know that when you printed them. Many of us who sent the stories knew they were false, but we had to write them for they were official releases from responsible military headquarters, and were released for publication even though the people responsible knew they were untrue.[24]

Laboratory experiments have shown that even stories that we know are fictions influence what we understand to be fact.[25] The various difficulties of sorting out facts and fictions lead to Lockwood's second objection, concerning the harm or harmlessness of comic book stories.

Harmful and Beneficial Consequences

The charge that reading comic books might have harmful consequences has remained a sensitive issue for some comics fans. During the period surrounding the Korean War, a public controversy raged over the possible effects of comic books on their young readers. At that time, many mothers threw away their children's bizarre and disturbing comic book collections, supposedly for their own good. A generation of outraged children grew up hotly rejecting the idea that comic books could "influence" their behavior.

It seems reasonable to suppose that this body of texts—Korean War comics, which impressionable readers hoarded, traded, minutely studied, acted out, copied, scribbled on, dreamed about, or even plagiarized for classroom writing assignments—had some impact on their readers' thoughts, attitudes, feelings and behavior. It also seems probable that young readers found much of what went on in these comics baffling or irrelevant.[26]

Propaganda in the Comics

In the years approaching the United States' entry into World War II, several writers had recognized comic strips and comic books as powerful propaganda media. The article "Propaganda in the Comic Strips," prepared by the Institute for Propaganda Analysis, appeared in *Scholastic* magazine in May 1940, illustrated with a panel from the *Superman* comic strip.[27] It reported that:

> Propaganda in the comics which is definitely planned and which utilizes the devices of name-calling, glittering generalities, and card-stacking is fairly new. However it has not been able to escape the eye of the editors who believe that the comics should entertain but not influence opinion. But you have probably discovered that a great deal of effective propaganda is unintentional. Probably we have all had mind pictures formed by the comics which we are not aware of.

Shortly before the attack on Pearl Harbor that brought the United States into World War II, two more articles summarized the case for regarding newspaper comic strips as a significant, unsuspected medium for propaganda.[28] As with the work of the Institute for Propaganda Analysis, most of their arguments could also apply to the war comic books of the early 1950s (especially since some comic books continued to be reformatted reprints of newspaper comics). In "Comic Strip Propaganda," Gerald W. Movius compared the subtle propaganda in comic strips (a popular, simple-to-understand, cheap and frequent medium) to the better-recognized "dangerous and insidious pro-war propaganda" that appeared in other media:

> Newsreel propaganda is sharp, shocking; radio propaganda is delivered in an authoritative tone; newspaper columnists twist arguments around like pretzels and leave less widely read persons confused; the magazines prey on sentimentality.
> But comic strips catch readers in their most relaxed moments.[29]

In "Propaganda in the Funnies," Fred Latimer Hadsel noticed that serial comic strips were reproduced in huge numbers across the whole nation, and were eagerly read by an uncritical, unsuspecting audience who turn to them, not to consciously examine the political themes and ideas they carry, but simply as a form of "entertainment." Hadsel proposed that comic strips were an extraordinarily powerful propaganda medium for shaping their readers' prejudices and sympathies: "Since more people are reached through the comics than by any other part of a newspaper, what is to be found there may well be more effective in molding public opinion than anything written by reporters, editors and columnists."[30]

Interpreting the Comics

Because we make our own meanings when we read a comic book story, rather than merely unwrapping neatly packaged messages that the author has put into it, we cannot deduce from the content of Korean War comic books exactly how they were understood or regarded by their original readers. Judging from published letters to editors, readers interpreted the various war comics in various ways. Some readers were encouraged by war comics to become or to fall in love with soldiers.[31] Some gained a warm feeling of patriotic belonging. Some found in war comics a message about war's futility.[32] Many seemed to focus narrowly on how accurately the weapons and uniforms were illustrated.

Despite the differences in how people read them, the overall messages in war comics are not completely invented in the minds of their readers. Of all the possible stories that can be told, comic books keep coming back to a few basic images that, through massive repetition, become normal, accepted, and taken for granted.

No reliable way exists to infer the "effects" of these comics on their first readers. It has become hard to even determine who read them. Many decades have passed. Rather than being unique to comic books, the political perspectives that they conveyed also appeared in booklets, pamphlets, radio broadcasts, film and television and the news media, and so the comics must be understood as having been elements in a larger media landscape.[33] The content of the comics cannot even serve as a reliable guide to what the artists and writers who churned them out were thinking.

Radical cartoonist Spain (Spain Rodriguez, 1940–2012) included a sequence in his autobiographical comic "My Cold War" in which he remembered how he had been influenced by war comics. In one panel, he represents his father and his "cousin who had been in the Air Force in WWII" reading one of his *Blackhawk* comic books. (Based on its cover, Spain suggests that they were looking at the June 1950 issue.) His father says "They really want a war. You can even see it in these comic books." In the next panel, Spain describes becoming an anti-communist at about this time, and insightfully comments that rather than understanding where he had acquired such notions as that "factory owners should be free to do whatever they want with their own property," these had "seemed like original ideas."[34]

Education and the Comics

Many writers considered the possibility that comic books, in addition to their function as entertainment, also might have "good" effects, as an educational medium.[35] One of comic books' most frequently mentioned, unambiguously "good" educational services was to support the American war effort in World War II.[36] By the time of the Korean War, the military had found many uses for cartoon illustrations. For example, teachers were using specially designed, fill-in-the-balloon comic books at the Army's language school in Monterey, California.[37] American soldiers received heavily illustrated, cartoony pamphlets to explain what they were doing in Korea.[38]

During this period, Will Eisner, one of the most celebrated cartoonists in the history of comic books, while working for the Army created some of the most important examples of educational cartooning. When Eisner had served in the Army during World War II, he had been assigned to work on *Army Motors*, a publication to teach proper methods of maintaining equipment. Eisner improved it by adding comics-format instructional features.[39] An adjutant general in charge of technical manuals objected to the comics format, but repeated testing proved Eisner's comics to be easier to read, understand and remember compared to the standard technical manuals.[40] *Army Motors* ended with the end of World War II, but the Korean War led to a successor publication, *P.S.: The Preventive Maintenance Monthly*. Eisner won a contract to create six issues of this magazine.[41] The first issue appeared in June 1951, and rather than ending with the armistice in Korea as originally intended, it continued until 2019. Eisner served as art director for its first two decades.[42]

Educational comic books were used not just to aid the military effort, but also to explain the stakes of the Cold War competition between communism and capitalism to civilian readers. After the Second World War, business interests who felt threatened by government regulation and by labor unions conducted major (and highly successful) "economic education" propaganda campaigns to promote "free enterprise," using every available medium, including (in a minor role) comic books.[43] As with Eisner's work for the Army, this campaign produced an example of the effectiveness of comic books as an educational medium being formally tested and verified. The Bemis Brothers Bag Company hired The Psychological Corporation of New York to do a study which confirmed what the company had found with its 10,000 employees:

> That the comic-type booklet [...] entitled "How Stalin Hopes We Will Destroy America" [...] prepared by Pictorial Media, Inc. of New York under supervision of the Gardner Advertising Agency, had a distinct effect in changing the attitude of Bemis employees and their families.[44]

In the early 1950s, thinking about media in terms of their "effects" received a large boost. With the recent experience of "total war" in World War II, and at a time of intense ideological conflict between "East" and "West," scholars focused on mass communication in relation to "psychological warfare."[45]

Social Responsibility

Lockwood's third question ("Dean Wilderness a question of journalistic responsibility?") raises the issue of ethics. Comic book writers do not share journalists' responsibility to communicate reliable information that can be recognized as factual even by people who interpret it differently. The responsibilities of cartoonists included getting their pages in on time and providing a dime's worth of enjoyment in a ten-cent comic book. Beyond these professional obligations, Harvey Kurtzman, the editor of the two most celebrated Korean War comic book series, thought comics had a responsibility to present a more realistic view of the *costs* of war:

> ...you *have* a responsibility, and these guys feeding this crap to the children that soldiers spend their time merrily killing little buck-toothed yellow men with the butt of a rifle is terrible....[46]

A cartoonist's "social responsibility" does not consist in conformity to a particular political agenda. Although many comic books fed the political "paranoia" and "hysteria" that these times are remembered for, their irresponsibility came in how they told their stories rather than who they chose as their villains. Cartoonists had good reasons to draw anti-communist comics. During the early 1950s, the Soviet Union, led by Joseph Stalin, had begun building an arsenal of atomic bombs. Under his rule, over a million Soviet citizens had been executed, 16–17 million had spent time in in forced labor camps, and 3–5 million had died in (or been killed by) famines in the Ukraine.[47] Under Stalin, the Soviet Union had forcibly relocated entire nationalities, beginning in 1937 with an order which led to all ethnic Koreans in the Russian Far East (over 170,000 people) being put in filthy freight cars and deported, mostly to distant Uzbekistan, Turkmenistan and Kazakhstan.[48] Nevertheless, Stalin was idolized by the worldwide communist movement as a great leader of a noble experiment. His weapons programs had progressed faster than expected thanks to networks of spies. The Soviet Union had just completed establishing its power over Eastern Europe.[49] Under Mao Zedong, communists had won the Civil War in China in 1949, which would have comparably bloody consequences. The Communist Party of the USA. took its orders from Moscow, and in 1949, in a Manhattan courtroom, its leaders were judged guilty of conspiring to advocate the violent overthrow of the U.S. government (at some unspecified time in the future). The Party recently had been exposed as involved in Soviet espionage against the United States.[50]

From a different perspective, cartooning against nuclear weapons, colonialism, white supremacism, militarism, fascism, monopoly capitalism, and other ills could express a cartoonist's sense of social responsibility as well. Still, the extent to which the politics of Korean War comic book stories represented the deliberate intentions of ideologically sensitive writers (and the extent to which cartoonists could freely express their own views through their work) can easily be exaggerated.

John Gardner has proposed that a fiction writer performs morally when he or she creates a thought experiment and then allows it to work itself through without imposing on it a predetermined outcome that conforms to the author's own preferences.[51] The comic book industry limited cartoonists' freedom to write morally responsible fiction in this sense. Mass-circulated children's stories must conform to *conventional* morality, and entertainment for soldiers must not damage morale.[52]

3

◇◇◇◇◇◇◇◇◇

The Business

Understanding Korean War comic books requires knowing something of the industry that created the war comics and the people who read them. Generally speaking, war comics were published for quick profits as cheaply produced, disposable entertainment. In old comic books, we rarely encounter stories that were designed to have lasting value but find instead a rich record of a culture babbling to itself.

The Industry

Publishing war comics has never been a separate business. War comic books were published as a part of varied lines of comics, and the comics lines themselves were frequently part of larger chain publishing enterprises. For example, the comics line that became Marvel was part of Martin and Jean Goodman's Magazine Management Company, which also published confession, movie fan, sports, detective, and other kinds of magazines, including the pocket-sized news magazines *Quick* and *Focus*, which sometimes printed Korean War news and photographs.[1] That company published 320 issues of 25 war comics titles from the summer of 1950 to the spring of 1955. This was more than their next seven competitors' war comics added together.[2] Stan Lee, who edited their war comics during and after the Korean War (and wrote some of the stories himself), has provided an explanation of how they came to be the publishers of the most war comics titles in that period:

> We worked according to what the trend was. If there was a trend for cowboy books, we did two dozen cowboy titles. When romance books came in, we did two dozen romance books. We were just a volume publisher. Whatever was trendy at the moment, we published. We did teenage books[....] We did fantasy books[....] We did war stories—Combat Kelly, Combat Casey, Battlefield, Battlefront, Battleground, Combat. We did romance[....] And those are just a few examples, the tip of the iceberg. Just whatever was a name, we threw in and did the books. None of them were particularly good, none of them were particularly bad. They were just production jobs.[3]

Magazine Management Company, like others in the comic book industry, followed the pattern that they had used with pulp magazines, and created many shell companies. They did this for tax reasons and so that any of them could declare bankruptcy to escape its debts without bringing down the rest of their operations.[4] During the Korean War, rather than creating a subdivision dedicated to war comics, they spread their war and espionage comic books (mixed with titles in other genres) across many such paper entities. The "Atlas" logo that appeared on the Korean War comic books which fans now categorize as "Marvel" referred to Martin Goodman's distribution company.[5]

Blake Bell and Dr. Michael J. Vassallo, co-authors of *The Secret History of Marvel Comics,* argue that "All of comic books' founding fathers rose up from the fetid swamp of cheap magazine and pulp publishing."[6] Bell and Vassallo's lavishly illustrated volume shows that in the late 1930s, Goodman had joined the sleazy trend of publishing "shudder pulps," a sadomasochistic genre of "torture porn" based on graphic depictions of sexual violence against women.[7]

Meanwhile, Harry Donenfeld, who would co-found the company that became DC, publisher of Superman and Batman, had been publishing "girlie" pulps including lurid "spicy" pulp magazines.[8] The spicy pulp covers commonly featured half-dressed white women, sometimes in bondage, being threatened by men of color holding knives, swords, spears, guns or whips.[9]

The New York Society for the Suppression of Vice, founded by Anthony Comstock in 1873, repeatedly arranged for obscenity charges to be brought against printers, publishers and newsstand dealers. One such obscenity trial resulted in Donenfeld pleading guilty to publishing obscene material.[10] When psychiatrist Fredric Wertham identified "the formula" of crime comic books as "an obscene glorification of violence, crime and sadism," he named the recipe that leading comics publishers had previously used in their pulp magazines.[11]

Beyond the larger magazine industry, the comic book business also had ties with comic strips, television and film, through licensing agreements. In *John Wayne's Adventure Comics,* for example, a story appeared in which Wayne (a popular film star of westerns and combat films, and a tremendously influential male role model) starts out as a cowboy, receives a letter calling him out of the reserves to return to active duty, and ends up fighting in Korea.[12] Comic book heroes sometimes appeared in animated films or were played by live actors. Television shows and films were sometimes adapted to comic book format.[13]

The publishers kept their attention on the bottom line. As Will Eisner described the business philosophy of Everett M. (Busy) Arnold, the publisher of some of the finer war comics:

> Busy's artistic standards were based on sales…. If it sold it was good; if not, it wasn't good. … We agreed that he knew damn little about art, but he was a heck of a salesman.[14]

The Format

Comic books in their still-familiar American format began in 1933 when Harry I. Wildenberg, a sales manager for a company that printed newspapers' Sunday comics sections, had the idea of folding the standard Sunday newspaper comics section in half again to make a smaller-format booklet that children would be able to handle more easily.[15] At first companies bought these reformatted comics to give away as free advertising premiums. Then Wildenberg and his salesman Max C. Gaines successfully experimented with selling comic books on newsstands. By 1938, comic book companies were running out of newspaper comic strips to republish and were hiring cartoonists or contracting with studios that employed "commercial artists" to create original material.[16] Soon after that, the content of comic strips and comic books began to diverge, especially with the rise of superheroes and funny animal comic books, as cartoonists explored the possibilities of presenting multi-page comics stories as magazine features.[17]

The large Sunday newspaper comic pages had been created for a general audience, and parents and children often shared them, reading through the comics together. When these comics were reprinted and sold as small, inexpensive magazines, the opportunity arose of targeting a narrower audience, including (but not limited to) comics specifically created to be sold to children. The general titles of the first generation of comic books, like *New Fun Comics*, *Famous Funnies*, or *Popular Comics*, gave way to themed comics like *Detective Comics*, *Walt Disney's Comics and Stories*, and *War Comics*.[18] The typical comic book in 1951 included a cover, advertising for other comic books and general advertising, text pieces, puzzles and games, and (on three fourths of its pages) self-contained comic book stories.[19] A study of comic books that were distributed in Washington State from January through March 1954 found that the average comic book story was 6.8 pages long. That report listed war comics as the sixth most popular genre, with 4.3 percent of the market.[20] (At this point, the war had ended, and the war comics genre had already passed its peak.)

Like the Sunday funnies that spawned them, comic books were printed on newsprint with four colors of ink. In the early 1950s, when newsreels and newspaper photos pictured the Korean War in shades of gray, the war comics' bright colors stood out boldly.

Distribution

In the 1950s, comic books were distributed by the same companies that handled magazines and paperback books. Jean-Paul Gabilliet's excellent history of American comic books explains that these distributors were often themselves comic book publishers.[21] A distribution system based on specialty shops devoted to selling comic books existed only in the far, unimagined future.[22]

The dates printed on comic books' front covers or inside covers indicated, not the exact release date, but when the comic would be taken off the racks to make room for the next issue. Comic books typically came out two or three months before their cover dates. For many reasons, calculations from a published cover date to when the comic had been written and when it had been sold cannot be more than crude approximations.[23]

The distributors succeeded in boosting comic book circulation to incredible heights. The New York State Legislature study of comic books in 1952 reported that "The comic book industry has, since the termination of World War II, achieved the greatest volume of circulation of any type of book or magazine that this country has ever known."[24] They estimated that a billion comics were sold in one year. A University of California report interpreted this to mean that the United States was spending on comic books: "four times the combined annual book-purchasing budgets of all public libraries in the country, and more than is spent on textbooks for all the nation's elementary and secondary schools."[25] An investigating Senate subcommittee's later figures indicate that during the Korean War, the number of comic book titles, the average circulation, and the comics' annual revenues all more than doubled, reaching peak numbers.[26]

During this period, more comic books were published than could be displayed on the available shelf space and display racks. This glut contributed to the collapse from the record high of 650 titles in 1954 to less than half that many in 1955.[27]

Cartoonists

Will Eisner remembered that in the early days of comic books in the 1930s, when he had organized one of the first "shops" to supply comic book art to publishers, "Nobody saw any future in this thing. It was just a quick buck." The comic book artists "all wanted to be illustrators, nobody wanted to be a cartoonist."[28]

During World War II, "schlock houses" hired young beginners who could produce a lot of pages quickly.[29] Understandably, the public criticized comic books most frequently on aesthetic grounds, as crudely written and drawn, immature and unsophisticated.[30] This same crudity, though, could appeal to fans as vital, unpretentious and energetic.

With some glorious exceptions, those who *wrote* comic books in the 1950s were not the same people as those who *drew* comic books. In most cases, the names of those who wrote Korean War comic books remain unknown. Paul S. Newman, the most prolific writer in the history of American comic books, over the course of half a century wrote over 4,100 published comic book stories totaling about 36,000 pages. (He estimated that he submitted an additional 5,000 comic book plots that were rejected.[31]) Newman's work appeared, uncredited, in Korean War–era war comics that included *G.I. Joe, Men in Action, Young Men on the Battlefield, Battle, Battle Action, War Comics, Battlefront, Combat, Attack!*, and *Combat Casey.*[32] Newman wrote comic books to make a living, and wrote for any genre that was selling well. In his spare time, and with much less success, he pursued his real interest: writing plays for stage and screen.[33]

The cartoonists who drew war comics also drew whatever genre of comics the people who hired them thought might sell. They did not necessarily have any special interest in the stories that they illustrated. For example, Joe Kubert, one of the comic book artists most associated with American war comics because of his three-decade run on the best-selling *Sgt. Rock* comic, did not have a particular affection for war comics, but drew them as his job.[34] The cartoonist Jack Kirby, on the other hand, has been revered as the most centrally important superhero comic book artist, but according to his widow he would probably have been happier to have been drawing war comics instead of superheroes.[35]

As the war comics genre took shape during the Korean War, rather than relying as heavily on continuing characters (such as the Blackhawks or "Rip Carson") as World War II comics had done, most war comics drafted a fresh cast for each story. Although this anthology format was ideal for encouraging experiments in style and content, most of the published work appeared on casual inspection to be almost interchangeable. Cartoonists, doing their jobs on the artistic equivalent of an assembly line, were encouraged to be fast and reliable, not daring and unconventional.[36]

Those who drew comic books have left some blunt descriptions of their working conditions, and they mostly remember the relentless pressure to finish their pages by their deadlines. Comic book creators had little contact with their readers, and usually received little respect from their publishers. Joe Simon, co-creator of Captain America and an originator of the romance comics genre, spoke for many when he said about World War II comic books: "At that time we weren't interested in art. We felt that the comic business was the lowest rung on the ladder. We were interested in making money. Our only purpose was to get the stuff out as quickly as possible."[37]

During the Korean War, cartoonist Bernie Krigstein argued that comic book artists should demand to be taken more seriously. In 1952, at the first meeting of the Society of Comic Book Illustrators, which he had organized and been elected president of, Krigstein had taken the position "that comics was a great art, that we are in fact fine artists and illustrators."[38]

The Society of Comic Book Illustrators had a difficult time deciding whether to act as a union (threatening to strike for a decent minimum page rate, group health insurance, and return of the artwork to the cartoonists after it had been used) or as a professional society, cooperating with the publishers. Over Krigstein's objections, the Executive

Committee invited editor/writer Robert Kanigher to address a meeting. (Around this time, Kanigher was editing the first issues of *Our Army at War*, *All-American Men of War* and *Star-Spangled War Stories*. With the addition of *Our Fighting Forces* in 1954 and DC's *G.I. Combat* in 1957, Kanigher became the longtime editor/writer of all five of DC's enormously successful, long-running war comic book series.[39]) Krigstein remembered that Kanigher had used the opportunity to deliver "a diatribe on our ignorance and arrogance in assuming the title of *artist*. In a verbal assault he attacked the idea that we might be anything more than commercial craftsmen producing a product on demand."

As Kanigher remembered that same meeting:

> In an economic move, Fawcett elevated ignorant typists and sex-retaries to editorship. [...] One of the new "editors" was speaking when I entered. She called the assemblage unappreciated genius artists. I doubt whether she knew anything more about art than coloring her toenails. [...] When I arose, I described the group for what they were: illustrators of the written word. The word, the thought always came first. They weren't artists.[40]

By fall 1953, the Society of Comic Book Illustrators, still unable to decide between acting as a union or a professional society, came to an end. These were difficult years for forming a trade union because unionism connoted communism.[41]

Krigstein drew several war comics for DC, including some written by Kanigher. Soon after the Society of Comic Book Illustrators disbanded, Kanigher fired Krigstein for missing a DC deadline while he had been drawing for DC's competitor Atlas.[42]

Many of the comic book artists during the Korean War had served in the military a few years earlier during World War II. Partly due to those experiences, the representations of the Korean War differed greatly from the more fantastic stories in World War II comic books, when American superheroes in tight-fitting costumes had punched enemy agents, spies and saboteurs on the jaw. The cartoonists depicted the soldiers in Korea as men like themselves, stuck with a job that they had to do (but still, sometimes, as punching enemy soldiers on the jaw).

Readers

Not much can be said with certainty about who read war comics in the 1950s. Academic studies have usually steered around the subject of children consuming war stories and "playing war."[43] In 1951, Harvey Kurtzman replied to a woman who had written a fan letter to one of his comic books that "Our mag is designed for both sexes, young and old."[44]

The letter columns in the 1952 issues of Ziff-Davis's pioneering war comic *G.I. Joe* suggested that they too were aiming at a wide audience. Their fans included the mother of a soldier stationed in Germany, the wife of an Army veteran, the girlfriend of a soldier, a 22-year-old serving in the Army, a corporal stationed in Germany, a sergeant in Germany, a 16-year-old who was already a "five month veteran of Korea," and several young boys who needed their mothers' permission to read it.

Several bits of evidence suggest that most comic book readers in 1950 may have been teenagers and adults.[45] If so, this would seem especially true of war comics. Some clues that war comics were intended for adult men include pin-up features of scantily-clad women in enticing poses (as seen in *Tell It to the Marines*, *Fighting Leathernecks*, and *Monty Hall of the U.S. Marines*), pen-pal sections for lonely GIs, and ads about hair loss, pills to break the smoking habit, and for expensive products.[46]

Comics Readers in the Military in World War II

Film and theater critic Stanley Kauffman has described his experiences as a comic book editor at Fawcett Publications during World War II, and confirms that even a series that strongly appealed to children like *Captain Marvel* (which he discusses under the pseudonym "Major Mighty") was sold largely to men in the military:

> Magazines of every kind sold well during the war, and comic books sold phenomenally. Besides the children and others whom they pleased and who now had plenty of pocket money, comic books were the favorite reading of the armed forces. There was a [Captain Marvel] Club, with membership cards and secret code; there were hundreds of thousands of members, about half of whom were servicemen. I saw many a letter from a serviceman overseas confiding his troubles to [Captain Marvel] because there was no one around he could really talk to. [...] I saw more than one letter from a serviceman overseas applying for membership and asking [Captain Marvel] to rush the membership card so that the soldier or sailor could have it before he went into combat.[47]

Perhaps the most frequently cited statistic in the comic book controversy claimed that "At post exchanges comic books outsold the *Saturday Evening Post, Life,* and the *Reader's Digest* combined, by a ratio of 10 to 1."[48] Still, comics maintained their reputation as kid stuff. One Canadian soldier, wounded three times fighting in Europe, remembered that on his return home:

> ...when we came off the ship here's the Red Cross or the [Salvation Army], some girls, they give us a little bag and it has a couple of chocolate bars in it and a comic book.
>
> Here we had gone overseas not much more than children but we were coming back, sure, let's face it, as killers. And they were still treating us as children. Candy and comic books.[49]

Comics Readers in the Military in Korea

Like the soldiers of World War II, the soldiers in Korea also read comic books. A widely-published Associated Press photograph of a soldier reading a comic book while on duty in Korea was captioned:

> Neither war nor reds can interfere with a GI's favorite literature and 25th Division machine gunner Pfc. David Singleton, Lynchburg, Va., is no exception. Hand on gun trigger, he concentrates on inevitable comic book on Korea's southern front on Sept. 9, 1950.[50]

When asked about this picture many years later, David Singleton remembered, "I was just 17 years old. It was just a staged photograph. I *was* behind a machine gun. We'd had an attack that morning." Singleton speculated that the press staged this photograph "to make light of what was going on at the time." Rather than reading comic books in Korea, he added that "I don't recall reading *any* books over there. We were going up and coming back so fast."[51]

A Korean War veteran who organized a "mail from home" campaign, Sergeant Wilbur R.H. Radeline, suggested that "folks with boys in Korea should write more often" and "send little gifts such as home-town newspapers, comic books and candy." The chairman of the Los Angeles Junior Chamber of Commerce's annual "Operation Gift Lift," which sent hundreds of thousands of Christmas gifts to soldiers in Korea, said that the GIs had requested "practical gifts such as candy, cookies, sweaters, comic books and magazines."[52]

Letter Columns

Letters to the editor columns in comic books of the 1940s and 1950s were rare compared to what they would become later. EC war comics made them a regular feature. In the letter column of *Two-Fisted Tales* (#22, July–August 1951), Cpl. Walter Kosneki wrote that: "I somehow obtained a battered, old copy of TWO-FISTED TALES here in Korea, and during a lull, found time to read it. Needless to say, I enjoyed it so much that I felt I had to write and compliment you on the realism of your battle sequences." He followed this with a story about his "personal battle experiences," which editor Harvey Kurtzman replaced with an ellipsis, and promised in an editorial reply to use "as the basis of a future story." He also invited "any of you other Joes over there who want to write and tell us your war stories" to please do so. In the next issue, he reported that "Many letters from you readers who are stationed in Korea have contained useful facts and information that have enabled us to more accurately portray in our war stories conditions and situations as they truly exist!"

"Battlefield Bivouac" in *War Adventures on the Battlefield #4* (October 1952) was the only letter column that appeared in that Atlas series. It began with a letter from Joe Wallace, a Private First Class in Korea, who demonstrated his discerning taste by singling out a story that comics historians have remembered as truly extraordinary:

> "I never wrote to a magazine before, but I got such a charge out of the stories—if you know what I mean—they're the kind that makes a guy think. Especially the one called Atrocity Story (wow), and that Paul Reinman sure can draw. Let's have more like that. You can bet that *Battlefield* is my favorite war book."[53]

That same column also published a letter from Berlin, in which Corporal Harold Minetta complained that unhappy stories do not provide the escapist, emotional satisfaction that he seeks in a war comic:

> What's with so many unhappy endings in the stories in *Battlefield*? I think that the stories are great, but I think every story should have a happy ending. Even though it doesn't happen that way in combat, that's the way I like to read them—so that it leaves me with a good feeling at the end. Let's have more stories like "5 HOURS 'TIL DAWN" where you think it's going to end bad, but everything works out O.K.

The column concluded with a letter from Hank O'Brien in Dayton, Ohio, who (in contrast to Corporal Minetta) appreciated that this series did not try to "kid" its readers with happy war stories:

> I don't usually read Comic Magazines about war because most of the time the stories they print are just for kids, and they read as if the writers hadn't been within a thousand miles of a battlefield. But I picked your magazine up in my cousin's house and started to read it. Now, I must say that I was surprised to see the stories were adult, accurate, and had all the flavor of battle. The stories in *Battlefield* had to be written by guys who were in the army (am I right?) … and that's the kind of magazine I'm going to read. I like the stories because they show war for what it really is. And it's certainly no picnic, like a lot of other magazines would have you believe. You don't get happy endings in war, so why should we try to kid ourselves? Keep up the good work. In a sense, what you're doing is accurate reporting.

The editor (an uncredited Stan Lee) answered that O'Brien had been correct about the military background of *Battlefield*'s writers: "Most of 'em have seen action and they don't sugar-coat the facts … the people back home have got to realize what the G.I.'s are going through."[54]

"The Only Reading Matter"

A British anti-comics crusader said in 1951 that:

…we have the authority of The Times for saying that these comic strip magazines form the only reading matter for the American troops in Korea. Lest we should feel superior, we should note that Army padres […] state that young British soldiers spend most of their Sundays on their beds reading American comics.[55]

In 1954, an Australian article, datelined New York, ("[Fredric Wertham] Sees U.S. Comics as Textbooks of Crime"), reported that "millions of semi-literate adults no longer read anything more serious than a comic book," and gave as an example that "in the armed services it is notorious that a book means a 'comic.'"[56] The soldiers entered the war with comic books, and they left still reading them, for example, in military hospitals.[57]

Connections to Korea

The comic book industry was based in New York City, which in those days of propeller airplanes was even farther from Korea than it is today.[58] The Korean population in the United States at the beginning of the Korean War was only a tiny fraction of today's 1.7 million people of Korean descent living in the United States.

New York–based cartoonists were usually forced to rely on their imaginations and the pictures in newsreels, newspapers and magazines to create their images of Koreans. Still, some comic book artists gained direct experience by visiting Korea on tours to help boost military morale. Irwin Hasen remembered that:

I belonged to the National Cartoonists Society and we had U.S.O. trips to Korea during the war. I went to the front lines with six cartoonists. They flew us in helicopters over each base, and we were all in full packs, with our drawing boards over our shoulders, and we would entertain the troops.
    We arrived the day the peace accord was signed but it gave me a perspective on what the Korean war was. It was one of the bloodiest things. Vietnam was bloody, of course, but Korea was one of the bloodiest wars. We went to the hospitals and everything…[59]

Cartoonist Lew Sayre Schwartz retired from drawing comic books after what may have been the same junket to Korea. He recalled: "When I got back, I couldn't stand drawing another page" of *Batman*.[60]

Comics as Mass Culture

Even if the contents of comic books had never been violent or salacious, they still would have been controversial because of how they were made and consumed as commercial products. Comic books appeared to embody in an extreme way the faults that intellectuals had already found in other mass media.[61] Dwight MacDonald, as both an anti-totalitarian leftist and a cultural conservative, developed "A Theory of Mass Culture" which provided one influential explanation of what was wrong with mass media, including comic books.[62] In columns serialized from 1944 to 1945 and re-edited and republished in 1953, MacDonald argued that unlike High Culture (the difficult works that individual artists create for the cognoscenti) and unlike Folk Art (which arises as the spontaneous expression of the common people themselves to suit their own needs), "Mass Culture" is "imposed from above":

> It is fabricated by technicians hired by business; its audiences are passive consumers, their participation limited to the choice between buying and not buying. The Lords of *kitsch,* in short, exploit the cultural needs of the masses in order to make a profit and/or to maintain their class rule....[63]

The "brutal" pervasiveness of mass-produced culture threatens to overwhelm the High Culture of the upper classes. Ironically, what began as their way "to make money from the crude tastes of the masses and to dominate them politically" ends with them "finding their own culture attacked and even threatened with destruction by the instrument they have thoughtlessly employed."

Mass culture not only threatens High Culture but erodes the possibility of people relating to one another as human beings, that is, as individuals or as members of a community. The new "mass man" has been homogenized by mass culture into "a solitary atom, uniform with and undifferentiated from thousands and millions of other atoms...."

MacDonald warned that the mass culture creates "adultized children and infantile adults":

> The homogenizing effects of *kitsch* also blurs age lines. It would be interesting to know how many adults read the comics. We do know that comic books are by far the favorite reading matter of our soldiers and sailors, and some forty million comic books are sold a month, and that some seventy million people (most of whom must be adults, there just aren't that many kids) are estimated to read the newspaper comic strip every day.[64]

MacDonald's pessimistic theory of mass culture provides a fuller expression of some ideas that had frequently popped up in the arguments against comic books during the Korean War.[65] MacDonald's theory and others like it added their weight to the widely-expressed worries that comic books and mass culture might be unintentionally feeding the menace of a domestic totalitarianism.[66]

4

◇◇◇◇◇◇◇◇◇

Strips

War comic books came into existence primarily as a form of entertainment. They inherited their styles of art and storytelling from the once-popular adventure strips on the comics pages of newspapers.[1] The generation that developed realistic adventure comic books frequently pointed to Roy Crane as an early and inspiring example and as a huge influence on the 1930s adventure comic strips.

The Roots of War Comics

A search for the predecessors of the war comics genre can go in several possible directions, depending on how we think of its defining characteristics. In the 1980s and 1990s, as a way of arguing for greater respect for comics, such cartoonist-theorists as Will Eisner and Scott McCloud defined comics by their formal properties, focusing primarily on the telling of stories or the communication of information through a sequence of juxtaposed images.[2] They built on earlier surveys that sought respectability for cartooning by inventing long pedigrees that ultimately go back to cave "paintings."[3] Several of the classic examples of the supposed predecessors of the comic strip have been stories of wars and conquests told through sequences of juxtaposed imagery, including Trajan's Column (finished in 113 CE), the Bayeux Tapestry (possibly completed in 1070), and the pre–Columbian Mixtec Codex Zouche-Nuttall (14th century).[4] Comic book publisher M.C. Gaines began his 1942 article on the history of the comics form by writing: "It seems that Little Orphan Annie isn't an orphan after all. Her ancestors include Sumerian army men whose exploits are celebrated in tablets long buried under desert sands…."[5] Even if the cartoonists who created war comics had heard of these earlier works, though, it seems difficult to imagine that they took much of their inspiration from them.[6]

If we think of war comics not primarily as sequential art, but as visual representations of war, this can lead to other precedents. Old battlefield images, in paintings, tapestries and lithographs, shared with some early newspaper comics an appeal based on what comics theorist Thierry Smolderen calls a "swarming effect." In this kind of bird's-eye view composition, the eye is led by zigzag paths through a large and intricate scene that teems with many figures engaged in various activities.[7] War comic books rarely immersed their readers in these kinds of complicated graphics because they were so difficult, time-consuming and labor-intensive to produce, and because they were less effective when reduced to the size of a comic book page, panel or cover. These practical considerations led the war comics to concentrate on faces of individual soldiers rather than panoramic views of a battle.[8]

A third way of defining war comics, other than by their form or subject, would be by their functions—for example, to promote a war effort. The history of American war propaganda goes back to our earliest cartoons. Variations of Benjamin Franklin's cartoon "Join or Die" were reprinted frequently during the United States' War for Independence, and the image of the Boston Massacre that Paul Revere engraved in 1770 provided a potent picture of British oppression.[9] Near the end of the Civil War, Abraham Lincoln recognized the power of cartoonist Thomas Nast's published editorial drawings by calling him "our best recruiting sergeant."[10]

During World War I, a "Bureau of Cartoons," meagerly funded by the government's Committee for Public Information, successfully mobilized "the cartoon power of the country" by sending a weekly bulletin to over 750 cartoonists with suggestions about what propaganda themes might best serve the war effort.[11] The founder and head of the Bureau of Cartoons was George Hecht, who went on to become the publisher of the comic book *True Comics* (which was filled with war stories during World War II, but which did not continue this tradition in the issues published during the Korean War).

Roy Crane

Roy Crane's comic strip *Wash Tubbs* began as a typical humor strip in 1924. Within a few years it began evolving by steps into a trailblazing adventure series. The cynical mercenary character Captain Easy joined Wash Tubbs in the daily strip in 1928 and got his own Sunday page in 1933, which began with a story set in the imaginary Central Asian "lost province of Gungshi," which "China, stripped of Manchuria [by Japan], is anxious to regain…."[12] After the attack on Pearl Harbor, Captain Easy enlisted in the Army.

In the 1930s, Crane's work inspired a new generation of "realistic," suspenseful, adventure stories that joined the earlier strips which had been based largely on funny gags and silly pictures.[13] Publisher William Randolph Hearst's powerful King Features Syndicate recognized the trend early, and in 1943 offered Roy Crane the opportunity to create a strip that he would own the rights to. Crane left *Captain Easy* and Cleveland's relatively minor-league NEA Syndicate to create a more realistic military strip, *Buz Sawyer*, about a Navy pilot who fought in the Pacific during World War II.[14] Buz Sawyer's adventures began appearing in comic books in 1945.[15]

It had been Crane's own idea to insert "propaganda" messages into his comic strip. In 1942, Crane wrote to the director of the recently established Office of War Information:

Those in Washington have almost overlooked one of the niftiest propaganda mediums to be found in the USA—newspaper comic strips. […] On my own initiative, I began some propaganda work about two years ago, in an effort to wake people up to the danger confronting us. It was necessary to be pretty subtle as office regulations did not permit any mention of war.

In that letter, Crane proposed that the government appoint someone to tell cartoonists which themes they should use in their stories.[16]

Crane eventually succeeded in winning military cooperation during World War II, and found personal satisfaction by continuing to attempt to use his comic strip "as an influence for good" through the Cold War.

Comics scholar/journalist Jeet Heer found that:

In creating *Buz Sawyer*, Crane repeatedly turned to the Navy for approval and ideas. He received special clearance to visit naval bases (and during the Cold War he was allowed to see ships and weapon systems that were classified "top secret" to civilians). While working on plotlines, Crane would send his stories to the Navy to make sure they were accurate and acceptable.[17]

Heer has looked through "a huge stack of letters from military and government officials giving Crane suggestions for story lines and propaganda points from 1943 till the early 1960s," and concluded that "Crane seems to have often (if not always) acted on these suggestions."[18]

Eventually the Cold War propaganda in the strip crowded out the qualities that had made Crane's work in the 1930s fresh and exciting, and editors began to complain. For example, in 1962, the *Toronto Star*'s editor wrote to King Features Syndicate to object to propaganda appearing in comics and said that little actual evidence supported the Buz Sawyer comic strip which had warned against "the flood of narcotic drugs from Red China."[19]

Frank V. Martinek

Captain Easy began as an adventurer, and not a uniformed member of the armed forces. Comics historian Ron Goulart has described the military adventure comic strip hero of the 1930s as having had a hard time getting started: "most of the paying customers didn't want to be reminded about anything pertaining to war and battle, certainly not fighting that was going to involve our own soldiers, sailors and marines."[20]

The first successful military adventure strip, *Don Winslow of the Navy*, was created in 1934 to promote military enlistment. Frank V. Martinek, a former Navy Intelligence Officer and a Lt. Commander in the Naval Reserve, decided to create this comic strip to help the Navy after he heard Admiral Wat Tyler Cluverius, Jr., describe the difficulties of Navy recruiting in the Midwest.[21] Martinek's friend Colonel Frank Knox, publisher of the Chicago Daily News, helped Martinek interest the Bell Syndicate in offering the strip. Martinek wrote the *Don Winslow* strip in the evening, while holding a day job as assistant vice-president in charge of personnel for the Standard Oil Company of Indiana.[22]

Martinek told Martin Sheridan, author of *Classic Comics & Their Creators* (first published in 1942), about how he organized the production of this comic strip, which had begun as a hobby project but soon became a success in newspapers, on radio, in books, as a comic book series, as a movie serial, and in more than 150 newspapers including papers published in fifteen foreign countries:

> In my situation as a business man, it is necessary for me to surround myself with a complete organization for the production of Don Winslow. [...] I create the episode and turn it over to my research director Carl Hammond. It is then put on paper roughly. Then it goes to the layout man, back to me for criticism, dialogue, etc., and thence to Lieut. Leon Beroth, U.S. N., who draws the strip.
>
> Since *Don Winslow of the Navy* is approved by the Navy Department, I cannot allow him to do anything that is contrary to the ideals, traditions or motives of the Navy.[23]

Milton Caniff

By far the most influential, most imitated newspaper comic strip for defining the look of the war comics was Milton Caniff's *Terry and the Pirates*.[24] This strip also was reprinted in comic book format.

The legendary head of the Chicago Tribune Syndicate, Captain Joseph Patterson, had hired Caniff in 1934 specifically to create an adventure strip set in China. Patterson had gotten his start in newspapering when he was in China in 1900, assisting a reporter who was covering the Boxer Rebellion.[25] Caniff accepted the job knowing almost nothing about China. He went to the library and checked out a stack of books, including Pearl S. Buck's recently published, critically acclaimed bestseller *The Good Earth*, and, on Patterson's recommendation, *Vampires of the China Coast* by "Bok," which gave him some of his first ideas.[26] Caniff quickly came up with a strip that featured a seductive Eurasian villain ("the Dragon Lady") and a Chinese interpreter/servant for comic relief ("Connie").[27] During his years on *Terry and the Pirates*, Caniff grew to become one of the true masters of the art of the comic strip.[28] In the years leading to America's entry into World War II, the strip may have influenced American public opinion in favor of China.[29]

Caniff told his stories with dramatically lighted panels that relied heavily on solid black areas, restlessly shifting angles and perspectives, and impressionistic brushwork that in some cases suggested photographs when his drawings were reduced for publication in newspapers. The most immediate and powerful influence on Caniff's style came from a cartoonist he shared studio space with, Noel Sickles.[30]

Syndicate head Joseph Patterson greatly admired Caniff's *Terry and the Pirates*, but became irritated when the strip seemed to be drumming up support for a war against Japan. On September 5, 1941, in a period when the *Chicago Tribune*'s editorial cartoons on the front page and inside the paper were agitating almost daily against the "war hysteria" being whipped up by the government "warmongers," the *Terry and the Pirates* strip showed in one panel a clearly-marked Japanese plane bombing a defenseless relief station. In response, Patterson called Caniff into his office to order him to drop the "politics."[31] Three months later, the attack on Pearl Harbor changed Patterson's mind.

Later Caniff told interviewer Studs Terkel that having set *Terry and the Pirates* in China made its transition into a war strip during World War II a simple matter:

> We laid the storyline in China because that was the last place anything could happen. The first strips were the usual adventure stuff. But when [World War II] began to loom—you could see it coming—I started using Japanese uniforms…. By the time Pearl Harbor hit, I was all armed and ready.[32]

By the time of the Korean War, Joseph Patterson had died, and Caniff had turned *Terry and the Pirates* over to another artist and started a new comic strip, *Steve Canyon*, for a different syndicate. Caniff left the Chicago Tribune syndicate because the Field Syndicate had offered him an irresistible chance to create a comic strip with full ownership of the rights and complete editorial control.[33] *Steve Canyon* began on January 13, 1947.

The Cold War flavor of the *Steve Canyon* strip was unusually strong. Steve Canyon's third adventure, beginning in July of 1947, took place in an unnamed Middle East country with large oil reserves that shared a border with the homeland of some villains who mistake the characters Steve Canyon and Happy Easter for "Yankee" spies "probably seeking data on oil in this area" so they can drill wells near the border, "thus weakening the flow of gas and oil into our storage tanks."[34] The previous year had seen one of the first Cold War conflicts flare up in oil-rich northern Iran, which bordered on the Soviet Union.[35] After several more Cold War adventures, Steve Canyon began 1950 in China by helping orphans escape from the "puppet government's" plan to put them in a Party school where they will be taught to hate the West.[36]

When "the business in Korea started," Caniff responded by having his title character, a Major in the Air Force Reserve, volunteer for active duty "like so many other World War II veterans," but at first Caniff sent Steve Canyon to Vietnam instead of Korea.[37] He later explained, "I didn't want to get involved in the Korean War at the beginning. It was an unpopular war—not as unpopular as Vietnam, but there was the same sense of it just not going anywhere."[38]

Besides permanently turning *Steve Canyon* into a military comic strip, the Korean War also pushed Caniff to move forward on an idea he had come up with earlier for a proposed hybrid comic/magazine series that would attract young people to support the Air Force. Caniff's proposal won enthusiastic support from the recently formed Air Force Association. He invented and copyrighted the character "Dart Davis," and envisioned that the stories about that teen character would carry the Air Force's messages in an entertaining way:

> The *Dart Davis* section can easily be the mouthpiece for any material the Air Force Association or the Air Force itself wishes to put over to the teenage boys. This does not have to take the form of propaganda in the Russian sense of the word, but can find great favor with educators and parents by urging the kids to stay in school until they receive full credits so that they can be certain of having the qualifications for aviation cadet training.[39]

Despite his great popularity as a cartoonist, Caniff was unable to successfully launch this comic, and it died after one issue. The first problem he encountered was that commercial comic book publishers he approached did not offer enough money to repay the extra effort that this project would require. At one point, Caniff convinced Marshall Field III to publish it, but Field was unable to get enough extra newsprint to print a comic book in addition to his newspaper. In November 1951, the Harvey brothers published the first issue of *Steve Canyon's Air Power* as a comic book without some of the magazine features that had been part of the original concept.[40]

The Air Force Association sent out many sample copies of *Steve Canyon's Air Power*, but only 155,000 copies were sold out of 400,000 printed, and it did not break even. The publishing arrangements were too cumbersome to make it worthwhile. Caniff, his syndicate, the artists he hired to imitate his style (at higher than average rates), the Air Force Association and the publisher all expected to make money on this project, and Steve Canyon's syndicate and the Air Force Association also shared in the editorial responsibilities. Ironically, at a time when the newsstands overflowed with war comics inspired by Caniff's style, Caniff's own war comic was not popular enough to successfully compete.

Unable to reach hundreds of thousands of comic book readers, Caniff put his messages in front of almost two hundred times more readers through his comic strip. Air Force Chief of Staff Nathan F. Twining remarked, "Steve [Canyon]'s occasional lectures put the Air Force's aims and problems and ideals before thirty million American citizens who follow him in the papers. I know of no other way to tell so many people so much about us, and what we are, and why we are."[41]

Since 1944, Caniff had made a Christmas tradition of putting small lectures in his comic strip, separate from his ongoing stories. In 1950, he addressed his readers on the subject of the Korean War by saying, "When we lick this thing and preserve the right to make our own decisions instead of getting the answers out of a dictator's rule book, remember that those good Joes buried in frozen Korean soil paid one more installment on *your* freedom."

The next year, a Steve Canyon adventure brought him to the fictional Maumee University, where he gave a lecture to the Department of Air Science and Tactics ROTC students. In response to the question "why are we in Asia," Canyon gave Caniff's standard explanation: "The military answer is the axiom of throwing your line of defense as far from your base as possible—as long as it can be supplied! … Our line of defense is the Western shore of the Pacific—or is it the Eastern! It's whether you want a fight in Korea—or California."[42] His readers might have imagined that Korea and China possessed troop ships that could carry the fight six thousand miles across the Pacific Ocean to the West Coast of the United States. If so, they would have been mistaken.

Decades later, Caniff reminisced about his own experiences in the Reserve Officers' Training Corps:

> …I couldn't wait until it was over. When I was in school, between the wars, nobody ever said "It's great to be in the ROTC." We *had* to be in the ROTC. If you went to a land grant school, you had to have two years of ROTC…. The minute it was over, I was done with it. I didn't sign up for a third year.[43]

In his Christmas 1951 strip, speaking in the voice of American soldiers in Korea's forgotten war, Caniff compared their job to fire fighters and wrote:

> We'll smother this thing, and do a good job of it too—but sometimes we look around and it's as if nobody's even watching us work—yet the flames are shooting in every direction….
>
> Look, citizen, we don't mind our number coming up to carry the hose, but it's *your* house we're keeping from catching fire….

Like others who have won high reputations for drawing war comics, Caniff paid scrupulous attention to "authenticity" and "realism" by accurately depicting uniforms, insignia, weapons, and military equipment. He assembled a personal library of reference books, manuals, textbooks and handbooks on military subjects, subscribed to military journals and magazines, collected military objects and model airplanes, corresponded with and received visits from servicemen who provided photo references, and made his own observations by visiting a military flight school several times. When he slipped up, his readers wrote in to bring it to his attention. His art studio contained so much technical military information for reference material that during World War II, his home studio had to follow the War Department's security procedures for handling classified documents. (Household members signed a log as they came and went.[44])

By the time of the Vietnam War, Caniff's *Steve Canyon* strip had become a target for anti-war protesters, but Caniff may have struck the first blow, introducing an obnoxious female war protester in 1967, "Felicia Lymph."[45] (Months earlier, Al Capp had added an obnoxious war protester character to his *Li'l Abner* comic strip, "Joanie Phonie," based on Joan Baez.) Newspapers began to drop Caniff's strip.[46]

According to comics historian Richard Marschall, by its last years, the thrill of Caniff's artistry had faded and his *Steve Canyon* strips became more strident, stagey, static, and lightweight: "To many readers, it seemed, at best, that Canyon was a seven-day-a-week recruiting poster and, at worst, that his creator had lost the magic formula for mixing plot, character, dialogue, and art as he had so supremely in *Terry and the Pirates*."[47]

Caniff's solution to his problem of drawing a military strip at a time of strong anti-military feeling included retiring his hero from flying fighter planes, keeping his strip's references to Vietnam to a minimum, and taking his hero out of uniform to have him work on special assignments for the Air Force Office of Special Investigations.[48] In his Christmas strips, however, Caniff's strip had hardly changed, and for many readers his message there was wearing thin. In the late 1960s and early 1970s he was still thanking American soldiers in Asia, now in Vietnam, for fixing it "so the folks at home never have to drop to their knees before a character wearing a red star" and doing it "there—instead of on Main Street!"; "manning fox holes in far places today—so you may walk tall and be free to choose your own destiny"; and "risking their lives, liberties and their sacred honor to insure *your* right to peaceful sleep tonight!"[49]

Bill Mauldin

Besides Caniff, the other big influence on the look of the war comics was Bill Mauldin's cartoons for the Mediterranean edition of *Stars and Stripes* during World War II, which were syndicated to several hundred newspapers while he was still in the Army.[50] Like Roy Crane and Milton Caniff, and many other successful cartoonists, Mauldin learned the basics of cartooning when he was a teenager by taking the Charles N. Landon correspondence course in cartooning.[51] Unlike Crane and Caniff, he worked with single panel cartoons instead of strips. Mauldin's characters, the laconic, unshaven, muddy, miserable combat infantrymen Willie and Joe, set a new standard for realism.[52] Several generals, notably including General George Patton, were outraged by these drawings of disrespectful soldiers in uncreased trousers, but with the support of other generals, especially General Dwight D. Eisenhower, Mauldin was allowed to keep drawing them.[53] Mauldin's highest-level political support had come indirectly, a few years earlier, when President Roosevelt, Secretary of War Henry Stimson and Chief of Staff George C. Marshall agreed in 1943 that the American people needed to see images of "the dangers, horrors, and grimness of War" so that they would understand the sacrifices being made overseas, discount false hopes about a quick victory, and be patient with wartime rationing and shortages.[54]

Still, Mauldin censored the amount of horror in his cartoons as a matter of course, since his job was to entertain, be funny, and raise frontline soldiers' dangerously low morale.[55] In Mauldin, these dispirited men found a champion who improbably turned them into an inspiring vision of the survival of human dignity.

The "realism" Mauldin's cartoons achieved consisted of allowing knowledgeable followers of his work to "read between the lines" and to imagine the corpses lying "outside of the frame." Certainly, Mauldin did not include in his drawings all that he had personally witnessed in the war, such as the sea littered with the floating pieces of men and machines destroyed in Operation Husky when he landed in Sicily, and destruction on a greater scale south of Salerno in Operation Avalanche; dead American parachutists caught in olive trees; the massive desertions, the massive corruption, or the reeking, decaying corpses of Italians killed by Allied bombing raids and of Germans and Americans spread across the roads and fields, green maggots crawling through their blackened faces.[56]

No comparable American cartoonist appeared in the military papers of the Pacific war zone, either during World War II or the Korean War, partly because those papers had less editorial freedom.[57] Mauldin's World War II cartoons were not reprinted there.

Mauldin wrote and illustrated a book about the fighting in Italy which he intended to be disturbing, but, in his view, the War Department censors in Washington, D.C., took the "teeth" out of it before publication. The softened text, *Up Front*, became a bestseller in 1945.[58]

In June 1945, Mauldin returned to the United States. He was tremendously popular, but wracked with guilt for having used his cartoons to turn the horrors of a vile war into mass entertainment.[59]

After World War II, Mauldin became an editorial cartoonist. After an uncertain start, he surprised his friends and fans by developing radical opinions, and speaking out in favor of public housing, price controls, labor unions, the United Nations, cooperation with the

Soviet Union, and against racial segregation, poll taxes, the American Legion, and the Red Scare.[60]

His January 8, 1946, cartoon showed Willie saying to a man who apparently preferred Nazi Germany over Communist Russia: "Accordin' to you, mister, I spent th' last three years helpin' my worst enemy kill my best friends." This cartoon became the first item of evidence of his supposed communist sympathies in Mauldin's FBI file.[61]

By 1946, furious newspaper editors, especially in the South, were refusing to print Mauldin's cartoons and threatening Mauldin's syndicate that they would cancel their subscriptions if they continued to send such material. After publisher Roy Howard accused Mauldin's cartoons against anti-communist politicians of "following the Communist Party line," the collapse in the number of papers carrying his cartoon was as rapid as his recent rise had been meteoric.[62] The syndicate protected its property by altering Mauldin's drawings, rewriting his captions, and withdrawing from circulation those unfixable cartoons which they knew would offend subscribing editors.

Mauldin was infuriated by his syndicate's interference, but soon put his efforts into improving his cartooning skills. He withdrew from communist front groups, and began mixing cartoons sincerely criticizing the Soviet Union and the Communist Party with the ones criticizing the red-baiters.[63] Nevertheless, the limits on his work during the postwar Red Scare drove him to temporarily retire from editorial cartooning in 1949.[64]

In 1951, *Collier's* magazine offered Mauldin the large amount of $3,000 each for seven articles if he would report on the war in Korea for them.[65] Mauldin would have preferred to do something else, but his other writing projects were not succeeding, and with a growing family to support, he agreed to go. After clearing up a problem with his visa (the Defense Department, based on information in the FBI's files, had initially refused him a security clearance), Mauldin visited Korea from January to April 1952.

Mauldin's series of feature articles about his experiences in Korea were published by *Collier's* magazine and then collected as his book *Bill Mauldin in Korea.*[66] The material took the form of an imagined correspondence between his two World War II characters, with Joe as a war correspondent and Willie as the one receiving and answering his letters. The introduction begins as "Joe's" words ("if they ever threaten to draft you again just tell them your uncle is a communist and they won't touch you with a ten foot pole") but ends in Mauldin's own voice:

> It's a slow, grinding, lonely, bitched-up war, but [the combat man in Korea] goes on fighting in it, not happy, but in good spirit, not in a frenzy of hatred against an enemy which is as pitiful as it is vicious, but efficiently and with purpose.
>
> In the minds of many people the phrase "professional soldier" has a stigma very much like "professional politician." It implies cynical and mercenary motives. Yet soldiering is as necessary and legitimate a profession, in a world which still makes war, as are politics in a world which still needs laws.
>
> I think that, due to the Korean war, we have a professional army for what may be the first time in our history, and maybe we'll have reason to be grateful for it in the years ahead.

Military Humor

Sgt. George Baker's *The Sad Sack* counts as another outstanding comic strip chronicle of World War II. Baker had been on the picket line during the Disney animators' strike of 1941, when he was drafted into the Army.[67] His *The Sad Sack* strip of pantomime humor began with the first issue of *Yank—the Army Weekly*, in June 1942. The character originated as Baker's self-portrait of "the way I felt the first day I was on K.P. [...]. That was before Pearl Harbor when I was in the Signal Corps at Fort Monmouth, N.J."

As the strip went on, the Sad Sack's character changed. The cartoonist explained:

> He became hardened to the knocks of Army life and he learned not to take the harsh words of the sergeant too seriously. Terrible things continued to happen to him every week, of course, but instead of crawling quietly into a corner and dying of humiliation he found himself taking it philosophically, as everybody does after six months in the Army, and coming back to stick out his chin for more.[68]

Baker designed his character "to refute the ads that were then beginning to make their appearance, in which soldiers always looked bright and cheerful, bedecked in tailored uniforms immaculately pressed and shined," and to try to remedy the "appalling" civilian ignorance about what Army life was like. Unlike the Hollywood image of a soldier, "my character looked resigned, tired, helpless, and beaten. Going the whole hog, he looked clumsy and even a little stupid, but these last two elements were actually unintentional and only slipped in because I was still a bit rusty in my drawing."

After the war, *The Sad Sack* became a syndicated newspaper comic strip, but the old formula did not work as well after the title character had left the Army. R.C. Harvey explains that:

> it was a somewhat depressing feature. As a portrayal of civilian life, the strip seemed unduly cynical and bitter: here the Sack encountered nothing but predatory con men, crooks, and heartless, conniving women, and he was victimized by their malevolent premeditation rather than by the uncomprehending and therefore comic blunderings of monumental military inefficiency.

The Sad Sack began appearing in his own comic book series in 1949, drawn by Fred Rhoads. After surviving twenty-one issues as a civilian, in the "22nd fun packed issue" of February 1951 The Sad Sack was "back in the Army again!" Teenagers made the *Sad Sack* comic book a bestseller during the Korean War.[69]

This strip was an obvious influence on Mort Walker's *Beetle Bailey* comic strip, which began in 1950, and which has also appeared in comic books. After the Korean War had started, Walker's character Beetle Bailey, then a college student, joined the Army. *Beetle Bailey*, a strip about the laziest private in the U.S. Army, eventually became a huge success, reaching 200 million readers in more than 50 countries. Circulation of the strip received a big boost beginning in 1954, thanks to publicity about the Pacific edition of the U.S. military paper *Stars and Stripes* banning the strip for mocking officers and encouraging laziness, and again when that paper banned the strip in 1970, fearing that the addition of its one black character, Lt. Flap, would stir racial tensions.[70]

Walker drew *Beetle Bailey* for a record-breaking 68 years.[71] In 1994, Walker, who had served in Italy during World War II, joked to a college audience that "I always tell people that I spent four years in the Army and 40 years getting even."[72]

Like Steve Canyon and the Sad Sack, who had rejoined the military during the Korean War, Beetle Bailey remained in the military from that point on. Another World War II character who returned to duty during the Korean War was Vic Herman's "Winnie the WAC," a morale-booster for the Women's Army Corps.[73]

Most war comics did not use humorous styles of cartooning, but some war comic books did, usually in the back of the book. Humor strips in war comics were about military life, but usually not about combat.

5

World War II Comic Books

While Korean War comics, like other "adventure" comics, inherited their basic approach from adventure comic strips in newspapers and from pulp magazines, their most immediate predecessors were earlier comic books.[1] Although only five years separated the end of World War II and the start of the Korean War, Korean War comic books differed in many ways from World War II comic books.

Comic book historians continue to take pride in the role that American comic books played in urging American participation in World War II. Although in his first comic book appearance, in 1938, Superman had foiled the plot of some men who had been trying to embroil America in another European War, by the time Japan attacked Pearl Harbor on December 7, 1941, and Germany and Italy had declared War on the United States on December 11, Superman was ready to support the American war effort along with the rest of America's many superheroes.[2] Between his first appearance and this turnabout, Superman had responded to one of the pivotal events of the century: the beginnings of World War II in Europe.

Superman and the Nazi-Soviet Nonaggression Pact

In August 1939, Nazi Germany and the Communist Soviet Union signed an agreement that they would not attack each other, either by themselves or in combination with other nations.[3] The Nazi-Soviet agreement included a secret division of Europe into German and Soviet spheres of influence, and practically immediately after it was signed, the Germans and then, after two weeks, the Soviets began seizing control of what had been Polish territory. France and Britain had responded immediately to Germany's invasion of Poland by declaring war on Germany.

The following February, *Look* magazine published an original story in which Superman's creators answered the question "How would Superman end the war?" In two pages, Superman simply grabs Hitler and Stalin ("the two power-mad scoundrels responsible for Europe's present ills") and then, rather than taking the law any further into his own hands, delivers them to the League of Nations, where they are convicted of "modern history's greatest crime—unprovoked aggression against defenseless countries."[4]

The Soviet Union had already been firmly opposed to Western-style comics since 1934.[5] The *Look* magazine Superman story attracted memorable criticism from Nazi Germany. A writer for *Das Schwarze Korps,* the weekly newspaper of the Schutzstaffel (the

German paramilitary organization that would soon administer the Holocaust's death camps) pointed contemptuously to the Jewish identity of Superman's original writer:

> Jerry Siegel, an intellectually and physically circumcised chap who has his headquarters in New York, is the inventor of a colorful figure with an impressive appearance, a powerful body, and a red swim suit who enjoys the ability to fly through the ether.
>
> The inventive Israelite named this pleasant guy with an overdeveloped body and underdeveloped mind "Superman." He advertised widely Superman's sense of justice, well-suited for imitation by the American youth.
>
> As you can see, there is nothing the Sadducees won't do for money![6]

Like a typical war comics fan, the *Das Schwarze Korps* writer quibbles with the accuracy of the story's technical details: "We see several German soldiers in a bunker, who in order to receive the American guest have borrowed old uniforms from a military museum."

The writer emphasizes that "Superman" deserves attention because of his influence on young American readers: "Instead of using the chance to encourage really useful virtues, he sows hate, suspicion, evil, laziness, and criminality in their young hearts. [...] Woe to the American youth, who must live in such a poisoned atmosphere and don't even notice the poison they swallow daily."

Superheroes Go to War

Pioneering comic book creators Joe Simon and Jack Kirby co-created the comic book superhero Captain America, with their first issue of *Captain America Comics* reaching newsstands on December 20, 1940 (a year before the U.S. entered the war in 1941).[7] Simon has described how he came up with the idea for the character:

> There never had been a truly believable villain in comics. But Adolph was live, hated by more than half the world. [...] I could smell a winner. All that was left to do was to devise a long underwear hero to stand up to him. [...] This was an opportunity for big money if I could make the right deal, not to mention the chance to make a mockery of the Nazis and their mad leader.[8]

American supporters of Hitler were infuriated. Joe Simon claimed that for representing Hitler as "a buffoon—a clown" in comic books "we were inundated with a torrent of raging hate mail and vicious, obscene telephone calls" which demanded "death to the Jews."[9] (Simon and Kirby were Jewish.)

Cartoonist Jack Kirby remembered of his political feelings during that period that "the only real politics I knew was that if a guy liked Hitler, I'd beat the stuffing out of him and that would be it."[10] Thousands of "guys" in New York supported Hitler. The German-American Bund, founded in 1936 to fight "Jewish Marxism and Communism," filled Madison Square Garden in February 1939 with 20,000 people for a "True American-ism" rally. The event also attracted 10,000 protesters who demonstrated to "keep the Nazis out of New York."[11]

In June 1941, Germany broke its 1939 Nazi-Soviet agreement by invading the Soviet Union. That December, the Japanese attack on the American naval base at Pearl Harbor brought the United States fully into the war. The comic books gave the war effort everything they had.

With the United States allied with the Soviet Union against Germany, several comic book stories appeared which supported America's Russian allies.[12] Still, American comic books, during the war and afterwards, did not make clear that the majority of Hitler's victims were citizens of the Soviet Union. Like Hollywood movies, they also grossly underestimated the Soviet Union's and Britain's roles in defeating Nazi Germany.

Britain and America

A shared language favored British propaganda efforts to enlist American support in World Wars I and II.[13] Despite this advantage, as World War II approached, America's military support for Britain had been far from a sure thing.[14]

The British campaign to enlist American help in World War II included an unusual example of a foreign government secretly convincing an American cartoonist to alter his work. The British Embassy sent an officer to meet with *Joe Palooka* cartoonist Ham Fisher and convinced Fisher to replace his unsympathetic strips about England with pro–British stories.[15]

Comic book artists' bias in favor of England was cemented during World War II, when the U.S. and the U.K. fought as allies against Germany. The prominence of immigrant Jews and the children of immigrant Jews in the comic-book industry assured that American comic books would be unsympathetic to Germany's anti–Semitic Nazi regime.[16] In other examples of the political influence of religion, on a more elite level, Christian religious affiliations would solidify American support for South Korean president Syngman Rhee and Chiang Kai-shek, president of the Republic of China on Taiwan (both Methodists), and Ngo Dinh Diem, the president of South Vietnam (a Catholic), in nations where Christians were small minorities.[17]

War Comic Books

Two years after the explosive growth of the comic book medium triggered by the appearance of Superman in 1938, a separate genre of war comics began to appear.[18] In 1940, Dell began a series called *War Comics*, and followed it with *War Heroes* and *War Stories*. Fiction House began *Wings*, and war themes also soon became prominent in adventure comics like *Fight Comics*.

War stories also appeared in several nonfiction comic book series. Parents Magazine Press began *Real Heroes* in 1941. Nelson Rockefeller's Office of Inter-American Affairs commissioned Spanish-language editions of *Real Heroes* war stories in 1943 for distribution in Latin America.[19] The reality-based *Heroic Comics* began in January 1943. It was continued after World War II by *New Heroic Comics*, featuring "stories of truly heroic men and women chosen by this publication for their daring actions in hazardous tasks." During the Korean War, *New Heroic Comics* reverted to war stories, relating the circumstances under which medals were won in Korea.

Koreans' struggle against Japan for national self-determination received support from a few American comic books during World War II, including a 1942 story of the multinational superhero team "The Girl Commandos." In that story, drawn by Barbara Hall, a Korean grandfather provides this background information:

That was when the Japanese overran our land ... plundering and murdering... [...] Over all Korea flew the hated flag of Japan! [...] But Koreans waged continuous warfare against the Japs ... sabotaging factories and killing many of the invaders! [...] December 7, 1941.... At last, the arrogant Nipponese made a fatal step ... they attacked our powerful friend, *America*!!![20]

In 1943, student teachers at Humboldt State College in northern California surveyed children about ages 9 to 14 about what they thought about comic books. They discovered that comics about the Army, Navy, and "Aviation" were "not very popular." The only comment about war comics that they printed was from a child who said, "If we are going to read about the Army, aviators, or mechanics, we want things to be very accurate."[21]

Total War

Comic books had represented World War II as a conflict in which each American was expected to contribute to the war effort.[22] The "limited" Korean War produced no comic book comparable to the World War II one-shot comic *How Boys and Girls Can Help Win the War* (1942). That comic began with an editorial from publisher George J. Hecht, who told his readers:

> OUR COUNTRY is engaged in a total effort to win a total war. That means that we all ... soldiers and civilians, grown-ups and children alike ... share in the responsibility. I am sure that every boy and girl is eager and anxious to do his or her part....

World War II comic books (and comic strips and cartoons) repeatedly emphasized that even boys and girls could help win the war. Defense stamps in denominations as small as ten cents could be saved up to trade in for defense bonds to help pay for the war effort (and also to reduce the threat of inflation at a time when consumer goods were scarce but paid work was plentiful). Many comic book covers waved the flag and urged readers to buy defense stamps and bonds or used their characters to reenact Archibald MacNeal Willard's famous patriotic painting *The Spirit of '76*.[23] During World War II, cartoonists also reminded the public to grow food in "victory gardens," participate in scrap drives, cooperate in blackouts, and keep quiet about sensitive information. The Korean War offered American children fewer ways to become actively involved.

The Office of War Information

In the first months of the United States' participation in World War II, the American public received contradictory information from the various government agencies, and remained confused about why the world was at war. In June 1942, President Roosevelt responded by ordering the creation of the United States Office of War Information (OWI), to provide a central source for official wartime information and to conduct propaganda campaigns.

Nine days after Roosevelt had announced the creation of the OWI, representatives of the American advertising company Young & Rubicam gave a presentation to the National Advisory Council on Government Posters, in the OWI's Graphics Division.[24] Based on previous studies which had found comics to be an extraordinarily effective medium for commercial advertising and promotional campaigns, the advertisers recommended "comic strips" as source material for the visual element in posters.

During the war, the OWI conducted several studies of how the war was being represented in syndicated newspaper comic strips and cartoons, and they found problems with the comics' images of the enemy, warfare, the goals of the war, American allies, and the importance of civilian sacrifice.[25] To communicate their messages in cartoon form, the OWI commissioned their own single panel cartoons, and sent them to two thousand newspapers and magazines weekly.

The OWI also sent comic book publishers copies of the "War Guide" which they had prepared to help magazines self-censor their war news (and the OWI discussed creating a similar guide designed specifically for comic books). Like the Bureau of Cartoons had done during World War I, the OWI also sent out a newsletter to artists (including editorial cartoonists, comic strip artists, comic book artists, poster artists and single-panel cartoonists) with suggestions for helpful themes to use when depicting the war.[26]

The OWI published several propaganda comic books for civilians overseas, but when, in 1943, a Republican Congressman criticized the OWI comic book *The Life of Franklin D. Roosevelt* as "purely political propaganda, designed entirely to promote a fourth term and a dictatorship," the OWI backed off from using comics for the rest of the war.[27]

The Writers' War Board

Paul Hirsch has investigated the collaboration during World War II of comic book publishers with the Writers' War Board (which was part of the Office of War Information).[28] These publishers included National Publications (later known as DC), Fawcett Comics, and Parents' Institute Press. Hirsch found that the Writers' War Board encouraged "racial and ethnic hatred" against Japan and Germany in World War II comic books. The Board hoped that strengthening comics readers' hatred of the enemy would increase their willingness to do whatever was needed for total victory.[29]

One story designed to stir hatred of the Japanese focused on Japan's oppression of Korea. "Japan's First Victim" appeared in *The United States Marines, Vol. 1, No. 3*, in 1944, with "Contents reviewed and cleared by the U.S. Marine Corps." The issue was edited by Vincent Sullivan, the first editor of what became DC Comics. Its catalog of Japanese crimes and atrocities against Korea begins with panels about "the Jap careerist Hideyoshi—known as Great Monkeyface" leading a failed invasion of Korea in 1592. The unusually violent illustrations include a picture of "the murder of Korea's last queen, Myung-Sung" in 1895; the Korean patriot Kim Ku getting revenge by choking to death "Captain Tsuchida," a Japanese trader whom Ku blamed (correctly in the comic book version) for the Queen's assassination; Japanese soldiers shooting young children; and scenes of torture from the 1919 suppression of the March 1 Movement for Korean Independence.[30]

The atrocity of "hooking" Korean protesters was widely reported in American newspapers, but these articles left the meaning of that term to the imagination. The cartoonist for "Japan's First Victim" imagined a Japanese soldier on horseback who has somehow pierced a Korean man through his shoulder with what looks like a giant fishhook attached to a rope and is pulling the man off his feet. In actuality, the term referred to the wounds caused by fire brigades, operating under police orders, who attacked crowds with the hooked poles that they usually used for pulling burning thatch off of the roofs of houses.[31]

"The First Victim" shows a familiar-looking drawing of an almost naked man nailed to a tall cross, as one onlooker tells the other: "Look! They crucify Korean Christians!" A 1919 Korean Red Cross pamphlet had reprinted a photograph of three fully-dressed Koreans who had been tied to short crosses in front of a crowd of spectators and executed.[32] In the year that it took to suppress the independence movement, Japanese police and soldiers would kill over 7,000 Koreans. ("Japan's First Victim" estimates the slaughter as 6,000 victims.)

The articles in American newspapers that mentioned "hooking" also reported that the Japanese stripped the clothes off of Korean women, especially relatives of the leaders of the insurrection, beat them in front of crowds, and tortured them. A 1920 collection of eyewitness stories about the suppression of the Korean Independence movement claimed that:

> A Korean woman would rather die than expose her naked body in ways not conformable to local customs. But it seems to be the common delight of official depravity just now to humiliate our Christian women by stripping them and beating them while naked. [...] the effect is maddening on the Korean masses.[33]

"Japan's First Victim" did not include stories about the enemy's sexual sadism. This kind of discretion characterizes war comics in general, and contributes to muting their readers' awareness of this important dimension of war's brutality.

The last panel of "Japan's First Victim" concludes:

> Today in Chungking [China], Korea has a Provisional Government. Its President is that same Kim Ku who strangled the Jap Tsuchida. And it is the burning desire of President Kim Ku and his followers to establish the Korean Declaration of Independence as a living document of freedom....!

As this story illustrates, Kim Ku did become a Korean national hero through that act of political violence, and the leader of a Korean Provisional Government in exile. He maintained a lifelong support for terrorism, political assassination and subversion, until he was himself assassinated in 1949. As a Korean nationalist, Kim Ku was fiercely against Japan and all those who had collaborated with Japan, and also fiercely against Russia and communism.[34] At the time of his death in Korea, he was opposing Syngman Rhee's decision to establish a government only in South Korea, arguing that if North and South Korea established separate governments, those governments would inevitably make war on each other.[35] Kim's right-wing assassin confessed 43 years later that he had acted after the head of South Korea's Army Counter-Intelligence Corps (and also a Korean-speaking lieutenant colonel of the United States' OSS) had told him several times that Kim Ku "should be removed."[36] (Ku had angered General John Hodge, the American military governor of occupied South Korea, by arranging the assassination of the head of the Korean political party that Hodge supported, organizing mass demonstrations to end the trusteeship over South Korea which Hodge administered, and attempting a coup d'état.[37])

The Writers' War Board was dissolved when World War II ended, and creators of Korean War comic books, except when working directly on government propaganda comics, had no formal organization to coordinate their work with the needs of the war effort. The Truman Administration repeatedly refused to set up a separate propaganda agency during the Korean War, reasoning that as a "limited war," the action in Korea did not call for a new Office of War Information like the "total war" a few years earlier had required.[38]

VD and War

During World War II, the American military conducted major health education programs for enlisted men to warn them about sexually transmitted diseases (which were called "venereal diseases," or "VD"). Near the end of his life, Stan Lee remembered that he had written training pamphlets and films when he was in the Army during World War II, but he got the most attention for drawing a cartoon to help enlisted men avoid getting VD:

> …they had what they called prophylactic stations, little one-room buildings with green lights inside. After you'd had carnal knowledge of a female, you would go to the pro station and get disinfected in the most horrible way. My mission was to tell the troops to go to the pro station after they'd had sex. So I drew a little cartoon of a soldier. There's the green light. Over his head there's a dialogue balloon that says, "VD? Not me!" They printed a couple million of them. I figure we probably won the war based on that.[39]

These "prophylactic ablution centers," originally conceived during World War I, were opened throughout Korea and Japan during the Korean War, but most troops did not use them and their effectiveness was questionable.

VD became much more common during the Korean War than in earlier conflicts or in other places, with a rate of infection three times higher than it had been in World War II.[40] War comic books could easily ignore this problem, since they concentrated overwhelmingly on battles, and usually imagined a world in which men revealed no sexual appetites and women were seldom seen.[41]

U.S. Government Cold War Propaganda Comics

Measured simply by circulation numbers, government-sponsored comic strips and comic books played a significant role in U.S. Cold War propaganda. Little has been written about them.

In 1949, the State Department's first anti-communist propaganda comic book for distribution in the Far East told life stories of famous Americans. It was designed for "areas under strong Communist pressure": South Korea, Thailand, Viet Nam (French Indo-China) and Indonesia.[42] M. Philip Copp, a 33-year-old former Manhattan art agent, had underbid the comic-book publishers to win the contract for this series.[43]

Stephen E. Pease's *PSYWAR*, a history of psychological warfare in the Korean War, mentions that more than 30 percent of the surrendering enemy soldiers were able to read only road signs and the simplest instructions, and most of the rest did not read much better. To get their messages across, the two billion UN PSYWAR leaflets used simple phrases, symbols, photos, and custom-drawn cartoons.[44] Most of the cartoon leaflets that showered over Korea were drawn at the Psychological Warfare Branch of the U.N. headquarters in Tokyo, by a small group of Chinese, Korean, Japanese, and American cartoonists.[45]

A "Pilot Model" of the propaganda comic book *Korea! The True Story* used 36 panels spread over 16 pages to celebrate the United Nations troops who "fought to protect the independence of the new nation [of South Korea], to repel the Communist aggression and to maintain world peace." The inside front cover introduction "Filipino Troops Fight Aggression in Korea" suggests that the plan might have been to produce localized versions for the various nations who had sent troops. Since the comic concludes with the UN troops pursuing "the few remaining North Korean Communist forces" while "The People of North Korea were happy to be rid of their Communist masters who had brought only lies and suffering," the comic must have been completed shortly after the UN troops swept through North Korea in October 1950, but before China entered the war. Perhaps the file copy was labeled "Pilot Model" because it became obsolete before reaching the printers.

A later chapter describes in some detail the propaganda comic *Korea My Home*.

The U.S. propaganda operations went through several bureaucratic changes, and in 1953 became part of the newly created United States Information Agency (USIA). The USIA continued to publish comics and cartoons as its predecessors had done.

The most successful of the USIA's five weekly or semi-weekly cartoon strips, the anti-communist humor strip *Little Moe*, ran from 1953 until January 1967. It appeared regularly in as many as 500 newspapers in 58 countries.[46]

After cancelling its own comics, the USIA continued to distribute cartoons by reproducing and distributing, with permission, commercially created political cartoons which suited its purposes.[47]

6

Harvey Kurtzman

Harvey Kurtzman has become one of the most acclaimed creators in the history of comic books. The Harvey Awards, among the oldest and most respected prizes given to recognize outstanding achievements in the comic book industry, are named in his honor.[1] As editor of EC's two war comics, *Two-Fisted Tales* and *Frontline Combat,* Kurtzman claimed (with good reason) to have been the first to attempt to tell realistic war stories in comic book format.[2]

As soon as the fighting started in Korea, with the second issue of *Two-Fisted Tales,* Kurtzman began converting what was originally conceived as a title for telling what he called "blood and thunder tales and rip-roaring high adventure" stories in the tradition of Roy Crane's *Captain Easy* and *Wash Tubbs,* into a war comic.[3] As the market for war comics grew, publisher William Gaines started a second war comic, *Frontline Combat,* and assigned Kurtzman to edit that one also.[4]

Bill Schelly, the author of *Harvey Kurtzman: The Man who Created MAD and Revolutionized Humor in America,* has described what made these two war-comics series artistically outstanding:

> Kurtzman's war comic books were special in many ways. There was the choice of subject matter, the sophistication of the story structure, the literary qualities (poetic elements) and the degree of authenticity. There was also the well-considered balance of text and visuals to tell the stories, the artistic clarity, the sensitive coloring and the cohesion that came from having one writer-artist at the helm. The result was nothing less than a new kind of comic book, one with extraordinary dramatic power in the early 1950s and with a potency that remains undiminished by the passage of time.[5]

Kurtzman's perfectionism drove him to create works that were not cost-effective in an industry based on selling cheap material at low prices. Since Kurtzman was paid by how much he produced, the extra care he lavished on his books was not rewarded economically, but punished. His publisher, William M. Gaines, explained that:

> …Kurtzman was very slow. He was putting out two books in a two month period. [Al] Feldstein was very fast and he was putting out seven books in a two month period. By simple mathematics you can see that Feldstein was making three and a half times as much as Kurtzman. This rankled Harvey, because he felt that his books were better than Feldstein's books, and in one sense they were, but they weren't *selling* as well, so *that* was negated.[6]

Kurtzman understood that the way he approached his work did not fit with the comic book industry's demands for speedy production. He spent most of his career trying to put comic books behind him and to find work cartooning for a higher class of magazines.[7]

Like the cartoonists he worked with, Kurtzman was a World War II veteran, and he had strong feelings about his Army experiences. His wife, Adele, remembered that Kurtz-man "hated the Army": "He had nightmares from being in the Army, about having to go back. He really detested it. He was set to go overseas but never did because the war ended."[8]

The one time that I met him, I asked Kurtzman whether he ever regretted not having been in combat. He said "No," but first he gave me a look that seemed to say that he was try-ing to decide if I was simply crazy, pathetically naïve, hopelessly stupid or putting him on.[9]

In contrast to his Korean War comics, the relatively amateurish cartoons Kurtzman created during World War II demonstrated no sensitivity about the enemy's basic humanity. His nineteen-panel strip "Private Brown Knows," published as the front page of the June 10, 1944, issue of Camp Sutton's newspaper *The Carry All,* encouraged plain hatred for the "Nazis and Japs." As a reminder of the reasons to "hate their guts," the strip included a list of their atrocities: "Nanking, Warsaw, Holland, Pearl Harbor, Coventry, Lidice, Manila, Cor-rigedor [sic], Sevastopol."[10]

Kurtzman expressed the same attitude in a 1945 "Black Venus" story he created for *Contact Comics* while on leave.[11] His story begins with a caption that introduces the lead character:

> Black Venus—a modern Joan of Arc—imbued with the fury of a tigress, sets out to avenge the merci-less treatment administered to our prisoners of war [at Corregidor] by a conglomeration of heartless beasts—the dastardly and treacherous *JAPS!*

"Black Venus" was a white character who wore a black-leather, full-body, form-revealing flying suit. Kurtzman later explained the story's visual appearance by saying "I went through a period of imitating Milton Caniff because that's what the market wanted. And that was the only way I could get work."[12]

Kurtzman did not depict the communist enemy in Korea with the same simple hatred that he had directed against the "Nazis and Japs" during World War II. One reason that he emphasized that the Red enemy consisted of human beings may have been that he grew up with leftist parents whom he liked and admired.[13]

Kurtzman's stories usually stripped the war of its political context. Robert Crumb, a fanatic devotee of Kurtzman's satirical works, has explained Kurtzman's politics:

> He thought the whole left-wing thing was real dumb. He grew up with low-level communist ideology being thrown at him all the time, the sloganeering, the left-wing summer camps they used to have on the East Coast for Jewish kids. I could see where you could grow up turned off to the whole idea from that.[14]

The clearest expression of Kurtzman's attitude about the Korean revolutionary move-ment appears in his story "Dying City!"[15] There he shows a young Korean who took up the gun as "a symbol of freedom … of revolution" of "the youth of Korea […] joining the march of Russia and China to stamp out the enemies of the people." The story drives home the point that this young man has made a tragic error which leads only to destruction. The sole surviving relative, his grandfather, puts the entire blame for the war on his grandson's having introduced a pistol, and the military ambition it symbolized, into their peaceful lives:

> "You couldn't see what you were doing when you came home with your gun!"
> "Did you see then that your father would be crushed flat under the treads of a [Russian] war tank?"
> "Did you see that your mother and little sister would be torn to pieces by a [North Korean] hand grenade?"
> "Did you see our city broken and ruined? Did you see the destroyed homes and factories?"

"What does the future mean when everything you love is dead, my son?"
"What is left? What good is your Revolution? What good? What good? What good?"

Kurtzman's portrayals of war as a serious, painful matter but a civic duty did not raise a public controversy, even at a time when the comic book industry and his publisher in particular were under close scrutiny. Kurtzman's comics said nothing against the governments of South Korea or the United States and nothing in favor of North Korea or communism. In *Frontline Combat,* #12 (May–June 1953), he ran a story "F-94!" which dramatized the work of the Ground Observer Corps, and at the Air Force's request, ran a full-page appeal to his readers which asked them to help the U.S. Air Force by joining that volunteer organization.[16]

For *Two-Fisted Tales* and *Frontline Combat,* Kurtzman prepared detailed roughs of each story. Although he completed some of these roughs himself, he usually assigned the pieces to other comic book artists to be fully rendered in pencil and ink.[17]

Kurtzman had a legendary concern for accuracy of technical details.[18] As he said, "My schtick was always authenticity...."[19] He consulted books from the New York Public Library by the duffel bag load.[20] He remembered that "I'd go rushing around, trying to write stories and do research simultaneously. We had an enormous library of photographs of equipment and combat, and I'd use every chance I could get to go or send somebody to actually use the equipment, or see it used."[21]

Kurtzman also visited the Korean Consulate for information, where "the Consul General would sit and talk to me for hours."[22] He corresponded with and spoke with soldiers frequently. He promised readers to be as factual as possible, and reported his impression from the fan mail that his readers "enjoy the unvarnished truth."[23] As with other well-respected war comics artists, his attention to the authenticity of props was not matched by a concern with accurately describing the immediate causes, goals, or long-range consequences of war.

Kurtzman found appreciative readers who realized from reading his cheerless *Two-Fisted Tales* that war is "[a] terrible waste of human life inflicted on both sides." This led some of them to ask, "When will the civilized world learn to settle their differences by peaceful methods?" The first two times that Kurtzman addressed this question, he said that he had no answer.[24] When he returned to the question of the causes of war for the third time, Kurtzman told a reader that "War is like a tiny snowball rolling down a hill, picking up thousands of flakes. Soon the snowball achieves the size and momentum of an avalanche.... And then it's too late to stop it! The time to prevent a war is when it's still a little snowball!"[25]

More commonly, the readers' letters in *Two-Fisted Tales*' "Combat Correspondence" column suggested ideas for war stories they would like to see or quibbled with the few alleged inaccuracies in drawings of ships, planes, jeeps, and weapons.[26] Sometimes Kurtzman was able to correct his readers; sometimes he apologized for his errors.

Some letters angrily criticized Kurtzman's war comics for taking the North's side in stories about the American Civil War of 90 years earlier.[27] Kurtzman replied in his letter column that "We wish to make it clear that we do not mean to show more favoritism to the North than to the South. If our material appears to be slanted in favor of the North, it is quite unintentional. We plan to feature many heroes of the South in future issues...."[28] That his comics were biased in favor of South Korea's side in the current Korean Civil War went without saying.

Kurtzman's Korean War comics matched the tone set by the photojournalists' images in news magazines, which had also represented American soldiers in Korea as tired and sorrowful but usually stoical.[29] Although some later writers have imagined that Kurtzman's grim war comics must have stood out as daring "anti-war" statements during the Cold War, Kurtzman accepted the Korean War as necessary.[30]

Kurtzman's Korean War comic books influenced other cartoonists.[31] As a rule, though, the usual stories in war comics were not carefully-considered, polished, artistic compositions, but quickly knocked out variations on a story formula that was selling well.

Kurtzman's work should not be taken as representative of typical war comics, if for no other reason than that Kurtzman expressed disgust for other publishers' war comics. His feelings came out in a hilarious fashion when he became the founding editor of *MAD* magazine in 1952, and satirized his competitor's war comic *G.I. Joe* as "G.I. Schmoe!" in *MAD #10* (April 1954).[32]

Kurtzman's skills as a satirist had been nourished by the example of his mother, who had used the perspective she gained from her subscription to the communist *Daily Worker* to (in her words) "read between the lines and get to the truth" behind the stories in the Hearst and Pulitzer papers. Rather than searching between the lines for political reasons, Harvey Kurtzman made it a habit to "read between the lines" of popular culture for the humor of exposing the distance between what was said and what was real.[33]

EC's rivals did not appreciate *MAD*'s parodies of their characters (which included not only those in war-related comics like *Blackhawk* and *G.I. Joe*, but Superman, Archie, and Mickey Mouse). EC publisher William Gaines thought that their "cracks at some of the sanctimonious … 'old boy' publishers … beloved by the 'old boy' wholesalers" had led to wholesalers retaliating against EC comics by sometimes refusing to handle their controversial comics.[34]

7

◇◇◇◇◇◇◇◇◇

Critics

In 1954, an anti-comic book movement approached its peak. In that year, a Senate sub-committee held hearings to investigate possible links between comic books and juvenile delinquency; Fredric Wertham's *Seduction of the Innocent*—a book that attacked almost every aspect of the comic book industry—was published; the comic book publishers defended themselves from a rising tide of criticism by creating a self-censorship body, the Comics Code Authority; and a wave of local laws restricting comic book sales were considered or passed.[1] Comic book circulation collapsed sharply. These events marked the most dramatic turning point in the history of comic books.

Comics historians have commonly described those who attacked the comic books of the 1940s and 1950s as people who had tried to encourage conformity to law and order.[2] The Federal and the New York State hearings which investigated a possible connection between comic books and juvenile delinquency, and articles in American newspapers of that period, do leave this impression. Nevertheless, the main critics of comic books were not primarily concerned with making children more obedient. These critics usually expressed fears that comic books were (among other things) conditioning their young readers to passively accept the rise of a brutal, totalitarian system. Several reformers with little else in common arrived at the shared conclusion that the core problem with comic books came down to irresponsible publishers putting their own profits above the public's interests, without regard for the requirements of a democratic society.

Because of its relative wealth of documentary evidence, dramatic interest, colorful characters and crucial importance, the anti-comics movement of the 1940s and 1950s has become one of the most familiar stories in comic book history. Too often, though, it has been reduced in the retelling to a legend about the "unscientific" Dr. Fredric Wertham and his anti-comic book "crusade." Comics folklore has reduced Wertham's arguments against comic books, in turn, to a claim that comic-book reading "causes" juvenile delinquency.[3] Reconsidering the anti-comics movement in relation to 20th century totalitarianism, to the minor genre of war comics, to the Korean War, and to the Cold War puts the comics controversy in a much different light.

Although comic books may have been the least censored of the mass media in this period, their range of creative freedom was still fenced in on many sides. The most immediate limits on what comic books could do came from the working conditions under which they were created. This chapter surveys some additional forces which put limits on what appeared in American comic books.

The attacks on comic books during the Korean War focused primarily on super-hero, crime, horror, and romance comics, but the frequent criticisms against sadistic brutality in comic books also applied to the wisecracking war comics of that time, and some newspaper items criticized war comics directly.[4] Even when *verbal* criticisms focused on crime and horror comics, their accompanying visuals sometimes included Korean War comics.[5]

1. Early Criticisms

The earliest attacks on comic books had criticized them on explicitly political grounds. Sterling North, in the first published article to condemn comic books, wrote in 1940 that comics included sex, violence, and "cheap political propaganda" on almost every page, and warned that their message was along a "pre–Fascist pattern."[6]

Less than a year later, North's article had been republished in forty magazines and newspapers, and he estimated that requests for reprints were arriving at the rate of a thousand copies a day.[7] Looking to the next generation, North warned that the stakes in this question of whether children would identify with heroes of good literature or comic book heroes were whether we would "produce a liberal, livable democratic world or a ferocious Fascist society."[8]

The fear that superhero comics were teaching totalitarian, anti-democratic values became one of the central themes of the early anti-comics critics. Stanley Kunitz, editor of the *Wilson Library Bulletin*, acknowledged a debt to North's "blistering indictment" of comic books when he editorialized that the violent world of comics was "quintessentially fascist" and concluded that those raised on "the sensational adventures of grotesque and impossible creatures who seem to have crawled out of a cheap underworld of the imagination" can grow to become only "a generation of Storm Troopers, *Gauleiter*, and coarse, audacious supermen."[9]

James Frank Vlamos asked in 1941:

How deeply is this artistic and imaginative fare registering on the young mind? No one has as yet measured the impression. But certainly the "funnies" demonstrate all the arguments a child ever needs for an omnipotent and infallible "strong man" beyond all law, the nihilistic man of the totalitarian ideology.[10]

Superman first appeared in 1938, and quickly became popular on the radio, in animated cartoons, and in his own newspaper comic strip (through which he reached twenty million readers).[11] Superman's success also sparked the creation of many cheap imitations, and critics of the comic books did not usually distinguish between the original Superman and the superhero genre. For American intellectuals, the name "Superman" inescapably suggested Nietzsche's Übermensch (as that idea had been corrupted by German Nazis).[12]

Most American comic strip readers accepted Superman as a morale-boosting character in the fight for democracy.[13] Still, most who *wrote* about that character continued to argue that Superman's commitment to democracy was mere lip service. After all, as a Yale Divinity School student noticed in 1942: "Superman and these other [superheroes] never act through the channels of law but always rise above it or cut through it. Law is held in contempt as long as some superman, who is a law unto himself can crack a case wide open."[14] The student, Stephen A. Bachelder, developed this point at some length, equating the appeal of Superman to the appeal of Hitler, and warning:

This popular admiration of super-heroes in the comics seems to indicate that America is growing tired of her democracy, growing more and more discouraged with this type of government. America apparently is groping for some great leader to solve her problems, relieving the individual of his burdensome duty to society. The comics not only reveal this trend, but help to foster it, impressing it on opinionless minds.[15]

These early concerns about superheroes were expressed at a time when many Americans regarded the possibility of American fascism as a threat too serious to ignore. In 1944, Freeman Champney surveyed recent American novels (rather than comic books) in an article for the literary journal *The Antioch Review*, and reported that:

In the twenty-odd years since fascism began to be recognized as a phenomenon of universal importance and menace, there has been much speculation about the possibility of its emergence in America and the special forms it might be expected to develop here.[16]

Champney described Americans' gradually maturing viewpoint on this problem:

Our prewar attitude toward fascism focused on the fuhrer as the causative factor that brought all the evils of barbarism to his country by some kind of black magic. And if we could convince ourselves that Hitler and Mussolini were absurd psychopaths (which was easy enough) we felt foolishly relieved and superior.[17]

"The more realistic tendency of today," he added, was to notice that "we have several widespread and deeply-rooted habits of mind in America which are obstructive to a functional democracy and might be used to support a domestic fascism."[18] The question of which "habits of mind" comic books would cultivate, while outside the scope of Champney's article on "Protofascism in Literature," weighed heavily on the imaginations of those who wrote against comics. The next year, Walter J. Ong's article "The Comics and the Super State: Glimpses down the Back Alleys of the Mind" warned that comic books about Superman (a "super state type of hero" who remains "true to his sources" in Nietzsche's Übermensch) were being uncritically absorbed "on the level at which propaganda moves."[19]

As Superman's critics had observed, that character (in his early stories) had embodied the fascist ideal of the perfectly evolved man, skilled in violence and unbound by law. These critics were not impressed that the comic book Superman used his powers, not to dominate the weak, but to protect ordinary people from evil.[20]

The many comic book stories about American heroes defeating spies, saboteurs and "fifth columnists" demonstrated that the creators of World War II comic books were *also* deeply concerned about the fascist threat in America, but in their own violent way. Americans grew less comfortable with the paradoxical idea that anti-democratic superheroes would be necessary to defend democracy, even before the war ended.[21]

Besides their concern about fascism, the early critics of comic books also feared that comics were teaching race hatred. In 1942, Margaret Frakes wrote in *Christian Century* that American comic books were worse than the anti–Semitic children's books that had been distributed in Nazi Germany:

We looked with revulsion a few years ago at the primers created for German children, with their grotesque pictures of Jews as half-monsters, and decried the depravity which could place them in the hands of children whose concepts of people and events were just being formed. But those primers have nothing on the comics which today are eagerly devoured by most American schoolchildren, their picture of the Jew as impotent monster not half so terrifying as the ruthless, fanged Oriental or nazi monster in which the comic magazine specializes.[22]

Frakes claimed (with some exaggeration) that the Japanese in American comic books "always appear literally as beasts with fangs for teeth and bright yellow skin."[23] By the Korean War, there had been some progress in toning down comic book racism, although Chinese and Koreans were still sometimes colored pale yellow, as they had been during World War II.[24]

The year after Frakes' article was published, racist stereotypes of the enemy in comic books became even more brutal, as the OWI's Writers' War Board consciously promoted racist stereotyping of enemy nations to build support for a "total war."[25]

The arguments against comic books evolved by repeating their older themes while adding new ones. In 1943, Sister Mary Clare, S.N.D.'s pamphlet "Comics: A study of the effects of Comic Books on children less than eleven years old" was a wide-ranging and intemperate attack, warning Catholic parents that comic books had become the means by which "hare-brained money-mad pagans carry moral disease germs into the souls of their children."[26] She cited Dr. Matthew Luckiesh, the respected "Father of the Science of Seeing," to argue that reading comic books at too early an age was physically bad for the eyes.[27]

Clare also criticized comic books for indoctrinating children with hatred of other nationalities:

> Christ's injunction that we must love our enemies seems to have been lost in a wave of hate promoted either by the persuasive agents of propaganda or by the psychological effects of the news.
> An examination of 180 different "comics" reveals that 95% teach everything but the Christian and democratic way of life, and in the current crisis are, therefore, positively dangerous for they are injecting into our children a livid hatred for the people who find themselves, through no will of their own, opposed to us in the present conflict.[28]

The next year, the Catechetical Guild published "The Case Against the Comics" by Gabriel Lynn.[29] Although Lynn's brochure begins by introducing comics as a contributing factor to "juvenile delinquency," it quickly becomes apparent that his concern about comic books that weaken respect for the rule of law has little to do with small-scale criminality. Instead, he hammers away at the already familiar argument that comic books, with their glorification of vigilante violence, threaten to move the entire society away from democracy and toward "the type of oppression of which Adolf Hitler stands as a current symbol."[30] Comics teach the observant child their dangerous lessons through a series of steps:

> …the parent who hands a child an uncensored comic book is literally saying to that child: Meet these murderers, sadists and degenerates; observe and study how these inhuman monsters torture and kill their helpless victims; notice how inadequate the law enforcing authorities are in handling these criminals, and how necessary it is to set up illegal methods to bring about law and order.[31]

In 1948, a news article reported that because of "increasing and persistent demands by parents, church and civic leaders," nearly fifty cities in the United States already had responded to the menace of objectionable comic books. Usually this took the form of cooperating with wholesalers and dealers "in some plan of voluntary control or self-censorship." Some cities had enacted laws to control comic books.[32] In New York City, a group of large comic book publishers asked the city for recommendations and were told that if they did not self-censor more carefully, "it can be expected that society's indignation and insistence on the protection of children will result in efforts to regulate the industry" through city licensing ordinances.[33] The next year, New York State passed a law that would require each comic book to file an application for a permit which would be reviewed by a new office created for that purpose, and to state on its title page whether the application had been approved or denied.[34] Governor Thomas Dewey vetoed it.[35] (Eventually, in 1955, New York State unanimously passed a law against crime comic books that Governor Averell Harriman signed.[36])

2. Anti-Communistic Comics

In the folklore of comic book fans, the postwar American anti-comic book movement has been described as happening in a "McCarthyist" cultural environment of anti-communist paranoia, hysteria and "moral panic."[37] Although the controversy over comic book content happened at the same time that other entertainment media (film, radio and television) were blacklisting communists and their sympathizers, the comic book controversy differed in important ways.[38] At a time of widespread concern over communist infiltration of the entertainment industries, public attacks on comic books as a tool for indoctrinating children with communist propaganda were less developed than the continuing criticisms of "fascist" conditioning in comic books.

Jack B. Tenney

California State Senator Jack B. Tenney gave at least one speech warning parents about "Red" comic books. Tenney had begun his political career on the left, supporting communist front organizations, but became a dedicated anti-communist.[39] As chair of California's Fact-finding Committee of Un-American Activities from 1941 to 1949, Tenney presided over tumultuous and sensational public hearings which sought to expose subversion in Hollywood, the labor movement, the universities, and elsewhere.[40]

In 1946, one month after Winston Churchill's famous "Iron Curtain" speech that had marked the beginning of the Cold War, Tenney told a meeting of Republican women that "well camouflaged" communist doctrines were appearing in "comic or thrill-and-adventure, colored pictorial strips obtainable for a few pennies in magazine-like form." Among the problems he noticed, one comic book had pages supporting the communist front group "American Youth for Democracy" and others supported "racial consciousness," class-based resentment against landlords and greedy employers, or promoted "the idea of giving out the atomic bomb secret to all the world instead of keeping it for the protection of America."[41] (The educational comic book *Picture News #3*, which came out around the time of Tenney's speech, promoted international control of nuclear weapons. The comic books *Young Life Comics* and *Teen Life Comics and Adventure* published pages supporting "American Youth for Democracy.")[42]

Tenney was unusual in publicly linking comic books, communism, and alleged Jewish control of the media.[43] In 1953, Tenney wrote a report describing his tour of the Anti-Defamation League of B'Nai B'rith's offices. The Anti-Defamation League had been founded in 1913 "to stop the defamation of the Jewish people and to secure justice and fair treatment to all." In Tenney's report, he accused that organization of inserting communist propaganda into children's comic books:

> "This is the 'COMIC BOOK SECTION,'" we are told.
> "Does the ADL plant propaganda in children's Comic books?" we ask.
> "Comic books," our guide replies, ignoring the form of the question, "carry strips denouncing native fascists and their use of inter-group tension as a weapon against Democracy."

The phraseology is reminiscent of the *Daily People's World* and *Daily Worker* ... "Native fascist," "intergroup tension," "Democracy"—brain-blinding slogans from the dialectical lexicon of Marx and Lenin.[44]

Tenney's hostile interpretation of what he had seen seems ironic. In 1951, the anti–Communist American Jewish Committee had explained that they worked with the Anti-Defamation League to influence comic books and other media partly to break the anti–Semitic stereotype that did not distinguish between communists and Jews.[45]

Harry S. Toy

In 1948, Detroit Police Commissioner Harry S. Toy ordered that copies of all comic books sold in that city be examined for harmful material after claiming to have discovered that some comic books "contained liberal doses of Communist propaganda, racial prejudice and sexy and gory reading."[46] A brief filler item reporting this news received wide distribution.

Detroit was a leader in using the police to censor comic books, magazines and paperback books.[47] Commissioner Toy assigned the investigation of the comic books to Detroit's "Red Squad" and Police Censor Bureau, and promised to share their findings with the FBI.[48] "Red Squads" were police units in American cities that specialized in identifying, tracking, and harassing radicals.[49]

Simply by threatening to prosecute distributors and retailers for obscenity, the Detroit police could control what was sold there. When Detroit's officials found 80 objectionable comic book titles, they informed the distributor that these comics violated a Michigan statute, and that they could either remove them from circulation or defend them in court as a test case. Faced with that choice, the distributor agreed to stop selling those titles.[50]

Around the time of the Korean War, this kind of "informal" police censorship seemed to be growing rapidly. The unnamed author of the law article "Censorship of Obscene Literature by Informal Governmental Action" explained that:

> The most prevalent practice is to send letters to booksellers or distributors stating that the writer considers certain books objectionable, and intimating that criminal prosecutions under the obscenity laws will be initiated against all who sell them. More subtly, the police may make a "request for coöperation," implicit with a threat that non-coöperation will produce "trouble." Such "trouble" may include visits by building inspectors, fire inspectors, health inspectors, or any of a number of other officials who might find technical violations of some law or ordinance. Or it may involve a disrupting police raid, a withdrawal of police protection from the offender's place of business, or the stationing of uniformed policemen inside his store. These informal restraints—"informal" because they operate outside the normal legal machinery—may be classified together under the generic term "police censorship."[51]

Because the business of wholesaling and distributing magazines, paperback books and comic books was highly concentrated, police censorship could operate much more easily than if the police had to work with each store and newsstand individually.[52] Besides the threat of sending building, fire and health inspectors to visit warehouses, the authorities could ticket truck drivers for the brief violations of parking regulations that they committed when they unloaded their bundles.[53] If little has been written about such police censorship, it might be partly because the distributors had been so eager to cooperate with the authorities.[54]

J.B. Matthews

J.B. Matthews wrote only a few paragraphs criticizing comic books and focused on only one example. His comments deserve attention because of his leading role in exposing hidden communist influence during the Cold War. In 1949, Matthews wrote:

> As might be expected, the communists and their front organizations have not neglected comic strips and comic books. Naturally, the class struggle angle is worked into this powerful medium of propaganda.
>
> The most impressive attempt in the comic book field for left-wing indoctrination of children has been made by the *Protestant* magazine, a vehemently pro-communist and anti–Catholic publication cited as subversive by the Congressional Committee on Un-American Activities. The *Protestant's* comic books have appeared under the title of "The Challenger." The "party line" is deftly woven into them. On the back cover of the books, there is a plan for organizing children into "Challenger" clubs. "Get together at least 10 young people who have signed the Challenger pledge card," the cover urges. The pledge reads, in part, as follows: "In the name of democracy and our faith in the new world born out of the most tragic of wars, we pledge ourselves to challenge, fight and defeat fascism in all forms." The initiated will have no difficulty in recognizing the "Challenger's" *new world* as the bloc of Soviet states.[55]

Matthews' article "The Commies Go After the Kids," which included this attack on comics, was reprinted and widely distributed in pamphlet form by the National Council for American Education, a group devoted to the eradication of "Marxism, Socialism, Communism and all other forces that seek to destroy the liberty of the American people."[56]

Poet and activist Kenneth Leslie had created the monthly *Protestant Digest* magazine in 1938 and later the anti-racist/anti-fascist comic book series *The Challenger* because he had been disturbed by the rise of fascist, anti–Semitic attitudes in the United States. Leslie saw this danger as represented by Roman Catholic priest Father Charles Coughlin's hugely popular radio program; by organizations such as the German-American Bund, the Protestant War Veterans Associations, the Christian Mobilizers, the Christian Front, and William Dudley Pelley's Silver Shirts; and also by the appearance in the United States of Nazi methods like the "buy Christian only" movement.[57] With the support of advisors including Paul Tillich and Reinhold Niebuhr, he used his magazine to help organize liberal clergymen into an anti-fascist political lobby.

The Challenger was drawn by professional cartoonists including Joe Kubert and Lou Ferstadt.[58] The print run reached 400,000 copies.

It might surprise cultural historians that someone had felt a need to publish a comic book series dedicated to anti-fascism after the mainstream superheroes already had proven themselves to be so eagerly anti–Nazi, but *The Challenger* tried to be especially bold. Comics historian Mark Carlson describes the "The Challenger Club" as the comic's most interesting regular feature. That "club" included a white couple, Don and Margie, and a black couple, Tom and Sally, who challenged racism wherever they found it. For example, the comic showed Don and Sally dancing together, and Don and Tom openly hugging each other.[59]

J.B. Matthews, a former activist for improved race relations, had been fired from a teaching position in the 1920s because of a furor over a party in his home at which whites and Negroes had reportedly danced together. By this period, however, his main goal had become to make amends for his former role as a prominent "fellow traveler" of the Communist Party by exposing secret communist influence.[60]

Others

The Senate Subcommittee that investigated comic books' possible connection to juvenile delinquency (described below) cited several pieces which appeared to attack comic books as "communist." None of them developed this argument in detail.

In Rapid City, South Dakota, a wing intelligence officer at Ellsworth Air Force Base, Capt. William Wygocki, warned a conference of civilian and military law-enforcement officials in 1954 that fifty comic books sold on all local newsstands were "communistic." The local paper's summary of Wygocki's evidence for calling these comic books politically unacceptable was that they "show brutal police and FBI officers and are derogatory to people of high social status."[61]

In Orlando, Florida, an editorial concluded that "as propaganda agencies for Communist cells" comic books "are made to order."[62] The Senate Subcommittee quoted this conclusion and described the accompanying drawing of a communist hammer and sickle with the sickle poking "U.S. comic books," but the rest of this Orlando editorial had said nothing about communism or propaganda.[63]

The Senate Subcommittee also quoted a pamphlet, "Brain Washing: American Style," as asking:

> How long and how often can the American people be duped? Parents, wake up! The objective of communism is to despoil your children, to rob them of their respect for law and the teachings of morality, to enslave them with sex and narcotics. When that happens, the Seeds of communism will fall on fertile ground.[64]

On closer examination, though, that pamphlet turns out to be primarily concerned not with comic books, but with "filth-drenched pocket books and magazines of the girlie-gag variety." Rather than blaming communism for these obscene publications, the pamphlet explains that they are distributed because of "Money! Big money in this case. It is a multi-million dollar racket."[65]

In 1955, Eric Larrabee explained that people were casually lumping whatever publications they objected to together with "pornography […] Communism or homosexuality" so they could attack them as "indefensible."[66] Larrabee quoted as two of his examples people who had linked comic books and communism. (As seen in the anti-comic book movement, leftists made similarly loose accusations of "fascism.")

Communists and Comics

If the anti-comics movement had been seriously searching for communists in the comic book industry, they could have assembled and publicized an interesting list of suspects. They might have given greater attention to the political views of pioneering comic book publisher Lev Gleason, who had been Eastern Color Printing's advertising manager when that company published *Funnies on Parade* in 1933 and then started the first monthly American comic book series, *Famous Funnies*, in 1934.[67] Gleason became a comic book editor in 1936 and started his own successful comic book publishing company in 1939.[68]

J.B. Matthews's files indicate some of the range of Gleason's political activities. Matthews kept file folders on two organizations that Gleason helped to lead (the Joint Anti-Fascist Committee and the People's Radio Foundation), a folder on the political party he belonged to (the American Labor Party), and folders of the leftist magazines Gleason published (*Friday, Reader's Scope* and *Salute*).[69]

Gleason was unusual for a comic book publisher because he did not grow up poor, Jewish, or an immigrant, but rich, Christian, and with a family history in New England that went back to the early 1600s.[70] His most successful comic book was *Crime Does Not Pay*. He did not publish war comics during the Korean War.[71]

In 1945, an article in the *New York World-Telegram* identified Gleason as the "pro–Communist" editorial director of a magazine that "manages to adhere to the Communist line in political matters," and as a director of the People's Radio Foundation, a communist dominated group that attempted "to get in on the ground floor" of FM radio.[72] Gleason responded by suing the paper for libel, but dropped the suit when the defense filed a brief that, according to an FBI informant, "stated that under the name of ALEXANDER LEV, GLEASON became a member of the Communist Party in or about the year 1939." The FBI determined that Alexander Lev was employed by the Soviet Russia Today Publishing Company, Inc., located at the same address as Gleason's publishing business.

By 1953, FBI files described Gleason as "reported to have been" a Communist Party member and pro-communist, but now "definitely anti–Communist," and FBI agents approached him for information about one of his former writers who was under investigation for suspected espionage.[73] Noticing his cooperative attitude, the FBI agents asked about his own political history, and recorded this description:

> GLEASON stated that, in the early 1930s, he believed that the Soviet Union was the answer to the world's problems and he was sympathetic to the Soviet Union. He stated that he joined the CP in 1936 or 1937 and remained a member for approximately two years. He stated that he became disillusioned with the Party with the Soviet-Nazi Pact in 1939 and thereafter had nothing to do with the Party. [...] He stated that he is sympathetic to the work that the FBI is trying to perform but that he has no use for Senator JOSEPH MCCARTHY.

Because of his cooperation, in 1954 the FBI removed Gleason's name from their "Security Index program" list of important people in the media and other institutions "who have shown sympathy for Communist objectives and policies." That list identified those marked for imprisonment in "preventive detention" camps in the event of a war or threat of invasion.[74]

Several comic book artists also drew for the communist newspaper the *Daily Worker*. One was Louis Ferstadt, who had run a small studio that supplied material to a dozen comic book publishers during World War II.[75] Ferstadt had given Harvey Kurtzman his start in the comic book business.[76] Maurice Del Bourgo joined the comic book industry after nine years doing *Little Lefty*, the *Daily Worker*'s longest running comic strip.[77] (Harvey Kurtzman told historian Paul Buhle that as a teenager, he had drawn backgrounds for the *Little Lefty* comic.[78]) Comic book artist Dick Briefer moonlighted as the creator of another *Daily Worker* comic strip, *Pinky Rankin*.[79] Comic book artist Phil Bard previously had done gag cartoons in the 1930s for *New Masses*, the *Daily Worker*, and *Labor Unity*.[80] Syd Hoff, identified in the *Counterattack* newsletter as having been a Communist Party member, a supporter of Communist front groups, and as a cartoonist for communist publications under the pen name "A Redfield," created the Hearst syndicate comic strip "Tuffy" which appeared as a regular one-page feature in *King Comics* in 1943 and 1944, and then became a comic book series which appeared from 1949 to 1950.[81]

Superman writer Alvin Schwartz, a self-described "Norman Thomas socialist" and former "Trotskyite," wrote comic book stories that were "superpatriotic, which I wasn't" as "a way of making a buck." Many years later, he remembered that he and his editor would sit in the cafeteria having political arguments "all the time." Schwartz described his editor, Jack

Schiff, as a very decent, fair, principled, educated man, even though he was also a "lousy rotten communist" who took "Stalinist" positions in their discussions.[82]

The co-creator of Superman, Jerry Siegel, raised the issue of a major comic book publisher's communist connections in a letter that he wrote to the FBI in November 1952. Siegel suggested that they investigate the backgrounds of the publishers Jack Liebowitz, Harry Donenfeld, and Paul Sampliner of National Comics (now DC Comics), and claimed that before they became comic book publishers, they had "criminal or communist records" and had published lewd magazines.[83] More typically, the tips that the FBI received naming suspected communist stooges within the comics industry were sent by naïve youth and local groups and ignored.[84]

3. More Anti-Fascist Critics

Gershon Legman

Gershon Legman, a Marxist, anti-fascist, anti-militarist, self-educated folklorist (specializing in a lusty, scholarly appreciation of dirty jokes and smutty verses) "played an influential role in the fight against comic books."[85] Legman attacked comic books for being part of the "profit economy's" industrialized system of "manufactured entertainment," which was pulling the nation in the direction of war, death and sadism.[86]

In 1948, Legman delivered the well-received first presentation in the symposium "Psychopathology of the Comics" (organized by Fredric Wertham).[87] That year Legman's arguments against comic books were also published as his first contribution to the small magazine *Neurotica*, which he later went on to edit.[88]

In 1949, Gershon Legman's book *Love and Death: A Study in Censorship* attacked comic books as an addictive medium that provided children with the incompletely satisfying thrill of hating a "scapegoat."[89] Legman also argued that when censors forbid the representation of sex, the only substitute within reach of ordinary people is sadism.[90] In 1963, he would distill his philosophy into a pithy, unprintable phrase that he claimed had been the basis for the popular slogan "Make love, not war."[91]

Legman said, in effect, that American superhero comic books' glorification of violent avengers who work outside the law made Hitler's propaganda look like the work of a beginner:

> In the ten-year effort to keep supplying sinister victims for the Supermen to destroy, comic books have succeeded in giving every American child a complete course in paranoid megalomania such as no German child ever had, a total conviction of the morality of force such as no Nazi could even aspire to.[92]

EC comics publisher William Gaines accurately quoted an essential piece of Legman's argument against the comics in his satirical, editorial/house-ad "Are You a Red Dupe?":

> "The child's natural character ... must be distorted to fit civilization.... Fantasy violence will paralyze his resistance, divert his aggression to unreal enemies and frustrations, and in this way prevent him from rebelling against parents and teachers.... This will siphon off his resistance against society, and *prevent revolution.*" [Gaines' emphasis.][93]

Ironically, Gershon Legman, the man Gaines accused of trying to censor the comics in "Are You a Red Dupe?," had himself recently been forced into exile because of American censorship. Legman's manuscript that attacked American comic books had been turned down by forty-two publishers.[94] Legman then self-published it, beginning with an edition of 2,000 copies, but in June 1950, post office censors took away his right to receive mail to prevent him from receiving orders for those "indecent, vulgar and obscene materials."[95] Unable to continue his work in the United States, Legman moved to France.[96]

Postal censors have used their power over the distribution of publications through much of American history to suppress, not only obscenity, but also political ideas, including sympathy for the French Revolution, abolitionism, anarchism, and other causes. In 1951, in response to a barrage of Korean-War-era propaganda tracts and magazines from communist countries, which (among other things) called for peace, criticized American culture, and accused the U.S. of germ warfare and prisoner of war atrocities, American officials began a program to confiscate communist propaganda arriving by mail.[97] The banned material included the East German magazine *USA in Bild und Wort,* whose cover story on American comic books had reported that:

> Taking one of the picture books about the dirty war against the Korean people in hand, it becomes almost blood-curdling. Here the readers' unleashed murder instincts are stoked. On its pages, you can see nothing but brute atrocities of the US soldiers (of course the American criminals are always represented as "heroes") while the Korean and Chinese defenders of their homelands appear as subhuman. The "yellow Devils" are not captured, but gunned down by the hundreds, hanged, tortured, quartered or torn by bloodhounds.[98]

The same month that Legman had lost his mailing privileges, the idea of using postal censors to restrict the circulation of crime comic books was raised in federal hearings on Organized Crime in Interstate Commerce. The chairman, Senator Estes Kefauver, after expressing his "personal opinion" that "one of the substantial reasons for the great amount of juvenile delinquency today is that children are reading this kind of literature rather than something that is more wholesome," had suggested a new law to ban such comics from the mail.[99] Kefauver asked Clifton C. Garner, the Chief Post Office Inspector, whether, if such a law were passed, it would be practical for the Post Office to differentiate "crime comic books that encourage juveniles to try to commit a more perfect crime" from other comics. Garner's opinion was that "it would be a most difficult job to attempt to decide…."[100]

What may have been the only case of postal censorship against comics in this period did not target mainstream comic books, but pornographic comics-format booklets. The pornographic "eight-pagers" of that time included some with imaginary sex scenes involving people whose names were in the news: *Whittaker Chambers and Alger Hiss in Betrayal; Earl Browder in the Good Old U.S.A.; Joe Stalin in The Great Leader; Taft in Back to Work;* and *Judith Coplon in Overpaid Lawyer.*[101]

Even if no mainstream American comic books had their mailing privileges challenged for being too radical or sexy, the enforcement of policies to restrict "propaganda" and "obscenity" from the mails, and the possibility of new legislation to keep "crime comics" from the mail, can be counted as more sections of that invisible fencing that kept comic book content in line.[102]

Norbert Muhlen

In 1949, Norbert Muhlen's article in *Commentary,* "Comic Books and Other Horrors: Prep School for Totalitarian Society?," reasserted the old idea that comics were supporting the passive acceptance of fascist, racist violence, dismissing the newer idea, associated with Fredric Wertham, that they also could be breeding delinquency:

The real point is not that the children will tend to resort to violence themselves; it is rather that they begin to accept violence, when practiced by others, as "normal," just as Americans in the last war began to accept the idea of putting people in concentration camps, even when practiced by "their" side, as normal.[103]

Muhlen had begun his anti-totalitarian activism as an anti–Nazi in his native Germany and by this period had turned his focus to exposing communist fellow travelers.[104] For example, Muhlen faulted Wertham's leftist politics as insufficiently critical of East Germany and the Soviet Union.[105]

The editorial director in charge of Superman, Batman and the other "National" comic books, Whitney Ellsworth, attempted to rebut Muhlen's arguments.

Dr. Muhlen makes a great distinction between the "older, much-censored, and more refined newspaper comic strips," and the "dehumanized, concentrated, and repetitious showing of death and destruction" in the comics magazines. Actually, no such wide dissimilarity exists. [...] Dick Tracy, Kerry Drake, and a number of other crime strips are every bit as brutal and gory as anything that might be found in even the most violent comics magazines. [...] The fairy tales are replete with horror, fantasy, and gore. The classics similarly depict scenes of cruelty, murder, and mayhem. [...] Might I remind Dr. Muhlen that during their training for combat, our soldiers were trained to kill; yet they did not continue to kill on their return to civilian status. Toy manufacturers have produced the simulated implements of war, yet I seriously doubt that they are guilty of instilling in children the desire to fight.

Norbert Muhlen's reply repeated that he was not talking about comics' supposed role as a factor in juvenile delinquency:

What I tried to emphasize was the more general, less acute effect of comic books—their tendency to encourage the acceptance of violence as the basis of human relations. Mr. Ellsworth does not even attempt to answer this point. [...] When Mr. Ellsworth compares the effect of his comic books to the wartime military education when soldiers were "trained to kill," his opinion seems rather close to mine.[106]

Albert E. Kahn

Albert E. Kahn strongly criticized America's Korean War comics while the Korean War was still being fought. He described their contents vividly:

Featuring stories of frenzied, sanguinary battles, devastating air raids, murderous hand-to-hand combat and barbarous atrocities, with most of the action laid in Korea, the war comics overflow with pictures of grim-faced or grinning American soldiers smashing in the heads of bestial-looking Chinese and North Korean soldiers with rifle butts, blowing them to pieces with hand grenades, and slaughtering them with machine guns, hand grenades, and flame throwers.[107]

Like Gershon Legman and Geoffrey Wagner, Kahn devoted one book chapter to criticizing comics, a chapter which was also published as a magazine article.[108] Nevertheless, Kahn's work has seldom been quoted in histories of the anti-comic book movement.[109]

Albert Kahn was a blacklisted author. The company that published his book was one that he co-founded in 1952 to publish works by "writers who have not accepted and will not accept the orthodoxies of the witch hunters."[110] The government believed that Kahn was not merely "unorthodox," but a member of a Soviet spy ring.[111] The FBI's file on him, over 2,000 pages long, shows that FBI agents monitored his writings, lectures, travel and family, tapped his phone, opened his mail, and illegally entered his study and photographed or stole his documents.[112] The level of attention increased in 1955 when Kahn co-published the confessions of Harvey Matusow, an "expert witness" whose false testimony against leftists had sent some to jail and damaged the reputations of many.[113]

Geoffrey Wagner

Geoffrey Wagner, an Oxford-educated British expatriate living in Harlem, researched American comic books in the early 1950s. His essay on comics appeared as a chapter in his book *Parade of Pleasure*.[114]

Wagner denied—directly and unconvincingly—that he was simply an elitist revolted by vulgarity.[115] He explained that he wrote this book to help defend the America that he loved from America's popular culture:

> My view is simply that Americans are being imposed upon by those responsible for the production of drivel. Americans are all too kind, too well-intentioned, too quick to see the best in everything and everyone. As a consequence, small groups, certain individuals, become able to exploit good nature in the masses at large to their own financial advantage.[116]

American newspapers said of Wagner's first article on comics that it had appeared in "a leftist journal of opinion" in London, edited by a man who "is often cross with America, especially in the field of foreign relations."[117] Wagner noted in his book *Parade of Pleasure* that "it is apparently considered 'Communist' to criticize comic-books in the USA today," especially because so many of them have communist villains. As an outspoken anti-communist, Wagner refused to be deterred by this insinuation.[118]

Wagner focused at length on war comics, which "are one of the most popular of all kinds and also one of the most violent."[119] Wagner found that, in contrast to his own military experiences in North Africa during World War II, in war comics:

> the terror of war is forgotten. It is all a gorgeous carnage, topped off with a joke or two in dreadful taste. Anything, even a hint of the torment involved in calling up the necessary courage each time a man steels himself for such endeavours is totally ignored. [...] Indeed, I refuse to be restrained about these war comics, which give such a fantastically unreal picture of war that I once wondered whether they weren't sponsored by draft boards. No one, except the enemy, gets hurt.[120]

Wagner's comments about the superhero genre not only repeat and support the arguments connecting Superman with fascism but also acknowledge how commonplace this argument had become:

> Now this type of comic-book has already received its share of attention in the press and on the radio. The whole concept of 'super' and its function in the political philosophies of our age have received copious criticism.[121]

Two decades later, after the campus upheavals of the 1960s and early 1970s, Wagner would lament that the rise of college and university courses in popular culture (film, Edgar Rice Burroughs novels, jazz, etc.) and of lessons about homosexuality, ecology, peace studies, and Zen Buddhism signaled "the End of Education."[122] The heart of Wagner's book *The End of Education* consisted of a seemingly endless recounting of every intemperate, violent, nonsensical or deplorable deed committed by (or attributed to) leftists and anti-racist activists, and every craven response by administrators and teachers. He compiled these one-sided examples without mentioning the government's COINTELPRO (Counter-Intelligence Program) to crush these protests. The method of *The End of Education* resembles that of *Parade of Pleasure*, which also consisted of a formidable "hall of horrors," assembled to arouse disgust and disdain and, perhaps, provide a bit of titillation.

Fredric Wertham

Dr. Fredric Wertham was the most important leader of the movement against comic books. He wrote an entire book about them, for which his publisher chose the racy title *Seduction of the Innocent*.[123] For the first three decades of the medium, this was the *only* book-length study of comic books.[124] As the central figure in the fight against comic books' alleged brutalization of the imagination, Wertham comes up in several chapters of this book.

Wertham was a man with wide interests and numerous accomplishments, who had gradually become concerned about comics through his work with children at the Bellevue Hospital Mental Hygiene Clinic, which he directed, and at the Lafargue Clinic, a psychiatric clinic for low-income people that he co-founded in Harlem.

Wertham had an unusual interest in what his patients were reading.[125] When he found himself working with young people who read nothing but comic books, in large numbers and with great devotion, he slowly became alert to comic books as a possible, previously unexamined "factor" in shaping their lives.[126]

Wertham summarized his observations by saying that comic books were "brutalizing" young people, dulling their sensitivity.[127] In 1948, Wertham responded to the idea that comic books were "socially harmless" by retorting "On the contrary, they immunize a whole generation against pity and against recognition of cruelty and violence."[128]

The comic book industry attempted to blunt the effectiveness of Wertham's criticism by hiring a public relations firm to try to damage Wertham's reputation.[129] A publishing industry newsletter explained their plans in language that Wertham interpreted as a threat and reported to the police: "The immediate enemy is Fredric Wertham.... He cannot be reasoned with. He must be discredited and rendered ineffective. ... Will he go away? Probably not. He must be knocked out."[130]

Cartoonist Bob Fujitani remembered that when *Seduction of the Innocent* was published in 1954, Bob Wood, the co-creator of the *Crime Does Not Pay* comic book series, had said that he would "go find Wertham and kill him with his bare hands." Four years later, in a hotel room just one block south of Wertham's home in Manhattan's Gramercy Park, Wood did kill someone, Violette Phillips, by bashing her face in with a clothes iron. (Wood, in a drunken stupor, had been angry because Phillips kept demanding that he marry her. By then, after the collapse of the comic book industry, Wood had been reduced to selling gag cartoons to sleazy men's magazines to make a living.)[131]

Wertham chose to focus primarily on crime comics (a popular genre which he defined broadly enough to include superheroes and "many war comics"),[132] The focus on crime fit well with his professional interests, since (among many other credentials) in 1932 he had directed the Psychiatric Clinic of the Court of General Sessions in New York, which provided evaluations of the mental condition of all felons convicted by Manhattan's main criminal court, to assist judges in their sentencing.[133] Through his work as an expert witness in criminal cases, he had become a familiar name in tabloid newspapers, and through the books, articles and book reviews he authored, he was also a familiar name for readers of more serious publications.[134]

Wertham's opposition to comic books was not grounded in a desire to hold youth in tighter conformity with existing norms. Wertham counted himself as among those who "are part of the struggle on the frontiers of imagination where the progress of society takes place [...] guided by visions of a time when, as Freud put it, 'culture will not crush anyone any more.'"[135]

The concluding chapter of Wertham's 1949 book *The Show of Violence* suggests his left-wing political perspective. In that chapter Wertham mourns the political assassinations of the German communists Karl Liebknecht and Rosa Luxemburg and the revolutionary Kurt Eisner, the mass murders organized by Nazi psychiatrists, the viciousness of American racism, the railroading of the anarchists Sacco and Vanzetti, the starvation and misery that the British caused in India and King Leopold of Belgium inflicted on the Congo, the high death rate of the Navajo Indians, the thousands of women dying during childbirth for lack of medical attention, the thousands of workers being murdered by preventable industrial accidents and the growing military indifference to civilian casualties. He also notes the "progress" of the Soviet Union in reducing their murder rate.[136]

Still, in his anti-comics activities, Wertham usually avoided politically charged language, and presented himself as a doctor and an expert. He succeeded well enough to be quoted uncritically in both communist and anti-communist publications.[137] Even those in the comic book industry seemed confused about his political position.

Al Feldstein, writer, artist and editor for EC comics' beloved and shocking horror titles, had assumed that Wertham was "a fascist … a Nazi."[138] Feldstein was a liberal who sometimes wrote comic book stories with strong political messages against racism, bigotry and nuclear weapons.[139] He saw the attacks on comics as a piece of a larger attack, coming from the political right:

> There were a lot of forces at the time. […] There was one force that I was terribly afraid of, which was the "control the press" force, which was the conservative, anti-communist, anti-"opposite opinion" force. And they were looking for a foot in the door to censorship, so they could control the media. They jumped on this bandwagon, because there was a lot of stuff put on TV about these "terrible" comic books. It was kind of ridiculous; you look at some of those old black and white programs that they had, these supposed documentaries, on how our children were being destroyed. It was idiotic.[140]

In contrast to Feldstein's uninformed image of Wertham as a fascist, the FBI's files on Wertham included freelance writer Maurice Zolotow's assertions that at Wertham's house parties, the conversations were "always political, and WERTHAM always took a very strong Stalinist point of view." In 1947, the year that their "mild social acquaintance" ended, Wertham had allegedly replied to an anti–Russian statement Zolotow made by saying "I don't permit criticism of Soviet Russia in my house."[141]

Wertham's criticism of comics was firmly within the tradition established by the earlier critics, and incorporated most arguments that had been made against comics, but not the accusation of "Godlessness."[142] To this discussion, he added the claim that he had observed the effects of comic book reading on his own young patients (most famously, that comic books were a "factor" that contributed to juvenile delinquency), and a call for legislation to keep "crime comics" from being sold to children under the age of fifteen.[143] (Wertham supported the right of adults to read what they wanted to read.[144])

Wertham rejected experimental and survey research into the effects of mass media as too artificial, crude and unreliable. He insisted that only the "clinical method" could provide reliable insights. He provided examples of how this works in *Seduction of the Innocent* and through case studies he described in his books *The Show of Violence*, *The Circle of Guilt*, and *Dark Legend*.

Eventually many scientific studies of media violence would be conducted using the quantitative approach that Wertham had disdained. These studies have provided support for some of the arguments that Wertham and other critics of comic books had made.[145]

Wertham has been misremembered, not only as having allegedly claimed that reading comic books "causes" juvenile delinquency, but even as having made the "monistic" error of blaming comic books as the single cause of juvenile delinquency. The main reason for this has been the lasting influence of a paper by Frederic Thrasher, published in 1949, which attacked Wertham's argument that reading comic books could be a "factor" that sometimes tipped the scales in cases of juvenile delinquency. Thrasher set up the false dichotomy that comic books either "caused" juvenile delinquency or else they were being "scapegoated" for broader social problems. According to Thrasher, Wertham (despite his denial that he believed any such thing) had "in effect" argued that children who read comics "are necessarily stimulated to the performance of delinquent acts." Since Wertham had failed to prove this claim that Thrasher had falsely attributed to him, Thrasher concluded that Wertham had unfairly set up comic books as a "whipping boy."[146]

The first thing Wertham did in *Seduction of the Innocent*'s chapter about juvenile delinquency was to quote the prominent psychiatrist Adolf Meyer, his mentor, against the idea that we should be thinking in terms of identifying a single cause for human behavior: "'We do not know the cause.' Is it not absurd to think of 'the' cause? Should we, over that, neglect the facts we have?"[147]

Wertham's arguments reached their largest audience, not through his book, but through overheated articles in *Collier's, Saturday Review of Literature, Ladies Home Journal* and (especially) *Reader's Digest*. These mass circulation magazines embraced Wertham's arguments eagerly.[148]

In general, the comics industry defended itself by claiming that reading comics teaches support for law and order, ignoring the critics' charges that comics were teaching tolerance for "fascist" violence and Ku Klux Klan terrorism. To see why the comic book industry felt compelled to respond at all requires looking to the grassroots, where an activist campaign against comic books was being waged.

4. The Grassroots

The intellectual campaign against comic books, waged in opinion journals, gained political power from the citizen campaigns conducted by groups such as the National Organization for Decent Literature, the Parent-Teacher Association, the General Federation of Women's Clubs, the Citizens Committee for Better Juvenile Literature, and others.[149] In addition to their attempts to pass legislation, members of these groups took their fight directly to the retailers.

The National Organization for Decent Literature (NODL) had been founded by Roman Catholic bishops in 1938. NODL organized Catholics across the United States to demand enforcement of existing obscenity laws, promote stronger laws, prepare lists of disapproved popular literature, and visit newsstands and drugstores to get blacklisted publications removed from sale. Magazine publishers would ask for interviews with NODL's National Committee and agree to changes which would take their periodicals off the NODL blacklist.[150] NODL introduced to the anti-comics movement the techniques of literature surveys, blacklisting, and neighborhood canvassing, which almost all the other groups adopted.[151] Most of the comic books that NODL objected to were romance and crime comic books. It approved of some war comics and condemned others.[152] In almost every case, NODL's grounds for disapproving war comics were that they included "morbid emotionality."[153]

Private conversations between individual parents and retailers (and the possibility of more of the same) seem to have been an important factor shaping what comic books would be offered for sale. In practice, comic book censorship came largely from ordinary citizens, rather than being an unpopular policy imposed by government-appointed censors or "elitist" culture critics. A newspaper columnist advised parents that "When out-of-line comics are found in local shops, often a few words of soundly based complaint from regular customers are all that's required to encourage the dealer to watch his stock more carefully."[154]

Apparently, these customer-activists took a dim view of the war comics genre. In 1953, druggists at a pharmaceutical convention in Saskatchewan resolved to urge Canada's government to extend its ban on crime comics to also include war comics because of what was reported as "frequent criticism from parents and customers for displaying the books."[155] In 1954, presumably responding to similar pressures, California's Riverside County Pharmaceutical Association included war comics in their declaration that "WEIRD, CRIME, MURDER, SEX, HORROR, LOVE, AND WAR Comics are not the kind of magazines that children should read" and that they wanted any comic magazines with such material "eliminated from our Magazine Delivery."[156] In 1955, the chair of the Committee for Decent Literature in Shelby, Ohio, resigned after the committee had succeeded in "ridding the city of the horror, sex, and war comics through the co-operation of the dealers selling magazines."[157]

Retailers who tried to be selective about which comic books to carry risked offending the distributors they relied on (who held exclusive distribution rights for popular magazine titles).[158] Fredric Wertham argued that the big distributors were retaliating against small store owners who refused to carry comic books by delivering the "good" magazines either too late for them to sell or not at all.[159]

In April 1948, another organization, the General Federation of Women's Clubs, published an article on the very serious matter of "fun," which included a section on "Radio, Comics, and Moving Pictures." Mrs. Philip Marston argued, "Everyone is entitled to fun, as part of his rightful heritage. What kind of fun a child has depends on what kind of fun he is exposed to. [...] It is a grave responsibility for all adults who must know that the peace of the world depends on what those young people become."[160]

The Youth Conservation Committee of the General Federation of Women's Clubs organized a meeting that October in Washington, D.C., to discuss "What Are Our Standards" and "How We Realize Them." They invited "heads of Motion Picture Associations, the National Broadcasters Association, and the Association of Comics Magazine Publishers" as well as representatives of the Parent-Teacher Association, the American Association of University Women, church groups, the YWCA, YMCA, Scouts, and others.[161]

At that well-attended meeting, participants realized that simple lists of prohibitions were not enough (such as "no nudity; no glamorizing of alcoholic beverages; no contempt of law, family, or respected institutions; no torture; no detailed methods of youth crimes; [and] no obscene language..."). Instead, they hoped for entertainment media that would contribute positively to "vibrant mental and social health." The participants accepted comic magazines, movies, radio and television programs "as part of our new society," and concluded that: "This is a new age, with new resources. Together we can make it one of gay laughter and high culture."[162]

The Citizens Committee for Better Juvenile Literature was organized at a meeting which the Chicago Police Department's Censor Bureau convened to alert community leaders about the increasing flow of "objectionable" material into the city. (Cities and states used to support their own censorship bureaus, which might require shots or scenes to be deleted from Hollywood films or prohibit entire films from being shown in their areas, sometimes for frankly political reasons. In 1907, Chicago had organized the first of these local censorship bureaus.)[163] The Citizens Committee for Better Juvenile Literature failed to get off the ground for six months, but when Wertham's book was published, that sparked the *Southtown Economist* community newspaper to vigorously resume the anti-comic book campaign which it had waged back in 1945, and the combination of national and local publicity allowed the group to get on its feet.[164]

These various civic and religious groups worked to pass laws and ordinances putting restrictions on comics, following the precedent of local restrictions on movies. Most of these proposals were defeated in legislative committees.[165]

In 1955, Charles G. Bolte's article "Security Through Book Burning" condemned both the laws restricting crime comics ("most of them of dubious constitutionality") and "the current rash of extralegal censorship by citizens' groups," such as the National Organization of Decent Literature, who were asking newsstands and drugstores not to carry items on their lists of "objectionable" publications. He opposed the campaign against crime comics, not because he sympathized with the comics, but because suppressing them could lead to a larger censorship.[166]

Book Burning

Ironically, after years of published warnings that comic books were leading to fascism, some anti-comics activists, especially in parochial schools, organized public book-burnings, sending thousands of comic books up in flames.[167] When critics noticed how this echoed (on a smaller scale) the Nazi book burnings, some changed to collecting objectionable comics for recycling.[168]

In Germany and the nations it invaded, Nazis had burned an estimated hundred million books, especially books by Jews and by those who opposed their party.[169] After the Nazis were defeated, communist "cultural advisors" in East Germany supervised another destruction of millions of books from libraries, bookshops and schools, this time weeding out "obsolete reactionary and fascist literature."[170] In 1955, an East German paper announced plans to climax a drive against Western comic books and other "trash literature" with a public bonfire in East Berlin.[171]

In West Germany, the occupying powers had also rigidly controlled German media to eliminate all "undemocratic, militaristic and Nazi" materials.[172] Some felt that American comic books fell into that category.[173]

Fredric Wertham told readers of *Seduction of the Innocent* that these exported American crime comics raised the problem of how to deal in a democratic way with anti-democratic children's magazines. Red Cross officials in West Germany, fearing "re-Nazification," did not want to give the books to children, could not send them back, and did not want to burn them because of "old associations."[174]

In the United States, those who were concerned about comic book content usually recognized the importance of respecting "freedom of the press" and avoiding censorship. Book burning was not widely adopted as a solution to the comic book problem because it reminded Americans of the dangers of totalitarian thought control. A reporter who summarized the Senate Subcommittee's comic book hearings began by assuring his readers that the Senators had not desired to put dangerous books in "the bonfire," as they "were in no combustive mood."[175]

5. The International Opposition to American Comic Books

During the Cold War, an international anti-comic book campaign furthered the aims of the primary, global communist propaganda effort, which sought to drive wedges between the United States and its allies.[176] The worldwide communist propaganda against American comic books had potential military significance because representing the United States as a corrupting cultural influence could weaken the Cold War military alliances that the United States was building.[177] In the 1940s and 1950s, American comic books met opposition in at least twenty countries on four continents.[178] During the Korean War, the *New York Times* coverage of anti-comic book campaigns focused more on foreign criticisms of American comic books than on the supposed link between comic books and juvenile delinquency.[179]

The communists' attacks on deplorable examples of American popular culture not only exploited an apparent vulnerability, but also attempted to neutralize an American competitive advantage. Their own high-minded cultural productions held less appeal for the world's masses than Hollywood films, jazz (and later rock), and American comic strips.[180] Even during the "anti-cosmopolitan" campaign to purge Soviet culture of western influences that began in 1946, American jazz persisted in the Soviet Union, partly through black market channels.[181] (Comic books, though, did not have an underground following in the Soviet Union, since the thought of American comic books generally disgusted people there.[182])

Cultural arguments had been a key element of anti–American Nazi propaganda, but that propaganda focused more on the corrupting influence of jazz rather than comics.[183] After the defeat of fascism, arguments about American cultural inferiority were continued by communists. Instead of attacking Jewish cultural influences in America and celebrating art that "builds on the eternal culture-building values of race and blood," communists attacked "bourgeois" cultural products and celebrated works in the style of "socialist realism."

International anti-comic book sentiment became enmeshed with the Cold War in 1947, when the *Daily Worker,* the communist newspaper in New York City, published the first of several major articles condemning the Catechetical Guild's anti-communist comic book *Is This Tomorrow?*[184] The Catechetical Guild pioneered the publication of anti-communist comic books because communist atheists directly threatened the lives and religious freedoms of Catholics.[185] (A few years after the publication of *Is This Tomorrow?* the North Korean army arrested and killed Korean Catholic priests, monks and nuns. Shortly before the war started, North Korea also killed hundreds of Korean Protestant clergy who had not fled to the south.[186])

The conclusion of *Is This Tomorrow?* warns that all of the subversive and totalitarian techniques the comic describes had been used in "Poland, Hungary, Yugoslavia, and country after country, the world over. It is their plan for America." Because the entire story describes an imaginary future in the United States, the comic makes no comment on the role of fascism and World War II as contexts for the communist takeover in those nations. Since the future envisioned in *Is This Tomorrow?* bears no resemblance to what happened after 1947 in real life, this comic has been remembered mostly as an example of Cold War nuttiness .[187]

After the American publication of *Is This Tomorrow?* communists remained actively involved in opposing American comic books. In Soviet propaganda, "comic books" became shorthand for the supposed decadence of American culture.[188]

In October 1949, the *New York Times* summarized an article condemning Superman comics which had appeared in Moscow's *Literaturnaia Gazetta* the previous day. Under the headline "Russian Says Comic Books 'Fascisize' U.S. Children," popular children's author Korny Chukovsky was quoted as saying: "Mass fascization of the children fully corresponds to the perspectives of the present bosses of America. The children are the *army* of tomorrow. One must impress them with the help of these gangster booklets that gangsterism is norm [*sic*] of human relations." Chukovsky cited Dr. Wertham as an authority on the harmful effects of reading comics.[189]

In 1949, French communists, who had been criticizing American comic strips for glorifying debauchery and crime and being "likely to blemish the freshness and purity of our youth," charged American comics with "war-mongering." Paulette Charbonnel explained the position of the newly formed Union des Femmes Francaises: "Before dropping nuclear bombs, warmongers feel the necessity of preparing minds for a new conflict. Debasing, corrupting our youth, diverting them from work and the struggle of collective protest are also the means to recruit mercenaries for an imperialist war."[190] Anti-communist comic albums were prevented from being imported in France, including Buck Danny adventures by Belgian authors about American pilots fighting in Korea.[191] The review board that was set up to control French children's literature (including comic books) resulted from an unusual political collaboration between French communists, anti–American French conservatives, and French comics creators who resented the competition from U.S.-made comic strips.[192]

Martin Barker's research discovered that the people who started the British anti-comics crusade were communists. They had concealed this political connection at the time.[193] Their earliest objections suggest the importance of the war comics in solidifying their opposition. A co-founder of the British campaign, Peter Mauger, in 1951, saw in the napalming of Korea proof of the harmful effects of American comics:

> ...as for the "vicarious outlet" mumbo-jumbo, it is precisely those people who feel no repugnance at dropping petrol-jelly bombs on villages containing women and children who are most avid readers of comic strips. These young men must have been conditioned to these atrocities somehow—and I suggest that comic strips justifying violence and brutality must have been a considerable factor in this conditioning process[....] Hitler's Nazis had to debauch the minds of Germany's youth before sending them to burn, kill, and destroy throughout Europe. The same process is being carried out in America: the proof is Korea. We must not allow the same thing to happen to our youth, to allow them to be softened up to be willing, unthinking cannon fodder.[194]

In New York, the *Daily Worker* published a five-column article attacking that city's comic books on July 13, 1952. Under the title "It Ain't Funny: Comic Books a Billion Dollar Industry Glorifying Brutality," the writer refers to:

> the conscious role of the so-called "comics" in brutalizing American youth, the better to prepare them for military service in implementing our government's aims of world domination, and to accept the atrocities now being perpetrated by American soldiers in Korea under the flag of the United Nations.[195]

By this point, the Soviet Union had launched what the State Department called "a gigantic cultural offensive," in which they not only promoted their own paintings and films internationally but also tried to tear down "the idea that any laudable culture can exist in Western civilization and particularly in the United States." The March 21, 1952, issue of the *Cominform Journal* summed up their complaint against "the corrupt 'culture' of imperialism" this way:

> ...it mutilates man, depraves his mind, implants among people misanthropy, moral dissoluteness, appeals to the lowest instincts, cultivates criminal tendencies.... For this reason advanced and progressive people in all countries reject with disgust and hatred this "culture" of capitalism that is rotting alive.[196]

That year, an article by a Danish school principal, published in Denmark and republished in Sweden, contrasted the "more socially useful" Danish comics with American comic books that appealed "to the lowest instincts possible."[197] In 1956, Martin S. Allwood described the 1953–1954 anti-comic book crusade in Sweden as another communist campaign: "The comics are made out to represent the American aim of whipping Europe up into a frenzy of war hysteria, in preparation for a third World War. The Soviet Union, on the other hand, has no comics, and stands for peace and anti-militarism."[198]

Similarly, in Finland the debates of the 1950s over American comic books included some socialist newspaper articles and pamphlets that condemned American comic books as racist war propaganda. These arguments were usually conducted on a more general level about "violence" in comic books, as American war and horror comics were not published or distributed there.[199]

Anne Rubenstein's history of Mexican comic books goes into some detail about the response of Mexico's comic book censors, in May 1953, to Mexican republications of two Korean War comics series from the United States. Rubenstein described these issues as "containing much blood-splattered imagery of saintly blonde Yankee soldiers slaughtering sneaky, twisted, dark-skinned, communist Koreans." A majority of Mexico's classifying commission had already condemned the entire genre of North American Korean War comic books as unwholesomely violent, or even a thinly veiled attack on Mexico itself.[200] In his report on these two titles, Commissioner Nájera argued that "In children and youth, this type of reading arouses the aggressive instinct, the contagion of war that rules certain foreign countries[…]. They present deformed ideas of heroes and heroic action[…]. They are open propaganda for foreign political interests."[201]

In 1954, an article warning about recent communist propaganda in Japan listed comic books as one element among many in the attack on American popular culture:

> Pointing to the GI radio programs, to the Westerns, Tarzan, and gangster movies sent by Hollywood for showing in Japan, to comic books, and even to the cowboy suits and toy pistols worn by little boys of the American community, the Reds charged that Americans lacked culture. The arguments would have been laughable had they not been so convincing. The tawdriness, drunkenness and vice near army camps, the lack of any real effort to appreciate Japanese culture, the almost insulting assumption that everything American was good and all things Japanese were feudal, worked to Communist advantage.[202]

From the anti-communist side of the struggle, Chester Bowles, the U.S. ambassador to India, complained that American comic books were making anti–American propaganda seem believable. Condemning a Captain Marvel story in which a tribe of Mongolian vampires make a pact to aid the communists in Korea, Bowles wrote:

> In Asia it is impossible to explain such things away by pointing out that it is pure fantasy. The Communist propagandists themselves could not possibly devise a more persuasive way to convince color-sensitive Indians that Americans believe in the superior civilization of people with white skins, and that we are indoctrinating our children with bitter racial prejudice from the time they learn to read.[203]

6. *The Cincinnati Committee on the Evaluation of Comic Books*

The Cincinnati Committee on the Evaluation of Comic Books, organized in 1948, provided the only nationally published consumer ratings of comic books in the late 1940s and early 1950s.[204] Chairman Jesse L. Murrell explained that:

[a]t the outset the Committee adopted a policy of attempting to cooperate with publishers and distributors to improve the quality of comic magazines. It decided it would seek no censorship ordinances. If the publishers chose to ignore appeals to make better comics, the Committee would then do its best to persuade the public to be more selective in buying them.[205]

In 1952, the Committee's "Annual Rating of Comic Magazines" reported on the rise of war comics, a genre unsuitable for children, and shared its concern that a couple of these comics might have tended to weaken the war effort in Korea:

> …there appears to be a perceptible increase of comic books that deal with war and horror. Nearly all of these books rate as objectionable.
>
> The propaganda value of the comics is very great. They are used in political campaigns and by organizations that want to sell ideas. An illustration of this use of comics came to the Committee's attention in the form of two war comics. One was rated objectionable, the other very objectionable because in the opinion of the Committee, they represented the United Nations soldiers in Korea as being in a hopeless situation. Such comics could be construed as trying to make Americans want to pull out of the war and to discourage young men from enlisting.[206]

The article does not specify which two war comics had come to its attention. *Two-Fisted Tales* and *Frontline Combat*, the two war comic books edited by Harvey Kurtzman, and *War Combat* (a title that the Navy had objected to that year) all received a "C" for "Objectionable," the Committee's typical rating for war comics, and *not* a "D" for "Very Objectionable."

By the following year, the Committee expressed its concern about "propaganda" by adding several items to its revised list of evaluation criteria. In 1953, it now specifically objected to:

- Undermining in any way traditional American folkways.
- Propaganda against or belittling traditional American institutions.
- Prejudice against class, race, creed or nationality.
- Stories and pictures which might affect national defense adversely.

That year, using these more politically sensitive criteria, it gave Harvey Kurtzman's *Frontline Combat* an "A," making it the only non-objectionable war comic in 1953's Annual Ratings. Overall, though, the Committee reported feeling distressed by the "downward trend" in the proportion of comics suitable for children and young teenagers to which the growing war comics genre had contributed.[207]

In 1954, the last year that *Parents* magazine published the Committee's annual ratings, the Committee refined its reporting to explain the basis for its rankings. This makes it possible to see that its objections to war comics were most frequently based on these criteria:

27. Use of chains, whips or other cruel devices.
28. Morbid picturization of dead bodies.
30. The portrayal of maiming or disfiguring acts of assault or murder.[208]

Wertham saw government regulation as necessary to protect children from irresponsible publishers. In *Seduction of the Innocent*, Wertham argued that the "amateurish extra-legal committee activities" of private citizens who created a ratings system for comic books could not substitute for "efficient, legal, democratic protection for … children." Wertham added, incorrectly, that private citizens had remained focused exclusively on objectionable sexual content in comic books, and were ignoring the more important role of comics as a factor in both crime and violence:

Legal control of comic books for children is necessary not so much on account of the question of sex, although their sexual abnormality is bad enough, but on account of their glorification of violence and crime. In the reaction to my proposals I found an interesting fact: People are always ready to censor obvious crudity in sex. But they have not yet learned the role of temptation, propaganda, seduction and indoctrination in the field of crime and violence.[209]

7. *Congressional Investigations*

In the years between North Korea's 1950 invasion of South Korea and the failure of the 1954 Peace Conference to end that war, the Congress of the United States investigated American comic books three times. In 1950, Senator Estes Kefauver's Senate Crime Investigating Committee responded to "frequently heard charges" that an increase in juvenile delinquency had been "stimulated by the publication of the so-called crime comic books" by collecting expert opinion on this question from officials, experts, and comic book publishers.[210] In 1952, the House of Representatives looked at comic books while investigating "Current Pornographic Materials." By far the most well-known and important Congressional investigation of comic books, however, were televised hearings held in New York City in April and June of 1954, as part of a larger investigation focusing on juvenile delinquency.[211] The same Subcommittee to Investigate Juvenile Delinquency had also held forgotten hearings in Washington, D.C., Denver, Boston, and Philadelphia. After New York City, they would go on to hold hearings in Chicago, Miami, and other cities. Comic books came up for brief discussion several times in these other hearings on crimes by minors, but the subcommittee focused *primarily* on comics only in New York City, the heart of the comic book industry.[212]

When Senators Kefauver and Hendrickson had originally explained the purposes of their proposed investigation of juvenile delinquency, their statement made no mention of comic books or other media influences. They argued that "Juvenile delinquency, fostered and fed by World War II and the Korean conflict," had reached peak levels, and they proposed to "determine the nationwide extent and character of juvenile delinquency, and its cause and contributing factors."[213] When they finally got down to more specific concerns in the concluding paragraphs of their press release, Senator Hendrickson, "quoting responsible Narcotics Bureau Officials," warned that Communist China was exporting "extremely high" amounts of narcotics to the United States, possibly as a "Communist plot to undermine our youth" and make them unfit for the draft.

Six weeks later, in a letter to Senator Eastland, they repeated the concern about drugs from Communist China (and North Korea), and as the eighth item in their outline of the nine aims for the subcommittee added, [W]e should determine the extent to which means of general public communication, such as comic books, television and radio, and other fictional media, affect the rate of child delinquency.[214] The idea that this committee was originally inspired by the threat of communist drugs rather than comic books is supported by the fact that in their first set of hearings, they heard testimony from Harry Anslinger, the head of the Federal Bureau of Narcotics, on November 23, 1953, almost half a year before they got around to investigating media influences on juvenile delinquency.[215] Anslinger had been the most powerful and persistent voice blaming Communist China for using narcotics to corrupt American youth, but eventually Anslinger's charges would be widely recognized as unfounded, fantastic distortions, made without evidence apparently in the hopes of mobilizing public opinion against recognizing Communist China for admission to the United

Nations and to divert attention from the anti-communist drug traffickers who were cooperating with the CIA in attacking Communist China from Burma.[216] Anslinger's false charges received a tremendous boost when Milt Caniff's *Steve Canyon* treated the smuggling of Red Chinese heroin as established fact, building an exciting story around this issue that ran from December 18, 1953, until April 29, 1954.[217]

Although the main focus in the Hearings in New York was on the possible influence of comic book reading on juvenile delinquency, the committee's investigators were also aware of and concerned about the damage that comic books were doing to the United States' reputation abroad.[218] The Congressional committee's report on "Comic Books and Juvenile Delinquency" summarized the international criticism of American comic books in some detail.

From the Congressional Committee's Report on "Comic Books and Juvenile Delinquency"

It has been repeatedly affirmed that the comic book, native product of the United States, is provoking discussion in other countries. Many Americans have expressed indignation of the influence these books may have upon the children and young adults in other parts of the world.

Some hold the view that there is no way in which we could give the young people abroad a more unfavorable and distorted view of American values, aspirations, and cultural pattern than through crime and horror comics. The destructive potentials of the comic book must be recognized both within our domestic society and in consideration of our relationship to peoples abroad. Publishers of undesirable comic books should be made aware of the negative effects these books may exert upon the thinking and conduct of persons who read them throughout the work and of the deplorable impression of the United States gained through their perusal.

Several considerations stem from the impact of the comic books abroad. They are:

1. Information gathered by United States Department of State personnel in many countries reveals public concern over the spread of crime and horror comic book reading. As far as can be ascertained by the subcommittee, concern has been expressed in almost every European country over the problem posed by the introduction of American comics, or comics of that pattern, since World War II.

2. Crime and horror comic books introduced to foreign cultures a lowered intellectual milieu. Detective and weird stories, American style, present a hardened version of killing, robbery, and sadism.

3. Comic book are distributed in many countries where the population is other than Caucasian. Materials depicting persons of other races as criminals may have meanings and implication for persons of other races which were unforeseen by the publisher.

4. There is evidence that comic books are being utilized by the U.S.S.R. to undermine the morale of youth in many countries by pointing to crime and horror as portrayed in American comics as one of the end results of the most successful capitalist nation in the world.

...Soviet propaganda cites the comic book in support of its favorite anti–American theme—the degeneracy of American culture. ... It is represented in the Soviet propaganda that the United States crime rate, particularly the incidence of juvenile delinquency, is largely incited by the murders, robberies, and other crimes portrayed in "trash literature." The reason such reading matter is distributed, according to that propaganda, is that the "imperialists" use it to condition a generation of young automatons who will be ready to march and kill in the future wars of aggression planned by the capitalists.[219]

The hearings were held in front of a display of "Representative Comic Book Covers: Crime, Horror & Weird Variety." The 24 displayed comic books included on the top row the current issue of *Combat Casey #16* (June 1954), whose cover, drawn by Robert Q. Sale, showed "The Fighting Infantry's Red-bearded Riot" conking two ugly Asian men together on a Korean battlefield, and the current *T-Man #1* (April 1954), whose unsigned cover included a blurb (placed over a woman in a red dress who is tied to a chair and looking at a smoking pistol) that asked "Will a merciless RED bullet end the life of Treasury Agent PETE TRASK as it did Dr. Kredge?—See THE TRAITOR."

One of the main defenders of comic books at the government hearings, Dr. Lauretta Bender, argued that "Superman has had a good influence" on children. By contrast, she condemned *True Comics* for its depictions of war:

> The Parent[s] Magazine got out a comic called True Comics. They were really very bad. The reason that they were bad is that they showed historical situations of, let us say, sailors being thrown off the boat because the boat had been bombarded by the Nazis and they were jumping in an ocean of flaming oil. There was just no help for these people.

In response to questioning, she elaborated:

> Now this was history. Certainly it is history, but do our children need to be exposed to such things? This is not history. I see no excuse whatsoever for a parent magazine group or an approved group approving that sort of thing. It was quite contrary to the code which we eventually established for the comic people.[220]

Comic book fans (more concerned about superheroes than educational series like *True Comics*) later praised Bender as "one of comics' unsung heroes," partly for the "spirited defense of comics" in this testimony.[221] These fans have not expressed any discomfort that Bender reached her "reasonable" findings in support of superhero comics' good influence without control groups, using the same "clinical method" that Wertham had used.

The Committee had begun its comic book hearings with a statement of their purpose:

> We are not a subcommittee of blue nosed censors. We have no preconceived notions as to the possible need for new legislation. We want to find out what damage, if any, is being done to our children's minds by certain types of publications which contain a substantial degree of sadism, crime, and horror. This, and only this, is the task at hand.

The Senators agreed with the New York State Joint Legislative Committee to Study the Publication of Comics that "governmental regulation should be undertaken as a last resort and only after the industry itself has shown an inability or incapacity to do it, or has failed or refused to do it." The comic book industry clearly felt great pressure to control what the New York Joint Legislative Committee had called "the undesirable minority of stubborn, willful, irresponsible publishers of comics whose brazen disregard for anything but their profits [...] is responsible for the bad reputation of the publishers of all comics."[222]

The Senate Subcommittee's hearings investigating comic books ended at 5:00 p.m., Friday, June 4, 1954, at which point they disappear from most histories of comic books. At 10:00 a.m. the next morning, Saturday, June 5, the subcommittee reconvened and began their investigation of the effects of television programs on juvenile delinquency.[223]

8. *The Comics Code*

Not long after the Senate Subcommittee hearings, comic book publishers announced their plan to create an organization for self-censorship of comic books, modeled after Hollywood's Motion Picture Production Code and baseball's National Commission.[224] The publishers set up the Comics Code Authority and immediately banned "horror, terror and gory crime comic books."[225] Instead of agreeing to Wertham's demand that comics for adults and comics for children be distributed separately, the industry promised to make all their comics suitable for children.

The participating comic book publishers created their Code with the help of the public relations firm Ruder & Finn. The firm's co-founder David Finn later explained that their goal had been "to find a way to make the smallest possible concessions necessary to end the controversy."[226] In his 1969 book *The Corporate Oligarch*, Finn described this comic book controversy as illustrating in microcosm conflicts that arise between corporate trade associations and "the self-appointed critic of industry" who tries to check corporate power to defend the public interest. As a self-described "childhood comic-book addict myself," Finn had been "an enthusiastic member of the 'scorn Wertham' club," but later regretted "that those of us on the industry side of that debate [...] failed to show respect" for Wertham's judgment, and had evaded the serious issues that Wertham had raised.[227] (After helping the comic book industry overcome public fears that comic books were harmful, Ruder & Finn went on to advise the tobacco industry about how to counter public fears that cigarettes cause cancer and to help the oil, coal, gas and automobile industries to lobby against the Kyoto Climate Change Treaty.[228])

The Comics Code was greeted with skepticism at first. In the Comics Code's first year, 32 states, Alaska and Hawaii either passed or considered anti-comic book legislation.[229] The Comics Code continued for over 56 years, though it grew weaker before finally being abandoned in the 21st century. Comic book historian Nick Caputo has closely read the ten Jack Kirby comic book stories published in *Battle!* from June 1959 to June 1960 (including two stories set in the Korean War) and found evidence of the Comics Code's heavy hand.

In "The Invincible Enemy" in *Battle!* #67 (December 1959), Caputo noticed five last-minute changes in the writing (indicated by a different letterer inserting a few words) and four in the pictures (indicated by clouds of smoke added by a different artist), which revised this story to eliminate not merely blood and profanity, but references to death on the battlefield.[230] Ironically, part of the industry's response to public concerns that comic books were training a new generation of soldiers was to produce an even more sanitized vision of combat which made war itself seem less objectionable.[231]

9. Cartoonists vs. Crime Comic Books

Comic book fans remember the anti-comic book movements of the 1940s and 1950s as uninformed "crusades" against a harmless medium. At that time, however, more than a few cartoonists and comic book publishers also opposed violent comic books. Wertham's chapter in *Seduction of the Innocent* on the makers and making of comic books reported that his research team had communicated by interviews, phone calls and letters with:

> publishers, writers, artists, middlemen between comic books and radio and television, publicity agents, lawyers whom manufacturers of crime comic books consulted, members of financially related industries such as the pulp paper industry or publishers of erotic magazines or books, technical and office employees.[232]

Rather than blaming the workers who wrote and drew crime comic books, Wertham described them as "victims" who were "often [...] very critical of comics," but afraid of "the ruthless economic power of the comic-book industry."[233]

The Senate Subcommittee Hearings in New York heard testimony from three cartoonists, Walt Kelly (creator of *Pogo*, who had been newly elected as president of the
300-member National Cartoonists Society), Milt Caniff (creator of *Steve Canyon*) and Joseph Musial (education director of the National Cartoonists Society, and a cartoonist whose
work had appeared in comic books regularly from 1937 to 1948). They spent much of their
time at the hearings drawing friendly caricatures of the Senators and establishing a cordial
rapport with them.[234]

At the time of his testimony, Kelly's book *The Pogo Stepmother Goose* (which included
a parody that starred Senator McCarthy under the unflattering guise of "Simple J. Malar-
key" as the leader of an inquisition) was at the printers. Those fans who imagine these comic
book hearings as something like a McCarthyist "witch hunt," and remember Walt Kelly
as a daring champion of liberal anti–McCarthyism, might be confused by the cooperative
testimony that he gave there.[235]

As it happened, Kelly was personally opposed to comic books that showed "burning
down houses, shooting people, tearing the clothes off women[....]"[236] He began his testimony by explaining that at one time he had tried to "help clean up the comic book business"
with stories about "little boys and little animals in red and blue pants and that sort of thing."
(His Pogo characters had originally appeared in comic books, and included a human character wearing red shorts.) He had discovered that comic book readers' tastes were "a little
more rugged than what I drew," so after his comic book failed, he had "been in the strip
business, the comic-strip business which is distinguished from the comic books."

These prefatory remarks seemed to seriously undercut the National Cartoonists Society statement which he then presented. In that statement, the organization went on record
as opposing "any additional legislative action that is intended to censor printed material,"
arguing that "We believe good material outsells bad. We believe people, even juveniles, are
fundamentally decent. We believe, as parents and onetime juveniles ourselves that most
young people are instinctively attracted to that which is wholesome." After reading this
statement, Kelly answered a question by immediately agreeing that "it is even entirely possible, sir" that crime and horror comics might have some harmful effects, and he went on to
recognize not only the great danger of censorship, but also (in his words) "the great danger
of the magazines in question."[237]

The National Cartoonists Society's newsletter a few months later reported that "The
NCS is taking part in the campaign against bad comics. Cartoonists should remember that
comic books are next door neighbors to the newspaper comic strip, and you know how
an undesireable neighbor can louse up the sales prospects of your house."[238] The next year,
Dave Breger, whose popular cartoons during World War II were credited with originating
the name "G.I. Joe," made a case that comic books had already loused up the situation for
other cartoonists. In his book *But That's Unprintable*, he described and opposed the severe, arbitrary and growing editorial restrictions on the freedom of American newspaper
and magazine cartoonists. He attributes the editors' tougher "don't risk offending" policies
partly to "The relentless sniping at the comics from all sides—because of certain "comic"
books that are anything but comic." By these, Breger means the "strips and books exploding
with violence, crime, bloodshed, killing, torture, and other such traits of modern civilization [....]"[239]

The situation for comic book artists after 1954 had also changed for the worse. Decades
later cartoonist Ben Brown remembered (in contrast to what Wertham had heard about the
powerlessness of comic-book artists and writers) that:

Before the Kefauver hearings and the Comics Code, a cartoonist would go to an editor with an idea and invariably receive the go-ahead (with maybe a suggestion here, a change there) and go off to complete the project. The relationship between the comic-book house and the cartoonist was very loose. But, after the Code, the cartoonist received an already approved script from the editor. The cartoonist became just one step in a long process. So much for individual creativity, or at least small teamwork.[240]

10. Television

Comics fans have long complained that comic books were singled out as scapegoats. The concentrated attention on comic books in this chapter should not obscure that the same people who opposed objectionable content in comic books made similar criticisms of newspapers, magazines, pin-ups, novels, radio, film and television.

In addition to the explosion of comic book circulation, television viewership was also booming in New York (where most of the published culture critics were living).[241] The studies that have been made of what happens to a community when *television* is introduced can help us imagine the unsettling cultural changes of that period.[242]

Fredric Wertham, in *Seduction of the Innocent*'s chapter on television, mentioned the difficulty of studying television's effects clinically:

> My studies of the effects of television on children grew out of the comic-book studies naturally—I might say inevitably. More and more children told me that they did not read so many comics because they were looking at television. A few children gave up comic books for television. Many combined both. The study of the effect of television on children is more difficult and I marvel at the glib generalizations that have been made about its harmlessness.[243]

In that television chapter, Wertham made some of his most unfortunate generalizations. There he repeatedly contrasted his mixed verdict on television, which he calls a medium with "a dubious present" but "a glorious future," and his unequivocal position on "crime comic books, which have a shameful past, a shameful present, and no future at all."[244]

ILLUSTRATIONS

THE "remedy" was a treaty which made Korea a part of Japan's sphere of influence . . . In 1895, after Nippon's victorious war with China, Viscount Miura arrived in Korea and proceeded to develop "friendship" for Japan. His first step was to order the murder of Korea's last Queen, Myung-Sung . . .

I WILL HUNT THAT MURDERER DOWN IF IT TAKES A LIFETIME!

MORE LIKELY IT WILL TAKE YOUR LIFE, KIM KU---!

1. "Japan's First Victim." Page 2, panels 4–5. *The United States Marines*, vol. 1, no. 3, 1944. © Magazine Enterprises, published in cooperation with the United States Marines. Vincent Sullivan editor; writer and artist unknown. (Public domain. Webposted at The Digital Comic Museum and at Comic Books +. Thanks to Richard Graham for a high-quality scan of the copy held by the Government Comics Collection, University of Nebraska–Lincoln Libraries.)

Chapter 5: World War II

One of the most horrific stories in one World War II comic book was a fact-based summary of Japan's oppression of Korea. The atrocities illustrated in this four-page piece included a Japanese soldier plunging his sword all the way through Korea's Queen Myeongseong.

At the time this comic was produced, the United States government's Office of War Information was urging the publisher to stir up hatred against the Japanese and the Germans so that readers would be encouraged to support the policy of "total war."

The text of "Japan's First Victim" primarily consists of typeset captions, but also uses hand-lettered speech balloons in those panels which show people acting out the story. Typesetting the narration allows the writer to use more words than could have been easily and legibly hand-lettered, and lends the information credibility, because of typesetting's association with books, magazines and newspapers.

2. "Captain Marvel Fights the Mongol Blood-Drinkers." Page 1, panel 1. *Captain Marvel Adventures* #140, January 1953. © Fawcett Publications, Inc. Script by Otto Binder. Penciled by C.C. Beck, inked by Pete Costanza. (Author's collection.)

Chapter 7: Critics

American Ambassador to India Chester Bowles singled out the story "Captain Marvel fights the Mongol Blood-drinkers" as harmful to American interests. Its pictures seemed to prove the Communist propaganda claim that Americans were subjecting their children to racist indoctrination. The idea that this comic book story expressed a "racist" point of view gains support when comparing it to similar cartoons that have epitomized racist cartooning, such as the picture of a Jewish vampire-bat by Fips (Philipp Rupprecht) which had been published in Nazi Germany (1) or the anti–Chinese cartoons published in California in the 1890s which represented Chinese immigrants as a monstrous dragon with bat wings (2).

We can contextualize this story in different ways by making our own loose associations between the picture of the "Mongol Blood-Drinker" and other images. For example, as part of a history of sensationalist fiction, these bat-winged creatures can be imagined as descended from the humanoid "man-bats" that had been observed on the moon according to a false report in the *New York Sun* on August 28, 1835 (3; detail).

The visual appearance of these "scarlet vampires" in this Captain Marvel story look like something that the artist invented based on the writer's script, perhaps while referring to a dictionary or encyclopedia's illustration of a "vampire bat" for inspiration (4).

3. "Peril in Korea." Page 1, panel 1. *War Comics* #1, December 1950. © U.S.A. Comic Magazine
Corp. (Marvel). Writer and artist unknown. (Author's collection.)

Chapter 8: Origins of the Korean War

The North Korean invasion of South Korea on June 25th, 1950 seemed reminiscent of the Nazi
invasion of Poland in 1939, and therefore possibly the beginning of a new world war. The first panel
of the cover story in *War Comics* #1 shows the lone defender (literally "on our side" in this visual
composition) as hopelessly outnumbered and outgunned.

The defending soldier could be South Korean, or one of the soldiers of Task Force Smith, who,
on July 5, became the first Americans to fight the North Koreans. Neither the defending soldier's
nor the attacking soldiers' faces are shown, since the propaganda purposes of this story include
emphasizing the general principle that aggression must be resisted wherever it occurs and overcoming the idea that this war is an internal matter between Koreans.

The colors are badly out of register, providing an example of the poor printing quality which
some of the opponents of comic books complained about.

The **shadows** of the two men imply inconsistent light sources (one below and one above.) The lantern that the spy is waving is inconsistent with his shadow (and seems unlit, as it puts no shadows on his hat or coat.)

The waves continue right up to the submarine's railings, suggesting that the **inker** may have misinterpreted the **penciller's** drawing.

The bright **colors** (blue jacket, orange pants) result from the small number of convenient choices, and contribute to the feeling that this is a dream scene rather than a night scene.

The **perspective** is inconsistent, for example, with the planks of the boardwalk not converging on the horizon.

The wind stirs the waves but not the papers on the ground and does not prevent the man on shore and the man on the submarine from understanding each other, as they yell to each other about their need for secrecy.

4. "The Gray Shark." Page one *Spy Cases* #28, February 1951. © Hercules Publishing Corp. (Marvel). Edited by Stan Lee; penciled by Mike Sekowsky. (Author's collection.)
Chapter 8: Origins of the Korean War

The first page of "The Gray Shark" includes both "realistic" and unrealistic elements. This establishes it as a fantasy story set in the real world. The intended realism of the scene is established by the proportions of the men's bodies (who are not three heads tall, as in a humor strip or nine heads tall, like a superhero); by the human heads of the characters (instead of cartoon animal heads); and by the familiar features of the background (brick wall, wood fence, wooden barrel, etc.).

The dream-like instability of this world is suggested when the writer refers interchangeably to the F.B.I., the O.S.S., and the "Office of Secret Information." The name of the main character changes without explanation from "Thomas J. Scully" to "Mallory Ashworth." The cover blurb refers to "The Gray Shark" as the "Grey" Shark.

The supposed setting allows the writer to allude to contemporary Cold War controversies regarding the International Longshore and Warehouse Union (ILWU) and the San Francisco chapter of the National Lawyers Guild, but it makes no sense geographically for a Russian spy on a tight schedule to land near San Francisco for the purpose of visiting a traitor in Washington, D.C., over 2,800 miles away.

5. Excerpts assembled from *Korea My Home*, January 1952. Panels from pages 1, 2, 3, 4, 5, 6, 9, 11, 12, 13. Johnstone and Cushing (for the U.S. State Department). Penciled by Al Stenzel, inked by Bill Timmins.

Chapter 8: Origins of the Korean War

These panels, taken from the pages of *Korea My Home,* show the exterior of the main characters' farm house. The penciller Al Stenzel has skillfully used a variety of compositions to maintain visual interest and to strengthen the sense that this comic depicts a real place.

In addition to the architecture of the house, the reader sees an unusual number of informative, visual details, including a stone bridge, a horse-drawn cart, a split-rail fence, a carrying pole suspending square buckets, men hoeing a plowed field, an outside water pump, a baby carried in a sling on a woman's back, telephone poles, an unpaved road, and several species of trees. The cartoonist, working in the United States, presumably relied on photographic reference material, probably supplied by the comic book's sponsor, the U.S. State Department.

6. "Spirit of War," Page 3, panel 4. *The Horrors* #11 *(The Horrors of War),* January 1953. © Star Publications, Inc., 1952. Script and art, Jay Disbrow. (Author's collection. Available online at The Digital Comic Museum and Comic Books +.)

Chapter 8: Origins of the Korean War

Comic book publishers frequently combined genres, for example romance comics plus war comics, or superhero comics plus funny animal comics. "Spirit of War," the featured story in the first issue of *The Horrors of War,* made the seemingly natural but uncommon combination of horror comics and war comics.

In this story, the North Korean decision to invade South Korea was inspired by the ghost of Adolf Hitler (not identified as such until the end of the story), who then laughs "in sadistic glee at the terrible havoc he had caused." The wicked inspiration behind the war is simply "lust for conquest."

The colorful montage of war scenes showing "the awful carnage" were clichés of the war comics genre. Although the text repeatedly emphasizes in general terms the "terrible suffering and destruction," the visuals hold back from expressing the true horrors of the war.

7. "Perimeter." Page 3, panel 4. *Frontline Combat* #15, January 1954. © Tiny Tot Comics, Inc. (EC). Writer and artist: Wally Wood. (From the Russ Cochran reprint of the art; originally published in color.)

Chapter 10: African Americans

"Perimeter!" is an example of a Korean War comic book story designed to communicate a message of racial tolerance. This is one of only two panels in which the face of the one black character, Matthews, is seen clearly.

Even in this panel, however, a different character, the white racist southerner Miller, is placed in the foreground and drawn with more dramatic lighting and greater attention to detail. The third major character in "Perimeter!," shown in the background, is the handsome, southern anti-racist character Tex.

The main action takes place in a battle fought in the rain at night. Miller has taken off his helmet, and his face is covered with raindrops, an unusually ambitious artistic touch. The billowing cloud of smoke behind them suggests the ongoing battle.

The artist, Wally Wood, was particularly fond of the kind of dramatic, low-key lighting effects that were used in the film noir movies of that time. In this story, he used a special, chemically treated paper, which enabled him to brush on two different shades of gray by using two different developer fluids. The developing fluids revealed patterns, hidden in the paper, which could be clearly and cheaply reproduced. Miller's face is inked mostly (but not entirely) by hand with hatching and cross-hatching, while Matthews is largely shaded with this Doubletone method.

8. "Atrocity Story." Page 7, panels 2–6. *Battlefield* #2, June 1952. © Atlas (Marvel). Writer, Hank Chapman; artist Paul Reinman. (Author's collection.)

Chapter 15: Atrocities

One of the most celebrated Korean War comic book pieces was "Atrocity Story." After illustrating Communist atrocities in Korea, this piece asks the reader to imagine these things happening in their own cities, and then compares Communist war crimes to the atrocities that had been committed by the Nazis. The seven-page feature "Atrocity Story" concludes by asking the reader what it will take to stop the Reds from committing further war crimes in Korea.

The story invites readers to consider fighting atrocities with atrocities, and killing communist prisoners of war. That option is rejected because it would mean "shoving civilization back to the dark ages of barbarism and savagery!"

The remaining choices are to ignore war crimes as "just propaganda," to use the atomic bomb as a last resort to eliminate an evil enemy, or to take on the difficult work of trying to imagine some other solution.

In reality, the South Koreans had been slaughtering huge numbers of prisoners since the beginning of the war. The Korean War's descent into "barbarism and savagery" was not something that could still be prevented, but something that had already happened.

The use of the atomic bomb, an indiscriminate weapon of mass destruction, would have been a war crime to top all the others. Still, as frustrations with the war mounted, the atomic bomb option suggested by this story was gaining public support.

9. *The Robert Alphonso Taft Story.* Page 7, panels 1–4. 1952. Produced by Toby Press for a committee of labor leaders representing the American Federation of Labor, Congress of Industrial Organizations, Mine Workers, Railroad Workers, and the Machinists. (Author's collection.)

Chapter 16: Politics

Ohio Senator Robert Taft led the Republican opposition to President Truman's handling of the war in Korea. Taft condemned the comic book that the leaders of the labor movement published about him during his 1952 reelection campaign as "Perhaps the most infamous piece of political propaganda ever devised," accusing it of fanning class hatred.

The story takes place in the home of the fictional "J. Phineas Moneybags" (the wealthy "Chairman of the local Taft campaign committee"), where Taft's supporters are shown editing a campaign film about their candidate.

The visual appearance of "J. Phineas Moneybags" seems to be inspired by "Rich Uncle Pennybags," the mascot of the Parker Bros. board game Monopoly (introduced in 1936). That mascot's appearance, in turn, was reportedly inspired by capitalist J.P. Morgan (1837–1913). This may explain the marquee initials "J.P.M." on the roof of the house. (In the story, Phineas is repeatedly addressed as "J.P.")

The cartoonist draws J.P. with an unusual bullet-shaped head. "Bullet-headed" was slang for obstinate and stupid.

CPL. SLADE DIED AT THE FRONT FIGHTING FOR HIS COUNTRY... SGT. HART DIED FOR THE SAME CAUSE FAR BEHIND THE BATTLE LINE! IN A WAR *EVERY* SOLDIER IS *CANNON FODDER*... WHETHER HE BE A CLERK, A TRUCK-DRIVER, PILOT, DOUGHFOOT... OR A *FOUR STAR GENERAL!* THE DOG-TAGS NAILED TO FIELDS OF WHITE CROSSES IN KOREA ARE GRIM REMINDERS OF THIS!

THE END

10. "Cannon Fodder." Page 7, panels 6–7. *Man Comics* #11, December 1951. © Newsstand Publications, Inc. (Marvel). Hank Chapman, writer; Joe Maneely, pencils and inks. (Author's collection.)

Chapter 18: Subversives

In 1951, people on various American army bases became suspicious of the downbeat comic book stories about the costs and horrors of war that were being published. The Army's Intelligence Department, G-2, collaborated with the FBI to investigate whether comic book publishers were participating in an intentional, subversive effort to damage military morale.

One of the series that attracted suspicion was *Man Comics*. The cover of *Man Comics* #11 included a prominent blurb for the story "Cannon Fodder." The term "cannon fodder" itself offers a demoralizing way to think about soldiers, as "expendable" men forced to fight in seemingly hopeless situations.

The text for the final panel of "Cannon Fodder" at least gave the dead a reason for their sacrifice. (The Americans fighting in Korea as part of the United Nations forces had died for their country). It also argues against the idea that the infantrymen are "cannon fodder" by emphasizing that all of those who participate in the war, and not only those on the front lines, risk death. A less controversial way to make this point would have been to conclude with an infantryman learning his lesson and reconciling with his counterpart in the artillery after winning a battle together. In this morale-threatening story, by contrast, the infantryman rants against the artillery man with his dying breath, not knowing that the artillery man has already been killed.

PART TWO

THE KOREAN WAR
IN COMIC BOOKS

8

◇◇◇◇◇◇◇◇◇

Origins of the Korean War

Very few of the comics about the Korean War addressed the questions of how and why it started. Instead, war comics usually focused on Americans' experiences of battle and took for granted that the enemy started the war. In the United States, most people simply accepted that the Korean War began on June 25, 1950, when soldiers of North Korea, in an unprovoked act of military aggression, invaded South Korea.[1] Few comics considered the background to the war, including the years of Japanese colonial occupation and the recent division of the Korean Peninsula into separate states.[2]

To those paying attention, the war should not have been a complete surprise. Even those who got their information from comic books could have seen war coming. That possibility was raised in a twelve-page story published in the first issue of *Spy-Hunters* in December 1949–January 1950. In "Adventures of a Spy," an American colonel reveals, "Now that American troops have pulled out of Southern Korea, the army has left its equipment behind in a camouflaged depot—for emergency use in case the communists try to take over the new democratic government!"

If the Russian spies in this story succeed in discovering its location and destroying this depot, "That means the democratic regime in southern Korea will be defenseless—and open to invasion from the communist-held area in the north!" On the last page, an official in the "Korean Foreign Office" thanks the heroic American agent: "With the assistance of Americans like yourself—we can smash **any** communist plot! We have waited years for democracy—**and we will never give it up**!"

Calling the South Korean government of that time "democratic" stretched the meaning of the term beyond recognition. During the American military occupation of South Korea, which began in 1945, Americans created an anti-communist government rather than a democratic one. After three years of this military government, the Republic of Korea, set up as a national government in South Korea in 1948, had similar priorities.[3]

In "Adventures of a Spy," the Americans hide their weapons in a Buddhist temple, closed to "unbelievers," and filled with creepy "idols" of the Buddhist "gods," including their "god of war." The representations of Buddhism that appeared in American comic books of this period show how distant and mysterious "the Orient" must have seemed to American comics creators.

Examples of comics that *did* describe the origins of the war included the story "Peril in Korea" in *War Comics #1* (December 1950), the story "The Gray Shark" in *Spy Cases #28* (February 1951), the comic book *Korea My Home* (January 1952), and the story "The Spirit of War" in *Horrors of War #11* (January 1953). Comparing these comic book accounts with some versions of the war's origin that have been written by historians brings these comics' political content into focus. Most of these comics promise "the truth." "Peril in Korea," heralded as "A Real War Episode!," shouts in boldface that it will communicate "the **real** truth about the **war in Korea**." "The Gray Shark" pretends to reveal a "true story" from secret government files. *Korea My Home* promises to tell a "true to life" story. "The Spirit of War" merely suggests that the readers entertain the possibility that the ghost story it tells might be true.

"Peril in Korea"

War Comics #1, with its front cover showing Americans resisting a Red tank invasion and its six-page lead story "Peril in Korea," seems to have been the first Korean War comic book to reach the newsstands, with a cover date of December 1950. The story provides evidence that doubt and controversy accompanied America's first steps into that war.

"Peril in Korea" begins: "I want to give you the facts just the way they happened—no pretending, no make believe." The narrator, an army sergeant, explains that "It all began when the Reds crossed the 38th parallel and we were given orders to ship" from Japan to Korea. That sergeant's first response had been that "We're making one big mistake. Korea is none of our business. Since when does their civil war become **our** affair?" Another soldier argues back that "You got it all wrong, kid! There's 45 countries in the U.N. that see it our way."

Later war comics usually ignored the United Nations and represented the war as one fought between Americans and Korean or Chinese communists, but sixteen countries sent soldiers to fight in the Korean War as part of a United Nations effort, controlled by and originally requested by the United States, to stop aggression in Korea.[4] Even progressives, such as *The Progressive* magazine's editor, Morris Rubin, supported the decision to turn back the North Korean invasion as necessary for the credibility of the recently organized United Nations. Rubin editorialized:

> Given the naked reality of Red aggression and the violation of international agreement and the UN charter, the only meaningful reply by the rest of mankind could be armed resistance. Failure on the part of the UN, with or without U.S. prodding, to act decisively, would have been the death blow of the United Nations, and the crushing of all hope for collective action against aggression.[5]

The next month, *The Progressive* published A.J. Muste's pacifist response:

> The person who does not unequivocally reject war and organized violence as a means for resisting aggression and tyranny always ends up by supporting another war. […] There is always some factor in the situation which enables him to convince himself that *this* war is different and support of it is somehow inevitable and right.[6]

The sergeant in "Peril in Korea" argues that the Korean Civil War is not America's problem and that Korea (just "mud and rain") is not worth defending from the Reds. The counterarguments, as usual in such stories, take the form of dramatic action. After his friend is wounded in combat, the two soldiers take refuge in a house belonging to "an English plantation owner who had been operating in that part of Korea for years." Then "Red Korean soldiers" arrive at the plantation, where they get into a brief argument (conveniently in English, so the American who does not care about Korea is able to eavesdrop on it).

> Red soldier: "The Americans are fools. We shall win here and it will only be the first step. Next will be Formosa, Japan, the Philippines, Hawaii—stepping stones toward America itself!"[7]

English plantation owner: "I wouldn't be too sure, Captain. Others have tried it and failed. Your people have become a willing tool in the hands of an aggressor nation. You do not fight for Korea, but for its enslavement."

The logic appears irrefutable, because the Captain responds, not with further words, but by slapping the white man and then machine-gunning him to death. The narrator's caption tells that "In one blinding flash, the terrible truth came home. The taunting, smug words of the Red officer and the brutal slaying of the old man and the boy galvanized me into action…." The story concludes with a clearly stated moral: "I've seen the enemy in action and heard their plans. We're not just fighting for Korea but for Main St., U.S.A. and a free world. We've got to stop them … before it's too late!"

Showing the murder of a foreign plantation owner does get to the heart of what the sergeant in this story had referred to as "the Korean Civil War." To get the reader to take sides with the plantation owners, as the United States had done, the story implausibly represents that longtime owner of a Korean plantation as a hospitable, white *Englishman*. A more realistic representation of insurgents killing a Japanese landowner or a Korean who had collaborated with the Japanese would not have had the same persuasive power for American readers.[8]

Still, invoking a British plantation owner and the UN would have done nothing to impress the Republican opponents of the war, whose views were represented by the *Chicago Tribune*'s outstandingly clear and attractive editorial cartoons.[9] That paper consistently expressed contempt for England, the UN, and the English-loving East Coast political establishment, represented by Secretary of State Dean Acheson and the State Department.

The comic book publishers did not share this anti–British point of view. In August 1950, around the time that his company was publishing "Peril in Korea," editor Stan Lee's name made its first appearance in the *New York Times* when he was forced to apologize for a comic book story that took the wrong (anti–British) side in an eight-page story depicting South Africa's Boer War.[10] Lee "vigorously denied […] that the company was anti–British" and added that:

> If it has caused any ill feeling, we are more than sorry […] My wife is English and I am very fond of the English. We publish more than thirty magazines a month and if we were anti–British it would be apparent in our other stories. But this is the only one that has brought any complaints.[11]

In "Peril in Korea," the enemy confesses out of his own mouth that the point of invading South Korea was not to reunify their nation or to eliminate the vestiges of Japanese colonialism from Korea, but rather "only the first step" of an Empire-building project that will sweep across Asia and ultimately lead to the conquest of "America itself!" In comic books, rather than taking an enemy's actual words out of context, the writer can simply invent speeches in which the enemy characters confess evil intentions.

The idea that the invasion of South Korea signaled a step in the communists' master plan to conquer the world by force, stated directly in this story, was one that gave Americans a reason to fight in Korea. When the evidence in the Soviet archives was eventually released, it showed that the invasion of South Korea (across a line that Koreans had never recognized as a legitimate international border) had not originated out of a master plan of world conquest, but through the persistent urging of North Korea's Kim Il-sung, who had eventually won Stalin's and Mao's approval for his plan.[12] Stalin's generals had handled the details of the war planning, using the continuing border skirmishes as a pretext for their "counterattack."[13]

"*The Gray Shark*"

The second example of a comic book story about the origin of the Korean War, "The Gray Shark" in *Spy Cases*, focuses on the American background to the war rather than on events within Korea. "The Gray Shark" boldly proclaimed itself to be "the true story," "the inside story," "from official federal records." On the other hand, any reader who cared to check the fine print would learn that: "No similarity between any of the names, characters, persons, and/or institutions appearing in this magazine with any living or dead person or institution is intended and any such similarity which may exist is purely coincidental."

Dismissing this story as merely fiction or believing it as documentary fact would have been extreme responses. The story invents an appealing explanation for a real disaster that resonated strongly with the American political debates of the time. Using the conventions of popular fiction, it gives a satisfying behind the scenes explanation to account for the invasion of South Korea, which pits a square-jawed defender of "America, freedom and liberty" against an evil conspiracy to enslave the world.

Like "Peril in Korea," this story was published by Martin Goodman. "The Gray Shark" carries no credits, but the penciller has been identified as Mike Sekowsky.[14]

The plot of "The Gray Shark" celebrates those engaged in the rapidly growing area of covert operations:

> Agents of the "U.S. Office of Secret Information" are dispersed in February, 1950 to discover when and where World War III will flare up. One agent, disguised as a communist vagrant, is quickly inducted into a spy ring, and put to work at the submarine base where foreign spies are shipped secretly in and out of the country. A spy arrives and travels to the State Department to meet with a traitorous official. Thanks to expert intelligence work, however, the State Department traitor has been discovered and arrested, and an impersonator put in his place. The spy asks the traitor's impersonator "Where is America and the United Nations the least prepared? We can attack in India or in Korea, wherever they least expect it! Your word is sufficient for us to go ahead Comrade Robbins." The impersonator falsely informs him that Korea is the weakest link. After the spy reports this false information and the war begins, the government moves in to arrest the spy ring.

The spectacular initial success of the North Korean invasion seemed to show that, in reality, the United States and the members of the United Nations had not been well prepared to resist communist aggression there.[15] Although most American planners assumed that in the coming war, South Korea would be evacuated as indefensible, nevertheless, "The Gray Shark" does agree on that point with the contents of some "official federal records." A group within the State Department had examined the problem of where the United States was most capable of resisting communist aggression, and concluded that of all the world's trouble spots, Korea was the most convenient place for an American military response.[16]

"The Gray Shark" depicts the State Department as having been infiltrated by a dangerous enemy agent. This traitorous infiltrator aspect of the story would have struck a strong note of recognition for the story's original readers. On February 9, 1950, Senator Joseph McCarthy had delivered a speech in Wheeling, West Virginia, rehashing a speech that Congressman Richard Nixon had made two weeks before that. McCarthy had echoed Nixon's warning that the case of former State Department official Alger Hiss, compared to simple espionage, was "a far more sinister type of activity because it permits the enemy to guide and shape our policy." McCarthy then added: "I have in my hand a list of 205 card-carrying Communists who are now employed in the State Department and whose identities are well-known to the State Department as being members of the Communist Party."

This claim launched McCarthy into political prominence and international notoriety.[17] Editorial cartoonist Herbert Block ("Herblock") of the *Washington Post* created some of the most lasting and hostile images of McCarthy, and in one of his cartoons published in the month after McCarthy's speech, Herblock coined the word "McCarthyism," which remains in the dictionary as:

1. the practice of making accusations of disloyalty, especially of pro–Communist activity, in many instances unsupported by proof or based on slight, doubtful, or irrelevant evidence.
2. the practice of making unfair allegations or using unfair investigative techniques, especially in order to restrict dissent or political criticism.[18]

In fact, the State Department and other departments of the Federal Government had been infiltrated by communist spies *earlier*, in the 1930s, when the communists' "Popular Front" period emphasized cooperation with the United States, and during World War II, when the United States and the Soviet Union were fighting as allies against Germany. By the time of McCarthy's speech, though, the communist spy networks in the U.S. Federal Government had been exposed and shut down, thanks to a series of defections.[19] American military plans and secrets continued to be passed to the Soviet Union for one more year, however, through a British spy ring operating in Washington, D.C., that included Kim Philby, Donald Maclean and Guy Burgess.

"The Gray Shark" had a basis in the news that was more direct than McCarthy's speech. In August 1950, around the time this story was being written, Republican Senators accused Secretary of State Dean Acheson of having invited the attack on Korea, one calling Acheson a "Communist-appeasing, Communist-protecting betrayer of America...." Specifically, a speech Acheson had made the previous January, in which he defined America's "defensive perimeter" in Asia in a way that excluded Korea, was interpreted as signaling a "green light" for communist aggression.[20] The day after the invasion, Senator Malone of Nevada had charged that advisers of the State Department had deliberately brought about "what is happening in Korea."[21]

In "The Gray Shark" the idea that in the worldwide resistance against communist aggression, the United States was best prepared to resist in Korea, was neatly merged with the idea that a betrayer in the State Department had given the communists a green light to invade there.

"The Gray Shark" depicted the invasion of South Korea as the "first offensive in World War III." Most Americans, including top American officials, interpreted the invasion in similar, global terms, as though it had resulted from a conspiracy originating in Moscow.[22]

When the news of the invasion reached America, reporters rushed to get a statement from Assistant Secretary of State Edward Barrett. In response to their question of whether he thought the Kremlin had had any connection with the North Korean attack, Barrett quipped "Can you imagine Donald Duck going on a rampage without Walt Disney knowing about it?"[23]

Barrett later explained the origin of the Korean War in the political context he knew best, propaganda:

Few realize that the U.S.-U.N. decision to resist in Korea was, broadly speaking, a propaganda decision. On world military maps Korea was not strategically important. [...] What was important and what all hands recognized was that a U.S.-U.N. failure to resist unprovoked aggression in Korea would be interpreted world-wide as a sign of weakness—as a sign that other areas could not count on U.N.-U.S. help in defending themselves.[24]

In this statement, Barrett expresses the American elite's primary focus on the North Atlantic. In June 1950, American policymakers cared more about how their responses to Korean developments would influence the situation in Europe than about Korea's strategic location in old conflicts between Russia, Japan and China.

Korea My Home

Unlike most comic book stories about the Korean War, *Korea My Home* was created as government-sponsored propaganda. Nevertheless, it looks very much like a comic created for entertainment.

Several clues indicate that *Korea My Home* is not an ordinary, newsstand comic book: it does not use glossy paper stock for its cover; it has no price, indicia or copyright notice; the cover illustration lacks dramatic tension; and the text, while not word-heavy, is conceptually dense, with many panels making a political generalization or historical claim. Edward W. Barrett's 1953 book *Truth Is Our Weapon* unmistakably refers to *Korea My Home*, but does not mention it by name:

> To demonstrate the true nature of Communist "liberation" in gripping human terms, for people of minimum literacy, the Department [of State] and USIE Korea collaborated in producing a true-to-life cartoon story. Based on interviews with North Koreans, this cartoon book tells a dramatic story of a Korean farmer and his family and their sufferings—how the Russians drove out the Japanese and set up a North Korean "People's Republic" which seized crops, forced young men into the Army, introduced thought control, and finally plunged North Korea into a bloody, aggressive war. More than 700,000 copies are printed or in production.[25]

In this brief paragraph, Barrett has explained who sponsored the comic, who they were trying to reach, what they were trying to say, where they got their information, how many they printed, and even provided a plot summary. The USIE Korea, which he mentioned as collaborating on this project, was a part of the State Department's international information and educational exchange program. In 1951, the Department described the scope of this rapidly expanding program:

> Factual information on the lies and treacheries of international communism and on the strength, progress, and ideals of the United States and other free nations flows steadily into the press of all non-communist areas from USIE press operations in each country, expressing the basic themes in news, feature articles, photographs, and cartoons. Such material reaches approximately 100 million people through some 10,000 foreign newspapers and magazines, which among them print an average of about 400,000 column inches—equivalent to 2,500 full-size newspaper pages—of USIE materials per month.[26]

The plot, characters, assumptions about the readers' background knowledge, and arguments of the comic book *Korea My Home* all suggest that it was primarily intended for free distribution in a Korean-language edition by USIE Korea to people who actually did call Korea their home, rather than for American readers. The title of the Korean edition was *Uri Taehan Min'guk* (우리 대한 민국).

The State Department awarded the contract for turning the idea for *Korea My Home* into a finished comic book, not to a Korean cartoonist, but to the company of Johnstone and Cushing.[27] Johnstone and Cushing was at that time the major company producing comics (which they called "line art continuity") for advertisers. Their staff of 15 to 20 artists created advertisements in comic strip and comic book format for clients such as Ford, Chrysler,

U.S. Steel, Post cereal, Kellogg's, the Girl Scouts, and Lucky Strike cigarettes. These ads that they created appeared regularly in Sunday comics sections of newspapers.[28]

Johnstone and Cushing created several comic books for the State Department. According to Bob LeRose, who worked as an assistant production manager for Johnstone and Cushing then, the company was linked to the State Department by "a salesman who worked in Washington and lobbied for comic books to help send messages to where printed brochures didn't seem to get the readership." In the case of *Korea My Home*, the State Department script was broken into panels and laid out in pencil by Al Stenzel, and then finished in ink by Bill Timmins.[29]

Although densely packed with explicit claims about recent Korean history and politics, *Korea My Home* leaves out of the picture some of the most basic facts about the period it describes. The truthfulness of the comic can be tested by looking at three themes of particular importance: how it portrays the Soviet involvement in North Korea, how it describes the land reform programs in North and South Korea, and how it explains the division of Korea into two separate states.

This comic begins with the narrator-protagonist Chong Kim introducing himself to the reader as a North Korean farmer who had always dreamed of someday owning his own piece of land. Chong Kim begins his story in August 1945, with the schoolmaster running to bring him the "wonderful news" that "Communist Russia has freed us from the Japanese."[30] The family is filled with hope by Soviet promises, but the Russian soldiers disappoint them with their every action. First, they "commandeered all the food and livestock they could find, promising to pay for it later." Soon, "Each day brought new military orders, which we were forced to obey. Those who spoke against the new orders were seized, never to be seen again. Young girls of the village mysteriously disappeared." A cruel district agent, "trained in Manchuria by the Russians," is placed in power over them.

The Russians in *Korea My Home* act methodically and deliberately to enslave North Korea. Still, in some ways the comic book understates its criticism of Russian behavior. As in East Germany and Manchuria, the Soviet soldiers who occupied North Korea treated civilians violently, looting, pillaging, and raping.[31] According to historian Bruce Cumings' *The Origins of the Korean War*: "The accounts of rape and pillage were inflated in the South by fleeing Japanese.... But there remains no doubt that the behavior of Soviet occupation forces was largely uncontrolled in the early weeks and cast a pall upon the Soviet effort in the north."[32]

Cumings adds, though, that the Russians sent in military police in early 1946, and they enforced control over the troops. Cumings explains the early history of the Soviet occupation of North Korea as a progression from military crime to military discipline and as supporting popular policies, such as land reform, which gave people hope. Clearly, this way of organizing the story would not have served the purposes of *Korea My Home*. Instead, the comic describes a descent from hope and excitement, through failed promises, to the depths of suffering and disillusionment, and then concludes with the hope that the communists will be defeated and freedom will triumph.

The comic book's understatement of the early weeks of Soviet rape, executions, deportations and pillage serves several dramatic purposes. For one thing, not illustrating the rapes brings the story into conformity with standards of "decency."[33] Also, minimizing those early crimes keeps the storyline about the Soviet occupation moving along on a simple to follow path, from bad to worse. Downplaying the Russian troops' undisciplined behavior serves to keep the image of strictly regimented Soviet totalitarianism sharp.

Korea My Home's most fully developed anti-communist argument claims that the North Korean land reform is a sham. Historian Charles K. Armstrong, by contrast, describes it as "one of the most rapid and thoroughgoing land redistribution efforts in history, and yet [one that] took place with very little violence, certainly nothing remotely approaching the bloodshed that accompanied initial land reform in the Soviet Union, China, or Vietnam."[34]

American histories of the war scarcely mention land reform, yet it had great importance to Koreans. Most of the Korean population was living as tenant farmers.[35] In the *Korea My Home* comic book, the communists give the land not to the long suffering local peasants, but to the ones that the heartless district agent Sun Kwoon calls "the patriots—the partisans—the fighters for freedom."

When the United States military had entered Korea in September 1945, it refused to recognize the pro-tenant People's Committees that the Koreans had set up, which were acting as governing bodies. It worked instead with the defeated Japanese colonial officials and with wealthy Korean landlords, industrialists and businessmen to build a "bulwark" to stem the tide of Soviet influence, and to prevent the "chaos" of domestic revolution.[36] To many Koreans, in the North and South, this looked like the old collaborationist government, staffed largely by the same officials who had served under Japan, now being propped up by a new foreign sponsor. Under the American military government and then the Republic of Korea, the deeply-hated, cruel and violent, pro–Japanese policemen, who had controlled even the small details of people's lives, even in small villages, continued to beat and torture Koreans as before.[37]

By contrast, the Soviet occupation forces recognized the People's Committees in the North, but as quickly as they could, they centralized power while removing as "Japanese-collaborators," "traitors," "capitalists" or "reactionaries" those who resisted communist control.[38] Many Japanese, police officials, government officials and landlords fled North Korea and hundreds of thousands of other Japanese and Koreans were shipped to Siberian prison camps.[39] These developments made North Korea's land reform appear relatively peaceful and created a simplified political situation.[40] The Soviet occupation of North Korea went relatively smoothly also partly because the Soviets happened to have available many ethnic Koreans who had been living in exile in the Soviet Union, spoke both Russian and Korean, understood Koreans, and were communists.[41]

In *Korea My Home*, young Chung Yung returns from the South with news that they have had a land reform program of their own: "Before the Americans drove the Japanese out, less than a quarter of the farmers owned their own land. […] Now more than half are farm owners … soon nine-tenths will be farming their own land under the new government program." According to Kim Dong-Choon's *The Unending Korean War*, the South Korean government's land reform bill finally passed in March 1950, and by April, farmers had been notified about the lands to be distributed. A political purpose of the legislation was to prevent South Korean farmers who had heard good things about land reform in North Korea from welcoming the communists in case of an invasion. When the North Koreans did invade, rather than winning the tenant farmers' support with a land reform program, the Northerners learned that most of the farmland had already been distributed.[42]

The *Korea My Home* comic book condenses so many claims that its pictures invite thousands of words of commentary. One last centrally important point, though, requires close attention. This regards the origin of the line dividing North and South Korea.

The Korean Peninsula, north and south, had been a single nation for more than a thousand years, united by language, culture, history, ethnicity and government.[43] Koreans also regarded themselves as united by heredity, as a single, homogenous "race" with a pure bloodline.[44] At the end of World War II, the United States, concerned that the Soviet Union was in a position to occupy the entire Korean Peninsula, proposed to divide Korea at the 38th parallel for the temporary purpose of receiving the surrender of the Japanese troops there. The Soviet forces, who were already entering North Korea, would occupy Korea north of that line, and the Americans, who were unable to reach Korea for several weeks, would occupy the south.

The Soviet Union had entered Japanese-occupied Korea while fulfilling a promise that Marshal Stalin made at President Roosevelt's request at the Yalta Conference in February 1945: "In two or three months after Germany has surrendered and the war in Europe has terminated the Soviet Union shall enter into the war against Japan on the side of the Allies…."[45]

Germany surrendered on May 8, 1945. Three months later, on August 9 (the day that the United States dropped its second atomic bomb, on Nagasaki), the Soviet Union declared war on Japan. Soviet forces quickly destroyed Japan's Kwantung Army in Manchuria and also captured much of North Korea.[46] The Japanese surrendered on August 15.

Americans chose the 38th parallel because it divided Korea roughly in half and left the capitol Seoul in the American zone.[47] No Koreans participated in this quick, midnight decision. The Soviet Union, without making a formal statement about it, withdrew to the 38th parallel, and this dividing line quickly hardened into an international border.[48] Koreans in both north and south angrily denounced the division of their country and demanded reunification. The American propagandists who wrote *Korea My Home* had to tell the story in a way that blamed the unpopular division of Korea squarely on the other side.

In *Korea My Home*, old, wise Kim Han tells the narrator/protagonist Chong Kim that the responsibility for the continued division of Korea belongs to the Soviet Union:

> I have heard United Nations broadcasts, although we are forbidden to listen to them. They call for free elections all over Korea, but the Soviet Union always objects. The Russian communists would not allow U.N. representatives to enter North Korea. They do not dare to allow us to vote freely. After the years we have spent under communist rule, no sensible man would vote for this regime.[49]

At the same time, *Korea My Home* explains the outbreak of the war in the language of an international invasion. Chung Yung professes shock at the North Korean propaganda lie which had branded South Korea as the invaders:

> Invaders! How far can the truth be twisted? Listen, oh Chong Kim. When the Americans withdrew from the Korean Republic, they left a self-governed people seeking only to live in peace on the land which the reforms had given them. Then on June 25th … the North Korean armies, trained by Soviet officers, using Soviet weapons and planes, poured in force across the border. Our army, trained only for police work, was no match for them.[50]

This speech rightly denounces North Korea's false claim that their invasion of June 25 had been in response to an earlier South Korean attack that morning, but then pushes too far. In the statement that South Korea wished only to "live in peace," *Korea My Home* prints an outright falsehood. The leaders of both North and South Korea regarded the division of that country as intolerable. Both of them had vowed to reunify the country before the civil war broke out with the North Korean invasion in June 1950.[51]

The comic's explanation that Russians would not permit "free elections all over Korea" because they would be sure to lose became a major theme in the four-page, comics-format

U.S. propaganda pamphlet *The Korea Story*. The difficulty, however, as historians Stewart Peter Lone and Gavan McCormack put it, was that "The merging of a revolutionary and a counter-revolutionary regime could only be achieved by the surrender of one or other side, or by war."[52]

The United States had pushed for UN-supervised elections in South Korea, not to determine the preferences of South Korean voters, but as part of a larger project of containing Soviet influence by surrounding the Soviet Union with anti-communist governments.[53] The 1948 election in South Korea was organized under the control of the political party that the United States supported, the Korean Democratic Party. This party was dominated by large landowners, and also represented large industrialists. It included in its membership the police who were ruthlessly suppressing Korean leftists.[54]

"The Spirit of War"

This chapter's final example of a story about the origins of the war, "The Spirit of War," was signed by Jay Disbrow, and published by Star Publications in *Horrors of War* in January 1953.[55] When compared to "The Gray Shark," both the disclaimer and the truth claims in this story sound milder. The fine print said: "All characters and incidents described or depicted in stories (except those based on history or fact) are fictitious, and any similarity to persons living or dead, is purely coincidental." The text describes itself as "almost unbelievable," "fantastic," and "a gripping tale."

The story begins in 1945, when an unidentified man dies violently in Germany, and his ghost floats out across a ruined city. In 1948, the ghost passes above a battle in Haifa (where as part of Israel's war of independence, a Jewish massacre of Arabs had led to a larger Arab massacre of Jews, followed by another Jewish massacre of Arabs). Later it watches a patrol action in French Indochina (as Vietnam was known then).[56] Then, "using its powers of invisibility, the Spirit of Evil entered the councils of the North Koreans and planted the seeds of aggression in their minds."

As a result of this spirit possession, "the Korean War began, with its terrible suffering and destruction." On many moonless nights, "this weird, ghostly figure was sighted, standing in the midst of the awful carnage, laughing in sadistic glee at the terrible havoc that he had caused." At the conclusion of the story, an American chaplain confronts the ghost, gazing at him "with the eyes of righteousness," and forcing the ghost to "reveal yourself as the man you were when you were living." The ghost takes on the face of Adolf Hitler. Then there is an explosion. In the final panel, a soldier who had accompanied the chaplain reflects: "But I wonder—! The evil men do sometimes lives after them. I'm not at all sure that one can thus so easily destroy the spirit of that fiend! Perhaps he is even now abroad in the world spreading the evil he spawned in life!—I wonder!"

In tracing the origin of the war to the ghost of Hitler, the writer dramatized a truth about the origin of the Korean War. President Truman did take America to war partly to fight the ghost of Hitler's aggressions. In his memoirs, Truman explained his response to the news of the North Korean invasion this way:

> In my generation, this was not the first occasion when the strong had attacked the weak. I recalled some earlier instances: Manchuria, Ethiopia, Austria. I remembered how each time that the democracies failed to act it had encouraged the aggressors to keep going ahead. Communism was acting in Korea just as Hitler, Mussolini, and the Japanese had acted ten, fifteen, and twenty years earlier.[57]

To Truman, the North Koreans attacking the south looked like the Japanese imperialists attacking Manchuria, aggressors who had to be stopped. (A similar substitution of new enemies for old appeared in comic books when communists were plugged into rewritten World War II stories to replace the original Japanese villains.[58]) A few months later, the President would explain that the United States had "attained the position which no other country in the world has ever had," and had to use its new power to block communist aggression. Truman argued that "with great power goes great responsibility."[59]

Ironically, the North Koreans had *also* gone to war because of the Japanese imperialists who had attacked Manchuria. The North Korean leaders had been fighting against Japanese imperialists and their Korean collaborators in Manchuria since 1932, when Japan had created the puppet state of Manchukuo. The North Koreans saw "The Korean War" as merely a continuation of the earlier conflicts in which the Japanese and their collaborators had already taken the lives of more than 200,000 people, mostly Koreans, who had resisted their rule over Manchuria.[60] This history makes the comic book illustration of the ghost of a World War II Axis enemy laughing over the Korean battlefield truly haunting.

9

◇◇◇◇◇◇◇◇◇

Spies

Comic books in the late 1940s tried a variety of experiments, searching for a new fad to replace the fading superheroes. Taking inspiration from the news of the day and the old spy comics of World War II, several publishers created comic book series about heroic espionage agents. The Cold War espionage comics genre seems to have begun with *Spy and Counterspy* (August–September 1949) and *Spy-Hunters* (December 1949–January 1950), published by American Comics Group, followed by titles like *Admiral Zacharias' Secret Missions* (February, 1950), published by St. John, and *Atomic Spy Cases* (March–April 1950), published by Avon.[1]

The first story of the first issue of the first Cold War espionage comic book series, *Spy and Counterspy*, told of a newly trained counterespionage agent assigned to stop a spy from delivering to the Reds the missing piece they need to make atomic bombs. The American counterspy goes behind enemy lines, wins the love of an enemy agent, and, by preserving the atomic secret, prevents World War III. (The comic had a cover-date of August–September 1949. In August 1949, the Soviet Union successfully tested its first A-bomb and in September, Americans first learned about it.)

That issue's second comics-format story, "Report to the Nation," tells of a white American "master of disguises" who goes behind enemy lines in yellowface, tricks and defeats the Chinese Reds, wins the love of a Chinese woman, and prevents "a stunning setback to the [Chinese anti-communist] Nationalist cause." (The same week in September that Americans were learning about the first Soviet A-bomb, the People's Republic of China was proclaimed, in a stunning setback to the Chinese Nationalist cause.)

Rather than sending Euro-Americans in yellowface disguise, hundreds of Chinese agents were sent into China to help resistance groups and thousands of Korean and Chinese agents were dropped into North Korea during the Korean War. These agents in North Korea sought to find bombing targets, to assess bomb damage, and to determine what effect these bombings were having on the enemy. Most of these agents were caught and killed or abandoned their missions.[2]

The exciting stories of competent, knowledgeable and successful American spies in these comic books resembled the equally unrealistic spy stories of World War II comic books (which also could be counted on to include a beautiful woman of uncertain loyalties wearing a red dress, a fistfight, and climactic gunplay through which an American hero defeats the agents who support tyrannical world domination). These comic book stories bore no resemblance to the actual record of America's spy organizations, which had failed to effectively warn of the North Korean invasion of June 25 or the Chinese entry into the war.[3] Publishing nothing but dramatic success stories in spy comic books could easily have distorted readers' understanding of what intelligence agencies do and how well they do it.[4]

107

Several stories in the *Spy-Hunters* series of espionage comics used the Korean War as their background. In "Peril in Pyongyang" (*Spy-Hunters #21*, December–January 1952–1953), South Korean Colonel Kim Yung gladly accepts an assignment to infiltrate "a top secret meeting of communist big shots [that] will be held in Pyongyang next week—to discuss the entire strategy of the Korean War!" The plan is for him to impersonate his hated twin brother, the traitorous General Chiang Yung, who had "collaborate [*sic*] with Japanese—then go on Red Side!" Actually, in contrast to South Korea, by late 1946 the North Koreans had purged almost every Korean who had collaborated with the Japanese from any position of authority.[5]

In the next comic book story in that issue, "Intelligence Mission," a white soldier is told, "Since you speak both Korean and Chinese, Lt. Byrnes, you're the perfect man to send behind enemy lines!" Thanks to his successful mission, a Red attack is thwarted, and a column of Red infantry is strafed by American planes.

In "Destination Korea!," an incoherent story penciled and inked by Robert S. Pious (*Spy-Hunters #22*, February–March 1953), a white American steals the identification papers of communist reporter Cyril Barstow and rescues a beautiful Korean-American "advertising model" who had been engaging in anti-communist espionage.

The boom in spy comics followed a series of sensational spy cases, which included the Amerasia Case (with arrests in 1945 of a Soviet spy ring that had been stealing secret American documents), the exposure of a Soviet spy ring that included State Department official Alger Hiss (accused in 1948), and the exposure of a Soviet spy ring that passed atomic secrets to the Soviet Union, for which Julius and Ethel Rosenberg (arrested in 1950) received the death penalty.[6] The office of the journal *Amerasia* and the homes of Alger Hiss and the Rosenbergs were all within three miles of the Empire State Building, where the publisher of *Spy Cases*, *Spy Fighters* and *Spy Thrillers* had its offices.[7]

The anti-communist perspective of American spy comics did not prevail all at once. *Spy-Hunters* and others published a number of stories that featured apparent communist plots that were unmasked as plots by cells of surviving die-hard Nazis still scheming to seize power or by the Fascist-sympathizing government of Spain.[8]

After World War II, Spain, under the dictator Francisco Franco, had used scorched-earth tactics in a war against leftist guerrillas in Spain that lasted until 1951, had welcomed refugee Nazis, and had given Nazi war criminals Spanish citizenship.[9] It seems, though, that no stories appeared in the news about Spain spying on the United States. Consequently, comic book stories about Spanish spies in America soon looked like unrealistic holdovers from a previous conflict (or crackpot fantasies from the radical left) and faded away.[10]

American comic book stories about die-hard Nazi villains also faded when the rise of the Cold War and the outbreak of the Korean War led the United States to lose whatever interest it had in its program for the "denazification" of Germany. Instead, the United States supported a spy network organized by former Wehrmacht General Reinhard Gehlen, which regularly supplied alarming misinformation about aggressive Soviet intentions to the CIA, which then passed these influential reports on to the Pentagon, the White House and the media.[11]

A Spy Who Cartooned

A rare, real-life occasion on which an American counterespionage agent *did* get his hands around the neck of a spy for the Soviet Union happened at a dinner party on January

19, 1951. The story demonstrates in a vivid and unexpected way the emotional power of cartooning.

The party was hosted by Kim Philby, a British Secret Intelligence Service intelligence officer, who worked with the CIA and the FBI (and was secretly working for the Soviet Union).[12] A social disaster began when Guy Burgess (a second secretary at the British Embassy, and also a spy for the Soviet Union) crashed the party, very drunk. There Burgess met Libby Harvey, the wife of William Harvey (formerly with the FBI, but then with the CIA, and the most knowledgeable man in the United States government on the subject of Soviet espionage).[13] Libby Harvey was also very drunk. Burgess, an amateur caricaturist, said something to the effect of "Ah, how remarkable to see the face I have been drawing all my life suddenly appear before me."[14]

She asked him to draw her. The results have been described in several ways. Verne W. Newton's book *The Cambridge Spies: The Untold Story of Maclean, Philby, and Burgess in America*, says that:

> [Burgess's] eyes were a study of concentration as he went to work, his hands framing her face with a theatrical flair, as Libby preened. When he had finished he held up the result as if it were a placard. It was only of her head, and the hair, eyes, nose, and ears bore an identifiable likeness. But when it got to her jaw—and, to be truthful, Libby Harvey's jaw did protrude—Burgess had drawn it "like the prow of a dreadnought with its underwater battering ram."[15]

By contrast, David C. Martin in *A Wilderness of Mirrors*, called it, more plausibly given what followed, "an obscene cartoon of Libby, legs spread, dress hiked above her waist, crotch bared. Harvey swung at Burgess and missed."[16] Winston MacKinlay Scott told author John Barron, "Enraged, [William] Harvey jumped on Burgess and was choking him with both hands. It took Scott and Philby and one other guest to pull him off."

Harvey's suspicion of Philby was aroused that night by his odd connection to Burgess, and Harvey became the first to solve the puzzle and identify Philby as a spy.[17] The whole spy ring escaped arrest, and Maclean, Burgess and Philby defected to the Soviet Union.

In May 1949, the heads of the U.S. military branches created the Armed Forces Security Agency (AFSA). Although taken by surprise by the outbreak of the Korean War, the AFSA quickly solved the North Korean codes, and their ability to read the enemy's battle plans helped the UN forces from being driven off the Korean Peninsula in the first few months of the war.[18] Despite some successes, the AFSA, rather than bringing order to the rivalry between the different military services' and the CIA's signal intelligence groups, became a bureaucratic nightmare.[19] To solve this problem, President Truman secretly created the National Security Agency by an executive order on October 24, 1952.[20] The NSA eventually developed what Glenn Greenwald has called "the explicit policy that literally no electronic communication can ever be free of U.S. collection and monitoring."[21]

An Evil Conspiracy to Conquer the World

As a matter of convenience, the image of communists in comic books about Cold War espionage came to closely match the one in government pamphlets published at that time by the House Un-American Activities Committee. In 1950, the first question in the HUAC pamphlet "100 Things You Should Know about Communism in the USA" asked "What is Communism?" and its entire answer was "A system by which one small group seeks to rule the world." In its pamphlet "100 Things You Should Know about Communism and Education" the entire answer to the same question became: "A conspiracy to conquer and rule the world by any means, legal or illegal, in peace or in war." The sheer simplicity of these definitions suited comic books perfectly. The anti-communist hero *T-Man*, for example, with no need to learn any boring information about local political, social or economic conditions (or any foreign languages), could travel the globe in his comic book series, defeating evil conspirators in Italy, India, Hong Kong, Cuba, Iran, the South Pacific, the French Alps, Panama, Spain, Turkey, Egypt, Czechoslovakia, China, Holland, Honduras, "one of the six Moslem Kingdoms," Iraq, "Rumania" and so forth.[22]

In espionage comics, communists act as a force of pure evil, seeking to create chaos, poverty and desperation to make nations ripe for their takeover of power, which they crave for its own sake. The Reds are quick to pull and fire their guns, but unable to hit any targets. The stories provide an unending stream of stories in which the American agents are well-informed and victorious.

The American comic book secret agents usually take the rightness of the world order that they work so skillfully to maintain for granted. A defense of the existing colonial order found particularly explicit expression in "Menace in Madagascar," drawn by Ogden Whitney for *Spy-Hunters #6,* and published in June–July 1950 (as the Korean War was beginning). Its readers could easily have *underestimated* the accuracy of the small details in this story set on the large island nation off the East coast of Africa, or *overestimated* the story's overall truthfulness regarding the worldwide anti-imperialist struggles of that period. In "Menace in Madagascar," the American hero's chief presents him with this problem:

> We have reports that the Malagasy natives are on the brink of revolt, and being stirred up by a rabble-rouser who claims he is the godlike reincarnation of **Radama**, an ancient native hero! [...] there are vast sources of **betafite** in Ambatolampikely on Madagascar—practically all the known betafite deposits in the world! And betafite happens to yield 30 percent of **uranium**—while American sources never produce more than **2** percent! We **need** that betafite uranium—and the native revolt threatens to cut off our supply!

In fact, "Radama" was not an "ancient" memory, but the name of two of Madagascar's 19th century kings: Radama I and Radama II. The vast, uranium-bearing betafite deposits in Ambatolampikely, Madagascar, had ceased to be strategically important in 1923, when the cheaper and more reliable Katanga uranium deposits were discovered in the Belgian Congo.[23] Still, the Cold War competition for African uranium provided an easy-to-understand, comic-book rationale for American interest in suppressing that potentially "disastrous" native revolt.

After the American comic book hero ("the best trouble-shooter in the espionage corps") has literally unmasked the "paid agent of a foreign country" who had been stirring up the betafite miners, he tells the miners that "you were **tricked** into taking up arms against your benevolent French guardians! [...] Go—in peace and friendship!" They answer, **"We go back to the mines—to our French friends!"** In actuality, at the time this story was written the French had just finished suppressing a nationalist movement calling for the independence of Madagascar. That war had resulted in 10,000 violent deaths from 1948 to 1949, plus another 20,000 to 30,000 war-related deaths caused by disease and malnutrition.[24]

Meanwhile, in a bloody prelude to the larger war, the United States and its new South

Korean ally were crushing an uprising on an island 300 times smaller than Madagascar, off the coast of South Korea.[25] The United States and Syngman Rhee blamed North Korea, supported by the Soviet Union, for stirring up and organizing the rebellion on Cheju-do (now transliterated as Jeju Island).[26] U.S. intelligence reports, by contrast, said that the rebellion had been provoked when a right-wing, dictatorial governor from the mainland arrived and resorted to terrorism to suppress any opposition to Syngman Rhee on an island which was being peacefully self-governed by leftists.[27] The charge that communist outside agitators were responsible for the uprising provided a readily understandable rationale for America's interest in helping to suppress those who were refusing to accept the division of Korea.[28]

10

◇◇◇◇◇◇◇◇◇◇

African Americans

The Korean War marked an end to official racial segregation in the U.S. military, a point at which the military stopped resisting President Truman's Executive Order 9981, issued in 1948, which had called for full racial equality in the armed services.[1] Some argue that as the military pioneered American racial integration in that period, the genre of war comics became a leading edge for the inclusion of respectfully represented black characters in mainstream American comic books.[2] During the Korean War, however, the integration of the military went much faster than the integration of war comics. The shifting representations of African Americans in comic books, and the changing policies about the civil rights of African Americans in the United States, unfolded in a context shaped by World War II and then by Cold War foreign policy considerations. Taking a broader view, one that includes the previous decade's struggles to eliminate racist cartoons and to introduce anti-racist messages in comic books, puts the few comic book stories that focused on black soldiers in Korea in a larger perspective.[3]

Action Against Racism in Comic Books

In the 1940s and 1950s, American comic books typically showed white characters in charge, sometimes helped by comical non-white servants, natives or sidekicks. In the broader society, racist caricatures of black people appeared seemingly everywhere, from cookie jars to Valentine cards.[4] At the same time, however, these old racial stereotypes were becoming a national embarrassment. The pressures to get rid of offensive cartoon stereotypes of black Americans came both from high-level officials who saw these images as damaging America's international reputation and from African Americans who felt personally offended by them.

An example of high-level officials pressuring the publishers to fix this problem came in a 1955 Senate Subcommittee report which delicately warned that when American comic books "are distributed in many countries where the population is other than Caucasian," their stories "depicting persons of other races as criminals may have meanings and implication for persons of other races which were unforeseen by the publisher."[5] As an example of offended people acting to stop the publication of insulting imagery, in 1945, a student protest succeeded in ending the character "Steamboat." The cartoonist C.C. Beck, who had drawn "Steamboat" regularly since 1942, remembered that:

> ...this character was created to capture the affection of black readers. Unfortunately, he offended them instead and was unceremoniously killed off after a delegation of blacks visited the Fawcett editor's

office protesting because he was a servant, because he had huge lips and kinky hair, and because he spoke in a dialect. He was always a cartoon character, not intended to be realistic at all, but he was taken seriously by some, sadly enough.[6]

The interracial group that Beck remembered as a "delegation of blacks" who came to the Fawcett editor Will Lieberson's office to deliver their petitions consisted of students from Junior High School 120, representing the school's chapter of Youthbuilders, Inc.[7] The students refused to accept Lieberson's explanation that *Captain Marvel* comics use many kinds of caricatures "for the sake of humor," and succeeded in forcing Steamboat's retirement.[8]

DC Comics and "Anti-Minority Prejudice"

During World War II, two researchers did a short study of "anti-minority prejudice" in DC's comics (such as Superman, Batman and Wonder Woman). They discovered that— in contrast to some comic books from 1937 with their "Chink" villains—they could find "no indications whatever of any national, racial, or religious discrimination or prejudice in the treatment of the heroes and villains in the typical 'good-conquers-evil' plot of the fantastic-crime-adventure stories in the comic books."[9] The researchers interviewed "one of the leaders in the comic book publication field," who explained to them why the company had eliminated such "discrimination" from their comic books:

> ...the villains must not be members of minority groups (1) because they "had some trouble" in this connection and (2) because they could expect trouble from representatives of the groups affected. The rule now seems to be, according to this respondent, that Negroes never appear in a comic book (1) because it is difficult to draw them without stressing characteristic Negro features and (2) because it would be difficult to place them in any but comic roles. Finally, the respondent made clear the obvious commercial basis for such rules of thumb: "We are interested in circulation primarily, and hence we must give what the public wants to get. Can you imagine a hero named Cohen? Our heroes must be Rick Carters—we could not risk any innovations."[10]

Commercial concerns notwithstanding, the year that this study was published DC Comics *did* risk a serious innovation, and created a nonviolent hero without superpowers, whose primary mission was overcoming racial and national prejudices. "Johnny Everyman" ran as a backup feature in comic books that featured the company's most popular characters: Superman, Batman and Robin in *World's Finest Comics* and Wonder Woman, the Flash, and Green Lantern in *Comic Cavalcade*, from 1944 through 1947.

Johnny Everyman was created in an unusual collaboration with novelist Pearl S. Buck's East and West Association, a group that promoted a "critical internationalism." Critical internationalism advocated an anti-militarist perspective based on cooperation and dialogue between Americans and Asians, and on opposition to Western imperialism and racism.[11] Johnny Everyman was written by Jack Schiff, the longtime editor of the Batman comic books, and drawn by John Daly.[12] The East and West Association reprinted hundreds of thousands of copies of the Johnny Everyman stories for use in schools, and also created color cartoon supplements, "East and West in the Comics," which were distributed by newspaper syndicates.[13]

The first Johnny Everyman story to directly address racism in the United States appeared in *World's Finest Comics #17*, dated Spring 1945. The untitled story was "Dedicated to the millions of American Negroes who are doing their share in the armed forces, and on the home front, to win the war and usher in a new era of peace and understanding among men." It told of decorated military hero Sgt. Ralph Jackson returning to the United States and being refused service in restaurants because of racial prejudice. A headwaiter frankly tells Ralph that "Negroes are not allowed in this restaurant," and Ralph protests "that's against the law of this state!" (On a national level, this kind of discrimination remained legal until the passage of the Civil Rights Act of 1964.) Johnny Everyman appears, and invites Ralph and his black friend (who works in a defense plant "producing guns for us") to share his table. Johnny reassures his old friend Ralph that a growing number of organizations are fighting "to overcome the prejudices that spring from ignorance and misunderstanding." Before "real racial equality" can be achieved, however, the war against the fascists must be won.[14]

As the Cold War was beginning, the East and West Association tried to maintain a middle path between "the enthusiastic, sentimental glorification of the Soviet Union, which seeks to squelch all criticism" and the "bitter vituperation which sees in everything Russian a threat to Western civilization and all we hold dear." In the Johnny Everyman story "Room for Improvement" in the July–August 1946 issue of *World's Finest Comics*, Johnny Everyman says: "neither Russia nor America is perfect!" and that "the people of both lands must work to better themselves," and he agrees with the statement that "America has lots of luxuries but not enough racial tolerance—and Russia has lots of racial tolerance but not enough luxuries." Widely syndicated columnist George Sokolsky responded to this story by claiming that "when the United States is poo-boohed and Soviet Russia is made out to be better than she is, the minds of our children about their own country are corrupted." Sokolsky challenged the suggestion that a Russian visitor to the United States would notice only racial prejudice, and not Americans' much higher standard of living, and he faulted the story for mentioning not one word about "freedom of speech, of movement, of thought, of the press, of secret elections, of trial by jury and the privacy of one's home and possessions."[15]

The East and West Association's "middle path" became unsustainable, and Buck suspended the organization's operations in December 1950.[16] "Johnny Everyman" died out after a few years, not only because the feature raised political controversy, but because it did not tell exciting adventures of good overpowering evil, and even worse, it looked like something that a teacher would assign as required reading.

Buck had high hopes when she began working with comics.[17] By 1948, however (the year after Johnny Everyman's final appearance), Buck had concluded that magazine readers' craving for violent stories "hardens the soul and dulls the mind" and becomes addictive like a drug. She added that "The old bang-bang-bang ways of cowboys and comics are obsolete. To keep them alive is to suck our thumbs too long beyond childhood." To prevent "more scientifically deadly" weapons from destroying the world, to prevent the "militarization" of young people, and to produce the "different kind of humanbeing [*sic*]" that the new era of intercultural understanding requires, Buck put her hopes in the schools instead.[18]

Blood

During World War II, the quasi-governmental Writers' War Board, although it encouraged racist hatred against America's wartime enemy Japan, also expressed concern that "the rising tide of prejudice against racial, religious, and other groups here at home" could jeopardize the success of the war effort.[19] One of the eight comic book publishers that cooperated with the Writers' War Board, the Parents' Institute Press, published a couple of anti-prejudice features in *True Comics*, including the comics-format illustrated lecture "There Are No Master Races" (*True Comics* #39, October 1944).[20] In those days, people discussed race in terms of "blood" rather than genes. The story concludes: "Although their skin color may be very different, all men—of every country—are really 'brothers under the skin,' for all men are true blood relations." What's more, "Our soldiers' lives are being saved by blood plasma contributed by Americans whose ancestors came from all over the world."[21]

In 1944, Clifton Fadiman, the executive director of the Writers' War Board Comics Committee, suggested that M.C. Gaines publish a story celebrating the black 99th Pursuit Squadron, known as the Tuskegee Airmen. When the story "The 99th Squadron" appeared in *Comic Cavalcade*, Winter 1944, the story starred white pilot Hop Harrigan flying a racist Nazi prisoner of war to a POW camp. Hop Harrigan sets up a film projector in the plane and shows the captured Luftwaffe General a film of the 99th shooting down German planes. In a final reel, the Nazi prisoner sees his own plane shot down, and learns that while he was unconscious, blood transfusions from a Jewish soldier and a black volunteer had saved his life.[22]

In November 1950, the American Red Cross finally declared that they would stop segregating blood donations according to race. The main reasons for this change were Cold War competition for alliances with the newly-independent and non-white nations in Africa, Asia and Latin America (who saw the segregation of blood supplies as another example of American racism) and the increased need for blood supplies that resulted from the Korean War.[23] From 1951 to 1953, the government's National Blood Program took over blood-collecting efforts, and rather than publicizing that blood was no longer racially segregated, they did what they could to avoid calling attention to that fact (so as not to discourage donations from people who opposed the new policy).[24] After the National Blood Program ended, cross-racial blood transfusions became a controversial issue again.[25]

Comic books returned to blood as a symbol of a common humanity that transcends racial categories in EC's "Blood Brothers," published in *Shock SuspenStories #13* (February–March 1954). In this story, by Al Feldstein and drawn by Wally Wood, a bigot learns that as a child, a transfusion of "negro blood" had saved his life.[26] (This anti-racist "preachie" carefully explains that there is no such thing as "negro blood.")

Celebrated Individuals

Some comic books of the 1940s celebrated and respectfully represented high-achieving African American individuals. In 1946, Paul Robeson, the extraordinary and multi-talented left-wing activist, was featured in *two* four-page features: one in *True Comics #48*, and a piece called "Paul Robeson—All American Citizen," written by Jack Schiff, Mort Weisinger and Bernie Breslauer, which appeared in DC Comics' *Real Fact #5*. Other issues of *True Comics* celebrated Joe Louis, the "Brown Bomber: World's Greatest Fighter" (October 1941) and Jackie Robinson, baseball's "Rookie of the Year" (July 1948).[27]

In October 1949, *True Comics #79* put on its cover African American professor and diplomat "United Nations Peacemaker Ralph J. Bunche." The comic hailed Bunche as a "Hero of Peace" for being "the man who more than any other one person was responsible for peace in Palestine" between Jews and Arabs.

In 1947, the National Urban League republished six of the stories that had appeared in Parents' Magazine Press's *True Comics*, *Real Heroes*, and *Calling All Girls* as *Negro Heroes #1*. In its foreword, world heavyweight boxing champion Joe Louis told "kids" that this comic book is filled with "honest-to-goodness true stories of Negro Americans who are real Champs. Fighters! Folks who climbed into the ring punching, kayoed everything that tried to stop them, and stood up winners for the referee's count."[28] A second issue of *Negro Heroes* appeared in 1948, also published by the National Urban League but this time in cooperation with the Delta Sigma Theta Sorority. Some of its features had appeared in *True Comics.*

"Racial Consciousness"

Jack B. Tenney's objection to "racial consciousness" in comic books was quoted in a previous chapter. A 1951 pamphlet from the Christian Nationalist movement that Tenney was associated with explained "racial consciousness" as dangerous propaganda which encouraged "Negroes" to think about Negro heroes, Negro history, and the future of Negro people, rather than of themselves only as *individuals*:

> The Negro in America is being subjected to a campaign of intense propagandization from all sides of the political fence. [...] In all cases the Negro is being called upon to act not as an individual American citizen—but as "a Negro." In order to make each individual react from group considerations, rather than individual considerations, he must be shown that he has reasons to act similarly with other Negroes. [...] The result of this awakening of racial consciousness, of racial destiny and of a racial enemy will be that the struggle for world power that today appears as the warfare of "political" ideas for "political" domination will, tomorrow, appear as "racial" warfare for "racial" survival.[29]

The pamphleteer, Don Lohbeck, offers the opposite advice for white people: to think of themselves as members of an embattled race rather than merely as individual American citizens. Lohbeck summarizes the Christian Nationalist movement's racial philosophy as believing: "in racial purity, the superiority of the white race, that the white race is the bearer and protector of civilization, segregation of the races, that the danger to the white race comes from the aspiration of the Jewish race to dominate the world."[30]

The idea that black "racial consciousness" should be discouraged also had a more respectable, integrationist form. A comic book published in 1952 to support Dwight Eisenhower for the Republican nomination, *Ike's Story*, after quoting Eisenhower on the virtue of striving to eliminate the vestiges of prejudice from our hearts shows him appealing for African American support by asking, "About the year 2000, what will they be saying about the Negro race? I rather doubt at that time if it will occur to us to mention those words. We will just say Americans because that is what we all are!" In a narrow sense, Eisenhower had been correct, since "those words" ("the Negro race") had fallen into disuse before 2000. Eisenhower succeeded in winning 21 percent of the "Nonwhite" vote in 1952 and 39 percent of the nonwhite vote in his successful 1956 reelection campaign.[31]

In 1952, the Christian Nationalist Party nominated General Douglas MacArthur for President (without MacArthur's consent) and California State Senator Jack B. Tenney for Vice President (which Tenney accepted). That year, MacArthur's supporters hoped that he might win the nomination of the Republican Party if there were a deadlock between Eisenhower and Taft. Their hopes quickly deflated when MacArthur gave the convention's uninspiring keynote address.[32]

Matt Baker

The most remembered African American cartoonist drawing comic books during the Korean War (and one of the few mainstream black comic book artists of his generation) was the extremely talented artist Matt Baker. During the Korean War, his work appeared in western comics, crime comics, the war comic *Fightin' Marines* and many romance comics, including *Wartime Romances.*

For *Fightin' Marines,* Baker did not draw combat stories. He drew covers and the humor series "Canteen Kate," which was about a mischievous and sexy character who resembles a pin-up poster come to life.[33] In these stories, Baker did not draw any black characters. As was usually the case with war comics, the entire twelve-issue run of *Fighting Marines* did not include a single drawing of a black character in *any* of its stories or ads. (That series was unusual, though, in including South Koreans as regular characters: South Korean Buck Private "Duck Sing" in the stories about Sgt. Tripoli Shores, and "Gum," the "sidekick" to Leatherneck Jack.)

Cal Massey

Another African American cartoonist, comic book artist Cal Massey, worked for several publishers, but mostly for a company he knew as Magazine Management (now known as Marvel). His work appeared regularly in their war comic books, including *Battle, Battle Action, Battlefield, Battlefront, Combat, Man Comics, Marines at War, Marines in Battle, Navy Combat, Navy Tales, War Action, War Comics* and *Young Men on the Battlefield.*[34] Massey remembers that editor Stan Lee wrote most of the stories that he illustrated. Besides the Korean War, Massey drew stories set in other conflicts, including the Revolutionary War, the Civil War, the Spanish-American War, World War I, and World War II. (He had served in the U.S. Army Air Force during World War II as a pre-flight mechanic and radio mechanic.[35])

Massey drew comic books "as a matter of making a living," but he especially enjoyed working in the war comics genre. He recalls that "the fun part was researching it," and war comics required more research than other kinds of stories. He learned to draw various guns from memory. He not only penciled the stories that he was assigned but also inked his own pages. Eventually, he developed "battle fatigue" from all the war comics and moved on to other genres.

As the comic book industry collapsed in the mid–1950s, the rates paid for a page of comic book art plummeted. When the page rate dropped to $18, he left comic books to begin a successful career as a commercial artist and then as a fine artist.

I asked Cal Massey if he had drawn any black characters in his war comics, and he answered: "I was not particularly interested in doing it." In later years, however, his work included a variety of art projects celebrating the beauty and spirituality of black people.[36]

Orrin C. Evans

Comic books that directly addressed black readers were at a disadvantage during the Korean War, partly because African Americans were a minority (10 percent of the U.S. population, compared to 89.5 percent white, as measured by the 1950 census question on "race").[37] Also, black readers were more likely to buy a comic book with white heroes than white readers were to buy a comic book with black heroes.

African American journalist Orrin C. Evans sought to create a comic book not only *for* and *about* black people (like *Negro Heroes* which had appeared in Spring 1947) but also *by* black people. He published *All-Negro Comics* in June 1947. On the inside-front cover,

Evans wrote that "Every brush stroke and pen line in the drawings on these pages are by Negro artists. And each drawing is an original; that is, none has been published ANY-WHERE before."

This self-proclaimed "FIRST in Negro History" did not survive to a second issue.[38] Given the odds against any unusual comic book breaking even on its first appearance, and with the additional challenges of working without the resources of a large publisher or distributor or established cartoonists or well-known characters, this does not seem surprising. *All-Negro Comics* retailed for fifteen cents when most comic books cost a dime. Still, Evans' family remembers that the immediate reason for the series stopping after one issue was a problem getting newsprint:

> A second issue was planned and the art completed, but when Orrin was ready to publish he found that his source for newsprint would no longer sell to him, nor would any of the other vendors he contacted. Though Orrin was unyielding in his support of integration and civil rights he was moderate in his methods of achieving these goals. He believed in the general fairness of the system he had been born into. He was not a man given to conspiratorial thinking, but his family remembers that his belief was that there was pressure being placed on the newsprint wholesalers by bigger publishers and distributors who didn't welcome any intrusions on their established territories.[39]

At a time when demand for newsprint was larger than the supply, the newsprint industry focused on maintaining its long-term contracts with large publishers.[40] In 1951, a Senate report would list the most frequent sources of the "flood of complaints" it had received about newsprint shortages as "the publishers of small daily and weekly newspapers of general circulation, and of special group newspapers such as the Catholic and the Negro press."[41]

Evans was far from alone in having trouble finding newsprint to publish comic books. During World War II, paper had been rationed, and the government confiscated the press runs of dozens of comic book titles because their small publishers had gone ahead without the required "paper consumption quota."[42] Paper rationing was relaxed when World War II ended, and in the glut of new magazines that followed, the large publishers outbid the smaller and newer companies for scarce newsprint supplies.[43] The problem of getting newsprint, then, might be added to the list of factors that prevented a full range of views from appearing regularly in print.[44]

Jackie Ormes

Of the cartoonists who worked for African American newspapers in that period, the most remembered have been Jackie Ormes and Ollie Harrington. Although neither drew for comic books, the views they expressed in their newspaper cartoons and through their activism stand as reminders of some ideas that circulated only *outside* the limits of the comic book medium during the Korean War.

Jackie Ormes, recognized as the first African American woman cartoonist, drew the cartoon feature *Patty-Jo 'n' Ginger* and the comic strip *Torchy in Heartbeats* from 1950 to 1954.[45] The FBI became interested in Ormes because of her appearances at many Communist Party-sponsored events.[46] They interviewed her directly several times, and in 1953 her FBI file reported that: "The subject [Ormes] spoke of Korea, stating that we (United States and/or United Nations) were the aggressors in that conflict and should withdraw and permit 'Asians to fight Asians.'"[47]

In some of her cartoons, Ormes, in the words of her biographer Nancy Goldstein, would "boldly criticize U.S. weapons programs, American military adventurism, and government encroachment on privacy and on freedom of speech."[48] The 250-page FBI file on Ormes, while noting that she was a cartoonist, did not describe any of her specific cartoons.[49]

Ollie Harrington

Ollie Harrington (black on his father's side and with an immigrant Hungarian Jew as his mother) had a long and successful career as a very popular and strongly anti-racist editorial cartoonist for black papers. During World War II, Harrington had worked as a war correspondent/illustrator, sending reports to the black press about the conditions for black soldiers in training camps and in combat in Italy. He reported mostly on the Tuskegee Airmen, a group of African American pilots that he praised for never having lost to enemy fire a bomber that they were escorting.[50] Besides his articles, Harrington also celebrated the Tuskegee Airmen in a weekly series of comic strips that he drew for the *Baltimore Afro-American,* under the title *Jive Gray*. In the May 22, 1943, installment, their commanding officer concludes his briefing by reminding them: "Remember they say that they don't know whether Negroes make good pilots. You can make them liars! God bless you all…. **Man your ships!"**[51]

Some of the Tuskegee Airmen went on to participate in the Korean War and Vietnam War, no longer in racially segregated units.[52] A black jet pilot appears in one panel of the Korean War comic book story "Iron Curtains for Ivan," published in 1953. The Soviet pilot Ivan Petrovitch, sent to Korea "to learn modern tactics by actually fighting the planes of the United Nations," muses that his officers "tell us the Americans are fascists … that they persecute the minority races … and yet we see their colored soldiers fighting side by side with the white soldiers." Ivan watches as his arrogant flight instructor is outmaneuvered and shot down and then he sees that the successful pilot is "a negro! Can the leaders have been lying to us?" Unfortunately for Ivan, he learns the truth about American racial equality too late and is killed in action.[53]

After World War II, Harrington found that rather than winning acceptance as full citizens in recognition of their military service, black veterans were facing an intense backlash. While he was reporting on lynchings in Georgia in 1946, one black veteran told him: "They're exterminating us. They're killing Negro vets, and we don't have nothing to fight back with but our bare hands."[54]

That year, Harrington accepted an invitation to create a public relations department for the National Association of Colored People (NAACP), while continuing to draw his *Dark Laughter* cartoon on the side. During his year with the organization, the case that he became most involved with was that of Isaac Woodard, whom he came to know personally on Woodard's speaking tours.[55] When Walter White of the NAACP told President Truman about Sergeant Isaac Woodard and other similar stories, Truman's shock at hearing about a "negro Sergeant" who was "not only seriously beaten" by a small-town South Carolina police chief, but had "his eyes deliberately put out" inspired him to actively take on the issue of civil rights.[56] Among Truman's other actions to advance civil rights, on July 26, 1948, he issued Executive Order 9981 to desegregate the military.[57]

In 1952, on the advice of a friend in Army Intelligence, cartoonist Ollie Harrington moved beyond the reach of the communist-hunters in America and settled in France.[58] From there, Harrington moved to East Germany in 1961, and he lived in East Berlin (with annual trips to France and other trips to Ghana, Denmark, Switzerland, and the United States) until his death in 1995.[59]

Comic Books and the Segregated Military

Gerald Early argues that until Truman had ordered the armed forces to stop practicing racial segregation, a war comic book could not have added a token black but would have to draw a mostly black comic book story:

> The officer in charge of the black unit could be white, but he would be the only white, and the characters could not be in combat [since almost all African American men in the military were in "service units," for example, driving trucks]. This would have violated two important selling points of war comics—or any comics, for that matter: first, by depicting a large number of blacks as anything other than a jungle tribe, and second, by showing soldiers in wartime doing something other than engaging in combat, when precisely what attracted adolescent readers to depictions of war were images of carnage and heroism.[60]

Harvey Kurtzman solved the artistic problem of how to represent black soldiers without devoting an entire eight-page story to a black military unit by showing a black military unit and a white military unit, fighting the Chinese in Korea from opposite sides of the same hill. Segregated units had fought in the first year of the Korean War, but these units had become a thing of the past when the Army disbanded the all-black 24th Infantry Regiment in October 1951. By the November–December 1952 issue of *Two-Fisted Tales* (#30), when the story "Bunker" appeared, the army had become racially integrated. That context helps to explain this story's seemingly tacked-on (and counterfactual) introduction: "The war in Korea has quieted down! The guns are hardly louder than the haggling at the truce tents! But we can remember two years back when the whole Korean front was exploding with war! Back then our story took place…"

Kurtzman's most dismaying personal memories of his own experiences in the Army had centered on the white supremacism that he observed while serving in Army camps in the American South during World War II.[61] Still, fans do not mention his only war comic book story that focused on the issue of race when they remember his better efforts.

Some of the first American soldiers shipped to Korea to resist the North Korean invasion were member of the all-black 24th regiment, and they were widely criticized for being ineffective soldiers who "bugged out" when the enemy attacked, abandoning their weapons. (They were blamed and punished more for their shortcomings and less remembered for their successes than white soldiers.[62])

Kurtzman's story seems to suggest that "our Negro troops" perform just as well in combat as white troops. The Army's own study in 1951 found that all-black units did *not* perform as well, but not because black men were inferior soldiers. The problem was segregation itself, which created morale problems. A *Saturday Evening Post* article quoted "one hard-fighting Negro captain" who explained the advantages of integration this way:

> The trouble is you take a man who in his own country has always been treated as a second-class citizen, and you call upon him to fight as a first-class soldier. [...] You put him in a white regiment, and he looks around him and sees white men and black men both, and he feels in his heart, "Now they are treating me like an American, not like a Negro." But you put him in a Negro regiment, and he looks around him and sees nothing but Negroes, and he feels like somebody is using him as cannon fodder.[63]

Comic Books and the Integrated Military

After the high-ranking officers who had opposed Truman's Executive Order 9981 yielded to the practical need to find quick replacements for dead riflemen during the Korean War, the racial integration of the army went surprisingly smoothly.[64]

Around the time that the negotiators at Panmunjom were reaching the armistice agreement, in July 1953, EC artist Wallace Wood finally took on the topic of racial integration in the Army in "Perimeter!," the cover story of the last issue of *Frontline Combat*. It was one of the few EC war comic book stories that he had written himself.

Fellow EC cartoonist Joe Orlando remembered of Wood that "He wasn't just into comics, he was into politics."[65] Wood's politics were leftist, shaped by socialist ideals inherited from his mother, and by the music he enjoyed, by politically aware singers including the Weavers, Pete Seeger, Odetta, Paul Robeson, Miriam Makeba, Marian Anderson, and others.[66] Wood told cartoonist Al Williamson that he had overcome his racist views while serving in the racially integrated Merchant Marine during World War II.[67] Anti-racist and other leftist themes appeared in several of the stories he drew for EC's editor Al Feldstein.

In "Perimeter!," Americans are portrayed as "A mixture of all nationalities and racial origins in the world." The central characters in the story are two white Southerners, but a black soldier, Matthews—shown as always reading his Bible—and two South Korean soldiers also have speaking parts.

At the conclusion of "Perimeter!" a white Southern American soldier gives the white Southern racist in his squad a moving anti-racist Bible lesson from Malachi 2:10:

> Have we not all one father
> Hath not one God created us

This lesson distorted the prophet Malachi's original meaning by choosing only a few words out of context. Had that Bible quotation continued for even one more line, it would have turned into a curse against intermarriage.[68]

New Heroic Comics

The unusual series *New Heroic Comics* based its many Korean War stories on the experiences of actual fighting men who had received awards for their heroic actions on the battlefield. This series did not refer to black or white ethnicity in its captions or speech balloons (though its dialogue balloons included casual references to "Chinks" and "Gooks"). *New Heroic Comics* artists included more images of soldiers who could be visually interpreted as black than other series did. Judging by skin tone, hair, and the shapes of lips and noses, such characters appear, for example, on the cover of issue #69 by H.E. Kiefer—but the same characters become white when drawn by Frank Frazetta in the story that the cover is based on (November 1951). Possibly because the artists were drawing actual people without visual reference material, the series provided relatively few clues about what their main characters' faces looked like. They frequently showed main characters in silhouette or from a distance or with their back turned.

Fred McGee won a medal for bravery in Korea, for reasons dramatized in *New Heroic Comics #81*, published in March 1953. In two pages, cartoonist Sam Burlockoff showed how Cpl. Fred McGee had "for his gallantry and courage" been awarded the Silver Star.

When interviewed for the website Comic Book Resources over fifty years later, McGee remembered that:

> When I first heard it was coming out, I was pretty excited [...] I saw the comic while I was still in Korea in 1953. I looked at it, saw that my character was white, and felt it did not seem right. I was mad. I felt like someone else was getting the accolades for what I did. I think it was racially motivated.[69]

A wider look at this unusual series does not support the idea that the problem had been motivated by an editorial reluctance to recognize black heroism. Seven issues earlier, in August 1952, the series had clearly represented Medal of Honor recipient Sgt. Cornelius H. Charlton as African American, which was historically accurate. Charlton fought in the segregated 24th Infantry Regiment.

As a Medal of Honor recipient, Charlton was automatically qualified to be buried at Arlington National Cemetery, but according to Charlton family history, the horse-drawn buggy carrying his flag-covered coffin was blocked before it could reach that destination:

> As they were approaching Arlington Cemetery, they were stopped by some folks in pickup trucks with shotguns, pointing at them and telling them he wasn't going to be buried there. [...] They were just racists. They weren't military. They weren't Arlington [National Cemetery] representatives. They were just racists. They didn't want to celebrate—it wasn't time yet for the South to celebrate a black military hero.[70]

In 2008, Charlton's family decided to correct this injustice, and Cornelius H. Charlton's body was finally reburied in Arlington National Cemetery, which welcomed his remains.

The issue following the one that told Charlton's story also included a black hero. Chaplain Captain George W. Williams, who received a Silver Star.[71] Although the series included black heroes, the editorial approach focused on heroism rather than black pride. Issue #78 included a story in which a white First Lieutenant earns a Silver Star while the black soldiers under his command shout out "He *did* it! Singlehanded, he *did* it!" and "What an officer! *What a man!*"[72] In issue #87, white First Sergeant Willard W. Wolfe is awarded the Silver Star for rescuing two frightened black Americans from a mine field. Their only line of dialogue is "We set one [mine] off before ... and we're afraid to go back."[73]

Cold War Considerations

Anti-racist comic book stories were rare exceptions to the rule. The racism in American comic books attracted foreign criticism. Peter Mauger, a leader of the anti-comics movement in Britain, said in 1953: "In war comics and films ... the lesson drummed into receptive minds is that anyone coloured and/or non[-]European is, quite simply, subhuman—and so ripe for destruction."[74]

In the Cold War competition for international influence, Soviet and Communist Chinese propaganda emphasized American racism, and American leaders recognized this racism as a serious foreign policy disadvantage.[75] For example, the U.S. ambassador to India, Chester Bowles, told a Yale audience in 1952:

> A year, a month, or even a week in Asia is enough to convince any perceptive American that the colored peoples of Asia and Africa, who total two-thirds of the world's population, seldom think about the United States without considering the limitations under which our 13 million Negroes are living.[76]

Several of the comics codes and editorial policies that multiplied during this period banned "prejudice," "intolerance" and "ridicule" of racial groups. This curbed the worst abuses, but cartoonists usually found it easier to eliminate stereotyped images of minorities than to replace them with something better.

Wertham vs. Comic Book Racism

Fredric Wertham (an anti-comics activist described in an earlier chapter) was particularly concerned about the racist contempt taught in many comic books. As the head of an anti-racist mental health clinic in central Harlem, a community that was 98 percent black in 1950, he was especially attuned to this issue.[77] While testifying about the harmful effects of school segregation in Delaware in 1951, Wertham had pulled out a copy of the current issue of the jungle comic *Jumbo Comics* to demonstrate that, even though "segregation in schools assumes a very much greater importance" in children's minds than the racism in comic books, both school segregation and racist comic books were examples of a larger anti-black climate that was putting emotional and psychic strains on children, and interfering with their healthy emotional and mental development.[78]

In his book *Seduction of the Innocent*, Wertham wrote:

> If I were to make the briefest summary of what children have told us about how different peoples are represented to them in the lore of crime comics, it would be that there are two kinds of people: on the one hand is the tall, blond, regular-featured man sometimes disguised as a superman (or superman disguised as a man) and the pretty young blonde girl with the superbreast. On the other hand are the inferior people: natives, primitives, savages, "ape men," Negroes, Jews, Indians, Italians, Slavs, Chinese and Japanese, immigrants of every description, people with irregular features, swarthy skins, physical deformities, Oriental features [...]. The pictures of these "inferior" types as criminals, gangsters, rapers, suitable victims for slaughter by either the lawless or the law, have made an indelible impression on children's minds.[79]

In 1954, Wertham estimated that "More race hatred has been instilled in American children through comic books in the past ten years than in the preceding hundred years."[80] (This was not a conclusion based on data, but his personal impression.[81])

In *Seduction of the Innocent*, Wertham briefly criticizes war comics for teaching race prejudice:

> War comics, in which war is just another setting for comic-book violence, are widely read by soldiers at the front and by children at home. It seems dubious whether this is good for the morale of soldiers; it certainly is not good for the morality of children. Against the background of regular-featured blonde Americans, the people of Asia are depicted in comic books as cruelly grimacing and toothy creatures, often of an unnatural yellow color.[82]

Wertham's testimony against school segregation in Delaware in 1951 provided a scientific foundation for the landmark Supreme Court's *Brown v. Board of Education* decision which overturned the idea that schools could be "separate but equal."[83] The statement summarizing the social-scientific evidence of the harms caused by discrimination that the National Association for the Advancement of Colored People submitted to the Supreme Court in 1954 paraphrased Wertham's distinctive contribution to the argument. Nevertheless, Wertham had been excluded from the drafting of that statement, was not credited in it, and was not invited to sign it, for what Gabriel N. Mendes summarizes as "personal, professional/methodological, and likely political reasons."[84]

One methodological problem was Wertham's use of the clinical method. As Wertham freely admitted, "clinical test results and psychological test results may have the appearance of factual data," but they are professional opinions, "clinical judgements" based on an evaluation of the evidence, rather than "science in the sense of mathematical certainty."[85]

Mendes supplies a reason for thinking that Wertham's clinical findings were not reproducible. Wertham's Lafargue Clinic:

> offered a space in which African Americans and any others who sought treatment could express themselves freely, trusting that their feelings would be taken seriously and that they would receive professional care. No other psychiatric clinic in the country could make the same claim.[86]

When Wertham co-founded the Lafargue Clinic in 1946, the rate of juvenile delinquency in Harlem was over four times higher than in the rest of Manhattan.[87] Novelist Richard Wright, who helped Wertham get the clinic started, explained that without "mental hygiene clinics," Harlem's emotionally disturbed individuals had been turning to violent crime, gangs, thievery, and other unhealthy activities.[88] When Wertham wrote in *Seduction of the Innocent* that he had noticed "a thousand times" that the punishment of children by sending them to reformatories does not fit their crimes but rather causes them lasting harm, we may assume that many of those times he had been observing the mistreatment of individual African American children.[89]

The Civil Rights Movement and Comics

The Civil Rights Movement quickly picked up momentum soon after the Korean War. One of the organizing tools that helped build that movement was a comic book that the Fellowship of Reconciliation published in 1957 about the Montgomery Bus Boycott of 1955. That comic book, *Martin Luther King and the Montgomery Story,* provided the immediate inspiration for several demonstrations, including the historic sit-in at the Greensboro, North Carolina, Woolworth's lunch counter in February 1960.[90] As the historic events of the Civil Rights Movement unfolded, mainstream commercial comic books, however, were largely missing in action. After EC retired from the four-color comic book business, going out on a glorious note with a reprint of their anti-racist science fiction story "Judgment Day" in 1956, mainstream comics did not directly address segregation and racism again for years. When comic books returned to the subject, they did so more timidly than EC comics had done.

In 1961, the war comic *Our Army at War* anachronistically integrated a squad of soldiers fighting in World War II Europe with the addition of a black soldier, Jackie Johnson. Fredrik Strömberg's history of *Black Images in the Comics* recognizes this as one of "the earliest examples of stories featuring Black characters as equals."[91]

When asked about the introduction of this black military character, the artist Joe Kubert told an interviewer:

> Bob Kanigher was the editor at that time and he wrote most of the Sgt. Rock stories himself. The decision to publish the story was entirely his [...] and as far as I knew decisions were made solely on the basis of selling mags. You mentioned in your e-mail that you were wondering if the military had asked us to do this, but there was no political motive at all—certainly no government request.[92]

Immediately after saying it was "solely" about making money, he corrected himself: "It wasn't all purely money-making, however. There was an attempt to show recognition of problems that had existed. We knew there had been no integrated units in WWII but it was important to show how things were supposed to be."

The character made a second appearance in November 1965, in a story that *Our Army at War #160* promoted on its cover with an exciting blurb: "'**What's** the **Color** of **Your Blood**?' If you **think** you know the answer—you're going to get the **shock** of your life! Only **Sgt. Rock** dares to bring you the battle tale too hot for anyone else to handle!" As Joe Kubert remembered it, that issue (in which the black soldier proves to the racist Nazi enemy how wrong the Nazi had been by saving that Nazi's life with a transfusion of his own blood) did not provoke any negative mail.[93]

As for whether this tale had been "too hot for anyone else to handle," Sgt. Fury at Marvel Comics, DC's competitor, had been involved in a similar story in March 1964. In "The Fangs of the Desert Fox!," scripted by Stan Lee and penciled by Jack Kirby, the racist character George Stonewell is saved by the Jewish character, Izzy Cohen, and by a blood transfusion from the black character, Gabriel Jones.[94]

Integration in Fact and Fiction

When North Korea invaded South Korea, about eight percent of the U.S. armed forces were African Americans. Five thousand or more of the Americans who would die in combat in Korea were African Americans.[95] Perhaps more stories than the few in *New Heroic Comics* plus Harvey Kurtzman's "Bunker" and Wally Wood's "Perimeter!" address the experiences of black soldiers in Korea. If so, they remain to be discovered.[96]

The U.S. Army has become America's most desegregated large institution. Joe R. Feagin notes that by the late 1990s:

> black Americans made up about 11% of all officers, a figure much higher than that for executives in almost all large corporations or that for professors at almost all historically white colleges and universities. The 7,500 black officers there constitute the largest group of black executives in any historically white organization in the entire history of the United States. African Americans also make up one third or more of the sergeant ranks in the army, a proportion much higher than that for comparable supervisors in most other workplaces.[97]

The war comics genre faded away before it could catch up with this progress.

11

◇◇◇◇◇◇◇◇◇◇

Germs

One of the most passionate propaganda battles of the Korean War raged over whether the United States was using "germ warfare."[1] Communist governments formally accused the United States of the war crime of using biological weapons.[2] The United States denied the charge officially, repeatedly, unequivocally, utterly and angrily. Creators of popular culture on both sides of the Cold War took up the issue, dramatizing germ warfare charges in plays, films, editorial cartoons, and American comic book stories.[3]

The Korean War germ warfare allegations have been described as "perhaps the most audacious, elaborate and unscrupulous campaign in the history of psychological warfare" and as the "most highly organized, closely concentrated and virulent" of the "many hate campaigns waged by communist propagandists."[4] In 1998, handwritten copies of a dozen secret Russian documents surfaced which were presented as proof that the germ warfare charges had been a fraud based on faked evidence.[5]

Several comic book stories that took up the theme of germ warfare charges appear to have been loose fictionalizations of the story of General Crawford Sams, who conducted a mission in March 1951 to investigate a possible epidemic of plague behind enemy lines.[6] Comparing the various versions of Sams' activities that were presented as fact and as fiction helps to reveal the patterns that shaped the stories in Korean War comics.

"Danger Below"

Soon after General Sams' secret information gathering mission in North Korea, his story was publicized in a widely published United Press article, a *New York Times* article, and a *Collier's* magazine story, "Doctor Commando."[7] The following paragraph describes the common elements between "Doctor Commando," by Peter Kalischer, and a *Monty Hall* comic book story, "Danger Below," drawn by Mel Keefer:

> An officer leads a four-man team behind enemy lines in North Korea to learn the truth about an epidemic sweeping the enemy troops. They intend to visit a North Korean hospital. If they learn that the epidemic is plague, the UN forces will be able to take measures to defend themselves from that disease. As they approach the shore in a small, inflatable boat, they see a signal light from their confederate, but also the headlights of a convoy of trucks. They meet their Korean contact. Air Force planes bomb the enemy truck convoy. The officer, relying on experience he gained in the Middle East, evaluates the evidence and decides that the enemy's epidemic is not plague. They hide from the enemy soldiers and return safely.[8]

The comic book story has a publication date three months later than the publication date of the magazine and seems to have been based, in part, on the *Collier's* article.

Some of the differences include that the comic book story has the landing party arrive more dramatically, by submarine.[9] Also, the comic book exaggerates the role of white American characters. In the magazine story, two of the four men in Sams' landing party were Koreans, and they met six Koreans on the beach. In the comic, the white Major Martin is accompanied by the regular characters in the *Monty Hall* comics—"Tex," "Canarsie," and "Monty Hall"—and they meet only one Korean on the beach. Writers must simplify, but here the result puts the white characters in a four to one majority rather than a two out of ten minority. The comic book story adds more violent action, and grants the American heroes a more unequivocal success.

In the *Collier's* account, twelve of the fourteen "friendly" Koreans who had scouted the area for Sams were "caught, tortured and executed by the communists. They had been sold out ...." After the mission, Sams said "we learned the communists got wind of our visit and executed 25 men and their families in reprisal." Although action-packed, the Monty Hall story shows no carnage. It also invents a happier ending. In the comic, their contact says "I go with you. Family also." Monty responds, "Of course. You're right. There's bound to be reprisals for tonight's work." Although the submarine is crowded already, "we can't leave them behind to be shot by the Reds!" The story reemphasizes the humanitarian sentiments of the UN side after they sink the enemy destroyer. The heroes drag the "Gooks" out of the sea, rescuing them because "that's what makes the difference between us and them." The story suggests that the enemy has no mercy on old men, women and children, unlike the Americans.

Finally, the comic book story differs from the magazine story by concluding that the Americans' mission had succeeded in disproving the communist germ warfare charges:

> ...Major Martin, Monty, Tex and Canarsie were able to destroy a communist lie. The Major proved that the North Korean epidemic was not bubonic plague instituted by diabolical UN germ warfare, but intestinal disorder caused by the Red troops' own carelessness and poor living conditions.

In the *Collier's* article, the communists responded to this mission by publicizing "their own distorted version," that is, by renewing the germ warfare charges.[10]

The March 1952 issue of the communist-sympathizing *China Monthly Review* would look back on General Sams' mission as an early example of American germ warfare activities in Korea:

> The record of American preparation and use of bacteriological weapons in Korea is a long one. Last March, a US naval ship, under Crawford F. Sams, chief of the Public Health and Welfare Section of the UN Forces General Headquarters, sailed to Wonsan on the east coast of Korea. Although masquerading as an epidemic control ship, it was actually loaded with bacteriological installations and was used for testing germ weapons on North Korea and Chinese prisoners.[11]

For supporting the communist germ warfare charges, the U.S. government punished the editor of the *China Monthly Review,* John William Powell, in various ways. These included driving his publication out of business by blocking it from the American mails, preventing him from finding other employment, and indicting him and his collaborators for sedition for "deliberately false reporting" about events in China, including their reports on germ warfare in Korea.[12]

"Plague Patrol"

Most of the characteristics of Korean War comic book stories that are revealed by com-paring "Danger Below!" with the *Collier's* article "Doctor Commando" also can be seen in the comic book story "Plague Patrol," published in 1952 and then republished as "Get That Man!" in 1953.[13] "Plague Patrol" appears to be based on an aspect of Sams' mission which the other versions of the story left unstated: that Sams had intended to take a patient with plague back for testing.[14]

The main characters set out with the stated purpose of gathering evidence to disprove germ warfare allegations.[15] Rather than making any complicated travel arrangements, the two U.S. soldiers fight straight across the battlefield, enter a "gook hospital," kidnap a pa-tient, and carry him back to their own side. They are assisted, not by characters identified as South Koreans or anti-communist Korean guerrillas, but by a captured enemy Korean soldier. They shoot rifles and pistols, throw grenades, choke and sock barehanded, and hit the enemy with rifle butts.

The story "Plague Patrol" conveys the idea of a "dirty" war with unusual scatological frankness when one soldier comments about the corpse on the other's back, "why don't ya change his diapers, Sarge?" The strikingly crude art, with its sloppy anatomy, strange compositions, and heavy brushstrokes, effectively communicates gut repulsion towards this "screwy war."

For his mission behind enemy lines, General Sams was awarded the Distinguished Service Cross, with a citation that noted that the information he gathered was of "such sig-nificance as to affect the immediate conduct of the United Nations' armed effort in Korea." His foray had been preceded by nine similar attempts which had failed.[16] Sams' actions also seem comparable to some unsuccessful spy missions the following year which had also tried to learn about health conditions in North Korea.[17]

Red Germs

Several articles about germ warfare had appeared just as the Korean War was begin-ning. The newsletter *Science News Letter* for July 8, 1950, predicted that "Germ warfare may get a trial very soon, if the fighting in Korea continues. The situation might be considered by the Soviets as a good one in which to stage a trial of such a weapon, if they have developed a satisfactory method of using it."[18] The Soviet Union's germ warfare research had begun in 1928, to study how to use typhus as a weapon.[19] In November 1950, with Americans occupy-ing Pyongyang, the capital of North Korea, the *New York Times* ran an article claiming that Americans had discovered a "super-secret bacteriological laboratory operated here since 1947 under supervision of a Russian woman scientist."[20] In 1952, retired Navy Admiral Ellis M. Zacharias called the communists' germ warfare accusations "a gigantic smokescreen be-hind which the Soviet Union continued its own feverish preparations for a biological war," and claimed that Russia had four centers for producing and experimenting with biological warfare agents, including one in the Korean War theater.[21]

Despite such hints, I have found no examples in which either news reports or history books have claimed that the communists used germ warfare in Korea. The absence of such news reports did not stop the comic book writers.

In an unusual superhero story set in the Korean War, the FBI sends Plastic Man and his sidekick Woozy Winks to investigate the enemy's introduction of "a secret weapon that threatened the very existence of the U.N. Armies!"[22] They arrive at a "U.N. outpost" to discover that a mysterious contagious disease has sickened everyone there. The doctor reports "we feel pretty sure that the sickness is caused by **germs** being shot into the area by the enemy," and "the Top Brass is afraid that the enemy is using this outpost as a test for their biological warfare!" Plastic Man and Woozy Winks parachute down to the "enemy field research headquarters" to "get some of those germs in their original state" so the "base hospital" can develop an antidote. In the enemy's germ warfare laboratory, the enemy researchers demand that Woozy Winks drink a "vial of new germ" from a test tube. Plastic Man saves his friend and succeeds in bringing the sample back to the U.N. scientists, thus enabling them to "develop a cure that will protect the entire U.N. Army!"

The story "Silent Death," published the following month in *U.S. Paratroops #6*, had the Americans fighting "the most horrible weapon of modern war." The story, drawn by Mort Lawrence, begins with a radio operator failing to contact a "South Korean outfit." The paratroopers go to investigate and discover a pile of their Korean allies' bodies with "hardly a wound on any of these men." They "take some of these dead bodies" back to the base's "medical department," where the doctor's autopsies conclude that "the enemy is using germ warfare." Before being killed, the South Koreans had downed a MiG plane, and the surviving pilot confesses that they have "a big underground laboratory not far from their airbase at Rinchon." The U.S. paratroopers, after being immunized, find the enemy's germ warfare lab, plaster it with RDX explosive, and "When Captain Hale thought all the enemy soldiers were well inside the germ breeding laboratory, he gave the signal for the blast, and…. B-AROOM!"

Meanwhile, in the popular Western genre of comic books, Roy Rogers fought what Roy Thomas summarized as "Red efforts to poison the water supply of a new western defense plant with anthrax germs" and "the spread of aftosa virus [hoof and mouth disease] among western cattle ranches."[23]

Some Roots of Exterminationism

Although this chapter begins by describing a propaganda battle over whether the United States was using biological weapons in Korea, the actual communist charges usually placed the germ warfare allegations in the wider context of an American policy of exterminationism. The accusations grouped germ warfare with conventional bombing, napalm, poison gas, and atomic threats.[24] The Western response focused tightly on the issue of whether biological warfare was being used as a weapon.

The idea of Americans using germ warfare to massacre Chinese and Koreans has surprisingly deep roots in Anglo-American popular literature. British and American novelists had predicted it many years before their militaries had begun working to make it a possibility. The "yellow peril" literature, in which these genocidal ideas were developed, eventually provided the foundation for the comic book image of Asians.[25]

The British author M.P. Shiel wrote an immensely popular novel, incorporating items from contemporary headlines, which was serialized in 1898 and published in book format in 1899 as *The Yellow Danger: Or what MIGHT Happen if the Division of the Chinese Empire should Estrange All European Countries.*[26] In Shiel's novel, the Chinese and Japanese, predicting an eventual race war with the whites, decide to trick the European powers into warring with each other and then invade Europe, planning to overwhelm the survivors with the force of their superior numbers.[27] Near the conclusion of the novel, seven million of the Chinese invaders are destroyed when the hero arranges for 150 "Chinamen" to be taken aboard a boat, injected with cholera, and then disembarked two at a time at 75 European ports, to spread that disease among their people. In the happy ending, the Americans take over the administration of the continent of Asia and the English exercise their hegemony over Europe and Africa.[28] Although comic books received a lot of criticism for their brutal indifference to human life, clearly that problem existed in more respected types of fiction as well.

The "yellow peril" literary tradition that Shiel helped to establish seems to have provided a framework through which both sides in the Korean War misinterpreted each other. In Korea, Americans saw the Chinese as vast "hordes," greatly outnumbering the UN forces, and with the potential to swarm across the Pacific into California.[29] Chinese "human wave" attacks seemed to be an American nightmare come true, and such attacks were frequently pictured in the comic books.[30] On the other hand, the Koreans and Chinese saw the goal of the U.S. and UN forces to be their own extermination.

The main body of germ warfare charges, however, had to do not with boats (such as those in Shiel's novel or General Sams' epidemic control ship) but with bombers. Here, once more, a piece of fiction seemed to prefigure the alleged events. Jack London's short story "The Unparalleled Invasion," written in 1906 and published in *McClure's Magazine* in 1910, described a future war in which Americans defeat the Chinese by using germ warfare. The Americans in that story drop "tubes of fragile glass" loaded with "scores of plagues," including smallpox, scarlet fever, cholera and bubonic plague.[31] In this fiction, the Chinese are exterminated by "these bacteria and germs, and microbes, and bacilli, cultured in the laboratories of the West, that had come down upon China in the rain of glass."[32] In the happy ending to "The Unparalleled Invasion," the Europeans and Americans put to death all the Chinese survivors, colonize the resulting wilderness, and solemnly agree "never to use against one another the laboratory methods of warfare they had employed in the invasion of China." One of the avid readers of *McClure's* fiction during this period, Harry S. Truman, would serve as the Commander in Chief of the United States military for the first two and a half years of the Korean War.[33]

The idea of an "exterminationist" policy against them resonated with the communists' own "annihilationist" programs. Ruth Rogaski points out that the Chinese public hygiene campaign to eliminate flies, mosquitoes, mice and rats, lice, and bedbugs happened at a time when the communists similarly sought to eradicate their *human* enemies.[34] The new government in China launched its successful campaign to eliminate its remaining political enemies, the Zhenfan campaign of 1950–1951, at the same time that it entered the Korean War. Official Chinese sources estimate that 712,000 counter-revolutionaries were killed out of a population of 500 million. The numbers were probably higher, and this campaign was followed by others.[35]

A new twist in the germ warfare campaign began in 1952, when captured American fliers confessed to having participated in germ warfare atrocities. The U.S. responded that the POWs' confessions had been coerced and were worthless. Again, comic books dramatized this turn of events, participating in the conversion of anti–American propaganda into stories of communist barbarity. The next chapter explores these germ warfare confession comic book stories, and their historical contexts.

12

Brainwashing

Beginning in 1952, propaganda campaigns about germ warfare reached sensational heights. The communists announced that captured American fliers had confessed that they had been engaged in germ warfare in Korea.[1] Comic book stories, following the lead of the news media, showed that these prisoners must have been "brainwashed," and that their so-called confessions were lies dictated by communist propagandists.[2]

A comic book story simply titled "The Confession!," published in *Battle Cry #12* in May 1954, corresponds closely to the stories about the germ warfare confessions that had appeared in U.S. newspapers. Nevertheless, that comic makes no editorial boast about revealing a "true story," but instead offers the disclaimer that "No actual person is named or delineated in this fiction magazine."

"The Confession!" tells the story of Lieutenant "James Nelson," a character who "represents all men who fell from the skies into the hands of the enemy...." Nelson is captured, suffers anxiety about what his captors will do to him, and finally is informed that he must "confess to the crime of dropping bombs for your country's plan of germ warfare." Then a scene of relentless interrogation follows, in which Nelson is deprived of food and sleep for 34 hours while his interrogator tries to put words in his mouth. The pressure is symbolized by picturing Nelson in three separate poses within a single panel while images of the large, disembodied head of his tormentor multiply behind him. After several montages of grueling interrogations, Nelson breaks down and writes a confession, being careful to "put plenty of things in here that can be proven false." His confession is tossed aside and Nelson is then forced to write and sign a 24-page document, filled with dictated lies. The scene shifts to the United Nations, where the delegate from the USSR presents the confession as documentary proof of U.S. germ warfare in Korea. Next Nelson must repeat his confession to an investigative commission composed of "party members or fellow travelers." A film is made of his confession, which is shown in Eastern Europe. Finally, Nelson is released as part of "Operation Big Switch." Although he tries to forget the ordeal he has been through, he finds himself at the center of a public controversy. The story ends on a serious note: "Who are we to draw conclusions, for we were not in Jim's position.... Each man has his breaking point.... all the Jim Nelson's can tell you that! But, THIS IS YOUR ENEMY ... know them well!"[3]

Some of the elements of "The Confession" that are easily matched to factual accounts include the threat to execute the POW as a "war criminal," the hunger and sleep deprivation, the forced writing and rewriting of his confession, the Soviet use of the confession at the UN, the testimony to the investigative commission (clearly representing the International Scientific Commission for the Investigation of Facts Concerning Bacterial Warfare

131

in Korea and China), the internationally distributed propaganda film of the confession, and finally the return to face public controversy in the United States.[4]

The editorial message of "The Confession!" warns the reader to know "your enemy." One way that the story guards the credibility of its description of the enemy is by not pretending to reveal the enemy's thoughts. Even some of the angriest critics of the germ warfare propaganda campaign conceded that the communists appeared to sincerely believe the accusations they were making.[5] (One indication of their sincerity was that the Chinese and North Koreans had responded to the threat of germ warfare with a huge epidemic prevention campaign that included vaccinations and sanitation programs.[6])

The story does not describe the interrogator's inner thoughts, but it does reveal the thoughts of the prisoner. It establishes his innocence by showing him alone in his cell wondering whether to make a false confession.[7]

Confession

The comic book story "The Confession!" refers to the communist torturers as "masters of psychiology [sic]" who have "ways to make you talk ways you never dreamed of." Still, this story includes no hint of any mysterious new techniques for the disintegration of the mind.

The recently formed CIA had taken a keen interest in secret methods to elicit false confessions, which they suspected had been responsible for the unbelievable confessions of those accused in the "Moscow Show Trials" of 1937 and the confessions of Hungary's Jozsef Cardinal Mindszenty at his trial in 1948. The trial of Cardinal Mindszenty, a personal friend of New York City's Cardinal Spellman, especially angered American Catholics, and they prayed and rallied and organized for his release. Through the Catechetical Guild Educational Society, Mindszenty's supporters published an entire comic book devoted to his story, *The Truth Behind the Trial of Cardinal Mindszenty* (1949).[8] The large number of American prisoners of war in Korea who made confessions (including the few who confessed to germ warfare charges) or who signed peace petitions seemed to confirm that the communists were using special mind control techniques.[9]

The term "brainwashing" was invented and popularized by Edward Hunter, a CIA propagandist working undercover as a journalist, who introduced the term in an article for the *Miami News* in September 1950.[10] Hunter drew a distinction between brainwashing, which he described as "indoctrination, a comparatively simple procedure," and "brain changing," in which:

> ...a person's specific recollections of some past period in his life are wiped away, as completely as if they never happened. Then, to fill these gaps in memory the ideas which the authorities want this person to "remember" are put into his brain. Hypnotism and drugs and cunning pressures that plague the body and do not necessarily require marked physical violence are required for a brain changing.[11]

In the first of his books on brainwashing, *Brainwashing in Red China: The Calculated Destruction of Men's Minds*, published in 1951, Hunter suggested that the Chinese were brainwashing American POWs in Korea. He also devoted an entire chapter of this book to the role of cartooning in brainwashing the Chinese masses. According to Hunter, Chinese comic books (which he called "picture story books") had become "sharp weapons of propaganda, possibly the most effective medium the Communists possessed among the mass of the people."[12]

Hunter returned briefly to the problem of enemy comic books in his 1956 book *Brainwashing: The Story of Men who Defied It*.[13] He tells this story about how the communists used "horror comics" to instill in Korean children a lifelong hatred against white soldiers: "These kids had adored the foreign soldiers when the war began. Americans gave them the tastiest sweet-meats they had ever eaten—candies, chewing gum, and chocolate bars—they got a treasure trove, too, in colored pencils and notebooks." A girl changed her mind about the Americans, however, at a neighborhood meeting where the community was told that Americans were "giving out poisoned candies and explosive toys, even dropping them from airplanes for luckless children to pick up, and that many boys and girls had already been killed."

> The youngsters were horrified that people could be so evil. […] The children resolved voluntarily, just like the grownups, to never touch a thing given them by these hateful white people, and to remember them with loathing all their lives. I saw the colored horror comics and illustrated story books in which these lessons were graphically illustrated.[14]

Richard Condon's 1959 bestseller *The Manchurian Candidate* kept interest in brainwashing alive and made another surprising connection between Korean War "brainwashing" and comic books. Condon's Communist Chinese villain Dr. Yen Lo, described as a Fu Manchu–type with skin "the color of raw sulphur," lectures the visiting Russians that "For any of you who are interested in massive negative conditioning there is Frederic Wertham's *The Seduction of the Innocent*, which demonstrates how thousands have been brought to antisocial actions through children's cartoon books." The fictional Dr. Yen Lo supposedly delivers that speech in July 1951 (three years before *Seduction of the Innocent*'s publication date).[15]

Much of the American public seized on Hunter's ideas, and "brainwashing" entered the language as a word with two meanings. "Brainwashed" meant indoctrinated, but "brainwashing" also became the word for a mysterious new scientific technique with elements of torture, propaganda, psycho-pharmaceuticals, hypnotism, Pavlovian conditioning, and electrical stimulation of the brain. By the second definition, however, communist brainwashing simply did not exist.[16] Lawrence E. Hinkle, Jr., and Harold G. Wolf investigated communist interrogation methods for the United States Department of Defense from 1954 to 1956, and found that:

> In no case is there reliable evidence that neurologists, psychiatrists, psychologists or other scientifically trained personnel have designed or participated in these police procedures. There is no evidence that drugs, hypnosis or other devices play any significant role in them…. There is no reason to dignify these methods by surrounding them with an aura of scientific mystery, or to denote them by terms such as "menticide" or "brain washing" which imply that they are scientifically organized techniques of predictable efficiency.[17]

By then, however, the United States had secretly embarked on its own huge research program to master (or invent) the science of brainwashing. In April 1950, shortly before the Korean War, the CIA had begun "Operation Bluebird" to discover more effective interrogation methods. Under this unsuccessful project, they reviewed Nazi interrogation techniques that included "drugs, electro-shock, hypnosis and psycho-surgery" and undertook experiments dominated by their interest in LSD.[18] In the early years, much of this research was conducted on unwitting subjects, ranging from North Korean prisoners to children at a summer camp.[19]

Eventually, the CIA discovered that the most powerful, anxiety-provoking, long-lastingly destructive technique for breaking a person's mind did not involve physical torture, but a seemingly simple combination of sensory disorientation and self-inflicted pain. The method found its iconic representation many years later in the Abu Ghraib photo of a prisoner wearing a hood (for sensory deprivation) and forced to hold his arms extended (to cause self-inflicted pain).[20]

The war comics authors usually stayed clear of the more outlandish brainwashing stories.[21] Instead, they sometimes emphasized the role of brute force in communist treatment of POWs. Scenes of fiendish brutality were published. In "Blonde Double-Cross" (*War Report #2*, November 1952), the communists capture three soldiers and a blonde U.S.O. singer. As the interrogator swings a belt buckle across her cheek, he says "This just a sample! I'll cut that lovely face of yours to ribbons if I don't get the information I need!" In "The Quiet Guy" (*War Action #12*, March 1953), the enemy puts burning twigs under an American's toenails in an attempt to make him talk. In a carefully done story called "Brain Wash" (*Foxhole #11*, 1963), the prison authorities put a prisoner in a hole in the ground during winter and throw water over him, lock him in a box too small to stand or lie in, and beat him with a whip. Some of these tortures can be matched to actual atrocities committed against American prisoners of war. Nevertheless, A.D. Biderman's study of the methods by which the communists had extorted confessions from Air Force POWs pointedly omitted torture from his chart of "Communist coercive methods for eliciting individual compliance." Biderman explained:

> I have not included physical torture as a general category in this outline, despite the fact that many of our prisoners of war did encounter physical torture and despite the fact that a few of the specific measures in the outline may involve physical pain. I have omitted torture from the outline to emphasize that inflicting physical pain is not a necessary nor particularly effective method of inducing compliance. While many of our people did encounter physical violence, this rarely occurred as part of a systematic effort to elicit a false confession. Where physical violence was inflicted during the course of such an attempt, the attempt was particularly likely to fail completely.[22]

Biderman concluded that the communists had not extorted the confessions for "some purpose as rational as propaganda." Instead, and in contrast to "the cynical Nazis," their ultimate goal was to make their prisoners experience remorse and repentance. American comic book stories about American POWs strongly implied any remorse would be unnecessary, irrational, unmanly, and traitorous.

In Korean War comic books, only an enemy would torture prisoners. After the attacks of September 11, 2001, however, a flood of American games, films and television fictions showed Americans using torture as a normal and very effective technique for getting timely and accurate confessions. Alfred W. McCoy reports that by 2008 "these dramatizations dominated the political debate over torture," with the result that "the world's preeminent power grounded its most controversial policy decision of the early twenty-first century not on research or rational analysis but in fiction and fantasy."[23]

In the comic book story "The Confession," the drawings of the POW "Lieutenant James Nelson" all show either close-ups or medium shots. The characters are all grouped closely together indoors. This reinforces a sense of pressure and confinement appropriate to the storyline. Unfortunately, the comic book creators who dramatized the germ warfare issue also confined their presentation of the controversy within narrow limits, leaving out the larger perspectives that would have made the charges intelligible. The previous chapter put the germ warfare charges in the context of an exterminationist theme in Anglo-American popular literature. Two of the most important missing contexts were the American germ warfare programs and American bombing practices.

U.S. Germ Warfare Research

Although U.S. officials responded to germ warfare accusations with shock and outrage, the fact that the United States had a large biological warfare research program was a poorly kept secret.[24] During the Korean War, American defense spending on its germ warfare programs shot up from $5.3 million in 1950 to $345 million for 1951 to 1953.[25]

In 1941, reports of a Japanese attack on China using plague-infected fleas (an attack that would lead to 7,000 deaths) convinced Americans of the need to develop defenses against biological warfare. Days later, Japan attacked a half-dozen American and British territories in the Pacific and Asia, most famously including Pearl Harbor.[26]

Japan's biological warfare research was headed by Shiro Ishii. During World War II, the group that he led attacked at least eleven Chinese cities with experimental germ bombs, poisoned wells, and tested his germs on various animals and on prisoners of war, including some American prisoners.[27] The plagues he unleashed in China may have killed hundreds of thousands of people.[28]

During World War II, several American comic book stories dramatized the issue of Japanese bacterial warfare. The story "Captain Freedom and the Young Defenders," published in *Speed Comics #24* (December 1942), calls a bacterial warfare plan a scheme that "would surpass the most fiendish crimes of history!" At first, the story leads the reader to believe that the evil Doctor Deemon is actually "Silas Green, the famous chemical engineer … one of our leading citizens." Green appears ready to unleash the dread "Yellow Death" from a large, green, corked ceramic jug, labeled in large letters "bacteria." Captain Freedom stops him, and then tears off Silas Green's Caucasian mask, revealing "It's a Jap!" The Japanese spy immediately confesses that: "I and my comrades had been attending medical school when we heard that Green was experimenting with deadly bacteria. So we took over the house and continued the experiments…." When the real Silas Green thanks Captain Freedom for rescuing him and says "I wish there was some way I could repay you," the Captain answers: "You can destroy the Yellow Death! The United States would never consider using such an inhuman method of warfare."

The "Captain Freedom" comic prompts the question of whether Japan's program had taken some of its inspiration and basic knowledge from earlier programs in the West. It turns out that from 1928 to 1930, Shiro Ishii had traveled the world (visiting 20 nations, mostly in Europe but also including Egypt, the Soviet Union, Canada and the United States) to gather enough evidence of secret germ warfare programs to convince the Japanese military to begin their own biological warfare program.[29] In 1939, a Japanese student of Ishii who would go on to serve in Ishii's germ warfare program made a failed attempt to acquire a sample of yellow fever virus in New York.[30]

On November 15, 1942, Frank Tinsley's *Captain Yank* comic strip showed a Japanese plane dropping germ bombs in a "test raid" on "a defenseless village." In a following strip, published on November 17, a young Chinese girl dies from the fictional "mortis tropica," a disease never before seen in China. Days later Captain Yank marvels that "A full-scale raid with those bombs could wipe out a whole countryside in no time!"[31] (This story was reformatted and republished in the comic book *Big Shot* in 1944.)

In 1947, Theodor Rosebury and Elvin Kabat created a worldwide sensation when, with official permission, they had their 1942 secret report on bacterial warfare published in the *Journal of Immunology*.[32] Their purpose in making the information publicly available was to warn that to avoid the horrors of biological warfare, the world must abolish war.

In 1949, Rosebury, who had been the director of the Air-Borne Infection Unit of the Biological Warfare Program at Camp Detrick, Maryland, during World War II, followed up his 1947 publication with a book for a popular audience, *Peace or Pestilence: Biological Warfare and How to Avoid It*. Rosebury asked rhetorically:

> If an American-Russian war were in progress and particularly if things were getting tough for either side, do you suppose that either we or the Russians would hesitate to use against the other, say, pneumonic plague? This is the worst form of the great Black Death of Boccaccio's Florence.[33]

A comic book story in *Rulah—Jungle Goddess*, published in 1948, apparently took its inspiration from a news item about germ warfare.[34] In this comic, "an ambitious gangster" learns about "bacterial warfare" from a newspaper article, steals a hypodermic needle holding "enough minute bugs […] to kill everything in New York" from a U.S. laboratory, and sends his girlfriend to Africa with the infectious material for a research project that consists of poisoning Rulah's tribe so he can "learn this bacterial stuff" and then "take this town over." (Wertham mentioned this story in *Seduction of the Innocent* to warn that American comic books were depicting the American government as researching germ warfare.[35])

During the Korean War, while American officials were publicly dismissing as "unproven" the charge that Japan had conducted germ warfare in China during World War II, the Chinese and Koreans insisted that the Japanese *had* used these weapons, and, further, that the U.S. was "openly collaborating with Japanese bacteriological war criminals," including Shiro Ishii.[36]

Bombing Practices

Besides its germ warfare programs, people in the United States have also usually ignored a second context in which the germ warfare charges were made, that of American bombing practices. In March 1952, the *China Monthly Review* introduced the germ warfare charge as "one more bestiality" in a broader American policy of "extermination."[37]

At the time of the germ warfare charges, the war was decimating the population of the Korean Peninsula with conventional weapons and napalm. When Truman overruled MacArthur's strategy of annihilating the enemy's ability to wage war, the new American military objective, as described by General Ridgeway, became "not the seizure of terrain but the maximum destruction of hostile persons and material at the minimum cost to our troops."[38]

The measure of the progress of the war became the "body count." World War II hero Jimmy Doolittle, appearing at an April 1952 inter-service symposium held to coordinate the biological warfare program, had said, "In my estimation, we have just one moral obligation—and that moral obligation is for us to develop at the earliest possible moment that agent which will kill enemy personnel most quickly and most cheaply."[39]

Simple Morality

War comics could generally be relied on to present simple conflicts, purged of annoying shades of gray, in which good defeats evil without becoming contaminated by it. Even stories about atrocities can seem almost comforting when they reaffirm the enemy's moral inferiority.[40]

13

◇◇◇◇◇◇◇◇◇

POW!

In addition to the issue of the alleged brainwashing of American prisoners of war, Korean War comic books dramatized two issues that involved Korean and Chinese prisoners of war. An incident in which prisoners on Koje-do island took the commander of the camp as a hostage offered comic book creators another opportunity to transform well-publicized communist propaganda charges into anti-communist fictions. The more important prisoner of war issue, though, concerned whether the United Nations would force the POWs it held to return to North Korea and Communist China if they did not wish to go back. At the peace negotiations in Panmunjom, the United States insisted that they would not force prisoners to return involuntarily. The communists argued that international law required that all the prisoners should be returned.[1] While this disagreement continued, the war dragged on for an additional year and a half, during which more Americans became casualties than the number of prisoners resisting repatriation.[2]

Riots

On May 7, 1952, General Frank Dodd, commanding officer of the Koje-do POW camp, was taken hostage by his own prisoners. In a premeditated plot, some prisoners invited him to discuss grievances. As they argued through the fence, the POWs who had been emptying the latrine sewage grabbed him and pushed him into the compound, where they held him for three days.[3]

The prisoners succeeded in getting General Dodd's replacement, General Colson, to agree in writing to most of their demands.[4] After receiving his promises, the prisoners released General Dodd.

Comic books rewrote this humiliating propaganda defeat in a more satisfying form. One example was the story "PW Riot at Koje" in the comic book *Atomic Attack #6* (March 1953). The comic book story begins with Joe Metnik, a guard at Koje who is "completely disgusted" with his assignment because he craves "action." Then "the diehard Reds" take over the leadership of the compound, raise the red flag, taunt and throw food at the guards, and begin killing the anti-communists. The next morning a group of American officers walk into the prisoners' compound gate to talk with the Red leader and are seized by the POWs. The POWs threaten to kill the officers unless they are allowed to go free. Metnik wins permission to try an idea. He enters the compound with sticks of dynamite and forces the prisoners to release the hostages. "Minutes later" the guards reenter the compound,

137

wearing gas masks, to "show them who's boss." The POWs' rebellion is crushed and Metnik is cited for the Congressional Medal of Honor.

The events of June 10, 1952, when the Americans did use tear gas and other weapons to break the power of the communist leadership in the prisoner of war camps, provided the apparent basis for the conclusion of "PW Riot at Koje" and also for "Riot on Koje!," a text piece published in *Captain Steve Savage's Flight to Kill #7* (October 1952).[5] The plot of "Riot on Koje!" was straightforward:

> Two American soldiers guarding a "seething, screaming mob of enemy prisoners-of-war" on Koje Island are congratulating themselves on their own patience and discussing the relative merits of democracy and totalitarianism. The POWs display placards which claim they are rioting because of unbearable and inhumane living conditions, and begin throwing stones at the guards. At five that night, the soldiers lead a UN force into the compound, charging through the barbed wire fence with a light tank. The POWs fall back, then charge swinging barbed wire flails. The UN uses tear gas and quickly mops up "the weeping, coughing mob of prisoners who, just a few short moments before, had been howling, complaining madmen." The story concludes with the guards agreeing that "democracy is definately [sic] the best way—as long as it's a fighting democracy."

Wilfred Burchett and Alan Winnington's book *Koje Unscreened,* self-published in Communist China that year, introduced their account of the June 10th "riot" by suggesting that the guards who invaded the compound had been reading too many comic strips:

> On Koje there were no Heartbreak Ridges to storm, with well-entrenched and hardened soldiers awaiting. Here was a battle to gladden the hearts of students of Superman and Joe Palooka, a battle without danger, with certain victory at the end, but still plenty of blood.[6]

Soon Joe Palooka *did* get involved in suppressing the prison riots at Koje-do. The cover blurb of *Joe Palooka Battle Adventures #75* (January 1953) invites us to "Read the startling truth behind the Konje-do [sic] Island headlines ... the startling facts that caused the PRISON RIOT."

In the *Joe Palooka* version, the communist prisoners take an American inspection team hostage, and then taunt the General in charge of the camp, gloating that "While they alive, you not shoot us! So we not kill them ... we TORTURE them! Ha Ha Ha.... You not DARE to interfere!" Joe enters the compound, easily defeats the Red leader, exposes him as a coward, and leaves him to be beaten by the other prisoners. In the final panel, Joe presents the moral of the story: "All I had to do was show them what a PHONY he was! Once you show people what a Commie is REALLY like, they'll never fall for his HOOEY again!" By "phony," Joe referred to the Red thug's physical cowardice. A reader wanting to follow Joe's advice might be receptive to the back-cover's body-building ad, which offered to help you develop "HE-MAN power—the kind of power that forces bullies to FEAR YOU instead of SNEERING at You."[7]

Burchett and Winnington had mentioned "plenty of blood," but the comic book stories did not show it. The main violence in "Riot on Koje!" occurs when Tex "Red" Kramer brings his rifle butt down on the arm of a North Korean who had been swinging a whip made of barbed wire, leaving the man "yelping with pain." This lack of blood distorts what had happened, since even the lower estimates of the actual casualties counted that 38 POWs and one guard were killed in this operation.[8]

A study commissioned by the U.S. Army supplies the historical context that the comic book depictions of the POW riots lacked.[9] The researchers found that the conditions in the POW camps went through several stages. From the beginning, the United States did not assign sufficient manpower to control the large numbers of prisoners in their custody, and also lacked familiarity with Chinese and Korean languages and cultures. After a period of scarcity and hardship, leaders emerged among the prisoners. Many of them were "former gangsters or outlaws who knew how to exploit a relatively disorganized collection of men."[10] The United Nations sent investigators into the POW camps to determine whether any of the prisoners were guilty of war crimes. The POW leaders responded enthusiastically, and unleashed a reign of terror against prisoners who had been Communist Party members or officials. According to the army study, "the PW leaders resorted to torture in order to wring false confessions to war crimes out of communist PW's so that the authorities would remove them," thus consolidating their own power. The communists organized, largely in self-defense, and began to battle for control of the prison compounds. Although both the communists and anti-communists spied on, beat, confined in home-made jails, and even killed their opponents in these struggles, the study noted some differences between them: the communist leaders tended to "give the prisoners less impression of cruelty than did the anti-communists" and were not visibly corrupt, as their opponents often were. The researchers noted that only a minority of the "anti-communists" were influenced by liberal-democratic ideas as such.[11]

Repatriation

The comic book story "He Won't Go Back!," published in *Battlefield #11*, May 1953, stands out as an especially effective work of comic book propaganda on the subject of prisoners of war. The story, drawn by Louis Ravielli, is narrated by a Chinese-American character with the Anglicized name Bob Young. Young begins the story by telling how the Communist Chinese had sent a series of ransom letters to his father (similar to those that "other citizens of Chinatown received"), demanding thousands of dollars for the life of his sister and her family in China. Although his father mortgaged his restaurant to comply, he eventually learned that the ransom payments he had been sending were for nothing, as the communists had killed his relatives the first day that they marched into their village. In a rage, Bob Young had quit college and joined the Army. After proving his bravery on the frontline, he is assigned (against his wishes) to a prisoner of war camp as an interpreter. He witnesses a riot in which a large group of communist prisoners attack a smaller group of anti-communist prisoners, causing a dozen deaths. The guards decide "to separate the two groups." Young screens the prisoners, and learns why some would "rather die right here than ever go back to the Communists." A prisoner whom Young had captured when he was in combat tells him:

> Please inform the United Nations and your officers at Panmunjom not to send us, who do not wish to return, back to the Communists ... for I have been warned what will happen! The moment we are returned we will be separated by the list they have ... and instantly liquidated ... shot down in cold blood by the thousands!

After a replacement interpreter arrives, Young gets to reunite with his outfit and "go back into action" on the battlefield, fighting for "a humane principle," no compulsory repatriation, which "concerns all the freedom-loving people of all nations!"[12]

In another example of a comic book story inspired by the issue of voluntary repatriation, in *Captain America #77*, July 1954, Cap and Bucky go to Red China to retrieve a list of "reformed Chinese soldiers who've come over to our side." They need to deprive the communists of these names to prevent retaliation against the men's families.[13]

The idea of allowing POWs to choose whether or not to accept repatriation originated with Brigadier General Robert A. McClure, Army chief of psychological warfare. At first, American officials resisted the idea, pointing out that it would violate the Geneva Convention.[14] President Truman, however, supported the idea strongly, saying "The forced repatriation is repugnant to the West. We will not buy an armistice by turning over human beings for slaughter and slavery." President Eisenhower agreed, and so voluntary repatriation became a part of the eventual armistice agreement.[15]

The insistence on voluntary repatriation was based on events that had happened in Europe during and after World War II, when Stalin refused to recognize Soviet prisoners in enemy hands as anything more than deserters who deserved to be executed if they returned.[16]

Michael B. Petrovich, an American official stationed in Yugoslavia, where security police killed tens of thousands of returnees after the war, relates that the principle of voluntary repatriation, perhaps not by that name, had been put into practice there:

> It is not to be wondered that as evidence of this butchery reached Western Allied authorities, they refused to hand over any more Yugoslavs [for return to Yugoslavia].... Since the Soviets also followed the practice of summarily killing returnees who were suspected of having fought against the Soviet regime, many Americans concluded that Communists of whatever variety were bloody executioners, indifferent to notions of justice and due process.[17]

The insistence on voluntary repatriation led to an American propaganda victory. Of the surviving prisoners who had been captured by the communists, very few chose to remain with the other side, but almost 49 percent of the prisoners held by the UN forces refused to be repatriated.[18] This UN propaganda victory, however, was misleading in several ways. According to the Army history cited above, "the U.N. Command failed to create conditions under which the individual PW could make an uncoerced, unintimidated, informed choice."[19] Also, historian J.I. Matray cites evidence that:

> the vast majority of North Korean POWs were actually South Koreans who either had joined voluntarily or had been impressed into [North Korea's Korean People's Army]. Thousands of Chinese POWs were Nationalist soldiers trapped in China when the civil war ended who now had the chance to escape to Taiwan.[20]

General K.S. Thimayya of India, who led the Neutral Nations Repatriation Commission which oversaw the prisoner exchange, noted that the prisoners did not place a central importance on politics:

> The Chinese and Korean soldiers, like our own, were mainly simple village folk, barely literate, and completely unsophisticated. It was quite impossible for us to believe that they had made, or were even capable of making, the relatively intellectual choice between communism and capitalism. Moreover, whatever the reasons were for making them into non-repats, we could not believe that they desired anything so much as to go home.[21]

Other researchers agreed that these prisoners, caught in a storm of ideological struggle, were not particularly ideological. William C. Bradbury and Jeane J. Kirkpatrick studied the Chinese prisoners and concluded "By all odds the most striking aspect is ignorance about the nature of the struggle that was racking China."[22]

Studies of the Americans who were captured by the North reached similar conclusions. The prisoners did not know what they were doing there, and they wanted to go home.

14

Griping Against the War

On those occasions when writers have mentioned war comics, they often hasten to categorize their favorite ones as "anti-war." The tangled categories of "pro-war" and "anti-war" are difficult to apply. Some supposedly "anti-war" Korean War comic books editorially affirmed that we had no other choice than to fight for peace.

Comic book critics have used a variety of criteria when judging the attitude of comics about war. One common criterion has been the "realism" of the depiction of violence. "Realistic," ugly violence has been taken as evidence of an anti-war stance. By contrast, representing bloodless battle scenes with a cheerful emphasis on military teamwork, manliness, national glory, heroism or courage in combat has been thought to demonstrate a pro-war position. Another criterion asks how the comic depicts the enemy. Other things being equal, a comic that portrays the enemy as a murderous horde of fanatic and unintelligible "gooks" would be considered more pro-war than a comic that portrays the enemy as composed of individual soldiers with names, families and dreams. Cord A. Scott's book *Comics and Conflict*, which presents "anti-war" comics as a major category of war comics, describes anti-war comics as stories that emphasize terror, destruction, injustice and futility, and call for negotiation and peace rather than flag waving and hero worship.[1] Taken together, these criteria can bring into focus some of the complexities of the comics' responses to war.

The Stated Message

When deciding what a story means, its explicitly stated moral can provide a good place to begin. In the early 1950s, comic books sometimes spelled out their message in the first and/or last panel of their stories. In war comics, these messages linked instruction in masculine codes of behavior to pro-military attitudes. This allowed their messages to be built deeply into young men's conceptions of themselves.[2]

Comic book titles that featured the words "Man" or "Men" usually included combat stories. These included *Men's Adventures*, *Young Men on the Battlefield*, and *Man Comics*. Mark Gerzon has described "the Soldier" as the most deeply embedded of all the masculine role models, and has explained why men have found this model so appealing:

> Before we can understand the soldier as a heroic image of masculinity, we must recall his original function. He was the protector, the man who made the difference between survival and annihilation. He was the man who defended his loved ones and the entire community. He symbolized security[....] In virtually every cultural system, the Soldier was a hero because without him, that system could not endure[....]

Gerzon goes on to write that this version of masculinity required "brutality" and reconciled men to it:

> Although this image of heroic masculinity often led men to brutality, it nevertheless seemed vital to civilization. […] So men through the ages have measured themselves against what seemed to be male destiny. Rather than deny it, we have embraced it. Those who have not, we called cowards. What war required was, by definition, manliness. The men who were the best soldiers were, in effect, the best men.[3]

War promises the possibility, not only of becoming a "real man," but of becoming a hero.[4] Some comic books celebrated specific individuals for their heroic actions. In later years, the idea grew that anyone who serves in the armed forces deserves to be called a "hero."

William J. Astore, a retired U.S. Air Force lieutenant colonel, argues against "an almost religious veneration of U.S. service members as 'Our American Heroes.'" Among the harms of such indiscriminate hero worship, he warns that this attitude feeds a misleading impression of warfare: "the brutalizing aspects and effects of war will be played down" because heroes "don't commit atrocities."[5]

In addition to the directly stated messages attached to particular stories, occasionally an editor would present an explicit description of the moral intent of an entire war comic series. Harvey Features Syndicate introduced the fifth issue of *War Battles,* dated July 1952, with a brief editorial titled "No Punches Pulled." The editorial began on an anti-militarist note:

> Franklin Denalo [sic] Roosevelt once said: "We are not a warlike people…." That was true in the past; that's true, today. And in order to hate war we've got to see it as it really is! WAR BATTLES is devoted to that purpose!

The editorial quickly shifts gears, however, becoming a sales pitch that emphasizes the display of violence:

> The action, the horror, the tearing suspense, the blistering movement and pace of the battle front….
> The pulsating tension of the Korean War, the rip-roaring rocketing fury of World War II, and the murderous action in the trenches of World War I are found on these pages.

The editorial closes by describing American soldiers as "the boys next door, they're ordinary guys who give their all for the cause they believe in!"

The comic itself shares the ambivalence of this editorial, presenting the Korean War as a hateful thing contrary to the American spirit, as a thrilling spectacle, and as a cause that ordinary Americans believe in.

There are several reasons not to take the comics' explicit messages at face value. For one thing, sometimes these messages contradict the messages conveyed by their stories. The most effective propaganda in comics does not come in openly stated arguments, but in what they assume as beyond argument.[6]

Most war comics let their stories speak for themselves, without explicit moralizing. With or without editorializing comments, these works of entertainment taught lessons.

Gore and Glory

Critics sometimes judge a comic book's attitude toward military conflict by the manner in which it presents the destructiveness of war. On the one hand, images of "ordinary guys" in command of vast destructive power which they can use to take revenge against their enemies, to defend their friends, to create thrilling experiences, and to support national goals, can present an appealing, "pro-war" picture. Critics of violent images in the comics and other media have specified what makes a depiction of violence objectionable.

During the Vietnam War, Fredric Wertham objected to some of the most commonly accepted kinds of media violence, warning against stories that idealize violence by associating it with the good and the just characters, celebrate as heroic models the violent men who overcome all obstacles through brute strength, present violence as a solution, or encourage a "sneering sadism" in which the victims are treated with cynical contempt by those who are killing them.[7] Wertham argued that scenes of the war in Vietnam "conditioned" readers and viewers to accept war, even when they present no justification for the violence:

> The endless repetition of fragmented and fragmentary battle scenes, without indication of an over-all design, gives them a cliche-like character. What could be most moving scenes if presented in a sufficiently severe frame and with proper reverence for human life become a mere backdrop for violence and the expectation of violence. Our senses are being dulled: Big things become small.[8]

Although activists raised alarms about violent comic books being unsuitable for children, the verbal and pictorial descriptions of violence in the war comics were fantastically restrained compared to the actual violence of war. In most publishers' comics, bodily fluids rarely leaked out of any characters, and, if they did, then usually from the enemy. Even bodies that were tossed in the air by explosions in war comics remained intact as they flew, like boys jumping and falling in war play.

War comic depictions of napalm provide one measure of the understatement in comic book violence. During the Korean War, as in the Vietnam War, opposition to the use of napalm became a rallying point for those who tried to express the horror of the war.[9] Although Korean War comics frequently mentioned napalm, they did not show its full effects. Flame throwers appeared on comic covers, but rarely seemed to do more than burn uniforms.[10] Perhaps the limit of this trivialization of napalm's consequences was reached in a famous Uncle Scrooge story by Carl Barks in 1952, in which Scrooge McDuck arranges for the Beagle Boys' planned napalm attack to backfire on them.[11]

For a second measure of the war comics' understatement of the gruesomeness of wartime violence, consider the anatomical location of fatal wounds. Of the Americans killed in action in Korea, 37.9 percent received wounds in the head, and an additional 4.9 percent received wounds in the face.[12] In comics, disfiguring facial wounds were vanishingly rare, and instead, soldiers were shot (if at all) cleanly in the chest or shoulder.

Editors calibrate the amount of violence in war comics according to both political and commercial considerations. The level of graphic violence found suitable for publication rose during World War II, and the Korean War picked things up from where they had left off.[13] Editors require a certain degree of "action," yet too much blood would spark criticism and threaten sales. Thus, the level of comic book violence is kept within a shifting but limited range, as violence is demanded (especially by older readers) but also monitored (especially by younger readers' parents).

Mass market comics cannot honestly depict the destruction of war because that would alienate their audience. Even the shocking comics that Keiji Nakazawa created in Japan to communicate the horrors of the atomic bomb intentionally understated the violence to keep from scaring away his readers.[14]

Enmity and Humanity

Besides their stated messages and their representation of violence, a third criterion for distinguishing "pro-war" from "anti-war" stories asks how the comic depicts the enemy. A "pro-war" comic would reduce the conflict to one between good and evil, treating our side as well-intentioned and well-behaved against an enemy who lacks any redeeming qualities. Any material that challenges that simple picture suggests an "anti-war" position.

Representing the evilness of the enemy visually often came down to showing ugly individuals with nasty facial expressions behaving badly.[15] Because the war was fought in the name of protecting South Korea, American cartoonists (with varying levels of success) worked to create respectful visual conventions for representing Asians, and to come up with something other than simple racial stereotypes to dehumanize the North Korean and Chinese enemy.

In the early 1950s, the raw, racist stereotypes of Asians from the old pulp magazines were becoming unacceptably offensive. Cartoonist Joe Orlando, who collaborated on the comic book *The Mask of Dr. Fu Manchu*, which appeared in 1951, remembered that:

> We'd give an editor a drawing for a *Fu Manchu* cover, and he'd say "Get a good chink in there with slanty eyes and long fingernails. Do the Yellow Menace thing. It's the Korean War!" So we gave him what he wanted and he came back screaming at us because his boss yelled at him for creating this kind of image. He blamed it on us.[16]

As another example of the declining acceptability of the old caricatures, the stereotypical Chinese character "Chop-Chop," who had appeared in *Blackhawk* war comics since 1941 for comic relief, began to evolve in these years. Carla Zimmerman's article about the evolution of this character explains that:

> In the 1950's America's involvement in Korea against Communist China presented a serious problem to the writers. […] Chop-Chop's Chineseness became increasingly problematic. Blackhawk's creators adjusted by employing a number of strategems, including the anglicization of his features and speech, drawing him more often from behind, and ultimately, cutting down on his dialogue and number of appearances.[17]

By 1956, in her estimation, the character had changed into "a nondescript quasi-Caucasian...."

Despite these pressures for political correctness, some comic books openly taught that the enemy was not human, but "vermin."[18] Many comic book stories uncritically used the racist term "gooks."[19]

General William F. Dean, who spent almost the entire war as a prisoner, reflected afterwards that if he were to have the power to make the rules again, "use of the term 'gook,' or its many equivalents, by Americans would be an offense for military punishment." In his time as a prisoner, he had learned of the "terrific harm" done by the thoughtless use of this word:

> Through all the questioning and my many subsequent conversations with intelligent Koreans who had chosen communism after knowing something about our government in South Korea, ran one refrain: they resented being called "gooks," and the slighting references to their race and color more than any of our policies, ill-advised or not. Again and again I was told that this man or that one had come north because he had decided he could never get along with people who called him a "gook," or worse, among themselves; because he resented American attention to Korean women; or because he hated to see foreigners riding in his country in big automobiles while he and his family had to walk.[20]

While General Dean had been held prisoner, General MacArthur's headquarters did warn servicemen that those who used racial slurs were "unwittingly guilty of 'Giving aid and comfort to the enemy,'" but Americans in Korea continued to treat and to speak of Koreans with contempt. The Koreans fighting for South Korea were stereotyped as unreliable cowards; those fighting for North Korea as ruthless fanatics; and the Korean civilians (who suffered most of the casualties) as ungrateful.[21]

When General Dean had returned to America and was asked on the *Meet the Press* television program about the changes he had noticed in America when he returned, he did not mention race relations, but comic books:

> I sound rather like a purist but I am disturbed by the crime programs that I hear on the radio, on television, by the comic strips and the comic books that I see at every newsstand and by the emphasis on sex, suggestive pictures, and stories and so on. I don't feel that is good for the coming generation and although we cuss about Koreans, I lived very closely to the North Korean soldiers for 3 years, lived in the same room with them, and sex does not mean to them what it means to our youth.[22]

A comic book story that challenged the use of the word "gook" appeared in *Warfront* in August 1953. The beginning caption of "Ambush" tells that "'Gook' is a nasty word ... a word too often applied to our friends and allies in the Far East. Read why hard-bitten soldiers lost the word 'Gook' while caught in an ... AMBUSH."

In "Ambush," an unnamed Korean boy asks an American soldier not to call him "Gook" (on page one, page two, page three, and page five). In the story's penultimate panel, the dying American praises the boy, who has stopped a communist attack by using hand grenades and rifle fire, as "a good gook," and for the fourth time, the boy says "Please Joe ... don't call me gook." With his last words, the American says "You're right ... *soldier*! I know better n-now." The more correct terms for the enemy in this story are "the dirty rats" and "the rat-race."

"Enemy Assault" and All Quiet on the Western Front

Harvey Kurtzman's reputation as an anti-war cartoonist rests largely on the unusual degree to which he insisted in his stories that the enemy is as human as we are. Kurtzman insisted just as strongly, though, that recognizing this commonality did not absolve a soldier from his responsibility to fight. His celebrated story "Enemy Assault" in *Frontline Combat #1*, the July–August 1951 issue, brings this out clearly. Because "Enemy Assault" includes a sequence, set in a trench, in which an American soldier-narrator sees a photograph of his enemy's wife and child, it invites comparison with a scene in Erich Maria Remarque's classic novel about World War I, *All Quiet on the Western Front*, set in a shell hole, in which the German soldier-narrator also sees a photograph of his enemy's wife and child.[23] The comparison reveals the contrast between Kurtzman's "anti-war" comic book stories and pacifist literature.

Remarque's chapter could be summarized this way:

> Some German soldiers puzzle over why they and the French, both "simple folk ... labourers" have been sent to fight each other. Later, the narrator is on a battlefield, in a muddy shell-hole, when a body falls on him, and he stabs it. He then remains trapped for hours in that hole, while the enemy soldier he has stabbed slowly dies. The narrator then begs for forgiveness from the corpse, promising to support his dead enemy's wife, parents and child and to fight against war. While looking for an address to send these promises to his wife, some pictures of a woman and a little girl fall out of the Frenchman's wallet. Soon "the madness" passes, and by the next morning the narrator remembers his moving vows to the dead man as "mere driveling nonsense."[24]

Kurtzman's story is much different:

The American soldier narrator aims his rifle at an approaching horde of "nameless, faceless" Chinese communists. He shoots four of them, and is then knocked unconscious while killing another. When he awakens, he casually notices the body of one of the enemy soldiers he has killed, which has fallen across his lap. He gets up, and finds himself alone in his trench with a wounded enemy soldier. They begin to argue about who has captured whom. The American asks where the Chinese man learned to speak English, and it turns out they had both lived in the same neighborhood in New York City (the one as a houseboy for an American tea importer, the other as a university student). Eventually they pull out their wallets and show each other photographs of their wives and babies. Then, simultaneously, the Chinese and American armies renew their attacks. In quick succession, a Chinese soldier "aimed his gun at me" but is killed by an American soldier, who is then killed by the English-speaking Chinese soldier, "And then I knew what I must do. I had to choose sides! You can't fight a war by comparing baby snapshots!" The American kills the Chinese man. The story concludes as it began, with the narrator aiming his loaded rifle at the next group of Chinese "tiny figures" moving toward his position.

Both stories unite two lessons, that the enemy is human and that war requires men to kill their enemies. In Remarque's novel, a man kills an enemy soldier and then realizes he has killed a human being. In Kurtzman's story, a man realizes that his enemy is a human being and then kills him.

A greater cultural distance separates a Euro-American and a Chinese man than the one between a German and a Frenchman. This explains much of the difference between the stories. Remarque describes how the indisputable truth that the enemy is human becomes emotionally real. Kurtzman's tries to get across the concept that the enemy is human, in a medium that had traditionally depicted Asian soldiers as beasts or automatons. Kurtzman purposely begins his story with a variety of dehumanizing images of the Chinese. Then he explodes these images with the description of the Chinese draftee as "a living breathing *human being* with a *wife* and *children* and *hopes* and *plans just like me!*" This realization, however, changes nothing.[25]

Because Kurtzman remains resolutely "apolitical," focused on the experiences of soldiers rather than on the causes and prevention of war, he reaches the conclusion that it would be better if there were no war, but no further. Remarque's narrator, before surrendering to the same point of view, goes on to raise the question: who benefits from war?

In 1952, Classics Illustrated released a comic book adaptation of *All Quiet on the Western Front*, which included two pages summarizing this chapter of Remarque's story. The story was chosen for adaptation in 1951 by publisher Al Kanter and editor Meyer Kaplan, and adapted by Ken Fitch.[26] The art was the most harrowing work of one of Classics Illustrated's best cartoonists, Maurice Del Bourgo, who, in his own words, "had been tremendously moved" by Remarque's novel and was "delighted with the chance" to illustrate it.[27] Fitch's script and Del Bourgo's art faithfully convey some of the power of the original.

Classics Illustrated's adaptation of this anti-war novel was so powerful, in fact, that the publisher withdrew it from circulation in 1955, the year that it also stopped circulating several of its titles that a New York State Joint Legislative Committee investigating comic books had condemned for "brutality and violence."[28] Classics Illustrated's general sales strategy was to keep all of their titles in print continuously, but their comic book adaptation of *All Quiet on the Western Front* remained out of print for the next decade.

Kurtzman won a lasting reputation as an anti-war cartoonist, but he regarded the Korean War as justifiable. Kurtzman opposed the glorification of war. He did his research with the cooperation of the U.S. military, which allowed Kurtzman to gather information on their bases as he worked to make his stories more authentic.

Kurtzman said later, "I feel there are times when you have to fight…. To some degree I guess we have an obligation to support war. Although if we ever stand up on a hilltop and look at that kind of reasoning it all gets to look pretty weird."[29]

When popular culture excludes truly pacifist perspectives, readers can take even the acknowledgment that war means killing human beings (which Kurtzman repeatedly emphasized in his Korean War comic books) as profoundly daring statements, extremely "subversive" messages, or powerful expressions of "dissent."[30]

Korean War comics invariably fell short of depicting the enemy as fully human by not allowing any Chinese or Korean character to offer any reasonable-sounding explanation of why their side was fighting. Even in Kurtzman's extraordinary "Enemy Assault," the Chinese soldier's only reason for fighting is that "they took me into the Army!" In American comic books the enemy fights out of fear of punishment, for glory, for careerist advancement, from a cruel love of violence, through racial instinct, or to steal territory—motivations which comics did not accept as appropriate for the characters fighting on our side.[31]

Lonely Voices of Protest

The political meaning of a comic book story comes most fully to life in those cases where we see characters representing different positions working out their disagreements. The reader watches as the characters representing the preferred values directly confront and humiliate the representatives of opposing perspectives. In war comics, the general rule seems to have been that the more explicitly a character criticizes the war, the more forcefully he (or she) converts to seeing the falseness of an anti-war position.[32]

In the end, violence can only be answered with violence. Geoffrey Wagner, in his book *Parade of Pleasure*, gave this example:

> *War Report* for March 1953 […] kicks off with a story of a padre who learns that might is right and who at the end brings a sword, not peace, with a vengeance. Chaplain James Tucker at first hates carnage but in the last pictures he hurls a grenade, shouting "The Lord is my shepherd" and cracks a commie on the skull with his rifle-butt ("YAGGH!") remarking, "And the Lord has a long arm, my erring brother!"[33]

Usually the stories depicted the characters who criticized the war as part of an Army squad. Their conversion worked as a variation on the more general formula plot of a conflict between fellow soldiers who come into harmony through fighting the enemy together.[34] This formula functions as a strongly "pro-war" device.

"Face to Face with the Enemy"

The very propagandistic comic book story "Face to Face with the Enemy" (in *Battle #70*, June 1960) shows how an American isolationist learns to support the Korean War. The story, drawn by Don Heck, uses an unusual split-page layout which juxtaposes the experiences of the fictional American "Stan" and his counterpart, the Chinese Communist (with a Korean name) "Kim," with each of their stories running vertically down their halves of the pages. The story apparently responds to the much-discussed question of whether Americans have become too soft to succeed as fighters.

On page one, two American youths wearing suits and ties express isolationist sentiments. The newspaper that one of them reads carries the headline "WAR IN KOREA":

> [Enlist?] Are you nuts? I never heard of Korea before!
> Who cares what happens way over there! Let them wash their own dirty linen!

Meanwhile, the slant-eyed, yellow-skinned, wavy-haired Chinese youth Kim greets the news enthusiastically as a glorious opportunity to fulfill his life's mission: to conquer "First Korea … then the world!"

On the story's second page, to his mother's dismay, the isolationist Stan is drafted. (During the Korean War, over one and a half million Americans were drafted.)[35] The Chinese man, by contrast, eagerly joins the army.

Stan dislikes basic training and daydreams of home, while Kim delights in learning to shoot and thinks only of smashing the enemy. Then the artist composes a panel that puts the reader in the position of standing shoulder to shoulder with the American soldiers as we hear our officer lay out the situation: "A lot of you don't yet know what this is all about! It's a test, to see if the Reds can walk into a free country and make the people slaves to Communism, or if the free world can stop such aggression! If the Reds can make it stick, they won't stop here!"

Our next viewpoint is from behind the man who addresses the Chinese soldiers, who presents an interpretation that seems to confirm what the American had said: "We must show the world that the People's Army cannot be stopped! We are in great numbers … we are strong … we will win!"

Actually, the huge Communist Chinese propaganda campaign to "Resist America, Aid Korea" had made an argument that closely mirrored what the American officer in this comic book story had said: China, as part of the "democratic and peace-loving camp," must defend its ally North Korea and itself from aggression by a "decadent capitalistic camp which aims at war-mongering and world conquest" to prevent falling under "the enslavement of imperialistic exploitation."[36] The many propaganda cartoons that Chinese cartoonists drew in the period leading up to China's entry into the war depicted North Koreans as heroic younger brothers, fighting against Americans who had taken over the role of the old, hated Japanese imperialists.[37]

The Americans in "Face to Face with the Enemy" then walk through a village, noticing "the faces of these poor people … filled with fear and despair! Y'know, I was thinking…. This could be America … these could be our folks, our families!" Another American answers: "Yeah! And if we don't stop 'em it *will* be!"

The Chinese characters had a stronger claim to make these observations than the Euro-American soldiers who said them in this story. Before China joined the Korean War, American pilots on several occasions had crossed the border separating North Korea and China to drop bombs on Chinese territory.[38] As for feeling like family, tens of thousands of Koreans living in Manchuria had fought on the side of the Communist Chinese in the Chinese Revolution (commanded by Korean revolutionaries who had fought as allies with the Chinese against Japan).[39] Two of the divisions of the People's Liberation Army that China sent to participate in the Korean War were of Korean ethnicity.[40]

Instead of expressing solidarity with the Koreans as the Americans in the comic book story "Face to Face with the Enemy" do, the corresponding picture shows one Chinese man firing a rifle while another encourages him to "Burn…. Shoot…. We are warriors of the new world! In us can be no weakness, no conscience! This is war … for the glory of Communism!"

In the conclusion, "destiny" brings Stan and Kim into hand-to-hand combat in a Buddhist temple (where "the age-old idols look down without interest" on them). Stan quickly defeats Kim, for reasons that the narrator spells out, "This valiant fighting man *battles* this way to protect the freedom and ease he is heir to, for the dignity of man! His power and glory is one with freedom!"

The story ends with a reference to rebuilding from the ashes of war, each stone dedicated to "freedom, no matter what the cost!" Stan's masculinity turns out to be secure after all, since he has proved his toughness on the battlefield.

Immortal Hero Yang Ken-Sze

The story "Face to Face with the Enemy" makes an interesting contrast with a Communist Chinese comic book, first published in 1959 and republished in English as *Immortal Hero Yang Ken-Sze*. This biographical war comic tells the story of a Chinese soldier who died fighting in the Korean War.[41] The Chinese comic shows "scores of examples of Special-Class Combat Hero Yang's noble love of country, his proletarian internationalism and his revolutionary heroism, as one of the Chinese People's Volunteers" in the Korean War.[42]

When the Chinese story introduces the Korean War, the story explains Yang Ken-Sze's motivations as to "resist […] aggression and aid Korea": "The news that U.S. imperialism had unleashed a war in Korea came like a thunderbolt. Ken-Sze and his comrades who fought for the rebirth of their country now volunteered to join the struggle to resist U.S. aggression and aid Korea."[43]

In contrast to the American comic, which had imagined the Chinese boy as growing up in peace while hoping for a war to begin that would give him a chance to prove himself, the Chinese comic, more realistically, depicts the Chinese soldier growing up in a world torn by the war against Japan and the Chinese Civil War.[44]

A Rough Consensus

Korea War comic books supporting the Korean War expressed views ranging from crusading anti-communism to universal brotherhood. The "anti-war" attitude that sending Americans to fight in Korea had been a "mistake" (which, according to several polls had become a majority opinion in the United States by 1952) found its strongest expression only in stories that showed this position as short-sighted and incorrect.[45]

The comic book industry, generally speaking, had little sympathy for "isolationists." Ten years before the Korean War, comic book publishers like Lev Gleason and cartoonists like Jack Kirby had agitated for America to join the fight against Hitler and fascism, at a time when as many as 800,000 members of "America First," the largest popular anti-war organization in American history, were trying to keep the U.S. out of the coming World War.[46]

Typical Korean War stories were not happy with the war but supported it anyway. The March 1953, story "Peril Patrol" in *The Fighting Man #5* includes a scene in which a soldier stabs to death an enemy soldier who jumps into his hole and spends the night with a corpse, but its "pro-war" message differs sharply from Remarque's *All Quiet on the Western Front.*

In "Peril Patrol" the enemy kills the protagonist's buddy and is then killed in a frenzy of revenge. The protagonist, introduced earlier in the story as "you, Jim Dickson," then throws "the corpse of the Gook" out of the hole, and endures a "long vigil alone" with the dead body of the friend. "You, Jim" reflects: "Guess I better write his girl! Gladys, ain't it? She'd want to know just how it happened." As the sun comes up, the hero directly addresses the reader for the first time: "Good to see the sun! We've got to make sure it continues to shine down on the right kind of folks … even if it takes all of this to do it."

Despite the powerful outside pressures that constrained the publication of anti-war messages in comic books, in the end the comics expressed a war mentality which did correspond to the public's attitude toward the Korean War: unenthusiastic, fatalistic, simplistic, and afraid.

15

Atrocities

One of the staples of war propaganda has been the "atrocity story" about the enemy's barbarism. These atrocity stories serve as proof that the enemy represents a force so profoundly evil that it must be stopped by any possible means except compromise. This argument usually works by downplaying or ignoring "our" atrocities while highlighting or inventing "theirs." Sometimes it works by blaming "our" atrocities on "them." Atrocity propaganda stories in comic books can become deeply hooked into our imaginations.

Bruce Cumings (born in 1943) includes in his landmark book *Origins of the Korean War* his personal testimony about the lasting effects of the images of enemy cruelty that appeared in Korean War comic books:

> Growing up on comic books depicting North Korean and Chinese soldiers as rabid, bloody-fanged beasts, for years I could not purge from my mind the notion that fighting such people must have made the Korean War a horror. Yet all testimony points to the very same "Red Chinese" as the most disciplined and correct army in the war. That could be verified a thousand times, however, before it would erode the residual Orientalism infecting the Western mind, from the simplicity of comics to the august judgments of contemporary advocates of "the West."[1]

Cumings quickly adds that "The numbers game [of comparing atrocities] is nauseating," and that all sides in the Korean War "were guilty of unforgiveable atrocities (although none held a candle to the Germans or Japanese in the just concluded world war)."

One of the most repeated Korean War atrocity stories told of the North Koreans' murdering prisoners of war after they had tied the prisoners' hands behind their backs with the prisoners' own shoelaces. Apparently, such stories about the Hill 303 Massacre of August 17, 1950, inspired Harvey Kurtzman's second Korean War story, published in *Two-Fisted Tales* in March–April 1951, which he titled "Massacred!" The story, drawn by John Severin and Will Elder, begins with some American soldiers discovering the bodies of what appear to be UN soldiers ("some of our guys!" … "Our South Korean allies!") who had been murdered with their hands tied behind their backs.[2] The sole survivor of this massacre, an American soldier, unexpectedly warns the men not to "waste their pity" on these dead Koreans. He explains that these dead men were actually *North* Koreans who had massacred some South Korean prisoners, disguised themselves in South Korean uniforms, and then been killed by other North Korean soldiers. In a case of poetic justice, the cruel North Korean Colonel Jun in this story is killed by soldiers who had been following his own orders on the treatment of prisoners.[3]

In comic books and more generally, the communist atrocities in Korea that Americans most cared about were war crimes against American prisoners of war. After the truce, the chairman of the Senate Subcommittee on Korean War Atrocities opened his hearings by introducing the communists' "beast-like acts committed against civilized humanity" as including an incident in which "a Red Chinese nurse cuts off the toes of a GI with a pair of garden shears, without benefit of anesthesia, and wraps the wounds in a newspaper"; other incidents when "GI's were lined up in a ditch and shot in cold blood, with their hands wired behind their backs"; and cases when others "were put into small iron cages and starved to death like animals with maggots coming out of their eye sockets...."[4]

Charges of war crimes against the UN forces often focused on large-scale, indiscriminate slaughter. For example, the March 1952 report of the Commission of the International Association of Democratic Lawyers, which had conducted its own fact-finding mission, claimed that "beyond doubt" American planes had conducted germ warfare, "beyond question" Americans had used chemical weapons against Korean civilians, and according to "overwhelming" evidence, American troops committed "mass-murders, individual murders and bestialities" against Korean civilians. Less controversially, they reported that they had personally witnessed that every town they passed through had either been completely destroyed or reduced to a few standing buildings; that bombers had caused tremendous damage to North Korean cities that lacked military targets, destroying houses, churches, hospitals marked with a red cross, dispensaries, schools and public buildings; and that they had received an official report listing temples, palaces, pavilions and other sites of archaeological or historical value that had been destroyed.[5] The lawyers unanimously concluded that with "the fullest knowledge of and planning by the leaders of the government of the U.S.A. and of the High Command of the U.S. Forces," the American forces were "guilty of the crime of Genocide as defined by the Genocide Convention of 1948."

Stewart Lone and Gavan McCormack have found it remarkable that in the West, meting out "indiscriminate death to the civilian population by bombing, strafing, napalming, blasting dams or destroying food crops" is not usually understood as committing "atrocities":

> Instead, the torture and murder of civilians, prisoners, or combatants is generally considered an atrocity only when the act is carried out in direct, person-to-person, "low-tech" fashion, not when delivered by "high-tech," remote control from a bomber or as the result of a bureaucrat's decision.[6]

"Atrocity Story"

One highly unusual comic book piece about the Korean War focused directly on unforgivable atrocities and was titled simply "Atrocity Story." It appeared in *Battlefield #2* with a cover date of June 1952.[7] Comics historian Michael Vassallo has described "Atrocity Story," which appeared in one of the hundreds of war comic books that Atlas published in the 1950s, as "possibly the single most powerful Atlas war entry of all time."[8] Comics historian Ger Apeldoorn remembers its writer, Hank Chapman, as having written:

> some of the most horrifying stories of the period. ... Chapman seems to have known the reality of war, but he also hated the sacrifices it took and in many of his stories he questions out loud if those sacrifices are worth it. Nowhere more than in one of his masterpieces, *"Atrocity Story,"* beautifully illustrated by Paul Reinman.[9]

"Atrocity Story" begins with five examples of communist atrocities in Korea: the murder of 100 civilians near Haeju; the murder of 400 civilians near the Haeju airport; the execution of 200 U.S. Marine prisoners of war; a slaughter of over 25,000 civilians as the North Korean occupation of South Korea ended; and the execution of UN soldiers after tying their hands behind their backs. The first page of the piece is a full-page illustration of a couple of dozen dead, bleeding bodies with their hands tied behind them, receding into the distance, to represent 200 Marines who had been among the "GI Prisoners Butchered by Reds in Korea."

The main source for "Atrocity Story" was apparently Colonel James Hanley's well-publicized atrocity report of mid–November 1951.[10] At the time, some reporters thought that Hanley's statement was intended to sabotage a cease-fire agreement.[11] The suspicion that the United States wanted to prolong the fighting had been fed the previous month by a speech in which a deputy United States representative on the United Nations Security Council told reporters that a cease-fire in Korea could lead to a dangerous weakening of "the sense of urgency that has developed in the free world as a result of Soviet actions."[12] The suspicion had been strengthened when the Reds then yielded on the issue of where to draw the armistice line (agreeing to either an immediate ceasefire on the existing battle lines or on the 38th parallel) and UN negotiators responded by demanding more territory.[13]

After listing the communist war crimes, Chapman and Reinman's "Atrocity Story" goes on to ask the reader to imagine what if this were happening in Nevada; Atlantic City, New Jersey; or Inglewood, California. The page after that describes for comparison the crimes of Nazi Germany at Buchenwald, Dachau, Ravensbruck, and Linz:

> Buchenwald.... The butcher shop of Germany! Where millions of men, women and children died! Can we ever forget ... or forgive sins such as this?
> Dachau.... Hell on earth! Where humans were burned like cord wood in special-built human ovens....

The page about Nazi atrocities seems inaccurate since Buchenwald and Dachau were "concentration camps," and not *extermination* camps like the six death camps the Nazis built in occupied Poland (Auschwitz-Birkenau, Chełmno, Bełżec, Majdanek, Sobibor, and Treblinka). Buchenwald, though, had a special place in the American imagination. It was the first concentration camp the Americans liberated, an event broadcast over radio by Edward R. Murrow. Americans found and photographed piles of emaciated naked bodies there, which Paul Reinman redrew for this story. (The huge death rate at Buchenwald resulted mostly from sick, starving people being worked to death or shot by guards.[14]) More than this, Buchenwald became the symbol of Nazi barbarism in large part because of a table on which three men, apparently former prisoners, displayed evidence of Nazi atrocities, including human heads, with their skulls removed, that had been stuffed and preserved like the "shrunken head" war trophies of the Jivaro of Ecuador; pieces of human skin covered with tattoos, and a lampshade made of human skin.[15]

"Atrocity Story" concludes with a series of questions about what it would take to stop communist atrocities in Korea. One man asks, "Should we fight atrocity with atrocity, General? Should we start executing the Red prisoners we have in our stockades?" The General answers: "If we did that Colonel, we'd be shoving civilization back to the dark ages of barbarism and savagery! There must be another way to stop them!"

No extermination camps were set up in Korea, but the government of South Korea mass murdered its "Red prisoners" throughout the war. According to Kim Dong-Choon of South Korea's Truth and Reconciliation Commission, these massacres of leftist prisoners happened mostly before the events at Haeju that Chapman's story had illustrated:

> In 1950, approximately 30,000 political prisoners were imprisoned in South Korea. [...] Most of these prisoners would later "disappear" after the outbreak of war. It is believed that a majority of them were

secretly executed along with NGL members [former and converted communists who had been put on a list for preventive detention and rounded up shortly after North Korea attacked] from July to August of 1950. The killing of NGL members surpassed other atrocities of the Korean War in its sheer size and brutality.[16]

The Taejon Massacre

As "Atrocity Story" had warned, the Korean War shoved "civilization back to the dark ages of barbarism and savagery!" Between the 1953 armistice agreement and the 1954 peace conference, *Time* magazine published a column based on information supplied by the Army's War Crimes Division simply titled "Barbarity" to remind readers about the worst communist atrocities of the recent war.[17]

By far the largest atrocity of the ones that *Time* listed was the Taejon Massacre of an estimated 5,000 to 7,500 prisoners, described as "anti–Communists—soldiers, officials, business and professional men." According to the Army's report: "For murderous barbarism, the Taejon massacre will be recorded in the annals of history along with the rape of Nanking, the Warsaw ghetto and other similar mass exterminations.... Those responsible ... must be brought to judgment before the tribunal of civilized peoples."

Eventually historians learned that there had been *two* Taejon Massacres, a massacre of political prisoners ordered by the South Korean government in July 1950, shortly after the war began, and then the much reported (but smaller) North Korean massacre in September, which had been an act of retaliation.[18]

In 2009, South Korea's Truth and Reconciliation Commission announced that the South Korean military and police had executed at least 4,900 civilians at Taejon, out of fear that they would help the communists who were invading from the north.[19] Similar executions had been conducted across Korea, with the total number of such deaths estimated unofficially to be at least 100,000 to 200,000 or more.[20] The dead included those South Koreans that Kim Il-sung had been counting on to rise up and make his reunification of Korea a success, plus others who were unlucky enough to get swept up in South Korea's crackdown on leftists. In a much smaller massacre, a few days after the July Taejon Massacre and not far away, Americans strafed and shot civilians at No Gun Ri.

Kim Dong-Choon has written a history of the Korean War centered upon its forgotten massacres of civilians rather than its battles.[21] Using this framework, Kim judges "the most brutal massacre committed by the [South Korean] military and police" to have been actions that happened in 1948: the suppression of the uprising on Cheju Island and of the Yeosu-Suncheon mutiny.[22]

As for what that other way of ending communist atrocities without sinking to their level of barbarism might be, the concluding panel of Chapman's "Atrocity Story," divided into three parts, asks: "Is this the solution?" (illustrated by a mushroom cloud) "or this...." (illustrated by a man with a newspaper telling his wife "Ah, forget it.... It's just propaganda!") "or what?"

Journalist I.F. Stone argued for dismissing these reports as "propaganda." He had warned in one of his first articles about the Korean War that the conflict might spread to a larger nuclear confrontation, with apocalyptic results: "Hundreds of millions may die, great cities become smoky ruins, men prowl like sub-human beasts in the lonely debris of a planet wrecked by atomic war."[23]

Stone devoted a chapter of his book *The Hidden History of the Korean War* to examining the various, rapidly changing atrocity statistics that were presented in November 1951 about the number of American prisoners of war killed by the communists. For reasons that he describes in detail, Stone decided that "This is sheer statistical slapstick, understandable enough if the purpose was merely to stir up hate and upset peace talks, utterly inexcusable if intended as a serious accounting on the murder of American men by the enemy."[24]

Alleged UN Atrocities

Predictably, while the charges of communist atrocities in Korea received sensational news coverage in the United States, enemy charges of "high-tech" atrocities by American and other UN forces in Korea were handled differently.

In June 1952 (the same month that Atlas published "Atrocity Story"), *G.I. Joe*'s cover story apparently responded to accusations that American jets had been strafing Korean civilian refugees. (Eventually, documents came out that the U.S. Air Force had strafed Korean civilians at the Army's request, and that the U.S. Army also had a policy of shooting refugees as they approached the American lines. These policies grew out of fears, based on experience, that apparent refugees, including women and children, could, at a signal, pull guns and grenades from their bundles and attack the Americans, or that Korean refugees might include infiltrating North Korean soldiers dressed as civilians.[25]) *G.I. Joe #12*'s story "The Patchwork Quilt" made a clumsy attempt to reverse the blame for the war crime of strafing refugees. "The Patchwork Quilt" begins with six horrifying panels that show jets strafing a column of refugees, killing a father and a mother, as seen from the refugees' perspective. The caption identifies the planes, not as American jets, but as "Red MiGs." (The story makes this identification only this one time, buried in the middle of a fifty-word block of text.) Soon, some American soldiers arrive at the massacre scene and find a hungry, orphaned baby. They go into town to look for milk for the baby, holding a flag of truce.

Meanwhile, in the town, the Red Commissar is trying to get the villagers to reveal the location of their underground caves, but the villagers resist his plan to "use the caves to ambush and massacre the Americans." After all, the Americans "have done us no harm."

The Korean elder insists to the Commissar that "Americans do not murder!" A villager contradicts the elder, saying that he has just returned from the scene where "thousands of our people lie dead on the road," adding that "Communist has very few planes.... Americans has many," but he does not suggest that Americans had been responsible for these strafing deaths any more clearly than that.

At this point, the American soldiers arrive under a flag of truce asking for milk. The villagers, already sympathetic to the Americans, are impressed by the soldiers' kindness in seeking milk for a baby.

The communists, because of the villagers' lack of cooperation, attack the village. The Americans drive off the attackers in a struggle described in a caption as "bitter," but which includes the slapstick touch of an American conking the skulls of two enemy soldiers together.

In the conclusion of the story, the Americans give the orphaned baby to Yeh H'sien, a woman whose child had been killed by the Red attack on her village. One American soldier leaves behind the patchwork quilt that had been in his family since his great-grandfather had carried it as a soldier ("in the uneeform of Jeff Davis' gray" in America's Civil War) to comfort the orphaned baby.

Because this was published as morale boosting entertainment, the comic did not have to build a convincing case that the communists had been strafing refugees (let alone killing them by the "thousands" at a time) or that the Americans would never do such a thing. Some readers whose letters appeared in the following issues praised the *G.I. Joe* comic book series as "so, so real," "true to life," and "the truth about the war," but others thought that some of its stories were "impossible and silly" and "absolutely too fantastic."[26]

The six-page story "Scorched Earth!" in *Spy Cases #11* (also published in June 1952) can be read as another example of using fiction to rebut communist propaganda charges. The Soviet delegate to the United Nations had repeatedly accused the United States of carrying out a "Hitlerian" scorched-earth policy in North Korea.[27] From the opening lines of "Scorched Earth!" we see this policy from the point of view of those who carried it out:

> One of the dirtiest, hottest and most dangerous jobs in warfare is the scorched-earth detail ... where you leave nothing but ashes and shells to the enemy you're retreating from! Of course, in the process of blowing up buildings, warehouses, docks, equipment and ammunition, you must try not to become a cinder in the inferno you yourself make! But not always does a soldier succeed!

In this story, a soldier who had been made boiling mad by America's "crazy" scorched-earth policy and the way it causes "wanton destruction" of "all this stuff" learns that the apparent wastefulness is actually a military necessity. At first, the angry American accepts at face value the word of "commie prisoners" that "Reds no occupy city! Just fool you, send few patrols, snipers in! You tricked! You blow up docks, bridges! You big fool!"

The American chooses not to destroy the bridge he has been assigned to bring down, and then is brought to his senses by the communist who takes him as prisoner: "Now our divisions will pour across the bridge! Had you blown it, it would've taken us days to occupy the city!"

The American realizes, "(Groan!) What a fool I was! I believed those red lice! I–I wanted to believe them! I couldn't stand the destruction...." He redeems himself in a suicidal action to blow up the bridge.[28]

When the Americans evacuated from North Korea through Hungnam, they continued the scorched-earth policy of destroying anything that could be used by the enemy. Harvey Kurtzman dramatized this event in the story "Hungnam!," illustrated by Wally Wood, in *Two-Fisted Tales #26* (March–April 1952). This story was the final piece in a special issue presented as "a document of the action at the Changjin Reservoir!"

Kurtzman made the central character of "Hungnam!" a "pooch," a dog who "doesn't know a Korean from an American.... Doesn't know a single thing about politics!" The dog feasts on canned beef that soldiers throw to a group of dogs, "from a huge pile of food that will have to be destroyed on the docks!" and then falls asleep. The last two pages of the story begin with a wide panel captioned:

> On the afternoon of December 24th, 1950, at 2:30 p.m., the last man fighting under the flag of the United Nations left the deserted port of Hungnam, and the only useable materials they left behind were blocks of wired explosives placed under every structure that would be of any value to the Communists!

Then the exciting demolitions continue for next eight panels. Because Kurtzman wants his readers to feel regret for the sad irony of men "still killing their fellow men" on "the birthday of the Prince of Peace," he shows "the broken little body of a dog lying in the rubble." (The dog seems to be sleeping, as the dog that Wood sketched for that panel probably was.[29])

Comics critic John Benson saw the special issue of *Two-Fisted Tales* that this story concluded as a turning point in Kurtzman's war comics:

> Once Kurtzman had had a taste of being a general, he was never really a footsoldier again. After issue #26, there was a decided shift in the type of stories he wrote. "Anti-war" stories all but disappeared. In their place was an increasing number of historical epics, in which Kurtzman became fascinated (and fascinated the reader, as well) with the details and military lessons of history.[30]

Rather than being the work of soldiers on the ground, most of the destruction was dropped from the air. Shortly after the Chinese entered the war, General MacArthur ordered his planes to destroy "every means of communication, every installation, factory, city and village" between the Yalu River and the battle line.[31]

"Korea, We Accuse!"

The 48-page pamphlet "Korea, We Accuse! Report of the Commission of the Women's International Democratic Federation in Korea, May 16 to 27, 1951" summarized the findings of a delegation of women who, on the invitation of a North Korean women's organization, "made a thorough on the spot investigation of the monstrous crimes committed by the American interventionist troops and their 'UN' allies in Korea."[32] The women delegates' published demand that the U.S. government officials responsible for the atrocities in Korea be "charged as war criminals" was, in all likelihood, too little known in the United States to have inspired a comic book rejoinder.[33] Nevertheless, even if no comic book writers attempted to respond to its charges, "Korea, We Accuse!" still has a place in the history of Korean War comic books. Some private correspondence involving this pamphlet in Fredric Wertham's archived papers invites us to reconsider the meaning of Wertham's book *Seduction of the Innocent* (the core text of the anti-comic book movement) in relation to the Korean War.

"Korea, We Accuse!" began by charging that "The people of Korea are subjected by American occupants to a merciless and methodical campaign of extermination...."[34] More specifically, it charged that "U.S. soldiers and officers" and those under their command were:

- systematically destroying the food that North Koreans needed to prevent starvation
- systematically destroying "town after town, [...] village after village" to break Korean morale
- using banned weapons including time bombs and napalm, and "constantly machine-gunning civilians from low-flying planes"
- "atrociously exterminating the Korean population" in occupied areas through torture, beatings, burning people, burying people alive, or letting them die of cold and hunger in overcrowded prisons "in which they were thrown without charges being levied against them, without investigation, trial or sentence."

The delegates declared that "These mass tortures and mass murders surpass the crimes committed by Hitler Nazis in temporarily occupied Europe."[35] This women's delegation included in their report several stories about atrocities against women:

> Kang Bok-Sen's daughter […] told the Commission that the Americans made the Opera and the remains of the adjoining house into an Army-brothel. To this brothel they took by force women and young girls they caught in the streets. [….]
> Kim Sun-Ok, 37, mother of four children killed by a bomb, stated that […] she saw 37 people killed by the Americans, among them the secretary of the local women's organization. The Americans led her naked through the streets and later killed her by pushing a red-hot bar into her vagina. Her small child was buried alive.[36]

The pamphlet "Korea, We Accuse!" and a brief exchange of letters about it were almost the only items about the Korean War included in the 82,200 items in the Fredric Wertham Papers in the Library of Congress. (The only other item in his archived papers about the Korean War was a clipping from a 1952 *People Today* magazine article on Picasso's anti-war painting "Massacre in Korea."[37])

The "Chairman" of the pamphlet's sponsoring Commission, the well-known left-wing peace activist Nora K. Rodd of Ontario, Canada, had sent Wertham a copy of "Korea, We Accuse!" in 1954, at the request of an American friend. Mrs. Rodd quoted this friend as criticizing *Seduction of the Innocent* for what it did *not* say about the relation of comic book reading to the atrocities that Americans had committed in Korea:

> Dr. Wertham comes to the conclusion that his studies have convinced him that the immense growth of juvenile delinquency has its main causes in the demoralization of young minds by comic books (plus radio, television influences). What he seems not yet to have realized is the fact that children who have proven immune as long as they lived under normal conditions, in spite of having devoured this poison for many years, get out of hand as soon as all the fetters and restraints of civilized life have been loosed and—as in war—responsibilities toward human beings they have to regard as enemies are eliminated. The same will also happen if domestic upheavals and unrest should confront the young people of USA. Then also the way to unlimited savagery will be open.
> This lack of awareness of the author seems to me to be a defect of the valuable book. Perhaps he never heard or read of the behavior of "our Boys" in warfare and also as occupation soldiers.[38]

Wertham's draft of his succinct reply, dated August 16, 1954, defends the omission as nothing more than a failure to state the obvious:

> Dear Mrs. Rodd:
> My thanks for your letter and the interesting pamphlet. Of course I know your name, and was very glad to hear from you.
> As far as your correspondent is concerned, it is a pity that she has not understood my book. Of course special circumstances make the comic book factor even more virulent; that would seem to me to be self-evident.
> Kind regards,

Wertham's reply does not mention that a political calculation may have been involved in his choosing to defend despised, so-called "juvenile delinquents" as having been brutalized by their comic book reading but not to unpatriotically attack American soldiers with the same argument. Perhaps that, too, seemed self-evident.

Since Wertham almost completely avoided the subject of the Korean War, it can be tempting to read too much into this brief and unpublished note. Predictably, he would reject as a misinterpretation of his argument the idea that mass media are among the "main causes" of juvenile delinquency. Still, he adds that the application of his arguments about the effects of comic books to the behavior of American soldiers committing atrocities in Korea is "self-evident" (and that comic book violence would have a "more virulent" effect on soldiers in Korea than it has on civilian readers). Perhaps not only a reader who ignores his usually-careful distinction between "causes" and "factors," but also the one who misses this implicit point about the effects of a brutalizing culture on soldiers' bad behavior has "not understood" *Seduction of the Innocent.*[39]

16

∞∞∞∞∞∞∞

Politics

Comic books participated in political debates, over the Korean War and other issues, most directly as a medium of sponsored campaign advertising. Such comic books were published to support both Democratic and Republican candidates.

The first comic book created to support a candidate had promoted William O'Dwyer, who would become New York City's 100th mayor in 1946.[1] In this local election, the soon-to-be-familiar format of a 16-page, four-color, coverless newsprint comic telling a candidate's biography was established.

Malcolm Ater and The Story of Harry S. Truman

Malcolm Ater's company Commercial Comics in Washington, D.C., became the leading specialist in this area, working on over fifty major political campaigns, beginning with his comic book about Harry Truman in 1948.[2] Ater, though a Democrat, had first approached the Republicans, thinking that they needed comic books and also that they could afford to publish them. The Republicans rejected his idea as "too undignified," so he had Jack Sparling draw a comic book about Harry S. Truman, based on his script, and submitted it to the Democratic National Committee. The Democrats liked it well enough to publish three million copies, making this the first time that a comic book had been used in a national election. Jack Redding, the Democratic head of publicity, credited the comic book with having contributed to Truman's unexpected victory.[3]

The Story of Harry S Truman told Truman's life story and never mentioned the names of his opponents in the 1948 election: Thomas S. Dewey, Strom Thurmond, Henry A. Wallace, or Norman Thomas. The comic concentrated on establishing Truman's credentials, for example his veto of the Taft-Hartley bill, which had been overridden by Congress.

In this comic, a young man explains the reasons that the Republicans killed the Office of Price Administration and passed the "Taft-Hartley Act, strangling labor" this way: "All the Republicans think of is **big profits** for the **big guy**! But we'll show them in the November elections!"

Ater's pro–Truman comic also emphasized that at the conclusion of World War II "he made the awesome decision to use the atom bomb and thus saved untold numbers of American lives." At times, the comic looks like a war comic, with its graphic telling of Truman's military service during World War I and its depictions of World War II.

The Robert Alphonso Taft Story

A campaign comic book took up the issue of the Korean War within months of the North Korean invasion. Labor unions used the extraordinarily controversial comic *The Robert Alphonso Taft Story: It's on the Record* against Ohio Senator Robert Taft during Taft's overwhelmingly successful bid for reelection in 1950. Created at a time when the Korean War looked like a brief and successful police action, the comic book mocked Taft for having doubted Russia's plans for aggression and having voted against spending money on "Korea Defense."[4] (China entered the Korean War, ending the chances for a quick military victory, a week before Taft's reelection.)

An unusually large amount of information is known about this comic book because it became a focus of attention in the Senate Subcommittee investigation of the 1950 Ohio Senatorial race. The hearings were held to investigate that race because the defeated Democratic candidate, Joe Ferguson, had claimed that Taft had spent an excessively large amount of money, and Taft had countered that "My opposition wrote, published, and distributed the most defamatory, scurrilous and violent literature ever used in a political campaign." Of this unfair campaign material, so disturbing that it led Taft to consider proposing a new law against fraudulent misstatements in campaign materials, he said: "Perhaps the most infamous piece of political propaganda ever devised was the 16-page four-color comic book."[5]

After Taft had co-sponsored the 1947 Taft-Hartley Act, which had put important limits on union organizers, the labor movement had marked Taft for defeat. (Co-sponsor Frederick A. Hartley, Jr., did not run for reelection in 1948.)[6]

A committee of labor leaders who were organizing against Taft's reelection needed a way to get publicity when Ohio's newspapers would not take their advertising.[7] They thought of either producing a film or commissioning a comic as their "major effort" in the campaign, and decided against a film because they reasoned that a movie might not reach the public.[8]

For the cost of $16,039.35, Elliott Caplin's Toby Press in New York furnished them with a million copies of a custom-made comic book.[9] Jake Clayman, secretary-treasurer of the Ohio CIO Council, acknowledged that some thought that this price sounded too low, but testified that "I was told that was a routine charge. I am sure of this: There was no ideological affinity between the publisher and ourselves. It was purely a business transaction. They were out to make a profit."[10]

The comic, drawn in the style of Al Capp's *Li'l Abner* comic strip, tells an imaginary, behind the scenes story of a meeting in "the home of J. Phineas Moneybags, Chairman of the local Taft Campaign Committee," as the pro–Taft people edit a film to promote their candidate and attack his opponent. Taft accused this comic of fanning "class hatred," since it based its story on imaginary scenes of selfish rich people treating Taft as "a fine investment" who serves their interests. For example, the rich men in this story discuss how Taft cut corporate taxes for them and shifted the tax burden to "the *rest of the people in Ohio.*"[11]

The visual appearance of "J. Phineas Moneybags" seems to be inspired by "Rich Uncle Pennybags," the mascot of the Parker Bros. board game Monopoly (introduced in 1936). That mascot's appearance, in turn, was reportedly based on capitalist J.P. Morgan (1837–1913). The subtle association of Taft with J.P. Morgan offers a possible explanation for the vehement anger that this comic provoked from Taft's supporters.[12]

Pioneering organic farmer and author Louis Bromfield seemed to express their agitated mood:

> The peculiar and unscrupulous vindictiveness of the campaign of organized labor against Senator Taft in my own state of Ohio provides a truly frightening foretaste of what might happen to the rest of us in this country if we have a government wholly dominated by the organized labor czars. As the campaign progresses, the methods, the lies, the whispering campaigns have reached proportions never attained in any other American campaign I have ever heard of and equaled probably only by the kind of calumny and brutal propaganda for which Hitler and Stalin have set the pattern. Certainly nothing resembling it has ever occurred before in this country. [...] One of the most outrageous of methods is the distribution of an atrocious comic book, the likes of which I have only seen before in nazi-communist circles in Europe. The whole tone is vicious.[13]

On page four, the comic shows a series of Taft's statements on war and peace. In the last of these quotes, from September 7, 1949, Taft claims "There is not much evidence that the Russians contemplate military aggression!"[14] This is followed by a drawing of Korea, colored red, with a big tank on it. The comic goes on to call Taft one of the few remaining Congressional supporters of the old-fashioned and unpopular policy of "isolationism."

When Joe Ferguson's character speaks, he says things like "We must establish peace and freedom in our time and for all time," and "Every American must stand behind President Truman in his efforts to protect the peace of the world."

As commonly happens with comic books, the caricature of Taft in *The Robert Alphonso Taft Story* oversimplified his positions. Although called an "isolationist," Taft had supported the president's decision to intervene in Korea, but claimed the war would not have been necessary if it had not been for "the bungling and inconsistent foreign policy of the administration."[15] Taft became the leading political opponent of Truman's handling of foreign policy. For example, Taft accused the Secretary of State, Dean Acheson, of having failed to make clear that the United States would retaliate against an attack on Korea in his speech to the National Press Club the previous January.[16] In addition, Taft opposed the President having sent troops to Korea without a Congressional declaration of war, arguing correctly that it had been unconstitutional.[17]

At the time of the Senate Hearings on the 1950 Ohio election, President Truman had said, "We saw how the special interests had poured money into Ohio last year to elect a Republican Senator. Now they will be thinking that if money can win an election in Ohio maybe money can win a national election."[18] Taft called the President's comment "completely false" and explained why he had to raise a large amount of money and why it was not such a large amount after all, giving his unconvincing estimate that he had actually been outspent three to one.[19] In answer to the investigating committee's finding that $512,326.98 had been earmarked for his reelection campaign, Taft answered that with five million Ohio voters, this worked out to ten cents per voter.[20] Even after adjusting for inflation, the level of spending per voter has grown greatly since then.[21]

If the union leaders had done any testing of the effectiveness of their comic book before mailing copies to Ohio voters, clearly it had not been enough. Taft, by contrast, made a historic advance with his direct mail campaign in this election. Over the objections of his direct mail adviser, Walter H. Weintz, Taft insisted on focusing on the Taft-Hartley Act. To Weintz's surprise, the mailing focused on the Taft-Hartley Act was the most popular letter that they tested. It won a large number of votes from union workers, and brought in enough small contributions to more than pay for itself.[22]

The Chicago Tribune

By the 1952 Presidential election year, the Korean War had become a major political issue. Senator Taft and other Republican "nationalists" led the opposition to the war. That year, the skillful editorial cartoonists of the pro–Taft *Chicago Tribune* (Carey Orr, Joseph Parrish and Daniel Holland) graphically represented their position. Those cartoonists pictured corrupt "Washington Brass Hats" (armed with the sword of "militarism") working in collaboration with "Socialist Wasters," supporting a huge military budget, the draft, and "endless war and endless spending" in Korea. They condemned Secretary of State "Acheson and the 'soft-war' enthusiasts" for having a defeatist "Yalu Policy" (dictated by England, a nation they showed as "beggars" asking Americans for handouts and as chummy with Russia). In a *Chicago Tribune* cartoon, Acheson coddles prisoners of war in the "Koje Island Rest Home," while in the background Stalin oppresses American prisoners of war. The cartoonists scorned internationalists as "ashamed Americans" and "one worlders" for waving the United Nations flag (whose lines of latitude and longitude they always showed as woven by a spider). They mocked as "Me-Too" candidates the Republicans Willkie, Dewey, and Eisenhower that the "Wall Street Internationalists" supported.

The *Chicago Tribune* controlled one of the most important newspaper syndicates, with several comic strips that were spun off into comic book series, including *Terry and the Pirates* (which George Wunder had taken over from Milton Caniff in 1946), Sidney Smith's *The Gumps*, Frank King's *Gasoline Alley*, Chester Gould's *Dick Tracy*, Harold Gray's *Little Orphan Annie*, Zack Mosley's *Smilin' Jack*, Frank Willard's *Moon Mullins* and Martin Branner's *Winnie Winkle*. The *Tribune*'s comic books did not provide a forum for an anti-war, isolationist perspective on the Korean War, for several reasons. Most simply, almost all the comic books starring Tribune Syndicate characters had stopped publication shortly before that war started.[23]

The 1952 Presidential Election

According to a 1952 newspaper article, that year's crop of political comic books was scheduled to include three million copies of a Malcolm Ater comic that the Democratic National Committee commissioned about Adlai Stevenson (*A Man Named Stevenson*); two million copies of the Republican comic *From Yalta to Korea*, and more comics from labor unions, corporations, foundations, and political candidates.[24] Two comic books introduced the Republican candidate Eisenhower: *Ike's Story* and *Dwight D. Eisenhower and Richard M. Nixon—The Choice of a Nation.*

M. Philip Copp

The 1952 eight-page comic *From Yalta to Korea* was copyrighted by M. Philip Copp. The first panel shows a Russian tank invading South Korea. The story explains that the reasons for "this tragedy that has cost over 100,000 American casualties and countless billions of dollars" began "at the Cairo Conference in 1943" where President Roosevelt promised Chiang Kai-Shek that "All territories Japan has stolen shall be restored to China. In due course Korea shall be independent" and China "took the white man at his word."[25]

Also in 1952, Copp created the very competently drawn, informative, but hastily organized eight-page comic *Crime, Corruption & Communism*. The booklet carried the imprimatur of an obscure group, the National Committee of The Jefferson Party of Charlottesville, Virginia. It ends by endorsing Eisenhower and Nixon, but does not quote them, show their portraits or even put their names in boldface.

After a section on corruption and racketeering, the *Crime, Corruption & Communism* comic turns to the problem of communist infiltration on page five. It shows portraits of the "traitor and [...] spy" Alger Hiss; Democrat Secretary of State Cordell Hull, who granted diplomatic recognition to the Soviet Union, after which the Russians immediately set up "Communist cells in this country for several purposes: spying, sabotage, and the influencing of foreign policy"; Owen Lattimore, named by a Senate committee as "a conscious instrument of the Soviet conspiracy"; and William Remington, who had been "one of the men in charge of sending military aid to Chiang Kai-shek," but is "now under indictment for lying about Communist Party membership."

This comic booklet warned that by the time "the administration blundered into a war against the Moscow-dominated North Koreans" the United States was no longer the most powerful nation. In conclusion:

> ...After 20 years of power, the Democrat Administration has reduced the United States to its most dangerous position since 1812. The American people cannot trust their government to men who, like Acheson and Stevenson, defend the Alger Hisses. Let's join the crusade to save America by electing Eisenhower and Nixon.

Adlai Stevenson

The comic book for the Democratic presidential nominee, *A Man Named Stevenson*, was published in an unusual format, five and a half inches wide by seven inches high, and with a slick cover. The comic emphasized Stevenson's record as governor of Illinois, praising him for cutting waste, inefficiency, corruption, political favoritism, spending, and debt. It also credited him for building roads, supporting mental hospitals, aiding schools, and increasing unemployment and disability benefits. The issue of the Korean War came up in just one panel. After four panels listing Stevenson's activities in helping to promote and to create the United Nations, and one panel of Stevenson denouncing the hypocrisy and "phony idealism" of communism, the comic stated, "He firmly believes that our action in Korea was necessary to halt the march of communist tyranny and renew the faith of freedom-loving peoples in their common defense."

Dwight D. Eisenhower

Neither of the two Eisenhower comic books—*Ike's Story*, which was published before Eisenhower won the nomination in July, nor *The Choice of a Nation*, which was published after he was nominated—mentioned Korea. When Eisenhower had returned to the United States from Europe in June 1952, after serving as Supreme Commander of NATO, his views on the Korean War were almost completely unknown.[26]

Ike's Story was published by cartoonist Zeke Zekley's company Sponsored Comics in Los Angeles. On the subject of military matters, *Ike's Story* quotes Eisenhower as believing in "preparedness" and "strength," and supports his "stand against isolationism."

(Eisenhower had felt compelled to run for President in 1952 because he objected to front-running Senator Taft's relatively "isolationist" views on foreign policy.[27])

At the Republican convention, Eisenhower said, "I do not believe it a presumption for me to call the effort of all who have enlisted with me—a crusade."[28] The comic book *The Choice of a Nation* organized its arguments around this theme of a "crusade." For example, it said that Eisenhower and Nixon "crusade for Peace."[29] In the comic they also "crusade" for better government, labor, free enterprise, Social Security, civil liberties, the economy, freedom, education and enlightenment. Other campaign comics had used religious language, but the promotion of Eisenhower's campaign as a "crusade" marked something new.[30]

Walter H. Weintz, who had worked on Senator Taft's senatorial re-election campaign in 1950, took a leave from his job at *Reader's Digest* to run a direct mail campaign for Eisenhower's 1952 presidential campaign. They initially tested 10,000 each of ten possible letters. Nine of the letters did about the same, but the letter focused on "Korea" did several times better than any of the others.[31] Weintz remembered:

> I can't say that it was the direct mail results alone which convinced Eisenhower that Korea was the important issue, but Walter Williams [Chairman of the Citizens for Eisenhower-Nixon Committee, who passed these test results to the candidate] told me that it was decisive in helping Eisenhower make up his mind.[32]

Historians have credited Eisenhower's speech in which he promised that if elected "I shall go to Korea" (to find a way to end the war quickly and honorably) as having helped to decide the election.[33] In a speech a few days later, Truman had responded to Eisenhower's pledge to go to Korea by saying, "No superman is going to solve our difficulties for us. And anybody who poses and talks like a superman is a fraud."[34]

Shortly after Eisenhower won the election, the *New York Times* editorial "Man and Superman" also warned against imagining Eisenhower as a superman or miracle-worker: "If a democracy cannot operate without supermen, it is no longer a democracy. [...] We are not children. We are citizens of a great Republic and all of us, in one way or another, can take part in the government of that Republic."[35]

It seems possible that Truman might have been reminded of the article "How would Superman end the war?" published a dozen years earlier in *Look* magazine when he responded to Eisenhower's promise to end the Korean War. Truman made no direct mention of the comic book and comic strip character Superman (who had also been appearing on television, with his successful series *Adventures of Superman* beginning a month before Truman's speech). The *New York Times* editorial used the word "superman" to mean an undemocratic leader, with no apparent thought to the comics character at all.

Eisenhower visited Korea a few weeks after winning the election and reached an armistice agreement the next summer (after the death of Stalin in March 1953).[36]

17

◇◇◇◇◇◇◇◇◇

The Bomb

American policymakers considered using nuclear weapons throughout the Korean War. The possibility of using nuclear weapons came up at the first meeting President Truman held on June 25, 1950, to discuss America's response to Stalin's aggression in Korea.[1] After the ceasefire, the American Secretary of State claimed that President Eisenhower's nuclear threat to China had brought the fighting to a stop.[2] Nuclear war themes in comic books of the time provide evidence for reconstructing what people felt and thought about nuclear weapons during the Korean War, and comics commissioned by Civil Defense agencies stand as evidence of what those in power thought the public should know.

Comprehending the growing presence of nuclear weapons as a revolutionary development in the history of the human species required overcoming the belief that such world-shattering weapons were to be found only in comic strips. In a top-secret report to the Secretary of State in January 1953, a Panel of Consultants on Disarmament chaired by Robert Oppenheimer warned against feeling that a threat so terrible could not be real:

> Whatever else may be said of it, it is plainly unprecedented. The power which will exist is not the power to win an ordinary military victory. It is rather the power to end a civilization and a very large number of the people in it. [...] The cities and people of [Russia and the United States] are now in the front lines, with a certainty and finality that must not be obscured by any feeling that nothing so much like comic-strip fantasy can possibly be true.[3]

Comic book artists, deeply rooted in these *Buck Rogers* and *Flash Gordon* comic strip fantasies, had used atomic weapon themes in their work many times before the atomic bomb finally leaped into the headlines a few days before the end of World War II.[4] Nuclear war was such a frequent theme in science fiction that in 1944, when military intelligence agents warned John Campbell, the editor of the science fiction magazine *Astounding*, to stop publishing atom bomb stories, he replied that the sudden disappearance of atom bomb stories would send a clear signal that the United States was secretly developing nuclear weapons.[5] The wartime United States Office of Censorship had better luck with Superman, convincing DC to postpone a 1944 comic book story in which Superman survives Lex Luthor's "atomic bomb," and gaining the McClure Syndicate's voluntary agreement that they would not publish any more atomic themed Superman comic strips.[6]

Since the dawn of the 20th century, popular fiction had connected the idea of nuclear weapons with the "end of the world."[7] As World War II ended, people entered the new "Buck Rogers world" of nuclear weapons and atomic energy with powerful anxieties that soon found renewed expression in comic books.[8]

Nuclear Superheroes

The first comic books to respond to the destruction of Hiroshima and Nagasaki distantly followed the example of H.G. Wells' 1914 novel *The World Set Free*. They treated the atomic bomb as a warning that the entire world had become endangered, and that humanity (with new urgency) must learn to live in peace.[9]

Some of the first comic book responses took the form of short-lived new superheroes. In November–December 1945, "Atomic Man" was introduced in *Headline Comics*. In one adventure, he fought a "crazed scientist" in possession of a technology stronger than the atomic bomb who brags "I have the power to destroy you and the world … and I'm going to start with you!"[10] "The Atomic Thunderbolt" vowed, in February 1946 (his only appearance), to "devote my life to save mankind from itself."[11]

In October 1946, Superman took a photograph of an atomic test at Bikini Atoll (the site of 23 nuclear tests, beginning with two tests in July 1946), as "a warning to men who talk against peace."[12] That same October, Captain Marvel's remarkable feature story showed a global nuclear war stretching on for page after page. That story turns out to be an imaginary televised dramatization. A father watching Captain Marvel's show with his children explains its "lesson" to them, "The world just ***can't afford*** to have another war, because it would wipe out all civilization and all human life! *Remember that kids!*"[13]

Unlike Atomic Man, The Atomic Thunderbolt, Superman and Captain Marvel, "Atoman" seemed to see the most urgent atomic problem as preventing the privatization of nuclear energy. In Atoman's origin story in February 1946, an unspeakably evil, greedy businessman, Mr. Twist, steals the atomic secret and then tries to persuade an atomic scientist, Barry Dale, to "build and operate an **atomic power** plant for me!" offering "a thousand dollars a week … fame … position … wealth … power! Anything you ask!" The scientist refuses as a matter of principle. Barry Dale threatens to expose Mr. Twist and all his tricks, and Mr. Twist responds by having a henchman throw the obstinate scientist off his penthouse balcony. As a result of years working with radium and uranium, however, Barry Dale has become the indestructible "Atoman," who survives the fall and devotes himself to the cause that "Atomic power cannot belong to one man … or group of men … or even one nation! **It belongs to the whole world!** My own power must be used to help all people … regardless of race or creed or nationality…. **I am strong—therefore it is my duty to help the weak!**"[14]

A few months later General Electric contracted with the Navy to build a nuclear reactor near Schenectady, New York. GE's comic book *Adventures Inside the Atom* said that they expected "to use the tremendous heat-energy" of this experimental reactor "to generate electric power—perhaps."[15] In 1954, Congress revised the Atomic Energy Act to allow for private ownership of nuclear power plants, and soon GE was in the business of selling commercial nuclear reactors to generate electricity.[16]

The Bomb That "Won the War"

Besides the superhero stories, the atomic bomb appeared on the cover of two new nonfiction comic book series that appeared in January 1946. *Science Comics #1* presented the hopeful side of the atomic age in a cover story titled "The Bomb That Won the War." In its last drawn panel, a speech balloon coming from the bomber responsible for the huge explosion below them says "Good-bye Japs! If they don't surrender after this we'll wipe them off the earth!" A boxed caption then concludes:

Thus, the atomic bomb—supreme achevement [*sic*] of modern science—soon brought about the surrender of Japan and the end of the global conflict! In the hands of the peace-loving nations of the earth, atomic energy will help build a new world far more wonderful than man ever dreamed of a few brief years ago![17]

The idea that the atomic bomb forced Japan to surrender and ended the war made a deep impression on the millions of people in the U.S. military who had expected to participate in a bloody invasion of Japan. Their families, friends and children could point to them as individuals whose lives may have been saved by the atomic bomb.[18] Nevertheless, historians have questioned whether the atomic destruction of Hiroshima and Nagasaki (the 67th and 68th Japanese cities that the Americans bombed that summer) had really "won the war" against Japan.[19] Japan's leaders surrendered only after they had heard the news, not only of the atomic destruction of Hiroshima and Nagasaki, but also of the Soviet Union's declaration of war and invasion of Japanese-held Manchuria.

The Bomb That Endangered the World

In contrast to the optimism of *Science Comics, Picture News in Color and Action #1* captioned its cover illustration "Will the Atom Blow the World Apart? George Bernard Shaw warns: It's likely—if we don't watch our step!"[20] Oversimplifying the matter, Shaw explains the principle of a nuclear chain reaction by simply burning a sheet of paper. ("The flame touches off the paper's connected fiber which continues to ignite itself until the paper is burned up. This is the principle of chain explosion."[21])

The United States government and a movement led by nuclear scientists looked to international control of atomic energy as the alternative to nuclear war.[22] Their hopes were illustrated in comics format in *Picture News #3*, in March 1946. One panel was captioned: "Sanity in international control of the atomic bomb as recommended by Senator [Brien] McMahon would be the first step to save civilization. The big three could bring it about…."[23]

The accompanying illustration showed President Truman of the United States flanked by Clement Richard Attlee, the Prime Minister of the United Kingdom, and Joseph Stalin, Marshal of the Soviet Union. Truman's speech balloon says: "Let us agree to the international inspection of all atomic plants in the world!" Attlee's speech balloon adds: "Mankind should at last prefer to be sensible rather than risk extermination!" Stalin's speech balloon concludes: "Peace is the happy, natural state of man!"

In June 1946, the United States proposed at the United Nations international inspections as a step toward international control of nuclear weapons. The Soviet Union did not accept international inspections, a predictable response because of what George Kennan had called their "continued secretiveness about internal matters, designed to conceal weaknesses and to keep opponents in the dark."[24]

The Soviet Union countered with a proposal to ban the bomb. The two sides failed to reach an agreement. The Soviet Union tested its first nuclear bomb in 1949. Great Britain became the third nation to test a nuclear bomb, in 1951.

"The Black Avengers"

The initial comic book responses to the Hiroshima bomb included hope and fear, but some Americans also experienced shame that the United States had dropped this weapon on a city and killed civilians. A story published in *Spy and Counterspy #2* (October–November 1949) seems designed to dispel any American guilt for having been the first nation to use atomic weapons.[25] The story takes the inspiration for its first pages from the 9,300 "fire balloons" that Japan had launched in the winter and spring of 1944–1945, to be carried across the ocean on the winds of the jet stream in an attempt to burn North American forests. About 300 of these Japanese balloons were found or observed in North America during the war, one of which killed a minister's wife and five children who had gathered around to look at it in Oregon. American officials were concerned that Japan might try to use these balloons for biological warfare.[26]

This *Spy and Counterspy* story, "The Black Avengers," begins in the summer of 1944 as a Japanese-American woman in an Oregon meadow sees what she thinks is one of the incendiary bombs that Japan has been sending over. She reports it to the local military post, where a soldier from their "Atomic Research Station" (boldly named by a sign on their fence) comes out and discovers that the dud bomb is actually an experimental nuclear weapon. The next page begins at "an emergency meeting of the top brass," where one officer says, "There must be no leak about this! It won't do morale on the home front any good to reveal that *a Japanese Atomic Bomb has landed on American soil!*" Another officer answers: "We've held back until now—The Japs have given us no choice! We'll see what happens to *their* morale when we drop *our* A-Bomb!"

The next panel shows a mushroom cloud rising over Hiroshima, with an encouraging caption: "Days later—with a single shattering blast over Southern Nippon—the war is ended!"

The ruins of Hiroshima and Nagasaki provide "a fitting end to the grim adventure that began at Pearl Harbor!" Further, the bombed cities quickly bounce back "just as if there'd never *been* a war!" Meanwhile, the Japanese-American woman who had found the bomb has become inspired to become a secret agent, and under the code name "Saigon" she infiltrates a gang of Japanese fanatics who intend to drop a more advanced nuclear bomb that they had invented on Washington, D.C., for revenge.

The Japanese atomic bomb aspect of this story may have been partly inspired by a 1946 newspaper story which made the sensational claim that Japanese scientists, working in Hungnam, Korea, had "developed and successfully tested an atomic bomb three days prior to the end of the war."[27] In a detail reminiscent of the secret atomic arms race between the U.S. and Japan in the "Black Avengers" comic book story, Robert K. Wilcox's book *Japan's Secret War* speculates that Truman had been informed of Japan's A-bomb research program when he was deciding to use the atomic bomb on Hiroshima.[28]

John W. Dower's review of the first edition of Wilcox's book for the *Bulletin of the Atomic Scientists* strongly reaffirms the consensus view that Japan's World War II efforts to develop nuclear weapons had been "low priority and small-scale activities, plagued by dire material shortages as well as fierce inter-service rivalries" which had no realistic hope of success.[29]

Koreans and Hiroshima

The seventh volume of Japanese cartoonist Keiji Nakazawa's epic manga about the Hiroshima bomb, *Barefoot Gen*, included an unusually long speech designed to teach his Japanese readers a Korean perspective on the horrors of the nuclear bomb.[30] Atomic bombs killed at least 10,000 Koreans in Hiroshima and Nagasaki.[31] Some of them had come to Japan looking for work, and many had been drafted by the Japanese (who held Korea as a colony) and sent to Hiroshima and Nagasaki to labor in the war industries.[32]

Nagasaki

The second use of an atomic bomb, on Nagasaki three days after the Hiroshima bombing, became the basis for Harvey Kurtzman's well-remembered seven-page story "Atom Bomb!" drawn by Wally Wood. It appeared in *Two-Fisted Tales #33* (May–June 1953). Kurtzman built the story around two pieces of correspondence that cross in the mail: a postcard from a Japanese soldier, dying in a "Siberian Slave camp" as a prisoner of the Russians, and a letter that his mother had sent, informing him of the deaths of his wife and son and daughter from the atom bomb (which was dropped by the United States, though the story assumes this as background knowledge and never mentions America)

The grandmother's concluding reflections prevent the story from being mistaken for anti–American communist propaganda:

> Are not the workings of fate strange! When Toshio left for the army ... we were all afraid that he would be killed by the war machines while we were safe at home! But **we** have been killed by the war machines and **he** has remained ... or **has** he? If he dies in Siberia, how different would it be from dying in Nagasaki?

The story's cheerful final panel shows a young boy with a full head of hair running to school while his grandmother walks away with a bowed head and men rebuild the city. The caption, perhaps a little too hastily and insistently, reads:

> On August 9, 1945, the A-Bomb killed 29,793 people and destroyed 18,409 homes! But **hope** was not destroyed in Nagasaki! And life nurtured by hope, blooms again! Plants, buildings, children grow in Nagasaki, for there is **hope** in Nagasaki! There is **hope** in the whole world![33]

EC Science Fiction

Harvey Kurtzman had emphasized hope and survival in his one war comic book story about nuclear weapons, but in EC's science fiction comics, the company's other editor-artist-writer, Al Feldstein, repeatedly represented nuclear weapons as causing the death of civilization (or of all life on earth.) The cover Feldstein drew for *Weird Fantasy #14* (July–August 1950) pictured aliens witnessing Earth being blown to bits by a "Cosmic Ray Bomb Explosion" whose mushroom cloud rises thousands of miles high. Next, Feldstein co-wrote and drew the story "Destruction of the Earth!" for *Weird Science #14* (September–October 1950), whose comic book cover showed aliens finding a lifeless planet on which a charred newspaper headline, poking from the rubble, reports that "U.S. Threatens to Use Hydrogen Bomb to End Atomic War." In that issue, officials dismiss the warnings of an atomic scientist that the proposed test of the new "Hydrogen Bomb" would throw the earth out of its orbit, and lead to our planet being sucked into the Sun by its gravitational field. The story turns out to be a school lesson about how the planet Earth ceased to exist, taught on Mars to a classroom of Martians.[34]

The United States tested its first thermonuclear device two years later, on November

1, 1952. The first deliverable thermonuclear bomb would be tested by the Soviet Union on August 12, 1953.

Feldstein returned to the theme with the cover of *Weird Science* #5 (January–February 1951). This one showed a rocket leaving Earth with another impossibly huge mushroom cloud rising in the background. The speech balloon coming from the rocket announces the beginning of an urgent search for another inhabitable planet: "We've escaped **just in time**! The **Atomic War** has started! All life on earth will be destroyed! Now we scientists must find another planet and begin civilization anew … one of **peace**, not of **war**!"

On the cover of the March–April 1953 *Weird Science #18*, flying saucers ring another enormous mushroom cloud. Kurtzman's hopeful Nagasaki story came out two months later.

Paul S. Hirsch's dissertation *Pulp Empire* put Feldstein's EC comic books in a class of their own for the insistence with which they condemned nuclear war:

> In the few years that *Weird Science* and *Weird Fantasy* appeared, practically every issue contained a reference to atomic power. […] [T]hese stories always ended with dreadful finality; someone had foolishly dared to tamper with the atomic bomb, and now he, along with millions of others, was dead. Quite simply, the atomic bomb was synonymous with The End.[35]

Civil Defense

Although many seemed to interpret the dawn of the nuclear age as a warning that people must turn away from war, the Bomb itself and the huge industrial infrastructure that had been required to bring it into existence had pulled Americans toward further militarization: of the government, the economy, and the culture.[36] As hopes for a new era of international cooperation wilted, more "practical" people focused, not on eliminating nuclear weapons, but on preparing for their terrible arrival over American cities. Several Civil Defense comic books were published to inform civilians about how to survive a nuclear war. As the eight-page comics format booklet *If an A-Bomb Falls,* distributed by Delaware's Department of Civil Defense (1951), explained:

> All of us earnestly hope that no enemy A-Bomb will ever fall on American soil [tacitly exempting from concern allied A-Bombs falling on enemy soil], but in spite of our efforts for peace, the ambitions of Communist dictators make the danger of an atomic attack on our cities a grave possibility. It is everyone's duty to be prepared, and to know what to do to insure the greatest protection….[37]

The comic advises those with superhuman leaping abilities and others what to do if an attack comes without warning: "If you see a brilliant flash, leap behind a bank, sturdy building or in a doorway. Always drop to the ground or floor and cover your head, if possible, and hide your face in the crook of your elbow." The narrator tells the reader that "A great deal has been said about the dangers of radioactivity from A-Bombs, yet there were far less casualties from it in Japan than from blast and burn." This comic concludes:

> It is true that atomic weapons are the most powerful and most destructive ever contrived by man. The key to survival of such explosions is proper shelter and the knowledge of what to do. By following the advice we have given, you will have a better chance to survive an atomic attack.

In 1953 and 1954, the Soviet Union and the United States began using fission-based "A-bombs" as triggers for fusion-based "H-bombs." In 1954, the United States tested a bomb a thousand times more powerful than the ones that had destroyed Hiroshima and Nagasaki.

The messages in Civil Defense comic books bravely continued to prepare Americans for World War III.

The H-Bomb and You, a 16-page comic book disguised with a wraparound cover to make it look like a serious pamphlet, was distributed to Washington, D.C., and Maryland residents from 1954 to 1956. The introduction signed by Maryland's Governor, Theodore McKeldin, argued that being prepared for an atomic attack might deter a would-be aggressor from launching one. Besides, he noted, "Preparation will prevent panic, create order among those who must maintain order and instill in each of us the will to go on to victory." In the story, a young student (perhaps an EC comics fan) asks "Won't everyone be killed?" and his teacher cautions him: "No, Johnny, don't ever believe such rumors. That is the kind of talk an enemy would have you believe!" She adds, "no matter what the weapon is, there is a defense against it. The best defense against the H-Bomb is a well-trained, alert Civil Defense to back up our military forces!"[38]

The comic recruits its young readers to volunteer for the Ground Observer Corps to join "Operation Skywatch" so they can phone in reports when they see enemy bombers that have penetrated our air defenses: "We need over a million American civilians—men, women, and boys and girls of ages varying with local policy—to give 2 to 4 hours each week in this important work!"

Most commercial war comics pretended that nuclear weapons did not exist. One of the exceptions was the five-page lecture-in-comic-book-format "Atomic Warfare" in *Combat Casey #19* (December 1954), drawn by Robert Q. Sale. Although typical of the Civil Defense comic book genre, it stuck out in an entertainment comic like *Combat Casey*. This feature begins with "a Korean War veteran, Private First Class Penny P. Pennington" (a character that had appeared in several previous stories) explaining to the reader that although "you" probably think of atomic war as "the end of the world," in fact: "...the atomic bomb *can't* destroy the world! Military tests on the deserts of the West have proven that an atomic explosion *can't* even destroy a division and all its equipment!"

Stating its propagandistic message directly, the comic pictures the dreadful fantasy of our planet cracking apart while a fiery mushroom cloud rises to a height twice the diameter of the Earth while its caption warns: "*Don't* believe the people who go around wailing that civilization will be wiped out ... that the Earth will be erased from the universe when and *if* an atomic war comes...." Nuclear weapons turn out to be a sane investment because, "as long as there are twisted minds of greedy, powerful lunatics like the Kaiser and Hitler, then those of us in our right minds have to find ways to stop them ... and ways to survive in the event the lunatics unleash the fury of an atomic war upon the world." Fortunately, "the good ol' reliable foxhole provides protection from *atomic blast* from as close as 800 yards!" As for nuclear radiation (the "least dangerous" effect after blast and heat): "Marines taking part in the atomic tests were able to move out of their foxholes a few minutes after an atomic burst without being affected by radiation...."

In conclusion, "it'll be rough, but it *won't* be the end of the world if an atomic war does come!" We might even get lucky: "There's always the hope that even the power-mad Commies *aren't crazy* enough to start an atomic war!"

The "Atomic Warfare" story confidently emphasizes that the soldiers who participated in the nuclear tests in Nevada were not harmed by being ordered out of their foxholes a few minutes after an atomic blast. For many years, this confidence was preserved by the government's decision to do no follow-up medical studies of the 250,000 military personnel who participated in nearly 200 atmospheric nuclear weapons tests that the U.S. conducted from

1945 to 1962.[39] In 1990, the Radiation Exposure Compensation Act was passed as an apology to those individuals who contracted certain cancers after being exposed to radiation in atmospheric nuclear tests and uranium mines and mills, and—as a less expensive alternative to court cases—to compensate them for their injuries with standard lump-sum payments.[40]

Atomic War! Entertainment Series

During the Korean War, a subgenre of war comics appeared that focused on imagining nuclear wars in the near future. These included *World War III* (predicting a nuclear war in 1960), *Atomic War!* (predicting a nuclear war in 1960), and *Atomic Attack* (predicting nuclear war for 1972). *Atom-Age Combat* also predicted a nuclear war, but without naming a date.

The first of these was *World War III #1* (March 1952). Its date of publication suggests that this extraordinary comic had been inspired by an extraordinary special issue of *Collier's* magazine the previous October, which was entirely dedicated to warning "the evil masters of the Russian people" not to move forward with their "vast conspiracy to enslave humanity" because it would lead to a war that would destroy them.[41] That magazine, with illustrations that included cartoons by Bill Mauldin, was written as an imaginary look back from the year 1960 to a war that had begun in May 1952, when "the West" responds to a Soviet attack on Yugoslavia by dropping atomic bombs on strategic targets "round the clock" for three and a half months.[42]

The high political and military officials that *Collier's* consulted while preparing this issue must have included some who were familiar with the U.S. military's secret "scenario planning" for nuclear war, including 1949's "Operation Dropshot" which imagined a war in 1957 in which the U.S. would drop 300 atomic bombs and prevail.[43]

Like the editors of *Collier's* in "Preview of the War We Do Not Want," the editors of *World War III: The War that Will Never Happen if America remains Strong and Alert*, state their purpose very seriously and directly. The first story begins:

> Let the reason for publishing this shocking account of World War III be completely clear. We want only to awaken America … and the world … to grim facts. The one way to prevent this mass destruction of humanity is to prepare NOW. Only a super-strong and fully enlightened America can stop this onrushing horror of the future!

This unusually grim comic book was written by Robert Turner, as he mentions in his breezy autobiography about his career as a writer of spicy stories, pulp magazine fiction, comic books, television, and "sex novels." Tellingly, Turner remembers *World War III* comics mostly for the page count and payment:

> From late 1950 to 1952, I turned out reams of scripts for the horror-type comics. […] The crime comics titles were a little less juicy. […] I also refought World War II in the comics with such heroic titles as "Decision on Devil's Ridge," "Operation Abracadabra" and others.[44] I even arranged World War *III*. I wrote two complete issues of a magazine called *World War III Comics*, thirty pages in each for five hundred dollars. Right now I don't recall whether this magazine was ever published or if it died aborning. I have a vague memory that it did come out, though, at least for one issue.[45]

Atom-Age Combat #1 (June 1952), a more fantasy-oriented nuclear war comic, begins with "Commandos Blitz a Red Invasion." The background of the Korean War and the North Atlantic Treaty Organization provided inspiration for this scene-setting beginning:

> Global aggression by the ruthless, Red Asians had plunged the freedom forces of the world to the brink of chaos! Their only hope rested on the striking power of the Atlantic Police Commandos! With a sneak attack, the Asians had seized the Galapagos Islands, strategic defense post guarding approaches to South America and the Panama Canal....

Six small mushroom clouds appear on the first page of the story. The two bare-chested heroes defeat the Red invaders. The rest of the stories in this comic book take place in Korea.

The second issue of *Atom-Age Combat* (November 1952) begins with a story that continues to put a science fiction spin on the stalemated Korean War. "Yellow Peril in the Skies" starts out:

> The full-scale war unleashed by the masters of the Red hordes had reached a sinister stalemate. Freedom loving forces of the Western World had turned back the Reds' mass attacks, but the brutal barbarians began a new and more insidious phase of warfare, spreading virus bacteria from mile-a-second flying saucers over America's west coast!

The "suicide squad" of "Atlantic Commandos" destroys the flying saucer base on the South China coast and its germ warfare bombs and survives to fight another day until "total victory" is achieved.

The same month that this second issue of *Atom-Age Combat* appeared, *Atomic War!* #1 (November 1952), from the same publishers as *World War III*, provided another serious nuclear war comic. Its cover shows a mushroom cloud rising over Manhattan, with the Chrysler Building and the Empire State Building falling over. The lead story, "Sneak Attack," is set eight years in the future. The slogan of the series warns that "Only a Strong America Can Prevent World War III." In this story, a gullible diplomat responds to a Russian call for peace by saying "We face a new future! The Russians really mean it this time! There isn't a doubt in my mind!" In the next panel, the Russians gloat in private that "The Western fools do not suspect a thing!" After some scenes of American complacency, the Russians treacherously send nuclear bombers to destroy New York City and Chicago, which the comic dramatizes with realistic detail. In answer to the question "why?" a captured Russian ("after prolonged questioning") says, "Our high command tell us they capture U.S. plans! Plans show our country to be attacked this week by atom bomb! We must attack first! That is all I know!" Rather than building to a conclusion that nuclear weapons must be eliminated because fear of a first strike invites preemptive war, the story concludes with an implication that the manufacture of nuclear weapons must be accelerated: "Look upon the pictures of our giant cities hundreds of years in the building, smashed by the Atom-Bomb, and say: This shall not come to pass! More than ever today, only a strong America can prevent this from becoming a reality!"

The third issue of this very serious series includes full page ads on the inside front and back covers for U.S. Defense Bonds, featuring the stories of Medal of Honor winners who fought in Korea. The ad space was "donated by this publication in cooperation with the Advertising Council and the Magazine Publishers of America."

The more disturbing comic books about nuclear wars in the future were not highly popular, as most people had a limited appetite for realistic stories on this subject. As a fantasy theme, though, the incredible power of nuclear weapons continued to stimulate the imagination for many years. The full-page ad on the back cover of the April–May 1966 issue of Charlton's *Marine War Heroes* ("Special Issue: The Complete Action-packed History of the Korean War") offered a fiberboard "Polaris Nuclear Sub Over 7 Feet Long" for $6.98. The advertisement asked young readers to imagine: "What hours of imaginative play and fun as you and your friends dive, surface, maneuver, watch the enemy through the periscope and fire your nuclear missiles and torpedoes!"

The Bomb and the Korean War

At his first meeting to discuss the North Korean invasion of South Korea, held on June 25, 1950, Truman asked his advisors if the Air Force could "take out" Soviet air bases near Korea and was told that it could be done with atomic bombs. He ordered preparations for launching an atomic attack on the Soviet Union if it entered the war.[46] Before the end of that July, the CIA had prepared a report on "Utilization of Atomic Bombardment to Assist in Accomplishment of the U.S. Objectives in South Korea"; the Army had prepared a study of "Employment of Atomic Bombs Against Military Targets" suggesting their possible use against ports or enemy air bases; General MacArthur had visualized using an atomic bomb to cut off the bridges and tunnels that the Chinese or Russians would use if they intervened; a shipment was authorized to send the non-nuclear components for ten atomic bombs to Guam; and planes configured to carry nuclear bombs were sent to England as preparation for possible escalation to a war with the Soviet Union.[47] Plans to use atomic bombs stalled because of international anti-nuclear sentiment and because no appropriate targets could be found in North Korea that would not have spillover effects in China and the Soviet Union.[48] Also, using nuclear weapons in Korea probably would have shattered the NATO military alliance in Europe.[49]

One result of American atomic saber-rattling was that both China and North Korea went on to develop their own nuclear weapons. These programs were in response to both U.S. nuclear threats during the Korean War and to continuing American nuclear threats after that war.[50] Although much of the news coverage of Korea in U.S. media in recent years has focused on the issue of "denuclearization," North Korean proposals for how to achieve this have generally been treated as beneath discussion.[51]

Roger Dingman's study of nuclear weapons and the Korean War concluded that:

> The Korean War ended [...] as it had begun, with not a single American nuclear weapon deployed within usable distance of the fighting. That state of affairs encapsulated one important truth, namely, that Washington never came close to tactical use of the atomic bomb in Korea. But it obscured another equally vital one: American statesmen repeatedly attempted to use nuclear weapons as tools with which to manage the politics and diplomacy of the war.

Between the bombing of Nagasaki at the end of World War II and the beginning of the Korean War, President Truman had made a nuclear threat to force the Soviet Union out of northern Iran in 1946.[52] The pattern already established, the United States went on to "use" nuclear weapons many more times in the same sense that someone "uses" a gun when they point it and make a threat but do not fire it.[53]

Nuclear Danger

Although Civil Defense comic books of the early 1950s had warned against defeatist susceptibility to enemy propaganda claims about the apocalyptic nature of nuclear weapons, the public's fear that nuclear war could mean the end of civilization eventually received some scientific confirmation with the discovery of the possibility of a "nuclear winter." The nuclear winter idea predicts that a nuclear war could raise enough smoke and dust to block the sun for months or years, making the world cold and dark. In 1984, a graph illustrating Carl Sagan's chapter on the atmospheric effects of a nuclear war showed that when the Korean War began, the climate was "not at known risk" from the existing nuclear arsenals, but as the American nuclear arsenal skyrocketed during that war, a risk of climate disaster from nuclear war appeared, and by the mid–1950s, a climatic catastrophe would be "expected" in the case of nuclear war.[54]

Around the time when the first "nuclear winter" studies were published, an international movement had been clamoring for a "freeze on testing, production, and further deployment of nuclear weapons." Huge protests demanding an end to the nuclear arms race were held in New York City (with almost a million participants, one of the largest political demonstrations in U.S. history), Bonn, Brussels, London, Paris, Rome and Amsterdam.[55] Shortly after this, the nuclear arms race, which had been running since 1949, suddenly reversed, and the number of nuclear weapons held by the Soviet Union dropped as quickly as it had risen.

President Reagan said in 1985:

A great many reputable scientists are telling us that [a nuclear war] could just end up in no victory for anyone because it would wipe out the earth as we know it. [...] If one volcano can [change the weather so much], what are we talking about with the whole nuclear exchange, the nuclear winter that scientists have been talking about?

Mikhail Gorbachev recalled in an interview in 2000:

Models made by Russian and American scientists showed that a nuclear war would result in a nuclear winter that would be extremely destructive to all life on earth; the knowledge of that was a great stimulus to us, to people of honour and morality, to act.[56]

The "nuclear winter" scenarios were gradually confirmed and refined through normal scientific discussion, but also vehemently attacked as "a pernicious fantasy," enemy "propaganda," "Soviet disinformation," "a fraud from the start," and a "hoax," by those who feared that accepting nuclear winter as a possibility would make American threats to use nuclear weapons unbelievable.[57] In 2008, one updated report on the "Environmental Consequences of Nuclear War" concluded that "modern climate models confirm that the 1980s prediction of nuclear-winter effects were, if anything, underestimates."[58]

A Limited War

Because the United States did not use atom bombs in Korea, and because the war did not trigger a nuclear exchange between the U.S. and Russia, the impression from afar has been that the Korean War was a "limited war." One of the great anxieties of the time was that the Korean War was either a prelude to World War III or a sign that World War III had already begun.[59] On May 3, 1954, in Charles Schulz's *Peanuts* comic strip, Shermy commented on Charlie Brown's comic book collection. Over three panels, Shermy says, "You have a terrific comic book collection, Charlie Brown. [...] 'Revolutionary War Comics,' 'War of 1812 Comics,' 'Civil War Comics,' 'World War I Comics.' [...] 'World War II Comics,' 'Korean War Comics'".... In panel four, Charlie Brown says: "The next issue has really got me worried."

From the perspective of Koreans, it was an absolutely devastating war. The bombs at Hiroshima and Nagasaki killed 210,000 people (or more, by some estimates), which amounted to ten percent of the total number of Japanese military and civilian deaths from 1937 to 1945, and in less than a week.[60] By comparison, the destruction in Korea, where no nuclear bombs were used, may have killed more people than Japan lost in all of World War II.[61] The total explosive yield of the bombs that the U.S. dropped on North Korea was comparable to 40 Hiroshima bombs.[62]

North Koreans have lived for generations under American threats of nuclear annihilation. As East Asia scholar Gavan McCormack noted in 2003,

> starting with the Korean War in the early 1950s, when the US went so far as to dispatch solitary B-29 bombers to Pyongyang on simulated nuclear bombing missions designed to cause terror, Pyongyang has always viewed its nuclear programs as a response to a perceived US nuclear threat. The North Korean government still takes the view, not unreasonably, that the only defense Washington respects is nuclear weapons....[63]

The Bomb and Democracy

After World War II, continued reliance on nuclear weapons was defended as necessary to protect democracy, and yet the Bomb threatened to make democracy impossible. In August 1945, atomic scientist Dr. Harold C. Urey warned: "I do not see any way to keep our democratic form of government if everybody has atomic bombs. [...] If everyone has them, it will be necessary for our government to move quickly in a manner not now possible under our diffused form of government."[64]

Besides concentrating nuclear war-making power in the hands of the president, nuclear weapons threatened U.S. democracy in other ways. In 1950, writer and culture critic Gilbert Seldes discussed the new burdens that the existence of nuclear weapons placed on the mass media and their audiences. On the one hand, if mass media do not prepare citizens to take an active role in making informed decisions about the hydrogen bomb, but prepare them instead to "acquiesce, without question, in any decision made," this would mark "a step towards the authoritarian state, losing our rights and our responsibility." On the other hand,

> If the decision is brought to us, have we the qualities of mind and character to understand the problem and to find a good answer? Considering our absorption in mass media, can the problem be fully exposed without the use of radio, the movies, television, and comic books? Are these media capable of conveying the problem intelligently to us, and are we capable of receiving it from them?[65]

Seldes proposed that in a nuclear age, appropriate action must begin with the recognition that mass media (including comic books, which he mentioned several times, but only in passing) can create a dangerous cultural climate which threatens us all: "Nothing effective can be done so long as the old concept of a purely personal relationship between the citizen and his diversions remains unchallenged."[66]

18

◇◇◇◇◇◇◇◇◇◇

Subversive Comics

One of the limits that federal law placed on the content of Korean War comic books was that they could not intentionally damage the country's military effort.[1] During the Korean War, the question of whether some war comics were seditiously damaging the war effort came up in a secret criminal investigation in which the Army, the FBI and the Department of Justice participated. In a different, well-publicized case, a Navy base in California announced a boycott of comic books that it called "subversive" and a threat to morale. The Navy boycott apparently succeeded in intimidating the main publisher of war comics into drastically changing the way that its comics represented the Korean War (and war in general) for many years afterward.

By comparison to that period's blacklisting of communists from the film industry, radio and television broadcasting, concern about the possibility of subversives in the comic book industry played only a small role.[2] Still, the government had to rule out the possibility that comic books about the horrors of war were being published to promote the goals of the communist conspiracy. Also, some people with less stringent definitions of "subversive" than the one used by Department of Justice lawyers argued that comic books might be subverting the foundations of America's national strength, either intentionally or as a side effect of their publishers' search for profit.

Beginning in December 1951, people on army bases "from throughout the United States and overseas" had been forwarding copies of *Man Comics* (published by the company now known as Marvel) and EC's *Two-Fisted Tales* and *Frontline Combat* to G-2, the Army's intelligence department. The December 1951 issue of *Man Comics #11* featured on its cover the Hank Chapman story "Cannon Fodder."[3] Typical of Chapman's extraordinary work, "Cannon Fodder" featured a flood of attacking Reds ("Jen Hai … the human sea"), a protagonist who is "sore at the whole blasted army," and a conclusion that ends in death rather than victory. The final lines of the story are, "In a war *every* soldier is *cannon fodder* … whether he be a clerk, a truck-driver, pilot, doughfoot … or a *Four Star General!* The dog-tags nailed to fields of white crosses in Korea are grim reminders of this!"[4]

The Army notified the FBI in a letter dated April 29, 1952, that:

a review of the contents of these comic books reveals that some of the material is detrimental to the morale of combat soldiers and emphasizes the horrors, hardships and futility of war. These comic books portray the seemingly needless sacrifices due to blunders on the part of officers and demonstrate the lack of protection to the United States forces against the trickery of the enemy. G-2 considers these publications subversive because they tend to discredit the army and undermine troop morale by presenting a picture of the inevitability of personal disaster in combat.[5]

In this same letter, the Army, suspecting that EC's comic books might violate the Sedition Statutes, requested the FBI to also look into the background of EC's editor Harvey Kurtzman and publisher William Gaines, and to collect "background information which might be of assistance in determining the true purposes of the publications." They also asked for the names, addresses and military status of "any members of the Armed Forces [who] have received copies of these comic books."[6]

The crucial legal question was to determine not *whether* the content of the comics was demoralizing, but *why* people were distributing such grim comic books. Meanwhile, the Navy had also acted against "subversive" war comics.

The Navy's ban on morale-damaging war comics was described in a three-paragraph section on "War Horror Comics" in a 1952 Senate committee report. That report raised the question of whether some comic books might be "the subversive efforts of Communists" to interfere with the Korean War effort. In doing so, the report also pointed to the importance of enlisted men as a market for war comic books, and, approvingly, to the power that this gave the military to steer the content of commercially distributed comic books away from anti-war material:

> The mutations that have been wrought in the name of "comics" by profit-minded publishers are well illustrated by books classified in the trade under the anomalous designation "War Horror Comics."
>
> It has been brought to the committee's attention that the entire output of one such promoter had been officially banned from distribution among United States Navy personnel because some of the contents were deemed contrary to the best interests of our country. Specifically, it was charged that their objectionable features might be the work of a genuine pacifist organization, but they were much more likely the subversive efforts of Communists. The publishers have admitted that some of their stories were unconventional, but blamed the editor's poor judgement for their inclusion. "They were not pleasant reading," according to the publishers.
>
> One highly salutary effect has been the assurance of the publishers that all gory and pacifist features have been removed from their product.[7]

In his book *Seduction of the Innocent*, Fredric Wertham found another message in what seems to have been the same incident: "If these war comics which are widely read by children are too "gory" for sailors in an actual war, why is it permitted to display and sell them to boys and girls of six and seven?"[8]

The most helpful identifying clues for identifying the comic book that sparked this incident appeared in newspaper stories that were published in August 1952. The *San Francisco Chronicle* reported that:

> Two comic books were removed from sale in Navy stores at Moffett Field yesterday on grounds they are subversive, and contain material injurious "to the morale of men in Korea."
>
> Moffett Field spokesmen refused to disclose the titles of the books or the number of copies taken off the stands because that information, they said, is "classified" and not available to the public.
>
> They described the books as "stressing fear," and cited as an example one comic book panel showing two servicemen on grave digging detail.
>
> One says to the other, "All I've done since I'm out here in Korea is burying my buddies." The other replies, "Better than being shot at the front."
>
> Moffett Field spokesmen said the two books were termed "subversive" comics on a list compiled by the Twelfth Naval District Intelligence officer.
>
> […]
>
> Navy spokesmen would not confirm or deny the comic book ban of two months ago described by [comic book distributor W.J. Seeley, of the Golden Gate Magazine Co.][9]

Most comic book fans' first guess might be that the publisher of the controversial comic books had been EC. The July–August 1952 issue of EC's *Frontline Combat* (the issue on newsstands during this ban) had printed responses to "Miss" Margaret M. Credie's previously published letter criticizing *Frontline Combat*'s "gloomy" approach. Credie had written:

> It's far too gruesome to help anyone's morale—man, woman or child! [...] I realize that many of your readers are adults, but won't you please think of the younger generation when you print funny books. Perhaps YOUR minds can take those gruesome picture stories you print, but a good many people need a cheerful tonic of joy to help them.[10]

Several pieces of evidence point toward EC. For one thing, a letter survived in the files of EC editor Harvey Kurtzman responding to an as-yet-undiscovered earlier newspaper article about this censorship:

> August 1, 1952
>
> Dear Dave,
>
> Thank you for your letter and attached newspaper article!
> It has caused quite a disturbance here since this clipping is the first such criticism we have *ever* received.
> The same article wasn't printed in the New York papers to our knowledge and we would like very much to get in touch with the newspaper from which you took the clipping. Perhaps they can direct us to the Naval authorities who objected to our books.
> We would appreciate it if you'd mail us the name and address of the newspaper in the enclosed return envelope....[11]

Nevertheless, the complete EC war comics have been republished and contain no scene similar to the one described in the *San Francisco Chronicle*'s article. Apparently, the "Dave" who wrote to Kurtzman in 1952 jumped to a false conclusion that EC's comic books were the unnamed comics that the Navy had banned.

Members of the Timely/Atlas Yahoo newsgroup have identified one of the allegedly "subversive" comics banned by the Navy as *War Combat #3* (July 1952).[12] The quoted dialogue in the newspaper article is a simplification of the opening scene of the four-page story "The Final Grave," written by Hank Chapman and illustrated by Joe Sinnott:

> (First GI, in a hole in the foreground, referring to a soldier seen fighting and dying in the three previous panels):
> "An' now it's up to me to dig a hole for him! That's all I've been doing ever since the Army plopped me on this stinkin' peninsula!"
> (Second GI, replying with back to us, digging another hole, right midground):
> "Don't go flippin' your lid again, Corkin! This ain't exactly the kind of Army life that the Recruitin' posters promised, but it's a lot better than carvin' out a foxhole at the front an' dodgin' lead spitballs at the same time!"[13]

In the story's conclusion, the disgruntled GI is transferred to the front, where he refuses to dig a foxhole ("Let the other suckers dig if they wanna ... but not this boy! I got in enough shovel-time back at that G.I. cemetery to last me for the duration plus!") For not digging in, the character ends up face down in the mud with eight red spots on his back showing the places where he had been fatally hit.

Dutch researcher Ger Apeldoorn describes writer Hank Chapman's work this way:

> Starting from late 1951, Chapman wrote nothing but war stories. ... They illustrate the cruelty of war, but take the necessity of it as a given. So in Chapman's stories we have a lot of soldiers dying for their country heroically or just as often needlessly, parents getting letters about their sons dying, soldiers killing each other ... and ships going down due to mis-communication or stupidity.[14]

The *War Combat* series that had published "The Final Grave" ended quickly, after two more issues.[15] The message that the Navy sent about not endangering the war effort seems to have lasted much longer. In 1967, Stan Lee (editor of Marvel's comic books from 1941 to 1972) became furious with writer Roy Thomas over a small political button that one of the characters in one panel of the first issue of Marvel's *Not Brand Echh* was wearing on his hat: a picture of a mushroom cloud with the words "All the Way with LBJ." The argument had quickly heated up to the point where Thomas (who was "*not* anti-war") threatened to quit and then it quickly cooled down again. Then Stan Lee apologized and explained his over-reaction. Roy Thomas's memory of the occasion is worth quoting at length, partly because of Stan Lee's important role in comic book history as editor and writer, partly because the company Lee worked for dominated the war comics genre, and partly because of how well this story illustrates that war comics have been shaped by something more than the preferences of their readers:

> He spoke of comic books' severe problems during the 1950s ... not the establishment of the Comics Code and its review board per se, or even the furor over horror and crime comics, but problems specifically related to war comics. In those days before and after the 1953 truce that ended the Korean War, Timely, like EC and a number of other companies, had published comics set during that conflict. Some had starred continuing heroes, like *Combat Kelly*, but others had featured one-off stories that showed the grimmer, grittier side of war ... at least so far as it was likely to be portrayed in a kids' comic book of that era. The message at stories' end had often been that war is no damn good, or even tragic ... but never that the US or UN forces were violating anyone's sovereignty in Korea, or murdering civilians ... certainly not any kind of "anti-war" statement in the vein of the Vietnam protesters, the so-called "peace-niks." Even so, some of the '50s story endings had been real downers, with brave American soldiers dying, or at least slogging wearily through the mud to fight another day. Since our government proclaimed that it, too, hated war, Stan said he felt that kind of message was in line with the approved view, and that's precisely where he'd wanted to be.
>
> To its horror, however, Timely Comics—which meant publisher Martin Goodman—had soon discovered that its war comics, or maybe it was *all* its comics, were no longer being sold in PX's, those stores on armed-services bases where men in uniform went to buy their candy and cigarettes, to shoot pool, to hang out. A ban of that kind entailed a serious loss of revenue for any comics company ... even as it fed the growing public perception, stoked by Dr. Wertham and his ilk, that comics were bad, *evil* ... not just for children, but even for adult servicemen.
>
> And so, Stan said, when he'd spied that "All the way with LBJ"/mushroom cloud button.... Well, it had sort of pushed *his* buttons, and made him see visions of the wrath of self-appointed do-gooders again descending upon the collective head of the comic book industry.[16]

Thomas (who would succeed Stan Lee as editor-in-chief of Marvel Comics in 1972) accepted Lee's apology, and promised to be very careful to see that "neither I, nor anyone else, put anything of that type into an issue":

> After all, we were in the business of entertainment, not politics. And what went into a Marvel comic was ultimately Stan's responsibility—with everybody's jobs ultimately on the line if sales were adversely affected. If there'd been trouble with the government or over-zealous critics and censors, Martin Goodman would've been after Stan's head on a platter, not mine. I was too far down the food chain to even be noticed![17]

After his publisher had promised to remove "all gory and pacifist features" from their comic books, Chapman's work changed greatly. Ger Apeldoorn noted that after "The Final Grave," Chapman "also wrote a lot of gung-ho stories, about brave soldiers fighting the Communists and winning in the most remarkable way. Two of the heroes he created in that vein were *Combat Kelly* and *Combat Casey* [and their deeds] got more heroic and fantastical as the years went on."[18]

In his response to "Dave," Harvey Kurtzman had referred to the misinformation that the Navy had attacked his comics as "the first such criticism we have *ever* received."

Kurtzman, then, was likely unaware that Army Intelligence was keeping files on him, that the FBI had been investigating him, and that the Justice Department had not yet decided whether to charge him with sedition based on the war comics he edited. That December, the Department of Justice finally advised the FBI that they could not prove that Kurtzman and Gaines intended to harm the military effort, and "that in the absence of proof beyond a reasonable doubt of such specific intent on their part prosecution under the sedition statute is not warranted."[19]

If Kurtzman or Gaines had *intended* for their comic books to "interfere with, impair, or influence the loyalty, morale, or discipline of the military or naval forces of the United States" by distributing a publication that "advises, counsels, or urges insubordination, disloyalty, mutiny, or refusal of duty by any member of the military or naval forces of the United States," they could have been fined more than $10,000 and sentenced to up to ten years in prison.[20]

Fredric Wertham, the leader of the anti–comic book movement, saved some letters that warned that comic books might be subversive.

For example, one man wrote to him:

> This is planned and deliberate subversion by means of psychological "brainwashing." I don't mean to sound dramatic, or to have brought upon me the much-repeated and tiresome phrase, "seeing Reds under the bed." But I do think that there is much more behind the staggering volume of cheap literature and lurid comic books than profit and profit alone.[21]

Although Wertham had a habit of adding into his anti-comic book arguments any suggestion that he found reasonable, he remained unimpressed by the idea that American comic books were (in spite of their anti-communist propagandizing) actually part of a subversive communist plot to corrupt American youth. In fact, Wertham regarded his *own* intentions as subversive of an oppressive social order. A 1946 article quoted Wertham as frequently telling people it is "far better to be subversive than subservient."[22] Rather than trying to "help adjust people to a vicious environment," Wertham's "subversive" goal was to "give [his patients] the best in psychiatric care to help build strong citizens, fighters against this debilitating ghetto!"[23]

Far from Wertham's Harlem clinic, in Bellville, Texas (a town with a population that had recently soared past 2,000), Kay Zeiske campaigned vigorously against "subversive comics." Zeiske, the wife of the local newspaper publisher, had been alerted to the threat of comic books by Fredric Wertham's article in the November 1953 issue of *Ladies Home Journal*. A page one article in *The Bellville Times* of December 10, 1953, reported that as part of an animated, two-hour discussion of comic books at the Tri-County PTA meeting "She showed how [Wertham's] article brought out the perverting effect of so-called comic books which teach young people how to commit burglaries, sex crimes and murder, and create a disrespect for law and a cynical disregard of the traditions of American democracy."[24] The participants in the discussion generally agreed that "some of these books appear to be intentionally subversive to American ideals," and, for the benefit of the elementary and high school students present, defined subversive: "SUBVERT: To turn upside down, completely overthrow, or ruin, as a government, or a man's principles."

The organizations represented at the meeting "pledged to fight the evil, principally by the use of Christian principles of decency." The Council also went on record as "opposing the sale of obscene, crime, and subversive intent comic books, and to take steps to curtail the distribution in local communities."[25]

When Zeiske learned of the planned federal hearings on crime comic books, she urged her readers to become involved because "Senators can not be expected to carry this investigation or fight against subversive comic books unless we grass roots people want it and fight this evil too."[26]

One suggestion that communists would use comic books for subversion was made by an anti-communist who had once served on the National Committee of the Communist Party. On March 10, 1953, Dr. Bella V. Dodd testified that

> There is no doubt in my mind that the Communists will use the schools and every other educational medium, whether it be comic books or the radio and television; they will use every educational medium.

Dodd was variously reported to have claimed that seventy, seventy-five, eighty, or eighty-five percent of the comic book printed in the United States were being financed by Communist interests. One reader wrote to an editor to share his opinion that this "very important point" had not received sufficient attention. Another, though, wondered whether Dodd could provide any basis for this "highly questionable statement."[27]

Still, it seems doubtful that the Communist Party of the United States seriously considered the revolutionary possibilities of the comic book medium. Communists found American comic books more valuable as damning proof of the inferiority of American popular culture than as a potential medium for communicating their own subversive views.

The communists' leading voice on issues of popular culture was V.J. Jerome, and in 1947 he mentioned "children's comic magazines" once, as an expression of "the cult of brutality, violence, and fascist anti-humanism" which reaches "its lowest depths in its systematic spiritual debasement of our children."[28]

In Jerome's 1951 pamphlet *Grasp the Weapon of Culture!*, a comic book appears on a long list of "bourgeois" mass media experiences: "The worker sits down to read—a Western or a comic book, in which Bugs Bunny becomes the captor of a 'spy ring'; or a homicidal hair-raiser with a tough agency dick as hero—slick thrillers—glorifying violence, brutality, and war."[29]

When Jerome urged that communists "grasp the weapon of culture" and create something better than the "racist, brutalizing, and pornographic output that is ballyhooed as 'art' and 'cultural' amusement" (that is, something "vibrant with the Party spirit, the very essence of Socialist realism"), he apparently did not imagine that comic-book makers would have a part in that cultural project.[30] As the chair of the Communist Party's cultural commission, Jerome was convicted, with a dozen other Communist leaders, of conspiring to advocate the violent overthrow of the government at some unspecified point in the future. Their appeals failed, and Jerome was imprisoned for three years.[31]

The well-known Senate Subcommittee Hearings on comic books and juvenile delinquency touched only briefly on the issue of "subversion." The Committee's Chief Counsel, Herbert Wilson Beaser, asked Richard Clendenen, the Committee's Executive Director, whether his investigation had turned up "any evidence of subversion in the use of comics, crime and horror comics." Clendenen answered that they had not found "a deliberate and planned effort to use the crime comics as a medium through which you are going to subvert the minds and morals of youngsters." He went on to promise that they intended to investigate war comics and other genres to search for evidence of deliberate subversion:

> ...we have not gone into war comics, love comics, jungle comics, and the many other varieties of comics.

Now, we do plan and will be looking further at some of these other types of comics. They will be subject to careful evaluation and certainly, Mr. Beaser, we will be looking for such evidence of subversion in the course of that exploration.[32]

Such an investigation of comic books (and their editors, writers and artists) had already been completed the previous year. According to an FBI document:

> The Department of Justice advised on December 9, 1953 that 30 comic books which were published in 1952 by 14 companies [redacted] were studied and analyzed by the Criminal Division in conjunction with Bureau reports which were submitted concerning [redacted] as well as the editor of the comic books, and numerous other individuals whose stories and illustrations appeared in the comic books.
>
> The Department stated that this review has failed to disclose any evidence that the subjects of the investigation had the required specific intent toward the acts prescribed [sic] by Section 2387 and 2388 of Title 18, U.S.C.[33]

Sections 2387 and 2388 of the laws regarding "Treason, Sedition, and Subversive Activities" focused on "Activities affecting armed forces generally" and "Activities affecting armed services during war."

The issue of "subversion" in the comic book debate usually expressed anxieties about a national descent into "moral rot," "decadence" and "degeneracy" rather than a specific fear of communism. For example, an article by the influential journalist Dorothy Thompson, "'Comic Books' Subversive," published in response to the 1954 Comic Book Hearings in New York, warned that America's "lewd and brutalitarian" comic books, like "termites, go on gnawing away the foundations of civilization, culture and morality, in the name of 'freedom,' and for the sake of the profits of filth."[34]

19

◇◇◇◇◇◇◇◇◇

The Korean War
in Comics Since 1953

The American comic book industry came crashing down not long after the ceasefire in Korea. Controversy over wild comic book content had led many mothers of young children to ban comic books from their homes. At the same time, conforming to the new Comics Code made many of the surviving comics too tame for their older readers. Television arrived as a replacement. The distributor of more than half of the comic books on the newsstands, the American News Company, suddenly stopped carrying comic books in 1957. A few comics, notably *Walt Disney's Comics and Stories* and *Little Lulu*, survived in this period to enjoy terrific success with stories of lasting entertainment value, but an era had ended.

War comics struggled on, but on a smaller scale. As the bitterness of the Korean War faded from memory, most comic book stories set against that background celebrated military heroism and minimized the horrors even further. The remaining U.S. war comics focused their attention mainly on World War II in Western Europe, and the most commercially successful war comics of the 1960s featured characters whose names in the title assured their survival from one issue to the next: Sgt. Rock and Sgt. Fury.

In the 1960s, a new generation of professional historians, responding to the tragedy in Vietnam, "revised" the story of the Cold War that had first been written by American officials.[1] In most comic books, though, rather than becoming more nuanced, factual, detailed, or critical, the image of the Korean War if anything hardened into an ever-simpler reaffirmation of American righteousness. Those who tried to do something different in war comics found various obstacles raised by people who objected to any stories that might interfere with military recruitment. Reviewing some of these later stories in which the Korean War plays a central or a peripheral role shows the comic book medium falling short as an arena where diverse views can be expressed on a regular basis, but also uncovers some irregular works that shine as examples of what comics have achieved. The examples in this chapter also serve to illustrate some of the main currents in the development of comics, from the superhero revivals to underground comix to alternative comics to graphic novels to webcomics, as well as educational comics for studying history. The move to book format and to book distribution channels, the increasingly international production and circulation of graphic novels, and the invention of webcomics have helped to broaden the range of views expressed through comics.

185

EC

EC comics had marked "the very happy ending of hostilities in Korea" by cancelling one of its war comics and turning the other into an "adventure" comic. Harvey Kurtzman told his readers:

> After a successful run, and towards the end of the Korean conflict, our circulation began to sag, finally reaching the point where our expenses far exceeded our income. And so, with a truce in Korea, we've regretfully decided that it's time for the end of the war mags. We've decided to turn down the flame of Two-Fisted Tales, and to snuff out Frontline Combat.[2]

In the previous issue, Managing Editor William M. Gaines had announced that *Two-Fisted Tales* would be changing from bi-monthly to a quarterly publication schedule because editor Kurtzman was "not yet recovered from the siege of yellow jaundice that hospitalized him for several months" and was overwhelmed by the "exhausting and inconceivably time-consuming" work of researching and creating two war comics plus his new humor magazine, *MAD.*

When *Two-Fisted Tales* went quarterly, Colin Dawkins became the writer of all its stories and text pieces. Rather than doing research as Kurtzman had done, Dawkins wrote the comics in his spare evenings, drawing on his imagination to fill out ideas that he discussed with the title's conservative new editor, John Severin.[3] At the same time, Dawkins had a full-time job as a copywriter on the Ford account for the prestigious J. Walter Thompson advertising agency.[4] Dawkins created a series of stories for *Two-Fisted Tales* about "Ruby Ed Coffey." He later remembered the character as:

> ...designed specifically and consciously as Daddy Warbucks and his gang without Little Orphan Annie. Daddy Warbucks always fascinated me as a character, so I redesigned him and made him the world's richest man fighting a private war against the communists and evil, just as Daddy Warbucks did.[5]

Marvel "Commie Smashers"

At the time of the Korean War ceasefire, Marvel was planning a superhero revival, which would result in 23 issues of comic books beginning in fall 1953. These comics pitted World War II heroes Captain America, the Human Torch, and the Sub-Mariner against communist villains.

One example of this failed superhero revival, "Kill Captain America," begins when the Reds announce that their top goal worldwide is to kill Captain America. This story, drawn by John Romita, takes place in Korea, where "some die-hard Reds still haven't given up!" Captain America's immediate problem concerns the attitude of one of the returning American prisoners of war: "They're all happy except Pfc. Tim Potter! There's something funny about that boy ... and I don't like it!" Then we hear Tim say, "I'm glad this is over.... I don't want any more war! I've had enough ... and my nerves are shot! If the Reds started it all over again, I wouldn't lift a finger to fight back!"

The question for Captain America is whether this kind of talk merely represents the temporary effects of the dope that the Reds had drugged him with to sap his strength and weaken his fighting spirit, or whether their narcotics have really changed him into a Red. In this story, expressing an anti-war attitude rather than an eager willingness to keep fighting—even while being repatriated, exhausted, from a POW camp—raises suspicion of disloyalty.[6]

In a different comic book published that same month, Captain America was sent to Korea on a special mission to save Red prisoners dying in the UN prison camps. We over-hear the enemy, in his "hidden cellar in Washington," explain, "We planted the poison in the food of our own soldiers in the prison camps, just so we could accuse the U.N. of mistreat-ing them! We want them to die, as long as we can make a [propaganda] case out of it before the world ... and Captain America is not going to spoil it for us!"

The enemy's plans to destroy Captain America before he can reach the sick prison-ers in Korea fail, and Captain America holds the Red prisoners still so the camp doctor can inject them all with a life-saving drug. When the prisoners see that the drug has made them well rather than poisoned them, the Red POWs who had trapped Captain America and Bucky inside the fenced enclosure stop battling against them and bow in apology. Captain America concludes the story with a moral: "Now if we can only teach them the rest of the real truth! That their own masters are the real killers ... and that the United Nations are the only ones who can cure what ails them ... with freedom and democracy!"[7]

In the next issue, the Human Torch and his boy sidekick Toro "blazed to North Korea after the end of the war to find out if the Commies were lying when they said they weren't holding back any of our G.I. prisoners!"[8] Of course they were lying, and the superheroes free a hundred unreported prisoners from the "Redskis," the "Scummies," the "Commies." One communist exclaims when he sees what they have done, "In the name of Buddha! The tank is melting!" A communist also calls out "In the name of the Buddha" in another Human Torch story, "In Korea," where they save a captured American general who holds "the secret of the atomic cannon."[9] (The M65 atomic cannon was an actual American weapon, which had been tested the previous year. Although the armistice agreement had forbidden the introduction of nuclear weapons in Korea, the United States deployed the atomic cannon in South Korea in 1958.[10])

These heavy-handed, propagandistic comics sold poorly, and were cancelled at a time when the comic book industry in general was shrinking quickly. Stan Lee told comic book artist John Romita that the "Captain America: Commie Smasher" series had been cancelled "because of the backlash of the Korean War," which had made Captain America a "dirty name."[11]

Communist and leftist parents in the United States were especially unhappy with these comic books. Ronald Radosh has described the comics policy at the trade unionist Camp Wo-Chi-Ca (Worker's Children's Camp):

> The camp [...] took "culture" seriously; that meant no comic books at Wo-Chi-Ca. The campers sol-emnly recited, "We pledge ourselves to combat the influence of jokes, comic books, newspapers, radio programs that make fun of any people." During the great 1950s comic-book scare, in which a left-wing psychologist [sic] named Dr. Frederick [sic] Wertham testified before Congress on the evil effects of superhero comics, the camp's yearbook proudly reported that the campers were asked to turn in all their comics. It was important that Wo-Chi-Ca campers not be influenced by whatever patriotic atti-tudes they might inadvertently pick up from a pro–American superhero such as "Captain America."[12]

Marvel's parent company began a series of "men's magazines" which picked up from where the war comics had left off, and these magazines became the company's biggest suc-cess.[13] The magazines typically combined military and sexual themes, and eventually started to come up with cover blurbs that combined the two, attracting readers with such features as "Shanghai's Bawdy House Spies: The Streetwalkers Who Seduced an Army"; "WWII's Strangest Story: The G.I. Secret in the French Girl's Bedroom"; "To Capture Asia's No. 1 Red

Bandit.... They Baited the Trap with Suzy 'Lucky-Hips'"; "Yank Who Flew 20 Playgirls out of Red China"; "Queen of the Commie Call-Girls"; and so forth.[14]

These magazines focused mostly on World War II. Mario Puzo, who would go on to fame as the author of *The Godfather*, wrote war stories for *Male* and *Men*. Although he wrote several stories about Vietnam, Puzo found that "They were absolute poison. Readers hated it. Also, we weren't the heroes. Just like the Korean War. We used to call that The No Fun War. World War II was The Fun War. And you could get some mileage out of the Civil War and World War I."[15]

The editor of these men's magazines, Korean War veteran Bruce Jay Friedman, later remembered that the publisher had done some research and found that their readers had a terrific hunger for stories about "what was actual and real." To keep up with this demand, they resorted to "simply making up 'true' stories":

> ...Mario Puzo [...] would create giant mythical armies, lock them in combat in Central Europe, and have casualties coming in by the hundreds of thousands. Although our mail was heavy, I don't recall a single letter casting doubt on any of these epic conflicts. Many correspondents scolded us, however, for incorrectly identifying a tank tread or rifle designation in our documentation.[16]

Other Superheroes

Smaller companies than Marvel also failed with anti-communist superheroes when the comics industry collapsed. Ajax published *Black Cobra*, a short-lived comic about an anti-communist superhero who fought spies. His civilian secret identity was as an FBI agent. In the second issue (December 1954–January 1955), he is assigned to protect a Guatemalan air base. Its publication date suggests that the story was written around the time of the CIA's overthrow of the democratically elected Árbenz government in Guatemala.[17]

The Avenger, published by Vincent Sullivan's Magazine Enterprises, was created by writer Gardner Fox and artist Dick Ayers. Despite some dynamic Cold War comics art by Bob Powell, the series ended in 1955 after just four bi-monthly issues.[18]

Fighting American, by Joe Simon and Jack Kirby, lasted seven issues. It began in April–May 1954 as a serious attempt to out-compete Simon and Kirby's earlier creation Captain America with a knock-off, anti-communist superhero that they owned the rights to. Within weeks of the first issue reaching the stands, Edward R. Murrow made Senator Joseph McCarthy look foolish on television, and Simon and Kirby tried to transform *Fighting American* into a comic that made light of McCarthyism rather than a comic against communism.[19]

In separate interviews decades later, the co-creators of *Fighting American* remembered how they had hated Joe McCarthy. Joe Simon remembered that:

> We were doing Fighting American while McCarthy was going through all this crap. We hated McCarthy. Oh, God. You ever hear of Joseph [Welch]? He was our hero. Yeah. Hated McCarthy. Look, we started this Fighting American as Commie-bashers, the first comic book Commie-bashers. They were exposing McCarthy all over the place, and this one day—it was either after the first issue or before it—and we said, "Ah, the hell with it." It became a satirical book.[20]

Jack Kirby's thoughts were similar:

> I didn't like McCarthy. I didn't like his methods. I liked this other fellow—he was a gray-haired man from Maine I believe. He sat opposite McCarthy and challenged him. [Welch] was his name. [....] He sounded more logical to me, more temperate. You didn't feel like the stormtroopers were going

to knock on your door the next day when you listened to this guy. When you listened to McCarthy, you knew they were going to drag you away, or your parents. McCarthy sounded like a threat, and if you didn't fit certain specifications as an American—he laid down the specifications, he laid down the rules. That's what put the fear into everybody, because all of us are afraid that we're not going to fit certain rules.[21]

Joseph Welch attained lasting fame for confronting McCarthy during the nationally televised Army-McCarthy hearings (in a session held five days after the famous Senate Subcommittee Hearings on Comic Books and Juvenile Delinquency ended). McCarthy had accused one of the junior attorneys at Welch's law firm of having associated with an alleged communist front group, the National Lawyers Guild, while at Harvard's law school. (The National Lawyers Guild had been organized in 1937 as a pro-labor, racially integrated, progressive alternative to the American Bar Association.[22]) Welch objected to McCarthy's bringing up that damning association: "Senator, may we not drop this? We know he belonged to the Lawyers Guild. Let us not assassinate this lad further, Senator. You've done enough. Have you no sense of decency, sir? At long last, have you left no sense of decency?"[23]

Roy Lichtenstein

In February 1962, a gallery show of new paintings by Roy Lichtenstein pushed the style of American war and romance comic books into the faces of the nation's cultural elite in a way that they could not ignore, by creating perfectly executed, huge paintings based on comic book panels. Art critics of that time found the issues these paintings raised for art theory so absorbing that they had no time left over to seek out and read and describe, let alone study or appreciate, the comics that Lichtenstein had used as his source material. The comic book stories that he quoted in his paintings largely escaped critical attention, not only in the high arts community, but also in the publications of comics fans and the later-arriving comics scholars and comics historians. Instead, the comics communities' discussions of Lichtenstein's art have focused on the issue of disrespect for comic book artists and on whether Lichtenstein had legal or ethical obligations to acknowledge his artistic debts and pay royalties.[24]

Although some of Lichtenstein's most famous paintings represented or referred to jet combat during the Korean War between American and Russian planes (identified as MiG jets within the paintings themselves), art critics have mischaracterized his war paintings as based on World War II.[25] More recently, Thomas Crow has found that many of Lichtenstein's jet pilot images came from a single comic, DC's *All-American Men of War,* drawn by Irv Novick and Russ Heath and published at the beginning of 1962. Out of the three wars illustrated in that issue, Lichtenstein used panels only from the Korean conflict, the first war in which jet pilots fought each other.[26]

Sgt. Fury

In 1963, Marvel's Stan Lee and Jack Kirby created a long-running series set in World War II about the adventures of "Sgt. Fury and His Howling Commandos."[27] Those fictional characters reunited to fight in the Korean War one time only, in a Special King Size Annual in 1965. A dozen years after the ceasefire, the time had not yet come for a more objective look at the Korean War. A caption by Stan Lee set out the moral framework of this story: "There was no doubt about it—we were the 'good guys' as usual, fighting by the rules—stopping at the 38th parallel...."

In fact, the United States swept across the 38th parallel into North Korea as soon as the military opportunity presented itself. The U.S. even secretly attacked enemy planes in China, in violation of the rules the U.S. had set for itself.[28] Presumably, this caption reminded the comic's original readers about the enemy's "privileged sanctuaries" in the war then heating up in Vietnam.

In this story, the "Howlers" take a submarine to the "Red coast," hike ten miles inland, and destroy a MiG jet base. The way that they conk two Reds' heads together or ambidextrously punch two of them at once had been the invention of artist Dick Ayers. He explained his approach this way:

> ...as I interpreted the outline/synopses, I thought of them as my Baron Munchausen stories and did as I remember us guys in the 585th Bomb Squadron, 394th Bomb Group, would do: Embellish our accounts of what we did on pass or on a mission. [...] I didn't write dialogue or captions but I believe my drawings inspired the writers who did their writing to conform to my "Baron Munchausen" interpretations.[29]

The Howlers' raid succeeds. Broken into four captioned panels, the narration, in sober words that contrast with the lighthearted, heavily-accented dialogue in the rest of the story, comments on the action:

> Explosion after explosion wracks the Red base, as its capacity for illegal, murderous air strikes from a position of sanctuary is destroyed! There is no way to estimate how many hospitals, how many Korean villages, how many innocent lives are thus saved by the explosive holocaust! But, in those few brief minutes, the warlike, merciless Reds learn that never again can any aggressors attack a nation, and do so with impunity! They have been shown, in the only way they understand, that free men can *always* strike back!

To present the United States as the "good guys," this story simply reversed the two sides' historic roles, by imagining a war in which the communists bomb villages and hospitals and the American jets try to stop them. A few days after the 1953 ceasefire, North Korea estimated that enemy air power had destroyed (among other things) over 600,000 of their homes and 6,000 schools and hospitals.[30]

In 1965, when this story was published, Marvel comics were gaining tremendous momentum, with several successful superhero series saturated in Cold War themes, like the *Fantastic Four*, *The Hulk*, *Thor*, and *Iron Man*. Years later, Stan Lee, the man most responsible for these stories, admitted, "In those days we were of a more unsophisticated bent, seeing things in terms of black and white. The Communists were the bad guys and we were the good guys."[31]

This simplistic formula made it relatively easy to come up with new super-villains. By the end of 1965, however, Marvel had begun to tone down its Cold War themes.[32]

Blazing Combat

Beginning in 1965, the year that Sgt. Fury had been romping in Korea, *Blazing Combat* tried a different approach to war comics. *Blazing Combat*'s brief publication history reveals some limits imposed on that genre.

From October 1965 to July 1966, four issues of *Blazing Combat* appeared in magazine format (thus getting around the Comics Code). Fans and critics regard them as among the best written and best drawn war comics ever published.[33] The publisher, James Warren, eager for glory and a chance to serve his country, had enlisted in the army at the age of twenty, as soon as the Korean War broke out. The *Blazing Combat* stories were written by Archie Goodwin, who had been drafted at the age of twenty-three in 1960 and trained by Korean War veterans. Warren and Goodwin were thoroughly and openly indebted for their inspiration to the war comics that Harvey Kurtzman had created during the Korean War. Three of the series' twenty-nine stories were set in Korea: "MIG Alley" (drawn by Al McWilliams), "Holding Action" (drawn by John Severin) and "The Edge!" (drawn by Alex Toth). The editorial point of view stated that "war is hell."

Warren later described what his political ideas had been at that time:

> ...I was not a total liberal; I had a militant right-wing approach to many problems, but at the same time I was not a macho, gung-ho war fanatic. [...] I was against the war in Vietnam because I've never believed in limited war. Either you go to war to win—and win quickly and decisively or you stay out.[34]

Beginning with the second issue, which included a powerful story suggesting that the war in Vietnam was horribly futile and that the U.S. was killing innocent civilians, *Blazing Combat* was banned from sale on military bases. According to Warren, this "showed me the handwriting on the wall," but it was not yet the death blow for this "anti-war" magazine that he felt so passionately about that he was prepared to lose up to $2,500 per issue for five years if that were necessary to keep it going. The magazine was killed by the wholesalers, many of whom belonged to the American Legion. They refused to handle this "unpatriotic crap" and were threatening to boycott the rest of his existing line and anything else he published, which would put him out of business.[35]

James Warren never published another war comic, but found publishing success with the titles *Creepy*, *Eerie* and *Vampirella*, three magazine-format comics which revived the horror genre that the Comics Code had killed. In 1970, an unusual editorial appeared in those comics above his byline: "An Editorial to The President of the United States and All the Members of Congress—On Behalf of Our Readers, Most of Whom Are from 10 to 18 Years Old...." In it, Warren says:

> Both this company and our young readers have felt for some time now that our country is in deep trouble. Our first personal taste of this trouble occurred in 1965 when we came out with BLAZING COMBAT Magazine. Blazing Combat pointed out that war is hell, and inhuman—and not the glamorous, adventurous matter often depicted in the mass media. [...] We suspect that part of the reason it failed was because some of the people involved in the sale and distribution of our product didn't like the attitude we took on Viet Nam. [...] We were angry—that a magazine we thought deserved to live—had died, possibly because it proclaimed a message that said "War is hell—and the Viet Nam war is not only hell, it's absolute insanity for our country."

The 40-year-old Warren, identifying strongly with his young readers, concluded his editorial by demanding that the President and Congress end America's participation in the Vietnam War:

> Most of us readers are under 21. We can't vote—yet. But we don't have to be 21 to die in a war that was a mistake to begin with.
>   That's why we are angry with you adults, Mr. President and Members of Congress. You adults have let this drag on for half of our lives. [...]
>   Before another human life is wasted—give us PEACE, NOW![36]

Charlton Comics

During the Korean War, thanks to its business strategy of flooding the market with many titles in whatever genre was selling well, the company that later became Marvel Comics published more war comics titles than any other publisher.[37] Beginning in 1954, however, Charlton Comics quickly grew to become the publisher of the most war comics titles, and became the American publisher most associated with this genre. Most of Charlton's war comics stories were set in World War II and the Vietnam War, but for several decades they also published many stories set in the supposedly "forgotten" Korean War. These stories tended to be repetitious and simplistic, and focused on battles between Americans and Chinese Communists, with Koreans rarely making an appearance.[38]

In 1973, Charlton published *The Comic Book Guide for the Artist-Writer-Letterer* addressed to "budding young talent" interested in working for that company.[39] Their guidelines for war comics (the second listed of their eight categories of "Adventure" comics) said only this:

> 2. **War:** Details of war machines and uniforms must be accurate. Stories may be heroic or anti-war.

Not long before the publication of this guide, however, Charlton had fired a writer because his war comics were perceived as "anti-war." Publisher Roger Broughton told the story in the *Comics Buyer's Guide*:

> A draftee in the late '60s declared himself to be a conscientious objector. During the interview to assess why he requested such status, he indicated, among other things, that the strip ["The Lonely War of Willie Schultz," appearing in Charlton Comics' *Fightin' Army*] and its author [teenager Willi Franz] were among the strong influences on his decision.
> The recruiting sergeant, recognizing both name and stories (Charlton Comics were a staple at U.S. Army bases all over the world), wrote down both author and work.
> This brought within a matter of weeks, a phone call from Charlton to Franz, stating that it was discontinuing titles and that he should stop all stories and Charlton would pay him for what he had done.

Franz's comic-book writing career ended abruptly, yet *Fightin' Army* continued publishing original material for another seven years.[40]

Underground Comix

The underground comix movement of the late 1960s and 1970s played a crucial role in reinventing comics as a medium for uncensored personal expression and artistic experimentation. New artists, new publishers, different printers, new distributors, and different retailers worked to build an alternative to the New York–based comics industry. Celebrated cartoonists who participated in the underground comix movement included R. Crumb, Art Spiegelman, Gilbert Shelton, Trina Robbins, and many others. Although historians sometimes lump together underground comix and the movement against the Vietnam War, very few underground comix mentioned the ongoing war in Vietnam, and possibly only one made a fleeting mention of the Korean War.[41]

Mutants of the Metropolis was drawn by P. (Pete) Serniuk, a cartoonist on the fringes of the already fringy comix movement, and published in 1972 by L.A. Comics, outside of the movement's main center of activity in the San Francisco Bay Area. It was his only published comic book. Many years later, its publisher looked back on this comic as "a book so unique that no one bought it, assuring our demise."[42]

Mutants of the Metropolis tells a science fiction story that begins in the 1950s, when "In Korea, a G.I. prisoner, constantly brainwashed for years," mentally withdraws to the point where his face and fingerprints disappear, at which point the enemy sends him back to the United States where a doctor has him cryogenically frozen. He gets thawed out in the 1990s (twenty years in the future at the time of publication) and becomes Joe Zero, the hero of the story.

The underground comix movement crashed in 1973, brought down by a Supreme Court decision allowing local communities to determine their own obscenity standards, a paper shortage that drove up printing costs, the glutting of their retail outlets with non-returnable merchandise, the weakening of the counterculture (partly due to a government campaign of harassment and disruption), a campaign to shut down the "head shops" where most comix were sold, and aging hippies' fading identification with the counterculture after conscription ended in June 1973. By the mid–1970s, when the comix movement turned toward nonfiction and more overtly political and radical themes, most of their former readers were no longer paying attention. Then a new distribution system of specialty comic book shops quickly reshaped the comics industry toward focusing narrowly on superhero stories designed for hardcore comic book fans.[43]

G.I. Combat

One of the most successful war comics series, *G.I. Combat*, typically focused on World War II, but included an eight-page story written by Robert Kanigher in 1983 titled "The Forgotten War," which began as a wordy history comic to reintroduce the Korean War before turning into a war adventure story.[44] The unusually long, three-paragraph caption that begins the story emphasizes the scale of the losses:

> It was one of the bloodiest conflicts in history! In 37 months, more than 1 million civilians were killed, several million made homeless! It caused over a billion dollars worth of damage!
>
> One side suffered more than 1 and a half million casualties, the other 2 million killed, wounded or missing!
>
> And yet, because it erupted between World War II and Vietnam, the "police action" in Korea became *the lost battle*…

A few years later, shortly before the *Sgt. Rock* series ended, Kanigher sent Sgt. Rock and Easy Company, his most famous characters, to fight in the Korean War.[45] In those eight pages, four members of Easy Company are killed in combat.

Real War Stories

The comic book *Real War Stories* provides an especially clear example of the military acting to limit the distribution of comics that threaten recruitment. Sometime in the 1980s, Lou Ann Merkle of the Central Committee for Conscientious Objectors (CCCO) contacted me about putting together a comic book for teenagers to provide a point of view that they don't hear from military recruiters. I recommended that she contact Harvey Pekar, a brilliant comic book writer living in her state of Ohio.[46] An article in *Cleveland Magazine* picks up the story from there:

In the mid–1980s, Lou Ann Merkle, a Cleveland artist, peace activist and member of the Central Committee for Conscientious Objectors, came to Pekar for advice on designing a comic book telling the nefarious side of the military draft.

When Pekar outlined a design that looked a lot like American Splendor, [Pekar's wife Joyce] Brabner jumped in. "You are going up against the biggest advertiser in the United States—[the Army]," she said. "This is the Top Gun era." To compete, Brabner argued, the comic book had to be colorful, impactful and animated.

"If you know so much, why don't you write it?" Pekar asked. So she did.[47]

Brabner's original idea was to get the top talent in the comic book industry (such as Alan Moore) without sacrificing the freedom to be honest that characterized the underground comix tradition. The comic succeeded in realizing this vision.

Brabner remembers that the CCCO sold *Real War Stories* (published in 1987) in a number of ways, but when "they got them into some schools and they were used in classrooms," this became "enough to attract the attention of the Department of Defense and the Department of Justice." A controversy over the presence of *Real War Stories* and other peace materials at an Atlanta, Georgia, high school career counseling day led to the school banning the Atlanta Peace Alliance (APA) and the CCCO from participating. The APA and CCCO interpreted this as a violation of their rights and sued.

Brabner says the Department of Defense became involved "because the comic was interfering with the recruiting process, so it was considered a 'threat to national security.'" When, in a preliminary hearing, the peace groups produced court records that established the factual basis for the comic's most controversial story, the military withdrew their complaint to avoid negative publicity.[48] Still, the second and final issue of the series did not appear until 1991 (created in association with Citizen Soldier, a non-profit GI and veterans' rights advocacy group)

Addicted to War

Joel Andreas responded to the Persian Gulf War in 1992 by creating the educational comic *Addicted to War*. Andreas's *Addicted to War: Why the U.S. Can't Kick Militarism* has been the only comprehensive attempt to summarize the costs of, history of, and resistance to the war system using an informational comics format.

The publisher of the updated 2015 edition had succeeded in distributing 450,000 copies in "at least" 12 languages by 2020, according to the book's website (where it can be read for free).[49] In 2004, publisher Frank Dorrel listed *Addicted to War*'s distribution channels as including classroom use as a textbook in high schools and colleges; sales by peace organizations at rallies and teach-ins; churches; libraries; bookstores and comic book shops; and individuals who buy multiple copies to give to their friends, co-workers and relatives.[50] A Korean translation was published in 2003 by Chang Hae Publishing Co. in Seoul.

Addicted to War emphasizes how terribly destructive and inconclusive the Korean War had been:

U.S. warships, bombers, and artillery reduced much of Korea to rubble. Over 4,500,000 Koreans died; three out of four were civilians. 54,000 U.S. soldiers returned home in coffins. But the U.S. military, for all of its technological superiority, did not prevail. After 3 years of intense warfare, a cease-fire was negotiated. Korea is still divided and some 40,000 U.S. troops remain in Southern Korea to this day.[51]

The title "Addicted to War" came as an afterthought, and the comic does not tap the richness of the addiction metaphor as an explanation for *why* the people who pay the costs of militarism tolerate its continuance. Militarism, like a personal drug addiction, is a life-threatening system built on and sustained by self-centeredness, crisis orientation, dishonesty, confusion, denial, forgetfulness, defensiveness, tunnel vision, frozen feelings, ethical deterioration, and fear.[52]

The War in Korea: 1950–1953

Alerted to the upcoming 50th anniversary of the Korean War, Wayne Vansant, a comic book creator specializing in war stories, wrote and drew an extraordinary 96-page, square-bound history of that conflict, *The War in Korea: 1950–1953*, which was copyrighted in 2001. His pages differ from most war comics in having no dialogue balloons. Instead of dialogue, they use typeset captions to describe the war's history in close detail.

Although this comic introduces the Korean War as an inevitable "showdown between the ideologies of the *Democratic West* and the *Communist Bloc*," it pays attention to strictly military matters rather than ideologies. This comic seems to use as many statistics and as many names of the individual commanders, fighting units, battles, and war heroes as the whole Korean War comic book genre added together. Almost every panel shows military violence, soldiers on a battlefield, military leaders or military equipment.

On page 13, Vansant's comic takes a break from reporting on battles to describe some of the better-known atrocities of that war:

> When the North Koreans arrived in Taejon, they did as they had done in other South Korean villages. They rounded up the mayors and school teachers. The doctors and landowners. Anyone in a position of authority.
>
> These people were led to a trench dug in the earth, **then...** [shot dead, as the picture shows].
>
> The ROK and Americans were not completely innocent either. Under a railroad bridge near the town of **No Gun Ri** an estimated 400 civilians were machine-gunned by men of the **1st Cavalry Division** who believed there were NKPA guerilas among them.

Vansant's comic appeared years before South Korea's official Truth and Reconciliation Commission announced that most of those killed at Taejon had been political prisoners killed by South Koreans.[53]

Apocalypse Nerd

The spirit of underground comix found a new home in the "alternative comics" of the 1980s. In 2003, Peter Bagge, one of the luminaries of that movement, heard a North Korean diplomat "brag on the radio that his country now had the capability to hit Seattle with a nuclear bomb." Since he was living in Seattle, Bagge found this "unnerving," and responded by attempting to make a comic "much more honest and realistic" than a "last man on earth" fantasy, to imagine "what things would be like for someone like me," living after a nuclear attack "with little or no survival skills." The story, *Apocalypse Nerd,* came out less realistically and less effectively than Bagge's usual social satires, commentary strips and graphic biographies.[54] As in *Mutants of the Metropolis*, Korea figures in only one crucial panel. A store clerk explains to the main character that **"That lunatic,** Kim Jung II [*sic*], **nuked Seattle** this morning!"[55] The entire explanation for the nuclear disaster they are experiencing is contained in that one word: "lunatic."

Barefoot Gen

The shortcomings of *Apocalypse Nerd* as an attempt to realistically visualize a post–Bomb scenario appear most clearly when contrasting it with the comics created by an actual nuclear bomb survivor, Keiji Nakazawa. The tremendous power of Nakazawa's epic autobiographical graphic novel series *Hadashi no Gen* (*Barefoot Gen*) has been attested to in many surveys of the comics medium.[56]

The eighth translated volume of the Gen series (published in 1993) contains Nakazawa's unambiguously anti-war look at the Korean War.[57] In that volume, which begins on June 25, 1950, Nakazawa's child protagonist fights to defend a pacifist teacher who had been fired because of a "red purge" ordered by Japan's military governor Douglas MacArthur; fights against a right-wing mob that tries to break up a peace march; and violently attacks a Japanese businessman who is profiting from the Korean War. Nakazawa's unique style of two-fisted pacifism shows his boy-hero Gen in a series of fistfights, each of which illuminates and combats an aspect of the incomparably larger violence of war.[58]

Pyongyang

French-Canadian cartoonist Guy Delisle's *Pyongyang: A Journey in North Korea* describes his experiences during two months of 2001 supervising animators at a studio in the North Korean capital.[59] Because animation is a highly labor-intensive art, Western animation studios have subcontracted much of their work to low-paid cartoonists in Eastern Europe, South Korea, China, and even North Korea.

Delisle refers to the Korean War only once as a contributing explanation for what he witnesses in North Korea. He explains that the reason Pyongyang's architecture is "all new" is because "During the Korean War, bombs rained on the city for 3 years, flattening it." He illustrates this with a drawing of bombs falling on buildings. The next panel's caption reads "Afterward, the party obliterated anything resembling an opposition…." The picture shows bombs falling on people.[60] Through a series of close observations of daily life, *Pyongyang* succeeds in conveying the stultifying effects of living under a totalitarian dictatorship.

Near the end of the book, after failing to talk his way out of it, Delisle receives a tour of the "Museum of Imperialist Occupation," in which "all atrocities commited [sic] by Americans against the Korean people during the war" are documented. Delisle reports that:

> A number of horrifying paintings drive home the message.
> Soldiers forcing children to drink motor oil.
> Soldiers nailing anti–American propaganda to the author's forehead.[61] […]
> It goes on like that for two crammed floors.

The official North Korean government description of this museum says that:

> Sinchon County in South Hwanghae Province is a place where the US imperialists and their stooges committed the atrocities of mass murder while the Korean People's Army was carrying out a strategic temporary retreat during the Korean war (June 1950–July 1953).
> During their occupation of Sinchon for 52 days (October 17–December 7, 1950) the US aggressors slaughtered 35,383 people, a quarter of the total population of the county.[62]

Plans for a film based on the *Pyongyang* graphic novel were cancelled in December 2014, the day after the U.S. government made their controversial accusation that North Korea had been responsible for the hacking of Sony Pictures Entertainment.[63]

The Bridge at No Gun Ri

A 612-page Korean graphic novel about an American massacre of unarmed refugees at the No Gun Ri bridge in July 1950 was republished in French (*Massacre au pont de No Gun Ri*) and in Italian (*il ponte di NOGUNRI*) in 2006 but not in English.[64] Writer Chung Eun-yong (born in 1923) served as president of the association of survivors of the No Gun Ri massacre. Illustrator Park Kun-woong was born in 1973. The killings at No Gun Ri had taken Chung's five-year-old son Goo-phil and two-year-old daughter Goo-hi.[65]

Park's graphic novel adapts Chung's written novel *Do You Know Our Pain?,* which Chung had based on the story that his wife told him about this massacre. Park's drawings use a brush style not associated with Western comic book art and traditional, handmade *hanji* paper. The drawings movingly convey the horrors of war as seen from the perspective of Korean noncombatants.

Under Syngman Rhee's rule, survivors had been afraid to tell their stories, but after protesters drove Rhee into permanent political exile in 1960, Chung Eun-yong became the first of those who would petition the governments of the United States and Korea for investigations, apologies and compensation for victims' families.

History Comics

The genre of war comics had gradually faded away by the late 1980s, but the old genre of nonfiction comics rose again stronger than ever. Nonfiction comics have presented the Korean War in a very different way, with an emphasis on understanding what actually happened rather than using it as a setting for adventure stories.[66]

Larry Gonick's exemplary *The Cartoon History of the United States* (1991) and *The Cartoon History of the Modern World, Part II: From the Bastille to Baghdad* (2009) include chapters on the Korean War. Unlike the "freedom and democracy" sloganeering in comics of the 1950s, Gonick's work invites us to wonder about how a North Korean "dictator" differed from a South Korean "strongman."

In another example in educational cartooning, *The Complete Idiot's Guide to U.S. History* (2009), Kenneth Hite and Shepherd Hendrix use a dozen panels, drawn in one of the more traditional American comic book styles, to summarize the military history of this war.[67]

A very interesting few pages about the Korean War, drawn in the sketchy, humorous visual style characteristic of this genre, appear in famous Korean cartoonist Rhie Won-bok's *Korea Unmasked: In Search of the Country, the Society and the People* (2002).[68] Rhie's comics-format introduction to Korea shows, by contrast, what an embarrassingly small amount of information a reader could learn about Korea from reading American war comics.

Unfortunately, *Korea Unmasked*, the first of Rhie's works to be translated into English, received little critical attention in the United States. This book was ignored even when Rhie attained brief notoriety in the United States a few years later over his claim, which appeared in his comics-format introduction to the United States, that Jews control American media.[69]

The fourth and final chapter of *Korea Unmasked*, "The Long and Treacherous Road to Reunification," explains in 28 pages of comics why "the most ardent wish of the Koreans," the reunification of North and South Korea, remains out of reach. In a masterful demonstration of educational cartooning, Rhie presents the South Korean proposal for reunification, the North Korean proposal for reunification, and the reasons that neither side could accept the other side's proposals.

Most of the nonfiction comics about the Korean War have been published in Korea and in Japan. So far, little of this work has become available in English.[70]

Chosin

In their 2013 graphic novel *Chosin*, military veterans Richard C. Meyer, Brian Iglesias, Otis Frampton and Anton Sattler, with Korean-American cartoonist Thomas Jung, portrayed the experience of Fox Company, 2nd Battalion, 7th Marines in the battle of the Chosin Reservoir as one of "sacrifice and courage that contends with the story of the 300 Spartans at Thermopylae as one of the most heroic feats in history." They dedicated their graphic novel to "the men of Chosin and to all who served in Korea. Your victory will not be forgotten." Their story concludes with the evacuation of nearly 100,000 North Korean refugees that the U.S. brought with them while being forced out of North Korea. One soldier says to another, while watching the "BOOM! BA-BOOM! DOOM!!" explosion which blots out the city of Hungnam:

> Look around French. There are more people on these boats than in my home town. Those Commies wanted to wipe us off map [sic], but we're still standing. [...] And all of these people and their children and their children's children get to live free because of what we did. [...] I'd call that a victory.[71]

A story by Hank Chapman, published in *War Comics #4* in June 1951, had taken a similar position regarding the evacuation at Hungnam.[72] The story centers on a stubborn Colonel who learns that "sometimes there can be victory in defeat." After the evacuation, another soldier congratulates him: "More than 200,000 troops and civilians had been removed and only four artillery battalions kept back fourteen Red divisions while evacuation was going on! You and your tanks also played a great part in this retreat, Colonel!" The Colonel concludes with satisfaction: "and in a short time from now I shall return to Korea at the head of an armored division ... to fight for *victory* made possible by a *retreat*!

The victory promised "in a short time from now" did not arrive. Harvey Kurtzman's special issue on that retreat, published in 1952 (one year after the events it dramatized), admitted in capital letters "WE SUFFERED A DEFEAT," but Kurtzman also tried to put the best face on it:

> Make no mistake! We suffered a defeat, but it could have been a heck of a lot worse! The 8th Army and the 10th Corps had been saved ... intact!
> A miracle? We don't think so! You might call it a *wonder* ... a wonder of machinery, a wonder of factories and industry, a wonder of democratic constitutional law that has taken many hundreds of years of hard work and bitter experience to fashion!

The 2013 graphic novel *Chosin* was "inspired and based on the true stories of Chosin veterans, Korean civilians, and Chinese soldiers." Iraq War combat veterans Sattler and Iglesias "interviewed hundreds of men who fought in the Chosin Reservoir campaign during the production of [their] award-winning documentary CHOSIN." Unlike that moving documentary, the graphic novel adaptation condenses the events it represents into a clear contest between good Americans and evil Communists (who suppress freedom of thought, coerce Chinese men into joining the army, threaten to slaughter their own troops if they fail to achieve victory, fill mass graves with Koreans they accuse of sympathizing with "the democratic South," take food without paying for it, kill those who resist, and shoot at fleeing orphans).

Kurtzman's special issue had been titled "A Document of the Action at the *Changjin Reservoir!*," emphasizing the politically correct Korean place name. "Chosin" had been the Japanese place name for the location of that action.[73]

Webcomics

The possibilities of the Web as a forum for sharing anyone-can-do-it cartooning created with cartooning software are illustrated by a few Korean War comic strips. A formerly-web-posted, eighteen-panel *Korean War Comic Strip* was created in 2009 using Pixton. The art was created by positioning and modifying ready-made "click-n-drag" graphic elements, and so the strip included such anachronisms as an American receiving the news of the invasion on his cell phone while sitting in front of his flat-screen computer. Another amateur cartoonist's six-panel comic strip about the Korean War was made using the program Storyboard That. The creator of that comic explained that Syngman Rhee and Kim Il-sung were unable to agree about whether their nation should be communist or a republic, so the two of them decided to divide "China" at the 38th parallel and set up two different systems. (The unlabeled, pasted-in map that illustrates the supposed division of "China" into north China and south China actually shows North and South Korea.) At least nine students have web-posted comics that they made with the program stripgenerator, assembling simple stock illustrations of various, generic characters as they tried to explain the entire Cold War in one page. The graphics offer no clue about the subject matter of the strip, unless using a character in a wire cage to represent Cold war "containment" counts. Apparently, all these students had been told about the Korean War was that the 38th parallel is: "a line of latitude that divides North and South Korea. It was decided on before the Korean war started. The Korean war was a war between North and South Korea, in which North Korea had help from the Soviet Union and South Korea had help from the United Staes [*sic*]."

More encouragingly, the web also serves for sharing amateur hand-drawn comics. Beginning in 2009, a very skilled amateur cartoonist using the name MOLD123 drew *The Cold War Project*, subtitled "The history of foreign relations in the American perspective from the 1950's to the 1990's.... HETALIA STYLE."

"Hetalia style" refers to the web-comic *Hetalia: Axis Powers*, which began in 2006. Each of Hidekazu Himaruya's *Hetalia* characters personifies a nation, and the comic loosely represents events of World War II as the interactions between these stereotyped personalities.[74]

Of the twenty pages that MOLD123 had posted between 2009 and 2015, ten of them focused on the Korean War.[75] One way that her representation of the Korean War differs from others is that it gives a prominent role to the character that personifies France (a major character in the original *Hetalia* series). In their comments, readers expressed astonishment that the French fought in Korea with *bayonets,* and cheered for France with many exclamation marks.[76]

Despite the low barriers to a person entering the conversation about the Korean War by web-posting original comics on that subject, such web-posted comics have remained unusual.

Communications scholar/activist Robert W. McChesney remembers that originally, people expected the Internet to bring "a noncommercial zone, a genuine public sphere, leading to far greater public awareness, stronger communities, and greater political participation. It would sound the death knell for widespread inequality and political tyranny, as well as corporate monopolies.[77]

The DeviantART site which hosts MOLD123's *The Cold War Project* accomplished the easier part of this vision, by creating a noncommercial public meeting place. On a broader scale, however, the Web's democratic potential has been under sustained attack.[78]

20

◇◇◇◇◇◇◇◇◇

Conclusion

The Korean War, the comic books about that war, and the movement that rose up against comic books during the Korean War were all shaped by the Cold War. In that dangerous new age of nuclear terror, rather than urging their readers (who included both soldiers and children) to push for a victory in a "total war" effort as comic books had done in World War II, Korean War comic books supported no more than a "limited war" in Korea.[1] The comic book industry worked out ways to sell stories that represented fighting in wars as both a man's obligation and an unending struggle. Some participants in the movement that rose up against comic books at that time feared that repetitive, illustrated stories of good guys violently defeating violent bad guys, might, by eroding compassion and numbing sensitivity, raise a generation psychologically adapted to perpetual warfare.[2]

The Korean War and NSC-68

American support for the "limited war" in Korea had its own limits, and in 1952, Dwight D. Eisenhower was elected to put a stop to it. Over the objections of his Secretary of State and his Secretary of Defense, Eisenhower decided to conclude the war by accepting an armistice. To force Syngman Rhee to agree to stop fighting while Korea remained divided, Eisenhower cut off the ROK Army's fuel supplies and threatened to completely withdraw all U.S. forces from Korea and end all military and financial aid to his government. The armistice was signed by representatives of North Korea and China, and a U.S. Army Lieutenant General representing the United Nations Command on July 27, 1953.[3]

During the war, the idea of fighting without "fighting to win" had frustrated and confused many Americans. If the U.S. government's secret files contained one item that held the key to understanding U.S. strategy in the Korean War, it would be National Security Council Paper NSC-68, an enormously influential U.S. State Department document which had been presented to President Truman in April 1950.[4]

NSC-68 laid out the following analysis:

> First, the defeat of Germany and Japan and the decline of the British and French Empires have interacted with the development of the United States and the Soviet Union in such a way that power has increasingly gravitated to these two centers. Second, the Soviet Union, unlike previous aspirants to hegemony, is animated by a new fanatic faith, antithetical to our own, and seeks to impose its absolute authority over the rest of the world.[5]

That April, NSC-68's plea for "substantially increasing" the defense budget to meet this exaggerated Soviet threat failed to convince President Truman. (Truman had first attained national attention during World War II by chairing Senate investigations that exposed and prevented billions of dollars of waste, fraud and profiteering in U.S. war production.)[6] Resistance to a huge increase in military spending collapsed a few months later, when North Korea's invasion of South Korea was misinterpreted as the first step of Moscow's plan for global military conquest.[7]

NSC-68 warned that at the same time that the United States faced the threat of this hostile, aggressive, tyrannical new superpower, the dawning of a nuclear arms race had created a situation in which "every individual faces the ever-present possibility of annihilation" if the conflict with the Soviet Union enters "the phase of total war."[8]

The U.S. response to the invasion of South Korea followed NSC-68's recommendations in several ways: refusing to allow the communists to erase the line that the U.S. had drawn across the Korean peninsula in 1945 to hold them back; vastly increasing military spending; strengthening (anti-communist) international cooperation through the United Nations; keeping the war from turning into a direct military confrontation with the Soviet Union; and resisting both domestic political pressure to escalate the war into a nuclear conflagration and international political pressure to eliminate nuclear weapons.[9] The U.S. achieved all of these goals.[10] The goals that the Koreans fought and died for—to reunite their nation and free it from foreign control—were not accomplished.

The appearance in newsstand comic books of the same basic perspectives as those in a top-secret document that the comic book creators had not seen involves no mystery. Dean Acheson, who was Secretary of State at the time, described NSC-68 as a statement of those obvious facts, elementary ideas, and fundamental conclusions regarding the world situation that he had been "preaching" around the country in 1950.[11] The more confidential parts of the document did not appear in comic books. For example, NSC-68 suggested that the U.S. would pretend to negotiate seriously with the Soviet Union for the sake of appearances.[12]

Democracy and Decency

Those who criticized comic books as a threat to democracy in the 1940s were not only imagining dystopian future possibilities. Some Americans felt that in World War II and the Cold War, democracy as they had understood it was already slipping away. When Superman first reached the newsstands in 1938, the United States had a smaller military than Portugal.[13] At the same time that Superman was rising in popularity, the United States was rapidly becoming a "superpower." Sociologist C. Wright Mills observed in his 1956 book *The Power Elite* that during World War II and the Korean War the United States had already moved some distance toward becoming a militarized, propagandized "mass society" with a "seemingly permanent war economy."[14] Some of these same anxieties about war, media, and the loss of democracy can be found in the writings of the anti-comic book movement.

Rather than having to choose whether sincere concerns about comic books' supposed threat to democracy, or opportunistic anti–American propaganda, or fears about juvenile delinquency explain more of the anti-comic book activism in this period, a wider perspective suggests that the fundamental issue usually came down to something else: a simple matter of defending "decency and good taste."[15] The most damning moment for the comic book industry came when publisher William Gaines was quoted on page one of the *New York Times* as testifying that the cover of his *Crime SuspenStories #22* (which showed a man with a bloody axe holding a woman's head up which has been severed from her body) was in "good taste ... for the cover of a horror comic."[16] The Comics Code of 1954 promised to prohibit any "violations of good taste or decency."[17] Senator Kefauver, as a defender of decency and good taste, reported that the Senate subcommittee investigation of crime and horror comic books in 1954 had "paved the way" for his hearings the next year which investigated the "insidious filth" of outright pornography.[18] A 1956 survey found that all of the statewide laws restricting comic books had their roots in anti-obscenity statutes designed to restrict materials that encouraged "immoral thoughts and actions."[19] Relations between the anti-comic book movement and the larger cultural and legal struggles over maintaining conventional standards of taste and morality would be worth at least another chapter.

Fredric Wertham Revisited

Although Fredric Wertham seldom mentioned the Korean War, the contexts of the Korean War and the Cold War put a clearer light on the views of this much-maligned anti-comic book activist and the movement that he inspired. People sometimes spoke out against comic books, not just because they feared comic books might lead their readers to become juvenile delinquents, but because they feared that comics were leading their readers to become *war criminals*.

In his book *Seduction of the Innocent*, Fredric Wertham did not quote or repeat the communist propaganda theme that American comic books (and war comics in particular) were hardening young people to fight in Wall Street's imperialist wars. He may have been hinting at this, though, when he called the "superman" Adolf Hitler's request that his generals be brutal and merciless in their upcoming invasion of Poland "an accurate summary" of the "essential ethical teaching of crime comics for children."[20] Wertham's approach ran parallel to the communists' anti–American propaganda campaign, by repeatedly blasting the shortcomings of an American culture that exploited children for profit.[21] Wertham shared with other critics the thought that crime comic books' most harmful "effect" may be their possible contribution, not to raising the crime rate, but rather to deepening society's acceptance of officially condoned injustices.

Wertham concluded that comic books were "far more significant as symptoms" of social evils than as "causes" of violence.[22] His 1966 book, *A Sign for Cain: An Exploration of Human Violence*, showed more clearly how anti-fascism and opposition to war were important elements of Wertham's thinking about media violence.[23]

Fredric Wertham, *Corporate CRIME Comics,* and *Barefoot Gen*

Wertham made a permanent enemy of comics fans by treating the comic book medium with contempt. In *Seduction of the Innocent*, he approvingly quoted condemnations of crime comic books as " the lowest, most despicable and most harmful and unethical form of trash," "cheap junk," "worse-than-rubbish," the "offal of the magazine trade," "tripe," "extremely ugly in appearance," "inartistically drawn" "gutter muck" and "hack-work filth."[24] The way I remember it, though, when I first read that book in the mid–1960s, it seemed clear that what he was talking about had little to do with the Comics Code–era comic books that I was familiar with and cared about (or the kind of kids that I knew). Consequently, his harsh opinions of comic books did not bother me.

I first wrote to Fredric Wertham on February 2, 1979, on the stationery of Krupp Comic

Works, where I was working for comic book publisher Denis Kitchen as his associate editor.[25] I had read an interview of Wertham in the fanzine *Instant Gratification #1* and in my letter I proposed to "pictorially dramatize" (in comic book format) Wertham's story of how comic book publishers and book distributors had conspired against him. I hoped to use it in the third issue of a comic book series that I founded and edited, *Corporate CRIME Comics*.[26] I also asked for a citation of the clinical studies that formed the basis for his statement that although "the positive claim is made especially for ... war comic books that to show violence in gory detail is to combat it ... [c]linical studies show ... [t]hat violence cannot discredit itself."[27] I explained that I was interested in this question because "I'm currently negotiating for the rights to republish [in comic book format] a very violent Japanese comic book series [Keiji Nakazawa's *Barefoot Gen*] ... which has a strongly humane, anti-war, anti-racism, anti-class exploitation message" and which I hoped would be useful "as a pacifist organizing tool."

Wertham answered on February 14 that he had been referring to his own clinical studies, since "there are practically no other *clinical* studies." He added, "The saturation of people's minds with violent images in which war is used merely as a setting has to be distinguished from the presentation of violence with a clearly stated purpose of being against it." This sounded encouraging, but after he saw the copy of Nakazawa's *Barefoot Gen* book, which I arranged for the War Resisters League to send him, he concluded (on March 4), "I think anything that goes against atomic war deserves attention. But I have doubts whether the comic-book brutality in the first part of the book is effective as an anti-violence message."[28]

The *Corporate CRIME Comics* series never reached a third issue, and my correspondence with Wertham did not continue.[29] In 1980, I began serializing Keiji Nakazawa's story in American comic book format through my company EduComics under the title *Gen of Hiroshima*. Wertham died in 1981.

Wertham's guiding vision was not "law and order," but rather a revolutionary ambition to eliminate violence in general, including both violent crime and war, from human society.[30] He judged comic books by whether they were contributing to or interfering with progress toward that distant goal.[31] Nothing in "human nature" requires that people wage wars or commit murders, and eliminating such violence would prevent a huge amount of pain and suffering.

The Control of Comic Books

During the Korean War, people regarded the mass culture that was shared through mass media as a sometimes-embarrassing expression of a shared national identity; as a potentially powerful conduit for propaganda and psychological warfare; as an artistically inferior commercial product; and as an extraordinarily influential means of educating and shaping the coming generation. Consequently, they were unwilling to let publishers' pursuit of private profit have the final say about what would be made available. Still, the Constitutional guarantee of freedom of the press, which was slowly and uncertainly being extended to commercially produced entertainment at the time of the Korean War, greatly limited the possibilities for government regulation of comic book content.[32]

In 1954, some leaders of the comic book industry set up the Comics Code Authority, as a way to dampen the growing popular demand for government censorship, to satisfy the public that they were socially responsible businessmen, and to reduce overproduction of comic books by driving out "irresponsible" publishers.[33] Within a few years, they succeeded, and the surviving publishers maintained leading positions in a much smaller but no-longer controversial industry. Even before the Code's new restrictions, however, comic book content had been filtered in many ways. The movement against comic books organized itself on a household, neighborhood, city, county, state and national level and internationally. In that controversy, "brutal" and "violent" war comic books were condemned as a variety of "crime" comics. By contrast, the sanitized war comics that conformed to the Comics Code were tacitly accepted as harmless entertainment.

When the comic book industry, responding to pressures from all sides, drove the "irresponsible" publishers from their ranks, this not only eliminated the most tasteless, indecent, violent and salacious depictions, but also silenced any hints of political dissent. Beginning in 1954, the Comics Code assured that American comic books would largely cease to be a medium for adults.[34] Even younger comics fans felt this loss keenly for a generation. To lose adult, critical content, in any of its forms, means to lose part of that conversation on which human survival increasingly depends.

A Culture Appropriate for a Peaceful and Democratic Society

Calls for a greater diversity of voices, especially adult, critical voices, should acknowledge that some voices in this world are much more severely silenced than others. The 2020 Reporters Without Borders World Press Freedom Index ranked North Korea as the nation with the least press freedom on earth.[35] In practice, North Koreans lack the freedom to say, write, draw or publish things that go against the interests of the people, as interpreted by their government.[36] Their dismal situation deserves serious attention, preferably without yielding to the simplistic and dangerous idea that democracy can be promoted successfully by overthrowing undemocratic governments.[37] However incomplete, fraudulent, eroded or endangered our own "democracies" may be, the contrast with North Korea suggests that our existing human rights and freedom to organize and to dissent should be cherished and strengthened through regular exercise.[38]

As in the 1940s and 1950s, democracy in America appears fragile.[39] Threats include authoritarian mindsets; extreme economic inequality; campaigns to prevent majority rule through voter suppression and gerrymandering; laws stripping away governments' powers to regulate corporate abuses; news as profit-driven entertainment; massive surveillance; oligopolistic control over information; white nationalist conspiracy theories, and other factors. For defending against these actual, existing threats to American democracy, the huge military establishment plays no helpful role.[40]

Like the present, the late 1940s and early 1950s were a time when the world struggled to comprehend and respond to new, human-created possibilities for unprecedented devastation. The possibility of a world-shattering nuclear war sparked by the situation in Korea still remains, to which has been added a human-caused climate emergency.[41] Then as now, news and entertainment media act "responsibly" by pushing to the margins radically dissenting views, including perspectives, information and analyses that would help us to better understand our current crises and to effectively work together to avoid disasters.[42]

Understanding the limitations of the corporate media system clarifies the importance of interpreting its reporting critically while also supporting alternatives to that system.

Because of my background in underground comix, I still feel that a culture appropriate to a democratic society would be one that we participate in building ourselves. At a minimum, democracy requires a media system that has not been monopolized and distorted to serve the narrow needs of business or government.[43]

Opposing Violence

Part of the problem of organizing a movement against violence (military violence or media violence) has been imagining an alternative. This would be difficult enough in any circumstances, but especially if violent media degrade people's capacity to envision a world in which an act of violence would be interpreted as strange behavior.

The word "violence" has dozens of meanings, and literally hundreds of words have been proposed on the web as "the opposite of violence." Opposing violence seems uninspiring, wrong or even impossible when the antonym to being "violent" is to be, not just "gentle," but "compliant," "submissive," "deferential," "weak," "harmless," "dull," "tame," "subdued," "domesticated," "feeble," "powerless," "bland," "cowardly," and the web-posted lists go on and on.[44] Fredric Wertham named the opposite of violence with a concept that scarcely appears on these very long lists. He wrote that "Communication is the opposite of violence. Where communication ends, violence begins."[45]

The main voices against comic book violence in the 1940s and 1950s have often been misunderstood as calling for conformity and obedience. This interpretation seems backwards. They did hope that children would grow up to be decent and moral, but that does not mean "normal" and "docile." Underlying those critics' comments linking comic books and fascism, they were warning that when the times will require it, those who have been raised on comic books might fail to rebel.

Chapter Notes

Preface

1. DeBruyne, 2018.

Korea was called "the forgotten war" by *U.S. News & World Report* in October 1951. The name stuck ("Korea: the 'Forgotten' War," 1951).

2. John Tirman explores the difficulties of estimating war deaths in Chapter 11 of his book *The Deaths of Others*. For the Korean War, he cites and examines estimates of 770,000 to 5.5 million total deaths, of which 400,000 to three million were civilian deaths (Tirman, 2011). In 1956, as many as 590,000 widows were living in South Korea (Hata, 2018: 140). (Others have estimated that the war created about 30,000 widows.) (Lee, 2006: 108).

3. Wills, 2010: 57–102.

4. Walter Isaacson and Evan Thomas describe the small circle of friends who created America's Cold War policies as "staunch capitalists for whom liberal free trade was a creed; some had extensive financial holdings that would today be considered conflicts of interest…. Although their belief in the ideals of democracy was not always evenly applied, they were sincerely repulsed by the tyrannical tactics of the Kremlin and understandably anxious to keep them from spreading" (Isaacson and Thomas, 1986, 2012: 32).

Public opinion researchers reported that "the united and wholehearted support of public opinion which characterized the last war [World War II] is conspicuous by its absence in the Korean war" (Suchman, et al., 1953: 171).

5. I survey the war comics genre at chapter length in *The Routledge Companion to Comics and Graphic Novels* (Rifas, 2017).

6. Wagner, 1954: 79. Wagner specified *Famous Funnies #204*, which was the first of five consecutive issues with Korean War theme covers.

7. Eisner, 1985, 2008.

8. This put them in charge of 95 percent of the Korean Peninsula and 98 percent of its population (McCormack, 2004: 27).

9. The transliteration of 인천 as "Incheon" (instead of "Inchon") dates from the year 2000, when the South Korean government introduced the Revised Romanization of Korean. As further examples, the name "Pusan" is now written as "Busan"; "No Gun Ri" is now "Nogeun-ri"; and "Syngman

Rhee" is now "Yi Seung-man." In this book, I usually use the older spellings.

10. Dobbins and Hornung, 2017.

In 2018, a dramatic flurry of diplomatic activity promised to move toward making a peace agreement. American strategists argued that withdrawing U.S. and UN forces (as North Korea has demanded as a condition for peace) could lead to doubts about U.S. commitments that might trigger a destabilizing nuclear arms race in the region (Pinkston, 2018).

New Zealand-based academic Tim Beal argues that American resistance to ending the Korean War rests on the U.S. desire to maintain both Korean military bases near China and Russia and access to "a huge reservoir of [South] Korean military assets" including over five million personnel (in the service or in the reserves) (Beal, 2016: 8–10).

11. Wertham, 1966: 20.

Kim Dong-Choon's *The Unending War* agrees, in effect, with Wertham on this point (Kim, 2000: 23, 32).

12. Karl Marlantes writes that "The least acknowledged aspect of war, today, is how exhilarating it is" and that this dangerous feeling, "the transcendent realm one reaches through violence," is "one that society says it condemns but in fact celebrates everywhere, on film, on television, and in the news" (Marlantes, 2011: 62, 66). For more on the "joys" of war, see also Kindsvatter, 2003: 178–191; Edwards, 2018: 90–2; and O'Brien, 1990: 64–67, 77–78.

13. To see how long it takes to properly analyze the formal features of a comic book story, I recommend Martin Petersen's "Sleepless in the DPRK: Graphic Negotiations of 'Family' in *The True Identity of Pear Blossom*" (Petersen, *Korean Studies*, 2012). Petersen applies the analytic tools of focalisation, closure, metalepsis and braiding to an 80-page (A5-size) North Korean comic written by Kim Yong-hyon and drawn by Choe Chu-sop about the exposing of a CIA sleeper agent. Petersen also analyzes North Korean comics, this time with a focus on characters, plots and the social functions of these publications (Petersen, *Scandinavian Journal of Comic Art*, 2012).

For an aesthetic appreciation of Harvey Kurtzman's work, see the editorial matter in *Corpse on the Imjin* (2012) and Jason Sacks appreciation in *Com-*

ics Bulletin (Sacks, 2013). I thank Jason Sacks for his editorial advice on several of my chapters.

14. For an encyclopedic survey of Korean War movies, see Korean War Filmography by Robert J. Lentz (Lentz, 2003).

15. A combat photographer captures a shot of an American soldier plunging his bayonet into the chest of a Chinese soldier in the comic book story "The Fighting 'Eightball'" (Fighting War Stories #3, December 1952). An early collection of photographs of the Korean War was published by the Veterans' Historical Book Service, Inc. (Cassino and Adam, 1951).

Sixteen hours of video about the Korean War, primarily the series "The Big Picture" and "Combat Bulletin," have been released on three discs by Mill Creek Entertainment as Korea: The Forgotten War (2011). These same documentaries are accessible over the Web.

16. Horror comics expressed several Cold War anxieties. Jim Trombetta usefully explores relations between themes in horror comic books and nuclear war, brainwashing, and even Chinese "human wave" attacks in Korea, which he calls "the real zombie attacks" (Trombetta, 2010: 168).

William Savage has written a chapter describing Cold War themes in the popular genre of Western comics (Savage, 1998: 66–73).

17. I have focused on "assembling twigs" of information that connect the comic book controversies of the 1940s and 1950s with the Cold War and Korean War. While doing so, I learned that the arguments about comic books and juvenile delinquency played a smaller role than I had expected. I postpone sharing my general impressions about the relative importance of the various concerns held by those who opposed comic books until the conclusion.

18. The URLs for these great resources are: http://digitalcomicmuseum.com and http://comicbookplus.com/.

19. Joseph Witek's Comic Books as History: The Narrative Art of Jack Jackson, Art Spiegelman, and Harvey Pekar, a pioneering critical analysis of comics based on factual events, mentions Harvey Kurtzman's "grimly pacifistic" Korean War comics only in passing (Witek, 1989: 40, 42).

Just as I was finishing my MA thesis on these comics, William Savage's book Comic Books and America, 1945–1954 (later republished as Commies, Cowboys, and Jungle Queens: Comic Books and America, 1945–1954) appeared, which included a chapter about Korean War comic books. My review of Savage's Comic Books and America: 1945–1954 focuses on challenging his metaphor of comic book stories as "reflections" or "mirrors" (Rifas, 1991:45–47; Savage, 1998).

Examples of books about ideology in comics include Comics & Ideology, edited by Matthew P. McAllister, Edward H. Sewell, and Ian Gordon (2001); The Power of Comics: History, Form and Culture, by Randy Duncan and Matthew J. Smith (2012); Comics: Ideology, Power, and the Critics, by Martin Barker (1989); Secret Identity Crisis: Comic Books and the Unmasking of Cold War America by Matthew J. Costello (2009); War, Politics and Super-

heroes: Ethics and Propaganda in Comics and Film by Marc Dipaolo (2011); Comic Books and American Cultural History: An Anthology, edited by Matthew Pustz (2012); Comic Books and the Cold War, 1946–1962: Essays on Graphic Treatment of Communism, the Code and Social Concerns, edited by Chris York and Rafiel York (2012), and Anti-Foreign Imagery in American Pulps and Comic Books, 1920–1960 by Nathan Vernon Madison (2013). Madison's comments on Korean War comic books appear on his pages 177–195.

Cord A. Scott's Comics and Conflict: Patriotism and Propaganda from WWII through Operation Iraqi Freedom (2014) includes a section on the Korean War. I reviewed this book for the Journal of American History (Rifas, 2015).

Martin Barker's A Haunt of Fears: The Strange History of the British Horror Comics Campaign includes an Appendix, "The Forgotten Cause for Concern," in which he argues that: "Throughout this book I have been pretty scornful of the critics of the comics, and dismissive of their claims about comics' supposed influence. […] In fact, there was a type of comic in those years which should have been a real cause for concern: the Korean War comic" (Barker, 1992: 200).

Christopher Murray's Champions of the Oppressed? Superhero Comics, Popular Culture, and Propaganda in America during World War II has a chapter on "Postwar Propaganda in Comics," which briefly discusses Korean War comic books. The greater value of Murray's book is in its descriptions of how a society's "myths," as seen through their appearances as entertainment, change with changing political circumstances, and how these stories, in which old and new ideas clash dramatically, help to "manage" social transformations by making a world in flux seem both natural and stable (Murray, 2011).

20. Chris Pedrin's Big Five Information Guide, vol. 1, no. 1 is a book-length guide which lists the writers, pencillers and inkers of almost every story in DC comics' five big war titles. Chris Pedrin has informed me that "there were many stories about the Korean War in the early 50's issues" (Chris Pedrin, personal letter, Jan 2019). Inconveniently, their titles rarely indicate which ones these were. The valuable articles in the beginning of Pedrin's Information Guide mention the Korean War only once briefly and once more in passing. I thank Chris Pedrin for the gift of a mint copy of this rare book.

America at War: The Best of DC War Comics, edited by Michael Uslan, reprints 19 stories from the 1940s through the 1970s, adding a seven-page introduction and a bibliography of that publisher's war comics. None of the examples represent the Korean War (Uslan, 1979: 10).

The Mammoth Book of Best War Comics, edited by David Kendall, also consists primarily of reprinted stories and an even briefer introduction than Uslan had written. The 26 republished stories do not include any Korean War story, and the introduction does not mention that war (Kendall, 2007).

Mike Conroy's War Stories: A Graphic History

offers a serious, book-length overview of the war comic book genre. Its chapter on "Korean and Vietnam Wars" provides a lavishly illustrated survey and a detailed text, focused on the comic books but without much historical context about the war itself (Conroy, 2009).

Adam Riches' *When the Comics Went to War* gives a highly detailed, well-illustrated account of British war comics, beginning with war stories in Victorian story papers of the 19th century. I was unable to find the word "Korea" in it (Riches, 2009).

Examples from one of the war comics series published by the company now known as Marvel during the Korean War have been reprinted as *Marvel Masterworks: Atlas Era Battlefield, Volume 1* (Chapman and Rico, 2011).

DC Showcase: Our Army at War reprints the first 20 issues of that series, including nineteen Korean War comics stories from when that war was being fought. The stories in that series included almost none of the topical references that might have bored children (DC Showcase, 2010).

The two war-comics series created by editor/cartoonist Harvey Kurtzman, *Two-Fisted Tales* and *Frontline Combat*, were republished in 1980 and 1982 respectively as boxed sets with notes and comments by John Benson, Bill Mason and E.B. Boatner. More recently, Fantagraphics has republished these war stories organized by artist rather than by title, beginning with *Corpse on the Imjin*, collecting the stories that Kurtzman both wrote and drew (Kurtzman, 2012).

21. Edwards, 2018: 93–138 (Chapter VIII, "The Infidelity of the Storytellers").

22. Halliday and Cumings, 1988: 88, 89, 123 and 174.

23. For information, see: http://www.english.ufl.edu/comics/scholars/.

24. These include Elizabeth B. Dunn (Research Services Librarian, Duke University), Tessa Brawley (Research Assistant, Syracuse University Library), Maria Medina (Archivist for the Archdiocese of Hartford), Amy P. Muscato (Manuscript Reference Intern, Library of Congress), Jocelyn K. Wilk (Bureau of Applied Social Research Records, Columbia University), Joan R. Duffy (Archives Assistant, Yale Divinity School Library), Sharon Sumpter (The Archives of The University of Notre Dame), Susan Liberator (Curatorial Assistant, Ohio State University), Ken Stewart (Archives Research Administrator, South Dakota State Historical Society), and Kevin M. Bailey (Reference Archivist, Dwight D. Eisenhower Presidential Library and Museum).

25. I welcome mail c/o EduComics, Box 45831, Seattle, WA 98145–0831, USA.

Chapter 1

1. Frank Motler has created a remarkable "Korean War Pre-Code Checklist, 1950–1955" which lists "all known War Comics published after the 25th June 1950 invasion of South Korea by North Korean forces until Comic Code Approval, March/April 1955." I thank Frank Motler for sending me his updated list. Motler's list includes (by my count) 919 issues of 113 comic book series from 32 publishers which published war stories in that period. (This count does not include Motler's data for issues of war comic books published after 1955.)

In addition to the war comics mentioned above, I have separated out of Motler's combined list 40 issues of eight military humor titles (including, for example, *Beetle Bailey* and *Sad Sack*); 53 issues of four wartime romance comic book series; and eight giveaway comics that mention the Korean War. I calculated these totals using Motler's October 30, 2003 revision of his list, which updated information that had originally been published in the fanzine *From the Tomb #9*, Halloween, 2002. There it accompanied his illustrated article "Unsung Heroes: Pre-Code Comics of The Korean War" (Motler, 2002).

2. Regarding North Korea's reputation as the world's "most militarized" nation, Andrew Scobell argues that "There is little question that North Korea is the most militarized state and society in the world. This is true whether one calculates the number of uniformed personnel in the armed forces, reserves, and militia as a proportion of the total population, the percentage of government expenditures allocated for defense, or the share of the DPRK economy that the defense sector comprises" (Scobell, 2007: 117+).

Nevertheless, South Korea's military is stronger, and is backed by a military alliance with the United States. United States troops in South Korea are no longer necessary to defend against a North Korean invasion (Faux, 2018).

3. The Armistice Agreement had not been designed as a permanent solution, but as a cease-fire leading to a conference where the reunification of Korea and the withdrawal of all foreign military forces would be arranged. This conference was held in Geneva from April to June 1954. (Coincidentally these were also the months when the Senate was investigating comic books in New York City.) (Brands, 1987: 60.)

4. James I. Matray's survey of Korean War histories found a consensus that the Korean War marked "a watershed in post-war international affairs, militarizing the Soviet-American competition and extending the Cold War contest for dominance to the entire world" (Matray, 2011: 99; see also Lee, 2001: 4).

5. Gene Michaud has described differences between how his working-class and his middle-class students interpret combat films. I recognize the patterns he identified in my middle-class readings of the working-class genre of war comics (Michaud, 1997).

6. My father, like his brothers, served in the U.S. Army Air Corps in Europe during World War II. My mother's brother served in the Army in France, beginning in 1954.

7. Rand, 1967: 259. My first memory of wondering what the Korean War had been about was puzzling over Ayn Rand's incorrect prediction that "Not many men would volunteer for such wars as Korea or Vietnam. Without the power to draft, the makers

of our foreign policy would not be able to embark on adventures of that kind. This is one of the best practical reasons for the abolition of the draft."

8. I remember two of her writings that cooled my enthusiasm for Rand's work. One appeared in her magazine *The Objectivist*, which I had subscribed to, and was a public renunciation of her extramarital lover for having concealed his own love affair from her (Rand, 1968: 449–456). I concluded that I had been falsely imagining how smooth a life pledged to the principle of rationality would be. The piece that ended my interest in her writings was her 1971 collection of essays *The New Left: The Anti-Industrial Revolution*, which reprinted her opinions about the Free Speech Movement at my university, about ecology activists, and about hippies.

9. I wrote a long account of the circumstances surrounding my first self-published comic, *Quoz*, which appears (along with the comic) in *Treasury of Mini Comics: Volume One* (Rifas, 2013: 10–32).

I survey "underground comix" with a focus on their political content in an entry for the *Encyclopedia of the American Left* (Rifas, 1998 [Buhle, Buhle and Georgakas, eds.]), revised and expanded for the forthcoming third edition.

10. For example, *Food Comics* (1980) and *Food First Comics* (1982) supported small farms and opposed globalization of agriculture. *Energy Comics* (1980) supported local, renewable energy and opposed centralized energy production based on fossil fuels and nuclear power. Later, the World Trade Organization (WTO) was created, which forbade participating governments from giving advantages to local producers, and I responded by creating a comic against the WTO, *The Big Picture: Visualizing the Global Economy* (Rifas, 1999).

11. These included China Books (which championed the People's Republic of China), the Socialist Party bookstore (which focused primarily on Latin America), the Old Wives Tales bookstore (which specialized in feminist empowerment), and two large independent left bookstores (including Modern Times, where I felt at home). Other places that sold my comics in my neighborhood were Gary Arlington's San Francisco Comic Book Company (a comic book shop, historically important as the epicenter of the underground comix movement), the Galería de la Raza book display, and a punk bookstall. I once visited my neighborhood's Communist Party Bookstore (which championed the Soviet Union) and once visited a short-lived libertarian bookstore which had opened on the edge of our neighborhood, and I found my comic book about nuclear power on sale in both places.

12. I describe my experience of working for Denis Kitchen in a sidebar in *Kitchen Sink Press: The First 25 Years* (Rifas, 1994: 46).

13. I had been bothered by the reviewer's apparent assumption that I held strong political opinions and had turned to comic books as a medium for promoting them. I saw myself as a comic book fan, writing comic books about current issues as a way of *discovering* my political opinions.

14. I describe how anti-nuclear perspectives soon came to be accepted as nonpolitical "entertainment" in "Cartooning and Nuclear Power: From Industry Advertising to Activist Uprising and Beyond" (Rifas, 2007: 255–260). Fredrik Strömberg discusses my 1976 comic book *All-Atomic Comics* in *Comic Art Propaganda: A Graphic History* (Strömberg, 2010: 106–7). My thoughts on ideological analysis of comic books, with details about a mainstream comic book that had negatively portrayed anti-nuclear protesters, appear in my chapter "Ideology: The Construction of Race and History in *Tintin in the Congo*" (Rifas, 2012: 221–234).

15. Rifas, 1991.

16. Heonik Kwon challenges the consensus view that the Cold War ended with the fall of the Berlin Wall and the Soviet Union by denying that such a thing as "the" Cold War ever existed, and insisting that we must specify which dimensions of whose "cold war" we are talking about (Kwon, 2010: 6).

17. For a list of theses and dissertations about comics and other resources for comics scholarship, see Gene Kannenberg's website http://www.comicsresearch.org/.

At the invitation of its founding editor/publisher, John Lent, I wrote a piece about my career as a pioneering "comics scholar" for *The International Journal of Comic Art* (Rifas, 2015).

18. See, for examples, the videos produced by the Media Education Foundation (http://www.mediaed.org/).

19. The main controversy over political content in comic books since 2017 has been "Comicsgate," which Mark S. Miller explains as "an alliance of comic book fans, critics, and creators who have found common cause in standing up against what they see as a hard push by social justice warriors into their hobby." They unite around the principle that superhero comics are for escapist, apolitical entertainment and should not be corrupted or politicized by "political or ideological proselytizing" (https://whatiscomicsgate.com).

Richard C. Meyer, the most prominent instigator of the Comicsgate movement through his Twitter and YouTube accounts, is an Army veteran who, in 2013, had co-written a graphic novel commemorating the Korean War's Battle of Chosin Reservoir (Elbein, 2018).

Self-described leftist Aubrey Sitterson became a Comicsgate target and lost his job as the writer of *G.I. Joe* comic books.

20. Children's Fears…, 1984: 8; Nakazawa, 1982.

21. Near the end of his life, Keiji Nakazawa told an interviewer why he had tried to frighten Japanese children with his comics:

Some readers wrote to say "This is too terrible. You shouldn't draw this." But I believe you have to show those scenes of the Bomb. You can't just say it was terrible; you have to see its effects. You can't draw that without having experienced it. I lived through something awful and I wanted to convey that to the readers. So I drew without restraint. But I got that response from readers so

I toned it down quite a bit. Even so, people say it is frightening. One parent wrote a letter, "After my child read *Barefoot Gen*, he's too scared to go to the toilet. Stop drawing such frightening manga." I wrote a letter back to the parent: "You have a wonderful child. It'd be far worse to read the story casually and not be frightened by it." I'm glad when I hear that people are frightened. I hope to sow the seeds of resolve among my readers to never again take the path of war and to never use nuclear weapons. Reluctantly, I toned down my drawings [Ishida, 2011: 45:16–47:02].

22. Bliley's testimony describes Keiji Nakazawa's *I SAW IT* as a comic available at teachers' conferences and accompanied by a lesson plan. Although I had advertised the availability of a lesson plan, I did not actually get around to completing one because I received so few requests for classroom copies or for lesson plans.

I had been attempting to run an educational comic book company without depending on schools, since I preferred to be supported directly by my readers, and did not like the idea of selling comics to some people (teachers) who would force other people (students) to read them. Since then, I have learned that my college and university students greatly appreciate being assigned to read Nakazawa's comics and I have realized how unlikely it would be for these grateful students to have bought his comics on their own.

I imagine that the person most responsible for bringing my republications of Nakazawa's comics to teachers' conferences would have been Florence M. Hongo, founder of the Japanese-American Curriculum Project, which became the Asian American Curriculum Project. I remain grateful that the JACP encouraged my republications of Nakazawa's work and included them in their catalog (http://asianamericanbooks.com/).

23. I describe my experiences publishing Nakazawa's *I SAW IT* in great detail in "Globalizing Comic Books from Below: How Manga Came to America" (Rifas, 2004b).

24. I am grateful to Bob Beerbohm for his support for this project. Old war comics are one of his specialties.

25. Savage, 1998: 52; Wagner, 1954: 94.

26. Lent, 1995: 11. (I have not seen these Korean comics. I thank John Lent for a copy of this article.) John Lent surveys the history of Korean comics in a chapter of his book *Asian Comics* (Lent, 2015: 76–95).

27. "Comic books for sale in Korea," 1952.

28. Schramm and Riley, 1951: 760.

29. Zwetsloot, 2015. See also Fenkl (n.d.) and Strangio, 2011.

30. South Korea's "peak strength" of 602,902 out of a total UN peak strength of 972,334 would put South Koreans at 62 percent of the total. However, the Wikipedia "Korean War" article which provides citations for each nation's peak strength cautions that their "figures vary by source" and that "peak unit strength varied during war."

31. A writer surveyed the titles on the newsstands of the capital Peking (Beijing) and of Mukden (Shenyang) in 1951, and pronounced 80 percent of them to be "backward" and "reactionary" comic books, mostly dealing with sex and violence and other "stupid and ridiculous subjects," such as exaggerating the power of atomic bombs. Worse, readers preferred these "old, feudalistic and backward" adventure stories to the "new and progressive" comic books about heroes and model workers that the Communist Chinese government published (Chen, 1955: 59–62; "Chinese writer says...," 1952).

32. Wang, 2019: 82.

33. See the chapter on China in John A. Lent's *Asian Comics* (Lent, 2015: 34), and "Chapter 4: Liberation, Maoist Campaigns, and Cartoons, 1949–1976" from *Comics Arts in China* (Lent and Xu, 2017).

34. Wang, 2019: 82.

35. An unsigned journal article, "The Popularisation of War in Comic Strips 1958–1988," remembers British war comics, beginning in 1958, as "the only all-picture strip comics available to the 11 to 16 age group" ("The Popularisation of War...," 1996: 182). The same article claims that American war comics between World War II and the introduction of these British war comics "failed to gain any popularity, and were always among those left on the rack to be returned to the wholesaler when the new assortment arrived."

The website of the long-running British war comic *Commando* includes stories coded as taking place in the "Korean War era." The summary of "Reds!" by Ferg Handley (issue 4749; October 11, 2014) differs markedly from the plots of American war comics:

Young Joe Cooper was a convinced socialist. Sent to serve in the Korean War, the idealistic National Serviceman hated the idea that he might have to kill the Chinese communists he thought of as fellow socialists.

To keep his conscience clear, he decided only to shoot to wound, not to kill.

Faced with the grim reality of battle, though, could he stick to his convictions in the desperate struggle to survive?[http://www.commandocomics.com/collection/issue-4749-reds].

I thank Paul Sammut for a copy of that comic book. (In *Reds!*, young Joe Cooper learns the difference between socialists and communists.)

36. Riches, 2009: 26–9.

37. Bell, 2006: 43.

38. Bell, 2006: 92.

39. Bell, 2006: 95–6. See also Wertham, 1953, 1954: 273–284.

40. Bell, John and Michel Viau, 2002.

41. Bell, 2006: 96.

42. Benice, 2018: 9.

43. Benice, 2018: 12–13, 23–25.

44. "Muslims Celebrate 50 Years in Korea," 2005.

45. Ryan, 1979: 203.

I thank comics scholar Ronald Stewart for the further information in this section (Ronald Stewart,

Sept. 16, 2013, e-mail to author) I have not yet seen any Australian war comics.

46. *Tim Valour* covers, including some with Korean War themes, are webposted at: http://www.ausreprints.com/content/main/?series=2721&ms=16526.

Other Australian comics from the early 1950s, such as *Char Chapman: Phantom of the East* (written and illustrated by Kevan Hardacre) placed greater emphasis on Australia's involvement in the "Malayan Emergency," a military campaign waged by British Commonwealth forces (including Australia) against communist insurgents in Malaya (now Malaysia) throughout 1948–1960. I am indebted for this information to Kevin Patrick, creator of *Comics Down Under* (http://comicsdownunder.blogspot.com) (Kevin Patrick, August 31, 2013, e-mail message to author).

47. Shiell, 1998: 62, 143.

The editorial in the first issue of *Sky Hawk*, quoted by Shiell, presents the "typical Australian" hero: "There is nothing phoney about the leading characters in our stories. They are all fine chaps with a lust for life lived bravely and healthily—the sort of blokes we would all like to be. They are people of character and of ideals that soar high—just like a Sky Hawk."

48. In a survey of Australian comics scholarship, Kevin Patrick provides a guide to the research on these points (Patrick, 2010).

49. Docker, 1984: 198–199.

50. Cawelti, 1976: 16–17.

51. Here I extend the arguments that Richard Gid Powers has made about the representation of the FBI in American popular culture (Powers, 1983: xii–xiv).

52. Hazel Kepler explained the appeal of comic books' formula fiction in a 1952 guide for parents and teachers:"The very fact that the plot is stereotyped, the outcome predictable, that among the many moments of suspense there is certainly none over the ultimate triumph of good over evil, gives the child a sense of security. In other words, the very things that would bore you to death are the familiar props which give the child a feeling of comfort and content" (Kepler, 1952: 183).

53. Psychologist William Moulton Marston, the creator of Wonder Woman, wrote in 1943: "Nine humans out of ten react first with their feelings rather than with their minds; the more primitive the emotion stimulated, the stronger the reaction. Comics play a trite but lusty tune on the C natural keys of human nature. They rouse the most primitive, but also the most powerful, reverberations in the noisy cranial sound-box of consciousness, drowning out more subtle symphonies. [...] Comics speak, without qualm or sophistication, to the innermost ears of the wishful self" (Marston, 1943–1944).

Chapter 2

1. Lockwood, 1965: 45; Leab, 1965: 42–47. "Deen [sic] Wilderness" and "Happy Easter" were support-

ing characters in Milt Caniff's *Steve Canyon* comic strip, first appearing in 1947.

In "Cold War Comics," Leab had concluded: "One must ask whether the cold-war comics, directed at the least sophisticated part of the audience, and offering glib solutions to world problems and caricatures of contemporary personalities both East and West, do not actually do harm. A newspaper presents itself as a reporter of fact; these comic strips are misrepresentations of actuality. The cold-war comics raise questions of journalistic responsibility for newspapers and their editors."

2. In my master's thesis, a lengthy digression at this point in the text described a history of the entanglement of fact and fiction, and went on to cite what several philosophers and scholars have said against the idea that representations "mirror" realities. These included Richard Rorty, Ludwig Wittgenstein, Martin Heidegger, John Dewey, George Lakoff and Mark Johnson, C.G. Prado, Lennard J. Davis, Valentin Volosinov, and Martin Barker (Rifas, 1991).

3. Weintraub, 2000: ix, 63, 93; Pash, 2012: 91; Green, 2010: 112–113, 127; Edwards, 2006: 7; Ridgeway, 1967: 2; Harden, 2017: 18.

A quote, posted in large letters on the wall of a temporary exhibit in South Korea's War Memorial museum in August 2013, described the smell of that war differently. It quoted William Stableforth (not further identified) as remembering: "It was a beautiful country, wild, hills all purple and icy and the air was very fresh, clear, not like Tynesdale." Whether the smells remembered were of garlic, gunpowder, and gasoline fumes or something else, the point remains: comic books could not convey the smell of really being there.

4. *Buck Rogers of the 25th Century #100*, January 1951–May-June 1951, Toby Press. I thank Frank Motler for a copy of this piece.

5. That the villains were "Mongols" distantly echoes the traumatic Mongol invasions of the 13th century, which had created an empire that briefly stretched from Korea in the East to Central Europe in the West.

6. February 8, 1929; February 11, 1929; February 21, 1929; March 9, 1929.

The series is web-posted by Roland Anderson at: http://www.rolandanderson.se/comics/buckrogers/buckstrips.php.

The reference to "Mongol Reds" presumably was inspired by the recently established "Mongolian People's Republic."

7. Several comic book stories included women reporters in Korea, likely because the writers were thinking of Marguerite Higgins, one of the first war reporters to arrive in Korea. (See also "Marine Saves White Horse Hill" in *With the Marines on the Battlefronts of the World #2*, March 1954.)

8. Tucker, 2006: 125.

9. "War of Nerves," 1950.

10. Nowlan and Calkins, 2008: 8, 17.

11. Tucker, 2006: 135.

Eric Croddy's book on chemical and biological warfare speculates that the Chinese military leaders believed that the U.S. military was using chemical weapons even though the evidence shows that they were not because, "resultant off-gases from bombardments were no doubt responsible for respiratory distress and pulmonary edema among Chinese soldiers, symptoms that are largely indistinguishable from lung irritants found in chemical weapons" (Croddy, 2002: 160–161).

12. Tucker, 2006: 126–128, 136. During the Korean War, American nerve gas plans had been delayed by technical and management problems, but soon, after the armistice, the U.S. began producing thousands of tons of Sarin nerve gas. In 1997, the United States promised to decommission its chemical weapons, but has missed several deadlines to do so (Monbiot, 2013).

13. In 1950, "In the [Air Force School of Aviation Medicine's] far reaching research program, the possibility of travel through inter-planetary space is not regarded as a mere phantom of the comic-strip artist's imagination. Current rocket development indicates the possibility of flight beyond the stratosphere in the foreseeable future" (Woods, 1950: 54).

Others were less "far reaching." In 1959, Dr. Lloyd V. Berkner remembered that serious government interest in the possibility of artificial satellites had been retarded in the early 1950s because "Buck Rogers of the comic strips had so shrouded space exploration in fantasy that men were hard pressed to believe that the space age was here" (Berkner, 1959: 22).

14. *The New York Times,* February 19, 1951 (p. 1:7) and February 21, 1951 (p. 2:2), citing the current issue of *Naval Aviation News*; *Newsweek*, March 3, 1952 (p. 44).

15. In January 1951, *Don Winslow of the Navy #65* featured the three-part story "Flying Saucer Attack." Another flying saucer story, Alex Toth's "Seeley's Saucer" in *Jet Fighters #7* (1952), tells of an American pilot ridiculed for seeing flying saucers, but it turns out he has seen a top-secret American experimental aircraft. "Suicide Alley" in *War Report # 5* (May 1953) pictured an American pilot encountering flying saucers in Korea. A flying saucer story, in which the saucer turns out to be a Russian secret weapon appeared in *Wings Comics No. 124* in 1954.

According to Korean War historian Paul Edwards, at the time, UFO sightings in Korea were thought to be experimental Russian weapons. He devotes a chapter of his book *Unusual Footnotes to the Korean War* to "Unidentified Flying Objects over Korea" (Edwards, 1977).

Wikipedia summarizes the history of military-funded attempts to build a real flying saucer during the Korean War in its entry on the "Avro Canada VZ-9 Avrocar."

16. *Captain Marvel's Adventures #147*, August 1953, "Captain Marvel and the Riddle of the Space Reds."

17. Captain Marvel stories were directed at younger readers than the usual war comics, thus creating a situation which C.C. Beck, the cartoonist who drew Captain Marvel, later described, "Back in the comic book dark ages nobody got his name on a comic-book feature. This was because, our edi-

tors told us, readers believed that the stories in comic books were true, and putting the name of a writer or an artist on them would be an admission that they were 'made up' or fiction" (Beck, 1986: 7).

18. In 2006, World War II combat veteran Edward W. Wood, Jr., observed that "Not one of the men and women in the administration who so praise war and its positive consequences has ever been in war. [...] Imagination forms their wars, images that must be drawn from movies, books, and memoirs, images that never convey war's reality" (Wood, 2006: 7).

19. Similarly, "Fangs of the Tiger" in *Spy Cases #10*, April 1952, had a story in which Red radio accuses the U.S. of bombing the neutral zone. Eventually a satisfactory explanation is discovered: "That's why this spy somehow kidnapped Dunsany, killed him ... impersonated him and tried to bomb truce territory! To brand the U.S. before the world as a worthless negotiator!"

20. Matray, 2012: 240–241; Burchett, 1969: 190.

21. Stone, 1952: 318–319; Bevin, 1986: 438–439; Halliday and Cumings, 1988: 160–1.

For a detailed account of one such strafing, written by an Australian journalist who was reporting from the negotiation sites, see Wilfred Burchett's autobiography *At the Barricades*, chapter 17 (Burchett, 1981: 162–174). Presumably in retaliation for repeatedly and effectively contradicting Western official sources, the Australian Minister of Immigration denied Burchett a passport (Burchett, 2008: xiii, xvi–xvii; Burchett, 1969: 196, 279–294).

22. Regarding this kind of loyalty, cartoonist Milton Caniff told his biographer, cartoonist R.C. Harvey: "Of course we [military-themed comic strip creators Roy Crane, George Wunder and himself] were propagandists. ... Same reason you go and cheer your football team. You don't question anything about it. You went to school there, that's your team, and so you root for 'em. You're expected to" (Harvey, 1992: 18).

23. Miller, 1952: 3.

Miller's speech was republished by *Reader's Digest* in December 1952 as "We Haven't Been Getting the Facts About Korea" (29–31).

24. Miller, 1952: 3–5.

Miller gave as an example of a story that had been censored "the actions of the South Korean police who blackmailed innocent farmers, threatening to arrest them as Reds unless they paid off," with the result that hundreds of these farmers "fled into the mountains and joined guerilla units." (4) His examples of false news included casualty estimates ("both those suffered by us and inflicted by us") and a photograph of a bridge, supposedly cut in half by "pin point bombing," but actually blown up by army engineers (6).

Mason Edward Horrell has provided a chronological narrative of military-press relations during the Korean War with appendices detailing the various censorship regulations and listing war correspondents in Korea who had been killed, wounded or captured (Horrell, 2002).

25. Laboratory experiments on the effects of reading un-illustrated fictional short stories have

demonstrated that people add both true and the false knowledge that they learn from fictions to the "knowledge bases" that they use to interpret the world. Most stories (and Korean War comic books in particular) include a mix of reliable information, mistaken information and invented information. Experiments have found that even when readers already knew the correct information, reading a short story that they understand to be fictional increases the likelihood that their answers on a knowledge test will match the incorrect information in the story (Butler, et al. 2012: 488).

26. William Savage wrote that "here were yarns with geo-political points of reference baffling to the adolescent and irrelevant to the adults who read the comic books for whatever visceral enjoyment might come from pictorial Red-bashing" (Savage, 1998: 41).

27. Institute for Propaganda Analysis, 1940: 34. The Institute for Propaganda Analysis had been founded in 1937, to promote rational thinking. Its advisory board ended this Institute during World War II, for fear that teaching young people to recognize propaganda "might serve to disturb the unity needed for the war effort" (Glander, 2000: 22–25).

28. Movius, 1941: 17–20; Hadsel, 1941: 365–368.

29. Movius, 1941: 18. The magazine that published Movius' article, *Scribner's Commentator*, was devoted to keeping Americans from being fooled by "the Communist and New Deal warmakers" into joining World War II. After Pearl Harbor, that magazine folded quickly. Its last issue, published in January 1942, featured General MacArthur on the cover and called for "the complete victory of our armed forces over those of our enemies all over the world" ("George Teeple Eggleston…," 2018).

30. Hadsel, 1941: 365.

Young readers may have been more alert than Movius and Hadsel gave them credit for. In 1941, high school students in Reeseville, Wisconsin answered "the question, 'Do you believe there is propaganda in the funnies?' [with] a 2 to 1 affirmative vote. And there's the new skepticism for you!" ("Findings," 1941).

31. Ronald Archer (age 10) wrote to one of the few continuing characters in the war comics: "Some day when I get eighteen years old I will join up in the Marines like you. So that is why I read Monty Hall so I will be like you too." The editors encouraged him strongly. Lillian Roberts wrote to the same publication: "As a girl reader, please permit me to say that Monty Hall is the handsomest hero in any comic magazine. Not the namby-pamby kind of handsome, like most other heroes, but real masculine" (*Monty Hall of the U.S. Marines #5*, Toby Press, April 1952).

32. Savage describes this as his reaction to "Dien Bien Phu" (a seven-page story written by John Putnam, drawn by John Severin, and published in *Two-Fisted Tales #40*, December 1954/January 1955), which he re-read often as a child (Savage, 1998: 117–118).

33. In 1950, George Seldes wrote that neither opponents nor defenders of comic books "can isolate the effect of the comic books from the effect of the movies and radio, from the headlines and the pictures in tabloids, from conversations in the street and the particular tensions which a child absorbs from his surroundings" (Seldes, 1950: 273).

34. Spain, 2002, p. 1, panels 4–5.

35. For example, comic book publisher Lev Gleason's 1952 article "In defense of comic books" promoted comic books' "amazing potential" to "actually help mold their young readers into happier, more intelligent adults, if developed with that in mind." Gleason argued that comics had tremendous influence, and that this influence can help provide a "decent and ethical framework, foster a realistic understanding of life and a sense of discrimination in literature and art." He added, "One authority has told me that if he could control all the editorial material that goes into comics magazines, he would be able completely to shape the future thinking of this country. That may be an extreme viewpoint, but many agree with him." As for the comic books that critics were attacking, Gleason readily conceded that "The effect of brutality, sex, sadism and cruelty in children's reading matter is self-evident. No comic book which includes such matter can ever be acceptable."

Demonstrating his sincerity, Gleason announced that his company had recently begun a new comic book series, *Uncle Charlie's Fables*, which was designed based on a year's study of what child welfare experts had determined is best for children in a comic book. After a fair trial of five issues, this dull series was quickly forgotten, except perhaps by other publishers, who Gleason had predicted would be "watching its reception to determine whether there is a market for comic books specifically designed to meet the high standards of people working with children" (Gleason, 1952).

36. *Superman* editor Mort Weisinger wrote a 1946 article that included four paragraphs about Superman's activities during World War II to help recycling drives, teach illiterates in the Navy to read, and serve as a decoration on military vehicles (Weisinger 1946: 6).

In 1950, *Superman*'s co-publisher, J.S. "Jack" Liebowitz, explained in a letter to a Senate investigating committee that his company had served the community in various ways. He listed first their creation of special editions of their comic books using simplified vocabulary to help teach illiterates in the Navy to read during World War II; second, their production of (propaganda) comics for Nelson Rockefeller's Office of Inter-American Affairs, which were distributed in Latin America; and third, the contribution to the military effort that they had made through their ordinary newsstand comic books: "Our commercial editions carried important public relations stories for the Army, Navy, and Air Forces, in which the desired message was woven into stories using our regular well-known characters, notably Superman" (*Juvenile Delinquency…*, 1950: 152). See also Reynolds, 1951: 19–21.

37. "Army School …," 1951.

38. Briefly, the pamphlet explains that "Far around the world from where you were—North Korea at Russia's insistence invaded the Republic

of Korea without provocation and this is where you come into the picture." A failure to resist communist aggression in Korea and then Japan "would lead to the ultimate invasion and defeat of the United States," in which case "your wife and children would be hungry, dressed in rags..." "What Am I Doing Here?" Pamphlet prepared by HQ. U.S.A.F.F.E. APO 343, pp. 16–7 (http://www.authentichistory.com/1946-1960/2-korea/5-GI/index.html).

39. Schumacher, 2010: 87.
40. Schumacher, 2010: 93.
41. Schumacher, 2010: 120–135.
42. In 1968, Eisner explained his attitude about cartooning for the Army:

What I'm doing for the Army today is instructional and educational material. We're teaching people how to maintain their equipment. ... I don't feel the slightest feeling of guilt, or separation, or any relationship between that and what I might think about war as war, or warmongering as warmongering. Or even, for that matter, whether or not we should be in Vietnam or shouldn't be in Vietnam. ... I have been devoting the last 20 years, really, to developing the comic-strip medium, which I had always experimented with, into a legitimate teaching tool. This is really the thing I'm proud of. I'll teach anything with that tool. I'd teach how to conduct a peace march in that tool, if we had a customer for it, or if I felt it was useful, or if I had a place where it could be distributed. I'll teach ... do a comic strip on how to burn your draft card, if I felt that was an area ... fix an engine ... anything [Eisner, 1968].

Perhaps it goes without saying that when cartooning for the highest-paying clients, the Army would be able to outbid peace march organizers or draft card burners whenever it wanted to.

Eisner revisited this subject in a documentary video about his career: "Occasionally I would get criticism from my more liberal friends, particularly the ones that I knew while I was in school because when I was in high school, I was very radical and I hung around with revolutionary kids and so, many years later, they still get in touch with me and they said 'how can you produce work for the military? You are a merchant of death,' and I pointed out to them that what I was doing was teaching men how to save their lives. It wasn't necessarily teaching them how to kill. I'm very proud of what I did" (Eisner, 1999: 17:59–19:08).

In the most detailed account of this part of his career, Eisner remembered that he had been in Korea when he received this encouragement: "Once during the Korean War when I was on a field trip to Korea, I remember walking into a shop, and a big mechanic came over to me and shoved his big paw into mine and said, 'Thank you very much: you saved my ass.' And he explained how I had done something that nobody had ever explained quite that simply. He said, 'I got no time to read them manuals; I'm fightin' a war here'" (Harvey, 2001).

43. Sharon Beder wrote in "The Role of 'Economic Education' in Achieving Capitalist Hegemony": "Corporations, and the PR people hired by them, identified business interests with national interest and 'the traditional American free-enterprise system with social harmony, freedom, democracy, the family, the church, and patriotism' whilst they identified 'all government regulation of the affairs of business, and all liberals who supported such *interference*,' with communism and subversion" (Beder, 2006).

The 1948 comic book *We Hit the Jackpot* explained that Americans "have more than all the rest of the world put together" because of freedom. Other anti-socialist comic books included the National Association of Manufacturers' comic book *Fight for Freedom* (1949) which promoted NAM's "philosophy of freedom, individual rights, and personal initiative"; *America Under Socialism* (1950); and *Alice in Blunderland* (1952). ("These Comic Books," 1950) The URLs for these four comics appear in the bibliography.

44. "Advertising News," 1951.
45. Shaw, 2001: 59–76. In the United States, "media effects" research became an important part of the new academic discipline of Communications Research, which was nourished by millions of dollars in grants from the Department of Defense, the U.S. Information Agency and the CIA. For details, see Christopher Simpson's book *Science of Coercion* (Simpson, 1994). See also communications scholar Steven H. Chaffee's generally unfavorable review of Simpson's book (Chaffee, 1995).

Two studies of the possible effects of war comics, perhaps the only two such studies, concluded in the 1960s that war comics *did* influence their readers. Both seem to have been based on British war comics (Johnson, 1966; Lovibond, 1967).

46. Kurtzman, 1980. Page preceding No. 21, May-June 1951. In 2010, an interviewer asked Joe Kubert whether he approaches war comics "with a moral duty as an artist." He answered: "I try to be as honest as I can. Bob Kanigher [the writer/editor he worked with] and I used to discuss this at great length. [...] Neither one of us was in combat or anything like that, but we knew a lot of people who were. It ain't fun. It ain't fun at all. What we wanted to do was to portray that the people involved in these situations weren't there because they enjoyed it, but because they were called upon to serve. As a matter of fact, we started finishing each Sgt. Rock story with a bullet and the words 'Make War No More'" (Pedler, 2010). Kubert served in Fort Dix, New Jersey and then Germany, from 1950–1952 (Spurgeon, 2012).

47. Naimark, 2010: 130. Norman M. Naimark concludes his book *Stalin's Genocides*: "For a number of reasons, the Holocaust should be thought of as the worst case of genocide in the modern era. Nevertheless, the points of comparison between Stalin and Hitler, Nazism and Stalinism, are too many to ignore. ... Both—in the end—were genocidaires" (Naimark, 2010: 137).

Timothy Snyder reports that archival research in recent decades has shown that "the total number of noncombatants killed by the Germans—about 11 million—is roughly what we had thought," but the "total figure of civilians deliberately killed under

Stalinism, around six million, is [...] far lower than the estimates of twenty million or more made before we had access to Soviet sources" (Snyder, 2011).

48. Gelb, 1995. The deportation order, Resolution No. 1428–326CC, is quoted in Wikipedia's article "Deportation of Koreans in the Soviet Union." Victoria Kim has created a multimedia report on the horrific deportation of Koreans to Uzbekistan (Kim, 2016).

49. Applebaum, 2012.

50. Some of these examples appear in Haynes, 2000. With the Communist Control Act of 1954, passed (almost unanimously) and signed into law in August of that year, the United States outlawed the Communist Party as "an instrumentality of a conspiracy to overthrow the Government of the United States" by "any available means, including resort to force and violence." (The law was not enforced.)

51. Gardner wrote, "True art is by its nature moral. We recognize true art by its careful, thoroughly honest search for and analysis of values. It is not didactic because, instead of teaching by authority and force, it explores, open-mindedly, to learn what it should teach." Gardner compares writing fiction to conducting an experiment in a chemistry lab: "As a chemist's experiment tests the laws of nature and dramatically reveals the truth or falsity of scientific hypotheses, moral art tests values and rouses trustworthy feelings about the better and the worse in human action" (Gardner, 1978, 2000: 19; 115–6).

52. A field of radical children's literature did exist, and was (in the words of Jack Zipes) "dismissed and repressed" (Mickenberg and Nel, 2008: vii). The only comic book artist in Mickenberg and Nel's anthology of this literature, Walt Kelly, is not represented by his studiously apolitical comic books or his famously political comic strip, but by a 22-page comic-book-format piece he drew for one of his books, caricaturing Joe McCarthy in an *Alice in Wonderland* story.

Chapter 3

1. In Harriet A. Bradfield's 1950 article "The Chain Publishers and Their Titles," Goodman's Magazine Management Co. has 27 magazines listed and 32 comic book titles (Bradfield, 1950: 103–104). The number of comics titles doubled within five years (*Comic Books and Juvenile Delinquency*, 1955: 46).

An interview that Josh Alan Friedman conducted with writer/editor/cartoonist Mel Shestack powerfully conveys the atmosphere of that company in the early 1960s (Friedman, 1984, 2019).

2. These are my calculations, based on Frank Motler's data (Motler, 2003). The number of issues of war comic books published by their next seven competitors were: DC, 58; Harvey, 54; Ziff-Davis, 47; Farrell, 41; Toby, 41; EC, 34; and Fawcett, 30. Michael J. Vassallo, who has personally indexed all Marvel war comics from 1950 to 1960, counted that in that decade Marvel published "512 full war comic issues, with 21 additional partial war content issues [...] in titles like *Man Comics, Men's Adventures,*

Young Men, Spy Cases, Spy Fighters and *Kent Blake*" (Vassallo, 2011: third page [unnumbered]).

3. "An Interview with Stan Lee" (Pitts, 2007: 86–87). The vast majority of Stan Lee's many comic book writing credits during the Korean War consisted of scripts for *My Friend Irma, Millie the Model, Nellie the Nurse,* and *Hedy of Hollywood Comics* (www. comics.org).

4. Canote, 2007; Saunders, 2014. The Grand Comics Database (comics.org) can generate lists of the "indicia/colophon" names by publisher. In *Seduction of the Innocent*, Wertham pointed out the "ludicrous discrepancy" when stories with adult dialogue (such as "You know as well as I do that any water he'd drink'd pour right out of his gut! It'd be MURDER!") appear under the imprimatur of Tiny Tot Comics, Inc. (This example came from "Combat Medic!," which appeared in EC's *Frontline Combat #4*'s issue dated January–February 1952.)

5. Bell and Vassallo, 2013: 35–9.

6. Bell and Vassallo, 2013: 15.

7. Bell and Vassallo, 2013: 53.

8. Collier, n.d.; Saunders, 2014.

9. For examples, see http://www.coverbrowser.com/covers/spicy-adventure-stories.

10. "Harry Donenfeld's FBI Files," posted at Muckrock: https://cdn.muckrock.com/foia_documents/7-2-12_mr1054_RES-email.pdf. (Of these 218 pages, see pages: 27, 36, and 73–74.) For a different version of the story see Saunders, 2014.

Donenfeld's FBI files also include rumors and informants' allegations that thanks to his connections with gansters of the "underworld," a "strong arm crew" forced newsstands to handle his company's obscene magazines and harassed his competitors. (See pages: 68, 99, 118–119, 137–139, 162, 167, and 178.)

11. Wertham, 1953, 1954: 254.

12. *John Wayne Adventure Comics #12*, 1951. John Wayne fights in Korea again in issues #14 and #15.

13. Fred McDonald's *Television and the Red Menace* includes several tables of "cold war" programming. Most of the shows listed on the tables on pages 124, 194 and 196 became short-lived comic book series (McDonald, 1985).

14. Yronwode, 1985: 35. As for whether Busy Arnold knew anything about comic book "art," Ken Quattro has web-posted business correspondence between Arnold and his partner Will Eisner from 1940 and 1941. In the web-posted letters, Arnold orders changes in characterization, style, backgrounds, continuity, content, lettering, tone, composition, topicality, and choice of artist, in addition to discussing more purely business matters (Quattro, 2013).

15. "Comic Book Originator...," 1954. By the time of the Korean War, Wildenberg had disassociated himself from comic books and moved to Tampa, Florida, to manufacture cigars. In 1950, Wildenberg said of crime comics "I think they are pretty awful. They leave no residue of worthwhile knowledge with the young reader. The adult that reads them is beyond saving" (Adcock, 2014). In 1952, Wildenberg was quoted as saying that he regretted having

invented the comic book and would like to see them abolished (McReynolds, 1952) In 1954, Wildenberg was reported to have said that "practically none of the comics on the newsstands are good mental food for children" and that "he is in full sympathy with any effort to control the subject matter of comic books" ("Comic Book Originator…," 1954).

16. Gabilliet, 2010: 111–116, 125.

17. R.C. Harvey explains that Will Eisner came up with new ways of laying out stories in comic book format when he was reformatting material for republication in the 1930s. Eisner then applied what he had learned when creating his original comic book material. Harvey cites Kurtzman's opinion that "It was Eisner more than anyone else, who developed the multipage booklet story form that became the grammar of the medium" (Harvey, 2001).

18. Sanders, 2016: 11–12.

19. Malter, 1952.

20. The big three categories at the time of that study were humor, crime (including superhero comics) and romance (Graalfs, 1954: 4–5, 11).

21. Gabilliet wrote:

Of the thirteen active distributors in the comic book industry of 1954, there existed no less than seven publisher-distributors (Ace, Atlas [Marvel], Capital [Charlton], Fawcett, Gilberton, Independent News [DC], George A. Pflaum). The distributor would ship the comics to its regional clients (independent distributors) who served as wholesalers. There were around seven hundred of these in 1952. These independent distributors provided comics to retailers, not only newsstands but also grocery stores, pharmacies, and other neighborhood stores […] as well as roadside bus and railway stations, where numerous books and magazines of all types were sold to travelers. In 1952, there were approximately one hundred thousand press retailers in the United States [Gabilliet, 2010: 139].

22. Two comic book shops did exist during the Korean War. Pop Hollinger's basement-level used comic book store in Concordia, Kansas, operated from the late 1930s until 1971, when the insurance company for the food store upstairs made the closure of this basement fire hazard a condition for continuing the food store's policy (Hessee, 1982) Also, Claude Held began dealing comics in Buffalo, New York, in 1946 (Gabilliet, 2010: 260).

23. A study of comic books sold in Washington State in 1954 found that: 1. Comic books are published quarterly, monthly, and bi-monthly, although some have no stated schedule. 2. They are released irregularly so that it is not unusual to observe retail stands displaying in the same months books with different issue dates; e.g., in January may be found books dated February, March, April, or May. 3. The length of time a particular issue of a title remains on the stands varies. Some remain two weeks; others, ten weeks (Graalfs, 1954: 2).

24. This estimate was quoted in several places, for example by Albert E. Kahn (Kahn, 1954).

25. Quoted in Craig, 1956: 3.

26. Various estimates of the overall size of the comic book industry during this period are available, but the figures quoted here are especially noteworthy because these were accompanied by an explanation of how they were derived. They were published in *Comic Books and Juvenile Delinquency*: "in 1950, about 300 comic-book titles were being published with annual revenues of nearly $41 million. The upswing in the next three years brought the number of titles to over 650 and the gross to about $90 million. Average monthly circulation jumped from close to 17 million copies in 1940 to 68 million in 1953" (*Comic Books and Juvenile Delinquency*,1955: 3).

According to their notes, "No accurate figures are available. Many of the newer publishers of comic books do not report to the Audit Bureau of Circulations nor to the Controlled Circulation Audits, the two firms that compile circulation figures. The subcommittee, in making the above estimate, took the most conservative estimate." According to a rumor which I have not been able to substantiate, because comic book circulation was not audited, comic book publishing and distributing became attractive to organized crime as "a great way to launder money." If so, this would imply that comic book circulations were smaller than reported.

27. Schelly, 2008: 118–120. The numbers posted at Mike's Amazing World of Comics show the peak a few years earlier, in 1952, and a slower decline: http://www.mikesamazingworld.com/mikes/index.php?page=pubstats.

28. Harvey, 2017.

29. Feiffer, 1967: 50–51.

30. Gruenberg, 1944: 205.

31. "Comic Book writer…," 1999.

32. Metcalf, 1995. The Grand Comics Database identifies 1,350 of Paul S. Newman's stories, and this list of his Korean War comic books is taken from that source.

33. Metcalf, 1995: 150. The next generation of writers also worked on what sold. Roy Thomas (born in 1940) recalls that "I rarely if ever read war comics (one of the reasons it was such an irony that my first ongoing adventure-comics assignment at Marvel was SGT. FURY)" (Roy Thomas, July 2, 2011, e-mail to author). I thank Roy Thomas for his correspondence and encouragement and his contributions to comics history.

34. Schelly, 2008: 129. The Sgt. Rock series was one of DC's best-selling comic books (Schelly, 2008: 136). When asked in 2010 whether he had become associated with war comics as something he had pursued or just by chance, Kubert answered: "I've been asked that before, and the answer is: my business is one in which if I find success, you keep repeating it! I took on the war stories in the early '60s—Bob Kanigher was my editor and writer at that time—and the stories I did apparently sold magazines. So I was given more. It's not because I had a particular interest. Whatever work that I have on my table, whatever I'm currently working on, is my favorite story" (Pedler, 2010).

In a 1994 *Comics Journal* interview, Kubert had

been even more emphatic, denying that he had any particular interest in war comics at all: "No. Not really. It was a job. One that I was fortunate to get. And by taking that job on, I felt I had to do the best I could. Therefore, I did a lot of reference and research on the subject, and I tried to do each subsequent job better than the last one. But I've never had any special affinity for war stuff at all … the war stuff held no special love for me" (http://www.tcj.com/the-joe-kubert-interview/3/).

35. Evanier, 2008: 87.

The stories Kirby told about his wartime experiences appear in *Jack Kirby Collector #27*. Kirby concluded by saying: "There is nothing that you would call 'romantic' about war. Sure, in the movies and on television they paint a great picture of the fellowship that it creates. I've seen war bring lots of people together, but I can tell you that the cost is extremely high: Not just in terms of lives, but in the human spirit. … This country has always been at war—Perhaps that is how it will end" (Wyman, 2000).

Kirby also tells his war stories in a web-posted video interview: https://www.youtube.com/watch?v=866ToIkLksA. Jack Kirby often had nightmares about World War II that woke him in a cold sweat for the rest of his life (Evanier, 2008: 69). An exhaustive list of the comic book stories Jack Kirby drew during the Korean War consists entirely of romance comics, horror and western comics, with no examples of superheroes or war comics (Owens, n.d.).

36. Gabilliet, 2010: 121–124.

37. Simon, 1982: 22. Some other quotes from Will Eisner's series of interviews with pioneering comic book artists:

Jack Kirby: "We were factories and we were turning out products thick and fast because they wanted books rapidly and steadily" (*The Spirit*, Issue #39, February 1982).

Joe Kubert: "Many of us were working on scripts that we thought were terrible, absolutely *awful*. But that was the last thing we would tell an editor. That was like yelling sour grapes. And besides, it wasn't too difficult to find an immediate replacement who wouldn't complain about the script" (*The Spirit*, Issue #40, April 1983).

38. Sadowski, 2002: 120.

39. Mangus, 2002. Unlike most of the writers for these series, Kanigher was not a military veteran (Chris Pedrin, Jan 2019, letter to author).

40. Sadowski, 2002: 122.

41. Jack Kirby later said of this attempted organization: "It was something I knew would fail. Everyone was wary. Remember, this was a time when Communists marched through the streets, waving flags and shouting. The unions did the same thing, so you began to associate them" (Sadowski, 2002: 121).

Sebastian T. Mercier has written about the obstacles that prevented early comic book creators from forming or joining a labor union (Mercier, 2018: 110–136).

42. Sadowski, 2013: 256.

43. Tom Engelhardt notes the oddity that in the early 1950s and 1960s, when young boys were spending much of their playtime fighting imaginary versions of World War II, child development experts left the subject of "war play" largely untouched (Engelhardt, 1995: 82–83). In *The End of Victory Culture: Cold War America and the Disillusioning of a Generation*, Engelhardt remembers, "I avidly went to war films, read war comics, and amassed toy soldiers. […] Yet what I so often played at being, I never dreamt of becoming. As a middle-class boy, it did not occur to me that I might grow up to be a soldier" (Engelhardt, 1995; 76, 97). "Bob Levin remembers that when he and his friends read the "anti-war" comic book stories created by Harvey Kurtzman, "we were also avidly assaulting alleys, storming porches, playing war" (Levin, 2013).

44. Harvey Kurtzman, "Combat Correspondence." *Two-Fisted Tales #22*, July–August 1951.

45. The authors of "Reading of Comic Magazines in Dayton, Ohio—A Continuing Study" concluded that because adults form a larger percentage of the total population, even though a much smaller proportion of adults than children read comics, adult readers still outnumbered child readers (*Juvenile Delinquency…*, 1950: 172). Lev Gleason informed the investigating senators in 1950 that "Several years ago, we took a survey to determine the age of readers of Crime Does Not Pay and at that time found that 57 percent were over 21 years of age" (*Juvenile Delinquency…*, 1950: 136).

46. This list of clues is partly adapted from D. Melissa Hilbish, "Advancing in Another Direction: The Comic Book and the Korean War" (Hilbish, 1999: 213). One war comic ad that describes its intended reader with demographic detail appeared in *The Fighting Man #8* in July 1953: "For men in their 30's, 40's, 50's who want to look slimmer and feel younger." The ad offered an "Amazing New Health Supporter Belt" that could push their stomachs in, for $3.98 plus postage (the cost of over 40 comic books).

47. Kauffmann, 1980: 111–112. The clues in Kauffmann's chapter amply indicate that he was working for Fawcett Publications, publisher of Captain Marvel, and David Hajdu, who interviewed Kauffmann for *The Ten Cent Plague*, confirms this. Kauffmann adds that with the exception of one editor, he and his coworkers experienced their time there as a boring, undemanding job, and lacked even a remote awareness that they were working in comic books' "Golden Age." Kauffmann threw away all his comic books when he left the company, and only regretted being unable to imagine that they were worth saving (Kauffmann, 1980: 112–3, 119).

48. Zorbaugh, 1944: 196–203. Dr. Harvey Zorbaugh was a professor at the New York University School of Education, and an active defender of comic books. His article followed this statistic by adding "The Market Research Company survey revealed that of the men in training camps in this country, 44 percent read comic books regularly and another 13 percent read them occasionally. U.S.O. hostesses report comic books leave their reading tables first, officers in training camps that they are passed from man to man until there is nothing left of them" (Zor-

baugh, 1944: 198). *The New York Times* published a list of 189 magazine titles including almost 50 comic books that could be distributed to soldiers without the camp commanders having to check them for banned political content. (Soldiers could subscribe as individuals to any magazine they liked without restrictions on political content.) (Shalett, 1944.)

49. Broadfoot, 1974: 392 (quoting anonymous participant's oral history).

50. AP Images #5009091140, anonymous photographer, http://apimages.ap.org. *The Southeast Missourian* published this image on its front page on September 9, 1950, captioned "He's just a boy." The caption was edited to read: "Neither war nor Reds can interfere with a GI's favorite literature, and a 25th Division gunner, Pfc. David Singleton of Lynchburg, Va., on the front line in Korea, is no exception. Hand on gun trigger, he concentrates on the inevitable comic book. His youth apparent, the lad is like countless others in the fighting, even yet too young to vote." An earlier news item that followed the same formula told of Lloyd A. Hahn reading a Batman comic book (which he found merely "so-so, but it helps fill in the time") while a shell fell a hundred yards away from his forward command post (Boyle, 1950).

51. David Singleton, 19 Dec. 2011, telephone interview. When asked about the representation of the Korean War in comic books, Singleton answered "I never saw any war comic books." I thank David Singleton for his help.

52. "Drive Started …," 1952.

53. I describe "Atrocity Story" in Chapter 15: Atrocities.

54. In reply to one letter on the page, the editor answers simply "'Nuff said," a phrase which Wikiquote attributes to Stan Lee as an "Often-used line on 'Stan Lee's Soapbox' editorial pages, since the 1960s."

55. Mauger, 1951: 47. The comics remained popular with the military through several more wars. In 1973, Robert Jay Lifton quoted a USAF medic in Japan: "The most widely read literature among the guys that return from Vietnam, it's comics. Comic books and adventure stories…. These guys are just living in a dream world. They're young, easily influenced…. Cartoons! It's the good against the bad. It's always *gooks*" (Lifton, 1973: 204). Of the men who committed the massacre at My Lai in 1968, Seymour Hersh reported that "The favorite reading matter of Charlie Company like that of other line infantry units in Vietnam, was comic books" (Hersh, 1970: 18).

56. "Sees U.S. Comics …," 1954.

57. Americans brought comic books when they had left for Korea (Cochrane, 1950). Recently released American POWs, returning from Korea, read mostly comic books ("Prisoners Crave…," 1954).

58. Benjamin Woo's article "Is There a Comic Book Industry?" includes a hyperlinked map showing the addresses of 35 comic book publishers active in the 1950s which were tightly clustered in New York City (about one mile west of the location where the United Nations' new headquarters was under construction). Since then, comic book production and publication have become more dispersed (Woo, 2018).

59. Evanier, 2000. Hasen arrived in Korea "the day the peace accord was signed" (July 27, 1953). A 1954 cartoonist tour of Korea (in which participants included Jerry Robinson, Carmine Infantino, Wilson McCoy, Bill Holman, Al Posen, and others) is described at chapter length in Tom Gill's *The Misadventures of a Roving Cartoonist* (Gill, 2006: 107–115). The National Cartoonists Society was founded in 1946, evolving from the volunteer chalk-talks that some cartoonists had done during World War II to entertain American servicemen (http://www.reuben. org/?page_id=2; accessed August 20, 2012). Irwin Hasen has been most remembered for the comic strip *Dondi*, which he drew based on scripts by Gus Edson. Hasen said that "What inspired it was that during the Korean war, officers were adopting war orphans. That was where it started. And then we just made it World War II, instead" (Evanier, 2000). In 1954, U.S. military men's adoption of Korean "mascots" not only inspired *Dondi*, but also marked the beginning what soon became an industrial-scale system of international adoptions. This system evolved from *finding families* for mixed-race Korean children fathered by (mostly American) UN soldiers, to *finding Korean children* for American families to adopt (Oh, 2015: 2, 3, 35–36, 55, 165, 186).

60. Campbell, 2011. According to Mark Evanier, at that point Schwartz had been drawing almost all of the DC Comics published under Bob Kane's name (Evanier, 2011).

61. The tradition of "radical mass media criticism" attempts to disrupt the ways that the industrialization of culture threatens democracy. (Berry and Theobald, 2006). Bart Beaty has explored how the work of anti-comic book activist Fredric Wertham overlapped with but fit "only unevenly into the mass culture critique" (Beaty, 1999: 49).

62. MacDonald, 1944, MacDonald, 1945; MacDonald, 1953.

63. MacDonald listed the option of maintaining class rule as a possible purpose of mass culture partly to include the role of mass culture in the Soviet Union, which was not organized for profit, but for domination.

64. In 1945, MacDonald had worded this a little differently and added a footnote summarizing statistical findings from a recent "Survey of Comic Magazines in Hudson, N.Y." by Paul W. Stewart & Associates (MacDonald, 1945).

65. The journal *Partisan Review* published a lengthy symposium in 1952 on "Our Country and Our Culture," in which 24 intellectuals responded to questions, including how American intellectuals and writers might adapt to the crushing power and "the enormous and ever-increasing growth" of a "mass culture" that has turned American culture into an industrial product ("Our Country…," 1952: 284–286) The best thing most of them could say for "mass culture" was that eventually it might improve ("Our Country…," 1952).

66. Bart Beaty names some of the others who, in the 1950s, saw mass culture as a threat to democ-

racy or an incubator of totalitarianism: the Frank-furt School philosophers such as Theodor Adorno, anthropologist Hortense Powdermaker, political scientist William Kornhauser, and sociologist Leo Bogart (Beaty, 1999).

Chapter 4

1. In this chapter I have relied heavily and gratefully on a few authors, whose research seems definitive: Jeet Heer on the work of Roy Crane, Robert C. Harvey on Milt Caniff, and Todd DePastino on Bill Mauldin.

2. Eisner, 1985: 5–6; McCloud, 1993: 2–9.

3. Gaines, 1942; Hogben, 1949.

4. Trajan's column; n.d.; Bayeux Tapestry, n.d.; Codex Zouche-Nuttall, n.d.

See also Bridgeford, 2004, on the Bayeux Tapestry.

5. Gaines, 1942: 25. Presumably Gaines was referring to "The Standard of Ur" (2500 BCE), which was (and remains) in the collection of the British Museum.

6. Comics scholar Jean-Paul Gabilliet argues against the adequacy of such a "rambling inventory" of supposed predecessors and emphasizes that comics as such were created "in the context of mass publishing since the 1830s" (Gabilliet, 2010: xii–xvii). Joe Sacco did take inspiration from the Bayeux Tapestry for his unusual, wordless, 24-foot long, accordion-folded panorama the Battle of the Somme, published as *The Great War* (Kaneko and Mouly, 2013).

7. Smolderen, n.d. (Smolderen refers to battlefield paintings in this valuable article only once in passing.) Jonathan Barli has assembled a marvelous anthology of early examples of this style of cartooning (including a few representations of battle) (Barli, 2016).

8. Joe Sacco's very labor-intensive graphic novels about war *do* sometimes use (in addition to close-ups of individuals) zig-zag paths through complicated compositions. Sacco took inspiration from Bruegel (Salter, 2013).

9. See Kenneth Baker's thoroughly illustrated and highly informative *George Washington's War: In Caricature and Print* (Baker, 2009).

10. Paine: 1904: 69.

11. Creel, 1920: 226. Michael T. Coventry's analysis of the World War I Committee for Public Information's products (including those of its Bureau of Cartoons) noted that they: "emerge not as the output of a powerful, unified, and carefully organized media state, but rather as the result of multiple, imperfect negotiations between a relatively weak state and the interests and ideas of multiple actors and audiences" (Coventry, 2007).

12. Crane, 2010. Beginning in 1936, reprints of Crane's work on "Wash Tubbs" and of "Captain Easy, Soldier of Fortune," appeared regularly in American comic books. Towards the end of World War Two, Captain Easy also appeared in *G.I. Comics*, one of the free, weekly comic book compilations of newspaper comics that the U.S. Army published for those serving in the military. In 1947–49, Crane's character Captain Easy appeared in eight issues of his own comic book.

Around this time, adventure stories became a powerful presence in the comics. This included some humor strips, notably Elzie Segar's Thimble Theater, which the character Popeye joined in 1929, and Mickey Mouse, drawn by Floyd Gottfredson, beginning in 1930; science fiction strips, most memorably Flash Gordon and Buck Rogers; and jungle comics, with Tarzan.

13. The new trend toward adventure stories alarmed John K. Ryan, who warned in 1936 that sadistic, ugly, violent, sentimental comic strips had become both "an effect and a powerful contributing cause" of "the prevailing infantilism of the American mind." The dozen strips Ryan cited as examples were detective comics, jungle comics and science fiction comics, but not war stories (Ryan,1936: 301, 302).

14. Heer, 2011: vi.

15. Comas, 1997; Grand Comics Database.

16. Heer, 2015.

17. Heer, 2011: xii.

18. Jeet Heer, June 28, 2012, e-mail message to author.

19. Heer, 2015. In the February 23, 1962 *Buz Sawyer* strip, a lecturer tells his listeners that: "The flood of narcotic drugs from Red China is not a private business, gentlemen. It is a government monopoly for the purpose of demoralizing the people of free Asia. […] It finances countless Communist activities throughout the world. It pays the undercover worker who organizes student riots, or who infiltrates a labor union or a government office. It is a multi-million-dollar business. […] The 'hypodermic' war is one of the most subtle and vicious wars in history. Hidden! Horrible! But Effective!"

20. Goulart, 1989: 42.

21. Sheridan, 1942, 1973: 125.

22. Sheridan, 1942, 1973: 126.

23. Sheridan, 1942, 1973: 128.

24. Russel Nye wrote of this strip: "Milton Caniff's 'Terry and the Pirates,' begun in 1934, attracted more imitators than any other comic strip in history. Caniff put together [Roy] Crane's adventure-sex 'male mag' formula with the exotic locales of 'Tarzan,' the movie serial's strong story line, and a handsome adventurer, Pat Ryan. Then in 1937 he boldly sent his characters to the current Chinese-Japanese wars, the first major comic to follow the headlines" (Nye, 1970: 225–226). A *Newsweek* article called Caniff "the most widely aped artisan in a tirelessly copycatting trade" ("Dumas …." 1950).

25. Harvey, 2007: 181, 198.

26. Harvey, 2007: 198–9.

27. Sheridan Prasso identifies several possible inspirations for Caniff's Dragon Lady: Anna May Wong's role as Dr. Fu Manchu's daughter in *Daughter of the Dragon* (1931) and a 1930 book by Aleko E. Lilius which featured the female Chinese pirate, La Choi San (Prasso, 2005: 80–81). Sheng-mei Ma has described Caniff's "unmistakably stereotyped" character Connie as descended from Earl Derr Biggers' "clownish, harmless Charlie Chan" and R.F. Out-

cault's Yellow Kid: "Pat and Terry retained the service of a Chinese boy, Connie, short for George Webster Confucius [...] A feminine nickname conferred by his white masters who shortened and belittled the name "Confucius" [...] In the evolution of the strip, Connie graduated from a cook and porter to the protagonists' confidant, but his fundamental inferiority and marginality never varied" (Ma, 2000: 12, 14–15).

28. Caniff, 1982: 34–38.

29. Hadsel, 1941: 368.

30. Marschall, 1989, Chapter 12 "Milton Caniff (1907–1988)": 209–223. Comic book artist Alex Toth credited Sickles as the true inventor "the Caniff style": "Everything—lettering, panel layout, motion picture camera techniques, the design of blacks, locale, characters, the whole business, was Sickles inspired and based" (Toth, 2011: 9). The reason that comics people credited Caniff rather than Sickles for this style may be that Caniff remained active as an extraordinarily successful cartoonist while Sickles, after being turned down for a salary raise in 1936, moved on to a career in magazine illustration. Also, Caniff's strips were more memorable because he paid greater attention to his plots and characters. Finally, Sickles had been a restlessly experimental artist, and the style that Caniff adapted was only one of the ones that Sickle had used (Harvey, 2004).

31. Harvey, 2004:349–50.

32. Terkel, 1984: 354.

33. Harvey, 2004: 472–5.

34. Caniff, 2012: 81–91, August 1–24, 1947.

35. Mark, 1975: 51–63.

36. Caniff, 2012.

37. Caniff explained Steve Canyon's reenlisting in the October 16, 1950 strip (Caniff, 2012: 301).

38. Caniff, 1985: 1; Harvey, 2007: 633. An additional, practical reason for avoiding Korea as a setting, as Bruce Canwell notes, was that "the situation on the ground in Korea was still fluid and deadlines demanded that work be generated several weeks ahead of actual events" (Canwell, 2012: 15).

39. Harvey, 2007: 627.

40. The Cincinnati Committee on Evaluation of Comic Books found the *Steve Canyon* comic books "objectionable," probably for violating their guidelines against sexual situations, women criminals, weapons and slang (Harvey, 2007: 665). In 1948, the publisher Harvey Comics had reprinted the newspaper strips as six issues of the *Steve Canyon* comic book.

41. Harvey, 2007: 636. Schelly compares the peak circulation of 500,000 copies of *Our Army at War* with the twenty million or more readers that a popular strip could reach (Schelly, 2008: 167). Milton Caniff's popularity was so great because of his "Terry and the Pirates" strip, that when his new strip "Steve Canyon" debuted, the first episode appeared in newspapers with a readership of 31 million readers (Brunner, 2010: 169).

42. Caniff, 2012: 170, December 13–4, 1951.

43. Caniff, 2013: 16–7.

44. Caniff's research did not include first-hand observations in China, Korea or Vietnam: "Despite all the stories set in Asia, Caniff had never been there until 1960 when he got far enough ahead with 'Steve Canyon' to take a month's vacation" (Correll, 2013: 73).

45. The Felicia Lymph storyline is summarized and analyzed in Harvey, 1992: 6–7, 9–11. Although Felicia Lymph is remembered (when remembered at all) as resembling Jane Fonda, Jane Fonda did not become known for her antiwar work (which at first centered on supporting soldiers who opposed the war) until 1970, and she did not reach her peak of notoriety until 1972, when she visited North Vietnam (Ross, 2011: 227–269; Schumacher and Kitchen, 2013: 201–203).

46. Correll, 2013: 73. In addition to the unpopularity of military themes, comic strips like "Steve Canyon" which told continuing stories were being replaced by a revival of the gag strip genre which told self-contained jokes; strips were being printed smaller, which allowed less room for Caniff's visual art; and newspapers were folding, leaving most cities without competing daily newspapers (Harvey, 1992: 20–21).

47. Marschall, 1989: 221.

48. Harvey, 1992: 19. At the same time that Milton Caniff was adapting to what he called "a cycle of antimilitarism as old as the United States itself," other comic strip artists with military themes were making similar adjustments. Roy Crane, in response to papers dropping the Buz Sawyer strip, put his hero "into civvies." George Wunder, the cartoonist on "Terry and the Pirates" shifted to telling stories in which his U.S. Air Force lieutenant colonel character, Terry Lee, is on leave or "on assignment where the story itself is not concerned with military duty." Wunder explained: "It's quite simple. This Vietnam War thing is very unpopular. Since we're in the business of entertaining, there's no point in doing the sort of stories that are not going to be favorably received" (Berthelsen, 1971).

49. David Irvine's "Milton Caniff's Christmas Strips" was webposted December 19, 2012, by Tom Heintjes at http://cartoonician.com/milton-caniffs-christmas-strips. The quoted strips are from 1968, 1970 and 1971.

50. When Mauldin received a Pulitzer Prize in 1945, "his syndication doubled overnight to over two hundred papers reaching perhaps 40 million readers" (DePastino, 2008: 197). Regarding the distinctive look of his wartime cartoons, Mauldin later explained that "in wartime Sicily and Italy forty-odd years ago, engravers' equipment was worn out or wrecked, making it impossible for them to reproduce fine lines or fancy shading. So I drew heavy, bold, contrasty lines that even a cracked lens couldn't miss" (Mauldin, 1985: vii).

51. John Garvin has republished the 1922 edition of the Landon course: http://www.enchantedimages.com/landon_second/landon_second_edition.pdf.

52. Cartoonist Howard Nostrand told an interviewer: "[Jack] Davis borrowed from Willie and Joe by Bill Mauldin like you wouldn't believe. [I did also.] Every time you get two guys slogging through the mud, you start *thinking* Bill Mauldin. There was the guy with the dented helmet, you know.... Everybody

needed a shave. It seemed to me it was always rain-
ing. And there's just, you know, dirt and mud and
crud all over the place. I got that, more or less, into
the war stuff I did" (Nostrand, 1974: 38). Cartoonist
Ric Estrada has also described Mauldin's influence:
"the grimy, rumpled hopelessness of war he depicted
with such wry humor was unforgettable, his art facile
and superb" (Estrada, 1994–1995: 13 [unpaginated]).

53. DePastino, 2008: 185–195.
54. DePastino, 2008: 138–9.
55. DePastino, 2008: 142.
56. DePastino, 2008.
57. DePastino told an interviewer: "it's interesting that Mauldin's cartoons weren't reprinted in
the Pacific Stars and Stripes, and Douglas MacArthur made sure that they weren't. MacArthur didn't
like Mauldin any more than Patton did" (Lindley, 2008). Military cartoonists who worked in the
Pacific include Bill Hume and John Annarino, who
did several *Babysan* cartoon books, which were set
in occupied Japan, and Shel Silverstein's *Take Ten*
(Scott, 2010). Ssgt. Norval E. Packwood, Jr.'s book
Leatherhead in Korea collects his cartoons and functions as a cartoon-history of the first Marine Division in Korea from August 2, 1950 to April 22, 1951
(Packwood, 1952).
58. DePastino, 2008: 207.
59. DePastino, 2008: 197–201.
60. DePastino, 2008: 217–219; Kercher, 2005:
311–312.
61. DePastino, 2008: 220–222. Stephen E. Kercher
says the first cartoon in Mauldin's FBI file was the one
from the previous day that showed the office door
of the "Un-American Committee for Investigating
Activities (Free Speech Division)" and had included
a swastika that was edited out by his syndicate (Kercher, 2005: 312–313).
62. DePastino, 2008: 227–8.
63. DePastino, 2008: 233–234; Kercher, 2005: 313.
64. Kercher, 2005: 315.
65. DePastino, 2008: 248–253.
66. Mauldin, 1952.
67. Harvey, 2013.
68. Baker, 1944.
69. Harvey, 2013.
70. Bahrampour, 2018.
71. Bacon, 2010; Bahrampour, 2018.
Craig Shutt has written a detailed history of Beetle Bailey as a comic book character (Shutt, 2016).
72. Finger, 2018.
73. Harvey, 2015.

Chapter 5

1. To some extent the creators of pulp magazines and comics overlapped. David Saunders has
posted a *Field Guide to Wild American Pulp Artists*
(Saunders, n.d.). That guide's listing for the pulp artist Adolphe Barreaux describes with special clarity
the overlap between pulps and comics. During the
Korean War, Norman Saunders painted covers for
(among other publications) the pulp magazines *War
Stories* and *Cloak and Dagger*, and the comic books

GI Joe, Little Al of the F.B.I., Cloak and Dagger and
Atomic Spy Cases (Saunders, n.d.).
2. The first Superman story from *Action Comics
#1* has been web-posted at: http://xroads.virginia.
edu/~ug02/yeung/actioncomics/page1.html.
3. The *Text of the Nazi-Soviet Non-Aggression Pact*
has been web-posted at: http://www.fordham.edu/
halsall/mod/1939pact.html.
4. Siegel and Schuster, 1940.
5. Regarding the Soviet Union's 1934 embrace of
"Socialist Realism" and rejection of Western pulp literature (including comics), see Jose Alaniz' *Komiks*.
(Alaniz, 2010: 57). New York's communist newspaper, *the Daily Worker*, did publish its own comic
strips beginning in 1936, but these ended quickly
when the "Popular Front" period ended in 1945.
(Brunner, 2007: 184). Communist-affiliated comic
books published by New Age Publishers (which
consisted largely of text pieces with a few features
in comic book format) ended in 1946 (www.comics.
org).
6. The translated text of this article (from *Das
Schwarze Korps* 25 April 1940, p. 8) has been web-
posted by Randal Bytwerk at the German Propaganda Archive ("Jerry Siegel Attacks," 1940; Bytwerk,
1998). For background on the Schutzstaffel, see Webb
et al., 2008.
7. Superheroes had begun turning their attention to fighting foreign dictators and spy rings in
1939 (Fertig, 2017).
8. Simon and Simon, 1990: 50.
9. Simon and Simon, 1990: 52.
10. Kirby, 2011: 75–76. In this period, anti-Semites
in New York City held frequent rallies and indoor
meetings, picketed Jewish stores and businesses,
and sold the Christian Front's *Social Justice* newspaper at busy intersections, shouting "Read the truth
about the Jews" and loudly insulting those pass-
ersby that they assumed were Jewish (Norwood,
2003: 241–242). During World War II, anti-Semitic
Irish-American Catholic gangs in New York City and
Boston beat up Jews in the street (sometimes using
blackjacks or brass knuckles), threw stones at rab-
bis, broke Jewish storekeepers' windows and stole or
damaged their merchandise, broke synagogue windows and vandalized synagogues with obscene graf-
fiti, tore the clothes off of Jewish girls, tugged old
men's beards, and turned over pushcarts (Schneider,
1999, 2001: 52, 86; Norwood, 2003: 233, 235–237,
261–2, 265–267). In Harlem, Pastor Adam Clayton
Powell, Jr., called the harassment of Boston's Jews
a familiar "fascist inspired ... pattern of persecution." A majority of New York City policemen were
Irish-American, and many of them sympathized with
the Christian Front whose anti-Semitic propaganda
had inspired these gangs (Norwood, 2003: 233, 242–
243, 253, 264; Hart, 2018: 86). Rather than seeing
these terrorist gangs as "fascists," the police dismissed
the issue as one of ordinary "juvenile delinquency"
and "boyish pranks" (Norwood, 2003: 253, 255–256,
264, 267). Several factors fed Irish Catholic hatred
for Jews including differences over Nazi Germany,
which these Catholics saw as a better alternative than
the Soviet Union's militant atheism, and over Brit-

ain, Catholic Ireland's traditional enemy (Norwood, 2003: 247–248). By contrast, during World War II German-American support for Hitler dropped sharply (Norwood, 2003: 239).

11. Goldstein, 2010: 208–209. Paul Hanebrink's *A Specter Haunting Europe: the myth of Judeo-Bolshevism* analyzes and historically contextualizes the persistent power of "the belief that Communism was created by a Jewish conspiracy and that Jews were therefore to blame for the crimes committed by Communist regimes" (Hanebrink, 2018: 4–5, 7).

12. For example, *Master Comics #43*, October 1943 (webposted at The Digital Comic Museum), featured "Captain Marvel Jr. Battles for Stalingrad!" Another example appeared in *Prize Comics #39*, "Ted O'Neil of the Commandoes," drawn by E.C. Stoner. It includes such dialogue as "Long live the Soviet Union!" and "America, England, and the Soviet Union united—we cannot lose! Long live the United Nations!" Their three flags wave in the background, but the colorist has (by error or political protest or editorial decision or to tease the writer) made the Red flag (identifiable by its hammer and sickle) blue.

In "The Russian Hell-Hole" in the May, 1943 issue of *Captain America Comics* (vol. 1, no. 26), Captain America and Bucky conclude one of their adventures in the Kremlin, as Stalin's honored guests.

13. Peterson, 1939: 6.

14. Sidney Rogerson's book *Propaganda in the next war*, published in England in 1938, included a section about propagandizing "the United States—the Great Neutral" (pp.144–152). As Rogerson had predicted, becoming involved in a war with Japan brought the United States immediately into the war in Europe. With the Pearl Harbor attack, American public opinion finally swung in favor of war (Rogerson, 1938: 148; Schuessler, 2010: 159–161).

15. Cull, 1995: 176. One of Cull's footnotes cites evidence that "later in the war [British Information Services] fed pro–British material to Fisher through the senior U.S. OWI officer, Lew Cown."

During the war, some readers suspected the Joe Palooka strip served as a conduit for government propaganda. Stephen A. Bachelder wrote at the time: "I have recently been told by a friend of a friend of Ham Fisher who draws *Joe Palooka* that Mr. Fisher was paid a considerable sum by a government agency to have Joe enlist in the army. I have not been able to substantiate this" (Bachelder, 1942 [?]: 13, n3). Josef Goebbels, Germany's propaganda minister, called the *Joe Palooka* strip "the most vicious of anti-Nazi propaganda." During World War II, foreign comic strips were prohibited in Germany (Manning and Romerstein, 2004: 62).

16. The disproportionate importance of Jews in the American comic book industry has been explored sympathetically in several books, including Simcha Weinstein's *Up, Up, and Oy Vey: How Jewish History, Culture, and Values Shaped The Comic Book Superhero* (2006); Danny Fingeroth's *Disguised as Clark Kent: Jews, Comics, and the Creation of the Superhero* (2007); Paul Buhle's *Jews and American Comics: An Illustrated History of an American Art Form*

(2008); Arie Kaplan's *From Krakow to Krypton: Jews and Comic Books* (2008); and Harry Brod's *Superman Is Jewish? How Comic Book Superheroes Came to Serve Truth, Justice, and the Jewish-American Way* (2012). See also Christopher B. Zeichmann's analysis of Superman's "Jewishness" (Zeichmann, 2017).

Martin Lund's *Re-Constructing the Man of Steel: Superman 1938–1941, Jewish American History, and the Invention of the Jewish-Comics Connection* debunks supposedly Jewish elements in the comics. Lund argues that "some of the more active pre-WWII fighters and explicit anti-Nazi superheroes were published or created by non-Jews" such as William Moulton Marston, Bob Powell and Leverett Gleason (Berlatsky, 2016; Lund, 2016).

17. Hoopes, 1973: 78.

At the end of World War II, about 3 percent of the Korean population was Christian. (After the 1960s, that number would grow to more than 25 percent.) Many Korean Protestants served in high positions during the U.S. occupation government and then in Syngman Rhee's administration (Busswell and Lee, 2006: 13, 21–2, 239). Harold R. Isaacs' study *Scratches on Our Minds*, published in 1958, found that the thousands of missionaries America had sent to China played the dominant role in shaping American images of that nation (Isaacs, 1958: 67–68).

18. The Grand Comics Database "Advanced Query" allows you to search by genre (including "war") and sort by date (http://www.comics.org).

19. Simon and Simon, 1990: 171–172. Their covers are posted at comics.org, where we see that issue #4 featured on its cover Franklin Delano Roosevelt flanked by Winston Churchill and Chiang Kai-shek. As far as I know, Stalin did not appear as an ally on any American comic book cover during World War II. (Stalin had appeared as an enemy allied with Hitler and Mussolini on the cover of *Cat-Man #3* in July, 1941, which reached the newsstands around the same time as the news that Hitler had invaded Russia.)

20. *Speed Comics #24*, December 1942.

21. Frost, 1943: 331. The student-teachers' survey described some details of how comic books functioned in the children's barter systems, with girls "raiding the pantry" for food to exchange for the comic books that boys paid for with their allowances, and with exchanges of four to six comics for one copy of *Popular Mechanics*, and several comics in exchange for an issue of *Popular Science, Popular Aviation*, or *Boy's Life* (Frost, 1943: 330).

22. Bernard, 2015.

23. Gerber and Gerber, 1989–1990.

24. Chapman, et al., 2015: 102–3.

25. Only "Joe Palooka" presented the government's preferred messages (Barkin, 1984: 114–116).

26. Chapman, et al., 2015: 106–7.

27. Barkin, 1984: 116–117. The Grand Comics Database (comics.org) says that 561,491 copies of this comic were printed in twelve languages (including Chinese) in mid–1942, plus another 100,035 copies in English.

28. Hirsch, 2013: 46.

29. Hirsch, 2013: 42.

30. "Myung-Sung" refers to the Empress Myeong-seong, also known as Queen Min. Japan's minister plenipotentiary extraordinary to Korea, Miura Gorō, plotted the assassination, which took place on October 8, 1895, because the Queen powerfully resisted Japanese influence in Korea (Keene, 2002: 513ff). According to one version, "The Queen heard the commotion and ran into a bush to hide, but the assassins discovered her. She was stabbed on the back several times, stripped naked and then gang-raped. The assassins fondled her breasts and genitals laughing. Finally, they took her to a small woodland, poured kerosene on her and lit the fuel. She was burned to death still alive and moaning" (Kim, 2003).

31. Federal Council of. …, 1920: 15, 30–31.

32. This photograph was titled "From the Japanese domination: crucifixion in 1919," and captioned "This photograph was taken by the International Film Co. a few minutes after the execution by the Japanese soldiers" (http://digitallibrary.usc.edu/cdm/ref/collection/p15799coll126/id/5245) (Hyun, 1919: 20).

In 1920, B.C. Lyhm, private secretary to Syngman Rhee, president of the provisional government of the Republic of Korea, referred to the "well known fact that the Japanese have been in the habit of crucifying Koreans, especially Christians" (Lyhm, 1920). The persecution of Korean Christians has a long history. In the 19th century, when Korea had been an independent nation, a series of waves of persecution against Christians for their refusal to perform Confucian rituals and their danger to national independence, peaked with "the Great Persecution" of 1866–1871, in which 8,000 believers were executed (Grayson, 2006: 10–11). In response to the largely Christian-led "March First Movement of 1919" which had proclaimed "the independence of Korea and the liberty of the Korean people," Japan had blamed the Christians, and retaliated by closing churches, arresting many Christians, and shooting dozens of church leaders (Wi, 2007: 102–104). South Korean Christians were also imprisoned and tortured in the 1970s for leading the fight for democracy and human rights against South Korea's dictatorship (Grayson, 2006: 21).

33. Federal Council of. …, 1920: 104.

34. Millett, 2005. Mark Gayn reported a November 7, 1946 interview with "Kim Koo" in his book *Japan Diary*. There he says:

… Kim Koo and Syngman Rhee differ in one major respect. While Rhee speaks for the collaborationists and landlords—for the "haves" of the extreme right—Kim Koo speaks for the rightist "have-nots" who refused to play along with the Japanese, spent decades in exile, and came back only to discover that the collaborators were still in control. There is little love lost between the two camps, though from time to time they work in alliance. Syngman Rhee's men hint that Kim Koo is a Chinese stooge. Kim Koo's men delight in listing the records of the collaborators working with Rhee (Gayn, 1948: 434).

35. Kim, 2000: 6, 146.

36. "Assassin Squeals…," 1992; "Why Sing Now?," 1992. I'm indebted to William Blum for copies of these articles. Blum places the assassination of Kim Ku first on a forty-one-item, chronological list of "U.S Government Assassination Plots." This list includes a 1951 plot against Kim Il-sung (Blum, 2008; see also Jacobsen, 2019: 39–42). As the war ended, OSS founder "Wild Bill" Donovan passed to President Truman an offer for postwar cooperation from Kim Ku, chairman of the Korean Provisional Government, adding that Ku had been working with the OSS to install agents in Korea. Truman curtly warned Donovan against "acting as a channel for the transmission to me of messages from representatives of self-styled governments which are not recognized by the Government of the United States" (Waller, 20122: 323).

When *Time Magazine* reported the killing of Kim Ku, rather than identifying him as "graying Kim Koo, head of a Korean provisional government" (as they had done on March 13, 1944) or "earnest, graying Kim Koo," the President of the Korean Provisional Government at Shanghai (as they did on September 10, 1945), "Rightist chairman of the Korean Independence Party (April 5, 1948) or "former chief of the Korean government in exile" (May 17, 1948), they remembered him as "an intense Korean nationalist and ruthless political terrorist" (July 4, 1949). *Time* reported that before his death "the tired, 73-year-old terrorist" had "made a bitter fight against establishment of the U.S.-sponsored South Korean Republic, which he felt would permanently divide his homeland."

37. Cumings, 2005: 193, 197–8.

38. Casey, 2008; 88, 217.

39. Lee, 2014.

40. Fitzpatrick, 2015: 555–556, 558, 565, 575. The most common sexually transmitted diseases in Korea and Japan were gonorrhea, chancroid and non-specific urethritis (retrospectively understood as mostly caused by chlamydia), but not syphilis (Fitzpatrick, 2015: 558–559).

41. Comic book editor Harvey Kurtzman's first assignment for the publisher EC in 1949 was a government-supported, educational, giveaway comic about syphilis (Schelly, 2015: 136).

42. "U.S. to Use…," 1949: 25.

43. "The Press: East Meets West," 1949: Rutter, 1955. According to Mark Langer, in addition to his government-sponsored comics, Copp created and published promotional comic books for "corporations including defence contractors Lockheed Aircraft, General Electric, Douglas Aircraft, B.F. Goodrich, Republic Aviation and General Motors," and created the comic book *The Atomic Revolution* for General Dynamics (Langer, 1995: 70–71).

44. Pease, 1992: 37, 40, 51.

45. Hall, 2019: 93–104.

46. Elder, 1968: 8–9. In 1966, as the series was nearing the end of its run, an article in *The Machinist* reported that "Little Moe is still fighting, still punching holes in the Iron Curtain" in many more publications than before, but in fewer countries: "The strip is one of the most popular in the world. Each week

the USIA sends Little Moe to 48 countries. It appears in 940 newspapers and magazines. More than one hundred million persons see it every week" ("Little Moe…," 1966).

47. Elder, 1968: 8–9.

Chapter 6

1. The Harvey Awards and the Eisner Awards (named in honor of Will Eisner) were created in 1988 as successors to the Kirby Awards (which had been named in honor of Jack Kirby). The Harvey Awards and Eisner Awards websites are at: http://www.harveyawards.com/ and https://www.comic-con.org/awards/eisner-awards-current-info. The first award for comic books was created at the suggestion of Roy Thomas, and first presented in 1961 (Thomas, 2008). During the Korean War, no prizes or awards were given to recognize excellence in the comic book industry. Comic book publisher Gary Groth explains why: "Today, there is barely a sustainable market for art- or literary-comics; in 1950, there was no market whatsoever because no one—the buying public, the publishers, the artists themselves—had even considered the idea; it was literally unthinkable" (Groth, 2013).

2. Kurtzman said: "I did then feel very strongly about not wanting to say anything glamorous about war, and everything that went before *Two-Fisted Tales had* glamorized war" (Kurtzman, 1980: Volume 1, page facing issue No. 21). Henry P. (Hank) Chapman, another writer with an anti-glamorous approach to war comics, began writing war comics later.

3. Kurtzman, 1980: Volume 1, page facing issue No.19.

4. Harvey, 2012: viii.

5. Schelly, 2015: 211–212. Joshua K. Akers' third chapter in his M.A. thesis describes Kurtzman's war comics at length. I thank Joshua K. Akers for a copy of his thesis and for comments on an early draft of this chapter (Akers, 2013: 132–133).

6. Gaines, 1983. Kurtzman told an interviewer:

> I idealized my role and my purpose as a writer, and I used to work very hard at it. And we were working on a piece-work basis, and [Al] Feldstein would be turning the sausage machine and cranking them out, you know, and the thinking was, "well, it's perfectly fair—the horror stuff makes lots of money and you get the same per page rates." I couldn't accept that emotionally, for obvious reasons. I'd be piss-poor all the time, and Al would be raking in the dough. Now, many years later, I know there's some kind of extra value to what I did. But how the hell do I get my reward? (Kurtzman, 1982: text facing the cover of issue #3).

7. Schelly argues that Kurtzman's work was "too good for comic books" and details at great length Kurtzman's long struggle to "get into the slick magazines" and "go legit" (Schelly, 2015: 203, 315).

8. Bell, 2002: 91

9. Thanks to an introduction by Denis Kitchen, I interviewed Harvey Kurtzman in Kurtzman's home around 1987, but I did not transcribe the conversation or publish anything about it.

10. Schelly, 2015: 76, 82.

11. Schelly, 2015: 78.

12. Schelly, 2015: 78. The most direct inspiration for "Black Venus" was probably Tarpé Mills' weekly Sunday comic strip "Black Fury." "Black Fury," the first female action hero, was another white character in a form-fitting black costume, drawn in the Caniff style. ("Black Fury" was also the name of a white, *male*, comic-book action hero in a form-fitting black costume who, like Mills' character, began appearing in April, 1941. After 36 weeks, Mills' comic strip was renamed as "Miss Fury.")

13. Schelly, 2015: 24–5.

14. Crumb, 1988: 67. I read that quote to Harvey Kurtzman when I interviewed him and he enthusiastically endorsed its accuracy, but without elaborating. Bill Schelly describes Crumb's personal relationship with his mentor, Harvey Kurtzman (Schelly, 2015: 444–448).

15. "Dying City!," *Two-Fisted Tales* #22, July/August 1951.

16. When challenged about this issue by an interviewer, John Benson, Kurtzman eventually remembered: "We made a deal with the Air Force to pitch a message that would make kids volunteer for Skywatch. They didn't have enough volunteers" (Kurtzman, 1982: facing issue #13). Many more readers received encouragement to support the Ground Observer Corps earlier that year through a story in Milton Caniff's "Steve Canyon" comic strip. On February 3, 1953, Steve Canyon pitched the idea of using the cupola of a local high school to set up a Ground Observer Corps Post: "Potential enemy aircraft are picked up at sea on radar screens if they're flying above 5,000 feet, but an airplane carrying the A-Bomb could slip in under that altitude unless there are observers to see or hear it—and flash the warning!" On January 21, the Steve Canyon character had explained the importance of preventing a nuclear attack on the United States: "Terrible as it is, Korea is only a diversion! Destroying Detroit, Seattle, Dayton, Pittsburgh, Birmingham and such industrial cities would become the first Red objective in an all-out war!"

17. An example of Kurtzman's thumbnail sketches for the seven-page World War I comic book story "Lost Battalion" and two pages of Kurtzman's rough pencils for that story and the finished art that Johnny Craig based on them appear in Denis Kitchen and Paul Buhle's *The Art of Harvey Kurtzman* (Kitchen and Buhle, 2009: 52–55). Fantagraphics publisher Gary Groth, who has republished Kurtzman's war comics, has observed that Kurtzman preferred to work with "chameleons who could be both illustrative and cartoony as the story warranted—[John] Severin, [Wally] Wood, [Will] Elder, and [Jack] Davis. (Did you notice that the regulars in Kurtzman's war books and the standard against which he measured all other artists who tried out for him, were equally good at dramatic and comedic work? I wonder if it was the absence of this humanizing quality

that turned Kurtzman off to otherwise fine crafts-man like Alex Toth, Gene Colan, and Russ Heath" (Groth, 2013).

18. Kurtzman's perfectionism extended to all aspects of comic book production, but he allowed colorist Marie Severin more freedom than he allowed the artists who illustrated his scripts. Marie Severin remembered how she got her job as a colorist for EC comic books:

> Well, it all started when Harvey [Kurtzman] started doing the war books, and he was such a perfectionist, and my brother [war comics artist John Severin] also loved that uniforms were correct, and insignia, and all that jazz. So he said, "Well, my sister is talented, she could probably do the coloring." At that time the color was sent, with the art, up to Chemical Color Company in Bridgeport, Connecticut, and they had separators there that separated all the work that came in from Marvel or DC or whoever, and they did the coloring, and so forth. But a lot of times [it was] not talented people doing it, and they might put green suits and yellow sidewalks, stuff like that, that was plentiful, and was typical of comics. EC wanted it more accurate. Harvey was a stickler for having it realistic and upgrading the look of the books [Cassell and Severin, 2012; Schelly, 2015: 203].

19. Kurtzman, 1980: page facing issue No.19. See also Schelly, 2015: 202.

20. Kitchen and Buhle, 2009: 60.

21. Kurtzman, 1980: page facing issue No.27.

22. Kurtzman, 1980: page facing issue No.25.

23. Kurtzman, 1980: "Combat Correspondence," reply to Alvin S. Poffenberger, *Two-Fisted Tales* #23, September-October 1951.

24. In a letter published in the November–December 1951 issue of *Two-Fisted Tales*, Tod McReea wrote: "I wish to compliment you on TWO-FISTED TALES, and it companion mag, FRONTLINE COMBAT! They dramatize the futility, the horror, the needlessness of war! In future issues, please point out the reasons why men fight, the misunderstandings and other reasons behind war, and the obvious solutions to the problem." Kurtzman answered: "We agree, Tod, that war is needless. We have no solution. We can only hope that by showing how ugly war is, YOUR generation will work hard to find the solution" (Kurtzman, 1980).

Two issues later, reader Gary Zeltzer wrote: "After reading your magazine, I realized what war meant. A terrible waste of human life inflicted on both sides. When will the civilized world learn to settle their difference by peaceful methods?" Kurtzman replied: "A nice letter and a good question, Gary! We can't answer it, so we pass it along to our readers!" (Kurtzman, 1980: "Combat Correspondence," *Two-Fisted Tales* #24, March–April 1952).

25. Kurtzman, 1980: "Combat Correspondence," reply to Robert E. Lee, Jr., Harriman, TN, *Two-Fisted Tales* #27, May–June 1952.

26. Wright, 2001:146.

27. "Combat Correspondence," especially the let-ters from John White, Oakland, CA, *Two-Fisted Tales* #33, May–June 1952. See also "Combat Correspondence in issue #37.

28. "Front Lines," *Frontline Combat #11*, March–April 1953.

29. Huebner, 2008: 100–3. Schelly shows *Life* magazine photographer David Douglas Duncan's images of an American soldier crying in Korea that had inspired Kurtzman's story "Big If!" (Schelly, 2015: 197–199).

30. Kurtzman later said "we were in a justifiable war, more justifiable than wars since…" (Kurtzman, 1982: text facing cover of issue #13).

31. To a reader who reported seeing a war comic that had pictures copied from *Two-Fisted Tales*, Kurtzman replied, "Not only are they copying from ONE of our books… they're copying from ALL of our books! But we take it as a back-handed compliment! Imitation, you know, is the sincerest form of flattery!" (Kurtzman, 1980: "Combat Correspondence," reply to Tod McReea, Fallsington, PA, *Two-Fisted Tales* #26, March–April 1952).

32. The Yiddish word "schmoe" has been variously translated as a stupid, obnoxious, foolish, boring, or dull person. When I asked Harvey Kurtzman about Jewish elements in his work, he answered "I didn't want to make it in the Jewish world; I wanted to make it in the big world." As someone who had grown up Jewish in Northern California, I was surprised by this idea that there could be enough Jews to form a "world."

33. Schelly, 2015:24.

34. Wright, 2001: 147. Cartoonist Joe Orlando's explained EC's rebellious attitude as a product of their experiences as veterans of World War II: "We all had a hate for supercilious authority…. It was hard to even get [a job] interview right after the war…. There was very little housing, and the jobs, they were all taken…. Every time we went for a job, some son of a bitch who hadn't been in the army had been there first…. And that anger, in the end, was what spawned EC comics and *Mad*. We were all angry. We had all been screwed" (Di Menno, 2005: 109).

Chapter 7

1. Several important studies focus primarily on aspects of the anti-comic book movement. Examples include Nyberg, 1998; Lent, 1999; Beaty, 2005; and Hajdu, 2009. See also Robert A. Emmons, Jr.'s documentary *Diagram for Delinquents: Fredric Wertham and the Evolution of Comic Books* (Emmons, 2014).

2. This states the matter gently. Comics historians, including Bob Harvey, whom I thank for his comments on this chapter, have described the anti-comics "crusade" as the work of book-burning control freaks.

I also thank Patrick Galbraith and Paul Hirsch for their helpful comments on drafts of this chapter.

3. Although he was not perfectly consistent on this point, especially in his first public comments about comic books in 1948, Wertham wrote and testified that comic books were a "factor" in juvenile

delinquency and repeatedly denied that they were a "cause" (Rifas, 2013).

4. For example, a four-paragraph letter to the editor of the *Tucson Daily Citizen* from F. Meza of Davis-Monthan Air Force Base, published on September 19, 1952, proposed that "These fake comics have no place in stores or newsstands. I ask—Just what kind of war experience, if any, have these people had who put out such sloppy comics?" Meza suggested that these comics, in which "the American G.I. [...] can kill anywhere from ten to a hundred enemy soldiers singlehanded," had been dangerous to the boys who grow up on them and then bitterly discover in Korea that the enemy cannot be killed so easily (Meza, 1952). The next year, Grant Loftin's "Totah Topic" column in the *Farmington Daily Times* of Farmington, New Mexico (August 21, 1953) responded to seeing a comic book that advertised itself as "America's most popular war comics" (a line that appeared across the top of the February–March and the June issues of *G.I. Joe* that year) by picking that blurb apart word by word: "In the first place we fail to see anything about war which could by any stretch of the imagination be called comical. [...] In the second place, we can't see anything about war which should be popular. In the third place, we can't understand the mentality which would in any way attempt to glorify the most savage aspect of so-called civilized man's traits. When the people of this nation reach the point of war glorification they will have ceased to be worthy of the name of free men" (Loftin, 1953).

5. A 1955 television documentary about comic books shows young boys reading comic books together. The narrator, Paul Coates, explains that "They're reading stories devoted to sexual perversion, to adultery, to horror, to the most despicable of crimes." As he says "despicable," the comic book shown is *War Comics #30* (December 1954). This comes at minute 9:04 of the web-posted 25:30-minute documentary (Coates, 1955). Another example of war comics appearing in films that attack crime comics appeared in an archival film used in Robert E. Emmons, Jr.'s documentary *Diagram for Delinquents* about Fredric Wertham. [Update #28: http://robertemmons.blogspot.com/2012/11/diagram-for-delinquents-update-28-not.html.] In this example, Herbert Wilton Beaser, Chief Counsel to the Congressional Subcommittee Hearings that are described below, says while standing in front of a display that included a war comic and an espionage comic: "These crime comic books that you are seeing here are a sample of what the children of the United States are reading today. [...] They're full of crime, terror and horror." I thank Robert E. Emmons for identifying Beaser as the speaker, and the date of the recording as May 1, 1954 (Robert E. Emmons, December 13, 2013, e-mail message to author). As a third example, the first installment of the documentary series *Truth, Justice and the American Way* uses archival footage showing the work of the Comics Code Authority (Kantor, 2013). While the narrator says "Crime had to be depicted as sordid and unpleasant. Excessive violence was forbidden...," the

visuals show original art for *war* comic books being reviewed and censored. (This example begins at 50:16 of the documentary, which has been webposted by Films on Demand: Digital Educational Video.)

6. North, 1940.

7. North, 1941.

8. North, 1941: 17.

9. Kunitz, 1941: 670–671.

10. Vlamos, 1941: 411–416.

11. Martin Sheridan wrote that in 1941 *Superman* "was appearing in more than three hundred daily and ninety Sunday newspapers in forty States, Canada, Mexico, Hawaii, Brazil and the Philippine Islands, with a total circulation of more than 20,000,000" (Sheridan, 1942: 234).

12. For example, in 1932, years before the comic book character Superman appeared, Americans had read in the *New York Times* that "The three main parts of the Hitlerite program deal with the racial, economic, and political aspects of Germany reborn. The *superman* [emphasis added] of Nietzsche's dreams is to give National Socialist Germany a racial unity. Members of the 'inferior' races must be excluded. As a leader of the Hitlerites has declared, anti-Semitism is the spiritual background of the entire movement. Hitlerism assumes that the worst afflictions of the postwar period originated in non-Germanic blood. A strong sense of racial exclusiveness must take the place of the lack of race consciousness" (Lengyel, 1932: XX3). Back in 1909, the word "superman" had appeared once in Israel Zangwill's play *The Melting Pot*, with an opposite meaning. Rather than resulting from racial purification, the *American* "superman" will be the product of "the great Melting-Pot where all the races of Europe are melting and re-forming! [...] Germans and Frenchmen, Irishmen and Englishmen, Jews and Russians—into the Crucible with you all! God is making the American [...] the real American has not yet arrived. He is only in the Crucible, I tell you—he will be the fusion of all races, perhaps the coming superman."

13. Martin Sheridan's path-breaking book about comic strips praised *Superman*, saying: "With two-thirds of the world at war people take delight in following the adventures of a fictional being who can dictate to dictators and make tyrants say 'uncle'" (Sheridan, 1942: 236).

14. Bachelder, 1942 (?):11.

15. Bachelder, 1942 (?): 30.

William Moulton Marston, who wrote Wonder Woman for the same company that published Superman, defended those altruistic characters as "constructive": "What life-desires do you wish to stimulate in your child? Do you want him (or her) to cultivate weakling aims, sissified attitudes? [...] The wish to be super-strong is a healthy wish, a vital, compelling, power-producing desire" (Marston, 1943–4).

16. Champney, 1944: 338.

17. Champney, 1944: 347.

18. Champney, 1944: 347. A decade earlier, a little-remembered attempt at a fascist coup in the United States had been exposed (or "alleged," if you

prefer) by General Smedley Butler (Archer, 1973, 2007).

19. Ong, 1945: 47. A week after its publication, *Time* magazine summarized Ong's argument as an answer to the simply stated question: "Are Comics Fascist?" An unusually striking example of comic books being portrayed as a fascist threat to democracy appeared as the first item in the *Southtown Economist's* 1945 series on "'Comic' Books—Schools for Crime." The article described a Hitler-like conspiracy led by five high school boys in Jackson, Michigan to establish a totalitarian government in the United States and then "take over the world in 15–20 years." The police decided that their plans had been inspired by what they had read in their huge library of "Superman and similar 'comic' books." The boys had stolen weapons and other things, including a printing press which they used to produce anti-black and anti-Jewish leaflets that they distributed through the city. Their plan to spark a race riot was thwarted when they were arrested for assaulting black students. The article emphasized that the boys had studied comic books for practical ideas of how to commit their planned crimes (and for the details of their initiation rites.) It also condemned the hero Superman as just another "Nazi-type." Superman's triumphs of good over evil are the triumphs of "an evil good" since he "obtains the triumph of his good over their evil through un-American vigilante activities which are themselves criminal ("'Comic' Books—Schools for Crime," 1945).

20. Superman began as a class-conscious champion of the underdog, expressing the radical values of the Popular Front political movement (Zeichmann, 2017). During World War II, however, Superman was radically transformed into an establishment hero, wrapped in the flag (Andrae, 1987: 130–132). According to Thomas Andrae, when Superman's publishers finally realized that Superman was an outlaw, they ordered Jerry Siegel to make Superman a crime-fighter instead and to avoid all controversial social issues. Siegel lost control of the character to freelancers while serving in the Army during World War II, and all of his subsequent attempts to regain control of his creation failed (Andrae, 1987:131–132).

21. I thank Chris Gavaler for a draft of his paper "Superman vs. the Superman: The Rise and Fall of Fascist Superpowers." His paper was published in 2015 (Gavaler, 2015: 8–11).

22. Frakes, 1942: 1349. In his Senate subcommittee testimony, a dozen years later, Fredric Wertham responded to Senator Kefauver's introduction of Hitler's "Big Lie" technique into the discussion by making a similar statement: "Hitler was a beginner compared to the comic book industry. They get the children much younger. They teach them race hatred at the age of 4 before they can read" (Wertham, 1954 [testimony]: 95). Of the anti-Semitic Nazi children's books, the most notorious was *Der Giftpilz* (*The Poisonous Mushroom*), which had been republished in England in 1938 by anti–Nazis to help English-speaking people "form a just estimate of the Anti-semitism of the German State"

("Propaganda and Children During the Hitler Years," n.d.).

23. Frakes, 1942: 1349. "The World's Worst Villain: The Claw," published in Lev Gleason's *Silver Streak Comics* and *Daredevil Comics*, fit Frakes' description of a ruthless, Oriental monster with bright yellow skin and fangs.

24. Comic books typically colored Asian and Euro-American characters with different skin tones, although real-life differences between the ranges of Asian and Euro-American skin colors were too subtle to be captured by the methods used for comic book coloring, which limited colorists' choices to combinations of a few standard percentages of magenta, cyan and yellow plus black. (Their palette finally began to grow in the 1980s, and especially after computer coloring arrived.) The Western world did not begin imagining East Asians as having a yellow skin color until the nineteenth century (Keevak, 2011:1–9).

In 1942, Milt Caniff's instructional piece "How to Spot a Jap," in an attempt to find a racial difference between America's Chinese ally and Japanese enemy, falsely taught that by contrast to the Chinese (who are "dull bronze in color,") Japanese people are "more on the lemon-yellow side." This work appeared in first edition of the booklet *Pocket Guide to China,* which the War Department distributed to those in the Army and Navy who were stationed in China (http://www.ep.tc/howtospotajap/index.html).

25. Hirsch, 2014: 449; 454–455. Paul Hirsch reports that "WWB members concluded that the core traits of the comic book form—its broad popularity, comprehensibility, emphasis on raw emotion, and distinct lack of subtlety—marked comic books as a potentially useful delivery system for propaganda and education. Additionally, because comics, unlike most other major [451] forms of media, were not subject to external censorship, comic book writers and propagandists could freely utilize clear, unambiguous images and language; they did not need to obscure opinions beneath layers of allegory or abstraction" (Hirsch, 2014: 449–451).

26. Clare, 1943. This 40-page pamphlet republished material that originally appeared in Cleveland, Ohio's *The Catholic Universe Bulletin*.

27. Clare, 1943: 14 Josette Frank, who frequently presented a pro-comic book view at public meetings, wrote in a letter in 1943: "I think I have never gone to any meeting at which some parent has not said something to the effect that she has no objection to her children reading the comics except that they are dangerous to the eye-sight [because of poor lettering and poor printing]" (Quattro, 2014).

28. Clare, 1943:27–28. The next year, Josette Frank (who had been an Editorial Advisor for DC comic books since 1941) judged that a concern that war comics "will make children love war and forever hate Germans and Japanese seems farfetched. Children are naturally fierce partisans, and such stories are likely to serve rather as a release for their feelings of aggression already heightened by the war" (Frank, 1944: 220).

29. Lynn, 1944.

30. Lynn, 1944: 8. Around two years later, in a

brochure for teachers, Lynn condemned superheroes for using "the vigilante procedure, the Hitlerian method. It is Ku-Klux terrorism in a new garb" and warned that such stories condition young readers to accept "those ideologies upon which dictatorships are built" (Lynn, c.1946:10–11). Ken Quattro discussed and posted excerpts from this brochure on the Facebook Comics Historians group, June 14, 2019. Chris Gavaler argues in "The Ku Klux Klan and the birth of the superhero" that "the American vigilante hero who assumes a costume and alias to hide his identity while waging his war for good" was a literary model that Superman inherited from Thomas Dixon's novel celebrating the Ku Klux Klan, and that despite Superman's role as "champion of the oppressed," his purported social mission stands in conflict with his "ethics of vigilante extremism" (Gavaler, 2012).

31. Lynn, 1944: 20.

32. "Fifty cities Place Ban On Comic Book Sales," 1948. In 1954, Fredric Wertham suggested that the passing of eventually over a hundred local ordinances had come as a "response" to a talk he had made at the 1948 Annual Congress of the American Prison Association urging a prohibition of the display and sale of crime comics to children under fifteen (Wertham, 1953, 1954: 301–2).

33. "Comic Publishers Get City Warning," 1949; "New York & Comics," 1949: 43.

34. Dales, 1949: 17.

35. "Policing the Comics," 1952.

36. Adin, 2015: 118; Cooke, 1955.

37. Theorizing the anti-comics movement as a "moral panic" preemptively dismisses critics' arguments as irrational and as a cover for hidden motivations having to do with maintaining social control (Jensen, 2010). Adin includes a long and detailed footnote surveying the scholarly literature about "moral panics" (Adin, 2015: 126–127). Dwight R. Decker was one of the first to call the fannish interpretation of the comic book controversy as a case of "McCarthyite persecution" mostly "moosefeathers" and to reinterpret it as "an internecine conflict within the left" (Decker, 1988: 57, 76).

38. Caute, 1978: 484–535.

39. Scobie, 1974: 192. In November, 1938 Tenney had said in a speech at a rally of the Hollywood Anti-Nazi League (a group which he would later condemn as a communist front group): "Fellow subversive elements, I have just heard that Mickey Mouse is conspiring with Shirley Temple to overthrow the government and that there is a witness who has seen the 'Red' card of Donald Duck. When the Dies Committee stoops to calling President Roosevelt a Communist, and says that Mrs. Roosevelt is a front for subversive elements, then I think the rest of us should be flattered to be put in that category" (Pritchard, 1970: 310).

40. Caute, 1978: 77; Scobie, 1974: 190, 194; Pritchard, 1970: 310; Heale, 1986:10, 13–14, 17–18, 21.

41. "Tenney Warns…," 1946.

42. The AYD address was not only the editorial and business address for the *Young Life* and *Teen Life* comics, but also the address for several pro-Soviet publications and had been the address for Lev Gleason's comic book company. In 1947, the House Committee on un-American Activities warned that the AYD, a successor organization of the Young Communists League, was a subversive organization, working to turn youth away from "religion, the American home, against the college authorities, and against the American Government itself" ("House Unit Scores AYD…,"1947).

43. Kellman, 1951: 61.

44. Tenney, 1953: section II.

After the completion of his tour, Tenney summarizes what he has seen:

> We were back in the clear, clean air of America as the double doors marked *American Jewish Committee* and *Anti-Defamation League of B'nai B'rith* close behind us. We had just seen the inside working of a private espionage and propaganda agency an agency organized with and maintained by private contributions; the nerve center of a world-wide net-work whose tentacles reach into every Gentile activity.
>
> In the "Fact-Finding, Legal and Investigative Divisions" we learned of the organizations' second (and perhaps most important) activity—the collection of files on so-called "anti-Semites." We had a glimpse of the extensive rows of cabinets containing data on thousands of individuals who, for one reason or another, qualify by ADL standards as anti-Jewish, actually or potentially, YOUR name may be included [Tenney, 1953: section V].

As a consequence of a lawsuit against the ADL in San Francisco, I once received a letter that legally notified me that my name had appeared on an ADL list. Documents related to this case—which was settled without a trial and without admission of any wrongdoing, the ADL denying that it had "violated the law in any respect whatsoever"—are web-posted under the title "Criminal investigation and successful civil lawsuits against the ADL over privacy right violations—1992–1993" (http://www.irmep.org/ila/ADL-CA/). As part of my research interest in educational uses of comic books, I had mail-ordered about ten copies of each of two anti-Semitic comics (at a generously discounted, bulk price), including *New World Order Comix #1: The Saga of White Will,* by William Pierce. I had not added them to my catalog, advertised or distributed them. (The ADL describes *New World Order Comix* at: http://archive.adl.org/presrele/militi_71/2737_71.html.) Besides scripting this comic book, Pierce wrote *The Turner Diaries,* a novel credited with inspiring over 200 murders (Barnes, 2017).

45. Engel, 1950: 535. On the anti-Communism of the ADL and AJC, see Hanebrink 2018: 227. Tenney's report on the ADL had appeared in one of a series of anti–Zionist pamphlets he self-published with the royalties he had earned for writing the hit song "Mexicali Rose." In a collection of his writings published in 1965, Tenney regretted that "Zionist PROPAGANDA […] brought the United States into the war against Germany," since otherwise "Communist

Russia would have been crushed by Germany…," and he shrugged off the Holocaust as a "remarkable falsehood" and "big lie" (Tenney, 1965: 126–7).

46. "Manners & Morals: Americana," 1948; "Comic Book Probe," 1948.

47. "Censorship of Obscene…," 1954: 216, 218.

48. "Comic Book Probe," 1948.

49. Donner, 1992: 46; Horne, 2001: 20, 42, 62, 71.

50. "Censorship of Obscene…," 1954: 216, quoting from the Senate's 1952 Hearings on Current Pornographic Literature. In 1948, the only comic book publisher that had asked for a hearing to defend a banned comic was Jack Liebowitz's National Comics Group (DC). That company's line of 30 titles included the banned *Gangbusters Comics*. A reporter quoted Liebowitz as objecting, not to police censorship itself, but to the inclusion of one of their titles on the list of censored comics, "We're glad that something is being done to apprise those publishers who are not cognizant of their responsibility that things can't go on unchecked. But we feel that our book was mistakenly banned in Detroit as it is in Indianapolis, although we're willing to make changes." John Byrne, editor of the banned titles *Wings Comics, Jumbo Comics* and *Fight Comics*, explained that "We don't edit our magazines for children." Comic book publishers, interviewed individually, said that the crime comics of the previous two years were designed "to satisfy the appetites of ex-GIs" ("Publishers Say 'Crime Comics' Are for Adults," 1948).

51. "Censorship of Obscene…," 1954: 219, 220.

52. The author of a 1956 legislative report, by contrast, argued that going after individual retailers was the preferred, effective method of police censorship because such pressure "bears down primarily upon the man in the most exposed position" ("Restrictions Upon Comic Books," 1956: 25–26).

53. Gellhorn, 1960: 30.

54. Such "voluntary cooperation" seemed to cause no embarrassment. For example, a short newspaper article reported that beginning in August 1954, police in Holyoke, Massachusetts, censored reading matter for teenagers, including comic books and pocket books, "with the full approval and cooperation of the [Holyoke News Co.'s] officials […]" ("Holyoke Police Keep Up on Comic Books," 1954). This kind of "prior restraint" of requiring state approval before a work was offered to the public also existed for films in those cities and states with censorship boards (Wittern-Keller, 2008: 2–3).

55. Matthews, 1949:62. The full Challengers pledge, as preserved in J.B. Matthews' file on comic books, does not make an anti-Catholic statement. In its entirety, it reads:

All men are brothers. Freedom is our common heritage, and fascism our common enemy.

Those who would destroy us seek first to defeat us by setting Gentile against Jew—White against Negro—faith against faith. But the unity of free peoples cannot be broken.

In the name of democracy and our faith in the new world born out of the most tragic of

wars, we pledge ourselves to challenge, fight, and defeat fascism in all forms!

I hereby join hands with the youth of the world, in its fight against fascism and bigotry, and by so doing, declare myself a Challenger.

56. The founder of the National Council for American Education, Allen A. Zoll, also had been a founder of the Christian Front, a supporter of Father Coughlin, and in the 1930s, the founder of American Patriots Inc, which the Attorney General listed as a subversive fascist organization ("Education: Our Enemies," 1951). "The Press: Trouble for the Mercury," 1952; Atwell, 2003.

57. Devanney, 1979: 83–104. Fredrik Strömberg's *Jewish Images in the Comics* includes a four panel comics-format excerpt from a "Buy Gentile/Boycott Jew Stores" broadside published in Los Angeles by the Christian Nation-alist [*sic*] Crusade in 1947 (Strömberg, 2012: 110–111).

58. Carlson, 2006; Grand Comics Database (comics.org). Two of Kubert's stories for *The Challenger* have been reprinted (Kubert, 2012: 101–106, 113–130).

59. Carlson, 2006.

60. Matthews may not have seen this "Challenger Club" story, as it was not in the issue of *The Challenger* that he saved in his files (Elizabeth B. Dunn, Research Librarian, Duke University, e-mail to author). The United States decided that "front organizations" were a useful tactic, and, through the CIA, set up a variety of Cold War front groups of its own (Wilford, 2008).

61. "Number of…," 1954: 3. This was quoted by ACMP newsletters and, in turn, entered as exhibit 8a in the Subcommittee Hearings.

62. "Problems Comic Books Produce," 1954.

63. The occasion of the editorial had been that "the ladies of Leesburg" had collected 300 signatures on a petition which it described as asking "that the comic book menace be abolished for all time in this country" because the comic books degrade morals and contribute to juvenile delinquency.

64. The pamphlet appears as Exhibit 5 in the Transcript web-posted at http://www.american-buddha.com/hearingssenatecomicbooks1.1.htm. The "Brain Washing American Style" pamphlet argued that a defense of the nation's founding principles required a narrower understanding of free speech: "We all hate the taking away of any true inalienable rights of man, but certainly this spreading of indecency, of dangerous information, and of criminal teachings cannot come under the title of inalienable rights. […] If this Nation was founded on the principles of religion and freedom and a trust in God, and upon the inalienable rights of man coming from God, under His natural law, then that which would destroy God's moral code cannot claim protection under those freedoms He ordained for us as a free people."

65. In addition to the pieces cited by the Senate Subcommittee, George S. Schuyler wrote an anti-communist editorial in 1953 in which he said that "There have been periodic drives to sweep murderous "comic books" off the newsstands in order

to protect the young. The only people who complain against these actions are the publishers of this stuff. Good people applaud." Schuyler gave the suppression of comic books as an example to show that "reasonable people" agree "that there are some books which should be burned," but he made no argument that comic books had communist political content. Instead, he categorized them with "filthy sex books" confiscated by customs officials, "filthy motion pictures" produced for showing in brothels and private clubs, and racist school textbooks [Schuyler, 1953: 9]. Richard Gid Powers describes Schuyler as "the most important black in the history of American anticommunism" (Powers, 1995:59).

66. Larrabee, 1955: 681: "Often the 'liberal' argument, as a way of touching base with respectability, has allowed that 'smut for smut's sake' must be rigorously dealt with—forgetting that this is the only concession the would-be censor has ever needed to ask. As long as an exception is made for the indefensible or even the detestable—'Freedom for everybody, except Communists and pornographers'—then there will be people perfectly prepared to state that you or I are Communists and pornographers, or their dupes, until we prove the contrary. It is at such times that one remembers why freedom has been said to be indivisible."

67. Worcester, 2010.

68. Quattro, 2011.

69. Inventory of the J. B. Matthews Papers, 1862–1986 and undated, http://library.duke.edu/rubenstein/findingaids/matthews/.

In 1948, Lev Gleason's digest-size *Reader's Scope* magazine published a nine-page "Picture Story" with photographs describing the situation in Korea, where Koreans hungering for freedom and self-rule were being thwarted by American and Soviet policies: "Honest expressions of democratic attitudes have been effectively squelched—in the north, by a tight censorship and one party system advocated by the Russians, and in the south, by American concern for maintaining the status quo, regardless of co-operation with former collaborators, fascists and brutal policemen that that entails ("Squeeze-play in Korea," 1948).

70. Quattro, 2011.

71. Harvey Kurtzman later recalled that the excitement of being brought "nose to nose with reality" in the pages of *Crime Does Not Pay* had been a major influence on the war comics series that he edited (*Two-Fisted Tales* and *Frontline Combat*) (Kitchen, 2011: 16).

72. The *New York World-Telegram*'s Fred Woltman wrote that in response to his page one article published on December 11, 1945, Gleason announced that he intended to sue "the paper and me for $250,000 each." Woltman's letter of December 26, 1945, the part of his article describing Gleason, and a nine-item list of Gleason's pro-Soviet activities from March 1935 to June 1940 appear in the Billy J. Hargis papers at the University of Arkansas.

73. The writer under investigation may have been Walter Bernstein, a creator of the magazine that Gleason published for veterans, *Salute*. Another of Gleason's writers who was investigated for possible espionage was Albert E. Kahn, whose criticisms of comic books are described in this chapter. Gleason had published the book *Sabotage!* that Kahn had co-authored (Brett Dakin, August 4–5, 2012, e-mail messages to author).

Ken Quattro, "the comics detective," has web-posted Gleason's FBI file (Quattro, 2011).

74. Theoharis, 1999: 28. Twelve days after the beginning of the Korean War, FBI director J. Edgar Hoover formally proposed a plan for President Truman to suspend habeas corpus and proclaim mass arrests of the approximately 12,000 individuals whom the FBI had listed as threats to national security. The detainees would be held on military bases and in federal prisons. Unlike the Palmer Raids of 1919–1920, during which Hoover had coordinated the arrests of thousands of suspected radicals, his plan of 1950 was not carried out (Weiner, 2007; Ellis, 1994: 39).

The adoption of the McCarran Internal Security Act in September, 1950 resulted in six American internment camps being maintained in readiness for the preventive detention (in a case of national emergency) of as many as 15,000 persons "who may commit acts of espionage or sabotage" (Cotter and Smith, 1957: 20–33). This act passed over the veto of President Truman, who argued that this legislation would "put the Government of the United States in the thought control business," and that some of the provisions of the McCarran Act constitute "a long step toward totalitarianism" and "a mockery … of the deep American belief in human freedom and dignity" (http://trumanlibrary.org/publicpapers/viewpapers.php?pid=883).

75. Bails, 2006: Lou Ferstadt. (Bails says Ferstadt worked for the *Daily Worker* "ca. 1946.")

76. Kurtzman began working for Ferstadt at the age of 17, in 1942. Bill Schelly describes this in great detail (Schelly, 2015: 57–66).

77. Holtz, 2006.

78. Buhle, 2007: 349.

79. Buhle, 2007: 349.

80. Bails, 2006: "Phil Bard."

81. "Dear Subscriber:," Sept. 1953. See also Hoff's memorial website: http://www.sacreddoodles.com/SydHoff/index.html.

82. I thank Larry Tye for generously sharing the notes of his interview with Alvin Schwartz, December 6, 2008 (Larry Tye, Sept. 8, 2017, e-mail message to author).

83. Siegel wrote that these men "have maneuvered me to a point where I am destitute and they continue making enormous profits from my creation" (Ricca, 2013: 231–232).

84. I extrapolate this conclusion loosely from James Gordon Meek's report that as the Cold War continued,

"Dear Mr. Hoover" letters arrived from churches, Boy Scout troops and school kids demanding to know if MAD was communist propaganda. Meek quotes Maria Reidelbach, the author of *Completely MAD*, the magazine's official history, as saying that half of those who worked at EC were "Red-diaper babies raised in Communist homes," so if the FBI and others suspected them, "They were right—MAD was genuinely subversive" (Meek, 2002).

85. Legman was a self-described Marxist, but when the FBI investigated him in 1949, they found no political ties connecting him to any party (Davis, 2019: 24, 63, 75). He became antimilitarist in the 1930s, when he realized that the world economy required military spending and foresaw that his generation was "slated to die soon in puddles of our own guts" if they could not prevent the next war. He and his friends were expelled from high school for passing out antiwar leaflets in the hallways (Davis, 2019: 64). When World War II did come, Legman was classified 4-F, unfit to serve (Davis, 2019: 107). Gershon and his friends firmly opposed fascism and Nazism (Davis, 2019: 64).

86. Legman, 1949: 23, 27, 32, 34, 38, 44, 50–51.

87. Legman's conference paper "The Comic Books and the Public" was published in the *American Journal of Psychotherapy*, as were those of the other presenters (except for Wertham, whose presentation was the basis for an article in the *Saturday Review of Literature*) (Legman, 1948). Several comic book industry professionals present at this historic meeting were quoted in the summary of the discussion: "*Mr. Charles Biro*, an editor of comic books, stated vigorously that comic books are getting better. *Mr. Alden Getz* and *Mr. Harvey Kurtzman* suggested that comic books should be improved and made educational" (Legman, 1948: 490). In *Seduction of the Innocent*, Wertham wrote that for years he had taken every opportunity to meet people in the comic book business, so it seems likely to me that Wertham had discussed Kurtzman's and Biro's work with them, at least casually if not in formal interviews (Wertham, 1953, 1954: 252). Unfortunately, I am not a skilled interviewer and when I met Kurtzman, his Parkinson's disease added to our communication difficulties. When I mentioned Wertham, Kurtzman became agitated, and I backed off rather than digging in with further questions.

88. *Neurotica* included early work by Allen Ginsberg, Marshall McLuhan, Jack Kerouac, Kenneth Patchen, and other writers who would become well-known (Campbell, 1999; Davis, 2019: 206, 205–216).

89. Legman, 1949, 1963: 29. A previous article by Marya Mannes had warned about comic book "addiction," calling comic books "the greatest intellectual narcotic on the market" (Mannes, 1947: 20). The idea that comic books were "addictive" was common enough by 1949 for Henry E. Schultz to complain that "every youngster in difficulty" was being portrayed in newspapers as "a comic book addict'" (Schultz, 1949: 216). For a heavily-footnoted survey of newspaper articles that linked comic book reading with addiction, juvenile delinquency and crime in this period, see Fernández, 2018.

Recent research showing that web-streamed visual pornography "addicts" its users raises many points reminiscent of the comic book controversy (Gombry, 2019).

90. Legman, 1949, 1963: 7–9.

91. Cornog and Pepper, 1999; Davis, 2019: 302.

In 1950, Robert Warshow's review of Legman's *Love and Death* predicted that ending censorship of sex would not raise the moral level of American culture as Legman had expected but would probably result in "a flood of pornographic comic books no less violent than the present 'clean' ones" (Warshow, 2001: 280; Davis, 2019: 423).

92. Legman, 1949, 1963: 42. Legman's extended family in Hungary had died in the recent Holocaust (Lambert, 2014: 44).

93. *Juvenile Delinquency (Comic Books): Hearings...,* 1954:62.

Gaines' joke, suggesting that opponents of comic books were unwittingly furthering communist purposes, fell completely flat. All four Senators on the subcommittee that investigated comic books, Hendrickson, Langer, Kefauver and Hennings, Jr., had been collectively described in a 1953 issue of the anti-Communist newsletter *Counterattack* as lacking reputations for being able to see through Communist propaganda, and so the suggestion that they were "red dupes" seemed more outrageous than ridiculous ("Dear Subscriber:," Feb. 1953).

The problem with the parody ad "The Group Most Anxious to Destroy Comics are the Communists" seemed to be that Gaines (as the publisher of the most liberal comic books) had misunderstood the politics of the anti-comics movement and assumed that Legman and the Daily Worker were exceptions, and that most of, those who opposed comic books were right-wingers. Decades later Gaines explained the origins of this joke that backfired: "It just didn't come off. It turned out to be ill-conceived. But, what I was trying to do, as I have said many times... I have a friend who, as he was walking down the street and saw someone making a speech to a crowd who he thought was right wing, and he found that if he'd go up and taunt the guy for being a communist, it would throw him into a fury. The theory being that he last thing a right winger wants is for people to think he's a left winger! [...] When I said 'anybody who's against my comics must be a communist' I had this in mind. But everybody took it seriously" (Gaines, 1983).

94. Brottman, 2004: 13.

95. Brottman, 2004: 19–20; Paul and Schwartz, 1961: 177.

96. Landesman, 1987, 1990: 60, 186.

Chapter Five of *Bookleggers and Smuthounds: The Trade in Erotica, 1920–1940* by Jay A. Gertzman provides a history of postal censors (Gertzman, 1999).

Legman's first experience as a published book author had been interrupted even more dramatically. In 1940, the police raided the bookshop of Jacob Brussel, who had published Legman's book about heterosexual cunnilingus, *Oragenitalism* and a clandestine edition of Henry Miller's novel *Tropic of Cancer* that Legman had arranged. The police took and destroyed the printer's plates, and Brussel's books, pamphlets and mailing lists. Brussel was jailed for three years on obscenity charges (Brottman, 2004:6–7; Davis, 2019: 112–118). According to Susan G. Davis's biography of Legman, in addition to this jail sentence, Brussel was "banned from any further work in publishing" (Davis, 2019: 117).

97. Schwartz and Paul, 1959: 628–9, 644.

98. I thank Matthias Harbeck for a copy of this article. (Hoffmann,1952). The article was illustrated by a drawing of Superman with a halo and by the cover of the first issue of the Korean War comic book *G.I. Joe.*

99. Investigation of organized crime in interstate commerce…., 1950: 47.

100. Kefauver had backed up his opinion of crime comic books by citing the pamphlets and speeches of FBI Director J. Edgar Hoover and the findings of "Dr. Wertham, famous criminologist and juvenile psychiatrist in New York, who has made a very extensive study of the results and effects of some of these crime books…."

101. de Grazia, 1955: 615, note 30. (Inexpensive photocopied reprints of Tijuana Bibles are available from GB Graphics, PO Box 14547, Portland, OR, 97293.) In "Betrayed," Whittaker Chambers turns against Alger Hiss when it turns out that Hiss "ain't all together queer." In turning him over to the authorities, Chambers concludes: "After all I did for him he betrayed me by goin' to women for his sex pleasure. Well them feds can lock him up. I'll not have him but neither will any woman."

David K. Johnson's eye-opening book *The Lavender Scare* tells of the rumors of Chambers' homosexual jealousy which were circulating at this time (Johnson, 2004:31–33).

In 1950, many Americans regarded homosexuals in government as a greater threat to national security than the Communists (Johnson, 2004: 2).

102. Schwartz and Paul describe how the program mostly stopped unsolicited publications that were mass-mailed by communist-controlled agencies, but on thousands of occasions also stopped books which Americans (including American research libraries) had ordered (Schwartz and Paul, 1959: 621–666).

103. Muhlen, 1949: 80–87.

The question of whether comic book readers would passively accept the erosion of democracy became mixed with concerns about comic book readers becoming "passive bystanders" in general. An editorial in the *New York Herald Tribune* after applauding the American Red Cross's appeal to supply comic books to "help troops pass tedious hours on transports headed for the Korean war zone" as accomplishing a "good deed," quoted unnamed "critics of comic books" as saying that they "leave their readers 'inactive, passive and physically unreleased." The newspaper confidently predicted that, to the contrary, "far from passive," a "six-foot four-inch marine with a new bazooka" arriving in Korea "might be equated to a very reasonable extent with that of Superboy or Superman by delinquent Reds started north" ("The Comics' Influence in Korea," 1950).

104. Muhlen, 1946:12; Muhlen, 1948: 6; Muhlen, 1951:18.

105. Muhlen's review of Wertham's *A Sign for Cain* in 1966 continued this theme (Muhlen, 1966: 353).

In *A Sign for Cain*, Wertham's very brief and indirect reference to communist atrocities had said only that: "absolute political power leads to estrangement from the masses and creates the danger of off-with-his-head methods for the solution of vexing problems. There can be no doubt that Stalin, who in the words of John Gunther was 'probably the most powerful single human being in the world,' was isolated and corrupted by the excessive absolute power concentrated in one person" (Wertham, 1966: 45).

Wertham's comment came a decade after Khrushchev's famous "secret speech" which had condemned as "foreign to the spirit of Marxism-Leninism" the way that Stalin had been elevated and transformed to the status of a "a superman possessing supernatural characteristics, akin to those of a god."

106. In *Seduction of the Innocent*, Wertham would make a similar statement: "If comic books make people get rid of their aggressions, why are millions of them given to young soldiers at the front whom we want to be aggressive? Comic books help people to get rid not of their aggressions, but of their inhibitions" (Wertham, 1953, 1954: 246). I recommend Dr. Michael Vassallo's Timely-Atlas-Comic blog, on which I found Muhlen's reply and very much more posted: http://timely-atlas-comics.blogspot.com/2011_02_01_archive.html, 26 Feb 2011. His "History of Atlas War Comics" was posted on his blog on May 4, 2013. http://timely-atlas-comics.blogspot.com/2013/05/a-history-of-atlas-war-comics-1950-1960.html (Vassallo, 2010).

107. Kahn, 1953 ("Comics, TV…"): 38.

108. Kahn, 1953 ("The Game of…"):116.

109. Kahn's anti-comic book arguments did receive some attention in the 1950s. The Canadian periodical *New Frontiers* (which had featured Stalin on its cover as Man of the Century on his death in 1953) published Bobbie Marsden's "Children and the Cold war" in 1954, which quoted Kahn generously and approvingly. I thank John Adcock for web posting this article, and a similar editorial from the same issue (http://punchincanada.blogspot.com/2008/05/children-and-cold-war.html).

A brief sample of Kahn's criticism of comic books from *The Game of Death* was also quoted in federal hearings on the "Strategy and Tactics of World Communism." The hearings quote Kahn as arguing: "Not all of the comic books deal with crime, sex, corruption, war. A handful feature stories taken from the Bible and other literary classics; and the narratives of some comics are built around animals. Almost invariably, however, the animal comics are replete with instances of sadism and violence. Many of the classic comics stress grim and brutal episodes…. There are also some comic books of a progressive nature, which stress the importance of combating discrimination and feature other such democratic concepts. The number of these comic books, however, is infinitesimal in comparison with the quantity of the horror, crime, and war comics" (Strategy and Tactic of World Communism…, 1955).

110. Kahn, 1987: 289.

111. In 1945, Elizabeth Bentley told the FBI that

Kahn participated in Jacob Golos's communist spy ring. Herbert Romerstein and Eric Breindel discuss Kahn in *The Venona Secrets*, and their most serious charge against him is that Kahn wrote an introduction for and published a pamphlet in July 1952, which promoted a Soviet disinformation campaign that used out-of-context quotations from a stolen diary to charge Major General Robert Grow, the military attaché of the American embassy in Moscow, with desiring and promoting a war against the USSR (Romerstein and Breindel, 2000: 420–423).

As for whether Americans actually had been promoting a war against the USSR, Russell D. Buhite and Wm. Christopher Hamel found that in 1945–1955 "documentary evidence now available demonstrates that a great many Americans, some of them in the highest ranks of government, in the nation's most prestigious universities, and among the country's leading journalists, at one time or another advocated attacking the Soviet Union before the Soviets could endanger the security of the United States" (Buhite and Hamel, 1990:367). The State Department opposed such talk of preventive war to keep the idea of an inevitable nuclear war from becoming a self-fulfilling prophecy (Casey, 2005: 9–11, 21–23, 36–37).

112. Romerstein and Breindel, 2000: 115, 295.

113. After publishing Matusow's book *False Witness*, Kahn was subpoenaed to appear before the Internal Security Committee, which referred to him in their official report as a "pro-Soviet propagandist" and "an integral part of the International Soviet espionage and intelligence apparatus" (Kahn, 1987:202–3, 248–9).

114. Wagner, 1954.

115. Wagner wrote that he "thoroughly approves" the American system, and claims that his position stands in contrast to "Britishers" who call it vulgar: "But that is surely the point. Far from shrinking in aesthetic revulsion from such 'vulgarisation,' we ought to recognize—as some of America's greatest artists in all fields do—the underlying potential and sign this round robin delivered to us in the name of demos with joy" (Wagner, 1954: 13). Marshall McLuhan had expressed a similar idea more clearly (while discussing Stan Lee's *Writer's Digest* article "There's Money in Comics!" when he argued: "The great artist necessarily has his roots very deep in his own time—roots which embrace the most commonplace fantasies and aspirations" (McLuhan, 1951: 152).

116. Wagner, 1954: 13.

117. For example, "Comic Books Destroying a Nation?," *Daytona Beach Morning Journal*, 11 Nov. 1951.

118. Wagner, 1954: 71–72.

119. Wagner, 1954: 78. Wagner listed his research collection as including:

Men's Adventures, GI Joe, Atomic WAR!, War WAR Comics. The American AIR FORCES, Two-Fisted Tales, The Adventures of REX, Buddies U.S. Army, Joe Yank, Battle Stories, Battlefront, War Birds, YOUNG MEN on the Battlefield, MAN Comics, T-Man, GI in Battle,

Battle Brady, Fighting MAN, BATTLE!, Battle Action, GI Combat, Combat Casey, Combat Kelly, JET Fighters, U.S. Tank Commandos, Horrors of War, Fighting MARINES, Battle Cry, Our ARMY at WAR, WAR Stories, The Fighting MAN, RANGERS, WAR Report, WARFRONT, Star-Spangled WAR STORIES, Atomic Attack, Battle Report, U.S. Marines, Fighting AIR FORCE—growing tedious? This has been called the most thorough psychological preparation for war any generation ever had—Soldier Comics, War Action, BATTLEFIELD, This is WAR, Frontline COMBAT, Operation PERIL, All American MEN of WAR, WAR HEROES, and so on. In fact, so explicit is the mystique here that I even treasure in my comic library a booklet of these 'steel-tough battle tales' entitled WORLD WAR III.

True to the emphasis of his chapter, *Parade of Pleasure*'s book cover showed an assortment of twenty American comic books, twelve of which were war and espionage comics.

120. Wagner, 1954: 94.

121. Wagner, 1954: 86. Wagner had contributed to making this connection in 1951 in *New Statesman and Nation*: "Nearly all of these Superman personifications are strongly Fascist. Captain Marvel, the Lone Ranger, etc., all carry insignia on their sleeves and dress in uniforms reminiscent of the Gestapo. Blackhawk dresses exactly like an S.S. man, complete with riding boots and crushed cap, except that he goes in state trooper blue. The villains and enemies of these men are readily identifiable by their hook-noses, as opposed to the Aryan snub-noses of the hero" (Wagner, 1951: 617). Gershon Legman had used this Blackhawk example earlier (Legman, 1949: 42).

122. Wagner, 1976: 36–37; 114–115; 176; 205. Wagner's examples of "the most bizarre projects imaginable" that had requested government funding included "the substitution of the comics for the classics..." (118–119). Another sign of the collapse of higher education as Wagner understood it was the introduction of student evaluations of professors, through which "Joe Blow yawning his head off in the back row" and other "retarded" "dunces" and "dolts" were asked to judge, in effect, whether he and the other professors had been sufficiently clear and entertaining (Wagner, 1976: 31, 42–49).

123. Wertham had titled his manuscript "All Our Innocences" from a Henry Steele Commager quote: "The ideals that grown-ups think should obtain are to be found more readily in children's literature than anywhere else. All our innocences are there" (Beaty, 1999: 26).

124. The first book about newspaper comic strips, Martin Sheridan's *Classic Comics and their Creators*, referred to monthly and quarterly "comic magazines" only in passing (Sheridan, 1942: 18). Cartoonist Coulton Waugh's *The Comics*, published in 1947, devoted its 17-page final chapter to comic books. Waugh called comic books "purely ugly" works characterized by "soulless emptiness," "outrageous vul-

garity" and discordant coloring, but nevertheless important commercially and to children (Waugh, 1947: 333).

Waugh (like "so many people") condemned comic books' hooded heroes as suggestive of the Ku Klux Klan ("the very reverse of the process of democratic law"), and was glad that the fad for "super-people" seemed to be waning (Waugh, 1947: 350–351). Nevertheless, he managed to end that chapter on a very upbeat note. During World War II, he had worked on a U.S. government-sponsored propaganda comic book and was thrilled to see his drawings printed with the text in Chinese characters. This had impressed on him the universality of communicating with pictures and had given him a glimpse of the future: "when you pick up one of these ugly little books you may be sure you are looking at the crude ancestor of something great," which someday could become "the most natural, the most influential form of teaching known to man" (Waugh, 1947: 346–347, 351).

125. In *The Show of Violence*, Wertham described crimes that had been influenced ("touched off" but not caused) by homophobic medical textbooks and a violent novel, "delusional" interpretations of the Bible, and Will Durant's *Story of Philosophy* (Wertham, 1948, 1949: 33–5, 75–6, 121, 143–144, 160).

126. Wertham, 1953,1954: 11, 142. In 1954, Wertham wrote: "When I first became aware of comic books (while I was director of the Bellevue Hospital Mental Hygiene Clinic, the largest mental clinic in the country) I paid no attention to them. [...] Several years passed before I decided to study comic books systematically" (Wertham [*Religious Education*], 1954: 394). In his 1956 book about the case of Frank Santana, *The Circle of Guilt*, Wertham reconstructs the interview in which Santana told him that the only books he read were comic books (Wertham, 1956: 85ff).

127. For example, in 1949 Wertham wrote: "The influence of comic books may not be easily apparent in the behavior of a child. But if he doesn't break into a candy store, that does not mean that the comics have made no impression on him. The most dangerous effect they have is a subtle distortion of human values. What children get out of comic books is that kindness, sympathy, and regard for human suffering are all weaknesses; that cunning and shrewdness are the kind of thing that counts; and that women are not to be respected as persons but are luxury prizes like automobiles, distinguished chiefly by sexy attributes rather than any high ideal of womanhood" (Wertham, 1949: 17). Wertham's *Seduction of the Innocent* makes many references to comic books as having brutal content and a brutalizing effect (Wertham, 1953, 1954: 109).

128. Wertham, 1948.

129. David Finn, who was hired as public-relations counsel to the Comics Magazine Association at the time, wrote "It was a major crisis for the [comic book] industry, and no effort was spared in its defense" (Finn, 1969: 175).

Dr. Wertham told the editors of the comics fan magazine *Instant Gratification* in 1979 that:

One time I got a call from one of the big New York newspapers, and the editor asked me if I had been paying my income tax. I told him that I assumed so; I have an accountant who handles that. I asked him why he wanted to know. "Because," he said, "we have been offered a portfolio on you, including statements that you haven't paid your income tax, but we've turned it down, of course. Don't you know you're being followed by detectives?" I didn't know, but I asked some of my friends, and they said that someone had been asking questions. I later found out that the comic book publishers had hired two private detectives, and that they had made all kinds of inquiries about my private life and my friends. They noted, among other things, that I often had "Negroes" come to my house—people like Ralph Ellison and Richard Wright [Bethke, 1979: 37].

130. Beaty, 2005: 146.

Young comic book fans did not need the help of any public relations specialists to decide that the main enemy of their favorite reading matter must be some kind of monster. Even after better information began to modify his image, comic book fans continued to repeat Wertham's comments about Batman and Robin's homoerotic atmosphere (out of context) to make him appear ridiculous. In fact, Wertham cannot fairly be regarded as a McCarthyist, as a censor, as a homophobe, as a quack scientist, or as a research fabricator.

I defend Wertham's reputation, including from Carol Tilley's claims that Wertham "fabricated evidence... for rhetorical gain," in two articles published by *The International Journal of Comic Art* and web-posted at academia.edu (Rifas, 2006; Rifas, 2013; Tilley, 2012).

Although Wertham has frequently been mischaracterized as a censor, he was proud to have testified consistently against censorship, beginning in 1928, when he became "the first psychiatrist in the U.S. to be admitted in Federal Court as a psychiatric expert in the case of a book the government had banned" (Wertham, 1957: 249; Wertham, 1970: 15).

131. Hajdu, 2008: 242; Kitchen 2011: 20–21.

132. "In our clinical research on crime comic books we came to the conclusion that *crime comic books are comic books that depict crime*, whether the setting is urban, Western, science-fiction, jungle, adventure or the realm of supermen, 'horror' or supernatural beings" (Wertham, 1953, 1954: 20). "Many war comics belong to the same category [crime comics], with the crime and violence dressed up in patriotic disguise" (Wertham, 1966: 194–195).

133. In the clinic's early years, Wertham was responsible for evaluating roughly 500 felons a year (Schechter, 2014: 116–7).

134. Schechter, 2014: 116; Gilbert, 1986: 94. A 1951 *New York Times* article introduced Wertham as "one of the country's best known psychiatrists" (Dales, 1951: 23).

135. Fredric Wertham, "Introduction: The Dreams That Heal," in Aswell, 1947: xxiv.

136. Wertham, 1949: 241–266.

137. For an example of an anti-communist publication respectfully citing Wertham, see Lester David's "Who raised these Hoodlums?," *American Legion* 49:1 July 1950: 52.

138. Feldstein told Grant Geissman in an interview for *Tales of Terror! The EC Companion*: "I met a guy at a convention in Seattle who had done a very serious treatise on this whole thing, in which he felt that Wertham was a communist, not a fascist of all things, but a communist. I won't say he was a communist, but he was in that milieu, looking for control of the media. I always thought he was a fascist. I thought he was a Nazi, [laughs] and he wanted to control us, but it was the other way around, he was a liberal. That's what this guy who had done this treatise thought" (Von Bernewitz and Geissman, 2002: 88).

I met Feldstein only once, at a Seattle comics convention, told him about my MA thesis, and sent a short letter afterwards summarizing the argument that Wertham had been politically on the left, not the right. (For example, Wertham named his "Lafargue Clinic" after Karl Marx's son-in-law, Paul Lafargue.) I had not said and do not say that Wertham had been a Communist Party member. Like Feldstein, I would use the words that Wertham had been "in that milieu."

139. Qiana Whitted has explored at book-length EC Comics unusual "preachies," about a dozen celebrated comic book stories that "proselytized" for liberal values (most of them written by Feldstein), which the company published from 1952 to 1956. (Whitted, 2019: 3, 8).

According to Geissman, Feldstein's "E.C. Preachies" on taboo topics including "racism, bigotry, drug use, anti-Semitism, and Civil Rights" were "quite controversial for the time, especially in certain parts of the country" (Geissman, 2013:208).

140. Geissman, 2013: 282/ Feldstein's description of a "supposed documentary" sounds like Paul Coates' "Confidential File: Horror Comic Books," except that this documentary said nothing about communism and repeated the by-then familiar argument that these comic books existed because people were making big money from publishing them.

A description of the "Confidential File" television series indicates that comic books had a serious public image problem at this time: *"Confidential File.*—[…] A behind-the-scenes report on America, with candid close-ups of people and places dealing with such critical problems as kid gangs, child molesters, comic books, leukemia, medical quacks, mental breakdown, narcotics, phony charity rackets and pyromaniacs"(Television Inquiry, 1957: 2572).

141. The document is in Part 39 of 87 of the Julius Rosenberg papers in "The Vault" of FBI records. "Memo Re: Julius Rosenberg, et al., Espionage R.," by James P. Lee, SA, reporting on an interview of Maurice Zolotow by Roy Cohn on May 8, 1951, which Lee had personally witnessed. Memo NY 65-15348-1724. The damning statements

attributed to Wertham included that "there was no need for psychoanalysis in Russia as everyone is contented." (The capitalization of "WERTHAM" indicates that the FBI held a file on him. I have failed twice to obtain Wertham's FBI file through FOIA requests.)

Also, in 1947 Wertham reportedly expressed the culpably naïve view that the Soviet Union's practice of sending "thousands and thousands of patients [to] collective farms" for work therapy exemplified the superiority of the Soviet approach to psychiatry over the American approach, where psychoanalysis and psychotherapy are only for the rich (Friedman, 2014: 160).

142. As an example of this accusation of Godlessness, Gabriel Lynn's 1944 Catechetical Guild pamphlet "The Case Against the Comics" argued that comics present: "an almost totally irreligious world. Moral and Christian values are rarely to be found identified as such in the comics. Night clubs, gang hideouts, worldly scenes are to be seen with wearying frequency, but the church is practically never seen or referred to. The world of comics is an irreligious world. It is in the main, a Godless world" (Lynn, 1944: 29). A decade later. Harold C. Gardiner, S.J. argued that comic books' greatest damage came through how they "stunt" and "paralyze" the imagination and convey an "atmosphere of utter materialism": "The imagination is a wonderfully delicate and apt instrument to help one realize—make real for himself—the eternal truths. If the imagination is blunted and dulled, these truths may still be held with utter constancy and sincerity, but they may not be held with the vividness, the immediacy, the sense of personal possession which they should evoke" (Gardiner, 1954).

In his article for the same issue of *Religious Education* in which Gardiner's article appeared, Wertham wrote that "Not being versed in theology, I cannot discuss this from a theological point of view," but he gives his opinion that "to the extent that the Bible is great literature," comic book adaptations of the Bible have been "sheer blasphemy" (Wertham, 1954: 397). Wertham's family had been non-religious, assimilated, German Jews. (Beaty, 1999: 23)

143. Wertham lived in a period in which society, working through government, recognized its responsibility to protect children's health and well-being. Joel Bakan argues that this "century of the child" ended in 1980, with the victory of neoliberalism. Bakan gives as an example that in 1981 the new head of the Federal Communications Commission justified his opposition to regulating children's television by describing broadcasters' mission as simply to "determine the wants of their audiences through the normal mechanism of the market" (Bakan, 2011: 8–9, 35).

144. Wertham testified on several occasions against censorship of reading matter for adults. His first public condemnation of comics came in the course of defending the right of nudist magazines to be distributed through the mails: "At a Post Office hearing in Washington I had to give a psychi-

atric analysis of what constitutes obscenity. By way of comparison with nudity in art and photography, I introduced comic books which I called obscene. I pointed out that the picture of a nude girl *per se* may be the opposite of obscene, as compared to one of a girl in brassiere and panties about to be tied up, gagged, tortured, set on fire, sold as a slave, chained, whipped, choked, raped, thrown to wild animals or crocodiles, forced to her knees, strangled, torn apart and so on" (Wertham, 1953, 1954: 297–298).

145. As summarized in July 2000, in a joint statement by the American Academy of Pediatrics, American Academy of Child & Adolescent Psychiatry, American Psychological Association, American Medical Association, American Academy of Family Physicians and American Psychiatric Association, the media violence research demonstrated that:

- Children who see a lot of violence are more likely to view violence as an effective way of settling conflicts. Children exposed to violence are more likely to assume that acts of violence are acceptable behavior.
- Viewing violence can lead to emotional desensitization towards violence in real life. It can decrease the likelihood that one will take action on behalf of a victim when violence occurs.
- Entertainment violence feeds a perception that the world is a violent and mean place. Viewing violence increases fear of becoming a victim of violence, with a resultant increase in self-protective behaviors and a mistrust of others.
- Viewing violence may lead to real life violence. Children exposed to violent programming at a young age have a higher tendency for violent and aggressive behavior later in life than children who are not so exposed ("Joint Statement …," 2000).

Psychology professor Christopher J. Ferguson and Psychiatry professor Eugene Beresin argue, in opposition to the fourth of these points, that research findings regarding the claimed "causal connection" between media violence and real-life violence have been mixed, that no consensus on that point has been achieved, and that statements from "professional guilds" warning about the effects of media violence have been both wildly alarmist and grossly inaccurate (Ferguson and Beresin, 2017).

146. The title of Thrasher's article was "The Comics and Delinquency: Cause or Scapegoat." Thrasher defines the "monistic" fallacy on page 195, and, on page 201, dismisses Wertham's failure to produce a quotable, suitably simple-minded statement about comic books causing delinquency as merely a matter of Wertham's "complicated and pretentious" reasoning (Thrasher, 1949: 195–205; Rifas, 2013).

In this twelve-page article, Thrasher quoted Wertham directly in five brief phrases for a total of only 30 words. Although Thrasher cites six sources for Wertham's views, all of his quotations are taken from a 1948 article about Wertham's work by Judith Crist for *Collier's Magazine*.

147. Adolf Meyer's writings return repeatedly to the importance of dealing with the facts of a partic-

ular person's personality and history, without being seduced into the "facile spotting of causes" (Meyer, 1948: 372). Alfred Lief described the difference between Meyer's attitude and those of a layman or a medical student trained in "the so-called accurate or absolute sciences" who "assumes that a factor must act like a set dose of a chemical and produce certain effects, or *if* it does *not*, it cannot be considered as a cause and becomes unreliable and negligible" (Meyer, 1948: 389).

According to Lief, who makes a comparison to William Hogarth's proto-comic etchings "The Harlot's Progress" and "The Rake's Progress," Meyer trained his students to "get at the biographic determinants of the 'complaint.' In this way the illness would become sharply etched as a series of progressive pictures telling the story of 'how it happened,' each case a Hogarthian 'Progress,' faithful to life and strong in social implications" (Meyer, 1948: 372).

Wertham had immigrated to the United States in 1922 to accept a position working under Meyer at the Phipps Psychiatric Clinic at Johns Hopkins University in Baltimore, Maryland, where he remained for seven years (Beaty, 2005: 16, 20).

148. I recommend the websites http://crisisofinnocence.library.ryerson.ca/index.php and lostsoti.org for valuable and well-organized information regarding Fredric Wertham and the anti-comic book movement, including links to key articles and documents.

149. As an example of other groups that participated in the fight over comic books, in San Mateo, California, comic book censorship was originally demanded by the Knights of Columbus and 68 affiliated Catholic organizations ("100 Comic Books Sent to Cowgill for Ruling," 1948).

Later that month, John S. Cowgill, that county's Probation Officer in charge of evaluating the comic books, told the Parents-Teachers-Association chapter in the neighborhood where I would later grow up that comic books "never are the basic cause of committing a crime" but are time-wasters that "also teach the child a false philosophy by emphasizing the comic book moral that evil can be overcome only by the use of violent force" ("Parent-Teacher-Association News—Baywood," 1948).

150. Twomey, 1955:29. See also the entry under "National Office for Decent Literature (NODL)" in the *New Catholic Encyclopedia* (National Office…," 1967: 237–8) and under "National Organization for Decent Literature" in *The Encyclopedia of Censorship* ("National Organization…," 1990: 204).

151. Twomey, 1955:32.

152. In 1952-3, NODL repeatedly objected to *Man Comics* and to Harvey Kurtzman's *Two-Fisted Tales*, while finding acceptable *Don Winslow* and *(New) Heroic Comics*. (NODL, 1952–1953).

Other war comics they found objectionable once or twice in this period were *Blackhawk, Fight, Spy Cases, War* and *Warfront*. The other war comic they found acceptable once in this period was *Combat Kelly*.

In its evaluations of comic books of March 1955, *Heroic Comics #90* (which included five fact-based

Korean War stories but did not picture the war on its cover) appeared on its list of 121 comic book titles to which it had no objection. In that report NODL listed seven war comics among the 41 titles to which it had "some objection." It found most of the war comics it looked at "objectionable" (their lowest category). These included such titles as *Battle*, *Battle Action*, *Battle Attack*, *Battle Fire*, *Battle Ground*, and *Battle Squadron*.

153. NODL, 1954- 1955.

154. This advice came after the industry's Comics Code had gone into effect with the hope that "Mothers and dads and community groups long concerned with the comics problem" would continue to remain vigilant (Barclay, 1955: SM48).

155. "News in Brief," 1953.

156. Moody, 1954.

157. "Quits Post On Committee," 1955.

158. The monopoly power of the American News Company began disintegrating in 1955, but it was followed by regional monopolies. According to an analysis by Buchan and Siegfried, "With the demise of American News came the emergence of only a single wholesaler in almost every distribution area in the United States" (Buchan and Siegfried, 1978: 20–21).

159. Wertham, 1953, 1954: 260–263; Wertham, 1954 ("Testimony..."): 395. Although the Subcommittee received conflicting testimony, evidence showed that wholesalers sometimes did make threats to pressure dealers to "display and sell their entire line," including crime comics ("Crime Comics and the Constitution," 1955: 252–3; Goldstein, 2003: 8, 19, 23–24). An unspoken analogy in the case of "tie-in sales" was to Hollywood's practice of "block booking," which the Supreme Court had declared a violation of antitrust law in 1948.

The "package" delivered to some newsstand dealers included not only "nationally known magazines with established circulation" and romance and crime comic books, but also "sexy girly magazines." These indecent "girly" magazines had photographs of "girls in varying states of undress" and articles featuring "promiscuity, rape and abnormal sex relationships" (Banning, 1952: 115, 117–118).

160. Marston, 1948: 18.

161. Scurlock, 1948 ("Comic Books—Movies..."): 1.

162. Scurlock, 1948 ("Youth's Radio...":): 5.

163. Some of the earlier activities of Chicago's Censor Bureau had included suppressing films that criticized conditions in Nazi Germany and banning Charlie Chaplin's anti-Nazi film *The Great Dictator* (1940), apparently to respect the feelings of the city's large German-American population; banning newsreels that showed city police shooting at striking workers; and temporarily banning a 1950 drama against race prejudice, *No Way Out* (Sidney Poitier's first film).

Chicago's censors testified in a Supreme Court case that they prohibited "Coarse language or anything that would be derogatory to the government—propaganda" and that "Nothing pink or red is allowed." They argued that "Children should be allowed to

see any movie that plays in Chicago ... If a picture is objectionable for a child, it is objectionable period" Choper, 1984: 58–59).

The largely-forgotten extent of film censorship in the United States by local censorship boards (especially in the years before 1952, when, in the Burstyn decision, the Supreme Court recognized movies as deserving the right to free speech), provides some valuable context for understanding the controversies over freedom of expression in comic books in that period.

164. Twomey, 1955: 33–43; Twomey, 1955 ("The Citizen's Committee..."); Wolfe, 1954.

165. Feder, 1955: 23.

166. Bolte, 1955: 92.

167. For example, the *Southtown Economist* published a page-one invitation to an upcoming "crime book bonfire," organized by Pastor Clinton Cox, who argued that he was fighting against the brutalization of the imagination:

"Probably the worst thing about these publications is their corrupting effect on the imagination of young people."

The "bad comics" destined for the flames were comic books "devoted to murder, savagery, perversion, brutality, and cunning" (Wolfe, 1954).

168. On another occasion, a newspaper article noticed, though, that children would tear apart recycling bundles to look for comic books, and recommended burning comic books without ceremony instead ("Comic Books Menace to Scrap Paper Drive," 1954).

A map of sixteen "Comics Burnings: 1945–55" in the United States appears in Pyle and Cunningham, 2014.

169. Báez, 2008: 206–219; Orlean, 2018: 98–101. The Nazi book burnings became the symbol of Nazi Germany's totalitarian suppression of "'Un-German' literature, theater, art, music, film and architecture..." (Hill, 2008: 32).

170. "German Red Purge...," 1952.

171. "Comic Book Burning Set in East Berlin," 1955.

Until East Germany's Protection of Youth Act of October 4th 1955, children in East Berlin could legally buy Western comics in West Berlin and bring them home. In 1961, the building of the Berlin Wall prevented Berliners from crossing back and forth between the two parts of the city. I thank Matthias Harbeck for an e-mail of September 1, 2014 with this information.

172. "Germany: Read no Evil," 1946. Major General Robert Alexis McClure had been in charge of censoring German radio, press, film, theater and music and publications in the zone administered by the United States (Paddock, Jr., n.d.).

173. Morrow, 1948; "ECA Denies Approval of Comics for Germany," 1948; Bassett, 1948.

174. Wertham, 1953, 1954: 292–3.

175. Sloyan, 1954: 407.

176. Evans, 1955: 46. (Evans does not mention comic books, but does name the primary Soviet propaganda goal of this period.)

177. These included the Inter-American Treaty

of Reciprocal Assistance (1947), NATO (1949), the ANZUS treaty (1951), the Security Treaty Between the United States and Japan (1951), SEATO (1954), and CENTO (1955).

178. Lent, 1999; Rifas, 2000 ("Addressing…"): 93.

179. Rifas, 2000 ("International…"): 97.

180. Lefevre, 2004: 196–197; Barbu, 2003.

181. Tsipursky, 2016.

Similarly, foreign movies, television dramas, music videos and pornography currently circulate clandestinely in North Korea while North Korean cultural productions lack international appeal (Tudor, 2017: 67–72, 75–77, 86–87, 136, 201–202, 213, 215–216).

182. Alaniz, 2010: 33, 68–69.

183. A 1944 article in *Das Schwarze Korps* (where the Nazi attack on Superman comics had appeared four years earlier) described jazz as a "cacophony of animal howls, wild instruments, and foot-stomping Negro lust" which takes the listener "to the depths of prehuman apedom." That article described the more general problem by saying "The Jews have used jazz and movies, magazines and smut, gangsterism and free love, and every perverse desire, to keep the American people so distracted that they pay no attention to their own fate" ("The Danger of Americanism," 1944).

This piece and a wealth of additional information is webposted at the German Propaganda Archive, maintained by Randall Bytwerk, whom I thank for his e-mailed advice (https://research.calvin.edu/german-propaganda-archive/).

The Nazis contrasted German art and culture (the genuine expression of the life of a community), with the situation in America, where Jewish influence had reduced art and culture to money-making businesses ("Americanization…," 1944).

As World War II ended, Mme. Ninon Talon, who chaired a committee that supervised the distribution of packages of children's books to "European and Chinese youngsters," announced that they would not be sending "comic strip books" overseas to prevent people from getting the wrong idea about America: "Too much Fascist propaganda disseminated in Europe during the war was founded on willful misrepresentations of our comic strips, Mme. Talon observed. Fascist propagandists played up the 'rootin', tootin' qualities of many of our most beloved comic strip characters and distorted them to convey the impressions that 'the United States is a country of gangsters and shooting,' she said" ("Children Abroad to Get No Comics," 1945).

184. Sroog, 1947. (Arnold Sroog wrote that *Is This Tomorrow's* "purpose is to soften up the minds of American youth so that in the near future they could become candidates for a fascist storm troop organization.")

185. The Catechetical Guild had been publishing comic books since 1942, distributing them through Catholic schools as a wholesome alternative to commercial comic books. Reportedly, four million copies of *Is This Tomorrow?* were circulated, mostly through church groups (Murray, 2010: 105).

The comic book *Is This Tomorrow?* featured some of the first published comic book work by Charles Schulz, who would later go on to create the comic strip "Peanuts" (Michaelis, 2008: 167).

186. Grayson, 2006:18–19, and Yi, 2006: 239.

An estimated third of North Korean Christians had joined the pro-government Korean Christian Federation (Armstrong, 2003: 94).

187. An interesting example of Cold War nuttiness appeared in a newspaper article in 1948, apparently in response to page 30 of *Is This Tomorrow?* Under the headline "Boston Police Say Comic Book Contains Communist Propaganda," the article reported that Mrs. Lenore McPherson had complained to the police that in a comic book her son bought on a newsstand "Communist doctrines were spread […] in the pretense of describing conditions that would prevail under Communism": "I object particularly to the passages that said 'Don't obey your parents: obey the state' and 'there is no God',… It seems the publishers of the magazine are trying to force their ideas of Communism on the youth of this country… If these books are permitted to be printed and sold … it won't be long before the youth of the country will become Communists."

It seems probable to me that Mrs. McPherson had been making a disingenuous attack on a comic that she disagreed with politically ("Boston Police…," 1948).

188. The Soviet criticism of America's commercial comic books had been anticipated. In 1948, Dave McGuire reported that "When Jacob Lomakin, the deposed Soviet Consul, sailed recently from New York City, one of the items in his luggage was a trunkful of comics magazines. Imagination conjures up a picture of Joe Stalin and the Politburo boys giving those publications the once-over, their brows beetling even more than usual in puzzled fascination. Any day now we may expect Pravda and Radio Moscow to quote from some of the worst as examples of democratic decadence" (McGuire, 1948).

189. "Russian Says…," 1949. Chukovsky's article was republished in 1955 in a textbook used in Soviet schools. Under the title "Poison for the Minds of American Children," his article concluded:

> The present rulers of America do nothing to take this poison away from their children, because they want a new war. "Today's children are tomorrow's army," says Wall Street. According to the Wall Street imperialists, American children must be taught that banditism is a normal thing and that modern technique will help them to rob, kill and commit crimes.
>
> But there are progressive, peace-loving people all over the world, and in America too, who are fighting for democracy. Our country, the first Socialist country in the world, is the leader in this great struggle. In the end American children and all the children of the world will be saved from war and such fascist poison as American children's comics [Quoted in Parker, 1957: 231].

Soviet propaganda's view of American comic books was also summarized in the 1950 article "American

Through the Kremlin's Eyes" by Louis Jay Herman in *The American Mercury*. The Soviet view presents Americans as "recruiting future SS guards among the children, who are taught to read *Superman* magazine from the age of eight. The little tykes are thus indoctrinated with the idea that 'gangsterism is the norm in human relations'" (Herman, 1950: 595).

190. Crépin, 2001: 135, 137–138.

191. The banned Korean War stories were Jean-Michel Charlier and Victor Hubinon's *Ciel de Corée* and *Avions sans pilotes* (Crépin, 2001: 141). As a result of this ban, French-speaking Belgian cartoonists censored their own work to maintain access to the lucrative French market (Lefevre, 2004: 200).

192. I thank comics scholar Jean-Paul Gabilliet for helping me fix several errors in my draft of this section (Jean-Paul Gabilliet, June 19–20, 2014, e-mail messages to author).

193. Barker, 1984.

194. Mauger, 1951: 47. I thank Martin Barker for a copy of this article.

195. "It Ain't Funny...," 1952. Gaines quoted this paragraph in his house ad "Are You a Red Dupe?"

196. Sargeant, 1952: 535, 538.

197. Bjork, 2017: 180.

198. Allwood, 1956: 4.

199. I thank comics scholar Ralf Kauranen for this information, in an e-mail of August 31, 2008. Kauranen adds that Albert E. Kahn's and Fredric Wertham's criticisms of comics were republished in Finnish, but most Finns thought about comics as Disney comics: "In the Finnish debate, it was [...] often pointed out that the problem hasn't reached Finland, but that it's good to be prepared."

200. Although these Korean War comic books included nothing that Mexico's comic book censorship law specifically prohibited, the censors refused to approve them for publication. They were sold in Mexico without a license, but did not sell particularly well (Rubenstein, 1998: 119).

201. Rubenstein, 1998: 119–122.

202. The author, Harry Emerson Wildes, also reflected on the failures of American propaganda efforts in Japan: "...to people who had never tasted freedom, who knew nothing of justice in its Western sense, who had been taught that individualism was evil and that democracy was degeneration, and by whom Christianity was not generally accepted, we warned that Communism periled all those aims. [....] Certainly the Japanese were mistaken, but many of them saw but little difference between the Allied occupation of Japan and the Russian control of North Korea" (Wildes, 1954: 3).

203. Bowles, 1954: 297.

Bowles' example was quoted from his book *Ambassador's Report* in a report of the Subcommittee hearings, including his description of a "superman character [Captain Marvel] struggling against half-human colored Mongolian tribesmen who has been recruited by the Communists to raid American hospitals in Korea and drink the plasma in the blood banks. In every picture they were portrayed with yellow skins, slanted eyes, hideous faces, and dripping jaws." The story Bowles referred to but did not cite was "Captain Marvel Fights the Mongol Blood-drinkers," published in *Captain Marvel Adventures* in January 1953.

204. In St. Paul, Minnesota, a citizens' project, started in 1949 with representation from churches, parent-teacher associations, distributors, and other groups, issued a list of "best buys among the comics." Some of the comics recommended in St. Paul as among the most acceptable, were rated as "objectionable" or "very objectionable" by the Cincinnati Committee on the Evaluation of Comic Books ("Policing the Comics," 1952).

205. Murrell, 1950. Murrell reported that "The organizations represented on the Committee were the University of Cincinnati, Xavier University, the Woman's University Club, the Parent-Teacher Associations (public and parochial), the Boy Scouts, the Girl Scouts, the Y.M.C.A., the Y.W.C.A., the playground group, the juvenile courts, the Council of Churches, the libraries, the private schools, and the three major religious groups—Protestant, Catholic and Jewish. About one third of the members of the committee were men."

206. Murrell, 1952: 134.

207. Murrell, 1953.

208. Murrell had notified the FBI that the "very objectionable" comic books might be presenting "insidious communist propaganda" ("Comic Book Committee...," 1952). Of 19 war comics that the Committee evaluated that year, 16 received "C" ratings, none "D," and only one an "A" (*Our Army at War*). The average comic was judged objectionable for more than three reasons, and 22 of the 31 criteria were listed for at least one war comic. Several of the criteria added the previous year, such as harming national defense had been dropped (Murrell, 1954).

209. Wertham, 1953, 1954: 328.

The expression "crime and violence," which Wertham used several times, implicitly encompasses both criminal violence and state violence.

210. Hajdu, 2008: 172–74; The main findings of this opinion survey concluded that "anti-social acts spring from no single factor" ("Juvenile Delinquency: a compilation...," 1950). Wertham agreed that anti-social acts do not spring from a single factor, but also described this "favorite argument of the comics experts" as a straw man (Wertham, 1953, 1954: 242–245).

211. In addition to being televised, the Hearings of April 21,1954 were broadcast by WNYC radio, and can be heard in their online archive: https://www.wnyc.org/story/subcommittee-to-investigate-comic-books-and-juvenile-delinquency-morning-session/; https://www.wnyc.org/story/subcommittee-to-investigate-juvenile-delinquency-and-comic-books-afternoon-session/.

212. Senator Hendrickson explained: "We are conducting these hearings in New York, the heart of the comic-book industry, because of the thousands of letters we have received. We are vitally interested in evaluating the impact of horror and crime comics upon the young mind" ("Comic Book Hearing to Start Tomorrow," 1954).

213. Hendrickson and Kefauver, 1953.

Warren Bernard posted this and many interesting archival finds on the *Comics Journal* website on February 6, 2013 ("Warren Bernard's Citations and Fredric Wertham Documents," http://www.tcj.com/warren-bernard-1954/14-19530304-jointstatement-1-copy/).

In 1956, Hendrickson and his co-author Fred J. Cook proposed that the connection between juvenile delinquency and war, war tensions and the draft "is so elemental that it should hardly need to be said" (Hendrickson and Cooke, 1956: 73).

214. April 15, 1953, letter to Hon. James O. Eastland, Senate Judiciary Committee from Robert C. Hendrickson, http://www.tcj.com/warren-bernard-1954/15-hendricksonsb89-2/.

215. McWilliams, 1990:150–1; Hendrickson and Cooke, 1956: 169–172.

216. McWilliams, 1990: 152–153; Scott, 2010: 76–7.

Zheng, 2003: 34, 36–7; Chen, 1995: 263–264.

The story "Three in a Jeep," published in *G-I in Battle #3*, in December 1952 is a semi-coherent story involving a South Korean, a suspected communist spy, who turns out to be trafficking in opium.

On the cover of *Battle Cry #11* (March 1954), the cover shows two American soldiers crashing a jeep through the wall of a communist opium warehouse, but this issue contains no feature that corresponds to that cover.

217. Caniff, 2014: 170–227. The *Steve Canyon* comic strip of April 21, the day Caniff testified before that subcommittee, showed some Americans wrestling with the problem that every bit of evidence that the villainess "Herself Muldoon" had been smuggling heroin from Red China had been lost at sea. Canyon says: "Gentlemen, I contend that the hundreds of kids who will receive dope she sells, plus the millions of U.S. dollars it puts in Red hands, justifies holding the woman here!"

The lack of evidence problem is solved when a sergeant secretly plants heroin on Muldoon as she is leaving and tips off the customs officials in Indo-China about where to find it. The sergeant later explains: "Look, Col. Canyon, before you feel you have to get noble and report me … the dope pushers hooked my kid brother … he's a hopeless junkie! So between me and them it's *war*—and *all's fair*!...." (27 April 1954). On March 18, a Red Chinese man, in a brief appearance, had told Herself Muldoon that "We obtained 70,000,000 U.S. dollars from narcotics in 1952—more in 1953!" As she knows, they also have been exchanging heroin for "electronic devices" that they forward to "the Russians for their submarines." Herself Muldoon understands their position: "you need more users in North America to sweeten the Communist Party treasury!"

218. Concerns about comic books encouraging juvenile delinquency and comic books disadvantaging the U.S. in the Cold War overlapped. A month after the comic book hearings, the U.S. Ambassador to Ceylon (present day Sri Lanka) wrote to the Department of State that "I have been asked by responsible travelled persons if it is really true that gangs of children terrorize the slums of big American cities. I have then been shown U.S.-made comic books that obviously encourage exactly this type of juvenile crime" (Crowe, 1954).

219. Comic Books and Juvenile Delinquency. Interim Report…: 20–21.

For additional evidence of elite concern about the effect of American comics on the reputation of the United States, see "Private Media and Public Policy," by C.D. Jackson. Jackson, a leading American expert on psychological warfare, warned that certain American publications "and not only comic book publishers" were dumping their unsold copies in Europe "without regard to the impression that material may create" (Merkel, 1949, Jackson, 1951: 334).

220. As she remembered it on the stand, that code, which she had helped to prepare for Superman-DC comics "in the middle forties," had required that "no character in the comic with whom the children could identify themselves, or their own parents, their own family, or their own country, or their own side, should be irretrievably damaged, killed, or mutilated, and neither should such a person with whom the child could identify himself or anyone on his side irretrievably damage or injure anyone else regardless of whether they were the enemy or not. That is to say, they should not have to bear the guilt of feeling that they were responsible for this damage having happened."

Lauretta Bender's testimony on Day Two, Thursday, April 22, has been conveniently reposted (along with the rest of the testimony in those Hearings) by Jamie Coville at: http://www.thecomicbooks.com/1954senatetranscripts.html.

Bender might have been thinking of a panel representing the Battle of Dunkirk in *Real Life #4* (May, 1942). Parents' Magazine's *Real Life* comics, *True Comics'* sister publication, promoted itself as "not about impossible supermen." It regularly showed large military ships going down in flames.

221. Gilbert, 2009: 63–64.

222. Feder, 1955: 30; Report of the New York State Joint Legislative Committee…, 1954: 11.

In an article published after the hearings had concluded, Hendrickson suggested that the comic book problem had more to do with capitalist irresponsibility than communist subversion: "Why are such comic books published? Because there is money in it. Not even the Communist conspiracy could devise a more deadly way to demoralize, disrupt and confuse our future citizens" (Arne, 1954: 4).

223. When the same committee went on to investigate the possible influence of motion pictures on Juvenile Delinquency, they heard testimony from Ronald Reagan, a multi-term President of the Screen Actors Guild, and later a two-term Governor of California and then two-term President of the United States.

Reagan testified:

A little while ago I was in a picture based on the Korean war, called *Prisoner of War*. It came from the stories of the first 60 repatriated prisoners.

Some people complained because the picture was too brutal. Well, a lot of American kids went over to the war and a lot of them went through and lived through in reality what we tried to portray.

I am sorry, but I don't see what is wrong with letting the American public, who are free to either buy the ticket or not buy the ticket—what is wrong with letting them come in and see a sample of what the American kids in the Armed Forces went through who had to fight that war for them. You can't do that by flashing a notice on the screen and saying, "We don't want to show you this, it is terrible, but awful things happened to this fellow," and then go on with the story. You have to portray what took place and what happened to him.

Reagan praised Hollywood's "self-restraint" under the Production Code's strict "voluntary censorship" and concluded by saying that he was very disturbed by the prospect that the government might censor the movies because of their supposed effects on youth: "…I am very much worried about my children and all the other children their age, an entire generation that is going to grow up taking it for granted that it is all right for someone to tell them what they can see and hear from a motion picture screen, because when they grow up and take our places as adults, I am afraid they will be mentally conditioned to where then somebody can tell them it is all right to tell them what they can read and what they can hear from a speaking platform, and what they can say and what they can think. If that day comes, of course, we have lost the cold war" (Juvenile delinquency [motion pictures]…, 1955: 93–96; The film *Prisoner of War* is described in Lentz, 2003: 284–288).

224. "Comics Publishers Seek 'Czar' … 1954: 19. Elliott Caplin, a member of the committee that drafted the Comics Code, confirmed that he had relied heavily on Hollywood's Hays Code (Nyberg, 1998: 112).

225. Shawna Kidman's article "Self-Regulation Through Distribution" explains that the Comics Code was an "all-in-one" solution for the comic book industry's problems, aimed not only at reducing outside pressures for government censorship, but also at reducing overproduction by driving smaller "irresponsible" publishers out of the business (Kidman, 2015: 29).

226. Finn, 1969, Chapter 7: "His Conflict with the Public Interest," pp.155–190. Finn's discussion of the comic book controversy appears on pages 174–176.

227. Finn, 1969: 176.

228. Ruder & Finn helped create the Philip Morris public relations campaign that argued that cigarettes had not been proven to cause cancer. Decades of documents have been web-posted by the University of California San Francisco, including the undated proposal "PROJECT 'B' AN ALTERNA-

TIVE PROPOSAL TO PROJECT 'A'" (https:// www.industrydocumentslibrary.ucsf.edu/tobacco/ docs/#id=sxbg0145).

In 1997, *Mother Jones* magazine found that Ruder & Finn were helping "the major carbon-emitting industries" mobilize "phony grassroots troops on the ground to lobby against the global Climate Change Treaty being negotiated this week in Kyoto, Japan. And some of those troops would be right at home in Tim McVeigh's militia unit" (Hammond, 1997).

In his 1969 book, Finn admits to wondering "where open-mindedness ends and self-deception begins" when representing management's positions on controversial matters, such as the health effects of smoking and also lists ten other comparable controversies in which Ruder & Finn had participated (Finn, 1969:186).

229. "Comment: The Problem of the Comic Books," 1956; "Comic Book Curb…, 1955; Crime Comic Sales…," 1956: 29.

230. Caputo, 2012.

231. Don Thompson identified another possible example of Comics Code censorship of a Korean War comic book story. The cover story "The Lonely One," published in *Impact #4* in 1955, seems to have been intended originally as a powerful statement against anti-Semitism in the army, but its message against religious bigotry became obscured by naming the harassed soldier, not something easily identifiable as Jewish like Levy or Cohen, but "Miller." In 1966, Comics Code Administrator Leonard Darvin told a skeptical Thompson that the editor, Al Feldstein, might have made that change on his own. (Thompson, 1972: 11). For background on World War II experiences of Jews in the U.S. Army including their encounters with anti-Semitism, see Moore (2004).

232. Wertham, 1953, 1954: 252, 266.

233. Wertham, 1953, 1954: 264–265.

In his testimony later that day, Walt Kelly responded to Wertham by saying: "Despite the testimony given before, I would say right offhand that cartoonists are not forced by editors or publishers to draw any certain way. If they don't want to draw the way the publisher or editor wants them to, they can get out of the business" (Juvenile Delinquency [Comic Books]…, 1954: 110).

234. Soper, 2012: 120–121.

235. The Senate investigation of comics was led by Senator Estes Kefauver, an outspoken opponent of McCarthyism. (Gorman, 1971: 141).

236. Soper, 2012: 119.

An example of a comic book panel showing a villain "tearing the clothes off" of a woman appeared in *Thrilling Comics #19* (August, 1941, web-posted as page 29 of 68 at The Digital Comic Museum).

237. Juvenile Delinquency (Comic Books)…, 1954: 112.

When asked for a statement, Milton Caniff emphasized that newspaper strips, unlike comic books, are "precensored" by syndicates and editors. As for which comic books are unacceptable, Caniff called that a matter of taste. Later he added that the cartoonists present were not attempting to debate Wertham, "whose opinion we value very highly," but to be sure that "the good stuff" in newspaper comics is part of the Hearings' record, and not only "the horrible stuff" (Juvenile Delinquency [Comic Books]..., 1954: 114–115).

Joseph Musial, clearly more comfortable drawing than speaking, expressed his views in drawings that the record of the Hearings neither described nor reproduced. He also made a clumsy pitch that the Senators hire cartoonists to make an educational comic about the comic book problem (Juvenile Delinquency [Comic Books]..., 1954:, 112, 117).

238. NCS newsletter, July 15, 1954, p.7 (quoted in Soper, 2012: 120).

239. Breger, 1955: 9, 23.

Breger also includes this observation: "I suppose it's most impolitic of me to lump the capitalist and communist systems together, but at the risk of being dragged before some investigating committee I say there's this similarity: Cartoon jokes about business in our magazines and newspapers are like the cartoon jokes in Soviet Russia's humor magazine *Krokodil*—the jokes are okay as long as the *system* isn't lampooned."

240. Brown, Ben, 1984: 242–243.

241. According to an October 11, 1947 *Billboard* survey: "In 1947, there were only approximately 44,000 to 63,000 television sets operating in the U.S. (of which an estimated 30–40,000 were in the metropolitan New York area, ...)" (Quoted in Shagawat, 2011: 10).

242. Researchers who studied the consequences of introducing television (decades later) to communities in Canada, Fiji and Bhutan measured such effects as a decline in creativity, a rise in aggression and violence, slower acquisition of reading skills, anxiety about body size, and various forms of bad behavior (Rubens, 2009: 186–188). No comparable studies were done in New York City, when comic books and then television arrived in quick succession.

243. Wertham, 1953, 1954: 375. In his original response to the Senate Subcommittee on Juvenile Delinquency's invitation to testify, Wertham said that he was willing to testify not only about comic books but also about television and the problem of juvenile delinquency generally. See Herbert J. Hannoch's letter to Herbert Beaser, of 2 Dec 1953, web-posted at: http://www.tcj.com/tag/fredric-wertham/feed/.

244. Wertham, 1953, 1954: 369.

Chapter 8

1. Harvey Kurtzman provides an apparent exception. He began his first comic book story about the Korean War with this scrupulously neutral description: "June, 1950! The incendiary spark of war is glowing in Korea! Again as before, men are hunting men—blasting each other to bits—commiting [*sic*] wholesale murder! This, then, is a story of man's inhumanity to man! This is a WAR STORY!"

The illustration accompanying these words, however, tells a more partisan story, visually placing us with the American characters that are being targeted

by enemy machine gun fire (*Two-Fisted Tales*, Jan/ Feb 1951).

"War Story!" was the first comic book story that Will Elder drew for the publisher EC. Elder later explained to an interviewer his motivations for drawing Kurtzman's war comics: "it was a living, it was a chance to get into the business and work at it, and develop techniques" (Geissman, 2013: 201).

A different kind of exception to the convention of dating the beginning of the war to June 25, 1950 appeared in the April-May, 1966 issue of *Marine War Heroes* no. 13, a "special issue" telling "The Complete Action-Packed History ... of the KOREAN WAR." In that "complete" story, the background to the war is completely erased, and the conflict does not begin until the U.S. Marines arrive on August 2, 1950. Paul M. Edwards argues against a widely-circulated "myth" that the Marines were the first United States forces to arrive in Korea after the North Korean attack. (Edwards, 2018: 62).

2. One story that did refer to the years before the North Korean invasion, "His Fraternity Pin" (*Wartime Romances #16*, July 1953), describes a difficult romance between two Korean students, Kim Wang and Lee Pon, studying at a university in California from 1947 to 1950. Lee Pon briefly mentions the period of Japanese colonialism which ended in 1945: "They held us under subjugation for forty years!"

In this story, signed by Ric Estrada, Kim Wang becomes embittered by American racism, joins a leftist campus organization of "frustrated malcontents who followed the communist line to the letter," and when the war begins, he returns to Korea and becomes a military officer in the North Korean army. Lee Pon also encounters American racism but allows herself to be consoled by the explanation that racism is merely a problem of certain insensitive individuals. After the war begins, she returns to South Korea as a Red Cross nurse. In the final scene, they are reunited in a hospital in Korea. Kim Wang's last words, spoken in a weak voice tinged with venom and hatred, are "we will crush the Western imperialists—drive them from the earth!" She then returns his fraternity pin to his dead body.

As for whether anti-Korean racism in the United States really came down to a just a matter of a few insensitive individuals as this story would have us believe, at that time Koreans could not legally marry white people in fifteen states, own land in eleven states, or enter twenty-seven occupations in New York City. Restrictions on immigration from Korea were so tight that only ten Koreans immigrated to the United States in 1950. In addition to these legal restrictions, white Americans routinely discriminated against Koreans (and other Asians), denying them service in restaurants, hotels, barber shops, and theaters and admission to churches (Cumings, 2005, 452–456).

3. Cumings, 1981; Cumings, 1990. Michael J. Seth's *A History of Korea* explains succinctly how South Korean President Syngman Rhee governed as an autocratic authoritarian: "He carried an antagonistic attitude toward the National Assembly, where

his supporters numbered hardly more than a quarter of the 200 seats. To maintain his authority, he relied on the bureaucracy, the police, and the military, all dominated by members who had loyally served in their posts under the Japanese. [...] Since Rhee's own nationalist, anti-Japanese credentials were impeccable, he was able to shield his officials, and they in turn served him" (Seth, 2011: 318).

4. The UN neither supervised nor controlled the war against North Korea (Hauben, 2013).

5. Rubin, 1950: 2.

6. Muste, 1950: 9.

7. General MacArthur wrote a statement to The Veterans of Foreign Wars in which he argued that Formosa (Taiwan) must also be defended, since failure to do so: "would shift any future battle area five thousand miles eastward to the coasts of the American continents, our home coast; it would completely expose our friends in the Philippines, our friends in Australia and New Zealand, our friends in Indonesia, our friends in Japan, and other areas, to the lustful thrusts of those who stand for slavery as against liberty, for atheism as against God" (Brands, 2016: 134).

8. This story did not present an exaggerated view of North Koreans' atrocities during their occupation of South Korea. Some "reactionaries" were tried in People's Courts, but others were summarily executed, or killed after being brutally tortured first, together with their families (including women and children) (Kim, 2000: 166).

9. Orr, Parrish and Holland, 1953.

10. The two-year-old story "The Soil of Africa Weeps!" from *Ideal Comics #3* (November, 1948) had raised complaints in London that it had "a violently anti-British slant." Stan Lee was quoted as saying that letting the anti-British sentiments slip through and see print had been "very embarrassing" for Timely Comics ("London newspaper...," 1950).

"The Soil of Africa Weeps!" sides with the Boers, described as "a small group of honest, freedom-loving people" and "a harried race of God-fearing decent people ... in search of a democratic peace." The heavy-handed partisanship in this story continues from beginning to end.

11. Wertham referred to this incident in *Seduction of the Innocent* when he writes: "Inaccuracies in historical comics are common. [...] the end of the Boer War is wrongly presented, while the story has such choice bits as 'You dirty British swine!'" (Wertham, 1953, 1954: 310).

Thinking about how the *New York Times* put Stan Lee on the spot reminds me of the one time that the *New York Times* did an article on a comic book that I had edited, *Corporate CRIME Comics*. The *New York Times* reporter asked why *Corporate CRIME Comics* didn't publish stories about crimes in the Soviet Union. My publisher, Denis Kitchen, and I had never thought about it. We didn't see any reason not to except maybe that we hadn't seen stories about that. The reporter's article about *Corporate CRIME Comics* concluded by quoting Denis on this question: "We're not just focusing on American crimes. We're doing some historical stuff too and we're interested in doing stuff behind the Iron Cur-

tain, but it's hard to get information" ("Crime in the Suites," 1980: F17).

It would be impossible for writers and reporters to passively "reflect" the events of the world. Instead, they use questions that shape our understanding of the world.

12. Melvyn P. Leffler summarizes the evidence released from the Soviet, Chinese and North Korean archives as showing that although "historians once thought Stalin ordered the North Koreans to attack South Korea in June 1950 to test American resolve," the North Korean leader Kim Il-sung "relentlessly pushed and prodded the reluctant Soviet leader for permission" to re-unify the Korean Peninsula by force (Leffler, 1996: 120, 129).

American policymakers were more concerned that the attack on Korea was a prelude to a possible attack on Western Europe than with the unlikely island-hopping scenario proposed in "Peril in Korea," but the records revealed after the Cold War showed with near-certainty that Stalin had never intended a military attack on Western Europe (Mastny, et al., 2006: 268).

Evidence suggests, however, that America's strong response to the invasion of South Korea inhibited Stalin from escalating his attacks on Tito's Yugoslavia (in *Eastern* Europe) into a full-scale war. Because the U.S. and NATO were prepared to use nuclear weapons to defend Yugoslavia, an article in the NSA's journal *Cryptologic Quarterly* concluded that the United States "did nothing less than save the world from a global conflagration" when it moved to save South Korea from a Communist takeover ("Dodging Armageddon...," 1998).

13. Goncharov, Lewis, and Xue, 1993: 150.

14. Jim Vadeboncoeur, 26 June 2010, e-mail to author.

15. Kim Dong-Choon has summarized the Republic of Korea's astonishing degree of unpreparedness to resist the invasion of June 25, including suspiciously "strange" and "mysterious" military decisions "that no one could understand" (Kim, 2000: 42–44).

16. Detzer 1977: 99; Gaddis, 1982: 110; Acheson, 1969, 1987: 405.

17. Adams, 1983: 22.

McCarthy's charges against the State Department, including his main charge that Owen Lattimore, an occasional advisor to the State Department on Far Eastern matters, was both "one of the principal architects of our Far Eastern policy" and "the top Russian espionage agent in this country" were investigated by the Tydings Committee. The committee declared McCarthy's charges to be "a fraud and a hoax perpetrated on the Senate of the United States and the American people." (That conclusion was supported by the three Democrats on the committee but not by the two Republicans.)

During the investigation, Tydings begged for access to the secret documents that McCarthy had been using, but his plan to confront McCarthy with information from the files turned out to be impractical. In comic book stories like "The Gray Shark," the contents of the government's secret files supply quick, clear answers, but Committee-member Senator Henry Cabot Lodge discovered that actually "the files alone did not furnish a basis for reaching firm conclusions of any kind.... The files which I read were in such an unfinished state" that going through them "would be a waste of time" (State Department Loyalty..., 1950: 9–11, 149–152, 167).

18. Definitions from dictionary.com. The cartoon that introduced the word "McCarthyism" appeared March 29, 1950 (Kercher, 2005: 316–317).

19. Isserman and Schrecker, 2004: 169; Weinstein and Vassiliev, 2000: 297–299; Benson and Warner, 1996.

20. Acheson, 1969, 1987: 357–358, 365.

21. Donovan, 1982: 205/ The theory that Acheson had given a "green light" for the invasion of South Korea remained the consensus position among American historians for the next 30 years. Nevertheless, James I. Matray's analysis of declassified Soviet documents concludes that "Acheson's National Press Club speech had no perceptible impact on the events leading to the outbreak of the Korean War," and that "[u]ntil the moment North Korea attacked South Korea, Joseph Stalin and Mao Zedong worried about U.S. military intervention" (Matray, 2002).

In arguing that Acheson's "Green Light" had not been a factor, Matray says: "Stalin reluctantly approved North Korea's invasion plan despite this risk, gambling that Korea could be reunited before the U.S. would have time to enter the war, and out of fear that a delay would give South Korea preparation time for them to invade and destroy North Korea" (Matray, 2002).

22. Harry Rositzke debunks the idea of a global Soviet conspiracy and deflates the flattering image of the CIA in *The CIA's Secret Operations: Espionage, Counterespionage, and Covert Action.* Rositzke spent 25 years as a professional intelligence officer beginning in 1946, and specialized in the study of the Soviet Union. The bunk in "The Gray Shark" becomes evident when this story is compared to Rositzke's account. Rositzke wrote: "The image underlying the Cold War mentality was that of a powerful and aggressive Soviet Union [which was] remote from the reality of a country weakened by war: with a shattered economy, an overtaxed civilian and military bureaucracy, and large areas of civil unrest" (Rositzke, 1977: 14).

23. Barrett, 1953:156–7.

24. Barrett, 1953: 94.

25. Barrett, 1953: 331.

26. Barrett, 1953: 323.

The grand scale of the American psychological warfare programs does not imply, however, that there was a perfected science of manipulation at work in comic books such as *Korea My Home.* Analysts at the Operations Research Office of The Johns Hopkins University surveyed the field of psychological warfare in August, 1950, and were surprised and disillusioned by the field's lack of general doctrine and expertise (Dyer, 1959: 114).

Thomas C. Sorensen's history of American propaganda put Barrett's program in this perspective: "In the wake of the Korean outbreak, the world-wide propaganda operation grew rapidly. It was not without growing pains: some decisions were made hastily and carelessly; not all of the thousands of persons hurriedly employed were of top caliber; and some USIS posts were assigned more people than they needed. But the program had its effect, as the Soviets demonstrated indirectly through their increased attacks upon it.... By mid-1951 Barrett could boast of a number of accomplishments, although on examination they proved to be more accomplishments of growth than of persuasion"(Sorensen, 1968: 27).

27. Although *Korea My Home* was drawn by an American cartoonist, the United States has also sponsored or recruited cartoonists from other nations for propaganda purposes. For example, during World War II, an anti-militarist Japanese cartoonist working under the name Taro Yashima, who had escaped into exile in the United States in 1939, drew propaganda leaflets for the U.S. Office of War Information. Yashima's pioneering autobiographical graphic novel *The New Sun* (1943) describes in instructive detail how the militarists in Japan had crushed Japan's progressive movement. In one scene, the author describes a conversation in prison, where he was being held without charges. One cellmate, a Korean garbageman, had tried to steal one zinc pipe, but "As he said, this was nothing compared to Japan's seizure of all Korea" (Yashima, 1943; Shibusawa, 2005).

When the Korean War started, South Korean cartoonists drew for Korean military publications, drew propaganda flyers, and also drew a few anti-communist comic books (Lent, 1995: 11; Hall, 2019: 89–122).

28. For my information on Johnstone and Cushing I am indebted to Bob LeRose, who I interviewed by phone in March, 1990. On the use of comics in advertising, see Heller, 1988.

29. Bob LeRose, March 1990, phone interview.

30. By contrast, in North Korean propaganda Korea was liberated from Japanese rule, not by the Russians, but by "Patriotic General Kim Il Sung" (Armstrong, 2003: 87–90).

31. Armstrong, 2003 ("The Cultural Cold War..."): 42–44.

32. Cumings, 1981; 1990: 388–9.

33. The cartoon propaganda leaflets dropped by American planes did use rape stories "designed to create dissension" between China and Russia or between North Korea and China. A large collection of American propaganda leaflets used during the Korean War, including many cartoon leaflets, resides at the Hoover Institution on War, Revolution and Peace, Stanford, CA.

American and UN rapes of South Koreans during the war were common but not well documented. To protect "decent" Korean women, "camptowns" that included prostitutes and women in longer-term relationships with foreign soldiers were built near military bases throughout South Korea.

As in other wars, the Korean War "mass-produced" prostitutes, partly by creating huge numbers of homeless, unemployed, desperately poor orphans and widows. A 1953 U.S. government report calculated that about 350,000 prostitutes were working throughout Korea, mostly around military bases (Oh, 2015: 49–50, n.4, 226–227; Moon, 1997: 27–29; Cho, 2008: 67; Fitzpatrick, 2015: 566, 569).

American soldiers also committed many rapes in Europe during World War II, a topic that was highly tabooed for many years (Vronsky, 2018: 319–324).

34. Armstrong, 2003: 77.

Chomsky and Herman argue that high estimates of the scale of a land reform "bloodbath" in North Vietnam were fabricated as part of a propaganda campaign, and based on forged documents. They conclude that rather than 700,00 deaths, the number executed during Vietnam's land reform was probably closer to 5,000, or less than the number of Vietnamese noncombatants killed in the single American military operation SPEEDY EXPRESS (Chomsky and Herman, 1979: 341–345).

35. Cumings, 1981: 4, 425.

36. Cumings, 1981: 136, 144.

37. Kim, 2000: 192–203.

38. Cumings, 1981: 403–409, 411.

39. According to Allan R. Millett, The Soviet soldiers arriving in North Korea treated Koreans as a conquered people instead of as a people liberated from Japanese oppression. In addition to those executed immediately, they shipped an estimated 400,000 Japanese and Korean prisoners to labor camps in Siberia, of whom 95,000 eventually returned (Millett, 2005: 49).

40. Park, 1999: Chapter 11.

41. Jager, 2013: 20.

42. Kim, 2000: 47, 107.

43. Seth, 2011: 1–2.

44. Myers, 2010; Oh, 2015: 52–54, 68.

45. The text of the Yalta Agreement is posted at: http://www.ndl.go.jp/constitution/e/etc/c04.html. As a condition for their agreeing to join the war against Japan, the U.S. and Britain accepted that the Soviet Union would get back the territory that Japan had taken from Russia in the Russo-Japanese war.

46. Jager, 2013: 18; McCormack, 2004: 16; Asmolov, 2008; Achkasov and Iur'ev, 1985. Japan's prestigious Kwantung Army had been greatly reduced in strength, as its forces were gradually withdrawn to fight in China and then to prepare to defend Japan from invasion. The politicians advising Japan's Emperor, however, apparently overestimated its current power. Beginning just past midnight, August 9th, the Soviet Union went to war against Japan, capturing 594,000 Japanese prisoners (including 143 generals), and killing over 80,000 men and officers of the Kwantung Army in combat. In these operations, the Soviet Army lost 8,219 killed and 22,264 wounded. No matter how one apportions the credit between America's atomic bombs and the Soviet Union's defeat of the Kwantung Army, the Soviet Union substantially contributed to Japan's decision to surrender (Teague, 2016). Arguably, the loss of the Kwantung Army, more than the losses of Hiroshima and Nagasaki, convinced Japan to accept defeat (Ham, 2014: 350–351, 354–355, 474–475).

47. Barry, 2012. Brigadier General George Lincoln decided on the 38th parallel, and then gave Colonels Dean Rusk and Charles Bonesteel a half hour to see if they could think of a better alternative. They agreed on the 38th parallel (Barry, 2012: 44; Stueck, 2013: 11–12).

Rusk would go on to serve as Secretary of State from 1961 to 1969; Bonesteel served as commander of the US, UN, and South Korean forces in Korea from 1966 to 1969 ("General Forecasts…," 1969: 17).

48. Cumings, 2010: 103–104; McCormack, 2004: 16; Grey, 1951: 486.

49. *Korea My Home*, page 19, panels 4–5.

50. *Korea My Home*, page 25, panels 1–2.

The 16-page propaganda comic *The Free World Speaks*, drawn by Jack Sparling and published by Malcolm Ater, has similar wording (*The Free World Speaks*, page 13, panel 1).

51. Rhee said as early as 1946: "On my returning to Korea I advocated unification … so that we could drive the Russians from North Korea…. As soon as the time comes, I will instruct you. Then you should be prepared to shed blood" (Schaeffer, 1990:138). In late 1949, thirteen members of South Korea's first elected National Assembly were arrested for their political opinions, including (according to the indictment) that they had opposed "the invasion of North Korea by South Korean forces" (Cumings, 2005: 217).

52. Lone and McCormack, 1993: 100. The art for *The Korea Story* was supplied by M. Philip Copp, who had cooperated with the State Department on their first experiment in comic book-format international propaganda the previous year, *Eight Great Americans*. The State Department's September 25 1950 press release announcing the new leaflet *The Korea Story* concluded: "The earlier State Department 'comic book,' *Eight Great Americans*, was a pictorial history of the lives of Washington, Jefferson, and others. The success of the booklet, which is being produced in nine languages, has, Department officials believe, established the comic book technique as an effective method of telling the American story overseas" ("Color Cartoon…," 1950: 591).

53. Cumings, 2005: 210.

54. Cumings, 2005: 186, 193, 203, 211; Cumings, 1990: 70–78.

55. *Horrors of War #11*, January, 1953. For information on Star Publications, see Benton, 1989: 145. John Wooley praises Disbrow (and L.B. Cole, who drew the cover for this issue) in an article he wrote about what he called comics' "Age of Funk" (Wooley, 1978).

56. The reference to French Indo-China (Vietnam) was not unusual. For descriptions of American comic book stories about fighting communists in Viet Nam that were published in the early 1950s, see Rifas, 2001: 3–32. One of Secretary of State Dean Acheson's first responses to the North Korean invasion was to increase American support for the French war effort in Vietnam (Acheson, 1969, 1987: 406, 408). The comic book's reference to recent fighting in Israel/Palestine, on the other hand, *was* unusual.

57. Truman, 1956: 332–333. The phrase "Hitler, Mussolini, and the Japanese" identifies Nazism and

Fascism with individual personalities, yet identifies Japanese militarism simply as "Japanese." For discussion of the implicit racism see Dower, 1986: 78–79.

58. The story "Burma Raid of the Air Commandos" in *Rangers Comics #61*, published by Fiction House in 1952, was a revised version of a Suicide Smith episode from *Wings Comics #51*, published by Fiction House in November 1944. The revised, Cold War version of this story, makes only minimal changes in the art, but thoroughly rewrites the dialogue and story, making the Japanese enemy into Red Chinese.

"Burma Raid of the Air Commandos" sheds no light on what Americans were actually doing in Burma in 1952. After the victory of the Communist Chinese in 1949, many Chinese Nationalist soldiers had moved to northern Burma. The CIA supported these Nationalists in large and small attacks on China, hoping to thereby force China to divert some of its military forces away from the war in Korea. (Blum, 2003: 23–4). The CIA's alliances with opium warlords in Burma at this time led to the agency's becoming increasingly complicit in the drug trade (McCoy, 2003: 129).

59. The phrase "with great power goes great responsibility" appeared in a luncheon-talk that Truman delivered in Independence, Missouri on November 6, 1950 (Truman, 1950).

One of Stan Lee's most famous lines was Spider-Man's motto "With great power comes great responsibility." John Fousek's chapter "The Meaning of Responsibility" in his book *To Lead the Free World: American Nationalism and the Cultural Roots of the Cold War* says the "prevailing discourse" in the U.S. after World War II was that, as "indisputably the most powerful nation in the world," the United States now had "global responsibilities" (Fousek, 2000: 63).

60. Cumings, 2010: 44–5; 50–55.

Chapter 9

1. Other comics in this genre included *Spy Cases* (September, 1950), *Little Al of the F.B.I.* (November, 1950), *Spy Fighters* (March, 1951), *Kent Blake of the Secret Service* (ca. July, 1951), *T-Man* (September, 1951), *Top Secret* (January, 1952) *Cloak and Dagger* (Fall, 1952), *Spy Thrillers* (November, 1954) and Canadian reprints under the titles *Spy Secrets* and *Amazing Spy Adventures*.

2. Harden, 2017; Weiner, 2007: 54; Haas, 2009: 207–208; Johnson, 2010: 80; Finnegan, 2011: 57–70. Anne Jacobsen suggests that these CIA teams were "led by Americans" behind enemy lines (Jacobsen, 2019: 42–46, 49–51).

3. Dr. Clayton Laurie of the Center for the Study of Intelligence explains that CIA analysts of that time interpreted developments in the Far East in terms of the Soviet Union's alleged "grand design for world domination": "While analysts accurately and consistently reported current intelligence, the reports did not emphasize that the Korean situation represented anything extraordinary beyond routine Soviet mischief-making and proxy-sponsored "tests" of

American resolve [...] in a world menaced by communists everywhere, its reporting on Korea did not stand out" (Laurie, 2010: 7).

Blaine Harden reveals that the American spymaster Donald Nichols *did* warn of the North Korean invasion in a timely, accurate way (but did not warn of the Chinese intervention). The problem had been that Nichols's warnings, and those of others, had been "muzzled" by General Charles Willoughby, America's top intelligence officer in the Far East (Harden, 2017: 48–61).

4. Amy B. Zegart, discussing a more recent generation of "spytainment," warns that even "policymakers—from cadets at West Point to senators on the Intelligence Committee to Supreme Court Justices—are referencing fake spies [from movies and television fictions] to formulate and implement real intelligence policies" (Zegart, 2010: 600). She also quotes a CIA staff historian who reports that junior and mid-level CIA officers have been "shocked" to hear that "there is nothing in [the Hollywood film *The Good Shepherd* about the CIA's early years] that can be relied on—at least if you're interested in truth, in reality." Zegart concludes: "If CIA officials are caught in a twilight zone between what is real [about their own organizational history] and what is not [but comes from a movie], it should be no surprise that everyone else is, too" (Zegart, 2010: 605; 612–613).

5. Hart-Landsberg, 1998: 80. Blaine Harden reports the extraordinary case of Lee Whal, a vice-commander of North Korea's air force, whose father had been a wealthy landowner and who had served as a military pilot for the Japanese during World War II. Harden says that Lee Whal may have escaped the usual fate of people of his class background "because he volunteered to train pilots in North Korea and donated his own property as facilities for pilot housing and education." The remarkable American spy Donald Nichols claimed that General Lee Whal was his friend, and Harden presents evidence suggesting that this was possible (Harden, 2017: 134–135).

The one exterior view of Pyongyang illustrated in "Peril in Pyongyang" shows a large convertible stopping in front of the undamaged "Ministry of Intelligence" building. By the time this story was published, Pyongyang actually lay in ruins with almost no buildings left standing; its population (reduced from 500,000 before the war to 50,000) was living in holes in the ground; and its few remaining officials were meeting in underground bunkers (Pembroke, 2018: 148–149).

6. Fredric Wertham testified on behalf of Ethel Rosenberg, and provided help to the Rosenbergs' children, Michael and Robert Meeropol (Beaty, 2005: 84–86; Reibman, 1999: 249–250).

7. The Amerasia office was at 225 Fifth Avenue, half a mile from Timely's offices ("INVESTIGATIONS...," 1950). Rosenberg was arrested at his home in Knickerbocker Village, a housing-development that was three miles from Timely's offices. According to the New York Times, Alger Hiss lived, beginning in 1946, in an apartment near University Place in Greenwich Village. ("'I HAVE COME HOME'...,"

1954). ("Timely" is an older name for the company later known as Marvel.)

World War II comics were full of Nazi spies. In 1941, the FBI had arrested Nazi Germany's Duquesne spy ring, which was based in Times Square, less than a mile from the Empire State Building.

8. For examples of comic book spy stories which persisted in using Nazi or fascist villains after the end of World War II, see (at The Digital Comic Museum or Comic Book +):

"Brought to Bay," (*Spy and Counterspy #2*, October–November 1949)

"The Trail of the Family Heirloom," signed by Myron Fass (*Atomic Spy Cases,* Avon Periodicals, March 1950)

"Nazi Nemesis," penciled and inked by John Celardo (*Spy-Hunters #6*, June–July 1950)

"Jonathan Kent: Espionage Ace," penciled and inked by Charles Sultan (*Spy-Hunters #8*, October–November 1950)

"Patrol Perilous," penciled and inked by Leonard Starr (*Spy-Hunters #8*, October–November 1950)

"The Dragon's Claw," credits unknown (*Little Al of the F.B.I.,* No. 10, 1950)

"The Pulverizing Peril," credits unknown (*Spy-Hunters #8*, October–November 1950)

"Thunderbolt in Thuringia," possibly by Charles Sultan (*Spy-Hunters #14*, October–November 1951)

"Murder Stalks New York" penciled and inked by Lin Streeter (*Spy-Hunters #18*, June–July 1952)

"Cloak and Dagger, starring Al Kennedy in the Krosno Butcher," penciled and inked by John Prentice (*Cloak & Dagger* Vol. 1 no. 1, Fall 1952)

By *Spy-Hunters #21* in December–January 1952, the whole issue used communist villains (with three of the stories set in Korea, and one in Columbia).

9. Preston, 1994: 549–550, 558.

10. The Korean War opened the way for Spain to be accepted as an American ally in the fight against communism (Preston, 1994: 567, 594–595, 607, 622–624).

I thank Ignacio Fernández Sarasola, author of *La Legislación sobre Historieta en España* (2014, 2017), for an interesting e-mail correspondence about Spanish comic books. He tells me that the best-known war comic series in Spain was *Hazañas Bélicas*. (The first 29 issues have been web-posted at comicbookplus.com.) He also alerted me to the long-running Korean War comic book series *Episodios de Corea*. (I found its covers posted at https://www.tebeosfera.com/.)

11. Lee, 2000: 33–38, 66; Simpson, 1988: 63 ff.. Fearing that the outbreak of the Korean War was a prelude to a Soviet invasion of Western Europe, the United States tried to arrange an alliance with the newly formed West German government. When West Germany's political leaders demanded as part of the bargain freedom for the fifteen Nazi war criminals who had been sentenced to death, the U.S. High Commissioner for Germany, John McCloy, saved ten of the condemned men from hanging, and began a process that would free hundreds of other convicted Nazi war criminals (Simpson, 1988: 190–192).

12. Newton, 1991: 243.

13. Martin, 1980, 2003: 38.

14. Newton, 1991: 310. Bayard Stockton quotes an alternate wording in his book *Flawed Patriot*: "How extraordinary to see the face I've been doodling all my life" (Stockton, 2006: 30).

15. Newton, 1991: 243.

16. Martin, 1980, 2003: 48; Macintyre, 2014, 148–149. Ben Macintyre's book reproduces two of Burgess's "typically irreverent cartoons" (drawings of Lenin and of Stalin) facing page 115.

17. Martin, 1980, 2003: 56.

18. Budiansky, 2016: 134. In July, 1951, the North Koreans improved their procedures, making it impossible for the Americans to continue reading their messages (Budiansky, 2016: 142).

19. Budiansky, 2016: 142–144.

20. Budiansky, 2016: 144.

21. Greenwald, 2013. Greenwald clarifies that even the NSA "could not read every mail, listen to every telephone call, and track the actions of each individual" but knowing that they have the capability to watch any person's words and actions at any time destroys "a core condition of being a free person." Without privacy, people are unable to "truly experiment, to test boundaries, to explore new ways of thinking and being, to explore what it means to be ourselves" (Greenwald, 2014: 172–175).

22. The locales for T-Man stories frequently appeared in the story titles (e.g., "Death Trap in Iran") and, in other cases (such as the story "A Quick Freeze With Hot Lead," set in the Alps, also in issue #3) can be determined from summaries of Quality Comics' *T-Man* comic series posted at the Grand Comics Database (www.comics.org).

23. Bourret, 1988: 178.

24. Fremigacci, 2007.

25. Allen Millett argues that the casualty estimates for the conflict on Cheju-do: "remain controversial and are exaggerated by anti-Rhee historians in Korea, Japan, and the United States. The government claimed that it killed 3,560 rebels, but the revisionists insist that the actual number, including the massacre of villagers, could be at least 30,000. The census figures suggest losses of less apocalyptic proportions" (Millett, 2005: 303, n.74).

Bruce Cumings reminds us that the true number will remain unknown: "No one will ever know how many died in this onslaught, but the American data, long kept secret, ranged from 30,000 to 60,000 killed, with upward of 40,000 more people having fled to Japan (where many still live in Osaka). More recent research suggests a figure of 80,000 killed" (Cumings, 2010: 121). For intermediate estimates of the death toll see Katsiaficas, 2012: 96 and Hart-Landsberg, 1998: 87.

26. Cumings, 2010: 137.

27. Cumings, 2005: 219–220.

28. Cumings, 1990: 283; Jager, 2013: 49–54.

Chapter 10

1. President Truman's Executive Order 9981, issued on July 26, 1948, has been web-posted at

The Truman Library: http://www.trumanlibrary.org/9981.htm.

Melinda Pash cautions against regarding the end of segregation during the Korean War as complete. She wrote: "Throughout the Korean War, the Army maintained segregated units and even resegregated some units" (Pash, 2012: 86).

I thank Fredrick D. Kakinami Cloyd, author of *Dream of the Water Children*, for his valuable comments on this chapter. I also thank Qiana Whitted, author of *EC Comics: Race, Shock, and Social Protest*, for her valuable comments on this chapter.

2. For example, Hayton and Albright, 2012.

3. For a densely footnoted, wide-ranging discussion of racial representations in comics, focusing on underground comix, see my article Racial Imagery, Racism, Individualism, and Underground Comix" (Rifas, 2004).

4. Pilgrim, 2017.

5. Comic Books and Juvenile Delinquency: Interim Report…, 1955.

6. Bennett, 2009. Will Eisner's character Ebony White appeared as the young sidekick to The Spirit from 1940 to 1949. Like Steamboat, Ebony had inhumanly-thick lips, but that character raised less controversy back then. Eisner later explained: "Remember, Ebony was created in the '40s and, at that time, you still had Amos & Andy. That sort of humor was prevalent and acceptable at the time—but I always treated Ebony very differently. […] I got mail from both sides. I got a letter from the Afro-American papers in Baltimore complimenting me on the way I treated Ebony. On the same day, I received another letter from a couple of fellows I had gone to high school with (in my radical days when I was going to change the world) and they said I betrayed socialism because of the portrayal. Oddly, the letters both came on the same day—I should have saved them" (Cooke, 1999).

7. "Negro Villain in Comic Book…," 1945; Dier, 1945.

8. Hirsch, 2013: 62–63. Brian Cremins includes an incisive chapter about the character Steamboat with detailed information about the Youthbuilders project in his book about Captain Marvel (Cremins, 2006: 98–129).

9. Berelson and Salter, 1944: 1.

10. Berelson and Salter, 1944: 2–3.

11. Goodrum, 2013: 201; Shaffer, 2003:6, 11; Shaffer, 1999: 152.

12. To indicate Schiff's political opinions, his fellow-DC-editor Mort Weisinger colorfully described him as "the house Red" and "that crazy pinko" (Jones, 2004: 260).

13. Shaffer, 2003: 6, 11; Conn, 1996: 278.

A columnist for an African American newspaper wrote in 1945 that: "With deep understanding and with admirable courage, the East and west association has brought the problem forthrightly and concretely to the American public and has taken the most effective approach possible touching the kids in their pliable years and instilling in them a sense of racial understanding that will do more real good, I am sure, than a hundred inter-racial meetings. …

The funnybook is one of the most powerful propaganda weapons we have" (Shaffer, 2003:6, 12).

14. Wells, 2001; Grost, n.d. I also thank John Wells for clarifications in an e-mail of July 14, 2017.

15. Sokolsky, 1946; Shaffer, 2003:15; Armagideon…, 2012; Quattro, 2014.

16. Shaffer, 2013: 20; Conn, 1996: 338; Hunt, 1977: 58.

17. When launching her East and West Association, Buck wrote to the Institute of Pacific Relations' Edward Carter: "I want somehow to get down into the level of people who don't and won't listen to your programs and read your books… I want to get down to the level of the comic strip if I can […]!" (Shaffer, 2013: 11–12).

18. Buck, 1948.

19. Hirsch, 2013: 71.

20. Paul S. Hirsch lists the eight comic book publishers who cooperated with the Writers' War Board as DC (and related publisher All-American), Famous Funnies, Fawcett Publications, The Parents' Institute Press, Standard Magazines, Street & Smith Publications, and Ziff-Davis (Hirsch, 2013: 37).

21. During World War II, unlike the policies concerning blood sent to Europe, the U.S. Red Cross continued to racially segregate blood donations used for transfusions in the United States (Horne, 2017: 61, 120).

22. I rely for this description of the story on Paul Hirsch (Hirsch, 2013: 63–64).

23. Woo, 2017: 10–11.

24. Woo, 2017: 14.

25. Woo, 2017: 21.

26. The repeated, quasi–vampiric comic book plot of a white bigot saved by a transfusion of black blood worked better as an argument for human equality when blood symbolized common humanity.

27. In 1950, Joe Louis would also be featured in two issues of his own full-length comic book, which gave almost a blow-by-blow history of his career as boxing champion: *Joe Louis, Champion of Champions: the heroic story of the fightingest champion of all time.*

28. That page listed ten "Advisory Editors," who included E. Simms Campbell ("Artist and Illustrator"), who had already become the first African American cartoonist to appear regularly in nationally-distributed slick magazines, and Oliver W. Harrington ("Artist and Former War Correspondent"), who was also a well-known cartoonist and is described further below.

29. Lohbeck, 1951: 6–8.

30. Lohbeck, 1951: 10.

31. "Election polls….," n.d.

32. Brands, 2016: 387–389.

33. Baker, 2013.

34. This list adds his credits from the Grand Comics Database to his war comic credit at marvel.wikia.com.

35. The information on Cal Massey comes from an interview published in *Alter Ego* (Massey, 2011) and from a telephone interview, November 27, 2015.

36. An October Gallery webpage advertising Cal Massey's art lists prints, postcard magnets, coffee

mugs, posters and a painting all featuring beautiful black women and refers to an official Olympic medallion which he was commissioned to create that depicts a young black woman athlete. It also describes his painting of a black Christ in his home studio. The page says: "For years, Massey's work has represented the black community in the art world" (http://octobergallery.com/83827-2/).

37. Gibson and Jung, 2002. That year, no question identified "Hispanics," and the total population of "Asian and Pacific islander" was 321,033 (one and a half percent of the estimated 21.4 million U.S. residents who were Asian or part-Asian in 2016) (U.S. Census Bureau Newsroom, 2018).

38. Hayton and Albright, 2012, paragraphs 8–9.

39. Christopher, 2002. In an obituary of Florence C. Evans, the widow of Orrin C. Evans, her husband was remembered, not for the *All-Negro Comics* comic book he had published, but as "a pioneering black journalist, [who traveled] around the South, writing about discrimination against black soldiers for the old *Philadelphia Record*. The articles prompted President Harry S. Truman to issue orders that integrated the armed forces."

Racists had responded to Evans' articles by telephoning his house late at night with frightening death threats against his family and leaving "ugly notes" on his family's door (Cipriano, 1990).

40. Friedman, 1948 (?): 4.

41. "Study of monopoly power...," 1950: 3.

42. Publisher Lindsay L. Baird, for example, was found guilty in June 1945 of having published the comic books *Blazing Comics* and *Blue Circle Comics* on paper that he had not been authorized to use. Baird was sentenced to 60 days in prison and fined $20,000. The prosecuting attorney explained to the jury that "Newsprint quotas are important because the same material used to make newsprint is also used to pack blood plasma, K rations, vaccines, shell cases and bomb bands." Will Murray, who tells this story in his article "Black Market Comic Books of the Golden Age," wrote in 2003: "You can only imagine Lindsay Baird's feelings on the matter: he was going to jail for having published what must be one of the worst superheroes of the Golden Age of Comics, *Blazing Comics*' the Green Turtle!"

In 2014, the superb cartoonists Gene Luen Yang and Sonny Liew rescued the Green Turtle from obscurity and created a new Green Turtle adventure. They had been intrigued by the rumor that Chu Hing, the Chinese cartoonist who originally created that character, had not been allowed to create a Chinese superhero because his publisher didn't think that a Chinese superhero would sell. Supposedly, Hing had rebelled against the order to make the Green Turtle white by composing the panels in ways that keep us from ever seeing the Green Turtle' face, and whatever clues it might hold about the Green Turtle's race (Murray, 2003; Yang and Liew, 2014). I thank Will Murray for a copy of his article.

43. Murray, 2003.

44. George Tichenor, formerly a member of the Executive Committee of the National Organization of Small Publishers, resented seeing the news-print he had needed to stay in business diverted to print expanded Sunday newspaper comic strip supplements for the large publishers. He complained that "the lifeblood of the press—newsprint" was being diverted to: "a few huge organs of the press by contacts, contracts, or controls not available to little papers. A labor, fraternal, or religious paper is briefly missed; a critical competitor is removed from the scene; the public yawns and buys a copy of the 'Metropolitan Monolith,' now speaking without fear of contradiction, and with 16 more pages of comics" (Study of Monopoly Power..., 1950:1002). Almost 62 percent of the world's newsprint supplies were used in the United States. One can imagine that journalists in England, Russia, Italy, France, Belgium and Greece, where the average postwar daily newspaper had page counts of four pages or less because of newsprint shortages, might have been predisposed to regard American comic books as a waste of valuable paper (Friedman, 1948 (?): 8–17, Table 7).

45. Goldstein, 2008: 45.

46. Goldstein, 2008: 28–31.

47. Goldstein, 2008: 121.

48. Goldstein, 2008: 31.

49. I thank Deborah E. Whaley for this information in an e-mail of September 15, 2015.

50. Dolinar, 2012: 184–9. (In 2007, new research clarified that the Tuskegee airmen's record, while excellent, was not perfect. Dolinar says whether Harrington had known about these losses is "uncertain.")

51. Nine strips from the Jive Gray sequence about the Tuskegee Airman are reproduced in Warren Bernard's *Cartoons for Victory* (Bernard, 2015: 202–203).

52. Morelli, 2016.

53. This story is also noteworthy because the fact that Russian fighter pilots were participating in the Korean War was being kept secret from the American people at that time, out of fear that this knowledge would increase popular demands for a larger war against the Soviet Union (Harden, 2017: 98–99; Herken, 2014: 136; Cleaver, 2013: 47).

54. Dolinar, 2012: 202. The rise of organized, armed self-defense in the Black freedom movement came later, in the 1950s and 1960s (Umoja, 2013).

55. Richard Gergel tells Woodard's story in *Unexampled Courage: The Blinding of Sgt. Isaac Woodard and the Awakening of President Harry S. Truman and Judge J. Waties Waring* (Gergel, 2019: 39).

56. Gergel, 2019: 72–3, 156–7, 170, 199, 251. James, 2013: 228–237. The quoted words are from Truman's letter to Attorney General Tom Clark the day after he heard the story.

57. Truman had not been raised as an anti-racist. When he was twenty-seven, in 1911, he expressed his belief in white supremacy as a digression in a love letter to the woman who later would become his wife. After admitting that he hates "Chinese and Japs," he continues: "It is race prejudice, I guess. But I am strongly of the opinion that negroes ought to be in Africa, yellow men in Asia and white people in Europe and America" (Truman, 1983: 39).

Truman became a champion of civil rights for several reasons, including the growing number of black voters and the Soviet Union's effective use of

American racism in their propaganda appeals to unaligned nations. More basically, the treatment of black veterans turned his stomach. He told Democratic leaders who had asked him to drop his strong support for civil rights: "My forebears were Confederates…. Every factor and influence in my background—and in my wife's for that matter—would foster the personal belief that you are right. But my very stomach turned over when I learned that Negro soldiers, just back from overseas, were being dumped out of Army trucks in Mississippi and beaten" (Leuchtenburg, 1991). Truman's firm support for civil rights measures split the Democratic Party, and in 1948, South Carolina Governor Strom Thurmond won four states of the Deep South for the States' Rights Democratic Party (or "Dixiecrats").

58. Harrington, 1993: 104. Harrington had been an "avowed Marxist" but not a communist ("Ollie Harrington," 1993). Harrington's FBI files have been web-posted at: http://omeka.wustl.edu/omeka/exhibits/show/fbeyes/harrington.

59. Makemson, 2009: 258–259. I first learned of Harrington's work in 1974, when I found an example in *Ya te vimos, Pinochet!*, a cartoon anthology edited by the Mexican cartoonist Rius (Eduardo del Río) to benefit Chilean refugees in Mexico. (This anthology also included a cartoon that I had drawn and submitted at Rius's invitation.) I stared at Harrington's work for a long time, thinking it must have been a mistake to identify him as a cartoonist from the United States, since I was pretty sure that no American cartoonist could be that good without my being aware of his work. I would have known Harrington's work if I had been reading the communist papers (Rius, 1974).

60. Early, 2003. "Almost" all African American soldiers being in service units would not have been enough to stop cartoonists, who will focus on the atypical, the exceptional and, the unusual, if it makes a more appealing story. Also, cartoonists, as seen below, can imagine that segregated units had been integrated, since the requirements of historical accuracy bind them very loosely.

61. According to his biographers Denis Kitchen and Paul Buhle, Kurtzman's most vivid memories of his army service during World War II (when he had been stationed in Louisiana, South Carolina, North Carolina and Texas) were of the racism he observed. This bigotry "disturbed him enormously, in no small part because others around him seemed to take it for granted" (Kitchen and Buhle, 2009: 14, 18). "Bunker" was the first of two stories that Cuban-born Ric Estrada drew for EC. Estrada later remembered that for this story ("featuring the first Black hero ever in comics"), Kurtzman had "provided me, with his fastidious insistence on authentic detail, with a real steel helmet and an Army ammo belt…" (Estrada, 1994–1995: 13).

62. Lt. Col. Charles M. Bussey has fought for a more accurate history of black soldiers in the Korean War. He writes: "Many blacks growing up today have no idea of what it was like to live in a racist society and be part of a racist Army. They need to understand how it was, if for no other reason than to understand

how much progress has been made. And it is unfair to deny those who fought their dignity. […] After over forty years, many other Korean War veterans—both black and white—and I are still filled with rage at the failure to paint a full and accurate picture of black men's failures *and successes* in the Korean War" (Bussey, 1991, 2002, vii–viii).

The United States Army Center of Military History re-examined the record of the 24th Infantry Regiment in Korea in great detail, and determined that much (but not all) of their trouble had been a consequence of segregation, endemic and virulent racial prejudice, bigotry, open and covert racial bias and discrimination, and "downright bad" white leaders who blamed their own failures on the "supposed racial characteristics of their African-American subordinates" (Bowers et al., 1996: iii, v–vi, xiv, 263, 265, 267–8). White Korean War veterans were *also* unfairly criticized as weak, inferior soldiers, compared to World War II veterans (Edwards, 2018: 5, 42, 54, 114).

63. Martin, 1951.

64. On the other hand, the integration of recently-drafted, poorly-trained, non-English-speaking South Koreans into U.S. units created resentment. One American colonel complained: "These men had no idea of sanitation, let alone the more complicated activities of military life. Yet high-level policy dictated that we treat them as out equals in every respect. They were to receive the same clothing and equipment, the same treatment, the same rations. Later they even had to have chocolate bars and 'comic' books…. Except for menial tasks, they were a performance cipher" (Skaggs, 1974: 53–54).

65. Starger, Spurlock and Max, 2006: 117–119. Orlando was the artist for the famous EC anti-racist science-fiction story "Judgment Day," whose attempted suppression by the Comics Code's Judge Charles Murphy led EC to abandon comic book publishing in 1956 (Hayton and Albright, 2012: paragraphs 13–16).

66. Starger, Spurlock and Max, 2006.

67. Stewart, 2017: 30.

68. "Judah hath dealt treacherously, and an abomination is committed in Israel and in Jerusalem; for Judah hath profaned the holiness of the LORD which he loved, and hath married the daughter of a strange god." Malachi: 11.

69. San Giacomo, 2009. McGee's complaint was made at a time when black soldiers were concerned that acts of black heroism in Korea were only honored in black papers (Pash, 2012: 169). American cartoonists and readers have long assumed, unless specified otherwise, that sympathetic characters are white. Some of the printings of Paul Revere's famous engraving of the 1770 Boston Massacre showed Crispus Attucks, recognized retrospectively as the first martyr of the American Revolution, as white (Boston Massacre Historical Society, n.d.). (As usual, when looked at more closely things look less black and white. Attucks was of African descent on his mother's side and descended from Native Americans on his father's side.)

Two soldiers of the all-black 24th infantry, resisting the North Korean invasion in the comic book *General Douglas MacArthur: the Great American* (published by Fox in 1951) were represented as white. Similarly, when Marvel introduced Sgt. Fury and his Howling Commandos in May, 1963, the colorist for the cover made the black trumpeter in this historically-inaccurate, racially-integrated World War II squad a white man.

70. Berman, 2008. The quoted words are from Charlton's niece, Zenobia Penn. A different version appears in the book *Black Soldier, White Army* (Bowers, et al., 1996: 256).

The anti-racist story "In Gratitude," written by Al Feldstein and drawn by Wally Wood, told of a wounded white soldier who returns from Korea to discover that his parents have refused his wishes to have the soldier who had died saving his life buried in their family cemetery plot, but had yielded to community pressure and buried him in a racially segregated cemetery instead. It was published in EC's *Shock SuspenStories #11* in 1953, and sparked a discussion in that comic's letters column which concluded in issue #16 (Wright, 2001: 137–139, 312).

A high school freshman in Florida, with his teacher's permission, read he EC story "In Gratitude" to his classmates, a majority of whom supported racial segregation. It reportedly upset them but did not lead to a discussion (Hill, 1955: 29–30).

71. "Soldiers of Salvation," *New Heroic Comics #75*.

72. "At the Risk of Death," *New Heroic Comics #78*.

73. "Stranded in a Mine Field," *New Heroic Comics #87*. (The art by Frank Frazetta was excellent.)

74. "World Tension…," 1954: 10.

75. Chinese cartoons about American racism helped to mobilize Chinese support for North Korea during the Korean War (Nash, 2017: 79).

76. Quoted in Dudziak, 2002: 77.

77. A graph of the skyrocketing black population of Harlem from 1910 to its peak in 1950 and beyond appears in Roberts, 2010.

78. Mendes, 2015: 151–152.

Wertham had testified in Delaware on October 22, 1951, and used as his example a panel from "Lost Legions of the Nile" drawn by Robert Webb for the November, 1951 issue, *Jumbo Comics #153*.

79. Wertham, 1953, 1954: 101.

Wertham's arguments about the effects of racist entertainment resembled his arguments about the brutalizing effects of violent entertainment and were based on the same kinds of evidence. Most scholars have dismissed the value of Wertham's criticism of violent entertainment, accepting the reasoning in Frederic Thrasher's 1949 paper "The Comics and Delinquency: Cause or Scapegoat?" There Thrasher had redefined the problem of comic book violence as whether comic books have a measurable effect on the rate at which their readers committed acts of juvenile delinquency (Thrasher, 1949).

The faulty nature of Thrasher's attack on Wertham's methodology becomes apparent if we imagine what if Thrasher had used the same approach to criticize Wertham's later claims about the effects of

comic book representations of "different peoples" (In *Seduction of the Innocent*, Wertham reported that his clinical observations demonstrate how comic book representations of human difference teach and support feelings of racial superiority and inferiority.) If Thrasher had done so, then his analogous counter-argument would have looked something like the following. First, if a person makes an argument that racist images spread racism, that means that they think racist images are the main cause of racism. Second, to claim that racist images in comic books harm children requires that we first measure a difference between a randomly selected group of children who see such images and a control group which does not. Third, in some communities, racism is so familiar to children that racist images in comic books seem "rather tame by comparison." Fourth, focusing on a few extreme and offensive examples of racist images is worthless without a systematic content analysis to determine which comic book images are typical. And finally, without such objective research, criticizing comic books for including racist images amounts to scapegoating comic books rather than accepting our responsibilities "as parents and as citizens for providing our children with more healthful family and community living" (Wertham, 1953, 1954: 100–105; Thrasher, 1949).

Unlike contemporary controversies over extreme examples of offensive racist imagery, Wertham had criticized "the *saturation* of children's minds with violent images" as an unhealthy factor in child development (Wertham, 1957: 251–252). I defended Wertham from Thrasher's criticisms in an article for the *International Journal of Comic Art*, web-posted at academia.edu (Rifas, 2013).

80. Wertham, 1954: 499.

81. A *Daily Worker* article quoted a variation on this comment from a talk that Wertham gave to the Urban League five days after testifying to the Senate Subcommittee: "'Through comic books more racial prejudice, especially against Negroes, has been taught to American children than at any time in the previous 100 years,' he said" ("Comic Books Feed Racism Says Wertham," 1954).

82. Wertham, 1953, 1954: 105.

83. In Wertham's opinion, the Supreme Court had made a "political decision," based in significant measure on "the foreign reaction to racial discrimination in the United States." He also thought that, among other factors, his own participation as an expert witness in the Delaware case ("the first time" that clinical psychiatric testimony had been admitted in such an issue) had contributed to the final decision (Wertham, 1954: 497; see also Mosse, 1958: 573–574).

84. Mendes, 2015: 146–147, 149–150.

85. Wertham, 1953: 334; Wertham, 1954: 498.

86. Mendes, 2015: 138.

87. Wright, 1946: 49.

88. Wright, 1946: 50; Doyle, 2009: 180–3.

89. In *Seduction of the Innocent*, Wertham says that the particular case he was thinking of when he began to study comic books more systematically was that of a young comic book fan who had been sentenced to a reformatory, over Wertham's objec-

tions, for threatening a teacher with a switchblade knife. Since advertisements for switchblade knives were published in comic books and their stories showed how to use them, Wertham concluded "that I ought to be some kind of defense counsel for the children who were condemned and punished by the very adults who permitted them to be tempted and seduced" (Wertham, 1953. 1954: 11–13; Wertham, 1964: 31).

In that book, Wertham also uses the example of a boy who was fascinated by comic books that glorified and advertised guns and was then sentenced to a reformatory after being brought to court for having negligently fired a bullet which accidentally killed a spectator at a nearby ball game. Unfortunately (and especially in the *Reader's Digest* condensed version), Wertham fails to state clearly that he had reason to know that the boy had not fired the fatal bullet, and so, in this case, while trying to act as "some kind of defense counsel" for scapegoated children, he falsely suggests that his supposed client was guilty as charged. I thank Christopher Pizzino for his research on this case.

90. *Martin Luther King and the Montgomery Story* was written through a collaboration between FOR's Director of Publication Alfred Hassler and Benton J. Resnik, the former general manager of Toby Press, one of the comic book publishers that had gone out of business when the comic book industry collapsed. The final script included small changes recommended by Martin Luther King, Jr. (Aydin, 2013). The art was drawn by Sy Barry.

91. Hayton and Albright, 2012: 38; Strömberg, 2003: 121.

Earlier examples of non-racist war comic book stories may remain to be discovered. The four-page comic story "Seagoing Haymaker" in *War Heroes #6* (October–December, 1943) by an uncredited writer and artist, includes in two panels a very respectfully drawn jet-black "colored man" who has a name; speech balloons without dialect; a positive, active role; and a central position in the composition of the panel that introduces him. This was an exception to the rules, both during World War II and for many years afterwards.

92. Strömberg 2003: 120–121. Out of this World, 2010 ("African American…").

93. "Out of This World," 2010 ("Interview…").

94. "Out of This World," 2010 ("African American…").

95. "The Beginnings…," n.d.; Green, 2010: 124.

According to Michael Cullen Green, "By the time an armistice was signed, more than 25,000 black soldiers were stationed in Korea, 15 percent of the army's strength there" (Green, 2010:110).

96. I have not yet found in Korean War comic books any reference to the Ethiopian soldiers who fought in that war. Ethiopia, because of its experience of having been invaded by Mussolini's Italy, was strongly committed to the principle of international collective action against aggression. When these African troops arrived in Korea, they were placed under the command of a white American general who expected them to serve as porters rather than as fighters. They refused (Adeto, 2018: 371). The Ethiopian *Kagnew* battalion went into combat over 200 times in Korea and reportedly "won every encounter" (Adeto, 2018: 372).

97. Feagin, 2000: 251.

Chapter 11

1. Biological warfare (BW) agents are living organisms, or infective material derived from them, which are intended to cause disease or death in humans, plants or animals, and which usually depend for their effects on their ability to multiply in the person, plant or animal attacked (Geissler, 1986: 4–5).

2. North Korean Foreign Minister Bak Hun Yung protested to the United Nations on February 22, 1952, that U.S. germ warfare against the North Koreans and Chinese was "the most serious criminal act in the history of mankind, viciously violating all international conventions relating to war" ("Crime Against Humanity," 1952: 227). Mainland China also protested to the United Nations against alleged germ warfare attacks on both North Korea and on Chinese territory.

3. Estonian August Yakobson wrote "The Jackals," an anti-American "satire" which was published in November, 1952, adapted for the stage, and made into the film *The Silvery Dust,* which was released in Moscow in 1953. French playwright Roger Gaillard's "Le Colonel Foster Plaidera Coupable" (Colonel Foster Will Plead Guilty), about the moral dilemmas of an American guilty of atrocities in Korea, was shut by the Paris police after the first night (Clews, 1964: 200).

An American film about a germ warfare plot to "destroy the United States," *The Whip Hand,* was released in 1951. It had originally been filmed as an anti-Nazi story, but the head of the RKO studios, Howard Hughes, demanded that it be brought up to date by becoming an anti-communist story. The villainous German scientist, now working for the communists, promises that sinking America to its knees will benefit mankind by removing "all those who stand in the way of communists…. Communists will rule the world!" (1:02:01; 1:15:43; 1:20:38; AFI Catalog of Feature Films, n.d.).

4. Wint, 1954: 83; Clews, 1964: 179.

5. Document #8, for example, had said:

The Soviet Government and the Central Committee of the CPSU were misled. The spread in the press of information about the use by the Americans of bacteriological weapons in Korea was based on false information. The accusations against the Americans were fictitious.

For the view that the documents, even if genuine, do not prove the germ warfare charges to have been false, see Endicott and Hagerman's "Twelve Newly Released Soviet-era 'Documents' and allegations of U.S. germ warfare during the Korean War" (Endicott and Hagerman, 1998), Dave Chaddock's book *This Must Be The Place: How the U.S. Waged Germ Warfare in the Korean War and Denied It Ever Since.*

(Chaddock, 2013: 342–353), and articles by Thomas Powell (Powell, 2017; Powell, 2018).

6. In January and February of 1951, Americans in North Korea captured many thousands of prisoners who were ill with typhus, smallpox and typhoid. Epidemics had struck both civilians and military forces in North Korea. Conventional war spreads diseases in several ways, including by mixing large numbers of unwashed, malnourished people from great distances, who expose each other to germs for which they may lack antibodies (Sams, 1998: 246).

7. "Atherton General Honored as Hero in War in Korea," *San Mateo Times*, 9 May, 1951, 1:1,2; "Plague is Believed Raging Among Foe," *New York Times*, June 19, 1951, 5:1; Peter Kalischer, "Doctor Commando," *Collier's*, September 22, 1951.

Also, M-G-M studios announced its plans for a film to be known as "The General Sams Story" which would be written and directed by Richard Brooks, after his completion of his current project, "a film about the mobile hospital units of the Medical Corps under the title 'M.A.S.H. 66.'" Brooks' "M.A.S.H." film would be released in 1953 under the title *Battle Circus* (Pryor, 1952).

8. *Monty Hall of the U.S. Marines #3*, December 1951, Toby Press. The art director of this issue, Mel Lazarus, went on to fame with his syndicated newspaper strips "Miss Peach" and "Momma."

9. The one mission during the Korean War in which troops arrived and left by submarine was dramatized with unusual fidelity to fact in the comic book story "The Mission of the Pregnant Perch," published in *Attack! #3* in September 1952. The story's source could have been the November, 1951 *Life* magazine article by the same title, which had described "a new concept in submarine warfare: transporting specially trained troops under the sea, putting them ashore for a specific operation and bringing them back."

10. According to General Sams' report, "... following our 'medical raid,' the Communists ... charged us with introducing biological warfare. ... In their effort to alibi to their own people for their non-effectiveness, they of course accused us of having started the epidemics" (Willoughby & Chamberlain, 1954: 415).

11. "Crime Against Humanity," 1952: 226.

In contrast to this picture of Sams as an evil scientist, consider this description of General Sams' work for the U.S. occupation Government in postwar Japan, as presented by William Manchester: "Sams conducted a national sanitation campaign, followed by a massive immunization and vaccination program. ... In the first two years of the occupation, Sams estimated, the control of communicable diseases alone had saved 2.1 million Japanese lives—more than the country's battle deaths during the war, over three times the number of Nipponese civilians killed in the wartime bombings, including Hiroshima and Nagasaki (Manchester, 1978: 509). With equal extravagance, Sams estimated the number of lives lost to epidemics in North Korea during the Korean War because of communist incompetence as eight

million deaths out of an initial population of eleven million (Sams, 1998: 254).

12. Endicott and Hagerman, 1998: 39.

13. "Plague Patrol!," *Battle Report #1*, August 1952; "Get That Man!," *War Report #5*, May 1953.

14. Stanley I. Kutler tells that General Sams had written a document which revealed "that Sams had planned forcibly to enter a North Korean hospital, inject morphine in an unwilling patient who allegedly suffered from bubonic plague, and kidnap him for a physical examination. No provisions were made for returning the patient or for his subsequent welfare. Although Sams apparently did not carry out his plan, the Army preferred not to disclose that he conspired to do so, for it constituted a violation of the Geneva Rules of Land Warfare" (Kutler, 1982: 235).

Without using the words "forcibly," "unwilling," "kidnap," "no provisions...for his subsequent welfare," "conspired" and "Geneva Rules of Land Warfare," Sams confirms the basics of this account in his book *"Medic"* (Sams, 1998: 246–254).

15. "Plague Patrol!" explains that "The Reds are claiming we're waging Germ Warfare! We think it's to cover up bubonic plague. If we can get a prisoner with plague, we can prove it." By contrast, the mission in "Danger Below!" was primarily to gather information rather than to support propaganda efforts: "The Reds are saying we're using Germ Warfare. That's not true, of course, but something is very wrong there and we want to find out what it is. If it's bubonic plague, we want to know before it can spread to our forces."

An earlier comic book story about a mission to investigate health conditions in North Korea had appeared in *Warfront #5* in April, 1952. The story "Secret Mission" shows an old American doctor accepting an assignment to parachute into the Korean village where he had worked before the war to investigate "rumors of a big epidemic among enemy troops!" He returns with the militarily valuable information that "their crack Tiger Corps is below strength and shot with illness! And the Natives are friendly to us!"

16. "Plague is Believed...," 1951: 5.

17. According to a 1952 Chinese newspaper report, Han Chong-Ak entered North Korea with instructions to find out what epidemics had broken out, how many had died, and what health measures were being used to combat the epidemics. His sister persuaded him to surrender to the police and confess. Two and a half months after that, North Korean police arrested a man who soon admitted that he had been assigned to check on the occurrence of infectious diseases (Chaddock, 2013: 296–297).

These may have been the South Korean infiltrators that journalist Wilfred Burchett interviewed who had been "given the specific task of checking the counter-measures which were being taken and the effectiveness of the germ warfare campaigns" (Burchett, 1969: 216).

Yi Chang-gon's history of the Korean Liaison Office (*KLO ui Hangukchon Pisa*) describes an incident in which Koreans disguised in North Korean army uniforms went ashore in Wonsan to check on the accuracy of rumors of bubonic plague and suc-ceeded in taking away with them two patients from a hospital for examination by medical experts. A book review by Stephen C. Mercado has additional details, but does not mention the date of this operation (Mercado, 2012).

18. "Germ Warfare In Korea?," 1950: 22.

19. Lockwood, 2009: 139.

20. "Germ Carrying Rats Bred in North Korea," 1950. The "expensively equipped laboratory" held "more than 5,000 rats and mice [...] inoculated with such diseases as bubonic plague and encephalitis."

21. Hersh, 1969: 248–249. Seymour Hersh wrote in 1969 that Zacharias's series of articles for the Hearst newspapers "still signifies the only time any Pentagon official, past or present, has publicly written about Russian BW bases and development..." (Hersh, 1969: 249).

22. "The Fight Against Germ Warfare!," *Plastic Man #38* (November 1952).

23. Thomas, 2005: 70, 84, 91; Savage, 1990, 1998: 71. These stories were "Poisoned Water," *Roy Rogers Comics #57*, September 1952, and "Medicine Smoke," *Roy Rogers Comics #64*, April 1953.

24. See the statements of the Polish delegate to the UN on October 17, 1952; The Soviet delegate to the UN on October 18, 1952; the Czechoslovakian delegate to the UN on October 20, 1952; and the Byelo-russian delegate to the UN on November 12, 1952.

25. Wu, 1982.

The single most powerful pop-fiction influence on the American conception of the Chinese was British author Sax Rohmer's "Fu Manchu," described by Rohmer as "the yellow peril incarnate." The racism of Jack London and other well-known American writers is examined in Thomas F. Gossett's *Race: The History of an Idea in America* (Gossett, 1963: 198–227).

26. Shiel, 1899.

27. The novel mentions Korea as a minor participant in these plans (Shiel, 1899: 129).

At the time of Shiel's writing, in the wake of China's defeat in the Sino-Japanese war of 1894, Chinese intellectual reformers began to think of China as faced with aggressive aliens in a merciless international struggle for racial survival and supremacy. According to Frank Dikötter: "Kang Youwei (1858–1927), perhaps the most acclaimed Chinese philosopher of the last hundred years, expounded a utopian vision of the world in a work called *Datongshu*, or 'One World.' Kang wanted to eliminate the darker races in order to achieve universal harmony. Darker races were inferior and should be eradicated. He proposed to whiten the darker races by dietary change, intermarriage, and migration; those who resisted should be eliminated by sterilization" (Dikötter, 1999:153–155).

28. Shiel, 1899: 369, 375, 380–381, 387–388.

29. James Michener's novel *The Bridges at Toko-Ri* suggests they might swarm into Colorado (Michener, 1953: 25).

30. According to Alexander Bevin: "Although there were many stories about the Chinese using 'hordes of troops' in 'human wave tactics' to storm UN positions, it was not mass attack but deception, surprise and stealthy infiltration at night which made the Chinese formidable. The Chinese did use 'human waves' with platoons and companies to overrun well-chosen tactical positions in order to make critical penetrations, but these were usually to hold defending troops in place while other Chinese units flanked the enemy positions and set up roadblocks in the rear" (Bevin, 1986: 311, 302–303, 343–344).

31. London's fantasy is set in the bicentennial year, 1976 (London, 1910: 308–315).

Gorman Beauchamp judges this story as "among London's most artistically unified and effective, but also the one in which his apocalyptic imagination approaches almost psychopathic proportions. London's covering of the Russo-Japanese War for the Hearst newspapers in 1904 had fueled his already pronounced phobia of dark-skinned races, a phobia which his political [socialist] convictions did little to soften..." (Beauchamp, 1984: 28).

32. London specifically included Koreans as part of the Chinese empire. Two years before he wrote this story, Jack London had been in Korea as a war correspondent (Mancini, n.d.).

33. Franklin, 1988: 126; Truman, 1983: 126.

34. Rogaski, 2002: 381–415; Chaddock, 2013: 296–306.

35. Yang, 2008: 120.

Chapter 12

1. On October 1, 1952, the Soviet delegate to the United Nations circulated statements by four American Air Force Lieutenants, confessing that they had waged germ warfare in Korea. These were followed in March, 1953, with confessions by two Marine officers. At the end of the war, these six men were released, whereupon they all stated categorically that their "confessions" had been false and extracted by coercion. (Mayo, 1953: 643). In all, 38 American POWs confessed to germ warfare charges during the last year of the war, of whom ten signed recantations after being repatriated (Halliday and Cumings, 1988:183, 206). In addition, by 1953, almost two thirds of the seventy-two hundred American POWs had signed other confessions or petitions calling for an end to the war. (Melley, 2008: 146–147). The returned POWs explained that they had made their germ warfare confessions after the Chinese Communists had threatened to execute them as war criminals. Their recantations, however, were also made under pressure. The U.S. Attorney General had threatened to charge those prisoners who had collaborated with their communist captors in Korea with the capital crime of treason (Endicott and Hagerman, 1998: 166–167).

2. As an example of a germ warfare confession, POW Colonel Frank H. Schwable of the U.S. Marine Corps. made a detailed statement claiming that the purpose of the germ warfare attacks had been experimental:

The basic objective was at that time to test, under field conditions, the various elements of bacteriological warfare, and to possibly expand the field tests, at a later date, into an element of the regular combat operations, depending on the results obtained, and the situation in Korea.

The effectiveness of the different diseases available was to be tested, especially for their spreading or epidemic qualities under various circumstances, and to test whether each disease caused a serious disruption to enemy operations and civilian routine or just minor inconveniences, or was contained completely, causing no difficulties (Schwable and Bley, 1953: 4).

Secretary of State Acheson had charged that in earlier confessions, U.S. Air Force Lieutenants Kenneth Enoch and John Quinn had repeated what they were told to say, pointing as evidence to clichés "alien to American youths" (Waggoner, 1952). Photolithographic copies of Enoch's and Quinn's handwritten confessions appear as appendices of the *Report of the Scientific Commission* (*Report...*, 1952: 492–540). Beginning on page 536, Quinn went into a long diatribe against the greedy Wall Street imperialists. Other than Quinn's four pages of concentrated, anti–imperialist venting and the titles of their confessions, Enoch and Quinn's testimonies raise suspicion mainly for the great amount of detail that they claim to remember from the secret lectures they received about bacteriological warfare (and, in Quinn's case, atomic warfare).

3. Since the graphic accompanying the message "This is your enemy" is a close-up of the collaborator Jim Nelson, the conclusion seems to simultaneously build sympathy for and suspicion of the returned POWs.

4. The International Scientific Commission concluded that a coherent pattern of circumstantial evidence indicated that "The peoples of Korea and China have indeed been the objective of bacteriological weapons. They have been employed by units of the U.S.A. armed forces, using a great variety of different methods for the purpose, some of which seem to be developments of those applied by the Japanese army during the second world war" (*Report...*, 1952: 60). Commission member Joseph Needham said that he was 97 percent sure that the charges were true. In 1987, he said that "everything that has been published in the past few years has shaken the very 3 percent of doubt which I had before and has instead abolished it. So I am now 100 percent sure" (McDermott, 1987: 168–169).

Needham had given a detailed report to the British government in 1944 about the alleged use of bacterial warfare by Japan in China, having been convinced by reports from the Chinese Surgeon-General that Japan had dropped plague-infected fleas from the air which spread bubonic plague in districts where it had not been known (Chen, 2009: 227–228). The 1949 Khabarovsk trial of a dozen Japanese participants in that germ warfare program, found them guilty of human experimentation for which they received light sentences, presumably in exchange for their providing information about bacteriological weapons valuable to the Soviet Union's biological warfare researchers (Yudin, 2010: 69).

Needham supported the germ warfare charges against the Americans based largely on his trust in what Chinese scientists (men who had been trained at Oxford, Harvard, Yale, and Cambridge) told him. The Chinese scientists and physicians who participated in the germ warfare investigations were leading experts in their research fields of entomology, epidemiology, botany and bacteriology (Chen, 2009: 235, 238–239, 245).

5. Wint, 1954: 98; White, 1957: 170, 177. The Red interrogators in the story "Red Trap" (*G-I in Battle, #8*, May 1953" are depicted very differently. In that story, an American is captured while trying to deliver typhus vaccine to a group of sick, anti-communist guerillas in the North. His captor threatens to blind him by burning his eyes with a red-hot saber if he does not sign a false confession that he has brought "dangerous germs to be used against our people." He is told: "[We] both know, naturally, that it is vaccine! But world does not know! Your confession will be most useful at the United Nations! We will prove Americans are beasts!" Then the story takes an unusual turn. A seductive Colonel Yoo tries to drug and charm the pilot into signing the confession, but he lunges at her, accidentally knocking her wig off, after which he recognizes Colonel Yoo as "A man! A female impersonator! Clever, those gooks! Figured that if they plied with me [*sic*] with wine and women and a few drinks, I'd sign that confession!"

6. Lockwood, 2006: 166–7; Burchett, 1969: 214–216.

7. In "The Confession," the Communist interrogator single-mindedly focuses from the beginning on forcing the prisoner to confess to germ warfare. Because of the massively destructive bombing of North Korea, captured U.S. Air Force prisoners received the harshest treatment, and their captors especially prized germ warfare confessions (Carlson, 2002: 182).

This story includes no hint of either of the main two, endlessly-repeated themes of the Communist "brainwashing" (indoctrination program) that most of the prisoners of war were subjected to: (1) that the United States government is run by and for a wealthy few, and (2) that Communism is the one true form of democracy (Carlson, 2002: 179).

8. In the comic book, Cardinal Mindszenty prepares for being arrested by the communists by writing a letter to the bishops to warn them not to believe anything he confesses after he has spent time in their torture chambers and been drugged with "Actedron." The comic accurately reproduced Mindszenty's warning about Actedron as it had appeared in the international Catholic news-weekly *The Tablet* ("Trial by Actedron," 1949: 4). Wilfred Burchett reported that the allegedly "new sinister drug" Actedron, "can be bought at all chemist shops in Budapest without prescription. It is the Hungarian version of Benzedrine. Three tablets helped me sit out the first long day in court,

after having travelled for three days to reach Budapest from Berlin"(Burchett, 1951: 129). By coincidence, a related amphetamine, Dexedrine, was the drug blamed for William Gaines' disastrous testimony at the 1954 Senate Subcommittee Hearings investigating comic books. Gaines had been taking diet pills and they were wearing off during his testimony (Jacobs, 1973: 107). After World War II and during the early Cold War, the CIA and Army Counter-Intelligence Corps used electroshock, Metrazol (pentylenetetrazol), LSD, mescaline, amphetamines and other drugs in their interrogations (Kaye and Albarelli, Jr., 2010; Kinzer, 2019: 41).

9. The *Joe Palooka* comic book included a multi-issue story, reprinted from the newspaper comic strip, in which the communist falsely accuse the character Humphrey Pennyworth of spying against Russia, inject him with drugs and put on a show trial, with backfiring results (*Joe Palooka* #66, March 1952 and #67, April 1952).

10. Marks, 1980: 125.

11. Hunter, 1951.

12. Hunter, 1951. For a more sympathetic view of Chinese cartooning of that period see "Lien huan hua: Revolutionary Serial Pictures" by John C. Hwang (Hwang, 1978) and an anthology of Communist Chinese comics republished in English in 1973 (Wilkinson, 1973). For an extraordinarily well-informed and sympathetic view of Chinese cartooning of that period, see John A. Lent and Xu Ying's *Comics Art in China* (2017). One of Hunter's examples can be identified as Zhang Leping's "Sanmao the Orphan" comic strip.

13. Hunter, 1956.

14. Hunter, 1956: 223–4.

15. Condon, 1959, 2005: 82, 86.

16. The myth of North Korean and Chinese brainwashing had a factual basis in totalitarian educational practices. As Robert Jay Lifton explained in 1961: "…despite the vicissitudes of brainwashing, the process which gave rise to the name is very much a reality: the official Chinese Communist program of *szuhsianq kai-tsao* (variously translated as 'ideological remolding,' 'ideological reform,' or as we shall refer to it here, 'thought reform') has in fact emerged as one of the most powerful efforts at human manipulation ever undertaken" (Lifton, 1961: 4–5). Lifton uses italics sparingly, but he does employ them to emphasize two points. First, that "it was the combination of *external force or coercion* with an appeal to *inner enthusiasm through evangelistic exhortation* which gave thought reform its emotional scope and power" (Lifton, 1961:13). Second, that *"what we see as a set of coercive maneuvers, the Chinese Communists view as a morally uplifting, harmonizing, and scientifically therapeautic experience."*

Another precedent for such mental abuse of prisoners in Korea was the pressures that the Japanese used against the communists during their rule over Korea. As Bruce Cumings tells it: "…recalcitrant Koreans, whether leftist workers or intellectuals, had improper ideas winnowed out of their heads through totalitarian methods of interrogation until

they were ready to confess their sins in writing and join associations for those who had "reformed their thoughts" (branches in every province)" (Cumings, 1981: 28, 36).

17. Hinkle and Wolff, 1957. According to Robert McLean, who had been a Prisoner of War in Korea, one drug, cannabis (which the prisoners found growing wild around the POW camp, secretly gathered and smoked), helped the POWs to *resist* brainwashing. McLean also credited cannabis for saving many lives, since it served as an appetite stimulant for prisoners who had been unable to eat because they were too depressed or too repulsed by the awful food (Hopper, 2019).

18. McCoy, 2006: 26–29. Through its front group the Society for the Investigation of Human Ecology, in 1960 the CIA partially and secretly funded Dr. Lauretta Bender's experiments with injecting young "schizophrenic" children with LSD (which she did twice a day continuously for 5½ to 35 months.) Bender had been a leading defender of Superman comic books (Kaye and Albarelli, Jr., 2010; Rifas, 2013).

19. McCoy, 2006: 29.

20. McCoy, 2006: 5–6.

21. An unusual story in *Fight Comics #75* (July 1951) included an imaginary scene of scientifically-based mental destruction (but without using the words "brainwash" or "brain change"). The evil Ho-Tung (who has a red star marked with a hammer and sickle on his cap and a Fu Manchu moustache) brings prisoners to his "special laboratory." There they are strapped to tables and have metal hemispheres with multiple wires coming out of them attached to their heads. His batches of prisoners undergo "the trans-cranial-electra process" and "lose control of their minds!" Ho-Tung uses these "zombies" as "human bombs," hiding explosives under their clothes and then sending them to "mix with the real refugees" on roads that lead directly to the enemy lines.

22. Biderman, 1957: 618–620.

23. McCoy, 2012: 154–155. McCoy argues that thanks to these fictionalized portrayals, "torture was, for many Americans, transformed from an unthinkable barbarism synonymous with fascist or communist regimes into a weapon necessary for U.S. national security" (McCoy, 2012: 167). American torturers in Guantanamo were directly inspired by such misleading television shows.(O'Mara, 2015: 35–37), while in real life, successful interrogations rely on building rapport and *avoiding* conflict, entertainment, by contrast, relies on dramatic scenes in which the good character achieves domination over the villain (Leslie, 2017).

24. A 1948 Associated Press article on how supposed military secrets have been published in the Congressional Record (a public document) gave as an example funding for germ warfare research at Camp Detrick, Maryland ("Discussions in Congress Bare 'Secrets,'" 1948).

Circumstantial evidence suggests that five days after attempting to resign because of "ethical concerns," American Frank Olson (one of the first scientists assigned to Camp Detrick) was murdered on November 28, 1953 by his own government because they no longer trusted him to keep their secrets about the MK-ULTRA mind-control research program and about germ warfare (Shane, 2004; Shaw, 2018, Kinzer, 2019. Information about Frank Olson is collected at https://frankolsonproject.org).

25. Endicott and Hagerman, 2002.

26. Lockwood, 2009: 142–3; Hess, 2014: 24. A year before the first reports of Japanese germ warfare against China, an America comic book had published a germ warfare story with a *Chinese* villain: "Dr. Wang—master criminal, master spy… an Oriental fiend whose twisted giant intellect would have spread ruin and destruction in America's vital defense industries" ("The Shield," *Shield-Wizard Comics #2*, Winter, 1940).

27. In 1950, the United States refused Soviet requests to try Ishii as a war criminal and instead made a secret deal with him. In exchange for immunity from prosecution, Ishii delivered to the Americans a manuscript detailing 15 years of biological warfare research, 8,000 slides of human tissues (representing more than 200 prisoner autopsies), and more than 600 pages of reports on artificially disseminating disease (McDermott, 1987:122, 124, 127–138; Harris and Paxman, 1982:75–80; Van Ginnekin, 1977: 130, 135).

28. Harris: 1991. Boris G. Yudin cites information suggesting that these casualty figures were greatly exaggerated. (Yudin, 2010: 72–74). Jeffrey A. Lockwood's detailed chapters about the failures and successes of Japan's bacterial warfare program says that "As a result of experiments, field tests, and attacks with biological weapons during World War II, the Japanese killed a total of 580,000 Chinese—slightly more than three-fourths by entomological weapons" (Lockwood, 2009: 104).

29. Barenblatt, 2004: 4–5; Lockwood, 2009: 90–91.

Although "Bacteriological Methods of Warfare" had been outlawed by the Geneva Protocol of 1925, several nations began developing biological weapons soon after they had signed that agreement, including Belgium, Canada, France, Great Britain, Italy, the Netherlands, Poland, the Soviet Union and Japan (Riedel, 2004:401).

30. Lockwood, 2009: 97; Wu, n.d.

31. "Captain Yank," *Big Shot* Vol. 4, No. 44, March, 1944. In 1941, a comic book story about germ warfare was set in the Atlantic Ocean and the villains were vaguely German. "Dr. Grubles" anticipates that "the people will die like flies" when the germs he has been cultivating are released, but the hero, who has been secretly listening to his conversation, interrupts with a warning that "Chemical warfare is a violation of international law, gentlemen!" (*Smash Comics #27*, 1941).

32. The Soviet Union's Ilya Ehrenberg informed his readers that "The Associated Press reports the preparation of bacteria and toxic agents, including diseases capable of being spread by airplane or guided missiles, like anthrax, psittacosis, undulant fever, yellow fever and plague. Army spokesmen talk

of experiments on lethal ultrasound waves…. But in their desire to scare the world, they have infected their own countrymen with the bacillus of panic" (Roberts, 1948: 86–87).

33. Rosebury, 1949: 44.

34. "Silent Death" appeared in *Rulah #21*, Fox Features Syndicate, Inc., December 1948, and then was reprinted in *Terrors of the Jungle #17*, Star Publications, Inc., May 1952. I'm indebted to Stephen O'Day in an e-mail of May 22, 2010, for identifying this story.

According to the Grand Comics Database, "Alec Hope," the signature on this story, was a pseudonym sometimes used by A.C. Hollingsworth (one of the first African American comic book artists).

35. Wertham's description of the story begins "At a time when accusations of bacterial warfare cloud the international scene, children here in the United States and, through export, in many other countries, are instructed that the United States Government is carrying out secret researches on bacteriological warfare and that it is practiced on colored natives […]" (Wertham, 1953, 1954: 388–389). That comic book story ended with Rulah concluding "Perhaps the world can take warning from this. […] Such things should never be invented in the first place!"

36. "Crime Against Humanity," 1952: 229. In February, 1950, Shiro Ishii's name appeared in the *New York Times* in an article which reported that "The Allied command in more than four years of occupation has been unable to find any evidence that the Japanese plotted germ warfare […]" (Waggoner, 1950). Ishii's name did not appear in that paper again until 1980, when Japan admitted having used germ warfare during World War II.

37. "Crimes Against Humanity," 1952: 225.

38. Gartner and Myers, 1995: 377–395, 383.

39. Crane, 2002: 245.

40. North Korea's use of a VX nerve agent to assassinate Kim Jong-un's half-brother Kim Jong-nam at the Kuala Lumpur international airport in Malaysia in February, 2017, renewed interest in whether North Korea had developed chemical and biological weapons of mass destruction. Unlike its nuclear weapons program, which North Korea has acknowledged many times, North Korea has strongly denied that it has a program to develop biological weapons (Kim, Philipp and Chung, 2017: 1, 3–4). According to second-hand, unverified reports by defectors, North Korea has tested biological and chemical weapons on its political prisoners (Cooper, 2007; Kim, Philipp and Chung, 2017: 8; Chang, 2010: 77). Others have concluded that unclassified information supports no stronger conclusion than that North Korea has the capability to produce biological weapons if it chooses to do so (Choi, 2015: Kim, Philipp and Chung, 2017).

Chapter 13

1. According to an American law journal article that appeared while the negotiations were still going on, the problem was that the communists

were interpreting the Geneva Convention of 1949 literally rather than correctly. That 1949 agreement had specified that all prisoners were to be returned "without delay after the cessation of active hostilities." At the time of this agreement, the Soviet Union still retained an estimated hundreds of thousands of POWs (mostly German and Japanese) from World War II (Charmatz and Wit, 1953: 391, 393–396, 400–404).

2. Bevin, 1986: 452–3.

3. The prisoners issued a list of four demands, the first of which was the "Immediate ceasing the barbarous behavior, insults, torture, forcible protest with blood writing, threatening, confinement, mass murdering, gun and machine gun shooting, using poison gas, germ weapons, experiment object of A-Bomb by your command. You should guarantee POW human rights and individual life with the base on the International Law" (Song, 1980: 75). "Blood writing" referred to the practice of anti-communists forcing prisoners to sign petitions swearing that they would rather die than accept repatriation, which were sealed with a drop of the prisoner's own blood next to his name (Song, 1980: 75). The references to "germ weapons" and the "A-Bomb" accorded with communist propaganda accusing the United States of using prisoners for germ warfare and atomic bomb experiments (Song, 1980: 131).

4. The response to their first demand was: "With reference to your item 1 of that message, I do admit that there has [*sic*] been instances of bloodshed where many PW have been killed and wounded by UN Forces. I can assure in the future that PW can expect humane treatment in this camp according to the principles of International Law. I will do all within my power to eliminate further violence and bloodshed. If such incidents happen in the future, I will be responsible" (Biderman, 1963: 77).

5. Text pieces, one- or two-page stories laid out as simple columns of text, were included in comic books for many years to qualify for cheaper postal rates. They were generally the least attractive and least read part of the comic. (Eventually, they were replaced by letters to the editor columns.)

6. Burchett and Winnington, 1952.

7. I discuss self-defense ads in my article "Korean War Comic Books and the Militarization of U.S. Masculinity" (Rifas, 2015).

8. White, 1957:196. William Lindsay White wrote: "If this seems high, compare it with the 115 prisoner-lives which the Communist leaders had taken since September of '51 in order to win control of Koje."

9. Meyers and Bradbury, 1968.

10. Meyers and Bradbury, 1968: 246.

11. Meyers and Bradbury, 1968: 278, 287, 301, 337.

12. The "Chinese Ransom Racket" had been well-publicized, beginning with articles in Chinese newspapers published in the United States (Cheng, 2013: 160–172).

13. Thomas, 2005: 68, 109.

14. Kaufman, 1986: 238–240.

15. According to President Eisenhower: "To force

those people to go back to a life of terror and persecution is something that would violate every moral standard by which America lives. Therefore it would be unacceptable to the American code, and it cannot be done" (Song, 1980: 35).

16. Malia, 1994: 283–284.

17. Petrovich, 1982: 48.

18. As William L. White described it:

In this struggle between ways of life, let us look at the result. Of the 75,000 UN and South Korean soldiers captured by their Communist armies more than 60,000 were unaccounted for, but 12,700 were allowed to go home and, according to Communist tabulation, only 327 Koreans, 21 Americans, and one Briton were converted to Communism.

Now for our side: of the more than 171,000 prisoners we took, only 83,000 chose to go home. Of these, probably not half were really pro-Communist. But an astounding total of 88,000 men who had worn Communist uniforms, with no coaxing from us, refused to go back. It was a situation without parallel in human history [White, 1957: 231].

North Korea claimed in 1953 that about 70,000 of the prisoners that they held had voluntarily "elected to stay in the North." In the 1990s, evidence emerged that many of these prisoners had been held against their will and assigned to dangerous jobs, such as coal mining (Cha, 2016).

19. Meyers and Bradbury, 1968: 334; Thimayya, 1981: 90, 123.

20. Matray, 2011: 116.

21. Thimayya, 1981:91.

22. Bradbury and Kirkpatrick, 1968: 28.

Chapter 14

1. Scott, 2014: 137.

2. Rifas, 1983 ("War Makes Men"). For example, *Exciting War #6* (November 1952), began a Korean War story by asserting that: "Fear is an emotion, not a weakness. A man stands his ground and fights his fear—a coward runs away from it."

3. Gerzon, 1982: 30–31.

4. This message stands out in the titles of Parents' Magazine *Real Heroes* (1941–1946) and *Outstanding American War Heroes* (1944); in Dell's *War Heroes* (1942–1945); in *Jewish War Heroes* (published by the Canadian Jewish Congress in 1944); and *Navy War Heroes* (published by Almanac Publishing Company in 1945). Of the many Korean War comic books, the only one with "hero" in the title was Ace Magazine's *War Heroes* (1952–1953). In the 1960s, Charlton published the series *Army War Heroes, War Heroes, Marine War Heroes,* and *Navy War Heroes,* and Stanley Morse published *Battle Heroes.*

5. Astore, 2010.

6. Barker, 1984: 200–201, 204.

7. Wertham, 1966: 209. (Wertham refers here to violence in "mass media" in general, but clearly indicates that he includes comic books.)

8. Wertham, 1966 ("Is TV…").

9. According to Robert M. Neer, "Not only did the allies drop more bombs on Korea than in the Pacific theater during World War II—635,000 tons, versus 503,000 tons—more of what fell was napalm, in both absolute and relative terms"(Neer, 2013: 99–100).

10. Robert M. Neer mentions the use of napalm in Korea in portable flamethrowers (Neer, 2013: 95–96). An *unusually* graphic verbal description of the consequences of napalm appeared in "They've got to KILL me!," in *Battles Stories #5* (September, 1952). An American soldier with a flamethrower, creeping toward a red bunker, anticipates that "the Reds within will smell their hair burning as they die, and they'll feel and hear their skin crackle for a brief second before it turns to ash … and those of them that aren't barbecued like a side of beef will feel their lungs burst like balloons as the fire eats up the air and their dream of conquest blows apart in the searing blast!"

The artist who illustrated this script made no big effort to communicate this horror, but simply pictured enemy soldiers grimacing and flailing as the flames engulf them. The story rationalizes the use of napalm as something that the American soldier must do: "not only for myself, my buddies, my platoon and my company, but for … my girl, my folks, my home, my neighbors, my country! I've got to do this job right for my way of life!"

The soldier concludes the story by describing himself as "just a guy who'll keep trying to make the reds pay for the evil they have visited upon mankind!" (I thank Kevin Patrick for helping me identify this comic, which an anti-comic book article in Australia had quoted from during the Korean War.)

11. *Uncle Scrooge One Shot 386* "Only a Poor Old Man," March 1952 (COA I.N.D.U.C.K.S.—Worldwide database about Disney comics, http://coa.inducks.org/story.php?c=W+OS++386-02).

12. Reister, 1973: 43.

13. Roeder, 1995: 147.

14. Nakazawa wrote: "With each episode, as I drew pictures of maggots wriggling in burns or the putrefaction of corpses, readers grew increasingly uncomfortable. I became dejected and decided to change my drawing, even though the result wasn't realistic. If, merely because they get uneasy, people won't follow the story, why draw it? So I drew it in much softer fashion" (Nakazawa, 2010: 164–165).

15. In 1966, Wertham summarized the "racist indoctrination of children" in comic books. He listed the stereotypes for various groups, including "Oriental people" who are "shown as ugly, brutal, and threatening, even as subhuman" (Wertham, 1966: 197).

16. Reidelbach, 2003: 1.

17. Zimmerman, 1986: 39.

18. For example, in "Desperate Destination," a stock initiation-by-combat story in *The Fighting Man* #5 (March 1953), the protagonist decides: "Nothing so hard about this! Just like killing vermin!" The relatively crude art for this story does not use anti-Asian visual stereotypes, or even make the "gooks" look recognizably Asian.

19. For background of the ethnic slur "gook," see Roediger, 1992.

20. Dean, 1954: 163–164.

21. Green, 2010: 113–115, 119, 124–125, 128–129, 133.

22. General Dean's words about changes he had noticed in American mass media were quoted in Federal Subcommittee Hearings investigating Juvenile Delinquency, meeting in Washington, D.C., and by the New York State committee's report on comic books, which introduced them like this: "It is the belief of this Committee that Russia will not have to conquer us by arms if moral decay becomes the order of the day in America. With this in mind, the words of Major General William F. Dean, recently appearing on "Meet the Press," should serve as a warning and as a fitting conclusion to this report" (*Report of the New York State …* 1954: 33). Presumably, General Dean had been shown the first issue of *G.I. Joe Comics*, which included an unsigned, nonfiction text piece "The Fighting General" describing the circumstances under which he had become missing in action. That issue included a large number of sexually suggestive drawings of women displaying their cleavage or thighs.

23. Remarque, 1928. An exclusive revival of the 1938 film *All Quiet on the Western Front* at New York City's Park Avenue Theater began a month after the Korean War started (Crowther, 1950: 36). Bill Schelly confirms that Kurtzman's story had been directly inspired by this rereleased film of Remarque's novel (Schelly, 2015: 186–187). At these film showings, standing room audiences loudly applauded *All Quiet on the Western Front*'s anti-war message, presumably to express their opposition to the Korean War (May, 2000: 224, 333 n. 20).

24. Remarque, 1928: chapter 9.

25. Actually, experiencing such a revelation does change a person. David Grossman retells stories by one World War II veteran and by one Vietnam veteran who found photographs of a wife and children on the soldiers that they had just killed and had felt haunted ever afterwards. As Grossman explains, such images break down the emotional distance that permits "the killer to deny that he is killing a human being" (Grossman, 2009, Chapter 3: "Emotional Distance…").

26. Dan Malan, August 19, 1990, e-mail message to author. Malan formerly edited and published *The Classics Collector*, a quarterly publication promoting the hobby of collecting Classics Illustrated comics.

27. Jones, 2011: 131–133. I thank William B. Jones, Jr., for his information and advice. (William B. Jones, Feb. 27, 2012, e-mail message to author.)

28. Jones, 2011: 167.

29. *Two-Fisted Tales*, Russ Cochran. Publisher, West Plains, MO, text facing cover of issue 25.

30. Versaci, 2007: 159; Field, 2012: 46.

31. These generalizations partially reinvent an argument that I had first encountered in an issue of the *Bulletin of Concerned Asian Scholars* in the 1970s. Although all of that article's examples were

from movies, all of its illustrations were panels from comic books, so it made a strong impression on me. Tom Engelhardt described the non-white enemy in America's pop-culture war stories as "strange, barbarous, hostile and dangerous": "he is not acting out of any human emotion. It is not a desire to defend his home, his friends, or his freedom. It has no rational (i.e. 'human') explanation. It is not even 'bravery' as we in the West know it (though similar acts by whites are portrayed heroically). Rather, it is something innate, fanatical, perverse—an inexplicable desire for death, disorder and destruction" (Engelhardt, 1971: 5).

32. Rifas, 1983.

33. Wagner, 1954: 94.

34. Basinger, 1986: 73–75.

35. Selective Service, "Induction Statistics" https://www.sss.gov/About/History-And-Records/Induction-Statistics.

36. Chen, 1952: xi, 5.

37. Cathcart, 2004: 45–47. Chinese cartoonists followed models that the government published in the *Cartoon Propaganda Reference Materials* serial.

38. Chen, 1952: 11; Cathcart, 2004: 48.

39. Lee, 2013: 193 ("The Transformation…"). Despite Chinese assistance during the Korean War, North Korean leaders harbored some bitterness about "big brother" China. In the Minsaengdan Incident of 1932–1934, the Chinese communists had arrested thousands of Korean communists (including Kim Il-sung) and killed hundreds of those that they arrested, suspecting them of being Japanese agents. North Korea turned to the Chinese for help only after the Soviet Union refused to send in troops (Armstrong, 2013: 19, 43; Han, 2013).

40. Wada, 2010: 19–20.

41. *Immortal Hero Yang Ken-Sze*, 1959, 1965.

42. Mao renamed "the Northeast Border Defence Force" (regular soldiers of China's People's Liberation Army) as "the Chinese People's Volunteers" to make the existence of a state of war between China and the United States deniable at a time when he was attempting to gain recognition from the United Nations (Pembroke, 2018: 86, 88).

43. *Immortal Hero Yang Ken-Sze*, 1959, 1965: 85.

44. From a Chinese perspective, the idea presented in "Face to Face with the Enemy" that its youth had been dreaming of a chance to go to war in Korea held no plausibility. It may, however, have projected the attitude of some young Americans (in 1950 and in 1960 when the story was published) who had regretted being too young to fight in World War II.

45. On the unpopularity of the Korean War, see Erskine, 1970: 135, 138–141; Suchman, Goldsen and Williams, Jr., 1953; Monroe, 1975: 21-; and Simons, 1974: 175.

46. Kauffman, 2008: 81. America First was founded in September, 1940 with the support of wealthy Republican businessmen who opposed Roosevelt's New Deal policies. It became the country's best-known "isolationist" group, arguing against entering a distant war to save the British Empire since this would cost American lives, raise taxes, and risk leading to a "one-man government" emerging in the United States. When aviation hero Charles Lindbergh became officially involved with the organization in April, 1941, its membership soared, but many of the members it attracted had pro-Nazi and anti-Semitic views. When the United States entered World War II, America First dissolved and its leading members immediately joined the war effort (Hart, 2018: 161, 163–164, 176, 182–184).

Chapter 15

1. Cumings, 1990: 697–698. I sent Bruce Cumings a question about his comic book reading in an e-mail message. He replied: "I did indeed collect a lot of my comic books, which would be worth a fortune now, although I didn't focus on the Korean War; I was more of a Lash LaRue and Batman fan. Unfortunately I lost track of them in the many moves that my father made when I was growing up. […] What stuck in my mind are the images and the gross propaganda and racism, even if I didn't have categories to put those images in when I was in grade school" (Bruce Cumings, August 2, 2016, e-mail message to author).

2. Cumings says, without details, that this method of killing prisoners was used against Americans, but the "Treatment of [South Korean] POWs was considerably worse [….]" (Cumings, 2005: 272–273).

3. In a response to a letter of comment in *Two-Fisted Tales #28* (July–August 1952), Kurtzman wrote: "Sure… we've got rotten apples in our barrel. Americans commit atrocities too! But at least our government and Constitution condemn such practices, which is a lot more than can be said for some other governments!" Actually, the enemy's extrajudicial massacres of prisoners, which Kurtzman dramatized in several stories, were condemned by their government (Halliday and Cumings, 1988: 90).

4. Korean War Atrocities…, 1954: 2. Several of these atrocity stories were based on the testimony of Sgt. Wendell Treffery which appeared on pages 86–97. Treffery had been ambushed near the "Chosen" Reservoir. He testified that after being forced to march for sixteen days as a prisoner of war without proper footwear in temperatures that reached 20 degrees below zero, "all the meat had worn off my feet, all the skin had dropped off, nothing but the bones showing." A Chinese woman that the prisoners called a nurse ("but I don't think that she was") "crunched…off" his toes, except the big toes. Treffery later snapped off his own big toes when they began to decay. The Chinese soldiers also lacked proper footwear, some wearing thin, cotton sandals or even fighting with rags wrapped around their bare feet (Dikötter, 2013: 133). Chinese Communists had fought their recent, successful war against the Chinese Nationalists from bases in neighboring Manchuria, sometimes marching without sufficient food, clothing or shelter in weather that reached 40 degrees below zero (Tanner, 2015: 65, 70).

During the war, some soldiers of the South Korean

Army, short of supplies because of embezzlement, marched until their shoes wore out and then continued barefoot through snow and ice, dying of sickness, of starvation, of inhumane treatment, and by freezing to death (Kim, 2000: 65, 130). In 1951, *Life* magazine reported that thousands of Korean War casualties were "victims of frostbite, a trivial-sounding but terrible affliction in which the flesh freezes solid, then dies and decays." Frostbite took soldiers' fingers, hands, toes and feet, and attacked their ears and noses ("Medicine," 1951: 82–84). Cartoonist Jack Kirby frequently told the story of how he had developed severe frostbite on both legs while fighting in Europe during World War II, and had spent months in a London hospital worrying that he would lose his legs (Ro, 2004: 40, 213).

    5. Commission of…, 1952.

    6. Lone and McCormack, 1993: 119.

    7. "Atrocity Story" appears in the collection *Marvel Masterworks Atlas Era Battlefield* (Vassallo, 2011).

    8. Vassallo, 2011.

    9. Apeldoorn, 2010.

Paul Reinman had left Germany not long after Adolf Hitler's dictatorship began in 1933 (Remez, 2012).

    10. "U.S. Charges Reds…," 1951.

John Toland called this report "one of the biggest sensations of the war" (Toland, 1991: 494).

    11. Toland, 1991: 494.

    12. Stone, 1952, 1988: 321.

    13. Burchett, 1981: 166; Stone, 1952, 1988: 322. Stone repeatedly argued that Truman did not want to settle the war because his military buildup depended on the tension which the war had sharpened (Kaner, 1971: 253, 255–256).

    14. Farmer, 1995: 100.

    15. Jacobson, 2010: 103–106. The atrocities of Buchenwald provided material that was fictionalized in several "horror comics" of the early 1950s (Streb, 2016: 40–43). Steve Danziger argues that the Nazis' obscene desecration of human bodies also inspired the Holocaust-haunted EC horror comics (Danziger, 2018: 383).

    16. Kim, 2009; Kim, 2000: 163–6; 175–176.

    17. "Armed Forces: Barbarity," 1953. The column reported that "The communist enemy which waits behind the truce lines is a barbarous enemy, capable of savagery and sadism which rival any atrocities in the history of modern warfare."

    18. The South Korean massacre of political prisoners at Taejon had been witnessed and photographed by Americans, but their reports were kept secret for four decades (Cumings, 2008; Harden, 2017: 76–80; Kim, 2000: 162).

    19. Choe, 2009: A6; McCormack, 2004: 39–42.

    20. Kim, 2004: 535. Unsurprisingly, I have not found any comic book story in which South Koreans kill their prisoners, but the story "Prison Camp Slaughter" imagines a scene in which the Communist Chinese dig big trenches, and then machine-gun to death all of their American prisoners of war to avoid the inconvenience of having to feed them. (First, though, the Communists in that story use the prisoners in a charade to fool international inspec-

tors into thinking that "those rumors you hear of Red cruelty … they're just bunk") (*G.I. Combat #2*, December 1952). A year earlier, in, "Prisoner of War" by Harvey Kurtzman, North Koreans kill their American prisoners (*Frontline Combat #3*, Nov.–Dec. 1951).

    21. Kim, 2000: 147, 210, 217.

    22. Kim's summary of these "cruelest and most atrocious" massacres is that "the military and the police tortured villagers with electricity, stripped women and beat them with firewood, made family members slap each other on horseback, cut off women's breasts, murdered women after raping them, cut open the bellies of pregnant women, and stabbed them with spears, stabbed women's vaginas with bamboo spears, stripped men and their mothers-in-law naked and made them have sex before killing them, shot women and their newborns just after labor, and made people walk around the village with their children's livers in their mouths" (Kim, 2000: 173). Kim calls these atrocities "egregious," and yet he adds that South Korean soldiers continued to use "just as violent" methods in massacres even after the war (Kim, 2000: 154–155, 173). Hur Sang-Soo (like Kim) assigns the ultimate legal responsibility for these massacres to the U.S. Military Government in Korea (Hur, 2015; Kim, 2000: 187–188).

The sexual violence against women that Kim describes fits into a very long, large, and mostly untold story of rape as a war crime and military tactic (Brownmiller, 1975: 31–113; Milillo, 2006).

    23. Kaner, 1971: 245.

    24. Stone, 1952, 1988: 327.

    25. Hanley and Mendoza, 2007; Williams, 2011; Cumings, 2005: 268–269; U.S. Department of the Army…, 2001; Bellesiles, 2012:260–26; Halliday and Cumings, 1988: 84–85; Choi, 2008: 376; See also Bellesiles, 2012: 260. During the Korean War, several comic book stories had dramatized the use of refugees as cover for North Korean infiltrators. See "Bullets, Babies and Bombs!" *Warfront #1*, Harvey, September 1951.

    26. A similar *G.I. Joe* comic book story, presumably by the same uncredited writer, found a way to reverse the blame for other UN war crimes. "The 'Massacre' at Ku-Shi Bridge," appeared in issue #27 in November 1953. The story tells of an ambitious enemy Colonel who plots to blow up a bridge with Korean orphans on it and blame it on the Americans in order to stir the villagers into hating and killing Americans. As revealed in 1999, Americans had blown up two bridges on August 3, 1950, killing hundreds of refugee women, children and old men out of fear that the refugees included disguised North Korean soldiers. Several ex-GIs told reporters that North Korean uniforms and weapons were found on some of the bodies (Choe, Handley and Mendoza, 1999).

    27. Rosenthal, 1950: 7.

    28. "The City of Flame," a comic book story published in the first issue of *Monty Hall of the U.S. Marines* (August, 1951) begins when "Monty Hall, assigned to the scorched-earth detail, finds himself

cut off in a city of flames—a man-made inferno!" while evacuating from Seoul.

According to an official army history of this evacuation of Seoul, General Ridgeway, disturbed by the appearance of destruction for destruction's sake, announced that in any future withdrawals nothing approaching "scorched earth" tactics would be condoned (Mossman, 1990: 201).

29. I. F. Stone's *Hidden History of the Korean War* quotes a British military publication that described American soldiers' ruthless, unsympathetic indifference to Korean suffering "except of course in the thousand and one little kindnesses troops offer to children and lost dogs" (Stone, 1952, 1988: 312–313, n.1).

30. Benson, 1981: 20.

31. Harrison, 2009: 9.

32. Women's International…, 1951: 2. Two years earlier, a House Committee had charged that this women's group was composed of hard-core Communist Party members (Trussell, 1949). Callum Macdonald describes many terrible, large-scale atrocities committed by South Koreans and U.S. soldiers during the occupation of North Korea between October and December of 1950 (MacDonald, 1991).

33. Presumably the pamphlet "Korea, We Accuse!," printed in East Germany, was one of the "tracts purporting to document United States war atrocities in Korea" that was confiscated wholesale by post office censors as unmailable in the United States, under a program the United States set up in 1951 (the year this pamphlet was published) to protect Americans from enemy propaganda (Schwartz and Paul, 1959: 644).

34. Women's International…, 1951: 6.

35. Women's International…, 1951: 6. This comparison to Nazi atrocities seems less clichéd when we remember that the seventeen nations these women came from included Denmark, Czechoslovakia, Netherlands, France, Italy, Austria, German Democratic Republic, West Germany, Belgium, and Algeria, all of which recently had been under Nazi German or Axis domination in World War II.

36. Women's International…, 1951: 16.

37. I thank archivist Amy. P. Muscato for this information.

38. Letter from Nora K. Rodd of Windsor, Ontario to Frederic Wertham in New York City, July 30, 1954.

39. In a later book, Wertham clarified that war should not be understood as juvenile delinquency writ large:

> We must distinguish between individual killing, such as murder, and collective killing in war. War is not a mere addition of aggressive acts by individuals. It is on an entirely different plane. It is a collective action to be understood only if we consider the objective social and economic laws that determine it (Wertham, 1966: 17).

Chapter 16

1. According to James M. Haswell's article "Comical Campaign Coming": "The use of comic books in political campaigns has been growing steadily since Ambassador to Mexico William O'Dwyer first got one out in 1940, when he was running for mayor of New York" (Haswell, 1952). In the 1945 election for mayor of New York, both the Democrat (O'Dwyer) and the Republican candidate hired the same company to produce their campaign comic books (Mead, 1947).

2. "Malcolm Ater…," 1992. I learned of Malcolm Ater from the cover story of *City Paper: Washington's Free Weekly* when I was passing through Washington, D.C. in 1983 (Dinges, 1983). Ater told me on the phone he did not have time to meet with me, but I waited on a bench outside his offices for him to come out, and I caught him for a quick conversation as he left. I thought he seemed old (he was 68, more than twice my age) and that he seemed panicked about the deadline on whatever project he was working on that week.

3. Christopher, 2003, 2014. Neale Roach, who had been the manager of the Democratic National Convention that year, had a much less positive memory of that comic book. (He also seemed unaware that millions of copies had been printed.) When asked in 1969 whether the Truman campaign had made any strategic mistakes in 1948, his main example was:

> We spent money on printed matter that turned out to be a waste because some of it, I should say the bulk of it, wasn't even distributed. It was shipped out and we paid a lot of money on credit—most people refer to it as a comic book. It was about Mr. Truman and his life, and I thought it was an insult to the President of the United States to publish such a thing. It was very poorly done. The pictures weren't clear, and it looked just like a comic book. And they ordered hundreds of thousands of that particular item, and on election day bundles of this material was still in the state headquarters, and in the national headquarters in New York, unopened. They weren't even distributed [Roach, 1969: 81–82].

4. The comic says: "On ECA [Economic Cooperation Administration] and Korea Defense … NO! (Senate vote–May 25, 1950)" (Page 9, panel 7).

5. Taft clarified that he was not opposed to comic books as a medium, but that what he found wrong with this particular comic was its "straight appeal to class prejudice […] plus the five or six lies on specific matters" (Investigation Into the 1950 Ohio Senatorial Campaign…, 1952: 56). In 1952, the headquarters for Taft's presidential campaign reportedly issued a booklet "using comic-book techniques": "How the Taft-Hartley Law Protects You as a Worker" ("Policing the Comics," 1952).

6. Fred Hartley's son, Al Hartley, had, with his father's encouragement, followed his own path and became a comic book artist. During the Korean War, Al Hartley freelanced for editor Stan Lee in several genres, including war stories for *Spy Cases*, *War Comics*, *Battle*, *Men's Adventures*, *Young Men*, *Young Men on the Battlefield*, *Combat Kelly*, *Battlefield*, *War Action*, *War Adventures*, *Man Comics*, *Men in Action*,

and *Battlefront*. (Al Hartley had served in the U.S. Army Air Corps in Europe during World War II as a bomber pilot.) In 1967, Hartley became a born-again Christian, and he has been most remembered for his Christian-themed comic books of the 1970s and 1980s, including Christian comics that licensed the Archie characters (Grand Comics Database; Hartley, 2006; Butler, 1996).

7. Investigation Into the 1950 Ohio Senatorial Campaign…, 1952: 170–171.

8. Investigation Into the 1950 Ohio Senatorial Campaign…, 1952: 172.

9. Investigation Into the 1950 Ohio Senatorial Campaign…, 1952: 171.

10. Investigation Into the 1950 Ohio Senatorial Campaign…, 1952: 171. Toby, a company founded by Elliott Caplin, produced comics in several genres, including the war comics *Tell it to the Marines and Monty Hall of the U.S. Marines*. Elliott Caplin was the brother and business partner of "Li'l Abner" cartoonist Al Capp.

11. Taft later testified: "There can't be much doubt about the attempt to arouse class prejudice. Of course, the whole effort is to show that I am run by and the campaign is run by J. Phineas Money-bags, chairman of the local Taft campaign committee" (Investigation Into the 1950 Ohio Senatorial Campaign…, 1952: 45).

12. J.P. Morgan featured prominently in conspiracy theories. In a book that Populist Party leader Henry Loucks wrote to expose "the great conspiracy of the house of Morgan," Loucks described Taft's father, President William Howard Taft, as having willingly carried out to the letter the secret policies of the "money monopoly" (Loucks, 1916: 4, 89).

In 1935, communist John L. Spivak described J.P. Morgan as "Ultimate fountain-head of the whole fascist conspiracy of Wall Street" (Spivak, 1935: 9).

13. Bromfield, 1950.

14. Regarding evidence of Russian plans for aggression, Taft had made the defensible statement that "I know of no indication of Russian intention to undertake military aggression beyond the sphere of influence which was originally assigned to them. The situation in Czechoslovakia was indeed a tragic one, but Russian influence has predominated there since the end of the war" (Berger, 1971: 181–182).

15. Medhurst, 2000: 467.

Vernon Van Dyke and Edward Lane Davis's analysis of Taft's evolving ideas about national defense concluded in 1952 that "no longer an isolationist, [Taft's] departure from isolationism is nevertheless cautious and incomplete" (Van Dyke and Davis, 1952: 195).

16. The decision to exclude Korea from America's "defensive perimeter," though, had been made a few years earlier by the Joint Chiefs of Staff (Berger, pp.191–192).

17. Fisher, 1995: 32–35, 37–38.

18. Investigation Into the 1950 Ohio Senatorial Campaign…, 1952: 4–5.

19. Taft's testimony beginning on page xx.

20. Investigation Into the 1950 Ohio Senatorial Campaign…, 1952: 20.

21. Wallack and Hudak, 2014.

22. Weintz, 1987: 82–83; Viguerie and Franke, 2004: 88–89.

23. Usually, newspaper syndicates, including the *Chicago Tribune* syndicate, insisted that the strips stay away from political controversies to avoid cutting into sales. Nevertheless, the rumor that the *Chicago Tribune* syndicate distributed comics that "[b]y design or not, […] all seem to be in harmony with the editorial views of the cartoonists' bosses[….]," led one communications researcher to formally analyze the content of the unusually outspoken strip "Little Orphan Annie" during the period April 18, 1948 through July 2, 1950 (that is, the 109 weeks leading up to the Korean War plus the following week (which would have been drawn before news of the invasion). The sample included a 39-week sequence "spent in conflict with foreign agents whose identities were thinly disguised and presumably Russian" who threaten to rule the world and enslave their enemies. The study found that "Foreign spies and their radical American counterparts are far and away the wiliest opponents Annie meet," and among her most frequently encountered foes (Shannon, 1954: 169–179).

24. Haswell, 1952.

25. The first page of From Yalta to Korea (and covers of similar anti-communist comic books) is posted at: https://www.cgccomics.com/boards/topic/32980-post-your-anti-communist-comics/?page=3.

26. Medhurst, 2000: 469.

27. Pickett, 2000: 118–9.

28. Medhurst, 2000: 481. Eisenhower's "crusade" used the power of religion to unite Americans across different faiths. As he famously said that December, "our form of government has no sense unless it is founded in a deeply-felt religious faith, and I don't care what it is" (Kruse, 2015: 67–68).

29. In this eight-page comic, Eisenhower is shown giving his formula for peace, which had also appeared in *Ike's Story*: "Here is our formula for peace—first, justice, freedom and opportunity for all men; second, international understanding; third, disarmament; fourth, a respected United Nations." In *Choice of a Nation*, Eisenhower introduces this formula by saying: "*I know war!* That's why I hate war! I am in favor of peace—peace with honor—and I shall work for peace, No soldier welcomes war."

More than half of the Eisenhower quotations in *Choice of a Nation* had appeared in *Ike's Story*, but with differences in their framing, illustration and editing.

30. As examples of religious language in other campaign comic books, the 1948 comic for Truman showed him singing hymns in church as a boy, and ended with Truman saying: "This is the hour to rededicate ourselves to the faith in mankind that makes us strong … to the faith in God that gives us confidence as we face the challenge of the years ahead!" The 1952 comic for Stevenson concluded with Stevenson saying "Peace is the great unfinished business of our generation. To the end that I

may help open the door to that Golden Age, I ask my God to give me strength and nourish my spirit in this great undertaking." Besides describing him as a crusader, the *Choice of a Nation* comic illustrates that when Eisenhower was young his family "held weekly Bible readings and often sang hymns around the piano." *Ike's Story*, does not mention a "crusade," but it does conclude that "Ike has proven his qualities of vigorous, able and honest spiritual leadership!"

31. Weintz, 1987: 83–100; Viguerie and Franke, 2004: 90–91.

32. Weintz, 1987: 100.

33. Medhurst, 2000: 464, 480, 482.

34. Truman concluded his speech by warning that behind Eisenhower's bland assertions, the Republicans' goals remained unchanged: "to hack and hew away at the New Deal and the Fair Deal, to limit and restrict the things the government can do for the average man, to return the control of our economy to selfish private interests." Finally, to further their goal "to reduce the rich man's taxes," Truman predicted the Republicans would dangerously "reduce the size of our defenses and the strength of our alliances" (Truman, 1952: 28). As Truman had predicted, President Eisenhower did swiftly cut military spending (by relying on nuclear bombs and missiles rather than the more expensive land and naval forces) (Stockman, 2013: 213–215). On the other hand, contrary to the fears of some and the hopes of others, Eisenhower did not work to reverse the New Deal (De Santis, 1976).

35. "Man and Superman," 1952.

36. In the thick educational comic book *Life Stories of American Presidents*, published by Dell in 1957, the eight-page chapter on the current president, Dwight D. Eisenhower begins with his promise that "if elected, I will concentrate on the job of ending the war in Korea. If necessary I will go to Korea myself."

That comic book's chapter on Harry S. Truman, only two-pages long, supports Truman's military orders to aid South Korea against the "clear case of aggression" by North Korea as an act of "characteristic vigor." Two panels later, a dialogue between two men at a lunch counter explains that Truman disregarded popular demands to "end this war by dropping an atom bomb on the Kremlin" because "Truman is trying to end the fighting, not spread it into a new world war!"

The last panel of the chapter on Truman shows him walking down the street after retiring at the end of his second term, "still interested in politics [and] always ready to give reporters his forthright views." I met Harry Truman when he had returned to Missouri and was walking down the street in Kansas City. According to a story that I heard my mother tell, perhaps only once, he had looked into my baby carriage and congratulated her on her fine-looking boy. Truman had spent the previous 30 years in elected positions. And I imagine that even in retirement, complimenting little children had become an unbreakable habit.

Chapter 17

1. Dingman, 1988/89: 50–91.

2. Shepley, 1956; On Eisenhower's willingness to use nuclear weapons in the Korean War, see Ellsberg, 2107: 317–318.

3. FRUS … 1952–4.

Oppenheimer mentioned comics again, the next year, when looking for a way to explain that fission bombs are used to trigger the fusion reactions in H-Bombs without revealing any nuclear secrets: "Another example which will be difficult for me again to give because of security reasons, but I will try to guard my words—certain aspects of the so-called fission field are directly relevant, intimately related to the fusion field. If you wish to have an unclassified example of this, again it is widely known in the comic strips, that apparently some sort of primary bomb, trigger mechanism as it is called, is apparently required" (United States Atomic Energy Commission, 1954: 484). *The Progressive* magazine published this "secret" in 1979 in their article "The H-Bomb Secret: How We Got It, Why We're Telling It" by Howard Morland. The May 1979 issue of *The Progressive* included (on page 50) an editorial illustration that I drew for them, supporting Morland's position that "nuclear bomb secrets are a hoax and... public understanding of nuclear arsenals is a necessary step in the quest for nuclear disarmament" (Lueders, 2019; Morland, 1999, 2007).

4. Szasz discusses the role of "Buck Rogers" and "Flash Gordon" in introducing "atomic" ideas to a mass audience of Americans (Szasz, 2012: 15ff).

5. Szasz, 2012: 33.

6. Szasz, 2012: 34–35; Koop, 1946: 277. The author of the Superman comic strip, Alvin Schwartz, later remembered that "When I finished a continuity, I never sat around and looked for it to appear in the newspapers. So it wasn't until a few years later, after the war, that I happened to see a headline in the *New York Post*: 'Superman Had It First.' It was the story of how the FBI had censored Superman because the bomb was forecast in the Duste continuity. The FBI had even questioned Jerry Siegel, Superman's originator, thinking he had written that story" (Schwartz, 1997, 2006, 128–131).

According to Rick Yager, who wrote and drew the Buck Rogers comic strip, throughout World War II "the Army assigned an intelligence man to keep his eye on Buck Rogers lest some U.S. military secret leak through this medium" (Ritter, 1947).

7. Spencer Weart describes how in 1903 "Scientist, press and public had crafted a new thought" together: an atomic weapon, which became an instant cliché, decades before such weapons existed in reality (Weart, 1988: 25).

8. The first to experience the dawn of the Atomic Age with reference to Buck Rogers may have been the crew of the *Enola Gay*. As they circled back to see what they had done to Hiroshima, Co-pilot Robert Lewis remembered that "We were struck dumb at the sight. It far exceeded all our expectations. Even though we expected something terrific, the actual sight caused all of us to feel that we

were Buck Rogers 25th Century Warriors" (Walker, 1997: 76).

9. Brians, 1987: 5, 335; Szasz, 2004.

10. "Atomic Man," *Headline Comics #7*, May–June 1946.

11. *Atomic Thunderbolt #1*, February 1946. An even earlier nuclear superhero, "The American Crusader," had appeared in *Thrilling Comics #19* (August 1941). The American Crusader's origin story was that he had come too close to an "Atom smasher" and "it accidentally rearranged my entire atomic structure, giving me limitless power!"

12. *Action Comics #101*, October 1946. The November–December 1946 issue of the comic book *Picture News* included a six-page nonfiction comics-format piece "Atom Bombs Over Bikini," describing a series of atom bomb tests at the atoll which had been "selected as the atomic guinea pig." That story concludes by presenting a choice of "war or peace," a future world in which survivors live underground in caves "to protect themselves from atomic destruction" or one in which atomic power is usefully harnessed so that "peace and prosperity come to mankind at last."

13. *Captain Marvel Adventures #66*, October 1946.

14. *Atoman No. 1*, February 1946. The story was written by Ken Crossen and drawn by Jerry Robinson.

15. Millions of copies of GE's comic book *Adventures Inside the Atom* were printed, of which 250,000 were distributed at a New York "Power from the Atom" exhibit (Robin, 1949: 351–353).

16. Allen, 1977: vii–ix, 44, 48, Appendix.

17. *Science Comics*, January 1946. A two-page nonfiction feature. "Our Atomic Future," in the one-shot science fiction comic book *Rocket Ship X* (published in September, 1951) predicted that atomic energy could be used to power ocean liners, interplanetary passenger rockets, the "car of tomorrow," subways, trains and jet planes, and that "Atomic power plants could make electricity so cheap that it wouldn't pay to read the meters!" (The erroneous prediction that nuclear power would be "too cheap to meter" has usually been credited to a speech that the Chairman of the U.S. Atomic Energy Commission, Lewis Strauss, made three years later, in 1954.) "Our Atomic Future" concluded, though, that "the gigantic expense and the many still unknown facts to be learned about atomic energy put these possibilities far in the future."

18. Alperovitz, 1995. 1996: 423–424. I was surprised to learn some years after he died that my father had been one of the soldiers reassigned to Asia after the war in Europe ended. (Shari Rifas, personal e-mail to author, 2 Feb. 2020). The war ended before he was sent there. Although not a pacifist, my father wrote a letter to support my petition to be recognized as a Conscientious Objector when I was a teenager and he and my mother supported my republication of Nakazawa's manga about the Hiroshima bomb (for example, by letting me store pallets full of copies in their basement for many years).

19. Wilson, 2007: 162–163, 167; Linenthal and Englehardt, 1996. D. M. Giangreco, without claim-

ing that the bomb "won the war," approvingly surveys scholarly works which challenge (or "shred" or "demolish") the idea that dropping atomic bombs on Japan had been militarily unwarranted (Giangreco, 1998: 141).

20. *Picture News #1*, January 1946.

21. Three years later, in the overly-complicated educational comic book *Learn How Dagwood Splits the Atom*, writer Joe Musial used large blocks of text under each cartoon drawing, which allowed him to explain more clearly how this analogy between a nuclear "chain reaction" and a chemical chain reaction worked: "Actually, every time you strike a match you start a chain reaction. The friction of striking the match produces enough heat to raise the temperature of some of the substance of the match head to the point where it reacts chemically and releases more heat. This heat causes more chemical reaction, more heat, and very quickly the head of the match is ablaze" (*Learn How Dagwood Splits the Atom*, 1949: 25).

22. Miscamble, 2011: 132–133, 135–136, 140, 143–144.

23. *Picture News #3*, March 1946: 4.

24. The quoted phrase appeared in Kennan's famous "Long Telegram." Bernard Baruch, who Truman had appointed to present the U.S. plan at the United Nations, added the part about tough requirements for inspections (Miscamble, 2011: 144).

25. *Spy and Counterspy #2*, November 1949, American Comics Group, Art, "The Black Avengers," possibly by Leonard Starr (Grand Comics Database).

26. Whether or not the possibility of Japanese germ warfare against the U.S. using balloons really "scared them stiff," American researchers used that possibility to successfully argue for more biological warfare funding (Lockwood, 2009: 147).

27. Snell, 1946 (Hungnam was then known as "Konan"). The newspapers that reported on the *Atlanta Journal's* story about Japan's atomic bomb included responses from various officials, who dismissed it as "a complete lie," "most unlikely," "without foundation," and "not true" (For example, "Scoff At Report…," 1946).

28. Wilcox, 1995, 18, 160, 170.

Daniel Ellsberg emphasizes that the long public controversy over "the decision to drop the bomb" falsely assumes that such a decision had been made: "There was, in reality, *no debate or discussion whatever in official circles* as to *whether* the [atomic] bomb would or should be used, if it were ready in time before the war ended for other reasons." For the five months leading up to the Hiroshima and Nagasaki bombing, "the U.S. Army Air Force had been deliberately killing as many Japanese civilians as it could" (Ellsberg, 2017: 260–261).

Wilson D. Miscamble's book *The Most Controversial Decision: Truman, the Atomic Bombs, and the Defeat of Japan* confirms that "historians have given the decision to use this devastating weapon an importance that it didn't obtain at the time" (Miscamble, 2011: 45)

29. Dower, 1986 ("Review…"): 61–62.

30. Nakazawa had been friends with a Korean neighbor as a young boy in Hiroshima (Nakazawa, 2010: 22). In *Barefoot Gen,* Nakazawa's sympathetic Korean character Mr. Pak, explains to Gen why he is eager to cooperate with Gen's plan to acquire paper on the black market (the only available source) to print a dying Japanese reporter's ghastly exposé of what had happened in Hiroshima.

Nakazawa illustrates Mr. Pak's description of how Japan had cruelly and violently robbed Koreans of their country; took Korea's resources including the food that Koreans needed to live; forced Koreans to work for almost nothing in mines and factories; sent Koreans as soldiers to die on the battlefields; and then "The two bombs dropped on Hiroshima and Nagasaki killed fifty thousand Koreans, all of them brought to Japan against their will." (The list of injustices in Mr. Pak's speech did not include Japan's sexual enslavement of Korean "comfort women.") (Nakazawa, 2008: 42–46).

In Volume 9 of *Barefoot Gen*, Nakazawa discusses American nuclear threats against North Korea in 1950, 1953 and 1969, and credits international public outcry with stopping the United States from using nuclear weapons in Korea (Nakazawa, 2009: 89–91).

31. Cumings, 2005: 183.

32. Cumings, 2005: 176–7. By the time of the atomic bombings, almost two million Koreans were living in Japan, where they were a third of the industrial work force. Measured in miles or kilometers, Hiroshima and Nagasaki are closer to Busan, Korea, than to Tokyo.

33. As another indication of optimism, Kurtzman's unrealistically precise figure for the number of deaths caused at Nagasaki is lower than the current range of estimates: 40,000 to 75,000 immediate deaths (Doherty, et al., 2008: 5).

34. This story is republished in Grant Geissman's book about Feldstein (Geissman, 2013: 136–144).

35. Hirsch, 2013: 128–129. Besides their science fiction titles, William Gaines and Al Feldstein created horror comics. Eric A. Homes argues at length that EC publisher Gaines and Feldstein's belief that nuclear war would mean "complete annihilation suddenly" for both sides "found its way into the tales that they wrote and edited for their EC horror publications" (Holmes, 2014: 97).

36. Wills, 2010.

37. *If an A-Bomb Falls* and *The H-Bomb and You* were created by Malcolm Ater's company. *If an A-Bomb Falls* was also published on the front page of the *Washington Post* in July, 1951 (Christopher, 2003, 2014).

38. By contrast, Albert Einstein had warned in 1947 that when it comes to nuclear weapons, "there is no secret and there is no defense" (Einstein, 1947).

39. DoJ "Radiation Exposure Compensation Act" website; Dalager, Kang and Mahan (2000). The information that no follow-up tests were conducted comes from the Atomic Veterans website. My Junior High School (Middle School) science teacher Charles Mabie told our class that he had been one of the soldiers who had participated in such a test and that he

had not been harmed by it. He died many years later at the age of 76, after what his obituary described as "a brave battle with chronic health issues."

40. "Radiation Exposure Compensation Act (RECA)," n.d.; Sorrentino, 2016.

41. "Preview of the War We Do Not Want," 1952: 17.

42. "Preview of the War We Do Not Want," 1952: 17, 27.

43. Kaku and Axelrod, 1987: x, 61.

44. The two war comic book stories that Turner named were set in the Korean War, not World War II, and appeared in *War Heroes #2*, July 1952.

45. Turner concludes his comments on *World War III* comics by adding "If any reader is interested and has any information about this comic magazine, please write to me" (Turner, 1970: 155–156). The same year that Turner made this request, the first edition of the *Overstreet Comic Book Price Guide* appeared, an important landmark in the development of the comic book collecting as an organized hobby.

46. Dingman, 1988/89: 50–91.

47. Weintraub, 2000: 251–253.

48. Weintraub, 2000: 251–253.

49. Bernstein, 1981: 271.

50. Mazarr, 1995: 16–21.

51. Alexandre Y. Mansourov reported in 2014 that North Korea had listed its two preconditions for giving up its nuclear weapons as (1) an end to the "U.S. hostile policy" which would be demonstrated by withdrawal of U.S. troops from South Korea, lifting all sanctions and embargoes, and normalizing bilateral relations, and (2) global nuclear disarmament (which would include U.S. nuclear disarmament) (Mansourov, 2014). In 2018, based on information from Joel S. Wit, Gareth Porter reported that:

> in the private meetings with Americans, North Korean officials presented a concrete plan for a three-phase agreement with the United States on denuclearization in which each side would undertake a set of related steps simultaneously. The American participants were told that the first stage of North Korea's implementation would be a freeze on its nuclear weapons development, followed by disabling key facilities and finally dismantling the facilities as well the nuclear weapons. The U.S. steps would include diplomatic recognition, ending economic sanctions and removing the U.S. military threat to North Korea, in part by finally bringing the Korean War to a formal conclusion.
>
> It was the same approach to a denuclearization agreement to which North Korea had agreed in 1994 and again in 2005 and 2007, but which had failed primarily because of the reluctance of the Clinton and Bush administrations to commit to entering into a normal political and economic relationship with North Korea [Porter, 2017; Porter, 2018].

In 2020, Tim Shorrock reported that Professor Moon Chung-in has provided "the most specific explanation I have heard in years of covering the issue" regarding what North Korea means when they ask for an end of the U.S. "hostile policy" against North Korea. The four-point set of demands that Shorrock describes could be summarized most simply as saying that North Korea wants to be treated as "a normal country" (Shorrock, 2020).

52. Gerson, 2007: 27, 171–172.

53. Ellsberg, 1981: i.

54. Sagan, 1984: 28. In 1988, I adapted the warnings about nuclear winter to comic-book format and included them in the first issue of a comic book series that I edited for Fantagraphics: *itchy PLANET* (Rifas, 1988).

55. Schell, 2007; Wittner, 2010; Rothberg, 2012.

56. Robock, 2011: 275.

57. Sagan and Turco, 1990: 185, 312–316.

58. Toon, Robock and Turco, 2008: 37. According to Alan Robock, previous calculations had indicated that a nuclear war could put so much smoke into the atmosphere that "surface temperatures would plummet below freezing for months, killing virtually all plants and producing worldwide famine" but "[t]he newer research indicates that this climate catastrophe would last, not for months, but for years" (Robock, 2011: 275).

59. In July 1950, 53 percent of those polled by Gallup thought "the United States is now actually in World War III" and only 30 percent thought "the present fighting in Korea will stop short of another world war." Over the course of the next year, these results remained relatively stable (Crabtree, 2003).

60. Dower, 1986: 297–298.

61. Casualty estimates for the Korean War are cited in Tirman, 2011. Victor Davis Hanson contextualizes the Hiroshima casualties in relation to World War II as a whole, reminding that most of the sixty million who died in that war were Russian and Chinese civilians, killed by aggressors from Nazi Germany and Imperial Japan (Hanson, 2016).

62. William J. Astore adds that in addition to these explosives, the U.S. dropped 32,557 tons of napalm. Then, in a similarly unsuccessful effort, the U.S. went on to drop the equivalent of 450 "Hiroshimas" on Vietnam, Laos and Cambodia (Astore, 2016).

63. McCormack, 2003. In addition to their psychological impact, the simulated nuclear attacks on Pyongyang served American training purposes as realistic tests of "atomic sorties" (Hayes, et al., 1986: 50–52).

64. Franklin, 1988, 2008: 145.

65. Seldes, 1950: 281, 287.

66. Seldes, 1950: 294. Seldes argued that mass media inescapably "create the climate of feeling in which all of us live," and that "neither our indifference nor our contempt gives us immunity against them" (Seldes, 1950: 4) He also wrote of comic books and of mass media more generally, "you cannot, by avoiding them, escape their effects" (Seldes, 1950: 277).

Chapter 18

1. The Sedition laws forbade "falsely impugning the motives and aims of the government in entering into war, exaggerating the horrors of war, denouncing the enforcement of conscription for military service and falsely charging public officers with misconduct..." (*Federal Code Annotated, Title 18*, 1950: 396).

2. Caute, 1978. Around the time of the Korean War, the most memorable controversies over the political content of American popular culture concerned the blacklisting of communists from the Hollywood movie industry, supposedly to prevent them from using film to communicate "un-American ideas and beliefs." (The blacklisting controversy grew largely out of struggles between the studios and Hollywood's militant labor unions.) At around the same time, three former-FBI agents formed a business, funded by wealthy anti-communist Alfred Kohlberg, which had a great impact in purging leftists from radio and television by publishing the names of those in the broadcasting industry who had supported left-wing causes. Communists were also being removed from positions of responsibility in the government, labor unions, the armed forces, universities and schools. At this time, the mistreatment of *anti*-communists in newly-communist China happened on an incomparably more severe level (Dikötter, 2013: 49).

3. In 1918, socialist Eugene Debs was sentenced to ten years in prison because his speech in which he told workers they were "fit for something better than slavery and cannon fodder" had a tendency to obstruct military recruitment (Starr, 2004: 281–282).

4. In 1948, Wertham had used the phrase "cannon fodder" when he called comic books "perfect" ... "If you want a generation of half stormtroopers and half cannon fodder with a dash of illiteracy" (McCallum, 1948).

5. SAC, New York, to Director, FBI (100–383747), April 29, 1951.

6. Schelly, 2015: 207–209. I thank Bill Schelly for a copy of William Gaines' FBI files.

7. Report of the Select Committee..., 1952: 29.

8. Wertham, 1953, 1954: 393.

9. "Navy Bans Two Comic Books...," 1952; See also "Navy Censors Comic Books...," 1952.

10. Credie, 1952.

11. I thank Denis Kitchen for a copy of this letter from Kurtzman's archived papers.

12. I thank Francis Di Menno and Stephen O'Day for calling this example to my attention in e-mails in June 2011. That newsgroup has since migrated to Facebook.

13. By the time this story was published, the remains in the temporary cemeteries in South Korea had been disinterred and evacuated to Japan, with the exception of a few left in the United Nations Military Cemetery at Tanggok. All new American dead were shipped to Kokura, Japan, and then back to the United States rather than being buried in Korea. (Martz, 1954) As part of the Armistice agree-

ment, in September and October, 1954, the two sides exchanged the remains of enemy war dead ("Operation Glory," 1954).

14. Apeldoorn, 2010.

15. *War Combat* was replaced by another comic with the same postal permit two issues later (Michaël Dewally, Aug. 25, 2011, e-mail message to the author).

16. Thomas, 2010: 10–12. I thank Roy Thomas for a copy of this article and for his permission to quote it at length. I tried to contact Stan Lee for his side of that conversation, and heard from his Executive Assistant Michael M. Kelly. Stan Lee had received my interview request but did not have time for most of the interview requests that he received, "[h]owever, it looks like you've already spoken to Roy Thomas, who has a much better recall of these things than Stan does, so whatever he told Roy some years ago would hold true" (Michael M. Kelly, Nov. 21, 2017, e-mail message to author).

17. The same year that Stan Lee and Roy Thomas had this argument, Stan Lee was briefly quoted in a news article as promising that Marvel comics "try to back up the soldiers" and stood for "the good virtues." In this article, on the topic of comic books as an advertising medium, the reporter described comic book readers as "children, servicemen and semi-adults (a term used by some people in the trade to refer to those over 18 who may not always think at the same level as their chronological age)" (Sloane, 1967).

18. Apeldoorn, 2010. From July 19 to August 11, 2015, Ger Apeldoorn posted a remarkable and valuable series of blog posts about Hank Chapman's war comics, with links to Chapman's stories: http://allthingsger.blogspot.ca/.

19. Federal Bureau of Investigation, title: "[Redacted] Et Al] New York, 12/30/53.

20. *Federal Code Annotated, Title 18, section 2387,* 1950: 394. During a declared war, the maximum prison sentence for this crime was twenty years. The sedition laws in effect at this time were passed in 1948. An earlier Sedition Act had been enacted as an amendment to the Espionage Act of 1917 and had been repealed in 1920. In 1918, during World War I, socialist cartoonist Art Young and the editor, layout man and business manager of the magazine he drew for, *The Masses,* were tried twice under the Espionage Act on the charge of "conspiracy to obstruct enlistment." Young was required to explain to the court about a half dozen of his anti-war cartoons which had been entered as evidence. Young often quoted as an outrageously anti–immigrant statement something that a "well-meaning gentleman," juror number two of his second trial, had told him afterwards: "It was a good thing for you boys that you were all American born; otherwise it might have gone pretty hard with you" (Young, 1928: 295, 298). A less-remembered socialist cartoonist, Morris Pass, was tried in Seattle in 1918 for draft resistance and then in 1919 for "criminal anarchy" for his radical cartoons in support of the Seattle General Strike (a strike which the authorities had interpreted as an attempt to overthrow the

government by force and install a Bolshevik dictatorship). Pass, who had been born in Russia, went to prison (Rifas, 2017).

21. Another example: a woman who self-identified as a liberal, wrote to ask Wertham "Has anyone approached our lawmakers with the idea of comic books as a source of subversion?" (Friedman, 2014: 188–189).

22. Friedman, 2014: 162. Wertham's name had been listed in a 1944 government document that investigated "the diffusion within the United States of subversive and un-American propaganda" (Investigation of Un-American Propaganda...," 1944: 1150).

In 1956, Wertham remained opposed to subservience. He argued that comic books' glorification of the strong individual ("the superman image") causes young people to become "over-submissive." Comic book readers do not see dramas about how ordinary people become powerful by "working together." Wertham warned that comic books' failure to provide their readers with an understanding of labor solidarity and collective bargaining "tear[s] at the roots of unionism" (Strunsky, 1956).

23. Friedman, 2014: 162. In 1958, in a review published in the leftist *Monthly Review,* Wertham wrote, "In academic circles, psychoanalysis both here and in Europe was originally considered rather subversive. However, it proved to be not only harmless but even useful in instilling conformity into questioning youths and quietism in restless intellectuals." In that article, Wertham criticized statistical-questionnaire research (which overwhelms the unwary with its impression of "scientificness") as a tool that serves those who "want us to remain in doubt, reach no definite conclusions, have no point of view...." This new, elaborately statistical approach helps to perpetuate the *status quo* rather than helping those who still strive for "juster social values" (Wertham, 1958: 280, 276).

24. "So-Called 'Comic' Books Censured...," 1953.

25. "Tri-County P.T.A...," 1954.

26. Zeiske, 1954.

27. *Subversive Influence in the Educational Process...,* 1953: 21–22; Barry, 1954: 10; Burton, 1954; Monaghan, 1954; Theisen, 1954; Wilfred, 1954.

Speaking to a meeting of the League of Catholic Women, Dodd explained communist involvement in comic books by saying that "They want children to read only that which is gruesome" and attunes their minds to violence and evil (Barry, 1954).

28. Jerome, 1947: 26–27. This pamphlet, based on Jerome's address at a Marxist cultural conference in June, 1947, develops this theme at length (Jerome, 1947: 8).

29. Jerome, 1951: 3–4.

30. Jerome, 1951: 3–4.

31. "Victor J. Jerome...," 1965.

32. *Juvenile Delinquency (Comic Books): Hearings...,* 1954: 58. The Hearings reproduced a series of articles by Irving M. Kravsow for the *Hartford Courant.* Kravsow quoted William Gaines' response to what Gaines regarded as a "crank" letter which

had charged him "with being subversive and trying to undermine the minds and morals of the youth of this Nation." Gaines said "That's ridiculous. ... We try to entertain and educate. That's all there is to it" (*Juvenile Delinquency [Comic Books]: Hearings...*, 1954: 299).

I met William Gaines once, at a Chicago comic book convention in 1980. (He was sitting by himself in the hotel lobby, outside of the dealers' room, so I introduced myself and, with permission, sat next to him.) I showed him a copy of a comic book about motherhood, edited by Trina Robbins, which I had published. While he slowly thumbed through it, I asked him whether it didn't seem that Wertham's main target had been Lev Gleason. He replied simply "They came after us too."

33. Schelly, 2015: 207–9; Hirsch, 2013:167.

34. Thompson, 1954.

Chapter 19

1. Cumings, 2003: 548.

2. Kurtzman, 1980: "In Memoriam," *Two-Fisted Tales* #30, January, 1954.

3. Bill Schelly refers to John Severin as "the house conservative in the midst of a group of mostly liberals" at EC. (Schelly, 2015: 176).

4. Kurtzman, 1980: facing cover of Issue #37. Dawkins worked on the Ford account from 1953 to 1971 (http://library.duke.edu/rubenstein/findingaids/jwtdawkins/).

5. Kurtzman, 1980: facing cover of Issue #38.

6. Romita, John, Dick Ayers and Bill Everett, 2008: "Kill Captain America," *Men's Adventures* #28, July, 1954.

7. Romita, John, Dick Ayers and Bill Everett, 2008: "Captain America," *Captain America* #77, July 1954. Art by John Romita.

8. Romita, John, Dick Ayers and Bill Everett, 2008: "Playing with Fire," *Captain America* #78, September 1954. In 1996, news stories reported that in December 1953, five months after the armistice agreement, Eisenhower was informed that the Defense Department had the names of over 900 U.S. servicemen still being held by the North Koreans. (Accounting for POW/MIA's from the Korean War..., 1997; Shenon, 1996; Rochelle, 1996; Schlatter, 2018.)

9. Romita, John, Dick Ayers and Bill Everett, 2008: "In Korea," *Human Torch* #38, August 1954.

10. Lee, S., 2013: 185–195; Lee, J-B, 2009. The United States deployed nuclear weapons on South Korean soil from 1958 to 1991 (Ritter, 2016).

11. Romita, John, Dick Ayers and Bill Everett, 2008; Roy Thomas "Introduction," 2008. For longer quotes from Romita about this, see Thomas, 2005: 109–110.

12. Radosh, 2001: 18.

13. Bill Devine's comprehensive checklist of Men's Adventure Magazines, lists a half dozen other comic book publishers that also turned to publishing men's magazines (Parfrey, 2003: 281).

14. "Shanghai's Bawdy House..." *Male*, Decem-ber, 1958; "WWII's Strangest Story..." *Male*, January, 1959; "To Capture..." *Male*, July, 1959; "Yank who Flew..." *Male*, November, 1960; "Queen of..." *Man's Adventure*, November 1960. The website "StagMags. com Classic Men's Magazine Covers" does an admirable job of presenting this material: http://www.stagmags.com/.

15. Josh Alan Friedman has web-posted an audio file of the 1984 interview in which Mario Puzo told him this as podcast #10 on his website, https://blackcracker.fm/tales-of-my-dead-heroes/page/2/.

16. Friedman, 2003: 13, 16–17.

17. When the Korean War began in 1950, Guatemala's democratically elected government confused the State Department by offering full support for the UN action against North Korea's aggression, including military bases in Guatemala and men for the armed forces if needed. At the time of the armistice in 1953, however, a few Guatemalan newspaper editorials and political speeches honored the strong and heroic "peace-loving forces" in North Korea who had fought the warmongering, imperialistic Western aggressors (Gleijeses, 1991: 121–122, 179–181).

18. Markstein, n.d.

19. Harvey, 1996: 276.

20. Simon, 2011.

21. Kirby, 2011. In both the Simon interview and the Kirby interview, the *Comics Journal* transcribed Welch's name as "Walsh."

22. Lobel, 2003: 2.

23. A video of "McCarthy vs. Welch: 'Have you no decency?'" has been web-posted. M. Stanton Evans has described what he calls the myth and reality behind this incident ("generally viewed as the moral Waterloo of Joe McCarthy.") Evans claims that because six weeks earlier Welch had confirmed news reports that he had relieved Fred Fisher from his duties because of admitted membership in the National Lawyers Guild, Welch had already "outed" Fisher when he "caused this story to appear," and so was guilty of the evil thing which he had accused McCarthy of doing (Evans, 2007: 568–569).

24. These discussions became passionate, thanks especially to the work of David Barsalou, who, beginning in 1979, set out to identify the comic book source material for "pop artists" Roy Lichtenstein, Andy Warhol and Mel Ramos. Barsalou's webposted project "Deconstructing Roy Lichtenstein" showed that Lichtenstein had copied published comic book panels more closely than many people had imagined (Barsalou, n.d.).

25. For examples, see Waldman, 2003 and Rubin, 2008.

26. Crow, 2010: 38–39.

27. Comic book artist Dick Ayers said on a panel at a comics convention that Jack Kirby and writer/editor Stan Lee fought more over the Marvel war comic *Sgt. Fury* than anything else because Kirby thought that Lee was turning it into a superhero comic. Their differences were irreconcilable and Ayers replaced Kirby as the artist on that series (Chapell, 2008).

28. According to Mark O'Neill, U.S. Air Force planes did not attack across the Yalu until April, 1952 "when U.S. F-86 pilots—apparently on their own initiative, but with the knowledge of their commanders—began attacking MiG-15s in Manchuria" (O'Neill, 2000).

The comic book story "Revenge Above the Yalu," published in January-February, 1953, began: "Ever since the start of the Korean War, one thing has stopped American pilots cold … far more effectively than Communist planes or ack-ack! The *Yalu River* lies between North Korea and Red China— screening the lair of Chinese air power in Manchuria—thwarting the American pilots who have been ordered not to cross! It was the Communists themselves who tricked Captain Tom Harvey into breaking that order—setting themselves up for *Revenge above the Yalu!*" (*Soldiers of Fortune #12*, Jan–Feb, 1953).

29. Smith, 2001.

30. Sewell, n.d.

By 2010, North Korea's estimates of the damage had grown several times larger: "The atrocities committed by the U.S. imperialists on the ground and in the sea and air resulted in destroying 50,941 buildings of industrial establishments, 28,632 school buildings at all levels, 4,534 public health buildings including hospitals and clinics, 579 scientific research institutions, 8,163 printing and cultural institutions and 2,077,226 dwelling houses, 7,491 churches, chapels, cathedrals and other buildings for religious services disappeared ("KCNA on Tremendous Damage…," 2010). This same article lists many other categories of damage, including that "40,755,640 volumes of ancient and old books, documents and data including ancient books listed as national treasures more valuable than billions of dollars were burnt or plundered." (The North Korean article supplies no information about how any of these figures were compiled, but by every account North Korea suffered tremendous damage.)

31. Thomas, 2005: 142.

32. Thomas, 2005:147.

33. Goodwin, 2009.

34. Warren, 1999.

35. Warren, 1999; Goodwin, 2009: 3.

36. Warren, 1970. I am indebted to Michael T. Gilbert for sending me a copy of this editorial.

37. See Chapter 3. According to Ronin Ro, publisher Martin Goodman's war comics proved to be a commercial miscalculation since the comic books that Stan Lee edited about this unpopular war did not sell as well as expected (Ro, 2004: 49–50).

38. Joseph Witek cites "comics-history anecdotes" to explain that Charlton comics' notorious "indifference to quality control" was possible because they published comics to keep their presses running and they sold them through tie-in arrangements with their newsstand magazines (Witek, 2016: 40).

39. Wildman, 1973.

40. Broughton, 1990: 1. Craig Yoe has edited an anthology of Charlton's anti-war comic book stories, stories which he justly refers to as "virtually unknown" and "one of the field's best kept secrets." Of the 33 "anti-war" Charlton comic book stories collected in *The Unknown Anti-war Comics,* 29 had appeared in the science fiction and fantasy titles. These stories were published between 1955 and 1967, and typically deal with the threat of extinction posed by nuclear weapons. The four stories which had appeared in war comics were from the two-issue series *Never Again,* and the only mention of the Korean War in this collection supported the U.S. involvement in that conflict excitedly. Navy "Career Man" "Hutch" Hutchinson explains to "a bunch of boys" (sailors in uniform) that "We showed the Germans we wouldn't stand still for any conquering armies back in 1918 … and we showed 'em again in World War II! We been fighting the Cold War with the Russians, an' what with the Berlin Airlift an' all they know we aren't backing' down … an' best of all, we showed 'em in Korea that we're ready to fight, an' fight hard when we have to!" Hutch believes that thanks to nuclear weapons, no one would be crazy enough to start another war, but then an officer interrupts Hutch's story to order all men to report to the ship to sail to battle stations in the "Formosa Strait." (The story was published around the time of the 1954–1955 Taiwan Strait crisis.) "Career Man" qualifies as a mildly "anti-war" story only because of its weak conclusion that "all any of us can do is pray that old Hutch Hutchinson's theory [basically John Foster Dulles' policy of "massive retaliation"] is right!" (Yoe, 2018: 8).

41. In my article "The Politics of Underground Comix and the Environmental Crisis," I argue that "Judging from the evidence in underground comix, a sense that mainstream society was rocketing forward on a fundamentally suicidal, insane trajectory toward world destruction, created a rationale for 'dropping out' more fundamental than the war in Vietnam. Early observers noticed the important role of anxiety over nuclear annihilation in bringing the counterculture together" (Rifas, 2019).

42. Moore, n.d.

43. Underground comix never died, but slowed down dramatically. In 1980, Jay Kinney and Paul Mavrides created a comically unlikely story that humorously matched Kim Il-sung (leader of North Korea from its founding in 1948 until his death in 1994) and Betty [*sic*] Page (a beloved pin-up and fetish model from 1950 to 1957). The story did not see print until a decade later in the 20th anniversary issue of an irregularly published series Kinney had co-founded, *Young Lust #7* (1990).

44. *G.I. Combat #254*, DC Comics, June, 1983. This "special" issue on "The 4 Faces of War!" includes stories on World War II, Korea, Vietnam, and World War I.

45. Kanigher's explanation for this story seems to be that when he proposed to write his long-promised story about his characters dying at the end of World War II, he was denied permission to do it:

When Dick Giordano [DC comics' vice president/executive editor] turned thumbs down on my idea, I had already left my desk. I was no longer an editor. He knew nothing about story. He was an illustrator, an inker. [...] So I wrote "Sons of Easy" (ed. note, *Sgt. Rock* #417, #418). I anaesthetized my conscience. I allowed Rock and Easy to survive World War II. Serve time policing West Berlin. Return home. Serve in Korea. Retire—too old to fight in The Name [sic.] But their sons and daughters weren't. And I used them as surrogates. [...] The sons and daughters of the vets of Easy were doubles who fought and died to the last. But stand-ins aren't the originals [Kanigher, 1994–95: 2–3; unpaginated].

Not only is Sgt. Rock's son a mere surrogate, but his death in Vietnam turns out to be just a "real bad" dream.

46. Pekar launched his self-published *American Splendor* a few years after the underground comix scene had collapsed. He explained his decision to self-publish: "At that time [1976], the counterculture which had supported alternative comics was dying out. A lot of these middle-class kids who were part of the counterculture—as soon as they found out they weren't going to get drafted—they just went on and became 'straight' again. As a result, the alternative comics just didn't have much of an audience anymore. It was becoming difficult for me to get my stories published, so I thought 'What the hell?' You Know?" (Pekar and Brabner, 1993: 131).

47. Meiser, 2013.

48. Pekar and Brabner, 1993: 137–139. *Real War Stories* contributor Alan Moore's extraordinary successes in mainstream comics helped revolutionize the industry in the late 1980s (especially with his highly-acclaimed series *Watchmen*, from 1986 to 1987), but not into someplace where he was willing to stay. In 2010, he told an interviewer that he would ultimately like to achieve "A healthier culture and a culture that is more engaged with reality, in the real world, where there are no superheroes, [...] I think that we should stop projecting into these escapist fantasies. I think we should stop thinking about marvelous possibilities for life on other worlds and should actually focus upon human life on this world." Because he has "so many unpleasant memories connected with the comics industry," Moore said he will not further attempt to achieve his visions through channels where he would only expect "to feel unhappy, cheated, and abused" (Martin, N., 2010).

49. Andreas, 2004 (http://www.addictedtowar.com/book.html).

50. Andreas, 2004: "Publisher's Note."

51. Andreas, 2004: 13.

52. Schaef makes this argument, without directly naming militarism, in *When Society Becomes an Addict* (Schaef, 1987).

53. One of the witnesses who had testified to that Commission, former South Korean prison-guard Lee Joon-Young, remembered that "Ten prisoners were carried to a trench at a time and were made to kneel at the edge. [South Korean] Police officers stepped up

behind them, pointed their rifles at the back of their heads and fired" (Choe, 2009).

54. Bagge, 2008.

55. Korea also appears fleetingly in one less crucial panel when the main character repeats that "the Koreans" had been responsible.

56. "Beginnings," a three-page autobiographical comic by phenomenally popular, graphic novelist Raina Telgemeier, describes her life-changing experience of reading *Barefoot Gen* at the age of nine. "Beginnings" stands as a moving testimony to the impact that an anti-war comic can have, and also as a reminder of how rarely children encounter an anti-war message of comparable power (Telgemeier, 2015).

57. Nakazawa, 2009.

58. Although Nakazawa's *Barefoot Gen* has rightly attracted much positive attention from comics scholars, most readers stop with Volume One of his story, which takes things through the dropping of the Bomb on Hiroshima. The Eighth Volume with his commentary on the Korean War attracted little notice when Last Gasp republished it in the United States in 2009 in a print run of 2,500 copies. I thank publisher Colin Turner of Last Gasp for sharing this statistic, but mostly for republishing this entire series in English for the first time.

59. Delisle, 2005.

60. In 1956, some leaders of North Korea's ruling Workers Party of Korea, with support from the Soviet Union and from China, attempted to remove Kim Il-sung from power. (This was called the "August Faction Incident.") Kim's opponents were arrested, purged or executed, and by 1961 the only surviving political faction in North Korea was composed of those who remained loyal to Kim Il-sung.

61. This unbelievable atrocity is reminiscent of an incident that appeared in the report of an international delegation of lawyers who visited North Korea in March, 1952 to investigate war crimes:

On the very day American troops entered the locality Wuol San Ri of the Cho Ri Region, Sinchen Myen—they committed a particularly horrible murder against the Woo Mai Che family. ... The Americans pierced a wire through the hands, ears and nose of the witness' husband. On his forehead they fastened with a nail, a diploma for work found in the room and tortured him until he died. 11 children of the family Woo Mai Che ranging from 5 till 25 years of age were shot on the spot. Woo Mai Che's daughter-in-law seeing the American soldiers torturing her father-in-law tried to defend him. The Americans attached her by her hair to a tree, cut off her breasts, put a wooden club in her vagina, poured fuel-oil on it and set fire to it. They then poured oil over her and burned her alive. About 20 American soldiers took part in this murder [Commission of International..., 1952: 18–19].

62. The accuracy of Delisle's description of the Sinchon Museum of American War Atrocities (Massacre) North Korea can be judged by comparing it to webposted photographs of a tour taken by Ray Cun-

ningham and listening to a 41:55-minute web-posted recording of this museum tour from 2009. Delisle's Graphic Novel holds up well as a convincing report of this propaganda tour (Ray Cunningham, 2010).

The Sinchon Museum of American War Atrocities was renovated in 2016. Jean H. Lee reports that "The simple building on a grassy knoll was replaced by a palatial museum that is a veritable house of horrors, with room after room graphically bringing to life the gruesome atrocities attributed to the Americans." North Korean schoolchildren visit this museum on field trips (Lee, 2017). Travis Jeppesen argues that the new Sinchon Museum of American War Atrocities misrepresents a wartime period in which right-wing Korean Christians and Korean Communists had committed massacres against each other as "an imaginary battle" between "innocent-hearted Korean civilians" and "the heartless American bastard imperialists." By appealing entirely to emotion, this "fake historical museum" demonstrates "one of the key tactics that the system uses to infantilize its populace, teaching them to *feel* rather than *think*, where the only guiding principle is this primitive notion of *good* and *evil*. The same primitive notions that certain Western politicians like to promote when propagandizing against North Korea ('the axis of evil')" (Jeppesen, 2018: 139–146, 156–161).

63. Delisle, 2014. North Korea had condemned Sony Pictures' Seth Rogen film *The Interview* (2014) as tantamount to "an act of war," and threatened that its release would result in "a decisive and merciless countermeasure." During its final editing, that film had received advice from the State Department, RAND corporation and (according to its director) the CIA. Bruce W. Bennett, the main defense researcher advising the filmmakers, hoped that *The Interview,* when smuggled into North Korea, might spark a coup against Kim Jong-un by North Korean elites who would be willing to accept a place in a U.S-friendly unified Korea under South Korean control (Shorrock, 2017).

64. "Nogeun-ri tragedy retold in cartoon book," 2006.

65. Choi, 2008: 368, 385; D. Martin, 2014.

66. For background on educational comics, see Rifas, 2010.

67. Hite and Hendrix, 2009.

68. Rhie's series of educational graphic novels about the histories and cultures of European nations that he had visited had a "groundbreaking" importance in the history of Korean educational cartooning. They attracted the attention of children, adults and the Korean media when they began appearing in 1987, and led to educational comics being sold in bookstores (Lim, 2011: 43; Lim, 2012: 37–38).

69. In March, 2007, Rabbi Abraham Cooper of the Simon Wiesenthal Center went to Seoul to meet with cartoonist Rhie Won-bok and his publisher personally. Cooper protested to them that Rhie's educational comic about the United States included anti-Semitic statements reminiscent of the Nazi-era paper Der Stürmer's cartoons that had led to genocide. Cooper claimed to have won the publisher's promise to withdraw the book from circulation and make changes and to publish a Korean edition of the Simon Wiesenthal Center's book *Dismantling the Big Lie*. Rhie's book, unchanged, remained in circulation a year later (Mondello, 2007, 2008). *Dismantling the Big Lie* describes itself as "the only work to refute the *Protocols* [the classic anti-Semitic forgery *The Protocols of the Elder of Zion*] item by item" (Jacobs and Weitzman, 2003: xiii). To the claim of Jewish control of the media, *Dismantling the Big Lie* responds with staggeringly ineffectual arguments (Jacobs and Weitzman, 2003: 37–38, 79–81).

Will Eisner devoted his last graphic novel, *THE PLOT: The Secret Story of the Protocols of the Elders of Zion* (2005), to debunking this famous, persistent and pernicious hoax (Hagemeister, 2008: 95).

For a more valuable examination of the idea that "the Jews" control a major American mass medium, see Steven Alan Carr's *Hollywood & Anti-Semitism* (Carr, 2008).

70. An exception, has been Shigeru Mizuki's outstanding manga *Showa*. His chapter on the Korean War from a Japanese perspective appears in *Showa 1944–1953: A History of Japan* (Mizuki. 2014: 513–522).

71. Historian Wada Haruki writes that when the UN forces left North Korea: "A large number of refugees fled to South Korea by sea or overland on foot. Those evacuated by U.S. and ROK forces probably had worked for or cooperated with the U.S. occupiers in the North. Civilians who walked south had a range of motives, from antipathy to Communism and a desire to join family members in the South, to rumor-fed fear that the Americans would drop atomic bombs on the North. In the chaos, few families escaped together" (Wada, 2014:147).

72. "The Victory," *War Comics #4*, 1951.

73. *Two-Fisted Tales # 26*, 1952.

74. The archives of *Hetalia* can be found at http://www.hetarchive.net/. For discussion, see Miyake, 2013.

75. MOLD123's work, including "The Cold War Project," appeared on the DeviantART website, the 13th-largest online community at that time, a site devoted to sharing artwork. On average, each page of her comic was viewed over 23,000 times and accompanied by over 100 comments, many of which were the cartoonists' replies. (These figures were as of September 6, 2015, based on the statistics posted on the pages that carried MOLD123's pages.) The self-identified nationalities of those who posted these comments included Canadian, Croatian, Finnish, French, German, Hungarian, Iranian, Korean, Filipino, Polish, Russian and American.

76. At the peak of the UN Command's strength in the Korean War, France was represented by 1,119 combatants, or about 0.1 percent of the total (0.3 percent if not counting South Korea) (http://www.usfk.mil/About/UnitedNationsCommand.aspx).

77. McChesney, 2013: 218.

78. McChesney, 2013: 23–24. The Media Education Foundation's documentary *Digital Disconnect* (2018) summarizes McChesney's arguments very effectively.

Chapter 20

1. The word "victory" had appeared in the titles of a half-dozen comic book series during World War II, but in none of the titles of Korean War comic books. Unlike World War II comic books, which had personalized a fight to the finish to defeat Hitler, Mussolini and Tojo, in Korean War comic books, pictures of or references to the enemy leaders Kim Il-sung, Mao Zedong or Stalin were almost nonexistent.

2. The chapter on "Critics" provides examples. In 1955, a colorful speech about "Crime Comics" sadly asked in passing "what kind of dream of tomorrow … can [kids] afford other than to someday wear the military uniform?" (Higgins, 1955: 7).

3. Smith, 2012: 574–577.

4. NSC-68 was declassified in 1975 and is now web-posted.

5. NSC-68, 1950: 4.

6. McCullough, 1992: 335, 337–338; NSC-68, 1950: 60.

7. Casey, 2005: 14; Pierpaoli, 1999: 17, 26, 29–30.

8. NSC-68, 1950: 4.

9. John Lewis Gaddis discusses various ways that "American strategy in Korea was consistent with the spirit of NSC-68, even to the point of duplicating some of that document's contradictions" (Gaddis, 1982, 2005: 108, 87–124).

10. American policymakers of that time also achieved their larger goal: to establish a "liberal international order." This "order" involved building international institutions which would prevent repetitions of the nightmarish events of the recent past: the global economic depression of the 1930s, the spread of tyrannies, and the recent World War. For one expression of these goals, see the preamble of the United Nations, signed in 1945.

The new, multilateral institutions designed to liberalize trade and grow the world economy included the General Agreement on Tariffs and Trade (which evolved into the World Trade Organization), the International Monetary Fund, and the World Bank. In 1983, at the suggestion of Tim Shorrock, editor of the *Multinational Monitor* I drew a full-page cartoon that explained and criticized how the International Monetary Fund works (Rifas, 1983). I have already mentioned that I created a comics-format tabloid to protest the 1999 WTO meeting in Seattle (Rifas, 1999). I also distributed copies of a comic book against the World Bank (*The World Bank: A Tale of Power, Plunder, and Resistance*) that Alec Dubro and Mike Konopacki created in 1995.

11. Acheson, 1969, 1987: 374–375.

12. NSC-68, 1950: section IX, "The Role of Negotiation"; Gaddis, 1982, 2005:102–104.

13. In 1939, the U.S. had the world's 19th largest military (Selby, 2014).

14. Mills, 1956, 2000: 206, 212, 215, 216, 219–223, 298–305, 313.

Mills saw that the militarists, despite their distasteful message, had one clear advantage: "in all of pluralist America, there is no interest—there is no possible combination of interests—that has anywhere near the time, the money, the manpower, to present a point of view on the issues involved that can effectively compete with the views presented day in and day out by the warlords and by those who they employ "(Mills, 1956: 221).

Mills' only mention of comic books in *The Power Elite* was to quote approvingly from historian A.E. Bestor's 1953 book *Educational Wastelands* that we can tell that schools are doing their job properly when we will see "marked decline in such evidences of mental retardation as the incessant reading of comic books by adults" (Mills, 1956, 2000: 319).

15. For example, in 1956, Herbert A. Bloch and Frank T. Flynn dismissed Wertham's findings as "extreme views" which are not based on studies of "carefully drawn control groups, the *sine qua non* of any modern quantitative study of delinquency," but still urged that, while waiting for more definitive research findings, "the welfare of this nation's young makes it mandatory that all concerned unite in […] demanding adequate standards of decency and good taste" in comic books (Bloch and Flynn, 1956: 218–219). Even Josette Frank, the most public and persistent of the comic book industry's defenders, agreed that "whether damage can be proved or not, we do have community standards of ethical as well as aesthetic values. Savagery, brutality, and lewdness are clearly against public policy, and certainly have no place in what is offered to children" (Frank, 1955: 4).

Those who opposed violent, lurid, racist comic books saw them as self-evidently inappropriate for children. In 1954, C. Wright Mills' laudatory review of *Seduction of the Innocent* for the *New York Times* confidently asserted that: "Surely any careful reader of this book can only agree with Dr. Wertham when he says: 'Whenever I see a book like this in the hands of a little 7-year-old boy, his eyes glued to the printed page, I feel like a fool to have to prove that this kind of thing is not good mental nourishment for children!'" (Wertham had been referring to *Tegra Jungle Empress #1*, published by Fox in August, 1948.) Mills concluded: "It does not seem to me that 'further studies are needed' before action is taken against comic book manufacturers and purveyors, but further studies are needed" (Mills, 1954).

16. Kihss, 1954. In his testimony, Gaines clarified that "a cover in bad taste, for example, might be defined as holding the head a little higher so that the neck could be seen dripping blood from it, and moving the body over a little further so that the neck of the body could be seen to be bloody." Gaines actually *had* edited this infamous comic book cover, which Johnny Craig had drawn after an argument with his wife, to eliminate the bleeding neck as too gory for publication (Krassner, 2012: 32).

17. Nyberg, 1998: 113, 167. "Decency" referred especially to sexual modesty. In the Comics Code's first months, over a fourth of the thousands of changes that the code's administrator required involved redrawing heroines with "less obvious curves and more obvious clothes" ("The Press," 1955: 38).

18. United States Congress, Juvenile Delinquency (Obscene and Pornographic Materials)…, 1955: 40;

Obscene and Pornographic Literature…, 1956: 1–2; Strub, 2010: 21–22, 41–42. Kefauver's Interim Report on pornography in 1956 mentioned the notorious series "Nights of Horror," which had pictured "many forms of whipping, beating, bondage, and similar perverted acts" and which "a juvenile thrill slayer in Brooklyn, N.Y." had credited as the source of "all of his ideas for torturing and killing an elderly man" ("Obscene and Pornographic Literature…, 1956": 39). These "Nights of Horror" pornographic booklets were anonymously illustrated by Joe Shuster, the first Superman artist, who had fallen into despair after he and his partner Jerry Siegel had lost a lawsuit over the ownership of their character and DC had cut them off from any further work; his art style fell out of fashion; he went nearly blind; he went broke; and the comic book industry collapsed. The "juvenile thrill slayer" who had taken inspiration from "Nights of Horror," horror comic fan Jack Koslow, led the "Brooklyn Thrill Killers," a so-called "gang" of four Jewish boys (Yoe, 2009: 16–17, 23–27; Adin, 2014: 72; Mannes, 1955: 24–25; Hendrickson and Cook, 1956: 193–194).

19. Restrictions Upon Comic Books, 1956: 12–13, 17–19.

20. Wertham, 1953, 1954: 95–96.

In Hitler's Obersalzberg Speech of August 22, 1939 (which has been reconstructed from the notes of his generals), he said: "Be hard, be without mercy, act more quickly and brutally than the others. The citizens of Western Europe must tremble with horror. That is the most human way of conducting a war. For it scares the others off "(Halsall, 1998).

21. One chapter of *Seduction of the Innocent,* for example, focused on ads in comic books. He had a special concern about ads for weapons, and was quoted in one newspaper article as saying: "Look around and see how many young children carry guns and weapons. 'That's just good clean fun,' say the adults. But they make enormous profits from supplying these weapons and from fascinating children with mass media showing their use in earnest. […] Children and teenagers have to expend so much energy not to fall for the temptations and seductions we bombard them with! It is no wonder that some of them adjust too well to our crime-comic-book culture" (Granik, 1954). Wertham testified to the investigating Senators, however, that "I want to add to this that my theory of temptation and seduction as I told you, is very, very vague."

22. Wertham, 1953, 1954: 395.

23. Wertham, 1966. In *A Sign for Cain*, Wertham focused on three of the "social evils" that lead to violence: fascism, colonialism, and race prejudice (Wertham, 1966). Wertham had also expressed concern about the media's contribution to militarism (through stirring up feelings against Russia) in 1947, as the Cold War was beginning (Wertham, 1947 "War OR Peace,": 39).

24. Wertham, 1953. 1954: (trash) 22, 108, 239–240, 299, 355 (cheap junk): 267 (rubbish): 276 (offal) 282 (tripe) 292 (ugly) 90, 168 (inartistically-drawn) 36, 267 (gutter muck) 260, 276 (hack-work filth) 278.

25. I thank Carol Tilley for sending me copies of this correspondence, which she found (in Box 125, Folder 2) while doing archival research in Wertham's papers at the Library of Congress (Tilley, July 29, 2017; e-mail to author).

26. Wertham had said of *Seduction of the Innocent,* "There has been an organized effort to eliminate the book. The distributors completely prevented the publication of SoTI in paperback. They simply won't distribute the book" (Bethke, 1989: 37). In my letter to Wertham, I compared the comic book publishers sending detectives around to find information to discredit him to General Motors' response to their main critic Ralph Nader, which had prompted Nader to sue for invasion of privacy. I compared the book distributors' alleged conspiracy to suppress *Seduction of the Innocent* in 1954 to the film distributors' suppression of *Salt of the Earth* that same year, which had prompted "Hollywood Ten" member Herbert Biberman to file an unsuccessful antitrust suit.

27. Wertham, 1978: 40.

28. Wertham's letter of March 4, 1979 appeared as an illustration in the *Comics Journal* interview of me (Rifas, 1984: 98). Presumably his reservations about the value of *Barefoot Gen* were a response, at least in part, to the ultra-violent scene where Gen Nakaoka, the young hero of the story, bites off the fingertips of his rival, the Town Chairman's son.

The edition of *Barefoot Gen* that he saw had been published in book format by Project Gen in April, 1978. I was so wedded to comic book format, that I republished a story that had already appeared in English translation.

29. *Corporate CRIME Comics* ended after two issues. In 1984, publisher Denis Kitchen explained to interviewer Dale Luciano that: "I could not afford the extra costs of editing the book. Leonard was willing to work cheap, but even then the book consumed an enormous amount of research time … the bottom line was that sales [of 10–20,000 copies per issue] did not justify the labor to the end product required." Also, Denis "became quite concerned" when he realized that being factually accurate and without malice did not eliminate the possibility that "a corporate entity that wanted to get us could easily have papered us to death in the legal sense" (Kitchen, 1984: 107).

30. The documentary *Diagram for Delinquents* begins with footage of Wertham's appearance on William F. Buckley's television show (June 20, 1968) in which Wertham says "I think one has to have the goal and the belief … that eventually human violence can be completely abolished" (0:06–0:18).

31. In recent years, the story of the "anti-comic book crusade" has been retold as part of a defense of shooter-based videogames, to make it sound as though in both cases the central issue involves uninformed critics making pseudo-scientific claims about violent entertainment causing violent behavior. The deeper issues involve the teaching of militarist values and the blunting of empathy and imagination. In the documentary *Joystick Warriors*, narrator Sut Jhally ends with a long argument that closely resembles Wertham's arguments about crime comic books and concludes: "Videogames don't create violent people, what they do is glorify a violent culture, and shut down our capacity as a society to imagine anything

different. They short-circuit our ability to think in more productive ways about the real violence in our lives—that is their real tragedy" (Sorkin, 2013).

32. "Crime Comics and the Constitution," 1955; Restrictions Upon Comic Books, 1956.

33. In April, 1954 EC comics publisher William Gaines invited the other comic book publishers to a meeting to discuss sponsoring research which he expected would vindicate comic books as harmless. The other publishers proposed a comics code, and created the Comics Magazine Association of America (CMAA) to administer it (Nyberg, 1998: 108–110). Gaines had serious disagreements with how the CMAA was run, and in August 1955, EC's business manager Lyle Stuart wrote a letter to the general counsel of the Senate Subcommittee that had investigated comic books in which he asked them to investigate the CMAA as a "monopolistic instrument" which was working to drive small publishers out of the business (Nyberg, 1998: 122).

34. Wertham opposed the Comics Code, arguing instead for separate distribution for adult material. When the underground comix movement rose up in the late 1960s, some of its cartoonists demonstrated their own opposition to the Comics Code by creating works that were as violent and indecent as they could imagine. Wertham recognized that these "comix" were being distributed through different channels than children's comic books, and commented that: "They represent a reaction—or rather an overreaction—to the above ground comic books and to our mass media in general. Such overreaction is all too understandable in a society like the one in which we live at present" (Wertham, 1973: 60–61).

35. On the 2020 Reporters Without Borders list, North Korea ranked 180 out of 180 nations. South Korea ranked 42. The United States ranked 45. (Reporters Without Borders, 2020).

36. North Korea's official "White Paper on the Human Rights Violations in the U.S. in 2017" sloppily attempts to reverse the accusations of human rights violations. It portrays the United States as "an A-class human rights violator" in which "the absolute majority of the working masses, deprived of elementary rights to survival, are hovering in the abyss of nightmare." The report charges that in the U.S., "genuine freedom of the press and expression does not exist" as shown by such examples as President Trump tweeting "a video clip on Twitter, in which he, portrayed as a professional wrestler, threw his opponent marked with 'CNN' to the ground, making even the gangsters blush shame" ("White Paper…, 2018).

37. For an essay on how discussions of human rights in North Korea have functioned to rationalize policies aimed at "regime change" in North Korea, see Christine Hong's "Manufacturing Dissidence" (Hong, 2015) Arguably, regime change in North Korea could be a counterproductive way to improve the human rights situation there (Beal, 2005: 129–166).

38. For a feeling of life in North Korea's totalitarian society, I have already cited Guy Delisle and Travis Jeppesen. *Dear Leader*, written under the name "Jang Jin-Sung" by a North Korean propaganda nov-

elist who defected, tells a moving story (Jang, 2014). I also recommend Suki Kim's *Without You There Is No Us* (Kim, 2015) and Daniel Tudor's *Ask a North Korean* (Tudor, 2017). (I have never visited North Korea personally.)

39. American democracy also had seemed especially fragile in the 1930s (Lepore, 2020).

In 1947, Fredric Wertham publicly expressed his strong agreement with an author who had boldly warned that "there is little in America today which could prevent the establishment of a Nazi-like state" (Wertham, "A Psychiatrist Examines…" 1947).

40. *Can It Happen Here? Authoritarianism in America,* edited by Cass R. Sunstein, helps us think more clearly about undesirable political possibilities. I read it as a reminder of how little the military can do to defend against the realistic threats to democracy and freedom in the United States (Sunstein, 2018). The list of threats that I presented, though, was not taken from that book.

41. *The Bulletin of the Atomic Scientists* has used its iconic "doomsday clock" since 1947 to mark many changes in the level of danger regarding nuclear war. In 2020, the clock stood at "100 seconds to midnight," a level "more dangerous than it has ever been, even at the height of the Cold War." The *Bulletin* warned that "Civilization-ending nuclear war—whether started by design, blunder, or simple miscommunication—is a genuine possibility. Climate change that could devastate the planet is undeniably happening. And for a variety of reasons that include a corrupted and manipulated media environment, democratic governments and other institutions that should be working to address these threats have failed to rise to the challenge." As in 2019, the Bulletin warned that "information warfare" has created a dangerous situation in which fact is becoming indistinguishable from fiction (*Bulletin of the Atomic Scientists…*, 2020).

42. Jeff Cohen provides a compelling introduction to the issue of cable news networks' marginalizing left of center and anti-war views in his autobiographical account of his experiences with CNN, Fox News, and MSNBC (Cohen, 2006). The media criticism organization Cohen founded, FAIR, has a site at https://fair.org.

For news commentary from an anti-militarist perspective, I rely on several sources including Tom Engelhardt's TomDispatch blog (https://www.tomdispatch.com) and The American Conservative (https://www.theamericanconservative.com).

43. Green, 2005: 18. (I added the part "or government," which other parts of the book bring out more clearly.)

44. Word Hippo, "What is the Opposite of Violent?," https://www.wordhippo.com/what-is/the-opposite-of/violent.html; Thesaurus.com, "Antonyms for violent," https://www.thesaurus.com/browse/violent; Power Thesaurus, "violent, antonyms-opposite meaning-200," https://www.powerthesaurus.org/violent/antonyms; Merriam-Webster, "antonyms for violent," https://www.merriam-webster.com/thesaurus/violent.

45. Wertham, 1966: 50.

Bibliography

Multiple sources by the same author are listed chronologically.

(A) Books, Articles, Theses, Dissertations, Editorials, Letters to Editors, and Graphic Novels, (B) Comic Book Series and Comic Book Stories, (C) Films and Videos, (D) Hearings and Government Documents

(A) *Books, Articles, Theses, Dissertations, Editorials, Letters to Editors, and Graphic Novels*

"100 Comic Books Sent to Cowgill for Ruling," *San Mateo Times*, 6 Nov. 1948: 1–2.

Acheson, Dean. *Present at the Creation: My Years in the State Department*. New York: W.W. Norton, 1969, 1987.

Achkasov, V.I. and E.M. Iur'ev. "China's War of National Liberation and the Defeat of Imperialist Japan: The Soviet Role," *Soviet Studies in History*, vol. 24, no. 3, 1985: 39–68.

Adams, John G. *Without Precedent: The Story of the Death of McCarthyism*. New York: W.W. Norton & Co., 1983.

Adcock, John. "Wings Winfair and Gulf Funny Weekly," *Yesterday's Papers*, 16 June 2014, http://john-adcock.blogspot.com/2014/06/wings-winfair-and-gulf-funny-weekly.html.

Adeto, Yonas Adaye. "Africa in the Global Security Governance: A Critical Analysis of Ethiopia's Role in the UN Peacekeeping Operations," *International Relations and Diplomacy*, vol. 6, no. 7, July 2018: 369–380.

Adin, Mariah. *The Brooklyn Thrill-Kill Gang and the Great Comic Book Scare of the 1950s*. New York: Praeger, 2014.

"Advertising News," *The New York Times*, 9 June 1951: 28.

AFI Catalog of Feature Films, "*The Whip Hand*," n.d. https://catalog.afi.com/Catalog/moviedetails/50369.

Akers, Joshua K., "Limited War, Limited Enthusiasm: Sexuality. Disillusionment, Survival, and the Changing Landscape of War Culture in Korean War-era Comic Books and Soldier Iconography," MA thesis, History, James Madison University, 2013.

Alaniz, Jose. *Komiks: Comic Art in Russia*. Jackson: The University Press of Mississippi, 2010.

Allen, Wendy. Nuclear Reactors for Generating Electricity: U.S. Development from 1946 to 1963, Rand (R-2116-NSF), June 1977.

Allwood, Martin S. *The Impact of the Comics on a European Country*. The Institute of Social Research, 1956.

Alperovitz, Gar. *The Decision to Use the Atomic Bomb*. Vintage Books, 1995, 1996.

"Americanization Would Mean the End of Europe," "Parole 22: Amerikanisierung wäre das Ende Europas!," *Sprechabenddienst*, Sept./Oct. 1944. Webposted by Randall Bytwerk, 1998, at the German Propaganda Archive. https://research.calvin.edu/german-propaganda-archive/sprech44d.htm.

Andrae, Thomas. "The History and Historicity of Superman" (excerpted from *Discourse No.2*, Summer, 1980,) *American Media and Mass Culture: Left Perspectives*, University of California Press, 1987: 124–138.

Andreas, Joel. *Addicted to War: Why the U.S. Can't Kick Militarism*. AK Press, 2004, http://www.addictedtowar.com/.

Apeldoorn, Ger, guest blogger at Ken Quattro's The Comics Detective, 7 March 2010, http://thecomicsdetective.blogspot.com/2010/03/hank-chapman.html.

Apeldoorn, Ger. "War Is Hell (but necessary)," parts 1–20, 2015. http://allthingsger.blogspot.ca/.

Applebaum, Anne. *Iron Curtain: The Crushing of Eastern Europe, 1944–1956*. New York: Doubleday, 2012.

Archer, Jules. *The Plot to Seize the White House*. New York: Skyhorse Publishing Inc., 1973, 2007.

Armagideon Time. "Apples and Cabbages" [Review of *Johnny Everyman*] 8 Feb 2012, http://www.armagideon-time.com/?p=6827.

"Armed Forces: Barbarity." *Time* Magazine, vol. 62, no, 19, 9 Nov. 1953: 23.

Armstrong, Charles K. "The Cultural Cold War in Korea, 1945–1950," *The Journal of Asian Studies*, vol. 62, no. 1, Feb. 2003: 71–99.

Armstrong, Charles K. *The North Korean Revolution, 1945 –1950*. Ithaca: Cornell University Press, 2003.

Armstrong, Charles K. *Tyranny of the Weak: North Korea and the World, 1950–1992*. Ithaca: Cornell University Press, 2013.

"Army School Gives 24 Lingual Courses: Presidio Turns Out Graduates Up to Colonels with Fluency in Russian to Japanese," *New York Times*, 16 July 1951: 18.

Arne, Ingrid. "How to Deal with Sordid Comics Is National Problem," *Meriden Record*, 11 Oct. 1954: 4.

Asmolov, Konstantin. "Victory in the Far East," in *The Great War* (Bing automatic translation), 2008, http://militera.lib.ru/research/pyhalov_dukov/07.html.

"Assassin Squeals After 43 Years," *Newsreview* (Seoul), 18 April 1992: 6–7.

Astore, William. "'Our American Heroes': Why It's Wrong to Equate Military Service with Heroism," 22 July 2010, TomDispatch.com.

Astore, William J. "Dominating the Skies—and Losing the Wars: Air Supremacy Isn't What It Used to Be," 21 June 2016, TomDispatch.com.

Aswell, Mary Louise. *The World Within*. San Francisco: Whittlesey House, 1947.

"Atherton General Honored as Hero in War in Korea," *San Mateo Times*, 9 May, 1951, 1:1,2.

Atwell, Jared. "The Work of a Super-Patriot: Allen Zoll and the National Council for American Education," BA Thesis, University of North Carolina at Asheville, Department of History, Nov. 2003.

Aydin, Andrew. "The Comic Book That Changed the World," *Creative Loafing Atlanta*: 1 Aug. 2013, https://creativeloafing.com/content-185638-Cover-Story:-The-comic-book-that-changed-the-world.

Bachelder, Stephen, "Social Ills and Social Change as Revealed and Fostered by Current Comics," Social Ethics, Professor Liston Pope, Yale Divinity School (undated, but references stop in April, 1942).

Bacon, Jeff. "Beetle Bailey at 60: Iconic Comic, and Its Creator, Still Going Strong," special to *Military Times*, 9 Sept. 2010, http://www.marinecorpstimes.com/news/2010/09/offduty-beetle-bailey-at-60-comic-creator-still-going-strong-091310w/.

Báez, Fernando. *A Universal History of the Destruction of Books: From Ancient Sumer to Modern Iraq*. New York: Atlas & Co., 2008.

Bagge, Peter. *Apocalypse Nerd*. New York: Dark Horse Books, 2008.

Bahrampour, Ali. "Mort Walker, Whose 'Beetle Bailey' Was a Comic-Page Staple for Decades, Dies at 94," *The Washington Post*, 27 Jan. 2018.

Bails, Jerry. *Who's Who of American Comic Books, 1928–1999*. Last updated October 18, 2006. http://bailsprojects.com/whoswho.aspx.

Bakan, Joel. *Childhood Under Siege: How Big Business Targets Children*. New York: Free Press, 2011.

Baker, George, Sgt. "The Real Sad Sack," *The New York Times*, 9 July 1944: SM16.

Baker, Kenneth. *George Washington's War: In Caricature and Print*. Grub Street Publishing, 2009.

Baker, Matt. *The Lost Art of Matt Baker, Vol. 1: The Complete Canteen Kate*. Picture This Press, 2013.

Banning, Margaret Culkin. "Filth on the Newsstand," *Reader's Digest*, Oct. 1952: 115–119.

"Barbarity." *Time* Magazine, vol. 62, no, 19, 9 Nov. 1953.

Barbu, Bogdan. "Hollywood Movies, American Music and Cultural Policies Behind the Iron Curtain. Case Study: Cold War Romania, 1945–1971." *Crossing Boundaries: From Syria to Slovakia*, S. Jakelic and J. Varsoke, eds., IWM Junior Visiting Fellows Conferences (Vienna), vol. 14, 2003.

Barclay, Dorothy. "That Comic Book Question," *The New York Times*, 20 March, 1955: SM48.

Barenblatt, Daniel. *Plague Upon Humanity: The Hidden History of Japan's Biological Warfare Program*. New York: HarperCollins, 2004.

Barli, Jonathan. *The Gaze of Drifting Skies: A Treasury of Bird's-eye View Cartoons*. Seattle: Fantagraphics, 2016.

Barnes, Luke. "The book that lies at the heart of white nationalist violence," ThinkProgress, 12 Oct. 2017.

Barker, Martin. *A Haunt of Fears*, Verso Books, 1984. (Republished as *A Haunt of Fears: The Strange History of the British Horror Comics Campaign*. New York: Pluto Press, 1992.)

Barker, Martin. *Comics: Ideology, Power, and the Critics*. Manchester University Press, 1989.

Barkin, Steve M. "Fighting the Cartoon War: Information Strategies in World War II," *Journal of American Culture*, vol. 7, no. 1/2, spring/summer 1984: 113–117.

Barrett, Edward W. *Truth Is Our Weapon*. New York: Funk and Wagnall Company, 1953.

Barry, Les. "Newspapers Lead Fight on 'Comics,'" *Burlington Daily News* (Burlington, VT), 21 June 1954: 10.

Barry, Mark P. "The U.S. and the 1945 Division of Korea: Mismanaging the 'Big Decisions,'" *International Journal on World Peace*, vol. 29, no. 4, Dec. 2012: 37–59.

Barsalou, David. "Deconstructing Roy Lichtenstein," n.d., https://www.flickr.com/photos/deconstructing-roy-lichtenstein/.

Basinger, Jeanine. *The World War II Combat Film: Anatomy of a Genre*. New York: Columbia University Press, 1986.

Bassett Francis J. "Comic Books for Germany: Protest Voiced Over Giving Wrong Concept of Our Democracy," *The New York Times*, 11 Nov. 1948: 26.

Bayeux Tapestry. "High Quality Panoramic Image, Bibliotheca Augustana," n.d., http://www.hs-augsburg.de/~harsch/Chronologia/Lspost11/Bayeux/bay_tama.html.

Beal, Tim. *North Korea: The Struggle Against American Power*. New York: Pluto Press, 2005.

Beal, Tim. "The Korean Peninsula Within the Framework of US Global Hegemony," *The Asia-Pacific Journal: Japan Focus*, vol. 14, no. 1, 15 Nov 2016: 1–37.

Beaty, Bart. "Roy Lichtenstein's Tears: Art vs. Pop in American Culture," *Canadian Review of American Studies*, vol. 34, no. 3, 2004: 249–286.

Beaty, Bart. *Fredric Wertham and the Critique of Mass Culture*. Jackson: University Press of Mississippi, 2005.

Beaty, Bart H. "All Our Innocences: Fredric Wertham, Mass Culture, and the Rise of the Media Effects Paradigm, 1940–1972," PhD diss., Communications, McGill University, 1999.

Beauchamp, Gorman. *Jack London (Starmont Reader's Guide 15)*. London: Starmont House, Inc., 1984.

Beck, C.C. Interview, *The Comics Journal #110*, Aug. 1986.

Beder, Sharon. "The Role of 'Economic Education' in Achieving Capitalist Hegemony," University of Wollongong, Research Online, 2006.

"The Beginnings of a New Era for African-Americans in the Armed Forces," n.d., http://www.nj.gov/military/korea/factsheets/afroamer.html.

Bell, Blake. *"I Have to Live with This Guy."* Raleigh, NC: TwoMorrows Publishing, 2002.

Bell, Blake, and Dr. Michael J. Vassallo. *The Secret History of Marvel Comics: Jack Kirby and the Moonlighting Artists at Martin Goodman's Empire*. Seattle: Fantagraphics, 2013.

Bell, John. *Invaders from the North: How Canada Conquered the Comic Book Universe*. Toronto: Dundurn, 2006.

Bell, John, and Michel Viau. "Beyond the Funnies: The History of Comics in English Canada and Quebec," (Archived.) http://www.collectionscanada.ca/comics/027002-8400-e.html, 2002.

Bellesiles, Michael A. *A People's History of the U.S. Military: Ordinary Soldiers Reflect on Their Experience of War, from the American Revolution to Afghanistan*. New York: The New Press, 2012.

Benice, Ali. "100 Years of Blossoming: A Generic History of Comics in Turkey," *ImageText*, vol.10, no. 1, 2018.

Bennett, Steve. "Confessions of a Comic Book Guy—That's Just the Way Things Were," 12 Aug. 2009 (posted at ICv2.com).

Benson, John. "Is War Hell? The Evolution of an Artist's Viewpoint," *Panels* no. 2, by John Benson, ed. and publisher, Spring 1981: 18–20.

Benson, Robert Louis, and Michael Warner. *Venona: Soviet Espionage and the American Response 1939–1957*, National Security Agency, Central Intelligence Agency, 1996.

Benton, John. *Comic Art in America: An Illustrated History*. New York: Taylor Publishing Company, 1989.

Berelson, B. (Bernard), and P. (Patricia) Salter. "Writer's War Board Study: Comic Books and Anti-Minority Prejudice," (Columbia University Rare Book and Manuscript Library), 28 Dec. 1944.

Berger, Henry W. "Senator Robert A. Taft Dissents from Military Escalation," in *Cold War Critics: Alternatives to American Foreign Policy in the Truman Years*, Thomas G. Paterson, ed. New York: Quadrangle, 1971.

Berkner, Lloyd V. "An Address to the Annual Dinner of the American Geographical Society," January 20, Plaza Hotel, New York. Published in *The Next Ten Years in Space, 1959–1969. Staff Report of the Select Committee on Astronautics and Space Exploration*, 86th Cong., 1st sess, House Document No. 115, Washington, D.C., USGPO, 1959: 21–28.

Berlatsky, Noah. "Was Superman Jewish? Martin Lund on Anti-Nazi Superheroes and Interventionist Comics," *Literary Hub*, lithub.com, 22 Nov. 2016.

Berman, Mark. "A Hero's Long Journey to Arlington; For Family, Burial Ends an 'Injustice,'" *The Washington Post,* 13 Nov. 2008: B-1.

Bernard, Warren. "Warren Bernard's Citations and Fredric Wertham Documents," 6 Feb. 2013, http://www.tcj.com/warren-bernard-1954/.

Bernard, Warren. *Cartoons for Victory*. San Diego: Fantagraphics, 2015.

Bernstein, Barton J. "New Light on the Korean War," *The International History Review*, vol. 3, no. 2, April 1981: 256–277.

Berry, David, and John Theobald, eds. *Radical Mass Media Criticism: A Cultural Genealogy*. London: Black Rose Books, 2006.

Berthelsen, John. "When the Comics Kept Us Safe," *The Sacramento Bee* (Sacramento, CA), 29 Aug. 1971.

Bethke, Marilyn. "Conversation with Dr. Wertham," *Instant Gratification: The Magazine for Comic Book Fans Who Aren't Afraid to Grow Up*, no. 1, 1979: 36–37.

Bevin Alexander R. *Korea: The First War We Lost*. New York: Hippocrene Books, 1986.

Biderman, Albert D. "Communist Attempts to Elicit False Confessions from Air Force Prisoners of War." *Bulletin of the New York Academy of Medicine* vol. 33, no. 9, Sept. 1957: 616–625.

Biderman, Albert D. *March to Calumny: The Story of American POW's in the Korean War*. Chicago: MacMillan Company, 1963.

Bjork, Ulf Jonas. "American Infection: the Swedish Debate over Comic Books, 1952–1957," *International Journal of Comic Art*, vol. 19, no.1, Spring/Summer, 2017: 177–189.

Bloch, Herbert A., and Frank T. Flynn. *Delinquency: The Juvenile Offender in America Today*. New York: Random House, 1956.

Blum, William. *Killing Hope: U.S. Military and CIA Interventions Since World War II*. New York: Zed Books, 2003. Appendix III: U.S. Government Assassination Attempts," 2008, http://killinghope.org/bblum6/assass.htm.

Bolte, Charles G. "Security Through Book Burning." *Annals of the American Academy of Political and Social Science*, vol. 300, Internal Security and Civil Rights, July 1955: 87–93.

Boston Massacre Historical Society, n.d., http://www.bostonmassacre.net/gravure.htm.

"Boston Police Say Comic Book Contains Communist Propaganda: Told Youngster Read Volumes Which Urge Disobedience and Preach Atheism." *Lowell Sun* (MA), 19 April 1948: 15.

Bourret, Weston. "Uranium-bearing Pegmatites of the Antsirabe-Kitsamby District, Madagascar," *Ore Geology Reviews*, vol. 3, no. 1–3, April 1988: 177–191.

Bowers, William T., William M. Hammond and George L. McGarrigle. *Black Soldier, White Army: The 24th Infantry Regiment in Korea*. Washington, DC: Center of Military History United States Army, 1996.

Bowles, Chester. *Ambassador's Report*. New York: Harper & Brothers, 1954.

Boyle, Hal. "Comic Books, Novels, Golf Clubs Help Yanks Kill Boredom of Battle," *The Seattle Times* (Seattle, WA), 29 Aug 1950: 19.

Bradbury, William C., and Jeane J. Kirkpatrick. "Determinants of Loyalty and Disaffection in Chinese Communist Soldiers During the Korean Hostilities," in *Mass Behavior in Battle and Captivity: the Communist Soldier in the Korean War, Research Studies Directed by William C. Bradbury*. Samuel M. Meyers and Albert D. Biderman, eds. Chicago: University of Chicago Press, 1968.

Bradfield, Harriet A. "The Chain Publishers and Their Titles," in *Writer's Year Book: 1950 Edition*, Writer's Digest, 1950.

Brands, Henry W., Jr., "The Dwight D. Eisenhower Administration, Syngman Rhee, and the 'Other' Geneva Conference of 1954," *Pacific Historical Review*, vol. 56, no. 1, Feb. 1987: 59–85.

Brands, H.W. *The General vs. the President: MacArthur and Truman at the Brink of Nuclear War*. New York: Doubleday, 2016.

Breger, Dave. *But That's Unprintable*. New York: Bantam, 1955.

Brians, Paul. *Nuclear Holocausts: Atomic War in Fiction*. Kent, OH: Kent State University Press, 1987.

Bridgeford, Andrew. *1066: The Hidden History of the Bayeux Tapestry*. London: Fourth Estate, 2004.

Broadfoot, Barry. "Comic Books for Killers," *Six War Years 1939–1945: Memories of Canadians at Home and Abroad*. Toronto: Doubleday Canada Limited, 1974.

Brod, Harry. *Superman Is Jewish? How Comic Book Superheroes Came to Serve Truth, Justice, and the Jewish-American Way*. New York: Free Press, 2012.

Bromfield, Louis. *Mansfield News Journal* (Mansfield, OH). 22 Oct. 1950: 6.

Brottman, Mikita. *Funny Peculiar: Gershon Legman and the Psychopathology of Humor*. Routledge, 2004.

Broughton, Roger. "Suppressed 'Lonely War' to Conclude 20 Years Later," *Comics Buyer's Guide,* 20 July 1990:1.

Brown, Ben. "Comic Books and History: A Symposium," *Radical History Review* 1984: 28–30.

Brown, Slater. "The Coming of Superman," *New Republic*, 2 Sept. 1940: 301.

Brownmiller, Susan. *Against Our Will: Men, Women and Rape*. New York: Simon & Schuster, 1975.

Brunner, Edward. "Red Funnies: The New York Daily Worker's 'Popular Front' Comics, 1936–1945," *American Periodicals*, vol. 17, no. 2, Periodical Comics and Cartoons, 2007: 184–207.

Brunner, Edward. "'How Can I Tell My Grandchildren What I Did in the Cold War?' Militarizing the Funny Pages and Milton Caniff's *Steve Canyon*," in *Pressing the Fight: Print, Propaganda, and the Cold War*, Greg Barnhisel and Catherine Turner, eds. Amherst: University of Massachusetts Press, 2010.

Buchan, Russell P., and John J. Siegfried. "An Economic Evaluation of the Magazine Distribution Industry," *The Antitrust Bulletin*, vol. 23, 1978: 9-50.

Buck, Pearl S. "The Atmosphere of Education," *Journal of the National Education Association*, vol. 37, May 1948: 2823–.

Budiansky, Stephen. *Code Warriors: NSA's Codebreakers and the Secret Intelligence War Against the Soviet Union*. New York: Alfred A. Knopf, 2016.

Buhite, Russel D., and Wm. Christopher Hamel. "War for Peace: The Question of an American Preventive War against the Soviet Union, 1945–1955," *Diplomatic History,* vol. 14, no. 3, July 1990: 367–384.

Buhle, Paul. "The Left in American Comics: Rethinking the Visual Vernacular," *Science & Society*, vol. 71, no.3, July 2007: 348–356.

Buhle, Paul. *Jews and American Comics: An Illustrated History of an American Art Form*. New York: The New Press, 2008.

Buhle, Paul, and Denis Kitchen. *The Art of Harvey Kurtzman: The Mad Genius of Comics*. New York: Abrams Comicarts, 2009.

Bulletin of the Atomic Scientists, Science and Security Board. "Closer Than Ever: It Is 100 Seconds to Midnight, 2020 Doomsday Clock Statement," 23 Jan. 2020, https://thebulletin.org.

Burchett, W. G. *Peoples' Democracies*. Melbourne: World Unity Publications, 1951.

Burchett, Wilfred, and Alan Winnington. *Koje Unscreened*. Published by the authors (Peking), 1952.

Burchett, Wilfred. *Passport: An Autobiography*. Sydney: Thomas Nelson, 1969.

Burchett, Wilfred. *At the Barricades: Forty Years on the Cutting Edge of History*. New York: Times Books, 1981.

Burchett, Wilfred G. *Again Korea*. London: International Publishers, 1968.

Burchett, Wilfred G. *Rebel Journalism: The Writings of Wilfred Burchett*. London: Cambridge University Press, 2008.

Burton, Bill. "Clergymen See Comic Books Corrupting Youth of City," *The North Adams, Massachusetts Transcript*, 15 July 1954: 3.

Bussey, Charles M. Lt. Col. *Firefight at Yechon: Courage and Racism in the Korean War*. Lincoln, NE: Bison Books, 1991, 2002.

Busswell, Robert E. and Timothy S. Lee (eds.). *Christianity in Korea*. Honolulu: University of Hawai'i Press, 2006.

Butler, Andrew C., Nancy A. Dennis and Elizabeth J. Marsh. "Inferring Facts from Fiction: Reading Correct and Incorrect Information Affects Memory for Related Information," *Journal of Memory*, vol. 20, no.5, 29 May 2012: 487–498.

Butler, Nate. "Christian Comics Pioneers: Al Hartley," 1996, http://www.christiancomicsinternational.org/hartley_pioneer.html ©ROX35 Media, Inc.

Bytwerk, Randal, "German Propaganda Archive," 1998, http://www.calvin.edu/academic/cas/gpa/superman.htm.

Campbell, Eddie. "Lee Sayre Schwartz, 1926–2011," *The Comics Journal*, 21 June 2011.

Campbell, James. "Behind the Beat: Remembering 'Neurotica,' the Short-Lived Journal of the Beats," *The Boston Review*, October/November 1999.

Caniff, Milton. Interview, *Will Eisner's Spirit Magazine, #35*. Princeton, WI: Kitchen Sink Press, Inc., June 1982.

Caniff, Milton. *Milton Caniff's Steve Canyon #12*. Princeton, WI: Kitchen Sink Press, Inc., Sept. 1985.

Caniff, Milton. *Steve Canyon: 1949–1950*. San Diego: IDW Publishing, 2012.

Caniff, Milton. *The Complete Steve Canyon Volume 3: 1951–1952*. San Diego: IDW Publishing, 2013.

Caniff, Milton. *Steve Canyon: 1953–1954*. San Diego: IDW Publishing, 2014.

Canote, Terence Towles. "Superman's Pal, the Smut Monger, A Shroud of Thoughts, 29 Aug. 2007.

Canwell, Bruce. "Stage Dressing: 'A Return Ticket on the Armchair Express,'" "Introduction," *The Complete Steve Canyon, Volume 2: 1949–1950*. San Diego: IDW Publishing, 2012: 5–17.

Caputo, Nick. "More Kirby War: Battle," Friday, November 30, 2012, Marvel Mysteries and Comics Minutiae: A Place to Explore the Cobwebbed Corridors of Comics' Past," 2012, http://nick-caputo.blogspot.com/2012/11/more-kirby-war-battle.html.

Carlson, Lewis H. *Remembered Prisoners of a Forgotten War: An Oral History of Korean War POWs*. New York: St. Martin's Press, 2002.

Carlson, Mark. "'Hey! That Ain't Funny!' (Part 2): Religious Comic Books in the Forties," *The Nostalgia Zone*, vol. 2, no. 2, 2006.

Carr, Steven Alan. *Hollywood & Anti-Semitism*. London: Cambridge University Press, 2008.

Casey, Steven. "Selling NSC-68: The Truman Administration, Public Opinion, and the Politics of Mobilization, 1950–51," *Diplomatic History* vol. 29, no. 4, 2005: 655–690.

Casey, Steven. *Selling the Korean War: Propaganda, Politics, and Public Opinion in the United States, 1950–1953*. London: Oxford University Press, 2008.

Cassell, Dewey, and Marie Severin. *Marie Severin: The Mirthful Mistress of Comics*. Raleigh, NC: TwoMorrows Publishing, 2012.

Cassino, Jay Allen, and William R. Adam. *Pictorial History of the Korean War: the Graphic Record of the United Nations Forces in Action throughout Every Phase of the Korean Conflict; MacArthur Reports; Veterans of Foreign Wars Memorial Edition*. Veterans' Historical Book Service, Inc., 1951.

Cathcart, Adam. "Cruel Resurrection: Chinese Comics and the Korean War," *International Journal of Comic Art* vol. 6, no. 1, Spring 2004: 375–5, https://adamcathcart.com/2018/03/19/cruel-resurrection-chinese-comics-and-the-korean-war/.

Caute, David. *The Great Fear: The Anti-Communist Purge Under Truman and Eisenhower*. New York: Simon & Schuster, 1978.

Cawelti, John G. *Adventure, Mystery and Romance: Formula Stories as Art and Popular Culture*. Chicago: The University of Chicago Press, 1976.

"Censorship of Obscene Literature by Informal Governmental Action," *The University of Chicago Law Review*, vol. 22, no. 1., Autumn 1954: 216–233.

Cha, John H. "Unforgotten Soldiers of the 'Forgotten War," *The Korea Herald* (Seoul), 15 February 2016.

Chaddock, Dave. *This Must Be the Place: How the U.S. Waged Germ Warfare in the Korean War and Denied It Ever Since*. Bennett & Hastings Publishing, 2013.

Chaffee, Steven H. Review, *The Journal of American History*, vol. 82, no. 1, June 1995: 345–346.

Champney, Freeman. "Protofascism in Literature," *The Antioch Review*, vol. 4, no. 3, Autumn 1944: 338–348.

Chang, Gordon. "North Korea Might Test Biological Weapons on Its Citizens," (in Stefan Kiesbye, ed., *Biological and Chemical Weapons*, Greenhaven Press) 2010: 77–80.

Chapell, Richard. "Ayers, Heath & Tucci Talk War Comics," 20 Nov. 2008, http://www.comicbookresources.com/print.php?type=ar&id=18897.

Chapman, Hank, and Don Rico. *Marvel Masterworks: Atlas Era Battlefield*. Vol. 1, Marvel Worldwide, 2011.

Chapman, Jane, Anna Hoyles, Andrew Kerr and Adam Sherif. *Comics and the World Wars: A Cultural Record*, Palgrave Studies in the History of the Media, 2015.

Charmatz, Jan P. and Harold M. Wit. "Repatriation of Prisoners of War and the 1949 Geneva Convention," *The Yale Law Journal*, vol. 62, no. 3, Feb. 1953: 391–415.

Chen, Shiwei. "History of Three Mobilizations: A Reexamination of the Chinese Biological Warfare Allegations against the United States in the Korean War," *The Journal of American-East Asian Relations*, vol. 16, no.3, Fall 2009: 213–247.

Chen, Theodore H.E. (Principal Investigator). *The Propaganda Machine in Communist China: With Special Reference to Ideology, Policy, and Regulations, as of 1952*. Lackland Air Force Base, TX: Air Force Personnel and Training Research Center, 1955.

Chen, Wen-hui C. (Mrs. Theodore H.E. Chen). *Chinese Communist Anti-Americanism and The Resist-America Aid-Korea Campaign*. Lackland Air Force Base, Texas: Air Force Personnel and Training Research Center, 1952.

Cheng, Cindy I-Fen. *Citizens of Asian America: Democracy and Race During the Cold War*. New York University Press, 2013.

"Children Abroad to Get No Comics: Treasure Chest Donations of Books Will Bar Inclusion of Such Publications," *The New York Times*, 8 Nov. 1945: 19.

"Chinese Writer Says Children's Books Must Be Purged of Superstition and Feudalistic Influences," from *Jen-min Chiao-yu (People's Education)*, vol. 2, no. 2, 1950, as reproduced in "Information from Foreign Documents or Radio Broadcasts," Central Intelligence Agency, March 15, 1952.

Cho, Grace M. *Haunting the Korean Diaspora: Shame, Secrecy, and the Forgotten War*. The University of Minnesota Press, 2008.

Choe Sang-Hun. "South Korean Commission Details Civilian Massacres Early in 1950s War," *The New York Times*, 27 Nov. 2009: A-6.

Choe Sang-Hun, Charles J. Handley and Martha Mendoza. "Korean War: More Deaths Revealed," *Kitsap Sun*, 14 Oct. 1999.

Choi, Ha-young. "U.S.-ROK Reveals Investigation Result on Anthrax Delivery: 15 Times of Anthrax Entry Since 2009," *nknews.org*, 21 Dec. 2015.

Choi, Suhi. "Silencing Survivors' Narratives: Why Are We Again Forgetting the No Gun Ri Story?." *Rhetoric & Public Affairs* vol. 11, 2008: 369–370.

Chomsky, Noam, and Edward S. Herman. *The Washington Connection and Third World Fascism, The Political Economy of Human Rights: Volume I*. South End Press, 1979.

Choper, Jesse H. "Consequences of Supreme Court Decisions Upholding Individual Constitutional Rights," *Michigan Law Review*, vol. 83, no. 1, Oct. 1984: 1–212.

Choy Bong-youn. *A History of the Korean Unification Movement*. Institute of International Studies, Bradley University, 1984.

Christopher, Tom. "Orrin C Evans and the Story of All Negro Comics," first published in the *Comic Buyer's Guide*, 2002, http://www.tomchristopher.com/.

Christopher, Tom. "Malcolm Ater and the Commercial Comics Company," 2003, 2014, http://www.tomchristopher.com/comics2/malcolm-ater-and-the-commercial-comics-company/.

Chung, Eun-yong and Park Kun-woong. *Il ponte di NOGUNRI*. Bologna: Coconino Press, 2006.

Cipriano, Ralph. "F.B. Evans, 88; Preached Racial Unity," Philly.com, 30 May 1990, http://articles.philly.com/1990-05-30/news/25886740_1_death-threats-brotherhood-young-daughter.

Clare, Sister Mary, S.N.D. "Comics: A Study of the Effects of Comic Books on Children Less Than Eleven Years Old," *Our Sunday Visitor Press*, 15 Feb. 1943.

Cleaver, Thomas McKelvey. "Four Down!: The Korean Combat the U.S. Tried to Forget," *Flight Journal*, June 2013: 42–49.

Clews, John C. *Communist Propaganda Techniques*. New York: Praeger, 1964.

Cloyd, Fredrick D. Kakinami. *Dream of the Water Children: Memory and Mourning in the Black Pacific*. 2Leaf Press, 2019.

Cochrane, Walter. "Marines Take Ship for Korea Combat," *Los Angeles Times*, 13 July 1950: 2.

Codex Zouche-Nuttall. "Facsimile web-posted by FAMSI," n.d., http://www.famsi.org/research/graz/zouche_nuttall/.

Cohen, Jeff. *Cable News Confidential: My Misadventures in Corporate Media*. Boulder, CO: PoliPoint Press, 2006.

Collier, Beau. "Birth of the Girlie Pulp," *The Pulp Magazine Project*, n.d., https://www.pulpmags.org/contexts/essays/history-of-girlie-pulps.html.

"Color Cartoon Leaflet on Korea to Be Sent to Near and Middle East," *Department of State Bulletin*, 9 Oct. 1950: 591.

Comas, Martin. "Comic Strip Artist, Veteran of World War II Dies At 82," 14 Feb. 1997, http://articles.orlandosentinel.com/1997-02-14/news/9702130871_1_schlensker-buzz-sawyer-comic-strips.

"Comic Book Burning Set in East Berlin," *Lubbock Evening Journal*, 24 May 1955: 10.

"Comic Book Committee Gaining Far-Flung Fame," *The Cincinnati Enquirer*, 23 Nov. 1952: 81.

"Comic Book Curb Grows: 13 States Enacted Laws This Year to Control Sales," *The New York Times*, 11 July 1955.

"Comic Book Hearing to Start Tomorrow." *The New York Times*, 20 April 1954: 32.

"Comic Book Originator Tells How They Began," *Wichita Daily Times* (Wichita Falls, TX), 19 Sept. 1954: E-1.

"Comic Book Probe," *Long Beach (Calif.) Press Telegram*, 14 April 1948: A-3.

"Comic Book Writer Paul S. Newman Dead at 75," CNN, 7 June 1999.

"Comic Books Destroying a Nation?," *Daytona Beach Morning Journal*, 11 Nov. 1951.

"Comic Books Feed Racism, Says Wertham," *Daily Worker*, 29 April 1954: 7.

"Comic Books for Sale in Korea," Photograph by Hanson A. Williams, Jr., held by Pepperdine Digital Collections and accessed through the Digital Public Library of America, 1952, http://cdm15730.contentdm.oclc.org/cdm/ref/collection/p15730coll5/id/2885.

"Comic Books Menace to Scrap Paper Drive," *The Washington Post and Times Herald*, 18 Dec 1954: 11.

"'Comic' Books—Schools for Crime; Economist Indicts Them as Menace to Child Readers (Article No. 1: A Michigan Tragedy)," *Southtown Economist*, 21 March 1945: 1–2.

"Comic Publishers Get City Warning." *The New York Times*, 9 Feb. 1949: 35.

"The Comics' Influence in Korea," Republished from *New York Herald Tribune* in *The Montreal Gazette*, 21 Aug. 1950: 6.

"Comics Publishers Seek 'Czar' to Censor Books." *The New York Times*, 21 Aug. 1954: 19.

"Comment: The Problem of the Comic Books." *American Journal of Psychiatry*, vol. 112, no. 10, 1956: 854.

Commission of International Association of Democratic Lawyers. "Report on U.S. Crime in Korea," 31 March 1952, Pyongyang: International Association of Democratic Lawyers; Annexed to the Letter from the Permanent Representative of the Union of Soviet Socialist Republics, President of the Security Council, dated 30 June, 1952: Annexes 1, 2 &3, International Association of Democratic Lawyers, UN Security Council. S/2684/ADD/1. 30 June 1952. (This document appeared in the Korea Truth Commission Report for June 23, 2001, War Crimes Tribunal.)

Condon, Richard. *The Manchurian Candidate*. New York: Wheeler Publishing, 1959, 2005.

Conn, Peter. *Pearl S. Buck: A Cultural Biography*. London: Cambridge University Press, 1996.

Conroy, Mike. *War Stories: A Graphic History*. New York: HarperCollins, 2009.

Cooke, Alistair. "New York's Law to Suppress Obscene Comics: Old Dislike of Censorship Overcome," *The Manchester Guardian*, 24 March 1955: 9.

Cooke, Jon B. "A Spirited Relationship: Will Eisner Discusses His Experiences with Warren," interview conducted by & © Jon B. Cooke, *Comic Book Artist* #4, Spring 1999, http://twomorrows.com/comicbookartist/articles/04eisner.html.

Cooper, Simon. "North Korea's Biochemical Threat," *Popular Mechanics*, 22 Aug. 2007, http://www.military.com/forums/0,15240,146869,00.html.

Cornog, Martha, and Timothy Perper. "Make Love, Not War: The Legacy of Gershon Legman, 1917–1999," *The Journal of Sex Research*, vol. 36, no. 3, August, 1999: 31–67.

Correll, John T. "Up in the Air with Milton Caniff," *AIR FORCE Magazine*, April 2013.

Costello, Matthew J. *Secret Identity Crisis: Comic Books and the Unmasking of Cold War America*. New York: Continuum, 2009.

Cotter, Cornelius P., and J. Malcolm Smith. "An American Paradox: The Emergency Detention Act of 1950," *The Journal of Politics*, vol. 19, no. 1, Feb. 1957: 20–33.

Coventry, Michael T. "'Editorials at a Glance,' Cultural Policy, Gender, and Modernity in the World War I Bureau of Cartoons," *The Review of Policy Research* vol. 27, no. 2, March 2007: 97.

Crabtree, Steve. "The Gallup Brain: Americans and the Korean War," 4 Feb. 2003, http://www.gallup.com/poll/7741/Gallup-Brain-Americans-Korean-War.aspx.

Craig, Hardin. "Reading and the Growth of the Imagination," *South Atlantic Bulletin*, May 1956: 3–5.

Crane, Conrad C. "No Practical Capabilities": American Biological and Chemical Warfare Programs During the Korean War," *Perspectives in Biology and Medicine*, vol. 45, no. 2, Spring 2002: 241–249.

Crane, Roy. *Roy Crane's Captain Easy: Soldier of Fortune: The Complete Sunday Newspaper Strips 1 (1933–1935)*. Rick Norwood, ed., introduction by Jeet Heer. Seattle: Fantagraphics, 2010.

Credie (Miss) Margaret M., Letter to editor, *Frontline Combat*, March–April, 1952.

Creel, George. *How We Advertised America: The First Telling of the Amazing Story of the Committee on Public Information That Carried the Gospel of Americanism to Every Corner of the Globe*. New York: Harper & Bros., 1920.

Cremins, Brian. *Captain Marvel and the Art of Nostalgia*. Jackson: University Press of Mississippi, 2016.

Crépin, Thierry. "Le Comité de Défense de la Littérature et de las Presse pour la Jeunesse: The Communists and the Press for children during the Cold War," *Libraries & Culture*, vol. 36, no. 1, Books, Libraries, Reading, and Publishing in the Cold War, Winter, 2011: 131–142.

"Crime Against Humanity," *China Monthly Review*, March 1952: 225–229.

"Crime and the Comics," *The New York Times*, 14 Nov 1950: 30.

"Crime Comic Sales Reported Dropping." *The New York Times*, 3 Jan. 1956: 29.

"Crime Comics and the Constitution," *Stanford Law Review*, vol. 7, no. 2, March 1955: 237–260.

"Crime in the Suites." *The New York Times*, 17 Feb. 1980: F17.

Croddy, Eric. *Chemical and Biological Warfare: A Comprehensive Survey for the Concerned Citizen*. New York: Springer-Verlag, 2002.

Crow, Thomas. "For and Against the Funnies: Roy Lichtenstein's Drawings in the Inception of Pop Art, 1961–1962," in *Roy Lichtenstein: The Black-and-White Drawings, 1961–1968*, Hatje Cantz Verlag (Ostfilder, Germany) in association with The Morgan Library & Museum, 2010.

Crowe, Philip K. "Letter to the State Department," *Foreign Relations of the United States, 1952–1954. Africa and South Asia (in two parts): Volume XI, Part 2*, 20 July 1954: 1616–1618.

Crowther, Bosley. "The Screen in Review," *The New York Times*, 20 July 1950.

Crumb, R. "The Straight Dope From R. Crumb," *The Comics Journal*, no. 121, Seattle: Fantagraphics Books, 1988: 50–122.

Cull, Nicholas John. *Selling War: The British Propaganda Campaign Against American "Neutrality" in World War II*. London: Oxford University Press, 1995.

Cumings, Bruce. *The Origins of the Korean War, Volume I: Liberation and the Emergence of Separate Regimes 1945–1947*. Princeton: Princeton University Press, 1981.

Cumings, Bruce. *The Origins of the Korean War, Volume II: The Roaring of the Cataract, 1947–1950*. Princeton: Princeton University Press, 1990.

Cumings, Bruce. "'Revising Postrevisionism,' or, The Poverty of Theory in Diplomatic History," *Diplomatic History*, vol. 17, no. 4, 2003: 539–570.

Cumings, Bruce. *Korea's Place in the Sun: A Modern History*. Updated edition. New York: W.W. Norton & Company, 2005.

Cumings, Bruce. "The South Korean Massacre at Taejon: New Evidence on US Responsibility and Coverup," *The Asia-Pacific Journal Japan Focus*, vol. 6, no. 7, 2 July 2008.

Cumings, Bruce. *The Korean War: A History*. New York: A Modern Library Chronicles Book, 2010.

Cunningham, Ray. "Ray Cunningham, Collections, North Korea DPRK Photographs–September 2009, Sinchon Museum of American War Atrocities (Massacre) North Korea," 2010, http://www.flickr.com/photos/zaruka/sets/72157622514076596/with/3980945978/.

Dalager, Nancy A., Han K. Kang and Clare M. Mahan. "Cancer Mortality Among the Highest Exposed US Atmospheric Nuclear Test Participants," *Journal of Occupational and Environmental Medicine*, vol. 42, no.8, Aug. 2000: 798.

Dales, Douglas. "State Senate Acts to Control Comics," *The New York Times*, 24 Feb. 1949: 17.

Dales, Douglas. "Public Segregation Held Health Drag: Dr. Wertham, Psychiatrist, Aids Delaware Test Case—Hits New York City 'Custom,'" *The New York Times*, 23 Oct. 1951: 23.

"The Danger of Americanism" ("Die Gefahr des Amerikanismus"), *Das Schwarze Korps*, 14 March 1944, pp. 12. Webposted by Randall Bytwerk, 1998, at the German Propaganda Archive. https://research.calvin.edu/german-propaganda-archive/sk03.htm.

Danziger, Steve. "Malice, Metaphysics, and Mengele—Holocaust Motifs and the Renunciation of Evil in EC Horror Comics," *International Journal of Comic Art*, vol. 20, no. 2, Fall/Winter 2018: 373–398.

David, Lester, "Who Raised These Hoodlums?," *American Legion* vol. 49 no. 1, July 1950: 26–27, 51–52.

Davis, Susan G. *Dirty Jokes and Bawdy Songs: The Uncensored Life of Gershon Legman*. Urbana: University of Illinois Press, 2019.

DC Showcase: Our Army at War. Vol. 1, DC Comics, 2010.

Dean, William F. *General Dean's Story, As Told to William L. Worden by Major General William F. Dean*. New York: The Viking Press, 1954.

"Dear Subscriber:" *Counterattack: Facts to Combat Communism*, vol. 7, no. 6, 6 Feb. 1953: 3.

"Dear Subscriber:" *Counterattack: Facts to Combat Communism*, vol. 7, no. 37, 11 Sept. 1953: 3.

DeBruyne, Nese F. *American War and Military Operations Casualties: Lists and Statistics*. Library of Congress, Congressional Research Service, 2018.

Decker, Dwight R. "When Strikes the Senate," *Amazing Heroes #142*, 1 June 1988: 57–60.

Decker, Dwight R. "When Strikes the Senate, Part II" *Amazing Heroes #143*, 15 June 1988: 71–76.

de Grazia, Edward. "Obscenity and the Mail: A Study of Administrative Restraint," *Law and Contemporary Problems*, Autumn 1955.

Delisle, Guy. "Adieu Hollywood," 18 Dec. 2014, http://www.guydelisle.com/divers/adieu-hollywood/.

Delisle, Guy, and L'Association. *Pyongyang: A Journey in North Korea*. New York: Drawn & Quarterly, 2005.

DePastino, Todd. *Bill Mauldin: A Life Up Front*. New York: W.W. Norton and Company, Inc., 2008.

De Santis, Vincent P. "Eisenhower Revisionism," *The Review of Politics*, vol. 38, no. 2, April 1976: 190–207.

Detzer, David. *Thunder of the Captains: The Short Summer in 1950*. London: Thomas Y. Crowell Co., 1977.

Devanney, Burris. "Kenneth Leslie: A Biographical Introduction," *Canadian Poetry: Studies / Documents / Reviews*, Michael Gnarowski & D.M.R. Bentley, eds., University of Western Ontario, Fall-Winter 1979: 83–104.

Di Menno, "The Rise and Fall of EC Comics, 1950–1956: Cold War or Cultural War Casualty?," MA thesis, History, University of Rhode Island, 2005.

Dier, Richard. "Kids Crusade to Eliminate Stereotypes," *Afro-American*, 8 Sept. 1945.

Dikötter, Frank. "Group Definition and the Idea of 'Race' in Modern China (1793–1949)," in *Racism*, Martin Bulmer and John Solomos, eds. London: Oxford University Press, 1999.

Dikötter, Frank. *Mao's Great Famine: The History of China's Most Devastating Catastrophe, 1958–1962*. New York: Bloomsbury, 2010.

Dikötter, Frank. *The Tragedy of Liberation: A History of the Chinese Revolution 1945–1957*. New York: Bloomsbury Press, 2013.

Dinges, John. "Thanks to Democracy the Future Is Ours," *City Paper: Washington's Free Weekly*, vol. 3, no. 19, 20–26 May 1983: 1.

Dingman, Roger. "Atomic Diplomacy During the Korean War," *International Security*, vol. 13, no. 3, Winter 1988/89: 50–91.

DiPaolo, Marc. *War, Politics and Superheroes: Ethics and Propaganda in Comics and Film*. Jefferson, NC: McFarland, 2011.

"Discussions in Congress Bare 'Secrets': Information Open to All Who Want It, Including Russians," AP, *The Titusville (PA) Herald*, 24 May 1948: 1.

Dobbins, James, and Jeffrey Hornung. "Opinion: End the Korean War, Finally," *The New York Times*, 8 June 2017.

Docker, John. "Culture, Society and the Communist Party," in Ann Curthoys and John Merritt, eds., *Australia's First Cold War: 1945–1953*. London: George Allen & Unwin, 1984: 183–212.

"Dodging Armaggedon: The Third World War That Almost Was, 1950," *Cryptologic Quarterly*, 24 Feb. 1998: 85–95 (DOCID 3967119).

Doherty, Eamon, Joel Liebesfeld, and Todd Liebesfeld. *A New Look at Nagasaki 1946*. Bloomington: Author-House, 2008.

Dolinar, Brian. "Chapter Four, Battling Fascism for Years with the Might of his Pen: Ollie Harrington and the Bootsie Cartoons," *The Black Cultural Front: Black Writers and Artists of the Depression Generation*. Jackson: The University Press of Mississippi, 2012.

Donner, Frank. *Protectors of Privilege: Red Squads and Police Repression in Urban America*. Berkeley: University of California Press, 1992.

Donovan, Robert J. *Tumultuous Years: The Presidency of Harry S. Truman 1949–1953*. New York: W.W .Norton & Co., 1982.

Dower, John W. *War Without Mercy: Race and Power in the Pacific War*. Random House, Inc., 1986.

Dower, John W. Review: Japan's Secret War, *Bulletin of the Atomic Scientists*, August/Sept 1986: 61–62.

Doyle, Dennis. "'A Fine New Child': The Lafargue Mental Hygiene Clinic and Harlem's African American Communities, 1946–1958," *Journal of the History of Medicine and Allied Sciences*, vol. 64, no. 2, April 2009: 173–212.

"Drive Started for Gifts for GIs in Korea," *Los Angeles Times*, 28 Oct 1952: A-2.

Dudziak, Mary L. *Cold War Civil Rights: Race and the Image of American Democracy*. Princeton: Princeton University Press, 2002.

"Dumas from Ohio," *Newsweek*, 24 April, 1950: 58–61.

Duncan, Randy, and Matthew J. Smith. *The Power of Comics: History, Form and Culture*. New York: Bloomsbury Academic, 2012.

Dyer, Murray. *Weapon on the Wall: Rethinking Psychological Warfare*. Baltimore: The Johns Hopkins University Press, 1959.

Early, Gerald. "Race, Art, and Integration: The Image of the African American Soldier in Popular Culture during the Korean War," *Bulletin of the American Academy of Arts and Sciences*, vol. 57, no. 1, Autumn 2003: 32–38.

"ECA Denies Approval of Comics for Germany," *The New York Times*, 13 Nov. 1948: 7.

"Education: Our Enemies," *Time Magazine*, 16 July 1951.

Edwards, Paul. *Unusual Footnotes to the Korean War*. New York: Bloomsbury Publishing, 1977.

Edwards, Paul M. *The Korean War*. New York: Greenwood Press, 2006.

Edwards, Paul M. *The Mistaken History of the Korean War: What We Got Wrong Then and Now*. Jefferson, NC: McFarland, 2018.

Einstein, Albert. Fundraising Letter for the Emergency Committee of Atomic Scientists Incorporated, 22 Jan. 1947, https://fas.org/sgp/eprint/einstein.html.

Eisner, Will, 1968. "Will Eisner: Having Something to Say," Interviewed by John Benson on September 10, 1968, Trimmed from *The Comics Journal #267*, April/May, 2005. http://web.archive.org/web/20080429235436/www.tcj.com/267/i_eisner.html.

Eisner, Will. *Comics and Sequential Art: Principles and Practices from the Legendary Cartoonist*. New York: W. W. Norton, 2008. (Revised edition of *Comics & Sequential Art*, 1985.)

Elbein, Asher. "#Comicsgate: How an Anti-Diversity Harassment Campaign in Comics Got Ugly—and Profitable," *Daily Beast*, 2 April 2018.

Elder, Robert E. *The Information Machine: The United States Information Agency and American Foreign Policy*. Syracuces: Syracuse University Press, 1968.

"Election Polls—Vote by Groups, 1952–1956," Gallup, https://news.gallup.com/poll/9451/Election-Polls-Vote-Groups-19521956.aspx.

Ellis, Mark. "J. Edgar Hoover and the 'Red Summer' of 1919," *Journal of American Studies*, vol. 28, no. 1 April 1994: 39–59.

Ellsberg, Daniel. "Introduction," *Protest and Survive*, E.P. Thompson and Dan Smith, eds., *Monthly Review Press*, 1981.

Ellsberg, Daniel. *The Doomsday Machine: Confessions of a Nuclear War Planner*. New York: Bloomsbury, 2017.

Ellsberg, Daniel. 1998. "Twelve Newly Released Soviet-Era 'Documents' and Allegations of U.S. Germ Warfare During the Korean War," Cold War International History Project H-Diplo Discussions: The Korean War, 5 July 1999 (and following thread).

Ellsberg, Daniel. 2002. "United States Biological Warfare During the Korean War: Rhetoric and Reality." http://www.yorku.ca/sendicot/ReplytoColCrane.htm.

Endicott, Stephen, and Edward Hagerman. *The United States and Biological Warfare: Secrets from the Early Cold War and Korea*. Bloomington: Indiana University Press, 1998.

Engel, Irving M., "Report of the Executive Committee: Highlights of 1949," published in *American Jewish Yearbook*, 1951. American Jewish Committee and Jewish Publication Society of America, 1950.

Engelhardt, Tom. "Ambush at Kamikaze Pass: Racism in the Media," *Bulletin of Concerned Asian Scholars*, vol. 3, no. 1, Winter/Spring 1971. https://docs.wixstatic.com/ugd/63d11a_628019a62265464191dc1cb292d88cd5.pdf.

Engelhardt, Tom. *The End of Victory Culture: Cold War America and the Disillusioning of a Generation*. Basic Books, 1995.

Erskine, Hazel. "The Polls: Is War a Mistake?," *Public Opinion Quarterly*, 1 March, 1970: 134–150.

Estrada, Ric. "War, you said?" in *Chris Pedrin's Big Five Information Guide*, vol. 1, no. 1. London: Alton-Kelly Corporation, 1994–1995: 13–14 (unpaginated).

Evanier, Mark. Irwin Hasen interview by Mark Evanier, "P.O.V.: Point of View," 20 Oct. 2000, http://www.newsfromme.com/pov/col312/.

Evanier, Mark. *Kirby: King of Comics*. New York: Abrams, 2008, 2017.

Evanier, Mark. "Lew Sayre Schwartz, R.I.P.," 20 June 2011, http://www.newsfromme.com/pov/col312/.

Evans, F. Bowen (ed.) *Worldwide Communist Propaganda Activities*. The Macmillan Company, 1955.

Evans, George. "Working on DC's 'War' Comics," in *Chris Pedrin's Big Five Information Guide*, vol. 1, no. 1, Alton-Kelly Corporation, 1994–1995: 8–9 (unpaginated).

Evans, M. Stanton. *Blacklisted by History: The Untold Story of Senator Joe McCarthy and His Fight Against America's Enemies*. New York: Crown Forum, 2007.

Farmer, Sarah. "Symbols That Face Two Ways: Commemorating the Victims of Nazism and Stalinism at Buchenwald and Sachsenhausen," *Representations*, no. 49, Winter 1995: 97–119.

Faux, Jeff. "Why Are US Troops Still in South Korea, Anyway? Our Garrison Is No Longer Needed to Defend the South—and It Poses a Continuing Threat to the North," *The Nation*, 6 March, 2018.

Feagin, Joe R. *Racist America: Roots, Current Realities & Future Reparations*. London: Routledge, 2000.

Feder, Edward L. *Comic Book Regulation*. Bureau of Public Administration, University of California, Berkeley, Feb. 1955.

Federal Council of the Churches of Christ in America. *The Korean Situation: Authentic Accounts of Recent Events by Eye Witnesses*. Commission on Relations with the Orient, 1920.

Fenkl, Heinz Insu. "North Korean Comics." *North Korean Manhwa—Reports for Students, Truckers, and Avid Readers*, n.d., www.heinzinsufenkl.net/dprk_manhwa.html.

Ferguson, Christopher J. and Eugene Beresin, "Social Science's Curious War with Pop Culture and How It Was Lost: The Media Violence Debate and the Risks It Holds for Social Science," *Preventive Medicine* vol. 99, 2017: 69–76.

Fernández Sarasola, Ignacio. "Crime News: Blaming Comic Books for Crimes Committed During the 'Golden Age'," *International Journal of Comic Art* vol. 20, no. 2, Fall-Winter 2018: 493–517.

Fertig, Mark. *Take That, Adolf! The Fighting Comic Books of the Second World War*. Seattle: Fantagraphics, 2017.

Field, Christopher B. "'He Was a Living Breathing Human Being': Harvey Kurtzman's War Comics and the 'Yellow Peril' in 1950s Containment Culture," in *Comic Books and the Cold War: Essays on Graphic Treatment of Communism, the Code and Social Concerns*. Jefferson, NC: McFarland, 2012.

"Fifty Cities Place Ban on Comic Books Sales." *The Oregonian*, 25 Nov. 1948: 7.

"Findings." *The Clearing House*, vol. 15, no. 6, Feb. 1941: 341.

Finger, Stan. "Mort Walker, El Dorado Native Who Created 'Beetle Bailey, Dies at 94." *The Wichita Eagle*, 27 Jan. 2018.

Fingeroth, Danny. *Disguised as Clark Kent: Jews, Comics, and the Creation of the Superhero*. London: Continuum, 2007.

Finn, David. *The Corporate Oligarch*. New York: Simon & Schuster, 1969.

Finnegan, John P. "The Evolution of US Army HUMINT: Intelligence Operations in the Korean War." *Studies in Intelligence* vol. 55, no. 2 (extracts) June, 2011: 57–70.

Fisher, Louis. "The Korean War: On What Legal Basis Did Truman Act?" *The American Journal of International Law*, vol. 89, no.1, Jan. 1995: 21–39.

Fitzpatrick, K. Meghan. "Prostitutes, Penicillin and Prophylaxis: Fighting Venereal Disease in the Commonwealth Division During the Korean War, 1950–1953," *Social History of Medicine* vol. 28, no. 3: 555–575.

Fousek, John. *To Lead the Free World: American Nationalism and the Cultural Roots of the Cold War*. Chapel Hill: The University of North Carolina Press, 2000.

Frakes, Margaret. "Comics Are No Longer Comic," *Christian Century*, 4 Nov. 1942: 1349.

Frank, Josette. "What's in the Comics?" *The Journal of Educational Sociology*, vol. 18, no. 4, Dec. 1944: 214–222.

Frank, Josette. *Comics, TV, Radio, Movies—What Do They Offer Children?* Public Affairs Pamphlet No, 148, Public Affairs Committee, Incorporated, 1955. (Revised edition, Feb 1955.)

Franklin, H. Bruce. *War Stars: The Superweapon in the American Imagination*. Oxford University Press, 1988, Revised and expanded edition, Amherst: University of Massachusetts Press, 1988, 2008.

Fremigacci, Jean. "La vérité sur la grande révolte de Madagascar," *L'Histoire*, n°318, March 2007.

Friedman, Andrea. *Citizenship in Cold War America: The National Security State and the Possibilities of Dissent*. Amherst: University of Massachusetts Press, 2014.

Friedman, Bruce Jay. "Even the Rhinos Were Nymphos," in *It's a Man's World: Men's Adventure Magazines*, Adam Parfrey, ed. Port Townsend, WA: Feral House, 2003.

Friedman, Clara H. *The Newsprint Problem, Then Questions and Answers*. American Newspaper Guild, 1948 (?).

Friedman, Josh Alan. Black Cracker: #13: "Mel Shestack: Magazine Management Trickster" https://blackcracker.fm/mel-shestack-pulp-magazine-trickster/ (podcast; interview recorded 1984 plus introduction), accessed 3 July 2019.

Frost, Margaret F. "The Children's Opinion of Comic Books," *The Elementary English Review*, vol. 20, no. 8, Dec, 1943: 330–331, 341.

"A Further Document from the Hungarian Hierarchy." *The Tablet: The International Catholic News Weekly,* 22 Jan 1949: 12.

Gabilliet, Jean-Paul. *Of Comics and Men: A Cultural History of American Comic Books.* Jackson: University Press of Mississippi, 2010.

Gaddis, John Lewis. *Strategies of Containment: A Critical Appraisal of Postwar American National Security Policy.* London: Oxford University Press, 1982, 2005.

Gaines, M.C. "Narrative Illustration: The Story of the Comics," *Print,* Summer 1942: 25–38.

Gaines, William M. "Interview," *The Comics Journal #81,* May 1983.

Gardiner, Harold C., S.J. "The Comic Books! Most Insidious Poison—Materialism," *Religious Education,* 1 Nov. 1954: 419–421.

Gardner, John. *On Moral Fiction.* New York: Basic Books, 1978, 2000.

Gartner, Scott Sigmund and Marissa Edson Myers. "Body Counts and 'Success' in the Vietnam and Korean Wars," *The Journal of Interdisciplinary History,* vol. 25, no. 3, Winter 1995: 377–395.

Gavaler, Chris. "The Ku Klux Klan and the Birth of the Superhero," *Journal of Graphic Novels and Comics,* 10 Dec. 2012: 1–17.

Gavaler, Chris. "The Rise and Fall of Fascist Superpowers," *Journal of Graphic Novels and Comics,* 2015: 1–18.

Gayn, Mark. *Japan Diary.* New York: William Sloan Associates, 1948.

Geissler, Erhard, ed. *Biological and Toxin Weapons Today.* Oxford University Press, 1986.

Geissman, Grant. *Tales of Terror! The EC Companion.* Seattle: Fantagraphics, 2002.

Geissman, Grant. *FELDSTEIN: The MAD Life and Fantastic Art of Al Feldstein!* San Diego: IDW Publishing, 2013.

Gelb, Michael. "An Early Soviet Ethnic Deportation: The Far-Eastern Koreans," *The Russian Review,* vol. 54, no. 3, July 1995: 389–412.

Gellhorn, Walter. "Restraints on Book Reading," in Robert B. Downs, ed. *The First Freedom.* American Library Association, 1960: 20–39.

"General Forecasts Peace in Korea," *The Spokesman-Review* (Spokane, WA), 9 Sept. 1969: 17.308.

"George Teeple Eggleston and the America First Movement," *American Heritage Center Wyoming,* 6 Dec. 2018. https://ahcwyo.org/2018/12/06/george-teeple-eggleston-and-the-america-first-movement/.

Gerber, Ernst, and Mary Gerber. *The Photo-Journal Guide to Comic Books* (Two Volumes). Minden, NV: Gerber Publishing Company, Inc., 1989–1990.

Gergel, Richard. *Unexampled Courage: The Blinding of Sgt. Isaac Woodard and the Awakening of President Harry S. Truman and Judge J. Waties Waring.* New York: Sarah Crichton Books, 2019.

"Germ Carrying Rats Bred in North Korea." *The New York Times,* 6 Nov. 1950: 3.

"Germ Warfare in Korea?" *Science News Letter,* 8 July 1950: 22.

"German Red Purge Sweeps Out Books," *The New York Times,* 10 Feb. 1952: 1.

"Germany: Read No Evil," *Time Magazine,* 27 May 1946.

Gerson, Joseph. *Empire and the Bomb: How the US Uses Nuclear Weapons to Dominate the World.* New York: Pluto Press, 2007.

Gertzman, Jay A. *Bookleggers and Smuthounds: The Trade in Erotica, 1920–1940.* Harrisburg: University of Pennsylvania Press, 1999.

Gerzon, Mark. *A Choice of Heroes: The Changing Face of American Manhood.* Chicago: Houghton Mifflin Company, 1982.

Giangreco, Dennis. "To Bomb Or Not to Bomb," *Naval War College Review,* vol. 51, no. 2, Spring 1998: 140–145.

Gibson, Campbell, and Kay Jung. Historical Census Statistics on Population Totals By Race, 1790 to 1990, and By Hispanic Origin, 1970 to 1990, for the United States, Regions, Divisions, and States, Population Division, U. S. Census Bureau, 2002.

Gilbert, James. *A Cycle of Outrage: America's Reaction to the Juvenile Delinquent in the 1950s.* London: Oxford University Press, 1986.

Gilbert, Michael T. "Mr. Monster's Comic Crypt!; Dr. Lauretta Bender: Comics' Anti-Wertham—Part 4," *Alter Ego* no. 92, 2009.

Gill, Tom. *The Misadventures of a Roving Cartoonist: The Lone Ranger's Secret Sidekick.* New York: Five Star Legends, 2006.

Glander, Timothy. *Origins of Mass Communications Research During the American Cold War: Educational Effects and Contemporary Implications.* New York: Lawrence Erlbaum Associates, 2000.

Gleason, Leverett. "In Defense of Comic Books," *Today's Health,* Sept. 1952: 41, 52–54.

Gleijeses, Piero. *Shattered Hope: The Guatemalan Revolution and the United States, 1944–1954.* Princeton, NJ: Princeton University Press, 1991.

Goldstein, Andrew. "'Depravity for Children—Ten Cents a Copy!' Hartford and the Censorship of Comic Books, 1948–1959," *Trinity College Digital Repository,* 5 Aug. 2003.

Goldstein, Nancy. *Jackie Ormes: The First African American Woman Cartoonist.* Lansing: The University of Michigan Press, 2008.

Goldstein, Richard. *Helluva Town: The Story of New York City During World War II.* New York: Free Press, 2010.

Gombry, Pascal-Emmanuel. "A Science-Based Case for Ending the Porn Epidemic," *American Greatness,* 15 Dec. 2019, https://amgreatness.com/2019/12/15/a-science-based-case-for-ending-the-porn-epidemic/.

Goncharov, Sergei, John W. Lewis and Xue Litai. *Uncertain Partners: Stalin, Mao and the Korean War*. Stanford, CA: Stanford University Press, 1993.

Gonick, Larry. *The Cartoon History of the United States*. San Francisco: HarperCollins, 1991.

Gonick, Larry. *The Cartoon History of the Modern Worlds, Part II: From the Bastille to Baghdad*. San Francisco: HarperCollins, 2009.

Goodrum, Michael. "'Friend of the People of Many Lands': Johnny Everyman, 'Critical Internationalism' and Liberal Post-War US Heroism," *Social History*, vol. 38, no. 2, 2013: 203–219.

Goodwin, Archie. *Blazing Combat*. Seattle: Fantagraphics, 2009.

Gorman, Joseph Bruce. *Kefauver: A Political Biography*. Oxford: Oxford University Press, 1971.

Gossett, Thomas F. *Race: The History of an Idea in America*. Dallas: Southern Methodist University Press, Chapter IX: "Literary Naturalism and Race," 1963: 198–227.

Goulart, Ron. "Funnies in the Thirties: Part 8: In Uniform," *Comics Buyer's Guide*, 3 Nov. 1989.

Goulart, Ron. *Over 50 Years of American Comic Books*, New York: Mallard Press, 1991.

Graalfs, Mrs. Marilyn. "A Survey of Comic Books in the State of Washington: A Report Made to the Washington State Council for Children and Youth," June 1954 (unpublished).

Graham, Richard L. *Government Issue: Comics for the People, 1940s-2000s*. New York: Abrams Comicarts, 2011.

Granik, Theodore. What Our Teenagers Want to Know: Hot-Rodding, Delinquency Discussed," *Bluefield Daily Telegraph*, Bluefield WV, 12 Oct. 1954: 2.

Grayson, James Huntley. "A Quarter-Millennium of Christianity in Korea," in *Christianity in Korea*, Robert E. Busswell Jr., and Timothy S. Lee, eds. Honolulu: University of Hawai'i Press, 2006.

Green, Michael Cullen. *Black Yanks in the Pacific: Race in the Making of American Military Empire After World War II*. Ithaca, NY: Cornell University Press, 2010.

Green, Philip. *Primetime Politics: The Truth About Conservative Lies, Corporate Control, and Television Culture*. Lanham, MD: Rowman & Littlefield Publishers, Inc., 2005.

Greenwald, Glenn. "The Crux of the NSA Story in One Phrase: 'Collect It All': The Actual Story That Matters Is Not Hard to See: The NSA Is Attempting to Collect, Monitor and Store All Forms of Human Communication," *The Guardian*, 15 July 2013. http://www.guardian.co.uk/commentisfree/2013/jul/15/crux-nsa-collect-it-all.

Greenwald, Glenn. *No Place to Hide: Edward Snowden, the NSA, and the U.S. Surveillance State*. New York: Metropolitan Books, 2014.

Grey, Arthur L, Jr. "The Thirty-Eighth Parallel," *Foreign Affairs* vol. 29, no. 3, 1 April 1951: 482–487.

Grossman, Lt. Col. Dave. *On Killing: The Psychological Cost of Learning to Kill in War and Society*, Revised edition, E-Rights/E-Reads, Ltd. Publishers, 2009.

Grost, Michael E. "Johnny Everyman: A 1940's Comic Book Hero," n.d., http://mikegrost.com/everyman.htm.

Groth, Gary. "Entertaining Comics," *The Comics Journal*, 23 Jan. 2013, http://www.tcj.com/entertaining-comics/.

Gruenberg, Sidonie Matsner. "The Comics as a Social Force," *The Journal of Educational Sociology*, vol. 18, no. 4, Dec 1944: 204–213.

Haas, Michael E. *In the Devils' Shadow: U.N. Special Operations During the Korean War*. Annapolis: Naval Institute Press, 2000.

Hadsel, Fred Latimer. "Propaganda in the Funnies," *Current History*, Dec. 1941: 365–368.

Hagemeister, Michael. "The Protocols of the Elders of Zion: Between History and Fiction," *New German Critique* 103, vol. 35, no. 1, Spring 2008: 83–95.

Hajdu, David. *The Ten-Cent Plague: The Great Comic-Book Scare and How It Changed America*. New York: Farrar, Straus and Giroux, 2009.

Hall, Emily. *Kim Sŏnghwan's "Mr. Kobu": Editorial Cartoons As Genre Weapons in South Korean Search for Democracy, 1945–1972*. Unpublished doctoral dissertation, University of Washington, Seattle, History, 2019.

Halliday, Jon, and Bruce Cumings. *Korea: The Unknown War*. New York: Pantheon Books, 1988.

Halsall, Paul. "Adolf Hitler: The Obersalzberg Speech," *Internet Modern History Sourcebook*. July 1998.

Ham, Paul. *Hiroshima Nagasaki: The Real Story of the Atomic Bombings and Their Aftermath*. New York: St. Martin's Press, 2014.

Hammond, Keith. "How the Polluters' Lobby Uses Phony Front Groups to Attack the Kyoto Treaty," 4 Dec. 1997, http://www.motherjones.com/politics/1997/12/astroturf-troopers/.

Han, Hongkoo, "Colonial Origins of *Juche*: The *Minsaengdan* Incident of the 1930s and the Birth of the North Korea-China Relationship," in *Origins of North Korea's Juche, Colonialism, War, and Development*, Suh, J.J., ed. New York: Lexington Books, 2013: 33–62.

Hanebrink, Paul. *A Specter Haunting Europe: The Myth of Judeo-Bolshevism*. Cambridge, MA: The Belknap Press of Harvard University Press, 2018.

Hanley, Charles J. and Martha Mendoza. "Korean War Policy Let U.S. Troops Kill Refugees," *Toronto Star*, 15 April 2007.

Hanson, Victor Davis. "The Horrors of Hiroshima in Context," 21 April 2016, townhall.com.

Harden, Blaine. *King of Spies: The Dark Reign of America's Spymaster in Korea*. New York: Viking, 2017.

Harrington, Oliver W. *Why I Left America and Other Essays*. Jackson: University Press of Mississippi, 1993.

Harris, Rober, and Jeremy Paxman. *A Higher Form of Killing*. Random House, 1982.

Harris, Sheldon. "Japanese biological warfare experiments and other atrocities in Manchuria, 1932–1945, and the subsequent United States cover up: a preliminary assessment," *Crime, Law and Social Change*, vol. 15, no. 3, 1991: 171–199.

Harrison, Selig. *Korean Endgame: A Strategy for Reunification and U.S. Disengagement.* New York: University Press, 2009.

Hart, Bradley W. *Hitler's American Friends: The Third Reich's supporters in the United States.* Toronto: Thomas Dunne Books, an imprint of St. Martin's Press, 2018.

Hart-Landsberg, Martin. *Korea: Division, Reunification, & U.S. Foreign Policy.* New York: Monthly Review Press, 1998.

Hartley, Al. "'The Lord Gave Me the Opportunity to Do What I Wanted': Artist Al Hartley on Timely, Archie, Spire & A Famous Father—not to mention Nedor and ACG; interview conducted and transcribed by Jim Amash," *Alter Ego* vol. 3, no. 61, 2006: 75–76.

Harvey, R.C. "February 1967: Caniff's Private War to Save Steve Canyon," *Nemo: The Classic Comics Library,* no. 32, Seattle: Fantagraphics Books, Inc., 1992: 4–21.

Harvey, R.C. *The Art of the Comic Book: An Aesthetic History.* Jackson: The University Press of Mississippi, 1996.

Harvey, R.C. "Will Eisner and the Arts and Industry of Cartooning: Inventing Instructional Comics," *Cartoonist PROfiles #131*, Sept. 2001 (retrieved from Harvey's "Rants & Raves").

Harvey, R.C. "The Unsung Sickles," "Harv's Hindsights," 2004, RCHarvey.com.

Harvey, R.C. *Meanwhile … A Biography of Milton Caniff.* Seattle: Fantagraphics Books, 2007.

Harvey, R.C. "The Truth," Introduction to *Corpse on the Imjin! And Other Stories by Harvey Kurtzman*, Seattle: Fantagraphics Books, 2012.

Harvey, R.C. "George Baker and the Sad Sack," *The Comics Journal,* 20 Dec. 2013, http://www.tcj.com/george-baker-and-the-sad-sack/.

Harvey, R.C. "Winnie the WAC," *The Comics Journal,* 4 March 2015, http://www.tcj.com/winnie-the-wac/.

Harvey, R.C. "THE EISNER-IGER SHOP: How It Came to Be and How It Operated," (a transcribed interview with Will Eisner)," 14 July 2017, http://rcharvey.com/main.html.

Haswell, James N. "Comical Campaign Coming," *The Pittsburgh Press,* 27 Sept. 1952.

Hata, Ikuhiko. *Comfort Women and Sex in the Battle Zone.* Lanham, MD: Hamilton Books, 2018.

Hauben, Ronda. "The Role of the UN in the Unending Korean War. 'United Nations Command' As Camouflage," *Global Research,* 21 Sept. 2013.

Hayes, Peter, Lyuba Zarsky and Walden Bello. *American Lake: Nuclear Peril in the Pacific.* Penguin Books, 1986.

Haynes, John Earl. "Survey Article: The Cold War Debate Continues, A Traditionalist View of Historical Writing on Domestic Communism and Anti-Communism," *Journal of Cold War Studies,* vol. 2, no.1, Winter 2000: 76–115.

Hayton, Christopher J. and David L. Albright. "The Military Vanguard for Desegregation: Civil Rights Era War Comics and Racial Integration." *ImageText* vol. 6, no. 2, Spring 2012.

Heale, M.J. "Red Scare Politics: California's Campaign Against Un-American Activities, 1940–1970," *Journal of American Studies,* vol. 20, no. 1, 5 April 1986: 5–32.

Heer, Jeet. "Crane's Great Gamble," *Buz Sawyer 1: The War in the Pacific by Roy Crane,* Rick Norwood, ed. Seattle: Fantagraphics, 2011.

Heer, Jeet. "Pulp Propaganda," *The New Republic,* September 2015: 55–59.

Heller, Steven. "When the Comics Sold Soap: Advertising from the '30s and 40s," *Print* vol. 42, no. 6, Nov/Dec 1988: 164–171.

Hendrickson, Robert C., and Fred J. Cook. *Youth in Danger: A Forthright Report by the Former Chairman of the Senate Subcommittee on Juvenile Delinquency.* New York: Harcourt, Brace and Company, 1956.

Herken, Greg. *The Georgetown Set: Friends and Rivals in Cold War Washington.* New York: Vintage Books, 2014.

Herman, Lester Jay. "American Through the Kremlin's Eyes," *The American Mercury,* Nov. 1950.

Hersh, Seymour M. *Chemical & Biological Warfare: America's Hidden Arsenal.* Boston: Anchor Books, 1969.

Hersh, Seymour M. *MY LAI 4; a report on the massacre and its aftermath,* New York: Random House, 1970.

Hess, Gary R. *The United States at War, 1941–1945.* New York: John Wiley & Sons, 2014.

Hessee, Tim. "The Pop Hollinger Story: The First Comic Book Collector/Dealer," *Overstreet's Comic Book Price Guide #12,* 1982.

Higgins, Lois Lundell, AB, MSW, LLD. "Crime Comics: A Report," a speech delivered to the 24th Annual Governor's Conference on Youth and Community Service," Chicago, IL, 29 April 1955.

Hilbish, Melissa. "Advancing in Another Direction," *War, Literature & the Arts: An International Journal of the Humanities* vol. 11 no. 1. Spring/Summer 1999.

Hill, Leonidas E. "The Nazi Attack on 'Un-German' Literature: 1933–1945," in *The Holocaust and the Book: Destruction and Preservation,* Jonathan Rose, ed. Boston: University of Massachusetts Press, 2008.

Hill, Thomas J. "Early Teen Agers and Racial Prejudice in the South," *The Clearing House,* vol. 30, no.1, Sept. 1955: 28–30.

Hinkle and Wolff. "The Methods of Interrogation and Indoctrination Used by the Communist State Police," *Bulletin of the New York Academy of Medicine* vol. 33, no. 9, Sept. 1957: 609–10.

Hirsch, Paul S. *Pulp Empire: Comic Books, Culture, and U.S. Foreign Policy, 1941–1955.* PhD diss., History, University of California, Santa Barbara, March 2013.

Hirsch, Paul. "'This Is Our Enemy': The Writers' War Board and Representations of Race in Comic Books, 1942–1945," *Pacific Historical Review* vol. 83, no.3, 2014: 448–486.

Hite, Kenneth, and Shepherd Hendrix. *The Complete Idiot's Guide to U.S. History*. New York: Alpha Books, 2009.

Hoffmann, A. "Gift aüs Übersee," *USA in Bild und Wort*, no. 9, 1952: 12–13.

Hogben, Lancelot. *From Cave Painting to Comic Strip: A Kaleidoscope of Human Communication*. Chanticleer Press, 1949.

Holmes, Eric A. "Atomic Horror: Entertaining Comics and 'One World or None," *International Journal of Comic Art*, vol. 16, no. 1, Spring 2014: 90–124.

Holtz, Allan. "Obscurity of the Day: Little Lefty," *Stripper's Guide*, 18 April 2006, http://strippersguide.blogspot.com/2006/04/obscurity-of-day-little-lefty.html.

"Holyoke Police Keep Up on Comic Books," *Altoona Mirror*, 9 Dec. 1954.

Hong, Christine. "Manufacturing Dissidence: Arts and Letters of North Korea's 'Second Culture,'" *Positions: Asia Critique*, vol. 23, no. 4, 2015: 743–784.

Hoopes, Townsend. *The Devil and John Foster Dulles*. New York: Little, Brown and Company, 1973.

Hopper, Tristin. "Why Some Korean War Prisoners Spent Their Captivity Stoned Out of Their Gourd," www.thegrowhop.com, 8 Feb. 2019.

Horn, Maurice, ed. *The World Encyclopedia of Comics*. Philadelphia: Chelsea House, 1976.

Horne, Gerald. *Class Struggle in Hollywood, 1930–1950*. Arlington: University of Texas Press, 2001.

Horne, Gerald. *The Rise & Fall of the Associated Negro Press: Claude Barnett's Pan-African News and the Jim Crow Paradox*. Champaign: University of Illinois Press, 2017.

Horrell, Mason Edward. *Reporting the "Forgotten War": Military-Press Relations in Korea, 1950–1954*. Ph.D. diss., History, University of Kentucky, 2002.

"House Unit Scores AYD As Subversive: Youth Group on University Campuses Called 'Training School for Lawlessness,'" *The New York Times*, 16 April 1947: 19.

Huck, Charlotte Stephena. "The Nature and Derivation of Young Children's Social Concepts," PhD diss., Education, Northwestern University, 1955.

Huebner, Andrew J. *The Warrior Image: Soldiers in American Culture from the Second World War to the Vietnam Era*. Chapel Hill: The University of North Carolina Press, 2008.

Hunt, Michael H. "Pearl Buck—Popular Expert on China, 1931–1949," *Modern China*, vol. 3, no. 1, Jan. 1977; 33–64.

Hunter, Edward. *Brainwashing in Red China: The Calculated Destruction of Men's Minds*. The Vanguard Press, Inc., 1951.

Hunter, Edward. *Brainwashing: The Story of Men Who Defied It*. New York: Farrar, Straus and Cudahy, 1956.

Hur, Sang-Soo. "Truth and Reconciliation of the Investigative Report of the National Truth Committee of ROK Comparing with Some Critical Points of Jeju April 3rd, 1948 Grand Tragedy," vol. 5, no. 3, Oct. 2015: 259–272.

Hwang, John C. "Lien huan hua: Revolutionary Serial Pictures," in *Popular Media in China: Shaping New Cultural Patterns*, Godwin C. Chu, ed., East-West Center, 1978: 51–72.

Hyun, Soon. [Untitled Korean Red Cross pamphlet on March 1st Movement], 1919 (http://digitallibrary.usc.edu/cdm/ref/collection/p15799coll126/id/5245).

"'I Have Come Home': So Says Hiss as He Arrives at Greenwich Village Apartment." *The New York Times*, 28 Nov. 1954: 37.

"Independence Riots Sweeping Over All Korea," *Jacksonville Daily Journal* (Jacksonville, IL), 9 April 1919: 1.

Institute for Propaganda Analysis. "Propaganda in the Comic Strips," *Scholastic*, May 1940.

"Investigations: The Strange Case of Amerasia." *TIME Magazine*, 12 June 1950.

Isaacs, Harold R. *Scratches on Our Minds*. New York: The John Day Company, 1958.

Isaacson, Walter, and Evan Thomas. *The Wise Men: Six Friends and the World They Made*. New York: Simon & Schuster, 1986.

Isserman, Maurice, and Ellen Schrecker. "'Papers of a Dangerous Tendency': From Major Andre's Boot to the VENONA Files," published in *Cold War Triumphalism: The Misuse of History After the Fall of Communism*. New York: The New Press, 2004.

"It Ain't Funny: Comic Books a Billion Dollar Industry Glorifying Brutality." *Daily Worker*, 13 July 1952: 8.

Jackson, Ben. "'One Nation' Dream: Do Younger South Koreans Want Reunification?" *Korea Exposé*, 6 March 2018.

Jackson, C.D. "Private Media and Public Policy," in *Propaganda in War and Crisis, Materials for American Policy*, Daniel Lerner, ed. New York: George W. Stewart, 1951: 328–341.

Jacobs, Frank. *The MAD World of William M Gaines*. New York: A Bantam Book, 1973.

Jacobs, Steven L., and Mark Weitzman. *Dismantling the Big Lie: The Protocols of the Elders of Zion*. Simon Wiesenthal Center, 2003.

Jacobsen, Anne. *Surprise, Kill, Vanish: The Secret History of CIA Paramilitary Armies, Operators, and Assassins*. Boston: Little Brown and Company, 2019.

Jacobson, Mark. *The Lampshade: A Holocaust Detective Story from Buchenwald to New Orleans*. New York: Simon & Schuster, 2010.

Jager, Sheila Miyoshi. *Brothers at War: The Unending Conflict in Korea*. New York: W.W. Norton, 2013.

James, Rawn, Jr. *The Double V: How Wars, Protest, and Harry Truman Desegregated America's Military*. New York: Bloomsbury Press, 2013.

Jang Jin-Sung. *Dear Leader: Poet, Spy, Escapee—A Look Inside North Korea*. New York: Atria Books, 2014.

Jensen, Helle Strandgaard. "Why Batman was Bad: A Scandinavian Debate About Children's Consumption of Comics and Literature in the 1950s," *Barn*, 2010, vol. 28, no. 3, 2010: 47–70.

Jeppesen, Travis. *See You Again in Pyongyang: A Journey into Kim Jong Un's North Korea*. London: Hachette Books, 2018.

Jerome, V.J. *Culture in a Changing World: a Marxist Approach*. New York: New Century Publishers, 1947.

Jerome, V.J. *Grasp the Weapon of Culture!* New York: New Century Publishers, 1951.

"Jerry Siegel Attacks!," *Das schwarze Korps*, 25 April 1940: 8. Webposted by Randall Bytwerk, 1998, at the German Propaganda Archive. http://www.calvin.edu/academic/cas/gpa/superman.htm.

Johnson, Chalmers. *Dismantling the Empire*. New York: Metropolitan Books, 2010.

Johnson, David K. *The Lavender Scare: The Cold War Persecution of Gays and Lesbians in the Federal Government*. Chicago: The University of Chicago, 2004.

Johnson, Nicholas. "What Do Children Learn from War Comics?" *New Society*, 7 July 1966: 7–12.

"Joint Statement on the Impact of Entertainment Violence on Children," Congressional Public Health Summit, 26 July 26 2000, http://www2.aap.org/advocacy/releases/jstmtevc.htm.

Jones, Gerard. *Men of Tomorrow: Geeks, Gangsters, and the Birth of the Comic Book*. New York: Basic Books, 2004.

Jones, William B., Jr. *Classics Illustrated: A Cultural History*. 2d ed. Jefferson, NC: McFarland, 2011.

Kahn, Albert E. "Comics, TV and Your Child," *Masses & Mainstream*, vol. 6, no. 6, June 1953: 36–43.

Kahn, Albert E. *The Game of Death: Effects of the Cold War on Our Children*. London: Cameron & Kahn, 1953.

Kahn, Albert E. *Matusow Affair: Memoir of a National Scandal*. Mt. Kisko, NY: Moyer Bell Limited, 1987.

Kaku, Michio, and Daniel Axelrod. *To Win a Nuclear War: The Pentagon's Secret War Plans*. New York: Black Rose Books, 1987.

Kalischer, Peter. "Doctor Commando," *Collier's*, 22 Sept. 1951.

Kaneko, Mina, and Francoise Mouly. "Joe Sacco's 'The Great War,'" *The New Yorker*, 19 Nov. 2013, http://www.newyorker.com/online/blogs/books/2013/11/joe-sacco-the-great-war-interview.html.

Kaner, Norman. "I.F. Stone and the Korean War," *Cold War Critics: Alternatives to American Foreign Policy in the Truman Years*, Thomas G. Paterson, ed. London: Quadrangle Books, 1971: 240–265.

Kanigher, Robert. "All Men are Brothers—Starting with Cain and Abel," in *Chris Pedrin's Big Five Information Guide*, vol. 1, no. 1. London: Alton-Kelly Corporation, 1994–1995: 2–6 (unpaginated).

Kaplan, Arie. *From Krakow to Krypton: Jews and Comic Books*. Philadelphia: The Jewish Publication Society, 2008.

Katsiaficas, George. *Asia's Unknown Uprisings: Volume I: South Korean Social Movements in the 20th Century*. Oakland, CA: PM Press, 2012.

Kauffman, Bill. *Ain't My America: The Long, Noble History of Antiwar Conservatism and Middle-American Anti-Imperialism*. New York: Metropolitan Books, 2008.

Kauffmann, Stanley. *Albums of Early Life: Memoirs*. London: Ticknor and Fields, 1980.

Kaufman, Burton I. *The Korean War: Challenges in Crisis, Credibility, and Command*. New York: Alfred A. Knopf, 1986.

Kaye, Dr. Jeffrey S., and H.P. Albarelli, Jr. "The Hidden Tragedy of the CIA's Experiments on Children," *Truthout*, 11 Aug 2010.

"KCNA on Tremendous Damage Done to DPRK by US," *Korean Central News Agency of DPRK* (Pyongyang) via Korea News Service (KNS), 24 June 2010, https://www.globalsecurity.org/wmd/library/news/dprk/2010/dprk-100624-kcna06.htm.

Keene, Donald. *Emperor of Japan: Meiji and His World, 1852–1912*. New York: Columbia University Press, 2002.

Keevak, Michael. *Becoming Yellow: A Short History of Racial Thinking*. Princeton, NJ: Princeton University Press, 2011.

Kellman, George. "Anti-Jewish Agitation," *American Jewish Yearbook*, American Jewish Committee, 1952: 61–70.

Kendall, David. *The Mammoth Book of Best War Comics*. London: Running Press, 2007.

Kepler, Hazel (Cloughley). *The Child and His Play: A Planning Guide for Parents and Teachers*. New York: Funk & Wagnalls Company, 1952.

Kercher, Stephen E. "Cartoons as 'Weapons of Wit': Bill Mauldin and Herbert Block Take on America's Postwar Anti-communist Crusade," *International Journal of Comic Art*, Fall 2005: 311–320.

Kidman, Shawna. "Self-Regulation Through Distribution: Censorship and the Comic Book Industry in 1954," *The Velvet Light Trap* no. 75, Spring 2015: 21–37.

Kihss, Peter. "No Harm in Horror, Comics Issuer Says," *The New York Times*, 22 April 1954: 1.

Kim, Dong-Choon. *The Unending Korean War: A Social History*. Larkspur, CA: Tamal Vista Publications, 2000.

Kim, Dong-Choon. "Forgotten War, Forgotten Massacres—the Korean War (1950–1953) as Licensed Mass Killings," *Journal of Genocide Research*, vol. 6, no. 4, Dec 2004: 523–544.

Kim, Dong-Choon. "Uncovering the Hidden Histories of the Korean War: The Work of South Korea's Truth and Reconciliation Commission," 27 March 2009, http://www.kpolicy.org/documents/policy/090327dongchoonkimuncoveringhiddenhistories.html.

Kim, Hyun-Kyung, Elizabeth Philipp and Hattie Chung. "North Korea's Biological Weapons Program: The Known and the Unknown," Harvard Kennedy School Belfer Center for Science and International Affairs, October 2017.

Kim, Suki. *Without You There Is No Us: Undercover Among the Sons of North Korea's Elite.* London: Penguin Random House, 2015.

Kim, Victoria. "Lost and Found in Uzbekistan: The Korean Story," *The Diplomat,* 2016, http://thediplomat.com/2016/06/lost-and-found-in-uzbekistan-the-korean-story-part-1/.

Kim Young-Sik, Ph.D. "A Brief History of the US-Korea Relations Prior to 1945," A paper presented at the University of Oregon, sponsored by 'MeetKorea in Eugene,' 15 May 2003.

Kindsvatter, Peter S. *American Soldiers: Ground Combat in the World Wars, Korea, and Vietnam.* Lawrence: University Press of Kansas, 2003.

Kinzer, Stephen. *Poisoner in Chief: Sidney Gottlieb and the CIA Search for Mind Control.* New York: Henry Holt and Company, 2019.

Kirby, Jack. Interviewed by Will Eisner, *The Spirit,* no. 39, Feb. 1982.

Kirby, Jack. "Jack Kirby Interview," by Gary Groth, *The Comics Journal,* no. 134, February 1990, 23 May 2011, http://www.tcj.com/jack-kirby-interview/5/.

Kitchen, Denis. "The Fate of Corporate Crime Comics," *The Comics Journal,* no. 92, August, 1984: 107.

Kitchen, Denis. "Introduction," "Biro & Wood: Partners in Crime," in *Blackjacked and Pistol-whipped: Crime Does Not Pay.* New York: Dark Horse Books, 2011.

Kitchen, Denis, and Paul Buhle. *The Art of Harvey Kurtzman: The Mad Genius of Comics.* New York: Harry N. Abrams, 2009.

Koop, Theodore F. *Weapon of Silence.* Chicago: The University of Chicago Press, 1946.

"Korea: the 'Forgotten' War; Casualties Rise—No End to Conflict in Sight." *U.S. News & World Report,* 5 Oct. 1951: 21.

Krassner, Paul. *Confessions of an Unconfined Nut: Misadventures in the Counterculture.* New York: Soft Skull Press, 2012.

Kruse, Kevin M. *One Nation Under God: How Corporate America Invented Christian America.* New York: Basic Books, 2015.

Kubert, Joe. Interviewed by Will Eisner, *The Spirit,* no. 40, April 1983.

Kubert, Joe. "The Joe Kubert Interview" (by Gary Groth), *The Comics Journal,* 1994, http://www.tcj.com/the-joe-kubert-interview/3/.

Kubert, Joe. *The Joe Kubert Archives Vol. 1: Weird Horrors & Daring Adventures.* Seattle: Fantagraphics, 2012.

Kunitz, Stanley J. (as "S.J.K.,"), "The Roving Eye: Libraries, to Arms!" *Wilson Library Bulletin* vol. 15, April 1941: 670–671.

Kurtzman, Harvey. *Two-Fisted Tales.* New York: Russ Cochran, 1980.

Kurtzman, Harvey. *Frontline Combat.* New York: Russ Cochran, 1982.

Kurtzman, Harvey, and Gary Groth. *Corpse on the Imjin! and Other Stories.* Seattle: Fantagraphics Books, 2012.

Kutler, Stanley I. *The American Inquisition: Justice and Injustice in the Cold War.* San Francisco: Hill & Wang, 1982.

Kwon, Heonik. *The Other Cold War.* New York: Columbia University Press, 2010.

Lambert, Josh. *Unclean Lips: Obscenity, Jews, and American Culture.* New York: New York University Press, 2014.

Landesman, Jay. *Rebel Without Applause.* New York: Paragon House, 1987, 1990.

Langer, Mark. "Why the Atom is our Friend: Disney, General Dynamics and the USS *Nautilus*," *Art History,* vol. 18, no. 1, March 1995: 63–96.

Larrabee, Eric. "The Cultural Context of Sex Censorship." *Law & Contemporary Problems,* vol. 20, no. 4, Autumn 1955: 672–688.

Laurie, Dr. Clayton. "The Korean War and the Central Intelligence Agency," in "Baptism By Fire: CIA Analysis of the Korean War Overview," published under the imprimaturs of the Historical Collections Division of CIA's Information Management Services, Center for the Study of Intelligence, Harry S. Truman Library and Museum, and The Eisenhower Presidential Library and Museum, 2010, http://www.foia.cia.gov/collection/baptism-fire-cia-analysis-korean-war-overview#Daily Reports 1950.

Leab, Daniel J. "Cold War Comics," *Columbia Journalism Review,* Winter 1965: 427.

Lee, Jae-Bong. "US Deployment of Nuclear Weapons in 1950s South Korea & North Korea's Nuclear Development: Toward Denuclearization of the Korean Peninsula," *The Asia-Pacific Journal, Japan Focus,* vol. 7, issue 8, no. 3, 17 Feb. 2009: 1–17.

Lee, Jean H. "For North Koreans, the War Never Ended." *The Wilson Quarterly,* Spring 2017.

Lee, Jong-Seok. "The Transformation of China-North Korea Relations and Its Implications," in *Understanding North Korea: Indigenous Perspectives* (Google eBook), Han Jong-woo, Jung Tae-hern, eds. New York: Lexington Books, 4 Dec. 2013.

Lee, Martin A. *The Beast Awakens: Fascism's Resurgence from Hitler's Spymasters to Today's Neo-Nazi Groups and Right-Wing Extremists.* New York: Routledge, 2000.

Lee, Na Young. *The Construction of U.S. Camptown Prostitution in South Korea: Trans/formation and Resistance.* PhD. Diss., Dep't of Women's Studies, University of Maryland, 2006.

Lee, Stan. "The Playboy Interview: Stan Lee on Superheroes, Marvel and Being Just Another Pretty Face" (interview conducted by David Hochman), *Playboy*, April 2014.

Lee, Steven. "The Korean Armistice and the End of Peace: The US-UN Coalition and the Dynamics of War-Making in Korea, 1953–1976," *The Journal of Korean Studies,* vol. 18, no. 2, Fall 2013: 183–224.

Lee, Steven High. *The Korean War*. London: Pearson Education Limited, 2001.

Lefevre, Pascal. "The Cold War and Belgian Comics (1945–1991)," *International Journal of Comic Art*, vol. 6, no. 2, Fall 2004: 195–204.

Leffler, Melvyn P. "Review Essay: Inside Enemy Archives: The Cold War Reopened," *Foreign Affairs,* July/August 1996: 120–135.

Legion of Andy, "BEN DAY DOTS Part 8: 1930s to 1950s—The Golden Age of Comics," 26 Aug. 2016, https://legionofandy.com/2016/08/26/ben-day-dots-part-8-1930s-to-1950s-the-golden-age-of-comics/.

"Legislator Asks Comic Books Probe." *Holland Evening Sentinel* (Holland, MI), 4 Feb. 1954: 1.

Legman, Gershon. "The Comic Books and the Public," Proceedings of the Association for the Advancement of Psychotherapy, *American Journal of Psychotherapy*, July 1948: 473–477.

Legman, Gershon. *Love and Death: A Study in Censorship*. New York: Hacker (originally self-published in 1949), 1963.

Lengyel, Emil. "The Battlecries Of Hitlerism Modified as Election Nears: The Slogans That Drew Germans High and Low are Tempered by the Prospect of a Mandate from the Voters of the Reich," *The New York Times*, 10 July 1932: XX3.

Lent, John A., "Korean Cartooning: Historical and Contemporary Perspectives," *Korean Culture*, vol. 16, no. 1, Spring 1995: 8–19.

Lent, John A., ed. *Pulp Demons: International Dimensions of the Postwar Anti-Comics Campaign*. Teaneck, NJ: Fairleigh Dickinson University Press, 1999.

Lent, John A. *Asian Comics*. Jackson: The University Press of Mississippi, 2015.

Lent, John A., and Xu Ying. *Comics Arts in China*. Jackson: The University Press of Mississippi, 2017.

Lentz, Robert J. *Korean War Filmography: 91 English Language Features Through 2000*. Jefferson, NC: McFarland, 2003.

Lepore, Jill. "The Last Time Democracy Almost Died: Learning from the Upheaval of the Nineteen-Thirties," *The New Yorker*, 27 Jan. 2020.

Leslie, Ian. "The Scientists Persuading Terrorists to Spill Their Secrets," *The Guardian*, 13 Oct. 2017.

Leuchtenburg, William E. "The Conversion of Harry Truman," *American Heritage*, Nov. 1991, http://www.americanheritage.com/content/conversion-harry-truman.

Levin, Bob. "The Anti-War Comics of Harvey Kurtzman," *The Comics Journal*, 4 Sept. 2013, http://www.tcj.com/the-anti-war-of-harvey-kurtzman/.

Lifton, Robert Jay. *Home from the War: Vietnam Veterans: Neither Victims nor Executioners*. New York: Simon & Schuster, 1973.

Lifton, Robert Jay, M.D. *Thought Reform and the Psychology of Totalism: A Study of "Brainwashing" in China*. New York: W.W. Norton & Company, 1961.

Lim, Yeo-Joo. "Educational Graphic Novels: Korean Children's Favorite Now," *Bookbird*, no. 4, 2011: 40–48.

Lim, Yeojoo. "Seriously, What Are They Reading? An Analysis of Korean Children's Reading Behavior regarding Educational Graphic Novels," PhD diss., Library and Information Science, University of Illinois–Urbana-Champaign, 2012.

Lindley, Robin. "The Legacy of Pulitzer-Prize Winning Cartoonist Bill Mauldin: An Interview with Biographer Todd DePastino," Sunday, 8 June 2008, 21:56, http://hnn.us/articles/50199.html.

Linenthal, Edward T. and Tom Engelhardt, eds. *History Wars: The Enola Gay and Other Battles for the American Past*. New York: Henry Holt and Company, 1996.

"Little Moe Fights On," *The Machinist*, 16 June 1966: 8.

Lobel, Jules. *Success Without Victory: Lost Legal Battles and the Long Road to Justice in America*. New York: New York University Press, 2003.

Lockwood, George J. Letter to the editor, *Columbia Journalism Review,* Summer 1965: 45.

Lockwood, Jeffrey A. *Six-legged Soldiers: Using Insects as Weapons of War*. London: Oxford University Press, 2009.

Loftin, Grant. "Totah Topic," *Farmington Daily Times* (Farmington, NM), 21 Aug. 1953.

Lohbeck, Don. *Racial Aspect of the Coming Political Struggle*. London: Gerald L.K. Smith, 1951.

London, Jack. "The Unparalleled Invasion: Excerpt from Walt Nervin's 'Certain Essays in History,'" *McClure's*, 1910: 308–315.

"London Newspaper Wars on U. S. Comics, Ascribing 'Anti-British Slant' to Two Strips." *The New York Times*, 9 Aug. 1950: 24.

Lone, Stewart, and Gavan MacCormack. *Korea Since 1850*. New York: St. Martin's Press, 1993.

Loucks, H.L. *The Great Conspiracy of the House of Morgan Exposed, and How to Defeat It*. Watertown, SD: H.L. Loucks, 1916.

Lovibond, S.H. "The Effect of Media Stressing Crime and Violence upon Children's Attitudes," *Social Problems*, Summer 1967: 91–100.

Lueders, Bill. "The H-Bomb Case Revisited," *The Progressive*, Aug/Sept 2019: 44–48.

Lund, Martin. "Re-Constructing the Man of Steel: Superman 1938–1941," *Jewish American History, and the Invention of the Jewish-Comics Connection,* Palgrave Macmillan, 2016.

Lyhm, B.C. "Alien Rule Must Go, Says Korean," *The Evening Star* (Washington, D.C.), 26 Jan. 1920: 3.

Lynn, Gabriel. "The Case Against the Comics: A Study by Gabriel Lynn," St. Paul, MN, *Catechetical Guild,* 1944.

Lynn, Gabriel. "The Teacher and the Comics," St. Paul, MN, *Catechetical Guild,* c. 1946.

Ma, Sheng-mei. *The Deathly Embrace: Orientalism and Asian American Identity.* Minneapolis: University of Minnesota Press, 2000.

MacDonald, Callum. "'So Terrible a Liberation'—The UN Occupation of North Korea," *Bulletin of Concerned Asian Scholars* 23:2, April-June 1991.

MacDonald, Dwight. "A Theory of 'Popular Culture," *Politics,* Feb. 1944: 20–23.

MacDonald, Dwight. "Field Notes," *Politics,* April 1945: 112–114.

MacDonald, Dwight. "A Theory of Mass Culture," *Diogenes,* no. 3, Summer 1953: 1–17.

Macintyre, Ben. *A Spy Among Friends: Kim Philby and the Great Betrayal.* London: Crown Publishers, 2014.

Madison, Nathan Vernon. *Anti-Foreign Imagery in American Pulps and Comic Books: 1920–1960.* Jefferson, NC: McFarland, 2013.

Makemson, Harlen. "Cartoonists, Political," *Encyclopedia of Journalism: A–C., Volume 1,* Christopher H. Sterling, ed. London: SAGE Publications, 2009.

"Malcolm Ater, 77, Dies; Comic Books Publisher." *The Washington Post,* 12 May 1992: D8.

Malia, Martin. *Soviet Tragedy: A History of Socialism in Russia.* New York: Free Press, 1994.

Malter, Morton S. "The Content of Current Comic Magazines," *The Elementary School Journal,* vol. 52, no. 9, May 1952: 505–510.

"Man and Superman" (editorial), *The New York Times,* 8 Nov. 1952: 16.

Manchester, William. *American Caesar: Douglas MacArthur, 1880–1964.* Little, Brown & Co., 1978.

Mancini, John. "Jack London: War Correspondent," n.d., http://www.jack-london.org/05-mat-warcorrespodet_e.htm.

Mangus, Don. "In Memory of Robert Kanigher: 1915–2002," 2002, http://www.comicartville.com/kanigherobit.htm.

"Manners & Morals: Americana," *TIME Magazine,* vol. 51, no. 17, 26 Apr. 1948: 26.

Mannes, Marya. "Junior Has A Craving," *New Republic,* 17 Feb. 1947: 20–23.

Mannes, Marya. "The 'Night of Horror' in Brooklyn," *The Reporter,* 27 Jan. 1955: 21–26.

Manning, Martin J., and Herbert Romerstein. *Historical Dictionary of American Propaganda.* "Comics and Comic Strips," Greenwood Publishing Group, 2004.

Mansourov, Alexandre Y. "Kim Jong Un's Nuclear Doctrine and Strategy: What Everyone Needs to Know," NAPSNet Special Reports, 16 Dec. 2014, https://nautilus.org/napsnet/napsnet-special-reports/kim-jong-uns-nuclear-doctrine-and-strategy-what-everyone-needs-to-know/.

Mark, Eduard M. "Allied Relations in Iran, 19411–947: The Origins of a Cold War Crisis, *The Wisconsin Magazine of History,* vol. 59, no. 1, Autumn 1975: 51–63.

Marks, John. *The Search for the Manchurian Candidate: The CIA and Mind Control.* New York: McGraw-Hill Book Company, 1980.

Markstein, Don. "The Avenger," n.d., http://www.toonopedia.com/avenger.htm.

Marlantes, Karl. *What It Is Like to Go to War.* New York: Atlantic Monthly Press, 2011.

Marschall, Richard. *America's Great Comic Book Artists.* New York: Abbeville Press, 1989.

Marsden, Bobbie. "Children and the Cold war," *New Frontiers,* vol. 3, no. 3, 1954: 13–16.

Marston, Mrs. Philip, "Just for Fun," *The General Federation Clubwoman,* April 1948.

Marston, William Moulton. "Why 100,000,000 Americans Read Comics," *The American Scholar,* Winter 1943–1944, https://theamericanscholar.org/wonder-woman/#.

Martin, David C. *A Wilderness of Mirrors, Intrigue, Deception, and the Secrets that Destroyed Two of the Cold War's Most Important Agents.* San Francisco: HarperCollins, 1980, Lyons Press edition, 2003.

Martin, Douglas. "Chung Eun-yong, Who Helped Expose U.S. Killings of Koreans, Dies at 91," *The New York Times,* 22 Aug. 2014.

Martin, Harold, H. "How Do Our Negro Troops Measure Up?," *Saturday Evening Post,* 16 June 1951: 30–31, 139–140.

Martin, Nick. "Alan Moore Turns His Back on Comics," 20 Aug. 2010, http://www.blackbookmag.com/article/alan-moore-turns-his-back-on-comics/21622.

Martz, Colonel John D, Jr., QMC. "Homeward Bound," *Quartermaster Review,* May/June, 1954, http://www.qmfound.com/homeward_bound_korea.htm.

Massey, Cal. "'You Have to Earn Your Talent Through Discipline' … Artist Cal Massey Talks Candidly to Jim Amash About His Comics Career in the 1950s." *Alter Ego* vol. 5, no. 103, October 2011: 55–66.

Mastny, Vojtech, Sven S. Holtsmark, Andreas Wenger, eds. *War Plans and Alliances in the Cold War: Threat Perceptions in the East and West.* New York: Routledge, 2006.

Matray, James I. "Dean Acheson's Press Club Speech Reexamined." *Journal of Conflict Studies,* Aug. 2002, https://journals.lib.unb.ca/index.php/JCS/article/view/366/578.

Matray, James I. "Historiographical Review, Korea's War at 60: A survey of the Literature," *Cold War History,* vol. 11, no. 1, February 2011: 99–129.

Matray, James I. "Mixed Message: The Korean Armistice Negotiations at Kaesong," *Pacific Historical Review*, vol. 81, no. 2, May 2012: 240–241.

Matthews, J.B. "The Commies Go After the Kids: How the Reds Inject Their Poison Into Children," *The American Legion Magazine*, Dec. 1949: 14–15, 60, 62–63.

Mauger, Peter. "Children's Reading," *Arena, A Magazine of Modern Literature Special Issue: The USA Threat to British Culture*, Vol. II, New Series 8, June/July 1951.

Mauger, Peter. "The Lure of the Comics." *The International Women's Day Committee* (London), April 1952.

Mauldin, Bill. *Bill Mauldin in Korea*. New York: Norton, 1952.

Mauldin, Bill. *Let's Declare Ourselves Winners ... and Get the Hell Out*. San Francisco: Presidio Press, 1985.

May, Larry. *The Big Tomorrow: Hollywood and the Politics of the American Way*. Chicago: The University of Chicago Press, 2000.

Mayo, Charles W. "The Role of Forced Confession in the Communist 'Germ Warfare' Propaganda Campaign," *Department of State Bulletin*, 26 Oct. 1953: 643.

Mazarr, Michael J. *North Korea and the Bomb: A Case Study of Nonproliferation*. New York: St. Martin's Press, 1995.

McAllister, Matthew P., Edward H. Sewell and Ian Gordon. *Comics & Ideology*. New York: Peter Lang, 2001.

McChesney, Robert W. *Digital Disconnect: How Capitalism Is Turning the Internet Against Democracy*. New York: The New Press, 2013.

McCloud, Scott. *Understanding Comics*. Princeton, WI: Kitchen Sink Press, 1993.

McCormack, Gavan. "Sunshine, Containment, War: The Korean Options," 20 Feb. 2003, http://www.tom.dispatch.com/blog/420/.

McCormack, Gavan. *Target North Korea: Pushing North Korea to the Brink of Nuclear Catastrophe*. New York: Nation Books, 2004.

McCoy, Alfred W. *The Politics of Heroin: CIA Complicity in the Global Drug Trade, Afghanistan, Southeast Asia, Central America*. 2nd rev. ed. Singapore: Lawrence Hill Books, 2003.

McCoy, Alfred W. *A Question of Torture: CIA Interrogation, from the Cold War to the War on Terror*. New York: Metropolitan Books, 2006.

McCoy, Alfred W. *Torture and Impunity: The U.S. Doctrine of Coercive Interrogation*. Madison: University of Wisconsin Press, 2012.

McCullough, David. *Truman*. New York: Simon & Schuster, 1992.

McDermott, Jeanne. *The Killing Winds: The Menace of Biological Warfare*. New York: Arbor House, 1987.

McDonald, Fred. *Television and the Red Menace: The Video Road to Vietnam*. New York: Praeger, 1985.

McGuire, Dave. *Report on Comic Books* by Dave McGuire, City Director of Public Relations to Mayor Morrison and the Commission Council of the City of New Orleans, 18 Oct. 1948.

McLuhan, Herbert Marshall. *The Mechanical Bride: Folklore of Industrial Man*. New York: The Vanguard Press, 1951.

McReynolds, Bill. "Vulgarity Rules Racks," *The Daily Texan*, 26 Nov. 1952.

McWilliams, John C. *The Protectors: Harry J. Anslinger and the Federal Bureau of Narcotics, 1930–1962*. Wilmington: University of Delaware Press, 1990.

Mead, Ronald. "Comics Are Big Business," *The Advertiser's Digest*, vol. 12 or 13 (condensed from *Printing Magazine*), 1947.

Medhurst, Martin J. "Text and Context in the 1952 Presidential Campaign: Eisenhower's 'I Shall Go to Korea' Speech," *Presidential Studies Quarterly*, Sept. 2000: 464–484.

"Medicine." *LIFE* Magazine vol. 30, no. 6, 5 Feb 1951: 82–84.

Meek, James Gordon. "MAD AT THE FBI," *ATOMIC Magazine*, Summer 2002, http://www.atomicmag.com/articles/2002/fbi_mad.shtml.

Meiser, Rebecca. "Life After Harvey: Three Years After Comic Book Legend Harvey Pekar's Death, Joyce Brabner, His Widow, Fights to Preserve His Legacy and Emerges as an Artist in Her Own Right," *Cleveland Magazine*. October, 2013.

Melley, Timothy. "Brainwashed! Conspiracy Theory and Ideology in the Postwar United States," *New German Critique*, vol. 103, 2008: 145–164.

Mendes, Gabriel N. *Under the Strain of Color: Harlem's LaFargue Clinic and the Promise of Antiracist Psychiatry*. Ithaca: Cornell University Press, 2015.

Mercado, Stephen C. "Intelligence in Public Literature," *Studies in Intelligence*, vol. 56, no. 1, March 2012.

Mercier, Sebastian T. "'The Whole Furshlugginer Operation': The Jewish Comic Book Industry, 1933–1954," PhD diss., History, Michigan State University, 2018.

Merkel, Lester, ed., *Public Opinion and Foreign Policy*. San Francisco: Harper & Bros. for the Council on Foreign Relations, 1949.

Metcalf, Greg. "If You Read It, I Wrote It: The Anonymous Career of Comic Book Writer Paul S. Newman," *The Journal of Popular Culture*. vol. 29, no. 1, Summer 1995: 147–162.

Meyer, Adolf. *The Commonsense Psychiatry of Dr. Adolf Meyer: Fifty-two Selected Papers Edited, with Biographical Narrative, by Alfred Lief*. New York: McGraw-Hill Book Company, Inc., 1948.

Meyer, Richard C., Brian Iglesias, Otis Frampton, Adam Sattler, and Thomas Jung. *Chosin: Hold the Line*. n.p.: Veterans Expeditionary Media, 2013.

Meyers, Samuel M., and William C. Bradbury, Chapter V: "The Political Behavior of Korean and Chinese Prisoners of War in the Korean Conflict: A Historical Analysis," in *Mass Behavior in Battle and Captivity: The Communist Soldier in the Korean War, Research Studies Directed by William C. Bradbury*, Samuel M. Meyers and Albert D. Biderman, eds. Chicago: University of Chicago Press, 1968.

Meza, F. (of Davis-Monthan Air Force Base,) Letter to the editor: "Those Fake Comics" (letter to the editor), *Tucson Daily Citizen*, 19 Sept. 1952.

Michaelis, David. *Schulz and Peanuts: A Biography.* New York: Harper Perennial, 2008.

Michaud, Gene. "Class Conflicts: Teaching the War Film," *The Radical Teacher*, no. 50 (Spring) 1997: 12–16.

Michener, James. *The Bridges at Toko-Ri.* New York: Random House, 1953.

Mickenberg, Julia L and Philip Nel, eds. *Tales for Little Rebels: A Collection of Radical Children's Literature.* New York: New York University Press, 2008.

Milillo, Diana. "Rape as a Tactic of War: Social and Psychological Perspectives," *Affilia—Journal of Women and Social Work*, vol. 21, no. 2, May 2006: 196–205.

Miller, Robert C. "News Censorship in Korea," *Nieman Reports*, July 1952: 3–6.

Millett, Allan R. *The War for Korea: 1945-1950: A House Burning.* Lawrence: University Press of Kansas, 2005.

Mills, C. Wright. "Nothing to Laugh At," *The New York Times*, 25 April 1954: BR20.

Mills, C. Wright. *The Power Elite.* Oxford University Press, 1956, 2000.

Miscamble, Wilson D. *The Most Controversial Decision: Truman, the Atomic Bombs, and the Defeat of Japan.* Cambridge: Cambridge University Press, 2011.

Miyake, Toshio. "Doing Occidentalism in Contemporary Japan: Nation Anthropomorphism and Sexualized Parody in *Axis Powers Hetalia*." In "Transnational Boys' Love Fan Studies," Kazumi Nagaike and Katshiko Suganuma, eds., special issue, *Transformative Works and Cultures, no. 12*, 2013.

Mizuki, Shigeru. *Showa 1944-1953: A History of Japan.* Montreal: Drawn & Quarterly, 2014.

Monaghan, William E. "Reds and the Comics" (letter to editor), *The Record* (Hackensack, NJ), 27 Sept. 1954: 14.

Monbiot, George. "Obama Is Presiding Over the Biggest Rogue State in the World, Trampling Every Law It Demands That Others Uphold," 9 Sept. 2013, http://www.theguardian.com/commentisfree/2013/sep/09/obama-rogue-state-tramples-every-law.

Mondello, Joe. Various blogposts, http://monarrakorea.blogspot.com, 14–16 March, 2007, 16 March 2008 .

Monroe, Alan D. *Public Opinion in America.* Chicago: Dodd, Mead & Company, 1975.

Moody, Jay. "Druggists Cancel Objectionable Comic Books," *Corona Daily Independent*, 24 May 1954: 1.

Moon, Katherine H.S. *Sex Among Allies: Military Prostitution in U.S.–Korea Relations.* New York: Columbia University Press, 1997.

Moore, Deborah Dash. *GI Jews: How World War II Changed A Generation.* London: Belknap Press, 2004.

Moore, Michael. "Moore Collection Underground Comix," n.d., http://lib.calpoly.edu/spec_coll/comix/.

Morelli, Keith. "Tuskegee Pilot Fought Prejudice and the Enemy During 30-year Career." *The Tampa Tribune*, 12 Feb. 2016.

Morland, Howard. "The Holocaust Bomb: A Question of Time," 1999, rev. 2007, https://fas.org/sgp/eprint/morland.html.

Morrow, Edward A. "ECA Underwrites Laughter for Germans; Finances Comic as Well as True Love Tales," *The New York Times*, 6 Nov. 1948: 6.

Mosse, Hilde L. In "Proceedings of the Association for the Advancement of Psychotherapy," *American Journal of Psychotherapy*, vol. 12, no. 3, 1958: 573–574.

Mossman, Billy C. *United States Army in the Korean War: Ebb and Flow, November 1950-July 1951.* Center of Military History, United States Army, 1990.

Motler, Frank. "Korean War Pre-Code Checklist, 1950–1955," *From the Tomb #9*, 2002 (revised October 30, 2003).

Movius, Gerald W. "Comic Strip Propaganda." *Scribner's Commentator* 11. Nov. 1941: 17.

Muhlen, Norbert. "Submission to Moscow: A Fellow Travelog in the Empire of the Mind," *The New Leader*, 12 Oct. 1946: 12.

Muhlen, Norbert. "Hysteria in America?" *The New Leader*, 26 June 1948: 6.

Muhlen, Norbert. "Comic Books and Other Horrors: Prep School for Totalitarian Society?" *Commentary*, vol. 7, no. I, Jan. 1949: 80–87, plus responses, *Commentary*, March 1949: 29–35.

Muhlen, Norbert. "The Phantom of McCarthyism," *The New Leader*, 21 May 1951: 18.

Muhlen, Norbert. "*A Sign for Cain*" [review], *America*, 24 Sept. 1966: 352–353.

Murray, Chris. "Cold War," in *Encyclopedia of Comic Books and Graphic Novels*, M. Keith Booker, ed., New York: Greenwood, 2010.

Murray, Christopher. *Champions of the Oppressed? Superhero Comics, Popular Culture, and Propaganda in America during World War II.* New York: Hampton Press, 2011.

Murray, Will. "Black Market Comic Books of the Golden Age," *Comic Book Marketplace*, vol. 3, no. 108, Dec. 2003.

Murrell, Jesse L. "Cincinnati Rates the Comic Books," *Parents Magazine*, Feb 1950: 38–39, 83, 85–87.

Murrell, Jesse L., D.D. "Annual Rating of Comic Magazines," *Parents' Magazine*, Nov. 1952: 48–49, 134–135.

Murrell, Jesse L., D.D. "Annual Rating of Comic Magazines," *Parents Magazine*, Oct. 1953: 54–55, 101–102, 104–105.

Murrell, Jesse L., D.D. "Annual Rating of Comic Magazines," *Parents Magazine*, Aug. 1954: 48–49, 111–114.

Musial, Joe (writer.) *Learn How Dagwood Splits the Atom!* Educational Division of King Features Syndicate, Inc., 1949.

"Muslims Celebrate 50 Years in Korea," *Profile: Imam Abu Hanifa (Numan Ibn Thabit)*, 2005, www.islamawareness. net/Asia/KoreaSouth/ks_article001.html.

Muste, A.J. "The Pacifist Position on Korea," *The Progressive*, vol. 14, no. 9, September 1950: 9–11.

Myers, Andrew H. "Resonant Ripples in a Global Pond: The Blinding of Isaac Woodard," n.d., http://faculty. uscupstate.edu/amyers/conference.html.

Myers, B.R. *The Cleanest Race: How North Koreans See Themselves and Why It Matters*. New York: Melville House Publishing, 2010.

Naimark, Norman M. *Stalin's Genocides*. Princeton, NJ: Princeton University Press, 2010.

Nakazawa, Keiji. *I SAW IT*. San Francisco: Educomics (translation of *Ore wa Mita*, 1972), 1982.

Nakazawa, Keiji. *Barefoot Gen, Volume 7* (translation of *Hadashi no Gen*), San Francisco: Last Gasp, 2008.

Nakazawa, Keiji. *Barefoot Gen, Volume 8* (translation of *Hadashi no Gen*). San Francisco: Last Gasp, 2009.

Nakazawa, Keiji. *Barefoot Gen, Volume 9.* (translation of *Hadashi no Gen*). San Francisco: Last Gasp, 2009.

Nakazawa, Keiji. *The Autobiography of Barefoot Gen*. Richard H. Minear, ed. and translator. Lanham, MD: Rowman & Littlefield, Publishers, Inc., 2010.

Nash, Patrick. "Re-imagining the Ku Klux Klan in Chinese Media through the 1950s," *International Journal of Comic Art*, Fall/Winter, 2017: 78–96.

"National Office for Decent Literature (NODL)," in the *New Catholic Encyclopedia*. New York: McGraw-Hill Book Co., 1967.

"National Organization for Decent Literature," in *The Encyclopedia of Censorship*. New York: Facts on File, 1990.

"Navy Bans Two Comic Books as 'Subversive.'" *San Francisco Chronicle*, 30 Aug. 1952: 1.

"Navy Censors Comic Books 'Designed' to Peril Morale," *The Seattle Daily Times* (Seattle, WA), 30 Aug. 1952: 1.

Neer, Robert M. *Napalm*. New York: Harvard University Press, 2013.

"Negro Villain in Comic Book Killed by Youngsters." *The Chicago Defender*, 5 May 1945: 11.

"New York & Comics." *Tide: The Newsmagazine of Advertising, Marketing, and Public Relations*, vol. 23, no. 7, 18 Feb. 1949: 43.

"News in Brief." *Brandon Daily Sun* (Brandon, Manitoba), 25 June 1953: 2.

Newton, Verne W. *Cambridge Spies: The Untold Story of McLean, Philby, and Burgess*. Lanham, MD: Madison Books, 1991.

NODL Evaluation of Comic Books, 1952–1953…: United States Conference of Catholic Bishops Office of the General Secretary Records, Box 201, Folders 8, 15, and 27.

NODL Evaluation of Comic Books, 1954–1955. United States Conference of Catholic Bishops Office of the General Secretary Records, Box 201, Folders 8, 15, and 27.

"Nogeun-ri Tragedy Retold in Cartoon Book," 2006. *The Hankyoreh* (Seoul), 27 Nov. 2006, modified 28 Nov. 2006, http://english.hani.co.kr/arti/english_edition/e_national/174654.html.

North, Sterling. "A National Disgrace," *Chicago Daily News*, 8 May 1940.

North, Sterling. "The Antidote for Comics," *National Parent-Teacher*, 16–17 March 1941.

Norwood, Stephen H. "Marauding Youth and the Christian Front: Antisemitic Violence in Boston and New York During World War II," *American Jewish History*, vol. 91, no. 2, June 2003: 233–267.

Nostrand, Howard. *Graphic Story Magazine no.16*. Summer 1974: 21–39.

Nowlan, Philip, and Richard Calkins. *Buck Rogers in the 25th Century—The Complete Newspaper Dailies: Volume One 1929–1930*. New York: Hermes Press, 2008.

"Number of Comic Books on Newsstands 'Communistic,'" *South Dakota Daily Journal*, 18 Feb. 1954: 3.

Nyberg, Amy Kiste, *Seal of Approval: The History of the Comics Code*. Jackson: University Press of Mississippi, 1998.

Nye, Russel. *The Unembarrassed Muse: The Popular Arts in America*. New York: The Dial Press, 1970.

O'Brien, Tim. *The Things They Carried*. New York: Houghton Mifflin, 1990.

Oh, Arissa H. *To Save the Children of Korea: The Cold War Origins of International Adoption*. Los Angeles: Stanford University Press, 2015.

"Ollie Harrington," *Ebony*, Jan. 1993: 42.

O'Mara, Shane. *Why Torture Doesn't Work: The Neuroscience of Interrogation*. New York: Harvard University Press, 2015.

O'Neill, Mark. "Soviet Involvement in the Korean War: A New View from the Soviet-era Archives," *OAH Magazine of History*, vol. 14, no 3, Spring 2000, http://ushist2112honors.files.wordpress.com/2010/08/oneilkoreanwar.pdf.

Ong, Walter J. "The Comics and the Super State: Glimpses Down the Back Alleys of the Mind," *The Arizona Quarterly: A Journal of Literature, History, Folklore*, vol. 1 no. 3, Autumn, 1945: 34–48.

"Operation GLORY" Condensed from Graves Registration Division, Korean Communications Zone (KCOMZ), *Historical Summary*, Jul-Dec 1954.

Orlean, Susan. *The Library Book*. London: Thorndike Press, 2018.

Orr, Carey, John Parrish and Ed Holland. *1952 Cartoons*. Chicago: Chicago Tribune, 1953.

"Our Country and Our Culture: A Symposium," *Partisan Review*, vol. 19, no. 3, May–June, 1952: 282–326; vol. 19, no.4, July–Aug, 1952: 420–450; vol. 19, no. 5, Sept.–Oct. 1952: 562–597.

"Out of This World," African American History Month Reprise: Sgt. Fury 6—"The Fangs of the Fox" 3 April 2010, http://kb-outofthisworld.blogspot.com/search?q=sgt.+fury.

"Out of This World," "Interview with Joe Kubert re: Our Army At War 113 & 160," 26 May 2010, http://kb-outofthisworld.blogspot.com/2010/05/interview-with-joe-kubert-re-our-army.html.

Owens, Ray. "Jack Kirby: a By-The-Month Chronology," n.d. http://www.marvelmasterworks.com/resources/kirby_chronology1.html.

Packwood, Sgt. Norval E., Jr. *Leatherhead in Korea*. Quantico, VA: Marine Corps Gazette, 1952.

Paddock, Colonel Alfred H., Jr. "Major General Robert Alexis McClure: Forgotten Father of US Army Special Warfare," n.d., www.psywarrior.com/mcclure.html.

Paine, Albert Bigelow. *Th. Nast: His Period and His Pictures*. New York: The MacMillan Company, 1904.

"Parent-Teacher-Association News—Baywood," *San Mateo Times*, 20 Nov. 1948: 10.

Parfrey, Adam. *It's a Man's World*. Port Townsend, WA: Feral House, 2003.

Park, Young. *Korea and the Imperialists: In Search of a National Identity*. New York: AuthorHouse, 1999.

Parker, Fan. "The Teaching of English in a Soviet Middle School, *The Modern Language Journal*, vol. 41, no. 5, May 1957: 229–233.

Pash, Melinda L. *In the Shadow of the Greatest Generation: The Americans who Fought the Korean War*. New York: New York University Press, 2012.

Patrick, Kevin. "The Invisible Medium: Comics Studies in Australia," 2010. http://refractory.unimelb.edu.au/2010/07/18/the-invisible-medium-comics-studies-in-australia-kevin-patrick/.

Paul, James C.N., and Murray L. Schwartz. *Federal Censorship: Obscenity in the Mail*. New York: The Free Press of Glencoe, Inc., 1961.

Pease, Stephen E. *PSYWAR: Psychological Warfare in Korea, 1950–1953*. Harrisburg, PA: Stackpole Books, 1992.

Pedler, Martyn. "An Interview with Joe Kubert," *Bookslut*, June 2010, http://www.bookslut.com/features/2010_06_016203.php.

Pedrin, Chris. *Pedrin's Big Five Information Guide*, vol. 1, no. 1. Redwood City, CA: Alton-Kelly Corporation, 1994–1995.

Pekar, Harvey, and Joyce Brabner. "Harvey Pekar & Joyce Brabner By the People, For the People" in *Comic Book Rebels: Conversations with the Creators of the New Comics,* Stanley Wiater & Stephen R. Bissette, eds. New York: Donald I. Fine, Inc., 1993.

Pembroke, Michael. *Korea: Where the American Century Began*. New York: Oneworld, 2018.

Petersen, Martin. "The Downfall of a Model Citizen? Family Background in North Korean Graphic Novels." *Korean Studies*, vol. 36, no. 1, 2012: 83–122.

Petersen, Martin. "Sleepless in the DPRK: Graphic Negotiations of 'Family' in The True Identity of Pear Blossom." *Scandinavian Journal of Comic Art*, vol. 1, no. 2, 2012: 30–58.

Peterson, H.C. *Propaganda for War: The Campaign Against American Neutrality 1914–1917*. Norman: University of Oklahoma Press, 1939.

Petrovich, Michael B. "The View from Yugoslavia," in *Witnesses to the Origins of the Cold War*, Thomas T. Hammond, ed. Seattle: University of Washington Press, 1982.

Pickett, William B. *Eisenhower Decides to Run: Presidential Politics and Cold War Strategy*. New York: Ivan R. Dee, 2000.

Pierpaoli, Paul G. *Truman and Korea: The Political Culture of the Early Cold War*. Columbia: University of Missouri Press, 1999.

Pilgrim, David. *Understanding Jim Crow: Using Racist Memorabilia to Teach Tolerance and Promote Social Justice*. Oakland, CA: PM Press, 2017.

Pilgrim, David. *Watermelons, Nooses, and Straight Razors: Stories from the Jim Crow Museum*. Oakland, CA: PM Press, 2017.

Pinkston, Daniel. "Why declaring an end to the Korean War is more complicated than you might think: Five conflicts continue on the peninsulas—unsustainable peace will require an end to them all," *NK News* 12 Nov. 2018.

Pitts, Leonard, Jr. *Stan Lee: Conversations*. Jeff McLaughlin, ed. Jackson: The University Press of Mississippi, 2007.

"Plague Is Believed Raging Among Foe." *The New York Times*, 19 Jan 1951: 5.

"Policing the Comics," *CQ Researcher*, 21 March 1952.

"The Popularisation of War in Comic Strips 1958–1988." *History Workshop Journal* no. 42, Autumn 1996: 180–189.

Porter, Gareth. "How Cheney & His Allies Created North Korea Nuclear Missile Crisis," *Truthout.org*, 30 Dec. 2017.

Porter, Gareth. "How Corporate Media Got the Trump Kim Summit All Wrong," *Truthdig*, 11 June 2018.

Powell, Thomas. "Biological Warfare in the Korean War: Allegations and Cover-up," *Socialism and Democracy*, vol. 31, no.1, March 2017: 23–42.

Powell, Thomas. "On the Biological Warfare 'Hoax' Thesis," *Socialism and Democracy*, vol. 32, no. 1, 2018: 1–22.

Powers, Richard Gid. *G-Men: Hoover's FBI in American Popular Culture*. Urbana: Southern Illinois University Press, 1983.

Powers, Richard Gid. *Not Without Honor: The History of American Anticommunism*. New York: The Free Press, 1995.

Prasso, Sheridan. *The Asian Mystique: Dragon Ladies, Geisha Girls, & Our Fantasies of the Exotic Orient*. New York: Public Affairs, 2005.

"The Press: East Meets West," *Time Magazine*, vol. 54, no. 26, 26 Dec. 1949: 37.

"The Press: Trouble for the Mercury," *Time Magazine,* vol. 60, no. 23, 8 Dec. 1952: 42.

"The Press: The Dior (Horror) Look," *Time Magazine,* vol. 66, no. 1, 10 Jan. 1955: 38.

Preston, Paul. *Franco: A Biography*. New York: Basic Books, 1994.

"Preview of the War We Do Not Want: Russia's Defeat and Occupation, 1952–1960," (Multiple authors), *Collier's,* 27 Oct. 1951.

"Prisoners Crave Comic Books," *The New York Times,* 24 April 1954: 4:6.

Pritchard, Robert L. "California Un-American Activities Investigations: Subversion on the Right?" *California Historical Society Quarterly*, vol. 49, no. 4, Dec. 1970: 309–327.

"Problems Comic Books Produce." *The Orlando Sentinel*, 23 Feb 1954.

"Propaganda and Children During the Hitler Years," Jewish Virtual Library: A Project of AICE, n.d., https://www.jewishvirtuallibrary.org/propaganda-and-children-during-the-hitler-years.

Pryor, Thomas M. "2D Metro Film Due on Medical Corps." *The New York Times,* 1 March 1952: 9.

"Publishers Say 'Crime Comics' Are for Adults." *The Canyon News* (Canyon, TX), 12 Aug. 1948.

Pustz, Matthew. *Comic Books and American Cultural History: An Anthology*. London: Continuum International Publishing Group, 2012.

Pyle, Kevin C. and Scott Cunningham. *Bad For You: Exposing the War on Fun!* New York: Henry Holt and Company, 2014.

Quattro, Ken. "The Comics Detective: Mr. Gleason, Are You Now or Have You Ever Been…?," 9 July 2011, http://thecomicsdetective.blogspot.com/2011/07/mr-gleason-are-you-now-or-you-have-you-ever.html.

Quattro, Ken. "Sincerely Yours, Busy," The Comics Detective (blog), 24 Jan. 2013, http://thecomicsdetective.blogspot.com/2013/01/sincerely-yours-busy.html.

Quattro, Ken. "Josette Frank: Alone Against the Storm, Part 2," 10 March 2014, http://thecomicsdetective.blogspot.com/2014/02/josette-frank-alone-against-storm-part-2.html.

"Quits Post on Committee," *Mansfield News Journal* (OH), 16 March 1955: 44.

Radosh, Ronald. *Commies: A Journey Through the Old Left, the New Left and the Leftover Left*. New York: Encounter Books, 2001.

Rand, Ayn. "The Wreckage of the Consensus," in *Capitalism the Unknown Ideal*. New York: Signet, 1967.

Rand, Ayn. "To Whom It May Concern." *The Objectivist* vol. 7 no. 5, 1968: 449–456.

Rand, Ayn. *The New Left: The Anti-Industrial Revolution*. New York: Signet, 1971.

Reibman, James E. "Fredric Wertham: A Social Psychiatrist Characterizes Crime Comic Books and Media Violence as Public Health Issues," in *Pulp Demons: International Dimensions of the Postwar Anti-comics Campaign*, John A. Lent, ed. Madison, NJ: Fairleigh Dickinson University Press, 1999: 234–268.

Reidelbach, Maria. "Introduction," *Against the Grain: MAD Artist Wallace Wood*. Bob Stewart, ed. Raleigh, NC: TwoMorrows Publishing, 2003.

Reister, Frank A. *Battle Casualties and Medical Statistics: US Army Experience in the Korean War*. Washington, DC: The Surgeon General, Department of the Army, 1973.

Remarque, Erich Maria. *All Quiet on the Western Front*. New York: Fawcett Books, 1928.

Remez, Gideon. "A Find Unlocks Comics Mystery," *Tablet*, 8 Nov. 2012.

Report of the International Scientific Commission for the Investigation of the Facts Concerning Bacterial Warfare in Korea and China (With Appendices) (Peking), 1952.

Reporters Without Borders, "2020 World Press Freedom Index," 2020. https://rsf.org/en/ranking#.

Reynolds, Elzada M. "Comics: A Teaching Aid for Slow Learners," MS thesis, Education, New Jersey State Teachers College at Newark, April 1951.

Rhie, Won-bok. *Korea Unmasked—In Search of The Country, The Society and the People*. Seoul: Gimm-Young International, 2002.

Ricca, Brad. *Super Boys: The Amazing Adventures of Jerry Siegel and Joe Shuster—the Creators of Superman*. New York: St. Martin's Press, 2013.

Riches, Adam (with Tim Parker and Robert Frankland). *When the Comics Went to War: Comic Book War Heroes*. New York: Mainstream Publishing Company, 2009.

Ridgeway, Matthew B. *The Korean War: How We Met the Challenge, How All-Out Asian War Was Averted, Why MacArthur Was Dismissed, Why Today's War Objectives Must Be Limited*. New York: Doubleday & Company, Inc., 1967.

Riedel, Stefan. "Biological Warfare and Bioterrorism: a Historical Review," *BUMC Proceedings*, 2004.

Rifas, Leonard. "The International Monetary Fund in Human Terms," *Multinational Monitor*, July 1983: back cover.

Rifas, Leonard. "War Makes Men," *Bulletin of the Council of Interracial Books for Children*, vol. 14, no.6, 1983: 8–12.

Rifas, Leonard. "The Forgotten War Comics: the Korean War and American Comic Books," MA thesis, Communications, University of Washington, Seattle, 1991.

Rifas, Leonard. "Comic Book Reflections on the Red Menace, *Comic Books and America, 1945–1954*, a review." *The Comics Journal*, no. 140, Feb. 1991: 45–47.

Rifas, Leonard, in Dave Schreiner, ed. *Kitchen Sink Press: The First 25 Years*. Northampton, MA: Kitchen Sink Press, 1994.

Rifas, Leonard. "Underground Comix," entry in *The Encyclopedia of the American Left* (Mari Jo Buhle, Paul Buhle and Dan Georgakas, eds.,) 2nd edition, London: Oxford University Press, 1998.

Rifas, Leonard. *The Big Picture: Visualizing the Global Economy*. Seattle: EduComics, 1999.

Rifas, Leonard. "Addressing Lent's Demons: *Pulp Demons*," *The Comics Journal*, no. 221, March, 2000: 95–98.

Rifas, Leonard. "International Aspects of the American Anti-Comic Book Crusade," *The Comics Journal*, no. 221, March 2000: 98–100.

Rifas, Leonard, "Cold War Comics," *The International Journal of Comic Art*, vol. 2, no. 1, Spring 2001: 3–32.

Rifas, Leonard."Racial Imagery, Racism, Individualism, and Underground Comix," *ImageText*, vol. 1, no.1, Spring 2004, http://imagetext.english.ufl.edu/archives/v1_1/rifas/.

Rifas, Leonard. "Globalizing Comic Books from Below: How Manga Came to America," *International Journal of Comic Art*, v. 6, no. 2, Fall 2004: 138–171.

Rifas, Leonard. "'And Especially Dr. Hilde L. Mosse': Wertham's Research Collaborator," *International Journal of Comic Art*, Vol. 8, No. 1, Spring/Summer 2006: 17–44.

Rifas, Leonard. "Cartooning and Nuclear Power: From Industry Advertising to Activist Uprising and Beyond." *PS: Political Science & Politics*, vol. 40, no. 02, Apr. 2007: 255–260.

Rifas, Leonard. "Educational Comics," *Encyclopedia of Comic Books and Graphic Novels, Volume 1: A-L*, M. Keith Booker, ed. Santa Barbara, CA: Greenwood, 2010: 160–169.

Rifas, Leonard. "Ideology: The Construction of Race and History in *Tintin in the Congo.: Critical Approaches to Comics: Theories and Methods*, ed. by Matthew J. Smith and Randy Duncan. London: Routledge, 2012: 221–234.

Rifas, Leonard. "Quoz." *Treasury of Mini Comics: Volume One*, Michael Dowers, ed. Seattle: Fantagraphics Books, 2013: 10–32.

Rifas, Leonard. "Frederic Wertham: Scientist (?): A Transgeneration Paper in Two Parts," *International Journal of Comic Art*, vol. 15, no. 2, Fall 2013: 219–267.

Rifas, Leonard. "*Comics and Conflict: Patriotism and Propaganda from WWII Through Operation Iraqi Freedom*, a review," *Journal of American History*, vol. 102, no. 2, 2015: 595–596.

Rifas, Leonard. "Korean War Comic Books and the Militarization of US Masculinity," *Positions: Asia Critique*, vol, 23, no. 4, 2015: 619–632.

Rifas, Leonard. "'Struggling Independently to Understand the World': My Career in Comics Scholarship and Creation." *International Journal of Comic Art*, vol. 17, no. 2, 2015: 362–374.

Rifas, Leonard. "War Comics." *The Routledge Companion to Comics*, by Frank Bramlett et al. New York: Routledge, 2017: 183–191.

Rifas, Leonard. "Morris Pass: The Forgotten Cartoonist of the Seattle General Strike of 1919," conference presentation, 2017 Labor and Working Class History Association Conference, Seattle, WA 23 June 2017.

Rifas, Leonard, "The Politics of Underground Comix and the Environmental Crisis," *International Journal of Comic Art*, vol. 20, no. 2, Fall/Winter 2018: 128–150.

Ritter, Ed. "Many Moon Inhabitants are Alabamians with Buck Rogers in the 25th Century," *Montgomery Advertiser*, 10 May 1947.

Ritter, Scott. "Going Nuclear: U.S. Policy and Kim Jong-un's Bomb," *The Washington Spectator*, 3 Nov. 2016.

Rius (Eduardo del Rio), ed. *Ya te vimos, Pinochet!* México: Editorial Posada, 1974.

Ro, Ronin. *Tales to Astonish: Jack Kirby, Stan Lee, and the American Comic Book Revolution*. New York: Bloomsbury Publishing, 2004.

Roach, Neale, "Oral History Interview with Neale Roach," by Jerry N. Hess, 21 Jan 1969, https://www.trumanlibrary.org/oralhist/roachn.htm.

Roberts, Leslie. *Home from the Cold Wars*. Boston: The Beacon Press, 1948.

Roberts, Sam. "No Longer Majority Black, Harlem Is in Transition," *The New York Times*, 5 Jan. 2010.

Robin, Richard C. "The Adult Meets and Tries to Understand the Atom, IV. Power from the Atom," *Journal of Educational Sociology*, vol. 22, no. 5, Jan. 1949: 350–356.

Robock, Alan "Nuclear Winter Is a Real and Present Danger," *Nature*, vol. 473, no. 7347, May 2011: 275–276.

Rochelle, Carl. "Eisenhower Knew POWs Remained in Korea," CNN Interactive, 16 Sept. 1996.

Roeder, George H., Jr. *The Censored War: American Visual Experience During World War Two*. Hartford, CT: Yale University Press, 1995.

Roediger, David. "Gook: The Short History of an Americanism," *Monthly Review*, vol. 43, no. 10, March 1992, http://www.davidroediger.org/articles/gook-the-short-history-of-americanism.html.

Rogerson, Sidney. *Propaganda in the Next War*. London: Geoffrey Bles, 1938.

Rogaski, Ruth. "Nature, Annihilation, and Modernity: China's Korean War Germ-Warfare Experience Reconsidered," *The Journal of Asian Studies*, vol. 61, no. 2, May 2001: 381–415.

Romerstein. Herbert and Eric Breindel. *The Venona Secrets: Exposing Soviet Espionage and America's Traitors.* London: Regnery Publishing, Inc., 2000.

Romita, John, Dick Ayers and Bill Everett. *Marvel Masterworks: Atlas Era Heroes Vol. 2.* New York: Marvel Publishing, Inc., 2008.

Rosebury, Theodor. *Peace or Pestilence: Biological Warfare and How to Avoid It.* New York: Whittlesey House, McGraw-Hill Book Company, Inc., 1949.

Rosenthal, A.M. "U.N. Defeats Soviet Demand for Rebuke to U.S. on Raids," *The New York Times*, 8 Sept. 1950: 1.

Rositzke, Harry. *The CIA's Secret Operations: Espionage, Counterespionage, and Covert Action.* New York: Reader's Digest Press, 1977.

Ross, Steven J. "Movement Leader, Grassroots Builder: Jane Fonda" in *Hollywood Left and Right: How Movie Stars Shaped American Politics.* London: Oxford University Press, 2011.

Rothberg, Peter "The Largest Political Demonstration in American History: Thirty Years Ago Today, More Than One Million People Rallied In New York City's Central Park Against Nuclear Arms and for an End to the Arms Race of the Cold War." *The Nation.com.*, 12 June, 2012.

Rubens, Jim. *OverSuccess: Healing the American Obsession with Wealth, Fame, Power, and Perfection.* Austin, TX: Greenleaf Book Group Press, LLC, 2009.

Rubenstein, Anne. *Bad Language, Naked Ladies, & Other Threats to the Nation: A Political History of Comic Books in Mexico.* Durham, NC: Duke University Press, 1998.

Rubin, Morris. "The Consequences of Korea," *The Progressive*, vol. 14, no. 8, August 1950: 2–4.

Rubin, Susan Goldman. *Whaam! The Art and Life of Roy Lichtenstein.* New York: Abrams, 2008.

"Russian Says Comic Books 'Fascisize' U.S. Children." *The New York Times*, 16 Oct. 1949: 33:4.

Rutter, Richard. "Industry Turns to Comic Books: Not for Laughs or Thrills but as a Potent Technique for Achieving Goodwill," *The New York Times*, 16 July 1955: 19.

Ryan, John. *Panel by Panel: An Illustrated History of Australian Comics.* Sydney: Cassell Australia, 1979.

Ryan, John K. "Are the Comics Moral?," *Forum and Century*, vol. 95, no. 5, 1936: 301–304.

Sacks, Jason. "Classic Comics Cavalcade: *Corpse on the Imjin and Other Stories* by Harvey Kurtzman." *Comics Bulletin*, 20 June 2013, comicsbulletin.com/classic-comics-cavalcade-corpse-imjin-and-other-stories-harvey-kurtzman/.

Sadowski, Greg. *B. Krigstein: Volume One: 1919–1955.* Seattle: Fantagraphics Books, 2002.

Sagan, Carl. "The Atmospheric and Climatic Consequences of Nuclear War," in *The Cold and the Dark: The World After Nuclear War.* New York: W.W. Norton & Company, 1984.

Sagan, Carl, and Richard Turco. *A Path Where No Man Thought: Nuclear Winter and the End of the Arms Race,* Random House, 1990.

Salter, Jessica. "The World of Cartoonist and Journalist Joe Sacco: Cartoonist and Journalist Joe Sacco Talks to Jessica Salter about his Drawing Process, Bosnia, and Bruegel," *The Telegraph*, 29 Sept. 2013, http://www.telegraph.co.uk/culture/books/10334363/The-world-of-cartoonist-and-journalist-Joe-Sacco.html.

Sams, Crawford F. *"Medic": The Mission of an American Military Doctor in Occupied Japan and Wartorn Korea.* New York: M.E. Sharpe, 1998.

Sanders, Joe Sutliff. "How Comics Became Kids' Stuff," *Good Grief! Children and Comics*, Michelle Ann Abate and Joe Sutliff Sanders, eds., Columbus, OH: Billy Ireland Cartoon Library & Museum in partnership with Ohio State University Libraries, 2016: 9–28.

San Giacomo, Michael. "Frank McGee's True Heroics in Comics," *Comic Book Resources*, 19 Feb. 2009.

Sargeant, Howland H. "How Can We Defend Free Culture," *Department of State Bulletin*, 7 April 1952: 53–58.

Saunders, David. *Field Guide to Wild American Pulp Artists,* n.d., http://pulpartists.com/.

Saunders, David. *Norman Saunders,* n.d., http://normansaunders.com.

Saunders, David. "Field Guide to Wild American Pulp Artists," 2014, http://www.pulpartists.com/Donenfeld.html.

Savage, William W. *Commies, Cowboys, and Jungle Queens: Comic Books and America, 1945–1954.* Hanover, NH: Wesleyan University Press, 1998 (a paperback reprint of William W. Savage, *Comic Books and America, 1945–1954.* Norman: University of Oklahoma Press, 1990).

Schaef, Anne Wilson. *When Society Becomes an Addict.* San Francisco: HarperCollins Publishers, 1987.

Schaeffer, Robert. *Warpaths: The Politics of Partitions.* New York: Hill and Wang, 1990.

Schechter, Harold. *The Mad Sculptor: The Maniac, the Model, and the Murder That Shook the Nation.* Boston: Houghton Mifflin Harcourt, 2014.

Schell, Jonathan. "The Spirit of June 12: Twenty-five Years After the Largest Antinuclear Demonstration Ever, the Movement Has Dwindled. But the Threat of Mass Destruction Grows Greater," *The Nation*, vol. 285, no. 1, 2 July 2007: 4.

Schelly, Bill. *Man of Rock: A Biography of Joe Kubert.* Seattle: Fantagraphics, 2008.

Schelly, Bill. *Harvey Kurtzman: The Man Who Created Mad and Revolutionized Humor in America.* Seattle: Fantagraphics Books, 2015.

Schlatter, Joe. "MIA Facts Site: The Claims of MG Jan Sjena: Crafted Nonsense," www.miafacts.org/sejna.htm, 2018.

Schneider, Eric C. *Vampires, Dragons, and Egyptian Kings: Youth Gangs in Postwar New York*. Princeton, NJ: Princeton University Press, 1999, 2001.

Schramm, Wilbur, and John W. Riley, Jr. "Communication in the Sovietized State, as Demonstrated in Korea," *American Sociological Review*, vol. 16, no. 6, Dec. 1951: 757–766.

Schuessler, John M. "The Deception Dividend: FDR's Undeclared War, *International Security*, vol. 34, no. 4, Spring 2010: 133–165.

Schultz, Henry E. "Censorship or Self Regulation?" *The Journal of Educational Sociology*, vol. 23, no. 4, Dec. 1949: 215–224.

Schumacher, Michael. *Will Eisner: A Dreamer's Life in Comics*. New York: Bloomsbury USA, 2010.

Schumacher, Michael, and Denis Kitchen. *Al Capp: A Life to the Contrary*. New York: Bloomsbury, 2013.

Schuyler, George S. "Views and Reviews: The Question of Burning (or Not Burning) Books!" *Pittsburgh Courier*, 27 June 1953: 9.

Schwable, Colonel Frank H., and Major Roy H. Bley. "The U.S.A. Is Waging Germ Warfare in Korea: Statements of Prisoners of War, Colonel Frank H. Schwable and Major Roy H. Bley, U.S. Marine Corps," *Supplement to New Times* no. 10, 4 March 1953 (printed in the USSR).

Schwartz, Alvin. *An Unlikely Prophet: A Metaphysical Memoir by the Legendary Writer of Superman and Batman*. Rochester, VT: Destiny Books, 1997, 2006.

Schwartz, Murray L., and James C.N. Paul. "Foreign Communist Propaganda in the Mails: A Report on Some Problems of Federal Censorship," *University of Pennsylvania Law Review*, vol. 107. no. 5, March 1959: 621–666.

Scobell, Andrew. "Notional North Korea," *Parameters*. vol. 37., no. 1, 2007: 117+.

Scobie, Ingrid Winther. "Jack B. Tenney and the 'Parasite Menace': Anti-Communist Legislation in California 1940–1949," *Pacific Historical Review*, vol. 43, no. 2, May 1974: 188–211.

"Scoff At Report of Japanese Atomic Bomb," *Courier* (Ottumwa, IA), 3 Oct. 1946: 2.

Scott, Cord. "Frankly, Mac, This 'Police Action' Business Is Going Too Damn Far!" Armed Forces Cartoons During the Korean Conflict," Korean War Conference: Commemorating the 60th Anniversary June 24–26, Victoria, Texas. Hosted by: Victoria College / University of Houston-Victoria Library, 2010.

Scott, Cord A. *Comics and Conflict: Patriotism and Propaganda from WWII Through Operation Iraqi Freedom*. Annapolis: Naval Institute Press, 2014.

Scott, Peter Dale. *American War Machine: Deep Politics, the CIA Global Drug Connections, and the Road to Afghanistan*. Lanham, MD: Rowman & Littlefield Publishers, Inc., 2010.

Scurlock, Stella A., Director Youth Conservation Program. "Comic Books—Movies—Radio; We're Doing Something About Them!," *General Federation Clubwoman*, vol. 28, no. 7, Oct. 1948.

Scurlock, Stella A. "Youth's Radio—Comics—Movie Diet Is Our Job Too," *General Federation Clubwoman*, Dec. 1948.

"Sees U.S. Comics as Textbooks of Crime," *The Advertiser* (Australia), 22 April 1954: 4. ohdannyboy.blogspot.com.

Selby, W. Gardner. "U.S. Army was Smaller Than the Army of Portugal Before World War II," *Politifact, Texas*, 13 June 2014.

Seldes, Gilbert. *The Great Audience*. New York: Viking Press, 1950.

Seth, Michael J. *A History of Korea: From Antiquity to the Present*. Lanham, MD: Rowman & Littlefield Publishers, Inc., 2011.

Sewell, Stephen L. (Cookie), compiler. "Korean Air War and Surrounding Events," Department of Defense Korean War Air Loss Database, n.d., http://www.korean-war.com/AirChronology.html.

Shaffer, Robert. "Women and International Relations: Pearl S. Buck's Critique of the Cold War," *Journal of Women's History*, vol. 11, no.3, Autumn 1999: 151–174.

Shaffer, Robert. "Pearl S. Buck and the East and West Association: The Trajectory and Fate of 'Critical Internationalism,' 1940–1950," *Peace & Change*, vol. 28, no. 1, Jan. 2003: 1–36.

Shalett, Sidney. "189 Magazines Put on New Army List," *The New York Times*, 20 July 1944: 8.

Shagawat, Robert. "Television Recording—the Origins and Earliest Surviving Live TV Broadcast Recordings," 2004, updated http://www.earlytelevision.org/pdf/Television_Recording_Origins.pdf, 2011.

Shane, Scott. "A Father Lost," *Baltimore Sun*, 1 Aug. 2004.

Shannon, Lyle W. "The Opinions of Little Orphan Annie and Her Friends," *The Public Opinion Quarterly*, vol. 18, no. 2, Summer 1954: 169–179.

Shaw, Tamsin. "The Bitter Secret of 'Wormwood,'" *The New York Review of Books*, 18 Jan. 2018.

Shaw, Tony. "Review Essay: The Politics of Cold War Culture," *Journal of Cold War Studies*, vol. 3, no. 3, Fall 2001: 59–76.

Shenon, Philip. "U.S. Knew in 1953 North Koreans Held American P.O.W.'s," *The New York Times*, A1, 17 Sep. 1996.

Shepley, James. "How Dulles Averted War," *Life*, 16 Jan 1956: 70–72+.

Sheridan, Martin. *Classic Comics and their Creators*. New York: Cushman and Flint, 1942.

Shibusawa, Naoko. "The Artist Belongs to the People": The Odyssey of Taro Yashima," *Journal of Asian American Studies*, vol. 8, no. 3, Oct. 2005: 257–275.

Shiel, M.P. *The Yellow Danger: Or What MIGHT Happen If the Division of the Chinese Empire Should Estrange All European Countries*. London: R.F. Fenno & Company, 1899.

Shiell, Annette, ed. *Bonzer: Australian Comic 1900s—1990s* (catalog from a Monash University Australian comics exhibition). Melbourne: Elgua Media/Binara Publishing, 1998.

Shorrock, Tim. "How Sony, Obama, Seth Rogen and the CIA Secretly Planned to Force Regime Change in North Korea: The Secret Backstory to the U.S.-North Korea Standoff." AlterNet, 5 Sept. 2017, https://www.alternet.org/grayzone-project/how-sony-obama-seth-rogen-and-cia-secretly-planned-force-regime-change-north-korea.

Shorrock, Tim. "'Parasite' Has Opened American Eyes to South Korea's Reality: Now we need a film to cut through US myths about the North," *The Nation*, 23 Jan 2020.

Shutt, Craig. "Beetle Bailey's Secret Comic Book Life," *Hogan's Alley* #12, 2004: 42–49.

Siegel, Jerry, and Joe Schuster. "How Superman Would End the War," *Look Magazine*, 27 Feb. 1940.

Simon, Joe. "Shop Talk: Joe Simon," *Will Eisner's Spirit Magazine #37*, Kitchen Sink, Oct. 1982.

Simon, Joe. "The Joe Simon Interview," by Gary Groth. *The Comics Journal*, no. 134, February 1990, 19 July 2011, http://www.tcj.com/the-joe-simon-interview/.

Simon, Joe, with Jim Simon. *The Comic Book Makers*. New York: Crestwood/II Publications, 1990.

Simon, Rita James. *Public Opinion in America: 1936-1970*. Chicago: Rand McNally College Publishing, 1974.

Simpson, Christopher. *Blowback: America's Recruitment of Nazis and Its Effects on the Cold War*. London: Weidenfeld & Nicolson, 1988.

Simpson, Christopher. *Science of Coercion: Communication Research and Psychological Warfare, 1945-1960*. London: Oxford University Press, 1994.

Skaggs, David. "The KATUSA Experiment: The Integration of Korean Nationals into the US Army, 1950-1965," *Military Affairs*, vol. 38, no.2, April 1974: 53–58.

Sloane, Leonard. "Advertising: Comics Go Up, Up and Away." *The New York Times*, 20 July 1967: 60.

Sloyan, Gerard S. "The Senate Subcommittee Hearings on the Comic Books Industry," *Religious Education*, 1 Nov 1954: 407–415.

Smith, Andrew A. "Blast from the Past: Captain Comics: Fury's Munchausen View, by Dick Ayers," from *Comics Buyer's Guide* #1441, 29 June 2001, http://www.cbgxtra.com/columnists/andrew-smith-captain-comics/cbg-1441-furys-munchausen-view-by-dick-ayers.

Smith, Jean Edward. *Eisenhower in War and Peace*. New York: Random House, 2012.

Smolderen, T. "Why the Brownies Are Important," n.d., http://www.old-coconino.com/s_classics/pop_classic/brownies/brow_eng.htm.

Snell, David. "Japan Developed Atom Bomb: Russia Grabbed Scientists," *The Atlanta Constitution*, 3 Oct. 1946: 1

Snyder, Timothy. "Hitler vs. Stalin: Who Killed More?" *The New York Review of Books*, 10 March 2011.

"So-Called 'Comic' Books Censured at PTA Meeting." *The Bellville Times* (Bellville, TX) 10 Dec. 1953: 1, 12.

Sokolsky, George. "These Days: The Reading of Children," *Dubois Courier Express*, 29 June 1946: 4.

Song, Hyo-Sun. *The Fight for Freedom*. Seoul: Korea Library Association, 1980.

Soper, Kerry D. *We Go Pogo: Walt Kelly, Politics, and American Satire*. Jackson: University Press of Mississippi, 2012.

Sorensen, Thomas C. *The Word War: The Story of American Propaganda*. New York: Harper & Row, Publishers, 1968.

Sorrentino, Joseph. "Uranium Mine and Mill Workers are Dying, and Nobody Will Take Responsibility," *In These Times*, 15 Feb. 2016.

Spain (Spain Rodriguez), 2002, "My Cold War." Republished in *Cruisin' with the Hound: The Life and Times of Fred Toote*. Seattle: Fantagraphics, 2012: 7–8.

Spivak, John L. "Wall Street's Fascist Conspiracy 2. Morgan Pulls the Strings." *New Masses*, 5 Feb. 1935: 17–21.

Spurgeon, Tom. "Joe Kubert, 1926–2012," *The Comics Reporter*, 13 August 2012, http://www.comicsreporter.com/index.php/joe_kubert_1926_2012/.

"Squeeze-Play in Korea," *Reader's Scope*, vol. 5, no. 10, March 1948: 67–75.

Sroog, Arnold. "5 Million Hitlerite Comic Books to Flood the Country," *Daily Worker* (New York), 20 Oct. 1947: 3.

Starger, Steve, J. Spurlock, and Peter Max. *Wally's World: The Brilliant Life and Tragic Death of Wally Wood, the World's Second-Best Comic Book Artist*. New York: Vanguard, 2006.

Starr, Paul. *The Creation of the Media: Political Origins of Modern Communications*. New York: Basic Books, 2004.

Stewart, Bhob. "Against the Grain," in *The Life and Legend of Wallace Wood, Volume 1*, Seattle: Fantagraphics, 2017.

Stockman, David A. *The Great Deformation: The Corruption of Capitalism in America*. Public Affairs, 2013.

Stockton, Bayard. *Flawed Patriot: The Rise and Fall of CIA Legend Bill Harvey*. Washington, DC: Potomac Books, Inc., 2006.

Stone, I.F. *The Hidden History of the Korean War: 1950-1951*. Little, Brown and Company, 1952, 1988.

Strangio, Sebastian. "'You Are Followers of the Juche Philosophy, So I Can Put My Trust in You': Reading North Korea's Comic Book Propaganda," *Slate.com*, 21 June 2011.

Streb, Markus. "Early Representations of Concentration Camps in Golden Age Comic Books: Graphic Narratives, American Society, and the Holocaust," *Scandinavian Journal of Comic Art*, vol. 3, no. 1, Fall 2016: 28–63.

Strömberg, Fredrik. *Black Images in the Comics: A Visual History*. Seattle: Fantagraphics, 2003.

Strömberg, Fredrik. *Comic Art Propaganda: A Graphic History*. East Sussex, UK: Ilex Press, 2010.

Strömberg, Fredrik. *Jewish Images in the Comics*. San Diego: Seattle: Fantagraphics, 2012.

Strub, Whitney Vincent. "Perversion for Profit: The Politics of Obscenity and Pornography in the Postwar United States," PhD diss., History, University of California Los Angeles, 2006.

Strunsky, Richard. "Crime Comics Instill Anti-Union Ideas in Millions of Youngsters," *Labor's Daily* (Oklahoma City, OK), 9 April, 1956: 5.

Stueck, William. *Rethinking the Korean War: A New Diplomatic and Strategic History*. New York: Princeton University Press, 2013.

Suchman, Edward A., Rose K. Goldstein and Robin M. Williams, Jr. "Attitudes Toward the Korean War," *The Public Opinion Quarterly*, vol. 17, no. 2, Summer, 1953: 171–184.

Sunstein Cass R. *Can It Happen Here? Authoritarianism in America*. San Francisco: HarperCollins, 2018.

Szasz, Ferenc M. "Atomic Comics: The Comic Book Industry Confronts the Nuclear Age," in *Atomic Culture: How We Learned to Stop Worrying and Love the Bomb*, Scott C. Zeman and Michael A, Admundson, eds. Denver: University Press of Colorado, 2004.

Szasz, Ferenc Morton. *Atomic Comics: Cartoonists Confront the Nuclear World*. Las Vegas: University of Nevada Press, 2012.

Tanner, Harold M. *Where Chiang Kai-shek Lost China: The Liao-Shen Campaign, 1948*. Bloomington: Indiana University Press, 2015.

Teague, Paul S. "The Soviet Invasion of Manchuria and the Kwangtung Army," 2016. *MilitaryHistoryOnline.com*.

Telgemeier, Raina, "Barefoot Gen, Again and Again," 5 Aug 2015, https://goraina.com/blog/2015/08/barefoot-gen-again-and-again.

Tenney, Jack B. *Zion's Fifth Column: A Tenney Report on World Zionism*. San Francisco: Standard Publications, 1953.

Tenney, Jack B. *"Cry Brotherhood."* San Francisco: Standard Publications, 1965.

"Tenney Warns Parents on Red Comic Books," *Los Angeles Times*, 9 April 1946: A6.

Terkel, Studs. *"The Good War": An Oral History of World War Two*. New York: Ballantine Books, 1984.

Theisen, Louis E. "So That's Settled," *The Record* (Hackensack, NJ), 4 March 1954: 34.

Theoharis, Athan G. *The FBI: A Comprehensive Reference Guide*. Phoenix: The Oryx Press, 1999.

"These Comic Books," *Long Beach Press-Telegram*, 6 July 1950: 12.

Thimayya, General K.S. *Experiment in Neutrality*. New Delhi: Vision Books, 1981.

Thomas, Roy. "The Alley Awards for 1961: A Report from Roy Thomas, Secretary of the Academy of Comic Book Arts and Sciences." *Alter Ego* no. 4, October 1962. (Reprinted in Roy Thomas and Bill Schelly, eds., *Alter Ego: The Best of the Legendary Comics Fanzine*. Raleigh, NC: TwoMorrows Publishing, 2008: 48–49.)

Thomas, Roy W. "American Comic Books and Their Reflection of Cold War Attitudes, 1945–1970: A Study of the Depiction of Communism and of Communist Nations in U.S. Comic Books from the End of World War II Through the Height of the Vietnam War," MA thesis, Humanities, California State University Dominguez Hills, Summer 2005.

Thomas, Roy. "Introduction," *Marvel Masterworks: Atlas Era Heroes Vol. 2.*New York: Marvel Publishing, Inc., 2008.

Thomas, Roy. "ECHH Marks the Spot!" *Alter Ego* no. 95. July 2010: 3–47.

Thompson, Don. "The Spawn of Dr. Wertham's Innocents," *The Monster Times*, vol. 1, no. 10, 31 May 1972: 10–11.

Thompson, Dorothy. "'Comic Books' Subversive," *The Oregonian*, 29 April 1954.

Thrasher, Frederic M. "The Comics and Delinquency. Cause or Scapegoat," *Journal of Educational Sociology* vol. 23, no. 4, 1949: 195–205.

Tilley, Carol L. "Seducing the Innocent: Fredric Wertham and the Falsifications That Helped Condemn Comics." *Information & Culture*, vol. 47, no.4, 2012: 383–413.

Tirman, John. *The Deaths of Others: The Fate of Civilians in America's Wars*. London: Oxford University Press, 2011.

Tobey, James A. "Exaggerated Dangers of Germ Warfare." *The American Mercury*, vol. 71, no. 21, July 1950: 319.

"Tokyo Hurries Army to Curb New Rebellion," *Oakland Tribune*, 13 April 1919: 1.

Toland, John. *In Mortal Combat: Korea, 1950–1953*. New York: William Morrow and Company, 1991.

Toon, Owen B., Alan Robock, and Richard P. Turco. "Environmental Consequences of Nuclear War." *Physics Today*, vol. 61, no. 12, 2008: 37–42.

Toth, Alex. "Interview with Alex Toth from *Graphic Story Magazine*," conducted by Richard Kyle and Bill Spicer in summer/fall 1968 and republished in *Setting the Standard: Comics by Alex Toth 1952–1954*, Greg Sadowski, ed. Seattle: Fantagraphics, 2011.

Trajan's Column. "Complete set of images with Italian commentary," n.d., http://www.rome-roma.net/impero-romano/colonna-traiana-1.html/.

"Trial by Actedron." *The Tablet*, 15 Jan 1949: 4.

"Tri-County P.T.A. Urge Good Reading for Children." *The Brookshire Times* (Brookshire, TX,) 14 Jan. 1954: 2.

Trombetta, Jim, introduction by R. L. Stine. *The Horror! the Horror! Comic Books the Government Didn't Want You to Read!* New York: Abrams ComicArts, 2010.

Truman, Harry S. "280. Remarks in Independence at the Liberty Bell Luncheon," *Public Papers, Harry S. Truman, 1945–1953,* Truman Library & Museum, 6 Nov. 1950.

Truman, Harry S. "Text of President Truman's Speech in Chicago Attacking Eisenhower on Korea," *The New York Times,* 30 Oct. 1952: 28.

Truman, Harry S. *Memoirs by Harry S. Truman, Volume Two: Years of Trial and Hope.* New York: Doubleday & Co., Inc., 1956.

Truman, Harry S. *Dear Bess: The Letters from Harry to Bess Truman, 1910–1959.* Robert H, Ferrell, ed. New York: W.W. Norton & Company, 1983.

Trussell, C. P. "Women's Congress is Accused as Red: House Committee Charges It Is Composed of 'Hard Core of Party Members." *The New York Times,* 23 Oct. 1949: 44.

Tsipursky, Gleb. "Jazz, Power, and Soviet Youth in the Early Cold War, 1948–1953." *The Journal of Musicology,* vol. 33, no. 3, Summer 2016: 332–361.

Tucker, Jonathan B. *War of Nerves: Chemical Warfare from World War I to Al-Qaeda.* New York: Pantheon Books, 2006.

Tudor, Dan. *Ask a North Korean: Defectors Talk About Their Lives Inside the World's Most Secretive Nation.* London: Tuttle Publishing, 2017.

Turner, Robert. *Some of My Best Friends Are Writers but … I Wouldn't Want My Daughter to Marry One.* London: Sherbourne Press, Inc., 1970.

Twomey John E. "The Anti-Comic Book Crusade," MA thesis, Communication, University of Chicago, Sept. 1955.

Twomey, John E. "The Citizens' Committee and Comic-Book Control: A Study of Extragovernmental Restraint," *Law and Contemporary Problems,* vol. 20, no. 4, Obscenity and the Arts, Autumn 1955: 621–629.

Umoja, Akinyele. "From One Generation to the Next: Armed Self-Defense, Revolutionary Nationalism, and the Southern Black Freedom Struggle," *Souls: A Critical Journal of Black Politics, Culture and Society,* vol. 15, no. 3, 2013: 218–240.

U.S. Census Bureau Newsroom. "Asian-American and Pacific Islander Heritage Month: May 2018," 1 May 2018.

"U.S. Charges Reds Killed 5,790 Soldier-Prisoners Since Start of Conflict: 5,500 Americans Included in Atrocities Toll; Many North Korean Civilians Slain," *Ellensburg Daily Record,* vol. 42, no. 114, 14 Nov. 1951.

"U.S. Department of the Army No Gun Ri Review Report," 11 Jan 2001, https://en.wikisource.org/wiki/U.S._Department_of_the_Army_No_Gun_Ri_Review_Report.

"U.S. to Use Cartoon Books to Tell Asia Our Story," *The New York Times,* 20 Dec. 1949: 25.

Uslan, Michael, and Joe Kubert. *America at War: The Best of DC War Comics.* New York: Simon & Schuster, 1979.

Van Dyke, Vernon and Edward Lane Davis, "Senator Taft and American Security, *The Journal of Politics,* vol. 14, no. 2, May 1952: 177–202.

Van Ginnekin, Jaap. "Bacteriological Warfare," *Journal of Contemporary Asia* vol. 7, no. 2, 1977.

Van Sant, Wayne. *The War in Korea: 1950–1953.* New York: Quadre Enterprises, 2001.

Vassallo, Michael J. Timely-Atlas-Comics: A Blog About the History of Martin Goodman's Comic Book Line from 1939 to About 1961, 2010.

Vassallo, Michael, Dr. "Introduction: The History of Atlas War Comics," in Hank Chapman and Don Rico, *Atlas Era Battlefield: Volume 1.* New York: Marvel, 2011.

Versaci, Rocco. "Chapter 5: Guerilla Warfare and Sneak Attacks." in *This Book Contains Graphic Language: Comics as Literature.* London: The Continuum International Publishing Group, Inc., 2007.

"Victor J. Jerome Is Dead at 68; Writer Was a U.S. Communist," *New York Times,* 8 Aug. 1965: 64.

Viguerie, Richard A. and David Franke. *America's Right Turn: How Conservatives Used New and Alternative Media to Take Power.* New York: Bonus Books, 2004.

Vlamos, James Frank. "The Sad Case of the Funnies," *The American Mercury* vol. 52, April 1941: 41–116.

Von Bernewitz, Fred and Grant Geissman. *Tales of Terror! The EC Companion.* Seattle: Fantagraphics, 2002.

Vronsky, Peter. *Sons of Cain: A History of Serial Killers from the Stone Age to the Present.* New York: Berkley, 2018.

Wada, Haruki. *The Korean War: An International History.* New York: Rowman & Littlefield, 2014.

Waggoner, Walter H. "Acheson Calls Germ Charge Soviet 'Crime,' Scouts Talks." *The New York Times,* 8 May 1952: 1.

Wagner, Geoffrey. "Kids' Stuff," *New Statesman and Nation,* vol. 42, no. 1082, 1 Dec. 1951: 617–618.

Wagner, Geoffrey. *Parade of Pleasure.* London: Derek Verschoyle, Ltd. 1954.

Wagner, Geoffrey Atheling. *The End of Education.* London: A.S. Barnes, 1976.

Waldman, Diane. *Roy Lichtenstein.* New York: Guggenheim Museum, 2003.

Walker, J. Samuel. *Prompt and Utter Destruction: Truman and the Use of the Atomic Bombs Against Japan.* Chapel Hill: University of North Carolina Press, 1997.

Wallack, Grace, and John Hudak. "How Much Did Your Vote Cost? Spending Per Voter in the 2014 Senate Races," FixGov: making Government Work, Brookings, 7 Nov 2014.

Waller, Douglas. *Wild Bill Donovan: The Spymaster Who Created the OSS and Modern American Espionage.* New York: Free Press, 2011.

Wang, Y. Yvon. "Yellow Books in Red China: A Preliminary Examination of Sex in Print in the Early People's Republic," *Twentieth-Century China,* vol. 44, no. 1, Jan. 2019: 75–97.

"War of Nerves," *Time Magazine,* 1 May 1950.

Warren, James, President, Warren Publishing Co. "An Editorial to The President of the United States and All the Members of Congress—On Behalf of Our Readers, Most of Whom Are from 10 to 18 Years Old..." *Eerie* no. 29, September 1970.

Warren, James. "Wrightson's Warren Days, The James Warren Interview," Conducted by & © Jon B. Cooke, From *Comic Book Artist* no. 4, 1999, http://twomorrows.com/comicbookartist/articles/04warren.html.

Warshow, Robert. *The Immediate Experience: Movies, Comics, Theatre and Other Aspects of Popular Culture.* Enlarged edition. New York: Harvard University Press, 2001.

Waugh, Coulton. *The Comics.* Jackson: University Press of Mississippi, 1947.

Weart, Spencer. *Nuclear Fear: A History of Images.* London: Harvard University Press, 1988.

Webb, Chris, Victor Smart and Carmelo Lisciotto. "The SS, Himmler's Schutzstaffel: 'Loyalty is my Honor,'" H.E.A.R.T., 2008, http://www.holocaustresearchproject.org/holoprelude/aboutthess.html.

Weiner, Tim. "A 1950 Plan: Arrest 12,000 And Suspend Due Process, *The New York Times,* 23 Dec. 2007: 40.

Weiner, Tim. *Legacy of Ashes: The History of the CIA.* New York: Doubleday, 2007.

Weinstein, Allen, and Alexander Vassiliev. *The Haunted Wood: Soviet Espionage in America.* New York: Random House, 2000.

Weinstein, Simcha. *Up, Up, and Oy Vey: How Jewish History, Culture, and Values Shaped the Comic Book Superhero.* Fort Lee, NJ: Barricade Books, 2006.

Weintraub, Stanley. *MacArthur's War: Korea and the Undoing of an American Hero.* New York: The Free Press, 2000.

Weintz, Walter H. *The Solid Gold Mailbox: How to Create Winning Mail-Order Campaigns by the Man Who's Done It All.* New York: John Wiley & Sons, 1987.

Weisinger, Mort. "Here Comes Superman!" *Coronet,* July 1946: 3–7.

Wells, John. "The Racial Justice Experience: Diversity in the DC Universe: 1961–1979," 2001, http://fanzing.com/mag/fanzing32/feature1.shtml.

Wertham, Frederic [*sic*]. "*War OR Peace?*," *The New Republic,* 27 Jan. 1947: 37–39.

Wertham, Frederic [*sic*]. "A Psychiatrist Examines the Master-Criminals at Nuremberg," *New York Times,* 2 Feb 1947: BR 7.

Wertham, Fredric. "The Comics ... Very Funny!," *Saturday Review of Literature,* 29 May 1948.

Wertham, Fredric, M.D. *The Show of Violence.* New York: Doubleday & Company, Inc., 1948, 1949.

Wertham, Fredric, "What Are Comic Books?," *National Parent-Teacher,* March 1949: 17.

Wertham, Fredric. "Psychiatric Observations on Abolition of School Segregation," *The Journal of Educational Sociology,* vol. 26, no. 7, March 1953: 333–336.

Wertham, Fredric, M.D. *Seduction of the Innocent.* New York: Rinehart & Company, Inc., 1953, 1954.

Wertham, Fredric. "Nine Men Speak to You: Jim Crow in the North," *The Nation,* 12 June 1954: 497–499.

Wertham, Fredric, M.D. "The Curse of the Comic Books: The Value Patterns and Effects of Comic Books," *Religious Education* vol. 49, no. 6, 1954: 394–406.

Wertham, Fredric, M.D. 1954. Testimony, April 21st Senate Subcommittee Hearings on Juvenile Delinquency, http://thecomicbooks.com/wertham.html.

Wertham, Fredric, M.D. *The Circle of Guilt.* Dennis Dobson (London), 1956.

Wertham, Fredric, M.D. "Editorial: Psychiatry and Censorship," *American Journal of Psychotherapy* vol. 11, no. 2, 1957: 249–253.

Wertham, Fredric. "The Head-Fixers," *Monthly Review,* Nov. 1958: 275–282.

Wertham, Fredric, M.D. "The Huckster as Headshrinker," *Fact,* Nov.-Dec. 1964, vol. 1, no. 6, 1964: 28–31.

Wertham, Fredric. *A Sign for Cain: An Exploration of Human Violence.* New York: The Macmillan Company, 1966.

Wertham, Fredric. "Is TV Hardening Us to the War in Vietnam?" *The New York Times* editorial, 4 Dec. 1966: D23. (Republished in *Violence and the Mass Media,* 1968, Otto N. Larsen, ed., Harper & Row Publishers.)

Wertham, Fredric. "'His Name Is ... Savage'—Mine Is Not," *Quintessence No. 2,* Mike O'Neal, 1970: 15–16.

Wertham, Fredric, M.D. *The World of Fanzines: A Special Form of Communication.* Urbana: Southern Illinois University Press, 1973.

Wertham, Fredric, M.D. "Medicine and Mayhem," Reprinted from *MD, the Medical Newsmagazine,* June 1978; *Instant Gratification,* vol. 1, no. 1, 1979: 38–40.

White, William Lindsay. *Captives of Korea: An Unofficial White Paper on the Treatment of War Prisoners.* New York: Charles Scribner's Sons, 1957.

"White Paper on the Human Rights Violations in the US in 2017." The Institutes of International Studies of the DPRK (Pyongyang), 30 Jan. 2018.

Whitted, Qiana. *EC Comics: Race, Shock, and Social Protest.* Rutgers, NJ: Rutgers University Press, 2019.

"Why Sing Now?" *Newsreview* (Seoul), 25 April 1992: 8–9.

Wi Jo Kang. "Church and State Relations in the Japanese Colonial Period," in *Christianity in Korea,* Robert E. Busswell, Jr., and Timothy S. Lee, eds. Honolulu: University of Hawai'i Press, 2007.

Wilcox, Robert K. *Japan's Secret War: Japan's Race Against Time to Build Its Own Atomic Bomb.* Marlowe & Company, 1995.

Wildes, Harry Emerson. "The War for the Mind of Japan," *Annals of the American Academy of Political and Social Science,* vol. 294. America and a New Asia, July 1954: 1–7.

Wildman, George, ed. *The Comic Book Guide for the Artist/Writer/Letterer*. Derby, CT: Charlton Publications, Inc., 1973.

Wilford, Hugh. *The Mighty Wurlitzer: How the CIA Played America*. New York: Harvard University Press, 2008.

Wilfred, John. "Editorial Rays: Rotten Prints Destroy Morality," *The Catholic Advance* (Wichita, KS), 4 June 1954: 13.

Wilkinson, Endymion (translator.) *The People's Comic Book: Red Women's Detachment, Hot on the Trail, and other Chinese Comics*. Garden City, NY: Anchor Press, 1973.

Williams, Jeremy. "Kill 'em All! The American Military in Korea," BBC History, 17 Feb. 2011.

Willoughby, Major Gen. Charles A., and John Chamberlain. *MacArthur 1941–1951*. Chicago: McGraw-Hill Book Co., 1954.

Wills, Gary. *Bomb Power: The Modern Presidency and the National Security State*. New York: The Penguin Press, 2010.

Wilson, Ward. "The Winning Weapon? Rethinking Nuclear Weapons in Light of Hiroshima," *International Security*, vol. 1, no. 4, Spring 2007: 162–179.

Wint, Guy. *What Happened in Korea? A Study of Collective Security*. New York: The Batchworth Press, 1954.

Witek, Joseph. *Comic Books as History: The Narrative Art of Jack Jackson, Art Spiegelman, and Harvey Pekar*. Jackson: University Press of Mississippi, 1989.

Witek, Joseph. "'If a Way to the Better There Be: Excellence, Mere Competence, and The Worst Comics Ever Made," *Image [&] Narrative*, vol. 17, no. 4, 2016: 26–42.

Wittern-Keller, Laura. *Freedom of the Screen: Legal Challenges to State Film Censorship, 1915–1981*. Lexington: The University Press of Kentucky, 2008.

Wittner, Lawrence S. "The Nuclear Freeze and its Impact," *Arms Control Today*, 2010, https://www.armscontrol. org/act/2010_12/LookingBack.

Wolfe, Sheila. "Bad Comics To Go Up In Flames," *Southtown Economist*, 19 Sept. 1954: 1.

Woltman, Fred. Letter of 26 Dec. 1945, the Billy J. Hargis papers at the University of Arkansas (Box 24, Folder 21).

Women's International Democratic Federation in Korea. *Korea, We Accuse! Report of the Commission of the Women's International Democratic Federation in Korea, May 16 to 27, 1951* (Berlin), 1951.

Woo, Benjamin. "Is There a Comic Book Industry?," *Media Industries*, vol. 5, no. 1, 2018.

Woo, Susie. "When Blood Won't Tell: Integrated Transfusions and Shifting Foundations of Race," *American Studies*, vol. 55, no. 4/vol. 56, no. 1, 2017: 5–28.

Wood, Edward J., Jr. *Worshiping the Myths of World War II: Reflections on America's Dedication to War*. Washington, DC: Potomac Books, Inc., 2006.

Woods, Wayne L., "Advances in Aviation Medicine," *Army Information Digest, vol. 5*, U.S. Department of the Army, Sept. 1950: 53–59.

Wooley, John. "Age of Funk," 1946 to 1955, and "A Guide to Collecting Funk Comics," *Collector's Dream #5*, 1978: 73–75, 79–80.

Worcester, Kent. "Is There a Lev Gleason Expert in the House?," *The Comics Journal*, tcj.com, 19 June 2010.

"World Tension and Education: Proceedings of the Conference 'International Tension and Education' Held at the Holborn Hall, 29th and 30th December 1953," National Committee of Teachers for Peace (UK), 1954.

Wright, Bradford W. *Comic Book Nation: The Transformation of Youth Culture in America*. Baltimore: The Johns Hopkins University Press, 2001.

Wright, Richard. "Phychiatry [sic] Comes to Harlem," *Free World*, Sept. 1946: 49–51.

Wu, Tien-Wei. "Biological Warfare Unit 731: A Preliminary Review of Studies of Japanese Biological Warfare Unit 731 in the United States," n.d., http://www.fepow-community.org/uk/arthur_lane/html/biological_ warfare_unit_731_in.htm.

Wu, William. *The Yellow Peril: Chinese-Americans in American Fiction, 1850–1940*. San Francisco: Archon Books, 1982.

Wyman, Ray, Jr. "Jack Kirby On: World War II Influences," *Jack Kirby Collector* no. 27, 1 Feb. 2000, http:// twomorrows.com/kirby/articles/27ww2.html.

Yang, Gene Luen, and Sonny Liew. *The Shadow Hero*. New York: First Second, 2014.

Yang Kuisong. "Reconsidering the Campaign to Suppress Revolutionaries," *The China Quarterly*, vol. 193, March 2008: 102–121.

Yashima, Taro. *The New Sun*. New York: Henry Holt, 1943.

Yi Mahn-yol. "Korean Protestants and the Reunification Movement, in *Christianity in Korea*, Robert E. Busswell aJr., and Timothy S. Lee, eds. Honolulu: University of Hawai'i Press, 2006.

Yoe, Craig. *Secret Identity: The Fetish Art of Superman's Co-creator Joe Shuster*. New York: Abrams ComicArts, 2009.

Yoe, Craig (ed.) *The Unknown Anti-War Comics*. San Diego: IDW Publishing, 2018.

York, Christopher and Rafiel York. *Comic Books and the Cold War, 1946–1962: Essays on Graphic Treatment of Communism, the Code and Social Concerns*. Jefferson, NC: McFarland, 2012.

Young, Art. *On My Way*. London: Horace Liveright, Inc., 1928.

Yronwode, Cat. "When Partners Collide: or: How Busy Arnold kept Will Eisner in a Revolving Door While Editors Demanded the Head of The Spirit," *Will Eisner's Quarterly* no. 4, Kitchen Sink Press, Jan. 1985.

Yudin, Boris G. "Research on Humans at the Khabarovsk War Crimes Trial: a historical and ethical examination," Chapter 3 of *Japan's Wartime Medical Atrocities: Comparative Inquiries in Science, History, and Ethics*, Jing Bao Nie, Nanyan Guo, Mark Selden, and Arthur Kleinman, eds. New York: Routledge, 2010: 59–77.

Zangwill, Israel. *The Melting Pot.* 1909, http://www.gutenberg.org/ebooks/23893.

Zegart, Amy B. "'Spytainment': The Real Influence of Fake Spies," *International Journal of Intelligence and Counterintelligence*, vol. 23, no. 4, 2010: 596–622.

Zeichmann, Christopher B. "Champion of the Oppressed: Redescribing the Jewishness of Superman as Populist Authenticity Politics," *The Journal of Religion and Popular Culture* vol. 29, no. 2, Summer 2017: 132–146.

Zeiske, Kay. "Letter from Kay," *Bellville Times* (Bellville, TX,), 7 Jan 1954: 18.

Zimmerman, Carla. "From Chop-Chop to Wu Cheng: The Evolution of the Chinese Character in Blackhawk comic books," in *Ethnic Images in the Comics*. The Balch Institute for Ethnic Studies and the Anti-Defamation League of B'nai B'rith, 1986.

Zorbaugh, Harvey. "The Comics—There They Stand!" *Journal of Educational Sociology* vol. 16, no. 4, Dec. 1944: 196–203.

Zwetsloot, Jacco. "North Korean Comics and Their Visual Language in the Work Of Ch' oe Hyŏk," in partial fulfilment of a Master's program in Asian Studies (Korean Studies) at Leiden University, 2015.

B. *Comic Book Series and Comic Book Stories*

Comic book stories in the public domain that are posted at Comic Book + and The Digital Comic Museum are marked with an asterisk. Stories currently web-posted elsewhere are marked with a double asterisk and a URL is provided.

I am using "DC" and "Marvel" anachronistically, ignoring previous publishing names and colophons.

Publication dates for series that the text mentions in passing are taken from the Grand Comics Database (GCD). The GCD usually includes reproductions of covers and much additional information, including credits (when these are known.) I use the abbreviations (w) writer (a) art (penciller and/or inker) (p) penciller (i) inker, and (e) editor.

Online resources include the following websites:

Comic Book +, http://comicbookplus.com/

The Digital Comic Museum, http://digitalcomicmuseum.com

Grand Comics Database, http://www.comics.org/

Comics with Problems, http://www.ep.tc/problems/.

Action Comics #1 (1938, June), "Superman," (w) Jerome Siegel (a) Joe Shuster (http://xroads.virginia.edu/~ug02/yeung/actioncomics/page1.html.)**

Action Comics #101 (1946, Oct.), DC, "Crime Paradise" (aka "Superman Covers Atom Bomb Test") (w) Jerry Siegel? (p) Win Mortimer (i) George Roussos [Cited but not seen.]

Adventures Inside the Atom (1948), GE (a) George Roussos (https://archive.org/details/GeneralElectricCompanyAdventuresInsideTheAtom1948).**

Adventures of Rex the Wonder Dog, (1952–1959), DC (War theme covers #4–9, 1952–1953).

Alice in Blunderland (1952), Industrial Services (http://www.ep.tc/problems/32/01.html).**

All-American Men of War (1952–1966), DC (e) Robert Kanigher.

All-American Men of War #89 (Jan.-Feb. 1962), "Battle Aces of 3 Wars!" (a) Irv Novick and Russ Heath.

All-Negro Comics (1947, June), All-Negro Comics (e) Orrin C. Evans.*

All Quiet on the Western Front (1952, May), Classics Illustrated #95 (w) Ken Fitch, adapting the novel by Erich Maria Remarque (a) Maurice del Bourgo.

America Under Socialism (1950), National Research Bureau (http://www.ep.tc/problems/35/).**

The American Air Forces (Magazine Enterprises) 1951–1954.*

American Splendor (1976–1991), H. Pekar (w) Harvey Pekar.

Archie [For details search the character's appearance at comics.org.]

Army and Navy Comics (1941–1942), Street and Smith.

Army War Heroes, (1963–1970), Charlton.*

Atom-Age Combat (1952–1953), St. John.*

Atom-Age Combat #1 (1952, June), St. John, "Commandos Blitz a Red Invasion."*

Atom-Age Combat #2 (1952, Nov.), St. John, "Yellow Peril in the Skies."*

Atoman # 1 (1946, Feb.), Spark Publications (w) Ken Crossen; (p) Jerry Robinson (i) Mort Meskin?*

Atomic Attack (1953), Youthful Magazines, Inc.*

Atomic Attack #6 (1953, March), Youthful Magazines, Inc., "PW Riot at Koje," (a) Vic Carrabotta.*

The Atomic Revolution (1957), M. Philip Copp (w) Oliver Townsend et al. (a) Sam Citron et al.) (http://www.ep.tc/atmc/index.html).**

Atomic Spy Cases (1950, March-April), Avon.*

Atomic Thunderbolt # 1 (1946, Feb.), Regor Company (p) Mort Lawrence (as Larry Morton), Robert Peterson.*

Atomic War (19521–953), Ace.*

Atomic War #1 (1952, Nov.), Ace, "Sneak Attack," (a) Ken Rice.*

Attack! #3 (1952, Sept.), Youthful, "The Mission of the Pregnant Perch," (a) Vince Napoli(?)*

The Avenger (1955), Magazine Enterprises.*

Battle (1951–1960), Marvel.

Battle, #67 (1959, Dec.), Marvel, "The Invincible Enemy," (a) Jack Kirby, Christopher Rule (http://fantasy-ink. blogspot.com/2013_03_01_archive.html).**

Battle, # 70 (1960, June), Marvel, "Face to Face with the Enemy," (a) Don Heck.

Battle Action (1952–1957), Marvel.

Battle Attack, (1954–1955), Stanley Morse.*

Battle Brady, (1953), Marvel.

Battle Cry #3 (1952, Sept.), Stanley Morse, "To the Victors!" (a) Eugene Hughes (Republished in issue #14, Sept. 1954).*

Battle Cry #11 (1954, March), Stanley Morse, cover (a) Irv Novick?*

Battle Cry #12 (1954, May), StanMor Publications, Inc., "The Confession!," (a) Eugene Hughes?*

Battle Fire, (1955–1956), Stanley Morse.*

Battle Heroes, (1966), Stanley Morse.*

Battle Report #1 (1952, Aug.), Farrell, "Plague Patrol!"*

Battle Squadron, (1955), Stanley Morse.*

Battle Stories #5 (1952, Sept.), Fawcett, "They've got to KILL me!," (a) Clem Weisbecker.*

Battlefield (1952–1953), Marvel.

Battlefield #2 (1952, June), Marvel, "Atrocity Story," (w) Hank Chapman (a) Paul Reinman (https://timely-atlas-comics.blogspot.com/2013/05/a-history-of-atlas-war-comics-1950-1960.html).**

Battlefield # 11 (1953, May), Marvel, "He Won't Go Back!," (a) Louis Ravielli.

Battlefront (1952–1957), Marvel.

Battleground, (1954–1957), Marvel.

Beetle Bailey, [For details search the character's appearance at comics.org.]

Big Shot #44 (1944, March), Columbia Comic Corporation, "Captain Yank: The Synthetic Rubber Formula, Part 5," (w/a) Frank Tinsley.*

Billy Battle, Norman Clifford [Australian; cited but not seen.]

Black Cat Mystery #39 (1952, Sept.), Harvey, "The Witch Killer," (a) Rudy Palais.*

Black Cobra (1954–1955), Ajax-Farrell.*

Black Cobra #6 [second actual issue] (1954–1955, Dec.-Jan.), Ajax, "The Big Blast."*

Blackhawk (1944–1956), Quality.*

Blazing Combat (1965–1966), Warren.

Blazing Combat #2 (1966, Jan.), Warren, "Holding Action," (w) Archie Goodwin (a) John Severin.

Blazing Combat #2 (1966, Jan.), Warren, "MiG Alley," (w) Archie Goodwin (a) Al McWilliams.

Blazing Combat #3 (1966, July), Warren, "The Edge," (w) Archie Goodwin (a) Alex Toth.

Bool Geun Tang (Red Land) 1952 [Korean language; cited but not seen.]

Buck Danny #11—Ciel de Corée (1954, Jan.) Dupuis [French language; cited but not seen.] (w) Jean-Michel Charlier (a) Victor Hubinon.

Buck Danny #12—Avions sans pilotes (1954, Jan.) Dupuis [French language; cited but not seen.] (w) Jean-Michel Charlier (a) Victor Hubinon.

Buck Rogers of the 25th Century, #100 (January, 1951), Toby Press, "The Adventure of the Flying Discs," (a) R.T. Chatton.

Buddies in the U.S. Army, (1952–1953), Avon.*

Buz Sawyer (1948–1949), Pines.*

Calling All Girls (1941–1949), Parents' Magazine Press.*

Captain America Comics (1941–1949), Marvel.

Captain America (1943, May), Marvel, "The Russian Hell-Hole," (p) Syd Shores (i) Vince Alascia.

Captain America #77 (1954, July), Marvel, "Mission to a POW Camp," (a) John Romita.

Captain America #78 (1954, Sept.), Marvel, "Playing with Fire," (a) John Romita, Dick Ayers and Bill Everett.

Captain Marvel Adventures (1941–1953), Fawcett.*

Captain Marvel Adventures # 66 (1946, Oct.), Fawcett, "Captain Marvel and the Atomic War," (w) Otto Binder (a) C.C. Beck.*

Captain Marvel Adventures #140 (1953, Jan), Fawcett, "Captain Marvel Fights the Mongol Blood-drinkers," (w) Otto Binder (a) C.C. Beck, Pete Costanza.

Captain Marvel's Adventures #147 (1953, Aug.), Fawcett, "Captain Marvel and the Riddle of the Space Reds," (w) Otto Binder (a) Kurt Schaffenberger.*

Captain Steve Savage's Flight to Kill #7 (1952, Oct.), Avon., "Riot on Koje!"*

Cat-Man #3 (1941, July), cover (a) Charles Quinlan, Sr.*

The Challenger (1945–1946), Interfaith Publications [Cited but not seen.]

Chambers and Hiss in Betrayed [8-pager].

Char Chapman, Phantom of the East (1952–1953), Young's Merchandising Company (w/a) Kevan Hardacre [Australian; cited but not seen].

Combat (1952–1953), Marvel.

Combat Casey #16 (1954, June), Marvel, cover (a) Robert Q. Sale (https://www.comics.org/issue/202673/cover/4/).**

Combat Casey #19 (1954, Dec.), Marvel, "Atomic Warfare," (a) Robert Q. Sale (http://warpastpresentfuture.blogspot.com/2013/02/).**

Comic Cavalcade (19421–954), DC.

Comic Cavalcade (1944, Winter). DC, "The 99th Squadron," (w/a) Jon L. Blummer [cited but not seen].

Contact Comics # 6 (May 1945). Marvel, "Black Venus," (w/a) Harvey Kurtzman (http://atomic-surgery.blogspot.com/2011/11/black-venus-by-harvey-kurtzman-1945.html).**

Corporate CRIME Comics, 1977, 1979, Kitchen Sink (e) Leonard Rifas.

Creepy (1964–1983), Warren.

Crime, Corruption & Communism (1952), the National Committee of The Jefferson Party of Charlottesville, Virginia, [eight-page, giveaway political comic], M. Philip Copp.

Crime Does Not Pay (1942–1955), Lev Gleason.*

Crime SuspenStories #22 (1954, April-May), EC, cover (e) William Gaines (a) Johnny Craig (https://www.comics.org/issue/11216/cover/4/).**

The Crimson Comet (1949–1957) John Dixon [Australian; cited but not seen].

Desfile de Historietas (1953, May) [Spanish language; cited but not seen].

Detective Comics (1937–2011), DC.

Don Winslow of the Navy (1943–1951), Fawcett.*

Don Winslow of the Navy #65 (1951, Jan.), Fawcett, "Flying Saucer Attack, Part I."*

Dwight D. Eisenhower and Richard M. Nixon—The Choice of a Nation (1952), Commercial Comics [eight-page, giveaway political comic].

Earl Browder in the Good Old U.S.A. [8-pager].

Eerie (1966–1983), Warren.

Episodios de Corea, (1951–1952?), Ricart [cited but not read].

Exciting War #6 (1952, Nov.), Better, "Stand or Die," (p) Jack Katz (i) Aldo Rubano.*

Famous Funnies (1934–1955), Eastern Color.

Famous Funnies #204 (1953, Feb.), Eastern Color, cover (https://www.comics.org/issue/128482/cover/4/).**

Fight Comics (1940–1954), Fiction House.*

Fight Comics #75 (1951, July), Fiction House, "Rip Carson of Risks, Unlimited," (a) Ken Battefield?*

Fight for Freedom! (1949), General Comics, Inc. (National Association of Manufacturers), (a) Dan Barry (https://digital.hagley.org/PAM_08028157)**

Fightin' Army (1956–1984), Charlton.*

Fighting American (1954–1955), Prize.

Fighting Leathernecks (1952), Toby.*

The Fighting Man #5 (1953, March), Ajax-Farrell, "Desperate Destination."*

The Fighting Man #5 (1953, March), Farrell, "Peril Patrol."*

The Fighting Man #8 (1953, July), Farrell, "Amazing New Health Supporter Belt" ad.*

Fighting War Stories #3 (1952, Dec.), Story Comics, "The Fighting 'Eightball,'" (p) Tony Tallarico?*

Fightin'Marines (1951–1953), St, John.*

Fightin'Marines (1955–1984), Charlton.*

Foxhole #1 (1954, Oct.), Mainline, "Brain Wash," (a) Jo Albistur (reprinted in *Foxhole #11,* 1963).

The Free World Speaks (n.d.), published by Malcom Ater (a) Jack Sparling. [In the collection of Ohio State University Libraries.]

From Yalta to Korea (1952), Republican National, Congressional, & Senatorial Committees [eight-page, giveaway political comic, copyrighted by M. Philip Copp].

Frontline Combat (1951–1954), EC.

Frontline Combat #1 (1951, July-Aug.), EC, "Enemy Assault!" (w) Harvey Kurtzman (a) Jack Davis.

Frontline Combat #4 (1952, Jan.-Feb.), EC, "Combat Media" (w) Harvey Kurtzman (a) Jack Davis.

Frontline Combat #11 (1953, March-April), EC, "Front Lines" (e) Harvey Kurtzman.

Frontline Combat #12 (1953, May-June), EC, "F-94!" (w) Harvey Kurtzman (a) George Evans.

Frontline Combat #13 (1953, July), EC, "Perimeter!" (w/a) Wally Wood.

Funnies on Parade (1933) Eastern Color Printing.

Gen of Hiroshima (1979, 1980), EduComics (w/a) Keiji Nakazawa [Republication of *Hadashi no Gen* (*Barefoot Gen*).]

G.I. Combat (19521–1956), Quality Comics.*

G.I. Combat (1957–1987), DC (e) Robert Kanigher.

G.I. Combat #2 (1952, Dec.), Quality Comics, "Prison Camp Slaughter," (w) Robert Bernstein (a) Pete Morisi.*

G.I. Combat #254 (1983, June), DC, "The Forgotten War," (w) Robert Kanigher (a) Angel Trinidad, Jr.

G-I in Battle #3 (1952, Dec.), Ajax-Farrell, "Three in a Jeep."*

G-I in Battle, #8 (May, 1953), Ajax-Farrell, "Flaming Coffin."*

G-I in Battle, #8 (1953, May), Ajax-Farrell, "Red Trap."*

G.I. Joe (1950–1951), Ziff-Davis.*

G.I. Joe #12 (1952, June), Ziff-Davis, "The Patchwork Quilt."*

G.I. Joe #27 (1953, Nov.), Ziff-Davis, "The 'Massacre' at Ku-Shi Bridge."*

The H-Bomb and You (1954), produced by Malcolm Ater. (http://www.ep.tc/comics/h-bomb/).**

Headline Comics #7 (1946, May-June), Prize, "Atomicman," (p) Gil Kane; (i) Jerry Robinson?*

Hechos Heroicos (1953, May) [Spanish language; cited but not seen.]

Heroic Comics (1943–1946) Eastern Color Printing Company.*

Horrors of War #11 (1953, Jan.) Star Publications, "The Spirit of War," (a) Jay Disbrow.*

How Boys and Girls Can Help Win the War (1942), The Parents Magazine Institute.*

How Stalin Hopes We Will Destroy America (1951) (https://images.socialwelfare.library.vcu.edu/items/show/293).**

Human Torch #38 (1954, Aug.), Marvel, "In Korea," (a) Dick Ayers.

I SAW IT [*Ore wa Mita*] (1982, Dec.), Educomics (w/p) Keiji Nakazawa.

Ideal Comics #3 (1948, Nov.), Marvel, "The Soil of Africa Weeps," (a) Mike Sekowsky?

If an A-Bomb Falls (1951), produced by Malcolm Ater (http://www.ep.tc/comics/a-bomb/).*

Ike's Story (1952), Sponsored Comics.

The Illustrated Story of the Army (1959, May), Classics Illustrated, "The Korean War," 2pp (a) Norman Nodel.

Immortal Hero Yang Ken-Sze (1959, 1965), Foreign Language Press (Peking), story by Wang Hao, adapted by Yi Fan (a) Ho Yu-chih.

Impact #4 (1955, Sept.-Oct.), EC, "The Lonely One," (w) Jack Oleck? (a) Jack Davis.

Incredible Science Fiction #33 (1956, Jan.-Feb.), EC, "Judgment Day!," (w) Al Feldstein (a) Joe Orlando (https://atocom.blogspot.com/2013/01/reading-room-weird-fantasy-judgement-day.html).**

Is This Tomorrow? America Under Communism (1947), Catechetical Guild (w) F. Robert Edman, Francis McGrade; (a) Charles Schulz and others. (https://archive.org/details/IsThisTomorrowAmericaUnderCommunismCatecheticalGuild).**

itchy PLANET #1 (1988, Spring), Seattle: Fantagraphics, "U.S. Comic Books and Nuclear War," (w/a) Leonard Rifas.

itchy PLANET #1 (1988, Spring), Fantagraphics, "Nuclear Winter," (w/a) Leonard Rifas.

Jet Fighters #7 (1953, March), Standard Comics, "Iran Curtains for Ivan," (a) John Celardo.*

Jet Fighters #7 (1953, March), Standard Comics, "Seeley's Saucer," (p) Alex Toth (i) Mike Peppe.*

Jewish War Heroes, (1944), the Canadian Jewish Congress.*

Joe Louis, Champion of Champions: the heroic story of the fightingest champion of all time (1950), Fawcett.*

Joe Palooka #66 (1952, March), Harvey, "The Red Plot," "Behind the Iron Curtain," "The Confession," (w/a) Ham Fisher.*

Joe Palooka #67 (1952, April), Harvey, "Flight to Freedom," "Mogla's Plan," (w/a) Ham Fisher.*

Joe Palooka Battle Adventures #75 (1953, Jan.), Harvey, "Prison Riot."*

Joe Yank (1952–1953), Pines.*

John Wayne Adventure Comics #12 (1951, Dec.), Toby Press, "Link-Up in Korea," (p) Charles Sultan.*

Judith Coplon in Overpaid Lawyer [8-pager, approx. 1949].

Jumbo Comics #153 (1951, Nov.), Fiction House, "Lost Legions of the Nile," (a) Robert Webb.*

Kent Blake (19511–953), Marvel.

Korea My Home (1953), Johnstone & Cushing (p) Al Stenzel (i) Bill Timmins [In collection of Ohio State University Libraries.]

Korea! The True Story (1950), Unpublished [in collection of Ohio State University Libraries].

Learn How Dagwood Splits the Atom (1949), King Features (w) Joe Musial (a) Chic Young? (https://www.sparehed.com/2007/05/14/dagwood-splits-the-atom/).**

Life Stories of American Presidents (1957, May), Dell (a) John Buscema.

Life Story of Franklin D. Roosevelt, The (July, 1942), Office of War Information, (https://www.coldwarradiomuseum.com/members-of-congress-exposed-somestic-us-government-propaganda-in-1943/)**

Little Lulu (1948–1962), Dell.

Los Agachados (1968–1981?), Editorial Posada, [Spanish language] (w/a) rius.

Los Supermachos (1965–1982?), Editorial Meridiano, [Spanish language] (w/a) rius.

MAD (1952–2018), EC.

MAD #10 (1954, April), "G.I. Schmoe!," (w/e) Harvey Kurtzman (a) Wally Wood (http://comicmaniaforever.blogspot.com/2015/07/gi-schmoe-mad-tale-by-harvey-kurtzman.html).**

Man Comics (19491–953), Marvel.

Man Comics #11 (1951, Dec.) Marvel, "Cannon Fodder" (w) Hank Chapman (a) Joe Maneely (allthingsger.blogspot.com/ August 04, 2015 War Is Hell [But Necessary] 17).**

A Man Named Stevenson (1952), Democratic National Committee, produced by Malcolm Ater.

Marine War Heroes #13 (1966, April-May), Charlton Comics, "Complete History of the Korean War," (w) Joe Gill(?) (p) Charles Nicholas (i) Vince Alascia (i) Rocco "Rocke" Mastroserio.

Marines at War (1957), Marvel.

Marines in Battle (1954–1958), Marvel.

Martin Luther King and the Montgomery Story (1958), Fellowship of Reconciliation (w) Alfred Hassler and Benton J. Resnik (a) Sy Barry (http://www.ep.tc/mlk/index.html).**

The Mask of Dr. Fu Manchu (1951), Avon, cover (a) Wally Wood).*

Master Comics #43 (1943, Oct.), Fawcett, "Captain Marvel Junior Battles for Stalingrad!," (w) Otto Binder (a) Mac Raboy.*

Men in Action (1952), Marvel.

Men's Adventures (1950–1954), Marvel.

Men's Adventures #28 (1954, July), Marvel, "Kill Captain America," (a) John Romita, Dick Ayers and Bill Everett.

Military Comics (1941–1945), Quality.*

Monty Hall of the U.S. Marines (1951–1953), Toby Press, Inc.*

Monty Hall of the U.S. Marines #1 (1951, Aug.), Toby Press, Inc., "The City of Flame," (a) Mel Keefer?*

Monty Hall of the U.S. Marines #3 (1951, Dec.), Toby Press. Inc., "Danger Below," (a) Mel Keefer.*

Monty Hall of the U.S. Marines #5 (1952, April), Toby Press letters column.*

Mutants of the Metropolis (1972), L.A. Comics (w/a) P. (Pete) Serniuk.

Navy Combat (1955–1958), Marvel.

Navy Heroes, (1945), Almanac Publishing Company.

Navy Tales (1957), Marvel.

Navy War Heroes, (1964–1965), Charlton.*

Negro Heroes (1947–1948), Parents Magazine Press.*

Never Again (19551–956), Charlton.*

New Fun Comics (1935) DC: National Allied Publications, Inc.

New Heroic Comics (1946–1955), Eastern Color.*

New Heroic Comics #69 (1951, Nov.), Eastern Color, cover (a) H.E. Kiefer.*

New Heroic Comics #74 (1952, Aug.), Eastern Color, "Sgt. Charlton and Hill 543."*

New Heroic Comics #75 (1952, Sept.), Eastern Color, "Soldier of Salvation."*

New Heroic Comics #78 (1952, Dec.), Eastern Color, "At the Risk of Death."*

New Heroic Comics #81 (1953, March.), Eastern Color, "Hill 528," (a) Sam Burlockoff.*

New Heroic Comics #87 (1953, Sept.), Eastern Color, Stranded in a Mine Field," (a) Frank Frazetta.*

New Heroic Comics #90 (1955, March) Eastern Color.*

New World Order Comix #1: *The Saga of White Will* (w) William Pierce (a) Daniel "Rip' Roush (colorist) William White Williams (https://archive.org/details/NewWorldOrderComix1TheSagaOf..WhiteWill1993WilliamPierce).**

Not Brand Echh (1967–1969), Marvel.

Operation Peril, (1950–1953), ACG.*

Our Army at War (1952–1977), DC (e) Robert Kanigher.

Our Army at War #113 (1961, Dec.), DC, "Eyes for a Blind Gunner," (w/e) Robert Kanigher (a) Joe Kubert.

Our Army at War #160 (1965, Nov.), DC, "What's the Color of Your Blood?," (w/e) Robert Kanigher (a) Joe Kubert (https://kb-outofthisworld.blogspot.com/2010/02/war-comics-introduce-racial-integration_15.html).**

Our Fighting Forces (19541–978), DC (e) Robert Kanigher.

Outstanding American War Heroes, (1944), Parent's Magazine Press.

Picture News #1 (1946, Jan.), Lafayette St. Corp., "Will the Atom Blow the World Apart?"*

Picture News #3 (1946, March), Lafayette St. Corp., "To Save the World Make Atomic Energy Constructive Rather than Destructive."*

Picture News #9 (1946, Nov.-Dec.) Lafayette St. Corp., "Atom Bombs Over Bikini."*

Plastic Man #38 (1952, Nov.), Quality, "The Fight against Germ Warfare!"*

Popular Comics (1936–1948), Dell.

Prize Comics #39 (1944, Feb.) Prize Comics, "Ted O'Neil of the Commandoes," (a) E.C. Stoner.*

P.S. Magazine: The Preventive Maintenance Monthly (1951-present), Department of the Army (http://psmag.radionerds.com/index.php/Index_by_issue; https://www.nsncenter.com/Library/PSMagazine).**

Rangers Comics (19421–952), Fiction House.*

Rangers Comics #61 (1952, Oct.), Fiction House, "Burma Raid of the Air Commandos," (a) Ruben Moreira.*

Real Fact #5 (1946, Nov.-Dec.), Parents' Magazine Press, "Paul Robeson—All American Citizen," (w) Jack Schiff, Mort Weisinger and Bernie Breslauer (a) Jack Lehti? [Cited but not seen.]

Real Heroes (19411–946), Parents Magazine Press.*

Real War Stories, #1 (1987), Eclipse Comics, "Tapestries," part one: (w) W.D. Erhart and Alan Moore (p) Stan Woch (i) John Totleben; part two: (w) Alan Moore (a) Steve Bissette.

Real War Stories, #1 (1987), Eclipse Comics, "Elite of the Fleet: The story of Tim Merrill" (w) Mike W. Barr (a) Brian Bolland and Mark Farmer.

Real War Stories #2 (1991), Eclipse Comics and Citizen Soldier.

The Robert Alphonso Taft Story (1950).

Rocket Ship × (1951, Sept.), Fox Feature Syndicate, Inc. "Our Atomic Future."*

Roy Rogers Comics #57 (1952, Sept.), Dell, "Poisoned Water," (a) Albert Micale.

Roy Rogers Comics #64 (1953, April), Dell, "Medicine Smoke" (a) Al McKimson team.

Rulah #21 (1948, Dec.), Fox Features Syndicate, Inc., "Silent Death," (a) Alec Hope (A.C. Hollingsworth).*

The Sad Sack (1949–1982), Harvey.

Science Comics #1 (1946, Jan.), Ace Magazines, "The Bomb That Won the War." (a) Rudy Palais.*

(Admiral Zacharias') Secret Missions #1 (1950, Feb.), St John.*

Sgt. Fury (1963–1974), Marvel.

Sgt. Fury # 6 (1964, March), Marvel, "The Fangs of the Desert Fox," (w/e) Stan Lee (p) Jack Kirby (i) George Roussos.

Sgt. Fury and his Howling Commandos Special King Size Annual #1 (1965), Marvel, "Commission in Korea," (w) Stan Lee (p) Dick Ayers (i) Frank Giacoia.

Sgt. Rock (1977–1988), DC.

Sgt. Rock #417 (1987, Aug.), DC, "The Sons of Easy," (w) Robert Kanigher (p) Andy Kubert (i) Adam Kubert (e) Murray Boltinoff.

Sgt. Rock #418 (1987, Oct.), DC, "Part Two: The Sons of Easy," (w) Robert Kanigher (a) Andy Kubert (e) Murray Boltinoff.

Shield-Wizard Comics # 2 (1940, Winter), M.L.J., "The Shield," (w) Harry Shorten (a) Irv Novick.*

Shock SuspenStories #11 (1953. Oct.-Nov.) EC, "In Gratitude," (w) Al Feldstein (a) Wally Wood.

Sky Demons, Southdown Press [Australian; cited but not seen].

Sky Hawk, Southdown Press [Australian; cited but not seen].

Smash Comics # 27 (1941, Oct.), Quality, "Wings Wendall," (w/a) Vernon Henkel.*

Soldier Comics (1952–1953), Fawcett.*

Soldiers of Fortune #12 (1953, Jan.-Feb.), ACG, "Revenge Above the Yalu," (p/i) Edmund Good.*

Speed Comics #23 (1942, Oct.), Harvey, "The Girl Commandos" (a) Barbara Hall.*

Speed Comics #24 (1942, Dec.), Harvey, "Captain Freedom and the Young Defenders," (a) Arthur Cazeneuve.*

Spy and Counterspy (1949), ACG.*

Spy and Counterspy #1 (1949, Aug.-Sept.), ACG, "Jonathan Kent, Counterspy," (w) Richard Hughes (a) Charles Sultan.*

Spy and Counterspy #1 (1949, Aug.-Sept.), ACG, "Report to the Nation," (w) Richard Hughes (a) John Belfi.*

Spy and Counterspy #2 (1949, Nov.), American Comics Group, "The Black Avengers," (a) Leonard Starr?*

Spy Cases (1951–1953), Marvel.

Spy Cases #28 (1951, Feb.), Marvel, "The Gray Shark," (p) Mike Sekowsky? (e) Stan Lee.

Spy Cases #10 (1952, April), Marvel, "Fangs of the Tiger," (a) Bill Savage.

Spy Cases #11 (1952, June), Marvel. "Scorched Earth!" (a) Bill Savage.

Spy Fighters (19511–953), Marvel.

Spy-Hunters (19491–953), ACG.*

Spy-Hunters #3 (Dec.-Jan.19491–950, Dec.-Jan.), ACG, "Adventures of a Spy," (a) Charles Sultan.*

Spy Hunters #6 (1950, June-July) ACG, "Menace in Madagascar," (a) Ogden Whitney.*

Spy-Hunters #21 (1952–1953, Dec.-Jan.), ACG, "Peril in Pyongyang."*

Spy-Hunters #21 (19521–953, Dec.-Jan.), ACG, "Intelligence Mission."*

Spy-Hunters #22 (1953, Feb.-March), ACG, "Destination Korea!," (a) Robert S. Pious.*

Spy Thrillers (1954–1955), Marvel.

Star-Spangled War Stories (1941–1952), DC (e) Robert Kanigher.

Steve Canyon (1948), Harvey.

Steve Canyon's Air Power (1951, Nov.) Harvey.

The Story of Harry S Truman (1948), Democratic National Committee (w) Malcolm Ater (a) Jack Sparling (https://www.trumanlibraryinstitute.org/trumancomicbook/).**

SuspenStories #13 (1954, Feb.-March), EC, "Blood Brothers," (w) Al Feldstein (a) Wally Wood (https://www.cbr.com/ec-comics-al-feldstein-wallace-wood-blood-brothers-bigotry/)**

T-Man (19511–956), Quality.*

T-Man #1 (1954, April), Quality, cover.*

Tales of the Green Berets (1967–1969), Dell.

Teen Life Comics and Adventures (1945–1946), New Age Publishers, Inc.*

Teen Life Comics and Adventures #3 (1945, Winter), New Age Publishers, Inc.*

Tegra Jungle Empress #1 (1948, Aug.), Fox.*

Tell it to the Marines (1952–1955), Toby.*

Terry and the Pirates (1947–1951), Harvey.*

Thrilling Comics #19 (1941, Aug.), Pines, "The American Crusader," (a) Max Plaisted.*

Tim Valour (1948–1957), John Dixon [Australian; cited but not seen].

Tot'ori Yongsa (*Brave Soldier Tot'ori*), 1952 [Korean language; cited but not seen].

Treasure Chest of Fun and Fact, v.6 n.10, (1951, January 18), Geo. A. Pflaum, Publisher, Inc., "Where Do We Stand?" (a) Lloyd Ostendorf, (https://cuislandora.wrlc.org/islandora/object/cuislandora%3A12741#page/1/mode/1up)**

True Comics (1941–1950), Parents Magazine Press.*

True Comics #39 (1941, Oct.), Parents' Magazine Press "Brown Bomber: World's Greatest Fighter," (a) Sam Glankoff.*

True Comics #39 (1944, Oct.), Parents' Magazine Press "There Are No Master Races."*
True Comics #48 (1946, April), Parents' Magazine Press, "Paul Robeson."*
True Comics #72 (1948, July), Parents' Magazine Press, "Jackie Robinson: Rookie of the Year."*
True Comics #79 (1949, Oct.), Parents' Magazine Press, "Ralph J. Bunche: United Nations Peacemaker."*
The Truth Behind the Trial of Cardinal Mindszenty (1949), the Catechetical Guild Educational Society.
Tuffy (1949–1950), Pines (w/a) Syd Hoff.*
Two Fisted Tales (19501–955), EC.
Two Fisted Tales #19 (1951, Jan.-Feb.) EC, "War Story!," (w/p) Harvey Kurtzman (i) Bill Elder.
Two-Fisted Tales #20 (1951, March-April), EC, "Massacred!" (w) Harvey Kurtzman (a) John Severin and Will Elder.
Two-Fisted Tales #22 (1951, July-August), EC, "Combat Correspondence," (e) Harvey Kurtzman.
Two-Fisted Tales #22 (1951, July/August), EC, "Dying City!," (w) Harvey Kurtzman (a) Alex Toth.
Two-Fisted Tales #23 (1951, Sept.-Oct.), EC, "Combat Correspondence," (e) Harvey Kurtzman.
Two-Fisted Tales #24 (1951, Nov.-Dec.), EC, "Combat Correspondence," (e) Harvey Kurtzman.
Two-Fisted Tales #26 (1952, March-April), EC, "Combat Correspondence," (e) Harvey Kurtzman.
Two-Fisted Tales #26 (1952, March-April), EC, "Hungnam!" (w) Harvey Kurtzman (a) Wally Wood.
Two-Fisted Tales #26 (1952, March-April) EC, "A Document of the Action at the Changjin Reservoir!," (w) Harvey Kurtzman (a) John Severin, Jack Davis and Will Elder.
Two-Fisted Tales #27 (1952, May-June), EC, "Combat Correspondence," (e) Harvey Kurtzman.
Two-Fisted Tales #28 (1952, July-Aug.), EC, "Combat Correspondence."
Two-Fisted Tales #30 (1952, Nov.-Dec.), EC, "Bunker," (w) Harvey Kurtzman (a) Ric Estrada.
Two-Fisted Tales #33 (1953, May-June), EC, "Atom Bomb!," (w) Harvey Kurtzman (a) Wallace Wood.
Two-Fisted Tales #33 (1953, May-June), EC, "Combat Correspondence," (e) Harvey Kurtzman.
Two-Fisted Tales #37 (1954, April), EC, "Combat Correspondence," (e) Harvey Kurtzman.
Two-Fisted Tales #40 (19541–955, Dec.-Jan.), EC, "Dien Bien Phu!," (w) John Putnam (a) John Severin.
Uncle Charlie's Fables (1952), Lev Gleason.*
Uncle Scrooge #1 (1952, March), Dell, *"Only A Poor Old Man,"* (w/a) Carl Barks.
United States Fighting Air Force #3 (1953, Jan.), Superior Comic, "Panmunjom Treachery."*
The United States Marines, vol. 1, no. 3 (1944), DC. "Japan's First Victim."*
U.S. Paratroops (1952), Avon.*
U.S. Paratroops #6 (1952, Dec.), Avon, "Silent Death," (a) Mort Lawrence.
U.S. Tank Commandoes (19521–953), Avon.*
Vampirella (19691–983), Warren.
Walt Disney's Comics and Stories (1940–1962), Dell.
War Action (1952–1953), Marvel.
War Action #12 (1953, March), Marvel, "The Quiet Guy," (a) Manny Stallman.
War Adventures on the Battlefield #4 (1952, Oct.) "Battlefield Bivouac."
War Battles #5 (1952, July), Harvey, "No Punches Pulled."*
War Birds, (1952), Fiction House.*
War Combat #1, (1952, March), Marvel, "Behind the Lines," (w) Hank Chapman, (a) Bill LaCava.
War Combat #3 (1952, July), Marvel, "The Final Grave," (w) Hank Chapman (a) Joe Sinnott.
War Comics (1940–1941), Dell.
War Comics (1950–1957), Marvel.
War Comics #1 (1950, Dec.), Marvel, "Peril in Korea" (a) Mike Sekowsky.
War Comics #4 (1951, June), Marvel, "The Victory," (w) Hank Chapman (a) Gene Colan.
War Comics #8 (1952, Feb.), Marvel, "The Face of the Enemy," (a) Bill LaCava.
War Comics #11, (1952, Aug.), Marvel, cover (a) Russ Heath (https://www.atlastales.com/issue/4488)**
War Comics #30 (1954, Dec.), Cover (a) Russ Heath (https://www.comics.org/issue/203210/cover/4/).**
War Heroes (1942–1945), Dell.*
War Heroes (1952–1953), Ace.*
War Heroes (1963), Charlton.*
War Heroes #6 (1943, Oct.-Dec.), Dell, "Seagoing Haymaker."*
War Heroes #2 (1952, July), Ace, "Decision on Devil's Ridge," (w) Robert Turner (a) Jim McLaughlin*
War Heroes #2 (1952, July), Ace, "Operation Abracadabra," (w) Robert Turner (a) Lou Cameron.*
War Report #2 (1952–1953) Ajax-Farrell.*
War Report #2 (1952, Nov.), Ajax-Farrell, "Blonde Double- Cross."*
War Report #4 (1953, March), Ajax-Farrell, "Cross of Courage."*
War Report #5 (1953, May), Ajax-Farrell Publications, "Get That Man!"*
War Report #5 (1953, May), Ajax-Farrell, "Suicide Alley."*
War Stories (1940–1941), Dell.*
War Stories (1952–1953), Farrell.*
Warfront #1 (1951, June), Harvey, "Bullets, Babies and Bombs!," (a) Jack Sparling.*
Warfront #4 (1952, March), Harvey, "Secret Mission."*
Warfront #16 (1953, Aug.), Harvey, "Ambush."*

Wartime Romances (1951–1953), St. John.*

Wartime Romances #16 (1953, July), St. John, "His Fraternity Pin," (a) Ric Estrada.*

We Hit the Jackpot, (1948), General Comics, Inc. (printed for American Affairs), (https://digital.hagley.org/PAM_08023277)**

Weird Fantasy #14 (1950, July-Aug.), EC, cover (a) Al Feldstein (https://www.comics.org/issue/8383/cover/4/).**

Weird Science #5 (1951, Jan.-Feb.), EC, cover (a) Al Feldstein (https://www.comics.org/issue/8671/cover/4/).**

Weird Science #14 (1950, Sept.-Oct.), EC, cover (a) Al Feldstein (https://www.comics.org/issue/8480/cover/4/).**

Weird Science #14 (1950, Sept.-Oct.), EC, "Destruction of the Earth!," (w) Bill Gaines, Al Feldstein (a) Al Feldstein.

Weird Science #18 (1953, March-April.), EC, cover (a) Wallace Wood (https://www.comics.org/issue/10430/cover/4/).**

Wings Comics (1940–1954), Fiction House.*

Wings Comics #51 (1944, Nov.), Fiction House, "Suicide Smith," (a) Ruben Moreira.*

Wings Comics #124 (1954), Fiction House, "Death Below Zero," (a) Johnny Bell.*

With the Marines on the Battlefronts of the World! #2 (1954, March), Toby Press, "Marine Saves White Horse Hill," (a) Mel Keefer.

The World Around Us #9: The Illustrated Story of the Army (1959, May), Gilberton, "The Korean War," (a) Norman Nodel.

The World Bank: a tale of power, plunder, and resistance (1995), Public Services International, Alec Dubro (a) Mike Konopacki.

World's Finest Comics (1941–1986), DC.

World's Finest Comics #17 (1945, Spring), "Dedicated to the millions…" (Johnny Everyman) (w) Jack Schiff (a) John Daly.

World's Finest Comics #23 (1946, July-Aug.), DC, "Room for Improvement" (Johnny Everyman) (w) Jack Schiff (a) John Daly.

World War III (1952), Ace (w) Robert Turner (a) Ken Rice, Lou Cameron, Jim McLaughlin.*

World War III #1 (1952, March), Ace, "World War III Unleashed," (w) Robert Turner (a) Ken Rice.*

Young Life (1945), New Age Publishers, Inc.*

Young Lust #7 (1990), Last Gasp, "Guilt-Edged Bonds," (w/a) Jay Kinney and Paul Mavrides.

Young Men, (1950–1951, 1953–1954), Marvel.

Young Men on the Battlefield (1952–1953), Marvel.

C. *Films and Videos*

Coates, Paul. "Confidential File: Horror Comic Books," Confidential Telepictures Company, Inc., 1955, https://www.youtube.com/watch?v=1r1XeAswKHc

Eisner, Will. *Will Eisner, Profession: Cartoonist,* Part Three: "Master Class: Military Training & Industrial Cartoons," video directed by Marisa Furtado, Brazil: SCRIPTORIUM, 1999.

Emmons, Robert E. Jr. *Diagram for Delinquents: Fredric Wertham and the Evolution of Comic Books,* Sequart, 2014.

Ishida, Yuko, director. *Barefoot Gen's Hiroshima (Hadashi No Gen Ga Mita Hiroshima),* Siglo/Tomo Corporation, 2011.

Kantor, Michael. *Truth, Justice and the American Way,* Ghost Light Films, 2013.

Kirby, Jack. "Jack Kirby at War," 1983, https://www.youtube.com/watch?v=866ToIkLksA.

Korea: The Forgotten War, Mill Creek Entertainment, 2011.

Sorkin, Roger. *Joystick Warriors: Video Games, Violence & the culture of Militarism,* Sorkin Productions, 2013.

D. *Hearings and Government Documents*

Accounting for POW/MIA's from the Korean War and the Vietnam War: Hearings Before the Military Personnel Subcommittee of the House Committee on National Security, 104th Cong., 2nd sess., held Sept. 17, 1996, USGPO, 1997.

Children's Fears of War: Hearing before the House Select Committee on Children, Youth, and Families, 98th Cong., 1st sess., 20 Sept. 1983, USGPO, 1984.

Comic Books and Juvenile Delinquency. Interim Report of the Senate Committee on the Judiciary pursuant to S. Res. 89 and S. Res. 190, 83rd Cong., 1st sess.—83rd Cong., 2nd sess., A Part of the Investigation of Juvenile Delinquency in the United States, USGPO, 1955–1956.

Federal Code Annotated…. Title 18, The Bobbs-Merrill Company, Inc., 1950.

FRUS Policy of the United States with respect to atomic energy and the regulation of armaments; President Eisenhower's 'atoms for peace' proposal of December 8, 1953; other foreign policy aspects of U.S. Development of Atomic Energy, Foreign Relations, USGPO, 1952–1954, Volume II: 1056, 1058, 1068.

Hendrickson, Robert C., and Estes Kefauver. "A joint statement from the offices of Senators Estes Kefauver

(D-Tenn.) and Robert C. Hendrickson (R-N.J.) For release to afternoon papers of Wednesday, March 4, 1953." Records of the U.S. Senate, 83rd Congress Committee on the Judiciary, Accompanying Papers (SEN 83A-E11), S. Res. 88 and S. Res 89, Record Group 46, Box 72, National Archives, Washington, D.C., 1953.

Investigation into the 1950 Ohio Senatorial Campaign: Hearings before the Subcommittee on Privileges and Elections of the Senate Committee on Rules and Administration, 82nd Cong., 1st and 2nd sess., USGPO, 1952 (This can be found at the Hathi Trust Digital Library by using the keywords "Taft comic book." https://www.hathitrust.org/).

Investigation of Organized Crime in Interstate Commerce: Hearings before a Special Committee to Investigate Organized Crime in Interstate Commerce, US Senate, 81st Cong., 2nd sess., pursuant to S. Res. 202. Clifton Garner testimony on June 23, 1950, USGPO, 1950.

Investigation of Un-American Propaganda Activities in the United States: Special Committee on Un-American Activities, House of Representatives, 78th Cong., 2nd sess. on H. Res. 282, Appendix Part IX: Communist Front Organizations, USGPO, 1944.

"Juvenile Delinquency: a compilation of information and suggestions submitted to the Special Senate Committee to Investigate Organized Crime in Interstate Commerce Relative to the Incidence of Juvenile Delinquency in the United States and the Possible Influence thereon of so-called Crime Comic Books during the 5-year period 1945 to 1950," USGPO, 1950.

Juvenile Delinquency (comic books): Hearings before the Subcommittee to Investigate Juvenile Delinquency in the U.S., of the Senate Committee on the Judiciary, 83rd Cong., 2nd sess., on Apr. 21, 22, June 4, 1954, USGPO, 1954.

Juvenile Delinquency (motion pictures) Hearings before the Subcommittee to Investigate Juvenile Delinquency of the Senate Committee on the Judiciary, 84th Cong, 1st sess., on June 15, 16, 17 and 18, 1955, USGPO, 1955.

Juvenile Delinquency (national, federal, and youth-serving agencies): Hearings before the Subcommittee to Investigate Juvenile Delinquency of the Senate Committee on The Judiciary, 83rd Cong., 1st sess., pursuant to S. Res. 89 Investigation of Juvenile Delinquency In The United States, Part 1 November 19, 20, 23 and 24, 1953, USGPO, 1954.

Juvenile Delinquency (Obscene and Pornographic Materials): Hearings before the Subcommittee to Investigate Juvenile Delinquency in the U.S of the Senate Committee on the Judiciary, 84th Cong., 1st sess., on May 24, 26, 31, June 9, 18, 1955, USGPO, 1955.

Juvenile Delinquency (Philadelphia, PA): Hearings before the Subcommittee to Investigate Juvenile Delinquency of the Senate Committee on the Judiciary, 83rd Cong., 2nd sess., pursuant to S. Res. 89, Investigation of Juvenile Delinquency in the United States, April 14 and 15, USGPO, 1954.

Korean War Atrocities: Subcommittee on Korean War Atrocities of the Permanent Subcommittee on Investigations of the Senate Committee on Government Operations, 83rd Cong., 1st sess., pursuant to S. Res. 40, Part 1, December 2, 1953, USGPO, 1954.

NSC-68: A Report to the National Security Council by the Executive Secretary on United States Objectives and Programs for National Security, April 14, 1950.

"Obscene and Pornographic Literature and Juvenile Delinquency. Interim Report of the Committee on the Judiciary Made by Its Subcommittee to Investigate Juvenile Delinquency pursuant to S. Res. 62, and S. Res. 173 (84th Congress) Relative to the Investigation of Juvenile Delinquency in the United States." USGPO, 1956.

"Radiation Exposure Compensation Act (RECA)," US Department of Justice, n.d., http://www.justice.gov/civil/common/reca.html.

Report of the New York State Joint Legislative Committee to Study the Publication of Comics, Legislative Document No. 37, March 1954.

Report of the Select Committee on Current Pornographic Materials, House of Representatives, 82nd Cong, pursuant to H. res. 596, a resolution creating a select committee to conduct a study and investigation of current pornographic materials, USGPO, 1952.

Restrictions Upon Comic Books: Report Pursuant to Proposal 437 Sponsored by Representative Ralph T. Smith, Illinois Legislative Council Bulletin 258–5, April 1956.

State Department Employee Loyalty Investigation: Report No. 2108, Senate Committee on Foreign Relations, 81st Cong., 2d sess., July 20, 1950.

Strategy and Tactics of World Communism: The Significance of the Matusow Case: Hearing before the Subcommittee to Investigate the Administration of the Internal Security Act and Other Internal Security Laws of the Senate Committee on the Judiciary, 84th Cong. 1st sess., April 20, 1955, USGPO, 1955.

Study of monopoly power: Hearings before the Subcommittee on Study of Monopoly Power of the House Committee on the Judiciary, 81st Cong., v.6A-6B, June 23, 1950.

Subversive influence in the educational process; report of the Subcommittee to Investigate the Administration of the Internal Security Act and Other Internal Security Laws to the Senate Committee on the Judiciary, 83rd Cong., 1st sess., USGPO, 1953.

Television inquiry: Hearings before the Senate Committee on Interstate and Foreign Commerce, 84th Cong., 2nd sess., Part IV Network Practices, USGPO, 1957.

United States Atomic Energy Commission. In the matter of J. Robert Oppenheimer; transcript of hearing before Personnel Security Board, Washington, D.C., April 12, 1954, through May 5, 1954. USGPO, 1954.

Index

accuracy and inaccuracy of comic books and cartooning as history 110, 197, 199, 244n11; *see also* fact and fiction; realism

accuracy in depiction of weapons and uniforms 3, 38, 43, 45, 52, 117, 188, 192, 226n18, 251n61

Acheson, Dean 98, 100, 162, 163, 164, 202, 245n21, 246n56, 255–256n2

Actedron (Benzedrine) 256–257n8

Adcock, John 233n109

Addicted to War 194–195

Adventures Inside the Atom (GE) 167, 266n15

The Adventures of Rex (DC) 234n119

Advertising Council 174

Afghanistan 1

Africa 122, 130, 136, 250n57; *see also* Ethiopia; South Africa

African American cartoonists *see* Baker, Matt; Harrington, Ollie; Hollingsworth, A.C.; Massey, Cal; Ormes, Jackie

African American newspapers and journalists 249n13, 251n69; see also *Baltimore Afro-American*; Evans, Orrin C.; Harrington, Ollie

African American soldiers and veterans 112–125; 250–251n57, 251n60, 251n62, 253n91, 253n95

African Americans 90, 112–125, 230–231n65, 235n129

Air Force 37, 52, 155, 175, 255n1, 271n28

Air Force Association 37

Air Force Heroes (Murray Comics) 259ch14, 259n4

Akers, Joshua K. 225n5

Alaniz, Jose 222n5

Alaska 79

alcohol (and drunkenness) 67, 70, 74, 109, 256n5

All-American Publications *see* DC

All-American Men of War (DC) 28, 189, 234n119

All-Negro Comics (All Negro Comics) 117–118, 250n39

All Quiet on the Western Front (*Classics Illustrated*) 145–146

All Quiet on the Western Front (film) 260n23

All Quiet on the Western Front (novel) 145–146, 149

Allwood, Martin S. 74

alternative comics 185, 195, 272n46

alternative media 205–206

Amazing Spy Adventures (Bell Features) 247n1

Amerasia case 108, 247n7

America First 149, 261n46

American Academy of Child and Adolescent Psychiatry 237n145

American Academy of Family Physicians 237n145

American Academy of Pediatrics 237n145

The American Air Forces (Magazine Enterprises) 234n119

American Association of University Women 70

American Bar Association 189

American Civil War (1861–1865) 34, 52, 117, 156, 176, 188

American Comics Group (ACG) see *Spy and Counterspy*; *Spy-Hunters*

The American Conservative (website) 276n42

"American Crusader" (character) 266n11

American "establishment" ruling elite 1; *see also* Wall Street

American Federation of Labor 92

American Jewish Committee 59, 229n44, 229n45

American Journal of Psychotherapy 232n87

American Labor Party 61

American Legion 40, 191

American Legion 236n137

American Medical Association 237n145

The American Mercury 239–240n189

American News Company 185, 238n158

American Patriots, Inc. 230n56

American Prison Association 229n32

American Psychological Association 237n145

American Psychiatric Association 237n145

American Red Cross (for other national affiliates *see* Red Cross) 115, 233n103, 249n21

American Revolutionary War (War of Independence, 1775–1783) 1, 117, 176, 251n69

American Splendor (H. Pekar) 194, 272n46

American Youth for Democracy (AYD) 58, 229n42

Americans as gullible or soft 147, 174

amphetamines 256–257n8

Anderson, Marian 121

Andrae, Thomas 228n20

Andreas, Joel 194

Anglicization 139, 144

animation 196

Annarino, John 222n57

annihilationism *see* exterminationism

Anslinger, Harry 76–77

anthrax 129, 258n32

Anti-British sentiments 44, 98, 222–223n10, 244n10, 244n11

anti-comic book controversy 54–81; *see also* censorship and other forces; comic book effects

Anti-Communism (and anti-Communists) 66, 96, 188, 230–231n65

Anti-Defamation League of

West Germany (Federal Republic of Germany) 71, 238*n*172, 248*n*11

West Virginia 99

Western comics genre 14, 117, 208*n*16, 235*n*132; *see also* Rogers, Roy; Wayne, John

Western Europe 244*n*12

Whips 25, 75, 134, 138, 236–237*n*144, 274–275*n*18

White, Walter 119

White, William Lindsay 259*n*8, 259*n*18

white as default assumption 251–252*n*69

white Korean War soldiers and veterans 127, 251*n*62; *see also* African American soldiers and veterans

white supremacism 116, 120, 250–251*n*57; *see also* race; racial; racism

Whitney, Ogden 110

Whitted, Qiana 236*n*139

widows in Korea 207*n*2, 245*n*33

Wilcox, Robert K. 169

Wildenberg, Harry I. 25, 216–217*n*15

Wildes, Harry Emerson 240*n*202

Willard, Archibald MacNeal 45

Willard, Frank 163

Williams, George W. 122

Williams, Walter 165

Williamson, Al 121

Willkie, Wendell 163

Willoughby, Charles 247*n*3

Wings Comics (Fiction House) 44, 230*n*50, 247*n*58

"Winnie the WAC" (character) 41

"Winnie Winkle" (comic strip) 163

Winnington, Alan 138

Wit, Joel S. 267*n*51

Witek, Joseph 208*n*19, 271*n*38

Wolf, Harold G. 133

Wolfe, Willard W. 122

Woltman, Fred 231*n*72

Women's Army Corps 41

Women's International Democratic Federation 157, 263*n*32, 263*n*35

"Wonder Woman" (character) 113; *see also* William Moulton Marston

Wonsan 127, 254–255*n*17

Woo, Benjamin 219*n*58

Woo Mai Che family 272*n*61

Wood, Bob 67

Wood, Edward W., Jr. 213*n*18

Wood, Wally 90, 115, 121, 156–157, 170, 225*n*17, 252*n*70

Woodard, Isaac 119

Wooley, John 246*n*55

Workers Party of Korea 272*n*60

World Bank 274*n*10

world destruction 114, 166, 167, 170, 171, 172, 202, 266*n*12, 267*n*35, 271*n*40, 271*n*41, 276*n*41; *see also* nuclear winter; science fiction; World War III

World Trade Organization (WTO) 210*n*10, 274*n*10

World War I 34, 145, 160, 188, 220*n*11

World War II 21, 36, 42–49, 104, 105–106, 114, 140, 168, 176, 185, 188, 202, 207*n*4, 222*n*10, 226*n*34, 229–230*n*45, 232*n*85, 261*n*46, 268*n*61; comic books (and World War II *in* comics) 13, 21, 27, 29, 42–49, 51, 56–57, 62, 107, 113, 114–115, 118, 124–125, 199, 228*n*20, 259*ch*14*n*4, 274*n*1

World War III 74, 86, 99, 107, 172, 173, 174, 176, 268*n*59; restraining American desires for 202, 233*n*111, 250*n*53, 265*n*36; *see also* Korean War, as a first step toward World War III; world destruction

World War III (Ace) 173, 174, 234*n*119, 267*n*45; *see also* world destruction

World's Finest Comics (DC) 113–114

wounds 143

Wright, Richard 124, 235*n*129

Writer's Digest 234*n*115

Writers' War Board 46, 47, 57, 114, 115, 228*n*25, 249*n*20

Wunder, George 163, 213*n*22, 221*n*48

Wygocki, William 61

Xavier University 240*n*205

Xu Ying 257*n*12

Yager, Rick 265*n*6

Yakobson, August 253*n*3

Yalta Conference 104, 246*n*45); see also *From Yalta to Korea*

Yalu River (and border between North Korea and China; "Yalu Policy") 2, 148, 157, 163, 271*n*28

Yang, Gene Luen 250*n*42

Yank, the Army Weekly 40

Yashima, Taro 245*n*27

yellow as imagined skin color of East Asians 22, 57, 64, 74, 107, 123, 133, 144, 148, 228*n*23, 228*n*24, 240*n*203, 250*n*57

yellow fever 135, 258*n*32

yellow jaundice 186

yellow peril (and yellow menace) 129, 130, 144, 174, 255*n*25

Yeosu-Suncheon Mutiny 154, 262*n*22

Yi Chang-gon 254–255*n*17

Yiddish 226*n*32

Yoe, Craig 271*n*40

Young & Rubicam 45

Young Communists League 229*n*42

Young Life 58, 229*n*42

Young Men (Atlas) 234*n*119, 263*n*6

Young Men on the Battlefield (Atlas) 27, 117, 141, 234*n*119, 263*n*6

Young Men's Christian Association (YMCA) 70, 240*n*205

Young Women's Christian Association (YWCA) 70, 240*n*205

Youthbuilders, Inc. 113, 249*n*8

Yudin, Boris G. 258*n*28

Yugoslavia 72, 140, 173, 244*n*12

Zacharias, Ellis M. 128, 255*n*21

Zangwill, Israel 227*n*12

Zegart, Amy B. 247*n*4

Zeiske, Kay 182–183

Zekley, Zeke 164

Zeltzer, Gary 226*n*24

Zen Buddhism 66; *see also* Buddhism

Zhang Leping 257*n*12

Zhenfan campaign 130

Ziff-Davis 28, 216*n*2, 249*n*20

Zimmerman, Carla 144

Zoll, Allen A. 230*n*56

Zolotow, Maurice 68, 236*n*141

Zombies 208*n*16, 257*n*21

Zorbaugh, Harvey 218*n*48